STRATEGIC PUBLIC RELATIONS

An Audience-Focused Approach

Barbara Diggs-Brown

Associate Professor Emerita
American University School of Communication

President and CEO
*The Center for Strategic Research
and Communications*

WADSWORTH
CENGAGE Learning

Australia • Brazil • Japan • Korea • Mexico • Singapore • Spain • United Kingdom • United States

WADSWORTH
CENGAGE Learning

Strategic Public Relations:
An Audience-Focused Approach
Barbara Diggs-Brown

Senior Publisher: Lyn Uhl

Publisher: Michael Rosenberg

Development Editor: Laurie Dobson

Assistant Editor: Erin Bosco

Editorial Assistant: Rebecca Donahue

Media Editor: Jessica Badiner

Marketing Program Manager:
Gurpreet S. Saran

Content Project Manager:
Aimee Chevrette Bear

Art Director: Marissa Falco

Print Buyer: Douglas Bertke

Rights Acquisition Specialist:
Mandy Grozsko

Production Service: Mary Tindle, S4Carlisle
Publishing Services

Text Designer: Rokusek Design

Cover Designer: Riezebos Holzbaur

Cover Image: Shutterstock

Compositor: S4Carlisle Publishing Services

For product information and technology assistance, contact us at
Cengage Learning Customer & Sales Support, 1-800-354-9706

For permission to use material from this text or product,
submit all requests online at **www.cengage.com/permissions.**
Further permissions questions can be e-mailed to
permissionrequest@cengage.com

Library of Congress Control Number: 2011932343

Student Edition:

ISBN-13: 978-0-534-63706-4

ISBN-10: 0-534-63706-X

Wadsworth
20 Channel Center Street
Boston, MA 02210
USA

Cengage Learning is a leading provider of customized learning solutions with office locations around the globe, including Singapore, the United Kingdom, Australia, Mexico, Brazil, and Japan. Locate your local office at **international.cengage.com/region**

Cengage Learning products are represented in Canada by Nelson Education, Ltd.

For your course and learning solutions, visit **www.cengage.com.**

Purchase any of our products at your local college store or at our preferred online store **www.cengagebrain.com.**

Printed in the United States of America
1 2 3 4 5 6 7 15 14 13 12 11

Dedication

To Royce Frasier Duncan, born January 24, 2008, I dedicate this book and commit the rest of my life.

Meet the Author

Barbara Diggs-Brown is a communication strategist with more than 25 years of communication experience, specializing in strategic planning, social marketing strategies, qualitative research, integrated communication, and media relations. She is a prominent national researcher on the development of effective social marketing and communication campaigns as tools to address social change issues, including education, race, and health. As senior social marketing counsel and strategist, Diggs-Brown has designed, conducted, and reported qualitative research for a number of government, foundation, and nonprofit clients. As a communication counsel, she advises communication directors of large and small organizations on planning, qualitative research, audience segmentation, message development, and management.

Diggs-Brown is the President and CEO of The Center for Strategic Research and Communication, a 501(c)(3) organization. She frequently lectures and writes on race in the media and is coauthor of a critically acclaimed analysis of race relations in the United States, *By the Color of Our Skin: The Illusion of Integration and the Reality of Race* published by Dutton. She is the author of the only style guide for public relations students and professionals, *The PR Styleguide: Formats for Public Relations Practice,* in its second edition with Cengage Learning.

Her public affairs career in Washington has included Director of Public Affairs, Director of Government and Nonprofit Liaison, and Press Secretary for a presidential campaign. She is Associate Professor Emerita and the founding Executive Director of the American University School of Communication Institute for Strategic Communication for Nonprofits.

Brief Contents

Contents

Part 2   Foundations of Public Relations

Part 4   Guide to Public Relations Tactics

Part 5 Public Relations Practice in Context

Preface

More than 25 years of experience as both a public relations teacher and communication strategist informed and guided my writing of this textbook. My starting point was my unwavering belief that, to effectively practice public relations today in the United States and abroad, PR must be truly strategic. Being truly strategic requires being audience-focused, and being audience-focused requires acknowledging that effective public relations, or any effective communication, must begin with listening and hearing our audiences. To do this we must conduct formative, process, and evaluative research. Therefore, this book is based on the premise that once audience research is in place, only then can effective strategy follow.

Throughout this book I use the term *audience* instead of the more traditional term *publics* because I believe that the people with whom we communicate and with whom we build relationships are active participants in ongoing conversations. Although scholars in the field have rejected the term on the premise that it denotes groups that sit and receive a message or performance and are not active participants, the use of the word *audience* is consistent with the practice of public relations. For example, no doubt the words *key audience* are prominently featured in most communication plans produced by PR practitioners. Furthermore, there is some indication in the scholarly literature that there might be a shift in the field of PR that is likely to lead to change in terminology, moving away from using the term *publics* (Botan, 1997; Botan & Taylor, 2004).

Also, referring to our audiences as publics presents a semantics problem. The term *public* refers to a homogeneous group that largely does not exist in public relations practice. As discussed in this textbook, our audiences are very heterogeneous and require segmenting for effective communication.

Finally, this book takes the audience-centered perspective because, more than ever, the conversation is not always instigated by the organization. Organization-centered communication is not effective communication with today's audiences (if it ever was). Why? Because we live in an informed consumer culture and our audiences are aware often that someone is trying to persuade them to do something, so they depend more on their own connections—face-to-face and cyber—to help them decipher, decide, and act. Their decisions to take the desired action—whether it's purchase a material product or service, adopt an idea, stop or modify a behavior, enter into a relationship or experience, or something else—depends on how personal, relevant, and finely crafted and targeted a particular message is, and how well it demonstrates the benefit they gain from acting on it. It also hinges on how well informed our audiences are. There is a wealth of information available to our audiences today, and more and more, they depend on word-of-mouth and their networks to help them make informed decisions.

INTENDED AUDIENCE

This textbook is intended to be used for undergraduate courses in public relations, for both majors in the field and non-majors. It provides a comprehensive survey of public relations' foundations, processes, tactics, and contexts. In addition to highlighting audience-focused principles and techniques of audience research and recurring assessment, *Strategic Public Relations* is based on the premise that public relations is a management function and in order for it to be effective, it must be coordinated with an organization's other management divisions. The goal is a practical text that reflects and prepares students for the best, most effective public relations practice today—and tomorrow.

FEATURES

Without contributing another practice model per se (and so too a new acronym) to the field, *Strategic Public Relations* does present public relations as a four-phase process: Formative (focusing on strategic planning); Development (focusing on research-based strategy); Implementation (focusing on program management); and Evaluation (focusing on assessment and follow-up). Although I present these phases in a linear sequence in the text, I introduce the process of strategic public relations as one that is fundamentally recursive, and I highlight the points where a practitioner is most likely to encounter that recursive dynamic.

Students and teachers using this text benefit from the following features:

- **Practical process approach.** Figuratively and literally (it's presented in the third of five parts), the four-phase strategic public relations process is at the heart of this text. The process is introduced in Chapter 1 (What Is Public Relations?) and with a bit more detail in Chapter 4 (Strategy in Public Relations) and in full, step-by-step detail in the four chapters in Part III (The Process of Strategic Public Relations). Within Part III, to reinforce and facilitate students' familiarity with the recursive nature of strategic public relations practice, the text informs students of all **TYPICAL ASSESSMENT POINTS,** as well as *Process Milestones,* which flag tasks and deliverables in the process that commonly trigger reporting and, when appropriate, billing.
- **Logical and user-friendly overall organization.** The chapters in Parts I and II cover the *What and Why* of public relations; the chapters in Parts III and IV present the *How To* of the practice of strategic public relations, specifically the process and the tactics and the practice, and the chapters in Part V present the *Where* of PR, or the contexts of PR practice.
- **Solid foundations.** The book provides concise, up-to-date surveys of public relations' foundations with separate chapters devoted to its ethics, law, history, and theories, as well as strategy (see next bullet) and the core communication, information, and business skills and knowledge that every practitioner should possess.
- **A unique chapter on strategy.** Chapter 4, *Strategy in Public Relations,* introduces students to the concept of strategy to ensure that they understand this core concept of strategic public relations practice. The chapter begins with everyday strategies, and moves into a discussion of the critical thinking, reasoning, and decision-making skills basic to all strategy. It then surveys the role of strategy within organizations, and places strategic PR in context in general by providing snapshots of the full process it requires.
- **Emphasis on audience diversity.** Instead of marginalizing coverage of minority, or "special interest" audiences, the text consistently addresses diversity within audiences and teaches students how to develop inclusive audience profiles. It also addresses strategies for attending to the needs, concerns, interests, and behaviors of all audiences.

- **Engaging, purposeful box program.** The text includes three types of boxes to highlight key concepts, introduce related content, and give students opportunities to apply their growing knowledge of the material:
  - **Brief Case.** These boxes present a short case based on actual campaigns. Primarily intended for in-class group work or individual homework, these case descriptions and activities give students the opportunity to test their understanding of chapter concepts by applying them to the varied cases presented.
  - **Professional Point of View.** These boxes feature commissioned commentary or reprinted articles by current public relations practitioners on related topics, personalizing and bringing to life concepts and examples discussed.
  - **Engaging Ethics.** These boxes focus on relevant ethical issues and include a decision tree that comprises several questions to address potential outcomes.
- **Consistent attention to electronic research and communication technologies.** The text fully integrates coverage of electronic research and communication technologies, including emerging and mediated forms.
- **End-of-chapter learning resources.** Each chapter concludes with a substantial set of materials designed to improve retention and prompt further exploration: Summary and Review, Key Terms, Questions for Review and Discussion, and Web Links.

ANCILLARIES

Instructor Companion Website for *Strategic Public Relations*

This password-protected website contains the online Instructor Resour ce Manual, as well as chapter-level PowerPoint® lecture slides.

Instructor Resource Manual for *Strategic Public Relations*

The Instructor Resource Manual contains resources designed to streamline and maximize the effectiveness of your course preparation. This helpful manual includes suggestions for developing a course syllabus, chapter outlines, class-tested activities and exercises, technology resources, test items, and assessment tests. Each chapter includes a chapter outline; a list of key terms with definitions; suggestions for individual, group, and class activities; and true/false, multiple choice, fill-in-the-blank, and essay test items.

PowerLecture with ExamView® and JoinIn™ for *Strategic Public Relations*

This one-stop lecture tool makes it easy for you to assemble, edit, publish, and present custom lectures for your course, using Microsoft PowerPoint®. The PowerLecture lets you bring together text-specific lecture outlines and art, along with video and animations from the web or your own materials, culminating in a powerful, personalized, media-enhanced presentation. Additionally, the CD-ROM offers an electronic version of the Instructor Resource Manual, ExamView® software, and JoinIn™ on Turning Point® lecture slides.

ACKNOWLEDGMENTS

This author is indebted to many—spiritual and mortal. First, if asked, I can respond to the question of the existence of muses. There is but one muse—God. Thank you. Yet, I know that many mortals supported me—my loving family and friends, publishers, reviewers, editors, colleagues, clients, and critical friends. Thank you. So important to me are you, I will take the risk of naming a few and missing others.

Thank you to the Cengage Learning editorial team: Lyn Uhl, Senior Publisher; Michael Rosenberg, Publisher; Laurie Dobson, Development Editor; Erin Bosco, Assistant Editor; Rebecca Donahue, Editorial Assistant. Thank you to the early editorial team: Renee Deljon (Lynne); Pat Carr; Tamara Wilde; and Holly Allen (thank you for signing this book). Thank you to the production team: Aimee Bear, Cengage Learning Content Project Manager; Mary Tindle, Senior Project Editor, S4Carlisle Publishing Services; Jean Ives, Copyeditor, Words Unleashed; Mandy Groszko, Cengage Learning Rights Acquisitions Specialist; Lisa Jelly Smith, Permissions Project Manager, PreMediaGlobal.

Thank you to Bob Cochran and Kelli Wells of the GE Foundation for taking a chance on me. Anya Karavanov and Sharyn Sutton, thanks for teaching and learning with me.

To my family and friends—my life spring: Carrie Diggs, Cari-Shawn and Courtney, Royce, Roy, Antoinette, Stephanie, Renee and Leon. You encouraged, read, critiqued, and prayed. Thank you.

Thank you to Stephanie Sprow for her research and Lenore Gelb who read, reread, and read again.

Special thanks also to the many reviewers who helped shape the final version of this book:

Christina Baily-Byers, Southern Methodist University
Josh Boyd, Purdue University
Karen Buzzard, Southwest Missouri State University
Coy Callison, Texas Tech University
Jeffrey L. Courtright, Illinois State University
Gregory De Blasio, Northern Kentucky University
Elizabeth B. Dickey, University of South Carolina
Sandra C. Duhé, University of Louisiana at Lafayette
Mohan J. Dutta-Bergman, Purdue University
Michelle Ewing, Kent State University
Kathleen Fearn-Banks, University of Washington
Rochelle Ford, Howard University
Duane Franceschi, Canyon College
Elizabeth Hays, California State University at Fresno
Karen Hilyard, University of Tennessee
E. Dennis Hinde, South Dakota State University
Ann D. Jabro, Robert Morris University
Janice S. Jenny, Herkimer County Community College
Ric Jensen, University of South Dakota
Dave Junker, University of Texas at Austin
LeeAnn Kahlor, University of Texas at Austin
Majorie Keeshan Nadler, Miami University
Michael Kent, Western Michigan University
John Kerezy, Cuyahoga Community College and Kent State University
Gracie Lawson-Borders, Southern Methodist University

Charles Lubbers, University of South Dakota
Becky A. McDonald, Ball State University
Mary Mohan, State University of New York College at Geneseo
Marjorie Nadler, Miami University
David Ogden, University of Nebraska at Omaha
Seth Oyer, Bowling Green State University
Pamela Ann Parry, Belmont University
Gemma Puglisi, American University
Natalie Ryder Redcross, California State University, Northridge
Don W. Stacks, University of Miami
Douglas J. Swanson, University of Wisconsin at LaCrosse
Jeff Tyus, Youngstown State University
Christina G. Yoshimura, University of Montana

What Is Public Relations?

Often the perceived elements of PR can be seen on TV and in the movies. For example, during the final season of HBO's *Sex and the City*, the Samantha Jones character, principal of her own PR firm, transforms waiter Jerry Jerrod into Smith Jerrod, Absolut Hunk, to launch the aspiring young actor's career. Her strategy seems to work, as Smith's off-off-Broadway play *Full Moon* quickly becomes a hit and the director Gus Van Zant casts him in a film.

What exactly did Samantha do? At the very least we know that she changed Jerrod's common, folksy first name to one ready for tabloid covers; publicized both his physical beauty and his nudity in the play; won him a modeling job for Absolut vodka; and, apparently, negotiated a deal with MTV.

To many people, Samantha's efforts on Jerry's behalf typify the life of a public relations professional. Is this your view of public relations? If this fictional situation had been real, what kind of work would Samantha have been doing behind the scenes? Making phone calls, writing letters and emails, preparing and sending media kits, and attending meetings? Seeing public relations work portrayed in movies and television often leads viewers to think that "PR people" intuitively know what's hip and what works. In the real world, it is likely that Samantha would have done some research, analyzed the landscape of pop-culture icons, and carefully planned her strategy for introducing Smith to the media and his audience.

TV shows and movies stereotype the work of real-life public relations practitioners. These stereotypes, along with other factors we will address, mean that most people do not have a good grasp of what PR really is and does. Let's acknowledge common misunderstandings about PR *before* settling on a clear, correct definition and description of what PR really is.

Publicity, publicity, publicity is the greatest moral factor and force in our public life.

—Joseph Pulitzer,
journalist and newspaper publisher

Lucas Jackson/Corbis

Actress Kim Cattrall in her role of Samantha, a public relations practitioner

WHAT PUBLIC RELATIONS ISN'T

The term *public relations*, or *PR*, is used in myriad flippant, and sometimes negative, ways. You've probably heard the dismissive labels "public relations ploy" and "public relations stunt." Consequently, misunderstandings abound about what PR is. Looking at some of the most common misunderstandings of PR is definitely worthwhile.

Popular Misunderstandings

The most common misunderstandings about PR come from equating it with what are, strictly speaking, two PR activities—publicity and media relations. However, just as the hammer and saw help a carpenter get the job done but are not themselves the work known as carpentry, *publicity*, *media relations*, and sometimes *crisis communication* are tools that may help get public relations work done, but they themselves are not public relations. Although this text includes coverage of publicity, media relations, and crisis communication, these activities in and of themselves are more like *functions* within the more complex and essential profession we know as public relations.

A 2004 Super Bowl performance by Janet Jackson and Justin Timberlake concluded with Jackson's bared breast. Although the brief nudity could very well have been accidental, the fact that the incident coincided with the release of her eighth album led much of the public and media commentary to suggest that her "wardrobe malfunction," as Timberlake famously referred to it, was a "PR stunt," orchestrated to increase the public's awareness of the new album.

For decades, the popular understanding of public relations has been essentially publicity. **Publicity** is best understood as *information disseminated to the public, usually through the mass media, for the purpose of gaining positive attention for an organization, individual, product, or service*. It is also sometimes used to refer to the result of these efforts, as in, "The publicity *The King's Speech* garnered for winning four Academy Awards in February 2011 further increased its ticket sales." The catalysts for this type of public attention, which is often generated free of charge and usually the result of some public relations effort, are not entirely unlike Janet Jackson's "wardrobe malfunction," though not necessarily as shocking.

Since the news coverage Janet Jackson received was free, it was what the PR industry calls **earned media,** which is *public attention accorded to an event based on intentional efforts to bring its newsworthiness to light*, as opposed to **bought media,** which is *public attention that is purchased*, such as TV commercials, magazine ads, or banner and pop-up ads. While Ms. Jackson earned her media coverage through a physical act, other individuals and organizations often earn it by distributing *news releases* or *media advisories*, both of which are examples of written forms of public relations tactics (Chapter 14). Publicity remains one of the most common and tangible elements of public relations activity, but again, it is just one element of what public relations is.

Another element of public relations is **media relations,** *a specialty in which practitioners attempt to generate and maintain good relationships with the news media to* *gain positive news media coverage.* By developing and cultivating relationships with members of the various media industries (such as magazine, newspaper, television, and Internet) and providing them with news or other content, the person or group has a better chance of being presented favorably, gaining an advantage over other people or groups with similar and competing interests.

For example, the National Basketball Association (NBA) wants the media to cover basketball as much as possible. Therefore, its media relations strategy is to make men's basketball the easiest sport to cover. Signs of the existence of this strategy include the fact that the NBA's media relations department provides sports reporters anywhere in the world with 24-hour access to stats, shot charts, game notes, video news releases, and box scores. Additionally, other organizations in the league are committed to distributing news releases and feature stories to the media that include pertinent information to make fact gathering as easy as possible for reporters.

Another aspect of public relations is **crisis communication,** *the effort to restore the image of a corporation, celebrity, or politician when they misstep.* Crisis communication also can refer to communication provided after a tragic or disastrous event, like a terrorist attack, oil spill, or hurricane). While the attention of Janet Jackson's Super Bowl performance may have been good for music sales, the allegation of impropriety was disastrous both for MTV and CBS, the producer and broadcaster of the show, and each responded in various ways to curtail the damage. Crisis communication is a fascinating and challenging component of public relations, but assuming that smoothing over a crisis is the primary function of PR misses the strategic nature of the practice. It is another example of mistaking a part for the whole.

Janet Jackson and Justin Timberlake after the infamous wardrobe malfunction at the 2004 Super Bowl

AP Photo/Elise Amendola, File

Finally, some people associate PR with simply drumming up attention or trying to smooth over scandals. The term for people who try to change public opinion about events is *spin doctors.* **Spin** is *the human tendency, when one is on the spot and the stakes are high, to distort the truth so that the subject at hand is perceived as favorably as possible—more favorably than facts would cause it to be perceived.* By confusing or obscuring circumstances, truth essentially spun on its axis may mislead the public by influencing the public to not form negative opinions.

When then–Illinois Governor Rod Blagojevich was embroiled in impeachment hearings in 2009 following his arrest and indictment on 16 felony charges, including trying to sell the U.S. Senate seat vacated by the election of Barack Obama, he maintained his innocence. Stating that he "always behaved ethically" and fought corruption in government, he decided that a media blitz was the proper tactic to help defend his reputation and perhaps sway public opinion. He appeared on almost every talk show imaginable, from *The View* to *Larry King Live.* Before it was over, Blagojevich was drawing parallels between himself, Ghandi, and Martin Luther King Jr. That was major spin. In PR, spin has major practical, and ethical, implications, but again, it alone is not public relations. Politics, of course, provides many examples of spin and its aftermath.

Why These Distinctions Matter

These common misconceptions dominate our thinking about PR for good reason. Why? Because for decades PR *was* primarily focused on media relations and publicity (see Chapter 3 for a survey of the history of public relations). If publicity, media relations, and crisis communication are elements of what public relations practitioners do, then why make the distinction between them and the overall work of public relations? The reason is that, while an object may be equivalent to the sum of its parts, it should not be confused with or mistaken for just one of those parts. The most spectacular or most visible actions of people may be remembered and noticed, but that doesn't mean they tell the whole story. It is important that we understand that public relations is a complex field that involves many types of carefully planned and executed activities.

PR's Contribution to the Confusion

Popular misconceptions are only one source of confusion about what, exactly, PR is. Deliberately or inadvertently, the PR industry itself adds to the confusion. This problem is rooted in the proliferation of titles people and organizations use to identify the practice. Here's a quick sample of the names organizations use to identify their PR departments: Corporate Communication, Stakeholder Relations, Corporate Relations, Marketing Communication, Public Information, Public Affairs, Nonprofit Marketing, and University Relations. Many of the people who work in these departments have the same kinds of jobs, but the department names give the impression that they are different and contribute to our general confusion about what public relations is.

Similarly, PR practitioners' job titles add to the confusion about what they do. On one hand, some job titles—like *media relations specialist* or *press secretary*—clearly define the scope and specific responsibilities of the persons who fill the positions. On the other hand, some independent and small-agency practitioners aim to distinguish themselves from competitors or indicate their unique approach by using titles that don't really explain what they do. These practitioners' business cards have titles that refer to them as marketing public relations associate, strategic marketing communication manager, marketing communication account executive, and vice president for strategic communication. With these similar but varied department names and job titles abounding, how are we to understand what it is that these people do? If we pay attention, we may notice the most commonly used, or most frequently recurring, terms: *communication, relations, public*. However, unless you are in the PR field, you could easily be confused.

WHAT PUBLIC RELATIONS IS

Having cleared up the misunderstandings about PR, we can now focus on the full definition of public relations, in order to better understand the actual nature and scope of this challenging and rewarding profession.

Defining Public Relations

The most widely accepted definitions of public relations come from the Public Relations Society of America (PRSA) and the Institute of Public Relations, the profession's two leading national organizations.

Here's the "Official PRSA Definition": "Public relations helps an organization and its publics [or, *audiences*] adapt mutually to each other." This brief definition appears within an extraordinarily extensive, multipart document that sets the practice within the context of society, and delineates the activities, outcomes, and required knowledge for the practice. A longer excerpt from this extended definition is often referred to as the PRSA "Official Statement on PR" (Figure 1.1), and it highlights two important concepts. First, it acknowledges that the practice exists to help organizations understand the attitudes and values of their **audiences** (traditionally referred to as **publics**), which are *the people or organizations most likely to limit or enhance an organization's ability to pursue its mission*. Second, it states that public relations practitioners advise management on how to use PR strategy to help accomplish the organization's overall goals.

The Institute of Public Relations, a nonprofit organization that seeks to link the academic and the profession of public relations, supporting PR research and education, describes public relations practice as "the planned and sustained effort to establish and maintain goodwill and mutual understanding between an organization and its publics." This definition adds the concepts of planning and process to the

Public relations helps our complex, pluralistic society to reach decisions and function more effectively by contributing to mutual understanding among groups and institutions. It serves to bring private and public policies into harmony.

Public relations serves a wide variety of institutions in society such as businesses, trade unions, government agencies, voluntary associations, foundations, hospitals, schools, colleges, and religious institutions. To achieve their goals, these institutions must develop effective relationships with many different audiences or publics such as employees, members, customers, local communities, shareholders, and other institutions, and with society at large.

The managements of institutions need to understand the attitudes and values of their publics in order to achieve institutional goals. The goals themselves are shaped by external environment. The public relations practitioner acts as a counselor to management and as a mediator, helping translate private aims into reasonable, publicly acceptable policy and action.

As a management function, public relations encompasses the following:

- Anticipating, analyzing, and interpreting public opinion, attitudes, and issues that might impact, for good or ill, the operations and plans of the organization.
- Counseling management at all levels in the organization with regard to policy decisions, courses of action, and communication, taking into account their public ramifications and the organization's social or citizenship responsibilities.
- Researching, conducting, and evaluating, on a continuing basis, programs of action and communication to achieve the informed public understanding necessary to the success of an organization's aims. These may include marketing, financial, fund raising, employee, community or government relations, and other programs.
- Planning and implementing the organization's efforts to influence or change public policy. Setting objectives, planning, budgeting, recruiting and training staff, developing facilities—in short, managing the resources needed to perform all of the above.

Examples of the knowledge that may be required in the professional practice of public relations include communication arts, psychology, social psychology, sociology, political science, economics, and the principles of management and ethics. Technical knowledge and skills are required for opinion research, public issues analysis, media relations, direct mail, institutional advertising, publications, film/video productions, special events, speeches, and presentations. In helping to define and implement policy, the public relations practitioner uses a variety of professional communication skills and plays an integrative role both within the organization and between the organization and the external environment.

Figure 1.1
Public Relations Society of America (PRSA) Official Statement on Public Relations

SOURCE: Public Relations Society of America (prsa.org)

Mike Segar/Reuters

Shannon Stapleton/Reuters/Corbis

J.B. Nicholas/Splash News/Newscom

Corporate social responsibility programs and special events such as groundbreakings and grand openings are public relations activities.

PRSA definition. These concepts are essential and are central to today's most widely accepted definitions of public relations, including the one used in this textbook:

> **Public relations** is *an applied discipline within the field of communication that uses strategic thinking, planning, research and practice to help an organization or person establish and manage mutually beneficial relationships and interact with an audience or audiences that ensure success or failure; position an organization, person, or issue favorably within the marketplace of ideas; and/or affect the attitudes, opinions, and behaviors of the targeted audience or audiences.*

Separately and together these definitions are useful for providing narrow and concise language that identifies the field, but discussing specific descriptors and key phrases in more detail will help us to better see how the field functions.

A Survey of PR's Characteristics

The preceding definitions are worded differently and highlight different aspects of public relations, but each has much in common with the other. Pulling together these definitions, the following characteristics stand out: PR requires communication, planned and strategic thinking, audience knowledge and focus, and becomes a management function within or for an organization.

PR Is a Form of Communication

The purpose of public relations is often to position an organization in a positive light for the people with whom the organization is concerned. To interact with people successfully requires a knowledge of communication. Because PR professionals need this skill and their duties often revolve around communication activities like writing and public speaking, public relations is considered as a discipline within the field of communication. You may have noticed that many public relations degree programs are housed within a college or school of communication at most universities and colleges. PR involves knowing how communication occurs, what makes it effective, and how to ensure that people are listening and responding to what you are saying.

To understand how to make communication effective, it is important to understand how people communicate and react to different types of communication. This is why communication majors study human behavior to understand how communication works. They learn how to test messages, how to find best openings for their messages and consider potential barriers to successful communication—all activities that involve human behavior. This places communication within the domain of social sciences, the academic discipline based on the formal investigation of social structures, behaviors, and phenomena (its other domains include general areas of study such as humanities and biological sciences). Formal investigation is foundational to the social sciences, so PR is also recognized as a profession that employs the methodologies of social sciences to investigate and research communication strategies before implementing plans.

PR Is Planned and Strategic

Public relations is not something we can just *do* spontaneously. Devising creative ideas does not mean that we can simply create effective public relations plans. Effective public relations begins with understanding the audiences we want to reach and requires the development of a plan based primarily on what we learn from the research we conduct.

The element of public relations that is most crucial to effective communication is strategy. When we use the word *strategy* in discussing the overall mission of an organization or communication plan, we are talking about the need to use an organization's goals and mission to determine where it and its public relations work are headed. Being strategic allows organizations to make better choices about their future because it is completely informed about the possibility for success in its environment. Chapter 4 provides a more detailed introduction to strategy, especially as it pertains to strategic public relations.

Biotechnology firm MedImmune has learned the value of strategic planning. The company makes FluMist, a flu vaccine that is sprayed in the nose rather than given by a needle injection. MedImmune needed to increase the number of flu vaccines it sold after a lackluster sales year. The company looked at its sales and communication efforts and conducted research to determine the reasons for the poor sales. Its marketing and sales strategy had involved an expensive advertising campaign that focused on FluMist's advantages over the flu shot. When MedImmune considered its environment, it realized that its initial strategy was not effective for two reasons: FluMist was more expensive and harder to store properly, and doctors were hesitant to prescribe it because they didn't fully understand its benefits and risks.

MedImmune's strategic approach meant revamping its efforts to sell FluMist. This entailed lowering the price of the vaccine and using PR more strategically; its new communication plans targeted educating doctors about the vaccine's safety and effectiveness so they would feel comfortable prescribing it. In this case, not using strategic PR in the beginning resulted in ineffective sales, as often happens. The best communication is *integrated communication*, which is communication that uses a combination of strategies to implement a communication plan (see Chapter 4).

PR Is Audience Focused

PR exists to facilitate a relationship and interaction between an organization and the key group (or groups) of people who can greatly affect the organization—for better or for worse. As mentioned earlier, a key principle of public relations involves identifying that group of people—the *audience*, or *publics*—that is most likely to limit or enhance an organization's ability to pursue its mission. After Janet Jackson's Super Bowl incident, CBS was focused on its primary audience: concerned parents and others who were displeased with such a revealing stage show.

Another example of audience focus is an automobile insurance company such as Progressive focusing PR efforts on drivers who use cell phones while they drive because such drivers are involved in more accidents, thus adding a financial burden on the company. And a nonprofit organization might be formed to increase the number

ENGAGING ETHICS

Photos and Privacy: For Celebs, Too?

In 2009 photos reportedly of the battered face of pop singer Rihanna appeared in the news media. The police headshot reportedly showed the singer's face with cuts and bruises allegedly inflicted by her boyfriend, R&B artist Chris Brown, during a domestic incident. The photos first appeared online, then published or linked by several media outlets and later appeared on *Oprah*, where the alleged abuse was discussed. Journalistic standards and police require editors to omit the names and photos of victims from coverage.

1. Should protection of Rihanna's privacy be respected? Held to lower standards? Explain your response.
2. Should journalistic standards be adhered to by "celebrity news" organizations? Explain your response.
3. Do you think the photo of a high-profile politician or CEO would have received the same exposure if it had been leaked? Why? Why not?

of people who vote. All of these organizations have different motivation for using public relations, but they can pinpoint at least one audience they need to reach to be successful.

But the simple identification of an audience or audiences by itself isn't enough. If it were that simple, most organizations would have effective communication programs. In fact, most do not. The reason they don't is that they don't know anything about their audiences beyond who those audiences are—a particular advocacy group, or consumer demographic, or student body. When an organization is audience focused, it listens to its audiences and attempts to understand the audience's attitudes, beliefs, norms, values, desires, and actions. An organization that listens to and gets to know its audiences knows who the individuals are who comprise those groups and what is important to them.

Going back to the MedImmune example, the company realized that it hadn't paid enough attention to one of its audiences—doctors. Once PR professionals identified doctors' misconceptions about the FluMist vaccine and what they needed to know to feel comfortable prescribing the vaccine, MedImmune had a tool that allowed it to revise its PR efforts and be more successful in selling the product.

In our example of Progressive automobile insurance, the company surveyed cell phone drivers and wisely asked more than just their age, gender, and income. Progressive's survey discovered that most cell phone drivers are communicating with friends and family, not coworkers, while they are driving, and that they do so to catch up on personal business because they are pressed for time. This information allowed practitioners to design communication plans that helped the organization manage its relationship with these audiences.

PR Is a Management Function within an Organization

Because PR contributes significantly to an organization's success (or failure), the person managing an organization's public relations efforts should participate in the organization's overall strategic planning and decision-making processes, providing guidance about the effects of the organization's actions on its many audiences. In short, a PR practitioner should be a member of the organization's group of department executives or higher-level managers.

James E. and Larissa A. Grunig, in their study of excellence in public relations (2000), provide the best model for how public relations can (and should be) practiced. Grunig and Grunig found that public relations is most effective when the people with whom organizations are communicating "are identified within the framework of organizational strategic management and when the function is managed strategically at the level of the public relations department."

PUBLIC RELATIONS IN CONTEXT

Organizations in American society fall into three main categories: for-profit organizations, nonprofit organizations, and local, regional, state, and national government agencies. Public relations work can be found in each type of organization, although the job title and type of work may vary from one to another.

For-Profit Organizations

For-profit organizations are most commonly referred to as *businesses*, *companies*, or *corporations*; they deal in commerce, offering products and services to consumers for a price. They do not, however, exist only to provide a product or service; they exist to make money—that is, to be profitable. Clothing stores, gyms, and television stations are examples of for-profit organizations. Public relations agencies and independent practitioners are usually for-profit entities, also. PR agencies and individual practitioners conduct public relations activities in all three of the major categories (for-profit, nonprofit, and government).

Corporate or business public relations is a large and varied practice area, and so are the audiences to whom these organizations sell products and services. The practitioner in this area will listen to and communicate with consumers, employees, boards of directors, government regulatory agencies, competitors, consumer advocacy groups, and politicians. Industry today requires a practitioner in for-profit organizations to know a little about communicating in the political world as well. More and more consumers are very vocal about the companies with which they conduct business and they are highly likely to communicate concerns to their local, state, and national representatives, as well as neighbors, family, and friends.

Not surprisingly, corporations have responded to consumers' concerns about company social practices by expanding their public relations efforts into the community. As a result, corporate social responsibility, a PR area of specialization that acknowledges and demonstrates a corporation's responsibility to the communities in which they interact, is thriving.

To stay competitive, many corporations also include community relations activities in their day-to-day operations (Price, 1997). For example, Target stores encourage employees (or "team members," as they are called) to participate in volunteer activities in their communities. They also donate a portion of their sales to local communities. Corporations use various communication tools to make their community involvement known to their customers and other key audiences. As shoppers enter Target stores, they walk by bulletin boards filled with pictures of Target employees

BRIEF CASE STUDY

That's Entertainment and That's Media Relations for Publicity

B|W|R is Ogilvy PR's Hollywood-based entertainment practice chosen to help pitch a new Fox television series based on the British highly popular reality show *Pop Idol*. The new show would be called *American Idol (AI)*. The question was: Can another reality show, a summertime one at that, really succeed?

American Idol had a very unique feature in that it offered viewers the opportunity to "make" the next pop star as opposed to leaving the power with the judges, exclusively. Viewers call, text, or go online to vote for their candidate of choice. This distinguishing factor served as a plan for the optimum way to begin the build-up of the media relations campaign and to position the judges. Because the real contestants did not emerge biweekly until five weeks into the series, it was important to give each judge a personality to which viewers could relate. This tactic allowed viewers to remain engaged while awaiting the 10 "stars" (really the contestants) of the show. Paula, Randy, and Simon, the three judges, and an occasional guest judge were placeholders who kept viewer attention during the culling down to 10 phase and auditions in Los Angeles, New York, Chicago, Atlanta, Miami, Dallas, and Seattle.

B|W|R media relations activities included the following:

- Working with a *TV Guide* reporter to attend auditions "as a possible contestant" to create a feature story to run along with the show's launch
- Working with local news media in each market to report on auditions
- Contacting media to cover auditions to help promote other cities, as well as to promote the premiere

Media relations for the launch included the following:

- Encouraging the media to review tapes of the UK version
- Introducing news media and readers/viewers to the judges and hosts of the new show
- Leveraging initial coverage such as *USA Today* and *Newsweek* to build interest by other media

Results are legend, as *AI* remains one of the country's most popular television shows. It premiered very "modestly" but gained momentum, winning its time period and peaking at 28 million viewers for the finale. Front-page coverage included *USA Today*, *US Weekly*, *People*, *Entertainment Weekly*, *Billboard*, *Broadcasting & Cable*, *TV Guide*, and *Seventeen*. It generated spoofs on *Saturday Night Live*, debate on *The O'Reilly Factor* and a revival of *Star Search*.

Working the Case

1. All of the preceding activities are referred to as media relations tactics because they are intended to engage the news media and encourage coverage. This is one way of generating publicity. If we were to undertake this launch today, what technology might we use to engage the news media?
2. What activities other than engaging the news media directly might result in publicity for the show?

building playgrounds and helping at recycling centers. Around the holiday seasons, Target TV commercials remind shoppers of Target's generous giving habit.

The practice of public relations and corporate social responsibility has grown so large that the Public Relations Society of America has launched a Strategic Social

Responsibility professional interest chapter to bring together members from the corporate, nonprofit, and government sectors practicing in the areas of philanthropy, business ethics, corporate governance, human rights, and work-life issues.

As an employee or staff member of a corporation, the practitioner receives a salary paid on a regular basis for performing public relations assignments. The general purview of the assignments and tasks are usually spelled out in a position description. Public relations practitioners who are employed by a for-profit organization may have positions from as far up in the hierarchy as vice president for corporate communication to public relations generalists who prepare news releases for dissemination.

Nonprofit Organizations

Nonprofit organizations include many of the institutions we know that provide needed services to communities across the country and around the globe. Nonprofit organizations and advocacy groups are concerned with issues and services that range from the environment (the Sierra Club) and arms control (Arms Control Association) to health (American Cancer Society), alternative energy (the Apollo Alliance), emergencies (the American Red Cross), and education (Teach for America). Nonprofits also include professional organizations, churches, schools, and museums.

Nonprofit organizations, in contrast to for-profit organizations, exist to provide a service without making a profit that is distributed to shareholders (though they often strive to make a profit that then goes back to serving their cause). While some of the duties of public relations professionals in a nonprofit are similar to those at a corporation, nonprofits face unique challenges that affect this type of work.

In the tumultuous economy of the past years, nonprofit organizations have faced increasing competition for resources. Effective communication strategies and techniques are often key to the success of nonprofit causes as the organizations strive to secure funding, attract volunteers, and affect social change. As nonprofit organizations struggle to accomplish more with less, they increasingly use innovative and venturesome strategies to further their causes (Wallack, 1993).

Much public relations work is spent raising awareness of the organization's mission or cause. This might entail significant media relations work to encourage the media to cover the organization's issue, or publicity work to direct the public's attention to a particular issue. For example, the National Partnership for Immunization, a nonprofit group, sponsors National Immunization Month every August to highlight the importance of immunization and to remind parents to have their children immunized before they start school. They host a press conference with health officials to discuss recent news in immunization and disseminate materials for parents, children, and doctors. Acquiring funding and donations is a major part of life at a nonprofit, and public relations representatives often participate directly in fund-raising programs.

Working in PR at a nonprofit that is concerned with a social or health cause often involves developing programs to help people change their behavior or better their lives. The PR practitioner often must develop persuasive campaigns and educational materials for the audiences they are targeting. An approach called social marketing has emerged that uses the marketing concepts to persuade audiences to adopt healthier behavior. This model is often used by nonprofit organizations and will be discussed in Chapter 18.

Nonprofit employees are often paid less than their corporate counterparts, but they are often motivated and rewarded by the knowledge that they are serving a worthy cause. Working for a small nonprofit often means being understaffed and having to fill many roles—especially in these economic times. This provides a unique opportunity for PR professionals to participate in a higher level of public relations work that would take many years to reach in the corporate world.

Political and Government Organizations

These organizations include federal, state, and local government agencies, which conduct the daily business of executive, legislative, and judicial branches of the governments that serve the country's citizens. Government agencies include the offices that ensure that we have safe roads, clean water, and local police enforcement.

On the federal, state, and local levels, government has long been a sizeable employer of public relations practitioners. Despite the government's prohibition on allowing public relations activities, government agencies hire practitioners to help reach the citizens they serve. Chapters 7 and 19 include discussions of the ethical concerns regarding this practice. Press assistant, liaison specialist, public information officer, public affairs officer or specialist, special assistant, and community liaison are all titles

BRIEF CASE STUDY

President Richard Nixon at a press conference in the East Room of the White House in October 1973

Dennis Brack/Newscom

Watergate and Its Effect on PR

The misunderstanding of public relations as just media relations, crisis communication, and spin became part of popular culture in the 1970s when President Richard Nixon directed his White House staff to get the public relations people to fix the erupting negative results of Watergate.

The story is generally well known, continues to be a popular topic for books, and was even the subject of a major movie, *Frost/Nixon*, but here is a brief summary of what happened. On June 17, 1972, employees of the Committee to Re-Elect the President were arrested for burglary of the Democratic Party headquarters located in the Watergate building complex in Washington, DC. By 1973, after the employees were convicted, evidence showed that there was a connection between the burglars and top aides of the Nixon Administration. Allegations charged that the aides were involved in the break-in or in subsequent efforts to hide or "cover up" what had transpired.

Wiretaps had recorded Nixon imploring his aides to assign public relations staff with the task of handling the crisis and making it go away. The former president may have been correct about the situation requiring the skills of public relations practitioners, but he was very wrong in thinking PR efforts could make his administration's actions less damaging. A series of untruths and political blunders led to President Nixon's resignation on August 9, 1974.

The Watergate scandal was not good PR for the practice of public relations. The very public way in which the former president drew attention to public relations while in the midst of wrongdoing and covering up wrongdoing was unfortunate.

Working the Case

1. Research the Watergate scandal to find out what some of the specific PR activities were that the Nixon White House tried.
2. Review the definitions of *crisis communication* and *media relations*: In what ways, if any, are these terms applicable to the Nixon administration's activities during the Watergate scandal?

given public relations practitioners employed in the government. They conduct the same PR activities—from strategy to tactics—that are found in nongovernmental sector organizations.

Political communication is a practice of public relations that seeks to get a political candidate elected to public office in a given country, state, county, or municipality. Practitioners specializing in politics often continue to work for the candidate after an election, occupying positions such as press secretary, spokesperson, strategist, and speechwriter. These practitioners are often referred to as strategists and may work as independent practitioners or belong to public relations firms that specialize in handling political campaigns. They are usually well-versed in politics and have special professional experience in government, and know how to work with pollsters and within the unique structure of political campaigns.

Of course, government has a flip side. Just as there are practitioners working within government, there are practitioners working in organizations that seek to influence the government or work closely with the government. These practitioners work in the specialization area of government and/or legislative relations. Like some of their counterparts in the government, these practitioners who deal with the government on behalf of their organizations often carry the title of public affairs specialist. Their responsibility is to take care of an organization's problems that stem from or can be ameliorated by federal, state, or local officials.

Practitioners who are directly involved in government relations for an organization work closely with lobbyists. Lobbyists tend to be attorneys or former government employees or elected officials who are hired because of their past relationship with the government. Public relations practitioners are also sometimes hired as lobbyists. Their job is to work with government and legislative staff to ensure that lawmakers understand the impact proposed legislation may have on an entire industry and to influence lawmakers to look favorably on a particular industry or issue. Lobbyists work for corporations and industry, but there are lobbyists who specialize in special interest lobbying on behalf of citizens, and issues as varied as conservation, national health insurance, and human and civil rights.

International Organizations

Many organizations conduct public relations activities globally in all of the sectors discussed. International PR involves helping for-profit, nonprofit, and political and government sector organizations communicate and build relationships with international audiences that are crucial to the success of their missions.

Many organizations across the three major sectors we have just discussed must interact with audiences abroad and operate within foreign countries. As communication technology has helped make the world smaller, it has made it possible to conduct business globally at almost any hour of the day. As a result, the practice of public relations internationally—though complex and challenging still—has become easier and more successful. American corporations and businesses have been operating globally for a century, and as the economies of countries around the world grow stronger and consumers grow more plentiful, the opportunities for international PR practice grow.

As with political and government practice, international practice has two sides. Some international practitioners serve domestic clients by helping them to implement their programs and campaigns for audiences who are abroad. Other international PR practitioners assist foreign clients, including foreign governments seeking to meet and to communicate effectively with U.S. audiences.

The practitioner practicing internationally must become steeped in the cultures, customs, politics, media environment, PR practices, and languages of her organization's audiences. While she may conduct or manage many of the activities we find in domestic practice, the practitioner must be diligent in monitoring the programs or campaigns to be sure they are appropriate to the country.

Like all strategic PR, international practice requires the practitioner to conduct research or utilize the consumer research provided by the organization. Because corporations have been at the forefront of international PR practice, there are many examples of PR successes in product campaigns and product marketing sales internationally. Most people who travel internationally have felt themselves transported to the United States when they see a McDonald's restaurant.

The other side of the coin is the practice of public relations abroad by PR agencies native to India, Russia, China, Japan, South Africa, and many other countries whose counsel and services are sought by American clients. There are distinct advantages to working with agencies that have the expertise *and* are fluent in the languages, dialects, customs, and cultures of the audiences organizations want to reach.

Nonprofits communicate with global audiences frequently, also. Here the field of social marketing has played a lead, helping to facilitate social change through affecting social behavior. The campaigns to build educational systems, reduce infant mortality, promote health among children and teens, reduce and prevent HIV AIDS infection, and improve nutrition abroad are legendary. Many nonprofits, such as the March of Dimes (see Chapter 20 for a discussion of its international work), are just beginning to envision the impact they can have globally. Others, such as the International Campaign to Ban Landmines and Human Rights Watch, were created with international missions from the start.

Chapters 17, 18, 19, and 20 provide an in-depth look at the kind of work necessary for successful PR in each of these different sectors.

THE ECONOMIC REALITIES OF PUBLIC RELATIONS

Today's global economy requires that the public relations practitioner understand and appreciate the costs associated with running a business or organization. Both for-profit and nonprofit organizations have to work within budgets designed to make a profit or maintain a positive cash flow. An awareness of an organization's financial concerns and interest in a company's business model are important to being successful. More than ever, the economies of companies around the world are interrelated, and stock market changes have international effects. In order to be effective, PR practitioners must be knowledgeable about an organization's position in the marketplace and manage resources prudently.

Limited Budgets

The marketing budgets of some major corporations are larger than the economies of some small countries, but that doesn't mean PR gets much funding. Companies like Microsoft, Intel, and Procter and Gamble spend billions of dollars annually on marketing, with advertising the largest expenditure. However, while PR budgets are increasing, they are never a major part of these budgets. A PR budget is usually 10 percent or less of the advertising dollars spent by corporations. Independent practitioners can charge from $75 per hour to $350 to $500 per hour depending upon experience and business and political connections. One of the largest PR budgets on record is actually a nonprofit anti-smoking public education campaign targeting teens that launched in 2000, resulting from the Tobacco Master Settlement Agreement (MSA) (*PRWeek*, 2008). That said, most PR budgets remain modest and using resources wisely is crucial to success. Knowing what resources you need—human and capital—and the extent to which they are available within the organization or from the client is crucial to PR planning and success. Budgeting as a part of the planning process is discussed in Chapter 11.

Emphasis on Accountability

Accountability in the PR field is both practical (produce desired results on schedule and within budget) and ethical. Chapter 7 discusses ethics and professional standards, and "Engaging Ethics" cases in each chapter bring such issues to life. Meanwhile, it is important to note here that you are expected to be responsible in what you promise to do and produce. Clients and organizations expect you to be highly responsible for the wise investment of resources to produce a specific end. But being accountable is the *ultimate* responsibility. As President Harry Truman said, "The buck stops here." And you must recognize that in the end, clients and CEOs hold you accountable for promised results. Measuring accountability can be difficult, and the level of difficulty depends on what clients want to see as a measure.

Substantial measures of accountability can be applied if the proper research is conducted at the beginning of the PR process. We can measure changes in attitude, knowledge, and behavior. Behavior is often the easiest of these when actions are simplistic, as we can measure tickets sold, blood given, volunteers participating, and funds donated. Clients still rate frequency of *media hits* (appearances in the news media) among their top measures of result, but they have become more sophisticated in examining this measure in that they pay closer attention to the quality of the *mentions* (references made). They concentrate more on the type and quality of publications, websites, and stations, the tone of the reporting, and the information used. This increased attention to quality as well as quantity requires you yourself to pay closer attention to content analysis.

Accountability does not begin and end with the measure of the results of PR activities, including campaign activities. Organizations are paying closer attention to their accountability to a broad range of audiences that goes beyond their immediate audience. Here we find an element of the management function of PR. Many practitioners say that PR is the conscience of the organization, insisting that management act responsibly, and ultimately be responsible to its community, investors, volunteers, benefactors, consumers, employees, and other stakeholders. Acting responsibly toward the community means keeping an eye on improving, or at the least not endangering, the ecology, quality of education, and health and general well-being of the citizens and the environment in which they live.

Return on Investment

When corporations invest resources in the sale of products and services, their primary motivation is a return on the resources invested. In fact, all organizations that are managed well expect to profit in some manner from time and money spent. Public relations practitioners have always had to be concerned with **return on investment,** or **ROI,** *evidence or measure of the profit or cost savings experienced as a result of the use of resources,* because traditionally it was difficult to determine the value of public relations activities. Today, ROI is basically a debate about how to measure or evaluate the impact of public relations efforts on the bottom line. Public relations agencies have created tools for measuring the effects of PR activities on company results. Software, measuring hits on websites, computing the value of news clippings or "ad-value equivalency," and tracking sales against media coverage are all ways that practitioners attempt to prove the value of PR.

In some ways, the constant eye on ROI can negatively impact an attempt to produce a strategic public relations campaign. If managers are trying to save money, more often than not the funds needed for the proper research are cut from communication budgets. But strategic communication requires the right research to find the right audience with the right message, and a manager with a little foresight can see that the additional money needed to fund research is a good investment because it ensures more effective results. While research can be costly, it is less expensive than mistakes that result in loss of financial resources and audience goodwill.

Public relations is an exciting and rewarding field of study and practice. As a practice, it is like many others professions in that it has its ups and downs and detractors and supporters. Perhaps it has been least understood among equals but not to diminishing levels.

Communication Holds the Key to an Organization's Value

William Novelli was the CEO of AARP when he delivered the following speech to the Institute for Strategic Communication for Nonprofits at American University School of Communication.

Today, whether it is politics, public policy, business, or elsewhere, the role of communications is often undervalued.

Far too often, communications executives spend too much time doing damage control, trying to clean up a mess that could have been avoided if only they had more influence when the options were initially discussed and decisions were made.

In addition, communications is infrequently seen as a stepping stone to senior management. But communications is clearly good training for the vision, strategic thinking, and leadership that executive decision makers must provide.

Communications is at the core of any successful modern organization—for profit or nonprofit, whether a public-policy enterprise, a corporation, or any other entity. Communications is key because it's about strategy, about image, and about bringing a vision and a mission to life and connecting with key audiences. Most of all, it's about persuasion.

Some organizations have a more powerful tool than others for achieving all this—their mission. An inspiring mission helps attract talented people, motivates employees, attract partners, interest the media, and inspire target audiences.

What key roles do communicators play in all this? What does top management want and need from communications? As a communications pro, and now as a CEO, I've found that there are eight important responsibilities. Not necessarily listed in order of importance, these eight points are what communications is about. The better you are at carrying out these responsibilities, the more likely you'll attain personal and organizational success.

First, communicators are the primary guardians and promoters of the organization's image and reputation—the most valuable commodity it owns. Call it reputation enhancement, image building, or corporate branding, it is the process of creating, nurturing, and sustaining a beneficial, rewarding relationship with stakeholders.

Second, communicators have the responsibility of promoting the president and/or CEO. While it seems self-serving, studies show that a good portion of an organization's reputation is attributed to the public image of its CEO. Many CEOs are not brilliant communicators, though most are pretty good at it. For many, it is a learned skill, not an innate ability. Many top managers learned those skills from their communications staffers, agencies, or consultants, and they are better and more effective as a result.

Third, communicators must provide top-quality strategic and analytic thinking. Once the communications executive lays out the strategy or contributes to the management team's strategic thinking, then come the sound communications skills and tactics. But strategy is needed before tactics. That may seem elementary, but how often do we see stunts and gimmicks masquerading as strategy?

Fourth, communications experts must provide cool, professional help with crisis management. This is where communications professionalism has to rise to the occasion and the communications pros have to be calm and effective under fire. This is a critical role. No other group or individual can do it without communications.

Fifth is a clear and consistent focus on results. No organization will truly succeed—or be satisfied—without a mutual understanding of what victory is supposed to look like and without regular assessments on whether you're getting there or not.

The next important role that communicators must play is giving good feedback to top management and the rest of the organization. This includes providing a reading on how things are going among internal audiences and also among external constituents such as policy makers, grantees, opinion leaders, and the public.

The seventh role is to engage in genuine team play. Most organizations recognize that team building is key to success. Communications pros must be strong and true partners in management team building. This means aligning with the organization's goals, not setting your own.

The last of these eight requirements is creativity and entrepreneurship. Creativity can come from any corner of an organization, but most often comes from communications people who know how to find the fresh idea in any strategy and bring it to life in a way that creates interest, excitement, and enthusism.

When communicators deliver on these critical responsibilities, everyone wins. Smart executives should expect these roles and responsibilities from their communications pros. And communicators should be able to provide them within the senior decision-making circles of an organization. That's the true value of communication.

SOURCE: William Novelli, AARP, (1-888-687-2277), 601 E St., NW Washington, DC 20049

Summary and Review

What Public Relations Isn't

- Popular culture has glamorized and trivialized the work of public relations practitioners. As a result, many people don't understand the field or where it is practiced and how.
- Public relations is more complex than publicity stunts and managing crises. Effective PR is the result of careful planning and execution.
- Confusion about the practice of PR occurs within and outside the profession. The myriad titles and names for practitioners and their departments have added to the perplexity.
- Publicity, media relations, and crisis communication are all elements of PR, but they don't tell the whole story.

What Public Relations Is

- Public relations is an applied discipline within the field of communication that uses strategic thinking, planning, research, and practice to help an organization or person establish and manage mutually beneficial relationships and interact with an audience or audiences that ensure success or failure; position an organization, person, or issue favorably within the marketplace of ideas; and/or affect the attitudes, opinions, and behaviors of the targeted audience or audiences.
- Public relations serves a wide variety of institutions in society including businesses, trade unions, government agencies, voluntary associations, foundations, hospitals, schools, and religious institutions.
- Public relations serves as a management function within an organization to monitor and anticipate public opinion; to research, conduct, and evaluate communication programs; participate in overall strategic planning and decision making; and to assist in effecting policy change.
- Public relations professionals must be able to communicate effectively, think strategically, understand their audiences, and serve in a management role in organizations.

Public Relations in Context

- The role of the PR practitioner varies depending on the type of the organization or sector of the community: for-profit, nonprofit, and local, regional, state, and national government agencies.
- International PR for organizations occurs across these three major sectors and has become easier and more successful because of new information technologies.

The Economic Realities of Public Relations

- In order to be effective, PR practitioners must be knowledgeable about an organization's position in the marketplace and prudently manage what are often limited resources.
- They are expected to be highly accountable for their actions in both practical and ethical ways.
- And practitioners are required to demonstrate their effectiveness with an eye on the bottom line both fiscally and communally.

Key Terms

audience	media relations	return on investment
bought media	public relations	(ROI)
crisis communication	publicity	spin
earned media	publics	

Questions for Review and Discussion

1. How has the field of public relations suffered because of popular misunderstanding of the field?

2. Discuss publicity and media relations and why they are often thought of as the sum total of public relations.

3. Conduct research to find public opinion polls that rate occupations. How do Americans rate the public relations practitioner?

4. Given what you have read about organizations where public relations is practiced, which type of organization appeals most to you? Why?

5. Why is the PR process dynamic?

6. Why are public relations activities more costly if they are not strategic?

Web Links

American Idol
www.americanidol.com

FluMist
www.flumist.com

National Partnership for Immunization
www.health.gov

Ogilvy Public Relations
www.ogilvypr.com

PRWeek
www.prweek.com

Public Relations Society of America
www.prsa.org

Red Cross
www.redcross.org

Teach for America
www.teachforamerica.org

Who Are PR Practitioners?

The U.S. Labor Department's Bureau of Labor Statistics (BLS), estimates that there were approximately 275,200 public relations professionals in the American workforce in 2008. That number is expected to increase by 24 percent by 2018 to 341,300. According to its *Occupational Outlook Handbook, 2010–2011 Edition*, the prospects for employment in the field at the entry and management levels are expected to increase faster than the average of other occupations through 2014. While employment is projected to grow faster than in other fields, keen competition is expected for entry-level jobs. Opportunities are always best if you are well prepared academically and through a public relations internship or other related work experience. (We discuss preparation later in this chapter.)

WHERE DO PR PRACTITIONERS WORK?

As we discussed in the previous chapter, PR practitioners work in almost every type of organization that has audiences with whom it must communicate and interact and relationships it needs to build and maintain. While we discuss the practice of PR in specific sectors in detail throughout this textbook, this discussion is designed to give you an introduction to where practitioners work.

Circumstances may cause interruptions and delays, but never lose sight of your goal. Prepare yourself in every way you can by increasing your knowledge and adding to your experience, so that you can make the most of opportunity when it occurs.

—Mario Andretti, race car driver

Business, Nonprofit, and Government Sector Organizations

Public relations employees in business, nonprofit, and government organizations usually work in a department whose name indicates that public relations activities take place within its structure. As discussed in Chapter 1, the names abound—Public Information Department, Public Affairs Department, Office of University Relations, External Relations Department, Communication Department, to name just a few. The configuration of these departments or offices varies, but most have distinct organizational structures that reflect a hierarchy no matter how small the organization or flat the arrangement.

The practitioners are salaried employees who receive a regular paycheck for the hours they work for the organization just like their peers in accounting, legal, or human resources. The PR positions in business, nonprofit, and government usually follow a pattern of entry, mid-level, mid-level manager, and senior manager. Their compensation is based on a salary band for their levels and extent of responsibility and, sometimes, years of service. The practitioners may work in divisions within the department such as the news bureau, speakers' bureau, creative design, publications, legislative affairs, internal affairs, or many more. Practitioners may be generalists, meaning they work to accomplish many different types of tasks, or they may be specialists such as writers, graphic designers, and web publishers.

Public Relations Agencies

PR practitioners can apply their skills in distinctly business, nonprofit, or government organizations. Another option, however, is to work where all three sectors are served by working for a PR firm or agency. PR firms and agencies are in the business of public relations and therefore provide services to clients in many of the types of organizations we discussed previously, as well as political candidates, celebrities, and the governments of other nations. Table 2.1 below lists the 20 largest independent PR firms, their revenues, the number of employees they have, and their locations.

Because PR firms and agencies are businesses themselves, PR professionals who work for them are paid on terms similar to those who work for organizations. Employees receive regular paychecks based upon an agreed-upon salary, and they may also receive additional benefits such as cost-sharing and bonuses at the end of the year. Some large firms have many employees, including writers, account executives, media relations and corporate social responsibility experts, website developers, creative staff, and production facility employees. Smaller firms outsource many of the activities they need to service their clients, sometimes using freelance or independent practitioners and counselors.

Other firms specialize in providing research to organizations. This research can range from traditional polling and surveying to the evaluation and analysis of public opinion, tracking issues and trends, as well as audience and consumer research that requires talking to key audiences. Organizations often request research assistance to help them with strategic planning for their future. The idea is to learn what new developments or changes are on the horizon that will affect their mission and the relationships they have with their audiences. This research focuses on identifying trends that the organization may take advantage of or prepare to cope with to ensure continued success.

Table 2.1	2010 Rankings 20 Largest U.S. Public Relations Firms 2009 Revenues, Employees, and Location*			
Ranking	PR Firm	Revenues	Employees	Location
1	Edelman	$288,504,585	1,715	Chicago
2	Waggener Edstrom Worldwide	$94,999,000	628	Bellevue, WA
3	Ruder Finn	$71,071,000	342	New York
4	APCO Worldwide	$60,000,000	257	Washington
5	Qorvis Communications	$37,188,804	96	Washington
6	WCG	$25,811,000	134	San Francisco
7	Schwartz Communication	$293,085,774	158	Waltham, MA
8	ICR	$22,463,008	91	Norwalk, CT
9	DKC	$22,050,000	125	New York
10	Taylor Global	$19,100,000	96	New York
11	Text 100	$17,000,000	85	New York
12	Gibbs & Soell	$16,420,326	91	New York
13	Padilla Speer Beardsley	$15,195,259	98	Minneapolis
14	Allison & Partners	$14,662,255	80	San Francisco
15	Peppercom	$14,662,255	70	New York
16	Paine PR	$12,429,549	66	Irvine, CA
17	Cooney/Waters Group	$12,429,549	45	New York
18	French/West/Vaughan	$12,234,095	71	Raliegh, NC
19	Coyne Public Relations	$12,176,000	91	Parsippany, NJ
20	PCGCampbell	$11,768,722	85	Dearborn, MI

SOURCE: *PRWeek* 2010 Agency Business Report

*This ranking does not include the majority of agencies owned by holding companies, Interpublic Group, Omnicom, WPPGroup, Havas, and Publicis Groupe. Omnicom owns: Fleishman-Hillard, Ketchum, Porter Novelli, Brodeur Worldwide, Clark & Weinstock, FitzGerald, Gavin Anderson & Co., Cone, Mercury and Public Affairs.

Most large PR agencies are organized into *practice areas* whose names often reflect the industries in which they practice such as the following:

- Brand or Consumer Marketing reaches out to consumers of products to help companies build and reposition their brands or products, launch new products, and motivate the news media to talk about products.
- Corporate PR works with executives and managers to help companies interact and develop positive and long-lasting relationships with their key audiences—investors, government officials, employees, and communities.
- Sport and Entertainment leverages its understanding of the industry, usually through existing relationships with sports leagues, agents, performers, producers, and athletes to assist companies in developing messages and relationships through promotion, media relations, and events.

- Wellness Communication can straddle both consumer healthcare (from pharmaceuticals to hospitals) and increased quality-of-life (from spas to organic foods) industries. So the practice might include varied clients. PR activities might include such areas as developing health and wellness brand promotion for companies, or health and wellness messages from government health agencies and associations.
- Technology practices help clients reach consumer and business audiences in the ever-changing industry of high-tech products and services. Activities range from media relations to demonstrating thought leadership in the field.

If you go to the website of a major PR firm such as one of those listed on page 22 of this chapter, others such as Ogilvy & Mather, or Burson-Marsteller, you will find these practice areas and many others. In addition to the practice areas, PR firms apply many strategies and tactics used on behalf of clients within the practice, such as the following:

Corporate Social Responsibility

Corporate social responsibility consists of *strategy and activities designed to assist corporations in delivering their products and services in a manner that reflects good stewardship; respect for the environment, its employees, and citizenry; corporate philanthropy; and interest in solving social issues.* Starbucks farmers' stories, found on its website, are an example of a company's attempt to communicate its commitment to balancing its business need—to grow and buy coffee—with its responsibilities to the communities in which the coffee is produced.

Crisis Communication

Crisis communication consists of *strategic planning and implementation of communication for any situation that threatens the financial stability, veracity, credibility and/or reputation of an organization, or response when national disaster strikes.* You see this in action when companies or individuals are involved in a scandal or when fires and hurricanes hit communities. Everyone connected to the crisis works to keep the news media and the affected audiences up to date on casualties, activities, containment and prevention efforts, and other important information.

Events

Events are *special occasions and experiences used to amplify messages and bring attention to a public relations campaign such as grand openings, community health fairs, movie premieres, and rallies.* The event itself, such the Olympics, Super Bowl, or the Professional Golf Association and Ladies Professional Golf Association tournaments, or a city vying to host the event might be the center of the PR effort. The management of events requires very detailed planning, coordination, and implementation.

Media Relations

Media relations still dominates public relations activities. In order to be strategic, media relations must be based on knowledge of two target audiences—the news media themselves and the audiences to whom they speak. Media relations strategies can be national or local and are always based on knowledge of how the members of the news media perform their jobs. The efforts to generate good relationships and positive news media coverage include many activities: writing news releases, taking inquiry calls from reporters, developing media kits, and writing the many tools of the business such as fact sheets, media advisories, and bios. You see media relations in action whenever a new high-tech product we "cannot live without" is released.

Stories appear on television, radio, and the Internet as the release of the product is anticipated, bringing you tidbits of all the product's capabilities, followed by stories showing consumers waiting in line for the product. After the purchase frenzy, consumers are interviewed about "the experience."

Partnership Development

Partnership development entails *developing and maintaining alliances and cooperation between groups to accomplish objectives that are mutually beneficial to the parties involved*. There are a myriad of possibilities and they happen often: corporations partner with nonprofits, nonprofit organizations develop alliances with other nonprofits, government agencies select nonprofits with which to work, etc. Their shared objectives can create social change, deliver difficult messages, or amplify their individual voices in the marketplace. Examples include Nike, Lance Armstrong, and the Lance Armstrong Foundation.

Message and Materials Development

Message and materials development is *the creation of the campaign messages and collateral materials of a campaign*. The messages are often taglines, headlines, slogans, and lyrics. Materials can be brochures, billboards, giveaways, and a host of other products.

Public Awareness Campaigns

Public awareness campaigns are *public relations initiatives that bring issues, concerns, opportunities, or problems to the attention of members of the public who may be affected*. They are often used to attempt to influence the behaviors, attitudes, and opinions of these target audiences. The public awareness campaign is often the first strategy of a given PR program, but its strategic effectiveness is limited if it is directed toward the *general public*. Many of the accident, injury, and drug prevention campaigns with which you are familiar fall into this category, including safety belt use, buzzed and drunk driving, and tobacco cessation.

Social Marketing

Social marketing is the *application of consumer marketing principles to social issues*. Its hallmark is the use of consumer research to determine how to communicate with target audiences in order to get them to take the actions you want them to take. The most famous of these are "The Five-a-Day," "VERB," and "Red Dress" campaigns. All of these strategies and others are discussed in detail throughout the chapters of this textbook.

As we discussed previously, most practitioners who are employed by corporate or nonprofit organizations are paid a salary. Salaried employees are paid from the budgets of the organization either from profits, investments, donations, or membership fees. Practitioners employed by agencies log their active work on behalf of client as **billable hours,** *hours billed directly to client contracts and budgets by the PR firm*. Billable hours are the foundation of profit for agencies. Because of this, PR agencies hire employees with the expectation that their salaries will be paid through the time the employees spend working on a client contract.

The agencies make their money based on the difference between the amount they offer, or bid, to perform the work and what it actually costs the agency. Agencies mark up the cost of billable hours and services. It is just like the premise of the lemonade stand: In order to make money, you have to charge more than the lemons, sugar, water, and time to prepare cost. (Chapter 11 discusses program budgets in depth.) PR firms expect to assign employees to contracts so that the employees are "100 percent billable" to client accounts on which they are working. An employee does not have to be 100 percent on one account; she can be working on multiple accounts, but the percentage of hours worked and billed to combined accounts must total 100 percent. Employees who cannot be billed to a client account are part of overhead. Overhead means that the employee's salary is billed against what would otherwise be the agency's profit.

The Independent PR Practitioners

Independent public relations counselors are hired to provide advice and strategy to their clients. They usually have extensive experience in public relations and have senior status in the field. Often referred to as *counsel*, senior independent counselors establish the fee for which they will provide counsel and are always paid additionally for travel, accommodations, and other business expenses. Independent counselors are highly valued because their senior-level standing usually means that in addition to extensive experience, they are well connected and can call on other high-level professionals for advice. As well, their professional experience has resulted in keen and well-honed research and analysis skills. For example, public relations counselor Ofield Dukes is legendary in his professional and civic work and has been hired to offer counsel to organizations such as CBS Records, Warner Brothers Records, AT&T, Anheuser-Busch, the U.S. Department of Navy, National Bankers Association, and Don King Productions. He has also been heavily involved in civic work, helping to organize the first Congressional Black Caucus Dinner, serving as advisor to the late Coretta Scott King, and coordinating the first Stevie Wonder March to promote Martin Luther King Jr.'s birthday as a national holiday.

Counselors do not actually implement the plan or tactics that result from their advice. Generally, they present particular findings and recommendations that are then carried out by an organization's staff or the staff of a public relations firm or agency. Instead, the counselor investigates and observes, conducts interviews and research, analyzes, and recommends strategies and courses of action. Like most senior executives, counselors often specialize in specific areas such as political communication or government and congressional relations or offer advice in particular problem situations such as external or internal crises. Counselors are usually greatly valued by those who call them in to provide assistance and are sometimes viewed askance by internal staff, who feel the counselors perhaps have too much influence with those at the top of the hierarchy.

The independent practitioner at all levels—referred to as a freelancer—is usually engaged by clients on a project-by-project basis and is most often paid on a fee basis. Fees may be paid in a variety of ways. The practitioner may work for a flat fee, a fee plus expenses or a fee plus expenses and hours charged. Fee plus expenses and fee plus expenses and hours charged are the most advantageous to the independent practitioner. Flat fee rates can result in a loss of income to the independent because it can be difficult to determine the precise number of hours a project will require, and unexpected expenses will always arise during a project no matter how hard you try to anticipate and negotiate them in advance.

MORE ABOUT PR PRACTITIONERS

Now that you know where the practitioners work, let's discuss the skills they need and the actual work they do. The average day of a PR practitioner is busy with meetings, email, conference calls, planning, brainstorming, discovering and analyzing facts and information, and managing projects and teams.

Practitioners work in several different teams to accomplish varied tasks.

What Characteristics Are Most Common to PR Practitioners?

Stating that all public relations practitioners share the same personalities, skills, and abilities would be a gross exaggeration. And even if they did, no one personality is the "right" personality for a PR practitioner. But they do share some qualities. What does it take to be successful in public relations today?

- Curiosity and a natural desire to probe beyond the obvious
- An inclination toward and an ability to use words—written and spoken—effectively
- Inquisitiveness about a broad range of topics
- Ability to delve into previously obscure and sometimes complex topics and ideas and to make them clear and understood by various audiences
- Analytical, critical thinking skills that result in the ability to define problems and develop creative solutions
- Interest in current events, public opinion, and trends
- Ability to work with a team of people who represent diverse opinions, cultures, backgrounds, and professions

What Skills Do Most PR Practitioners Have?

Most executives at PR firms or agencies agree that they expect to train new employees. They will teach you the business and how to be successful in the business. The training includes the internal processes for success—developing proposals, pitching clients for new work, planning, budgeting, and other elements of the business. In fact, some agencies require that you take a series of courses offered internally. But when asked what skills they value most in employees entering the field of public relations, most employers respond that successful candidates must have excellent written and oral communication skills. These skills are important enough that many organizations require candidates to take written and oral tests before they are granted interviews. But there are other skills crucial to success of the PR professional. She must be able to:

- Analyze formative, process, and evaluation research that is used throughout the strategic PR process. (See Chapters 6 and 9 through 13 for detailed discussion.)
- Analyze internal and external problems and opportunities facing the organization or client.
- Recommend creative solutions to problems.
- Plan programs based on the research, problems, and opportunities uncovered.
- Brief management on internal and external situations requiring communication intervention on programs and activities.
- Plan activities, budgets, and personnel assignments for one or a myriad of activities.
- Establish and monitor timelines and deadlines.
- Manage the development of creative strategies based on research, process, and evaluation findings.
- Organize and coordinate people, resources, logistics, and events.
- Write and edit for many different audiences based on what you know about the audiences and the action you want the audience to take.

What PR Practitioners Do?

Obviously, the skills and abilities a practitioner must possess and the day-to-day functions he must perform in the practice of public relations are closely related. Now let's take a look at what is involved in the day-to-day functions of a PR practitioner. He is responsible for doing the following tasks, or managing them as his career progresses.

1. Plan, coordinate, and implement the partnership and relationship, corporate social responsibility, news media, and stakeholder programs of the organization or individual.
2. Write for the news media, including news releases, fact sheets, backgrounders, photo captions, and quotes for the daily, weekly, newsletter, and trade media.
3. Write speeches, talking points, quotes, columns, and op-eds for spokespersons and principal officers of the organization.
4. Plan and coordinate news conferences, stakeholder conferences, meetings, quarterly reporting calls, and events, and speakers and participants for each.
5. Write and edit publications for internal and external audiences, including focus group and other qualitative data reports, web copy, newsletters, magazines, annual and quarterly reports, brochures, and white papers.
6. Speak on behalf of the corporation in briefings and news conferences during crises and in the absence of the primary spokesperson.
7. Plan and conduct verbal and written briefings of organization principals and spokespersons, including the CEO or director.
8. Attend (or accompany spokespersons) news interviews, special events, speeches, conventions, meetings, and other external activities.
9. Direct creative activities and assist creative staff in selection of photographs, graphics, layout, and design.
10. Work successfully under tight and ever-changing deadlines and deliver on time.

BRIEF CASE STUDY

Florida Teens Tell the Truth

The state of Florida won a $13 billion settlement in 1998 in a lawsuit against the tobacco industry that resulted in the creation of a $200 million budget for a state-run pilot program to fight youth tobacco use. The Florida Tobacco Pilot Program (FTPP) began its operation at a time when nationwide statistics for smoking among teens reached an all-time high, with 36 percent of high school students reporting they used tobacco. Also, 70 percent reported having tried smoking and 35.8 percent of that group intended to continue.

Research showed that teens were well aware of the health risks associated with smoking but didn't consider it a "significant issue" in their lives. Further, teens still saw smoking as an expression of rebellion and a way toward self-identity. After additional research involving talking to teens, the FTPP created a campaign concept that relied on teen involvement in a grassroots advocacy movement against Big Tobacco and an edgy advertising campaign.

Its objectives were to reduce tobacco use among youth, change Florida teens' attitudes about tobacco *and* the tobacco industry, and increase young people's sense of empowerment through community involvement. FTPP wanted to increase its own brand awareness—public knowledge and understanding of the organization—to 85 percent. So the tobacco industry became the "adult establishment" and the youth began to spread the truth about tobacco addiction and the industry's manipulation of its consumers through pop culture and products.

The advertising campaign produced 70 television commercials, 28 radio spots, three cinema trailers, 15 outdoor billboards, and 25 print ads and posters. Campaign tactics used "truth-branded" merchandise distributed by a van that traveled the state, a website, a "Truth" tour, and celebrity spokespersons. It produced results, also. After five months, the FTPP brand awareness rose to 92 percent and youth reporting agreement with negative statements about smoking increased by 15 percent. Nonsmoking teens were more than twice as likely to say they were influenced by the anti-tobacco-industry message with which the industry was trying to manipulate them. More than 10,000 teens joined the Truth advocacy organization and within a year the "current smokers" among middle and high school youth dropped 19 percent and 8 percent, respectively.

Working the Case

1. Review the public relations strategies and tactics listed earlier in the chapter and identify them in this case.
2. What public relations skills are present in this case?

What Educational Background Is Typical of PR Practitioners?

For decades public relations practitioners came to the profession after practicing journalism. This was a logical career transition considering the former emphasis on publicity and media relations and the writing and editing skills needed for PR positions. Former journalists know how the news media work and have friends and colleagues working in the news business, ensuring attention for their story pitches. They also have valuable training at writing and editing to create messages that are clear and concise.

Today, while many of the senior practitioners are former journalists, the majority of PR professionals are trained in other disciplines, including communication and public relations. A solid liberal arts education is crucial to success in this field. Practitioners must have well-rounded educational backgrounds that include the arts, sciences, history, and economics. They should be versed in literature and the cultural arts, know how government functions, and have a keen sense of pop culture and public opinion.

There are almost 200 bachelor's degree programs in public relations in the United States to which liberal arts courses can be added. Many of these programs require a minor from the arts and sciences.

In addition to a degree, previous experience is essential to landing a first job in the field. While it is difficult to get the required experience on a salaried basis, unpaid internships are excellent for building a portfolio. Undergraduate students in our program at American University report that in addition to serving as interns for the one-semester course we provide, they engage in additional internships during the summer and semester breaks. These experiences help them to build significant knowledge and experience and expose them to the intricacies of business. Students find internships at PR and advertising agencies, corporations, nonprofit organizations, and in government. The great advantage of the internships is that they provide on-the-job experience during which they are given the opportunity to assume increased responsibility. As a result, students learn firsthand the roles, functions, and activities of public relations.

The Commission on Public Relations Education, Public Relations Education for the 21st Century released guidelines for education in public relations in 2006. In 2010 the Commission released a report delineating how public relations is being taught at the undergraduate and graduate levels around the world. The findings suggest that public relations curriculum frequently reflects the five-course standard suggested by *The Professional Bond—Public Relations Education and the Practice*, 2006, that identified the following "ideal" courses for undergraduate majors in public relations:

1. Introduction to public relations (including theory, origin, and principles)
2. Case studies in public relations that review the professional practice
3. Public relations research, measurement, and evaluation
4. Public relations law and ethics
5. Public relations writing and production
6. Public relations planning and management
7. Supervised work experience in public relations (internship)
8. Directed electives

For graduate students, the commission recommended mastering the following content areas beyond the undergraduate degree:

1. Public relations theory and concepts
2. Public relations law
3. Public relations ethics
4. Global public relations
5. Public relations applications
6. Public relations management

Beginning to practice before becoming a professional is excellent experience to augment your education. Volunteering to serve as public relations counselor to organizations on campus is also a good idea. Also, the Public Relations Student Society of America (PRSSA), created by the Public Relations Society of America (PRSA) in 1968, has 285 chapters on college and university campuses throughout the United States. The chapters provide preprofessional experiences such as creating campaigns for competition and awards and allows the more than 9,000 student members opportunities to network with each other and PRSA professionals. The PRSSA holds an annual conference and hosts an interesting website for students who are studying and preparing for public relation careers.

ENTERING THE FIELD OF PUBLIC RELATIONS

Representative Job Postings

Clearly, the starting salaries for entry-level positions will vary from organization to organization and from city to city, depending on cost of living and factors affecting business. The titles for entry-level positions in the field vary, but the duties are usually somewhat alike. The following job postings are created from actual listings available online. Take time to look at websites such as www.entrylevelpr.com and www.workinpr.com as often as possible—perhaps every time you are surfing the net. This will help familiarize you with the types of positions available and the titles they carry.

Entry-Level: Communication Assistant
Location: New York
Company: Large newsweekly publisher
Seeking a bright recent college graduate with strong public relations or marketing internships. This entry-level position will support public relations through administrative duties (scheduling, phone support, faxing, travel arrangements, department budget management, etc.) and assist management with public relations initiatives (screening media inquiries, drafting/distributing press materials, coordinating media clippings internally, developing and maintaining a media database, etc.). Must be able to understand and manage the dynamics of internal and external media relations. Requires ability to communicate with senior management and handle confidential information in an appropriate and professional way. A bachelor's degree in PR, English, or Communications is desired. A high energy individual with strong written and verbal communication is necessary in this role. Must be able to juggle multiple tasks simultaneously. Applicants should be highly organized with superb attention to detail. A can-do attitude is a big plus.

Entry-Level: Public Relations Junior Account Executive
Location: San Francisco
Company: Mid-sized public relations agency
Seeking an energetic and bright Junior Account Executive to join the San Francisco office. Junior AEs play an active role on an account team, implementing strategic programs and working closely with clients and account executives. Job duties span a wide range—from compiling and maintaining media lists to pitching media and securing placements to proactively drafting media pitches and suggesting new tactics within the context of ongoing campaigns. Identifying and pursuing new business leads and taking an active role in proposals is encouraged. A Junior Account Executive has formed a solid working knowledge of the media (especially media that cover their clients' industries) and has a well-rounded knowledge of general news trends. A minimum of one year work experience is required. Please send cover letter and resume to jobs@mid-sizedprfirm.com.

Entry-Level: Public Relations Writer
Location: West Bloomfield, MI
Company: Confidential
Public relations agency needs staff member with talent for creating exciting press releases and pitch letters about our clients and their products. Some experience is helpful, but our primary interest is in your ability to write clearly. You must love to write, and almost as importantly, have an understanding and appreciation of marketing. The job package starts in the $30s with a chance for advancement.

Entry-Level: Public Relations AE
Location: New York
Company: Large global PR agency
The large PR Agency's Global Issues Communication group, the industry leader in creating media-focused public relations programs for corporations and organizations to address international political, economic, environmental and human rights issues, seeks an account executive to contribute to high-profile accounts. We require one year or more PR experience along with strong writing, media relations, and organizational skills. PR agency experience preferred. A privately-held company, our agency understands the value of independence: We cherish the freedom to chart our own course, to be creative in our work, and to encourage autonomy in our people while providing the support they need to flourish. This synergy of collaboration and independence is invaluable in growing careers and client reputations.
Email: careers@largePRagency.com

(continued)

Entry-Level: Public Relations AAE
Location: Chicago
Company: Well-known PR firm
Position Type: Full-time regular
Start Date: Immediately
Salary: $30,000–40,000
Responsibilities: Assistant Account Executives execute day-to-day client work under direct supervision of a Senior Account Executive or a higher-level supervisor. Assistant Account Executives play an active role in coordinating and implementing daily account activity on behalf of our clients. Responsibilities include, but are not limited to, competitive analysis and trend tracking by monitoring client and market news coverage, providing instantaneous information using online news services, and collaboration in written materials including pitch letters, status reports, briefing books, biographies, memos, fact sheets, and press releases.
Qualifications/Skills: Skills required include good basic written and verbal skills, proven ability to effectively organize and manage multiple responsibilities, creativity in writing samples, demonstrated ability to work well with others in a team and independent environment, efficiency in word processing, database management and online research, and a positive, flexible attitude that will lend itself to client service. Some professional experience, preferably with agency background preferred. BA degree, preferably in Communications, Journalism, English or PR related discipline.

The PR practice is fascinating, in part, because it requires practitioners who have broad interests and a higher-than-average intellect. Also, it is within itself broad, interesting, and intellectually stimulating. You can become a practitioner in a particular area or line of work, or continue your education with graduate study or develop an expertise that is valuable across practice areas such as speechwriting, technical writing, qualitative and quantitative research design and analysis, and graphic design.

2008 National Graduate Survey

The number of bachelor's degree graduates reporting full-time employment on October 31, 2008, 60.4 percent, is down from 70.2 percent in 2007, reflecting the instability approaching the 2009 economic downturn.

According to the *2009 Annual Survey of Journalism and Mass Communication Graduates*, the median salary for journalism and mass communication bachelor's degree recipients who took a job in public relations remained at $31,000 from 2008. Following are the median annual salaries for 2009 bachelor's degree recipients with full-time jobs, as reported in the survey (see Table 2.2).

PRWeek 2010 Salary Survey

The field of public relations continues to grow and its practitioners tend to be well paid. While the recent economic downturn has resulted in fewer positions and therefore greater competition, the median salary overall has decreased only slightly, to $82,000, from $86,000 the previous year. Earnings depend on many factors. Practitioners in government and nonprofit practice tend to make less than practition ers in agencies and industry. But the financial strength of the organization and the geographic location influence the level of compensation, as well. Practitioners in the American Northeast and West had higher salaries than their colleagues in other parts of the country. Obviously, qualifications affect the salary of practitioners. The more highly educated and experienced make more money.

According to the Salary Survey 2010 sponsored by *PRWeek*, the average salary in public relations for a person with fewer than two years experience was more than $37,000. An account supervisor of a consulting firm earned upwards of $65,000. An account manager earned an average of $60,000, and the range for a senior manager for a large corporation was $100,000 and up.

Seasoned public relations executives earn salaries from $75,000 to more than $215,000 with outstanding benefits. These practitioners are usually the strategists, counselors, and business development employees and are vice presidents and executive vice presidents of the organizations.

Disparity Continues among Genders   Men with more than five years experience report a median salary of $130,000, while the median salary for women with similar experience is $90,000. While this can be partly explained by the fact that the average male respondent has been in PR for 15 years, while the average female has been in the industry for only 11.7 years, there is also a disparity when looking only at those who have been in the industry for under five years. For this group, the median male salary is $50,000, while the median female salary is just $43,000. Women make up 53.1 percent of those PR professionals categorized as "PR managers" by the Bureau of Labor Statistics.

Table 2.2	Median Annual Salaries of Bachelor's Degree for 2009
Job	**Annual Salary**
Internet	$31,200
Specialized information publishers	$32,000
Public relations	$31,000
Consumer magazines	$30,500
Advertising	$32,000
Cable television	$26,500
Television	$24,900
Daily newspapers	$27,000
Weekly newspapers	$25,000
Radio	$29,000

SOURCE: "The Professional Bond—Public Relations Education and the Practice," 2006, Commission on Public Relations Education for the 21st Century

Tips for Building a Successful Career in PR

Of course you have to get there first, so let's look at two of the most valuable experiences you can take into an interview—internships and portfolios.

Internships

Internships are absolute musts if you intend to build a career in public relations. The academic internship provided through your campus career center or the department in which your program is housed is one option. You should take full advantage of it. Many organizations are pleased to offer internships and many need the help. The competition for internships in larger organizations or public relations firms is stiff, but internships are possible to secure. You can find internships in smaller organizations that will provide great experience, also. Sometimes the experience you gain in smaller organizations can help prepare you for competing for the agency internships. Smaller organizations *really* need the help. They often have no public relations counsel, have only volunteer or pro bono assistance, or are using a how-to guide. An internship in these organizations can mean very meaningful work and experience you cannot get in larger organizations.

Interns receive professional experience while working.

If you are unable to secure the internships you want consider the following:

- Volunteer or work for just expenses. Many small and non-profit organizations can use the help.
- If you miss an opportunity to land your first job in a public relations department or agency, take a position that is allied to the practice with an advertising agency, design company, a marketing department, or a newsletter company.
- Begin requesting informational interviews right away. These are interviews in which you are not seeking employment but are just learning more about the field. Personal contacts can result in networking, and networking can result in jobs.

Portfolios

Portfolios were once the domain of art students, but not anymore. Public relations students and entry-level professionals should keep an up-to-date portfolio of the work they have developed. The portfolio is an excellent opportunity to demonstrate your professional work. Students at American University are required to volunteer for a nonprofit organization or for an aspiring artist or designer who cannot afford expert PR assistance. They then work with those clients to determine their public relations needs and create a limited number of public relations media or products for them. Your products should be contained in a binder with removable plastic sheet covers. Take advantage of the many table-of-contents systems available in office supply stores and create a professional looking table of contents with corresponding tabs that explain what is located behind each tab. You can also design impressive covers for your portfolio with a little creativity and help from online sources for images. The contents should include a professional quality resume and biographical sketch and products such as news releases, media advisories, newsletters, web page screen shots, brochures, ads, radio and television public service announcement scripts, fact sheets, backgrounders, speeches, media kits, and/or other PR items you have produced. Descriptions of these items and others are explained throughout the tactics chapters of this textbook (Chapters 14, 15, and 16).

Lastly, though very important, learn another language. Public relations is global domestically and internationally, as our population grows more diverse with every passing day. Practitioners with the ability to speak, write, and comprehend other languages are very valuable, and employers are more likely to hire candidates who speak at least one additional language.

After securing your first job, enthusiasm for your work, networking and maintaining relationships, flexibility in your schedule, and exploring new interests, cultures, and lifestyles will be crucial to success. You must be willing to do what must be done to get the projects accomplished. Remember, everyone has to make copies and stuff media kits sometimes. Also, take advantage of every opportunity to learn something new. Eventually, the diversity of skills, expertise, and background you accumulate will be impressive and will help you climb the ladder.

ENGAGING ETHICS

To Be or Not to Be PR Director

You have just completed a year as an administrative assistant to the executive director of a small, local nonprofit that assists battered women and children. You worked there two summers as the volunteer PR director, as well. You really want to get into PR and intend to apply for an entry-level position at a small public relations agency. The online ad states, "one year of professional experience required." Are you eligible for this position? Should you reflect your PR director position as "professional" experience? With whom should you talk to determine if you should apply for this position?

PROFESSIONAL POINT OF VIEW

True Diversity Starts with the Appropriate Mindset

Helen Ostrowski wrote this point of view for PRWeek *while global CEO of Porter Novelli.*

Move over Hilfiger and Lauren. FUBU, Phat Farm, and other urban brands are America's fastest-growing fashion segment. Rap's more popular than pop among young people. The metrosexual look, guayabera shirts, and Japanese manga are mainstream. Increasingly, the "edges" of American society are defining the mainstream—what we eat, what we read, what we watch, what we find sexy ("buttocks are the new breasts," per a recent *New York Times* article). More than ever, our world is defined and driven by diversity. While baby boomers grew up in a world where whites outnumbered nonwhites 4 to 1, the world of Gen

Y kids is 1.5 to 1. During their lifetime, the children of Gen Y will be living in a minority-majority country.

What does "diversity" mean? Diversity is the mixture of similarities and differences. Sure, it includes race, gender, and ethnicity, but also lifestyle, functional expertise, age, and thinking style. Diversity is white and Asian-American, straight and gay, quantitative and creative, urban and country.

For those of us who make our living communicating with the world around us, it is critical that we understand that world from the inside out. We must be representative of our clients and their constituents if we want to deeply understand them.

To make your organization more diverse, you have to foster a "diversity mindset." Certainly, racial and ethnic diversity are important. However, representation alone is not sufficient to foster an environment in which people with differences—and different ideas—thrive. Organizations need to embrace and value differences—proactively, enthusiastically, and naturally. That means moving beyond the natural instinct to relate to those who think like they do and reaching out to those who think differently and have different backgrounds or points of view.

Consider this: Before a minority candidate comes to your firm for an interview, she has already checked you out. Her network of friends and connections is at two degrees of separation, not six. Minority candidates don't care most about the numbers—numbers just tell you representation. They want to know: Is this an environment where people who are "different" can grow and build a great career?

Your company has a reputation for how diversity really plays out. Do you know what that is? How can you enhance the reality—and thus the reputation—of your organization?

The business rationale for diversity is something we as a profession understand. Creating an environment where a "diversity mindset" thrives can be easier said than done. Here are some starting points:

Talk about it. Tensions often go hand-in-hand with differences. But often, instead of using differences as a source of creative energy and new thinking, people avoid dealing with them. You might start by bringing staff together in an open, non-judgmental environment. Help them reach a shared perspective on what diversity is and what a diversity-friendly environment looks and feels like. Ask your staff: Do you feel accepted for who you are? What are we doing well in promoting diversity? What are some opportunities to improve? Just getting the subject "out of the closet" is a start.

Learn about it. Hold brown-bag sessions with outside speakers who can help de-mystify diversity and share best practices. Invest in diversity training. Bring people along and help them get comfortable with the fact that "diversity" includes everyone, and that everyone can gain from a diversity mindset.

Model it. Embracing differences, welcoming debate, and fostering new ideas starts at the top. It must be constantly reinforced in word and deed. You must make investments in recruiting and relationships that advance the ball on diversity—internships, partnerships, and new hires. You must insist on a culture that values each person's uniqueness and contributions. Commit to, and be accountable for, milestones like diversity training, a mentoring program, and affinity groups.

Diversity is not a trend or a "nice-to-have." It's a strategic imperative, especially in the PR profession. We must think about it broadly—as a transformational issue and a competitive advantage. It takes all kinds of people, styles, approaches, and ideas to ensure we have the human assets that are an organization's only point of sustainable advantage.

SOURCE: Helen Ostrowski, *PRWeek*, December 13, 2004

Summary and Review

Where Do PR Practitioners Work?

- Public relations is practiced in almost every type of organization and industry. Business, nonprofit, and government are the three major American sectors. But public relations is practiced globally as well, with practitioners working all over the world.
- Public relations practitioners can work as employees in organizations where they perform their jobs according to a position description. Other practitioners work for public relations firms and research companies who have organizations, individuals, and possibly the governments of other countries as clients. These practitioners are a part of teams, have position descriptions, and are paid by the firms for which they work. Other practitioners act as independent counsels to organizations and individuals and are paid for their advice and years of experience. The freelance practitioner usually works for clients on a fee-per-project or fee-plus-expenses basis, invoicing the client as particular milestones are accomplished.
- The various element, components, or activities of the strategic PR practice also help explain how practitioners work in the field. While the entry-level job descriptions in the chapter help you to understand the tasks performed by people entering the field, description of these activities, contained in other chapters, is helpful, also.
- PR practitioners work in organizations in the for-profit, nonprofit, and government sectors. They can work within the organizations, as employees of the public relations firms, or as independent counselors.

More about PR Practitioners

- Some characteristics shared by PR practitioners include analytical and critical thinking skills, probing nature, ability to make complex topics clear and easily understood, and ability to identify, solve, and prevent problems.
- While employers provide training for entry-level practitioners, most practitioners have at least a bachelor's degree with a substantial liberal arts focus, including the arts, sciences, history, and economics. Also, they should be versed in politics, public opinion, literature, and the cultural arts. They must have previous experience, including internships, to secure even entry-level positions.

Entering the Field of Public Relations

- Internships or volunteer experiences count as previous background in the field. Portfolios of products produced while working on your degree and in preprofessional experiences are good for presentation at employment interviews.
- Practitioners must have strong written and oral presentation skills and strong skills in working in collaboration with others.

Key Terms

billable hours

corporate social
    responsibility

crisis communication

events

message and materials
    development

partnership
    development

public awareness
    campaigns

social marketing

Questions for Review and Discussion

1. Look at the characteristics of most PR practitioners and the skills they possess. Devise a matrix that helps you understand how the characteristics relate to the skills. Discuss the personal characteristics public relations practitioners should have. How many do you think you possess? Which characteristics do you think you need to work on acquiring? What can you do to acquire them?

2. The prospects for positions in public relations look very bright through 2014. Consider the existing specialty areas described in this chapter, your own interests, and what you think the hot markets will be when you graduate. Discuss the areas you think will be most abundant and interesting to you.

3. Let's say you are a strategic thinker. How would you chart your PR career beginning with today? List the steps you would take, and assign deadlines to the things you need to accomplish before graduation.

Web Links

Porter Novelli (global public relations firm)
www.porternovelli.com

Public Relations Society of America
www.prsa.org

Public Relations Student Society of America
prssa.org/
commpred.org

Association for Education in Journalism and Mass Communication
http://lamar.colostate.edu/~aejmcpr/

Historical Perspective

FIRST FRUITS: PR IN THE COLONIES AND THE EARLY UNITED STATES

The roots of modern American public relations reach back more than 400 years to promotional, fundraising, and advertising campaigns, the earliest of which predate the first permanent settlements in the New World. The American Revolution was the result, in part, of a brilliant campaign to rally support for a war for independence. Likewise, the expansion of the country into the West and the growth of American industry in the 19th century depended on public advocates. In these efforts we can find the first flowerings of what would grow into the modern public relations industry.

The history of PR is . . . a history of a battle for what is reality and how people will see and understand reality.

—Stuart Ewen,
author of *PR! A History of Social Spin*

The three main elements of public relations are practically as old as society: informing people, persuading people, or integrating people with people. Of course, the means and methods of accomplishing these ends have changed as society has changed.

—Edward Bernays,
pioneer in public relations

Hyping the "New World"

Numerous New World explorers—and the owners of trading companies who sponsored them—produced promotional materials to lure English settlers to the colonies
and raise money for the ventures. Much of the publicity contained glowing descriptions of the land and exaggerated claims of its resources. The English navigators Philip
Amadas and Arthur Barlowe, exploring for Sir Walter Raleigh in 1584, brought back
this account of coastal North Carolina: "The soile is the most plentiful, sweete, fruit-
ful and wholesome of all the worlde . . . they have . . . the highest and reddest Cedars
of the world." Their descriptions were recorded by Richard Hakluyt in *The Principal
Navigations, Voyages, Traffiques & Discoveries of the English Nation* (1589). Raleigh's
attempt to establish the Roanoke colony provided material for Thomas Hariot's
A Brief True Report of the New Found Land of Virginia (1588), which contained similar reports. Other publicity brochures drew settlers to Maryland, Georgia, Florida,
and other colonies.

The First College Fundraisers

Fundraising was a major activity of the early colonists. The first college public relations
pamphlet was the product of a **"begging mission"**—*an early American fund raising
campaign*—organized in 1641 by the Massachusetts Bay Colony to raise money for
Harvard College. The preachers who went back to England on the mission sent word
to the college that they needed a "condensed document"—what we would now call a
fundraising brochure—to help sell the institution to potential contributors. The result
was "New England's First Fruits," published in 1643, the first college public relations
pamphlet. In 1758, King's College, now Columbia University, became the first to
use commencement exercises for publicity and fundraising. Almost 150 years later,
in 1897, the University of Michigan established the first campus public relations
office. In 1917, the group that was to become the Council for Advancement and
Support of Education was founded.

Selling the "New Republic"

The men who steered the American colonies toward the war of independence from
England understood the necessity of first winning the war for the minds of the colonists. They were brilliant strategists, and the existence of the United States is the
result, in part, of the success of their grand public relations campaign. During the
run-up to the American Revolution, when England's King George III refused to meet
the colonists' demands for fair taxation, the revolutionaries set about turning public
opinion against the British. Loyalists—those sympathetic to the crown—were in the
majority, so the dissenters had their work cut out for them. They popularized slogans,
such as "Taxation without representation is tyranny," to ignite public sentiment. They
made fiery speeches, organized events, and distributed newspapers, pamphlets, and
other correspondence to win their fellow colonists over to their cause.

The big names of the day included Samuel Adams, Alexander Hamilton, John
Jay, James Madison, who would become the fourth president of the United States,
Thomas Paine, and Paul Revere. Adams, who has been called the press agent of

the revolution, organized Committees of Correspondence to spread anti-British **propaganda**—described as *the party line*—throughout the colonies and helped stage events, such as the Boston Tea Party—during which pounds of English tea were dramatically dumped into the harbor—to build up revolutionary fervor. Paine wrote the now-famous pamphlets "Common Sense" and the "American Crisis" to urge colonists to fight for independence. Revere tipped off all his countrymen to the arrival of British troops along his midnight ride to warn Adams that he would soon be arrested.

After their victory over the British, the same group of colonists set about creating a new government. Delegates were sent by the states to the Constitutional Convention in Philadelphia, which completed drafting the Constitution on Sept. 17, 1787. Fierce fights over its ratification broke out in many of the states. The federalists, who supported the Constitution, mounted a campaign to sway public opinion, battling the opposition in the press. Under the pseudonym "Publius," Hamilton, Jay, and Madison wrote letters, now known as the Federalist Papers, to leading newspapers, recommending the Constitution and urging readers to support it. Their campaign succeeded. On July 2, 1788, when New Hampshire ratified the Constitution—bringing the total number of states ratifying to nine, the required number—the Constitution became formally accepted.

The Growth of Advertising

The first advertisements for products and services were print ads that ran in colonial newspapers. These ads ranged from commonplace announcements of goods for sale to notices of slave auctions or appeals for the capture of runaway slaves. The first regularly published colonial newspaper to carry ads was the *Boston News-Letter*, which began the practice in the early 1700s. Unlike today's eye-catching, bold designs, the first ads were lines of plain type. In the 1730s, Benjamin Franklin tried to make ads more readable by printing them with larger headlines in his *Pennsylvania Gazette*.

Daniel Acker/Bloomberg via Getty Images

The current Morton Salt Girl

The first advertising agency in the United States was begun in 1841, when Volney B. Palmer set up shop in Philadelphia as an agent, placing ads in newspapers. He used copy written by the advertisers, rather than writing original ads. In 1869, Palmer was bought out by Francis Ayer, who founded N. W. Ayer & Son, an agency that lasted until 2002. Ayer transformed the advertising business by charging commissions for space that he sold, conducting market research and writing advertising copy. The agency went on to become remarkable for coining some of the most memorable ad slogans in U.S. advertising history, including "When it rains it pours," for Morton Salt in 1911; "I'd walk a mile for a Camel," for R.J. Reynolds Tobacco in 1921; "A diamond is forever," for De Beers in 1948; "Reach out and touch someone," for AT&T's long-distance telephone service in 1979; and "Be all you can be," for the United States Army in 1981.

Celebrity endorsements for products started in 1870, when Henry Ward Beecher, a well-known orator and brother of writer Harriet Beecher Stowe, appeared in a *Harper's Weekly* magazine advertisement endorsing Waltham watches. In 1879, John Wanamaker, owner of Wanamaker's department store in Philadelphia placed the first full-page department store ad in a newspaper. Other large department stores, such as Macy's in New York and Marshall Field's in Chicago, followed suit and invented new advertising styles. Mail-order catalogs from Sears Roebuck and Montgomery Ward department stores sold everything from sinks to kits with blueprints and materials for building homes.

Modern advertising began in the 1880s, when industries from soap to cigarettes tried to find buyers for their brand-name goods. Prior to the 1880s, marketing had depended on wholesalers, who bought goods in large lots and sold them in smaller ones, putting their own names on the products. When advances in technology enabled manufacturers to make more goods at lower costs and to package them at the plant, brand names replaced wholesaler names, and national advertising emerged. Within a few decades, advertising became a key weapon in the arsenal of companies fighting for brand loyalty and market share.

Tall-Tale Tellers and Tricksters

Many of the 19th-century ad men were hucksters, who relied on exaggerated claims, outrageous promises or outright lies to win consumers' attention. One of the most notorious campaigns was the promotion of **patent medicines**—*potions and pills that, by virtue of their having been patented, were touted as cures for just about everything.* Bonnore's Electro Magnetic Bathing Fluid, for example, claimed to cure "cholera, neuralgia, epilepsy, scarlet fever, necrosis, mercurial eruptions, paralysis, hip diseases, chronic abscesses, and 'female complaints.'" One infamous group of patent medicines was liniments that allegedly contained snake oil, a supposed reliever of aches and pains. To this day, **"snake-oil salesman"** remains *a synonym for a charlatan.*

Several products, which are still on the market today, such as the over-the-counter drugs Bromo-Seltzer, Luden Brothers Cough Drops and Phillips' Milk of Magnesia, began as patent medicines. One of the most famous is Coca-Cola, which initially sold as a patent medicine for 5 cents a glass. Its name was derived from the original formula, which contained coca leaves, a stimulant, and kola nuts, a source of caffeine. Early Coke ads claimed the soft drink cured morphine addiction, dyspepsia, neurasthenia, headache, and impotence. Today, with its formula changed and advertisements revised, the "real thing" is, of course, still a top seller.

Vintage Coca-Cola logo

In addition to print advertisements, makers of patent medicines also hawked their wares at the **"medicine show,"** *a kind of traveling circus that combined vaudeville acts with sales pitches.* In a typical show, musclemen would tout the physical vigor offered by the potion, and then shills would step forward from the crowd to offer "unsolicited testimonials." Oftentimes, the potion was made and bottled in the show wagon! The medicine show lived on in American folklore long after it had vanished from the touring circuit.

The demise of patent medicines was precipitated, to a large extent, by the work of muckraker journalists, principally Samuel Hopkins Adams. (As described later in this chapter's section "Teddy Roosevelt and the Muckrakers," a **muckraker** is *someone who "rakes through the muck," meaning brings to light negative information about a person or organization*.) While the labels and ads for patent medicines often listed exotic ingredients, the potions often contained opium extracts, cocaine, grain alcohol, or other unlisted drugs. Taking the potions could result in drug addiction and even death. In 1905, Adams published an exposé entitled "The Great American Fraud" in *Collier's Weekly* that led to the passage of the first Pure Food and Drug Act the following year. The law required that all ingredients be accurately listed on drug labels and curbed fraudulent advertising claims.

Other examples of the American genius for promotion can be found in the publicity-making stunts of 19th-century publicists, who specialized in promoting circuses, theatrical performances, and other public spectacles. The master of them all was the legendary showman P.T. Barnum, whose publicity stunts made "the greatest show on Earth" an irresistible draw wherever it played.

Barnum began his career in 1836 by exhibiting Joice Heth—an old slave woman whom he claimed to be 160 years old—as "George Washington's childhood nursemaid." He aroused public debate about the stunt by writing letters—all signed with fake names—to the editors of New York newspapers. Some of the fake letters praised Barnum for public service; others of the fake letters criticized him as a bold-faced liar and a scoundrel. He kept the public guessing and coming to his show. When Heth died, an autopsy showed she was about 80 years old. Barnum claimed to be shocked by the way the woman had deceived him. What the man who said "There's a sucker born every minute" knew about publicity was that it did not matter what the newspapers said about him, as long as they said it often.

ENGAGING ETHICS

Jeremy Jaynes, Modern Snake-Oil Salesman

AP Photo/Loudoun County Sheriff's office

Jeremy Jaynes

In November 2004, Jeremy Jaynes and his sister, Jessica DeGroot, were convicted in the first U.S. felony prosecution of spam distributors. The team sent unsolicited emails with fraudulent, untraceable routing information to millions of America Online customers. Using various aliases, such as "Gaven Stubberfield" and "National Wealth Builders Corp.," the two peddled a variety of get-rich-quick schemes on the Internet.

One such scheme, the "FedEx refund processor," supposedly allowed people to earn $75 an hour while working from home. In one month alone, Jaynes received 10,000 credit card orders, each for $39.95, for the processor, and he quickly amassed a personal fortune. Samuel Fishel, the state prosecutor who brought the two to trial said, "This was just a case of fraud. This is a snake-oil salesman in a new format."

Jaynes and his sister were prosecuted under the CAN-SPAM Act of 2003 (Controlling the Assault of Non-Solicited Pornography and Marketing Act), which became effective January 1, 2004. The law establishes requirements for those who send commercial email, spells out penalties for spammers and companies whose products are advertised in spam if they violate the law, and gives consumers the right to ask emailers to stop spamming them.

As a public relations professional, you will be involved in mass emailing for legitimate purposes. What steps should you take to avoid spamming?

The Railroad Industry: Greasing the Wheels

The railroad, the first major industry in the United States, was also the first industry to use advertising and depend on public relations. In the early days, the railroad used public speeches, conventions, pamphlets, and newspaper articles to convince the public that railroad travel was better than other means, such as stagecoach and steamboat, and to attract investors. Beginning in 1830, when the Baltimore and Ohio train schedules were first published in Baltimore newspapers, the railroads used the press to attract customers. They promoted excursions and produced guidebooks. With the construction of the transcontinental railroad, the industry became a principal promoter of settlement in the western states.

Many public relations historians also credit the railroads with the first use of the press release. While public relations pioneer Ivy Lee is often credited with developing the modern press release (see later section on Lee for a discussion of his influence), earlier forms of the release had been around for several decades. In the late 1800s, railroad owners, who were often in conflict with their workers, used press releases to create a favorable public impression of the industry. Soon the release was adopted by most large organizations. Ohio Bell Telephone, for example, found that handing out releases kept reporters from coming to telephone rate hearings and asking questions about rates. But more often, releases were used to attract reporters to press briefings.

At first, press releases were considered a form of advertising, and some newspapers charged to publish them. But the release soon became accepted as a free source of news and information that reporters could use as they wished. The advent of television led to the development of video news releases, or VNR. Today, with the growth of the Internet, many public relations practitioners email their releases, and organizations with websites archive them online, making releases accessible to anyone who wants to read them.

The Rise of Big Business: "The Public Be Damned"

At the start of consumerism in the United States, business tycoons obviously did not care about their companies' relationships with consumers. When asked by a Chicago reporter if railroads should be run as a public trust, railroad magnate William H. Vanderbilt famously retorted, "The public be damned." The year was 1882. *The decades surrounding the turn of the 20th century*—the so-called **Gilded Age**—saw the rapid growth of railroads, utilities, and other industries, whose owners amassed significant power and wealth, often at the expense of the public and their own employees. Trade unions emerged to fight for decent wages, hours, and working conditions for laborers, and owners and organized labor often went head to head.

Two famous examples of labor disputes of the time were the Homestead and the Pullman strikes. The Homestead strike began on June 29, 1892, when workers from the Amalgamated Association of Iron and Steel Workers struck the Carnegie Steel Co. plant in Homestead, Pennsylvania, over wage cuts. General manager Henry C. Frick, determined to break the union, hired 300 Pinkerton detectives to protect strikebreakers and the plant. Fighting broke out between the workers and the detectives, leaving seven workers and nine Pinkertons dead and scores injured. The governor called out the state militia. The plant reopened, the "scabs"—nonunion workers—stayed on the job, and the strike was broken.

The Pullman strike started on May 11, 1894, when workers at Pullman Palace Car Co. outside Chicago struck to protest the company's cutting wages while refusing to lower rents in company-owned housing where workers were forced to live. The striking workers sought support from their union. On June 26, the American Railway Union called for a boycott of all Pullman railway cars. Within days, railroad traffic out of Chicago came to a standstill. The railroad owners sought federal intervention, and on July 4, President Grover Cleveland sent troops to Chicago. Rioting and bloodshed followed, but the strike and the boycott soon collapsed.

While both companies won their labor battles, in time the American public began to question the methods and motives of big business. Corporations found themselves in need of friendly messengers, and corporate public relations took hold. Stuart Ewen, author of *PR! A Social History of Spin*, describes the industry's beginnings cynically in this way:

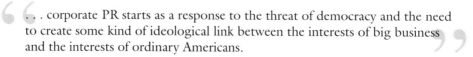

> . . . corporate PR starts as a response to the threat of democracy and the need to create some kind of ideological link between the interests of big business and the interests of ordinary Americans.

THE EVOLUTION OF MODERN PR

Modern public relations began to take shape after the turn of the 20th century. New corporations, eager for market share and positive media attention, quickly learned the benefit of using publicity to attract customers and investors and to court public favor. Public leaders and politicians also saw the value in media campaigns to win people over to their agendas. Companies and government agencies set up press bureaus, often hiring former newspapermen as their publicists, to circulate their views. Social activists also recognized the power of public communication to influence public thought and behavior. They mobilized the grassroots, using increasingly sophisticated public relations techniques. During the century, public relations evolved into an industry, shaping and being shaped by three interrelated arenas of modern life—corporate and nonprofit businesses, politics and government, and social reform movements.

The First Public Relations Firm

The first American public relations firm was the Publicity Bureau, established in Boston in 1900 by former newspapermen George V.S. Michaelis, Herbert Small, and Thomas O. Marvin. The firm gained national prominence in 1906, when it was employed by the nation's railroads to defeat the Hepburn Act, a regulatory measure that gave the U.S. Interstate Commerce Commission the power to fix railroad rates. The bill was supported by President Theodore Roosevelt, who understood that the media could be used as a tool to influence the public and Congress. Roosevelt mounted his own campaign, and the bill was passed. The Publicity Bureau closed down five years later, but not before it had made its mark. In the decades that followed, public relations consulting became an influential field.

Teddy Roosevelt and the Muckrakers

Roosevelt had a keen sense of news and knew how to use the media to advance the "Square Deal," his program based on the belief that government should represent all the people. So while the term *media relations* was not yet coined, the former president was employing it. In 1902, he helped settle a coal strike on terms favorable to the miners, the first time a president who intervened in a strike sided with organized labor. He sued several large corporations to break up monopolies and encourage competition. His slogan, "Walk softly, and carry a big stick," helped popularize his reputation as a trustbuster. He used the president's "bully pulpit" to refute the widely held notion that "what is good for big business is good for America."

But Roosevelt also believed that big business made good sense economically and that most large corporations should be regulated, not destroyed. He used his persuasive powers to push regulatory legislation such as the Hepburn Act. Roosevelt is also credited with naming the "muckrakers," as mentioned briefly earlier, a group of American journalists, novelists, and critics whose writings exposed corporate abuse and political corruption in early 20th century America. The name derives from the word "muckrake," which Roosevelt used in a 1906 speech. He compared the writers to a character in John Bunyan's *Pilgrim's Progress*—the man with the muckrake who could only look down at the filth on the floor with a muckrake in his hands and was only interested in raking filth and ignored the celestial crown offered him. While Roosevelt agreed with many of the writers' charges, he thought some of their *methods were sensational and irresponsible and that they were "raking filth" with their pens.* The movement lost support around 1912.

Among the most famous muckrakers were Lincoln Steffens, who exposed political corruption in Minneapolis, Ida Tarbell, who wrote a scathing history of Standard Oil, and Upton Sinclair, whose book *The Jungle* revealed in graphic detail the abuses of the Chicago meat-packing industry. Many of their stories where published in the first mass-circulation magazines, publications such as *McClure's*, *Everybody's*, and *Collier's*, which gave the writers financial backing for their investigations, as well as a wide readership. Their exposés put politicians and corporations on the defensive and encouraged the growth of corporate public relations departments.

Ivy Lee: Public Relations Pioneer

Ivy Ledbetter Lee—like most early public relations practitioners—was a former newspaperman. In 1904, he formed a partnership with another former reporter, George E. Parker. Their firm, Parker & Lee, lasted less than four years, but Lee went on to become a trailblazer in the industry.

Lee defined his philosophy of public relations in his **Declaration of Principles,** *the first articulation of the idea that public relations practitioners have a responsibility to the general public.* In theory, he believed that business should tell its story openly and accurately in order to win public understanding and support. In 1906, Lee wrote:

> This is not a secret press bureau. All our work is done in the open. We aim to supply news. This is not an advertising agency; if you think any of our matter properly ought to go to your business office, do not use it. Our matter is accurate. Further details on any subject treated will be supplied promptly, and any editor will be assisted most cheerfully in verifying directly any statement of fact. In brief, our plan is, frankly and openly, on behalf of the

Ivy Ledbetter Lee

> business concerns and public institutions, to supply to the press and public of the United States prompt and accurate information concerning subjects which is of value and interest to the public to know about.

His philosophy seemed a radical departure from Vanderbilt's "the public be damned" attitude. Lee said companies should strive to earn public confidence and be candid with the media. He suggested that good publicity be grounded in good corporate performance. He is credited with early efforts at building brand awareness and loyalty and with trying to engineer a more positive image for big business. He described the relationship between corporations and the public as a "two-way street" and the job of public relations practitioners as helping their clients listen to the public, as well as send messages to them.

In practice, however, Lee is often accused of propagandizing on behalf of powerful clients. His most famous client was the Rockefeller family, who engaged Lee's services after the so-called Ludlow Massacre, one of the most dramatic confrontations between business and labor in U.S. history. In September 1913, the miners at the Rockefeller-owned Colorado Fuel and Iron Company (CF&I) in Ludlow, Colorado, went on strike for improved working conditions, better wages, and union recognition. Coal miners in Colorado and other western states had been trying to join the United Mine Workers of America (UMWA) for many years but were bitterly opposed by the coal operators, led by CF&I. Once the strike began, the miners and their families were evicted from their company-owned houses; they set up a tent colony on public property.

On the morning of April 20, 1914, an accidental shot was fired at Ludlow. What followed was a bloody 14-hour battle, during which the miners' tent colony was hit with machine-gun fire and burned by the state militia. Several people were killed, among them two women and 11 children who suffocated in a pit they had dug under their tent. Ludlow is now a ghost town, and the site, owned by the UMWA, is marked by a statue in memory of the miners and their families who died that day.

The event caused a national scandal, and the deaths were blamed on John D. Rockefeller Jr., who hired Lee to help him with damage control. Lee produced a series of bulletins entitled "Facts Concerning the Strike in Colorado for Industrial Freedom," which he distributed throughout the country to editors, business and professional leaders, teachers, public officials, and other opinion leaders. According to Ewen,

> . the bulletins were designed to simulate objective evidence, proving that the pillage at Ludlow was not the work of the mine operators and their armies, but of 'well-paid agitators sent out by the union.'

The bulletins were widely dismissed as propaganda. The *San Francisco Star* reported that "Lee twisted facts, and invented some that he couldn't find outside his imagination." Another newspaper, the *Toledo Blade*, wrote that "It [the bulletins] swelled the postal receipts and added to the tonnage of houses that buy waste paper. But for education, there was none at all." The poet Carl Sandburg called Lee a "hired slanderer" and a "paid liar." Progressive journalist George Creel accused Lee of being a "poisoner of public opinion." The label "Poison Ivy" branded him for years.

Yet, Lee was able to depict Rockefeller as a benefactor. The Rockefeller family engaged in charitable giving but had done little to publicize the fact. Lee used every opportunity to get coverage by the newsreels that showed this side of Rockefeller in order to soften the image of a heartless and greedy businessman who was partly responsible for the massacre in Ludlow. Lee made a somewhat obvious public relations blunder when he agreed in 1934 to assist the German Dye Trust improving relations between Nazi Germany and America. He died with the accusation of being a Nazi sympathizer hanging over him.

World War I and the Creel Committee

Many of the first public relations professionals got their start serving on the *Committee for Public Information*, better known as the **Creel Committee,** during the years of the United States' involvement in World War I, 1917–1919. President Woodrow Wilson established the committee on the advice of his longtime friend, journalist George Creel. Wilson had been reelected to the White House in 1916 on the promise that he would keep the country out of "the bloody conflict that had been raging across Europe since 1914." When it became clear that involvement in the war was inevitable, Creel convinced Wilson that he needed to advertise a "coherent pro-war policy." The Creel Committee published more than 75 million pamphlets and books, educating the American public on everything from "Why We Are Fighting" to "What Our Enemy Really Is." The committee was the *predecessor to the U.S. Office of War Information, the government's propaganda arm during World War II.*

Edward Bernays: "Father of Spin"?

While some historians consider Ivy Lee the first practitioner of modern public relations, Edward Bernays is generally regarded as the industry's founder. After working on the Creel Committee, Bernays opened his office for "counsel in public relations" in New York in June 1919. In 1922, he married Doris Fleischman, and together they ran their firm and counseled major corporations, government agencies, and several U.S. presidents from Calvin Coolidge to Dwight Eisenhower. He taught the first college-level course in public relations at New York University and became a proponent of licensing public relations professionals in order to regulate the profession.

Edward Bernays

Born in Vienna in 1891, Bernays was the nephew of Sigmund Freud. "When a person would first meet Bernays," Cutlip writes, "it would not be long until Uncle Sigmund would be brought into the conversation. His relationship with Freud was always in the forefront of his thinking and his counseling." Another historian, Irwin Ross, remarked, "Bernays liked to think of himself as a kind of psychoanalyst to troubled corporations." Bernays drew many of his ideas from Freud's theories about the irrational and unconscious motives that shape human behavior. He saw public relations as an "applied social science" that uses insights from psychology and other social sciences to "engineer consent," or manipulate how an irrational and "herd-like" public thinks and behaves. In his book, *Propaganda*, written in 1928, Bernays wrote:

> The conscious and intelligent manipulation of the organized habits and opinions of the masses is an important element in democratic society. Those who manipulate this unseen mechanism of society constitute an invisible government, which is the true ruling power of our country. . . . We are governed, our minds are molded, our tastes formed, our ideas suggested, largely by men we have never heard of. This is a logical result of the way in which our democratic society is organized. Vast numbers of human beings must cooperate in this manner if they are to live together as a smoothly functioning society. . . . In almost every act of our daily lives, whether in the sphere of politics or business, in our social conduct or our ethical thinking,

we are dominated by the relatively small number of persons . . . who understand the mental processes and social patterns of the masses. It is they who pull the wires, which control the public mind.

In addition to *Propaganda*, Bernays authored several other important books, including *Crystallizing Public Opinion* in 1923 and *The Engineering of Consent* in 1947.

In contrast to Lee, who claimed to be very open, Bernays was quite candid about the closed and manipulative nature of some public relations work. One of his favorite techniques was the use of "third-party authorities" to plead for his clients' causes. "If you can influence the leaders, either with or without their conscious cooperation, you automatically influence the group which they sway," he said. A case in point: When Bernays was asked by the Beechnut Packing Company to improve its bacon sales, he devised a campaign to turn bacon and eggs into the quintessential American breakfast. First, he surveyed a group of medical professionals to get their recommendation that people eat hearty, nutritious breakfasts. Then, he sent the survey results to 5,000 physicians, along with publicity touting bacon and eggs as a nutritious breakfast.

One of Bernays' legendary publicity stunts occurred in 1929, when he persuaded a group of New York City debutantes to march down Fifth Avenue in the Easter Parade, openly smoking cigarettes. At the time, smoking was considered unfeminine and inappropriate for women with any social standing. Only prostitutes smoked cigarettes in public. He sent photographs of the event, which he dubbed the "torches of liberty contingent," to newspapers, implying that the young women's lighting-up was a statement of rebellion against the norms of a male-dominated society. What Bernays did not say was that he had been paid by the American Tobacco Company to find a way to help break the taboo against female smoking. The campaign had its desired effect. Many women began to equate smoking with women's rights, and some women went so far as to demand membership in all-male smoking clubs. It's no wonder that two historians of the public relations industry, Ewen and Larry Tye, see Bernays as the master of "spin."

The Origins of Propaganda

As we have read, Bernays entitled one of his major works *Propaganda*. The word has an interesting evolution. It gained currency in the 17th century, when the Roman Catholic Pope Gregory XV established the Congregatio de Propaganda Fide (the Congregation for Propagating the Faith) to centralize the church's missionary activity under his control. The congregation, referred to informally as "propaganda," was a group of cardinals charged with directing church affairs in non-Catholic countries.

The word itself has its roots in the Latin verb "propagare," to reproduce or spread a plant by cuttings; the church used the word rather symbolically to describe missionary activity. By the 1790s, its use in English had expanded to include advancing secular causes. One writer described leaders of the French Revolution as "a new race of pretenders . . . disciples of propaganda." By the mid-19th century, the religious sense of "propaganda" had been replaced by the political, and the word had taken on negative connotations. *The Dictionary of Science, Literature, and Art*, published in 1842, included this definition:

> Derived from this celebrated society [for propagating the faith], the name propaganda is applied in modern political language as a term of reproach to secret associations for the spread of opinions and principles, which are viewed by most governments with horror and aversion.

The modern use of "propaganda" is pejorative and means to spread biased information or falsehoods to promote a cause or serve an agenda. It is used to describe presentations aimed at influencing public opinion, rather than providing impartial information. We can find many examples of the modern use of propaganda. During the great world wars of the 20th century, both sides used propaganda to rally public support and undermine the enemy. In the 1930s and 1940s—before and during World War II—Joseph Goebbels, German leader Adolf Hitler's Propaganda Minister, mounted a chilling mass propaganda campaign to advance his evil "Final Solution" for the extermination of the Jews in Europe.

During the Cold War that followed World War II, the United States and the Soviet Union fought a war of words, as well as proxy wars in developing nations, to determine whether democracy or communism would rule the world. Before the two recent wars that the United States fought in Iraq, the government used propaganda to raise public support for its actions. (For more detailed descriptions of these events, see later sections of this chapter.)

Bernays understood that what we define as propaganda depends on our perspective. What's propaganda to one side is truth to the other. In his 1923 book, *Crystallizing Public Opinion*, Bernays wrote:

> The only difference between "propaganda" and "education," really, is in the point of view. The advocacy of what we believe in is education. The advocacy of what we don't believe in is propaganda.

When he opened his office, Bernays decided to call his practice "counsel in public relations" rather than propaganda. "I decided that if you could use propaganda for war, you could certainly use it for peace. And propaganda got to be a bad word because of the Germans using it. So what I did was to try to find some other words, so we found the words "Council on Public Relations."

Walter Lippmann: Manufacturing Consent

Another prominent 20th-century journalist and author, Walter Lippmann, is also important for his contributions to public relations theory. Born in New York City in 1889, Lippmann was educated at Harvard University, where he edited the "Harvard Monthly" and flirted with socialism. A supporter of Theodore Roosevelt and the Progressives, he took a job as secretary to muckraking journalist Lincoln Steffens in 1911. Three years later, he helped establish the political weekly, "The New Republic." With the publication of his book, *Drift and Mastery*, in 1914, Lippmann rejected socialist ideas, and he became a strong supporter of Woodrow Wilson and the Democrats in the election of 1916.

Like Bernays, Lippmann served on the Creel Commission. When World War I was over, he helped draft Wilson's Fourteen Points Peace Program and the covenant for the League of Nations. In 1920, he left "The New Republic" to join Joseph Pulitzer's newspaper the *New York World*. After the paper closed in 1931, Lippmann wrote for the *New York Herald Tribune*. He went on to become one of the nation's most widely read syndicated columnists.

His experience as a propagandist during World War I taught him about using propaganda and public relations to influence popular opinion. His two most controversial books, *Public Opinion*, published in 1922, and *The Phantom Public*, in 1925, raised the idea that true democracy is impossible in modern society and that the masses need to be guided by enlightened experts. He coined the phrase "manufacture of consent" to describe the process by which public opinion is formed.

Arthur W. Page: First Corporate Public Relations Officer

Arthur W. Page, who served as vice president of public relations for the American Telephone and Telegraph Company (AT&T) from 1927 to 1946, was the first public relations practitioner to serve as an officer and board member for a major corporation. A former writer and editor, he took the job on the condition that he would be involved in the development of company policy. He outlined five principles of corporate public relations for the company to follow:

- To make sure management thoughtfully analyzes its overall relation to the public
- To create a system for informing all employees about the general policies and practices
- To create a system giving contact employees the knowledge needed to be reasonable and polite to the public
- To create a system drawing employee and public questions and criticism back up through the organization to management
- To ensure frankness in telling the public about the company's actions

Page believed that "all business in a democratic society begins with public permission and exists by public approval." His principles have influenced thousands of practitioners who have followed him. In 1983, before the breakup of AT&T, several company executives founded the **Arthur W. Page Society** *to promote the principles of this public relations icon; its membership now includes leading corporate public relations officers and counselors.*

John W. Hill: Father of a Giant

Hill & Knowlton, a firm that would become one of the world's largest public relations corporations, was started by Cleveland journalist John W. Hill in 1927. Six years later, he formed a partnership with Don Knowlton. In 1934, he moved the company's headquarters to New York to serve as public relations counsel to the American Iron and Steel Institute. Known for his philosophy of teamwork, Hill skillfully managed his firm's growth until 1962. During World War II in the 1940s, the agency gained firm footing by representing war industry groups, such as the Aviation Corporation of America and the American Shipbuilding Council. In the 1950s, Hill & Knowlton, as well as Burson-Marsteller, another large public relations firm, opened offices in Europe, becoming the first transnational public relations firms. In the 1960s, Hill & Knowlton began offering lobbying services to its clients, beginning a new trend. Now most major public relations firms have a "government relations" practice. In July 1980, Hill & Knowlton was acquired by the advertising firm J. Walter Thompson (JWT), becoming one of several large public relations firms to merge with advertising. In 1987, the communication conglomerate WPP Group bought JWT. Today, the subsidiary Hill & Knowlton has offices around the globe, serving industry, government, and nonprofits.

Hill's legacy was tarnished by his role in aiding the tobacco industry in its fight against public health experts. In December 1953, Hill & Knowlton designed the tobacco industry's strategy for countering evidence linking cigarette smoking to lung cancer and helped organize the Council for Tobacco Research, a front group established by tobacco giant Philip Morris. A **front group** is *a group of citizens and so-called "experts" who claim to represent the public interest but are really a cover for promoting the interest of the issue or corporation.* As a result, the firm was named a co-defendant of Philip Morris in tobacco lawsuits.

ENGAGING ETHICS

Hill & Knowlton and the Run-Up to the First War in Iraq

Justification for the first Gulf war, fought in 1991 and 1992 during the administration of George H. W. Bush, rested, in part, on a public relations campaign on behalf of Kuwait run by Hill & Knowlton. A group of Kuwaiti professionals who called themselves Citizens for a Free Kuwait retained the firm following Iraq's occupation of their country in August 1990. At the time, Hill & Knowlton's Washington office was run by Craig Fuller, one of Bush's closest friends.

In October 1990, the Congressional Human Rights Caucus held public hearings on alleged Iraqi human rights violations in Kuwait. Since many of those testifying did not speak English well, Hill & Knowlton's staff helped prepare their statements. One of the most emotional testimonies came from a 15-year-old girl, identified in public only as Nayirah, who said that Iraqi soldiers went into a hospital in Kuwait City, took babies from incubators, and left them to die. The story was repeated many times, including by Bush, on radio and television talk shows and in the U.N. Security Council. It may have swayed some members of Congress, which voted by a slim margin to go to war.

The story turned out to be a fabrication in which both the Kuwaiti government and Hill & Knowlton were involved. More than 90 percent of the funding for Citizens for a Free Kuwait came from the Kuwaiti government. While Hill & Knowlton identified Nayirah in a written submission to the caucus as Nayirah al-Sabah, the daughter of the Kuwaiti ambassador to the United States, neither the firm nor the caucus made the relationship public for a while. Worse, a Hill & Knowlton vice president coached Nayirah in the story, which Kuwaiti investigators later confirmed was false.

1. Did Hill & Knowlton breach professional ethics in representing Citizens for a Free Kuwait? If so, why?
2. Could you describe Citizens for a Free Kuwait as a front group? If so, what ethical issues do front groups raise? If you were consulted regarding the setting up of such a group, what would you advise?

The Start of the Political Consulting Industry

The first U.S. political consulting firm was started by Clem Whitaker and Leone Baxter, a husband and wife team. Based in California, Whitaker & Baxter, sometimes functioning as Campaign, Inc., was something new in American politics. From 1935 to 1958, the firm managed 80 political campaigns and won all but six. The agency changed the way America campaigns and is credited with the "media blitz" in the final days of the campaign.

The First Black-Owned PR Firms

Joseph Varney Baker started the first black-owned public relations firm in 1934, when he left his position as city editor of the *Philadelphia Tribune* to provide counsel to the Pennsylvania Railroad Company. Baker became the first African American to be accredited by the **Public Relations Society of America**—*the world's largest public relations society founded in 1947*—and to serve as president of a PRSA chapter. His firm's clients included Chrysler, Gillette, Procter & Gamble, and NBC. During the firm's 40-year history, it specialized in targeting the black consumer market.

Calvin Coolidge and the First Photo-Op

Calvin Coolidge, U.S. president from 1923 to 1929, is often credited with beginning the photo-op. *Short for photo opportunity*, the **photo-op** is *a carefully planned news event that yields an effective photograph.* The term is often used to describe events engineered by politicians to generate good publicity. Unlike the news conference, the photo-op is not an opportunity for journalists to ask questions. Thus, politicians can—and do—milk the chance to look good while avoiding having to answer potentially difficult or embarrassing questions.

On July 4, 1927, while vacationing in South Dakota to celebrate his 55th birthday, Coolidge donned a cowboy suit and posed for news photographers. The shy Coolidge enjoyed the fact that he did not have to talk during the photo session, yet the amusing photos still endeared him to the public. Later, Coolidge posed as an honorary Sioux Indian and as a Boy Scout.

At the time Coolidge posed for news photographs, the use of photos in newspapers was very new. The date generally given for the birth of photography is 1839, when French photographer Louis Jacques Mandé Daguerre invented the daguerreotype—a method for transferring camera images to copper plates. The technology for transferring photos to paper for mass production, however, did not come into use until the turn of the century. On January 21, 1897, the *New York Tribune* published the first photo. By the end of the first decade of the 1900s, photographs were common in newspapers and magazines.

Franklin Roosevelt and the "Fireside Chats"

Franklin D. Roosevelt, U.S. president from 1933 until his death in 1944, was a skillful communicator who introduced radio as a venue for political public relations. His **Fireside Chats,** *a series of 30 evening radio talks, were designed to give his fellow Americans a feeling of pride and hope in their country during the hard times of the Great Depression.* After the Japanese attacked Pearl Harbor, pulling the United States into World War II, Roosevelt continued his Fireside Chats to explain wartime policies to the American people.

World War II and American Propaganda

"Uncle Sam wants you!" was the slogan Americans read on posters during World War II. To coordinate the war propaganda, Roosevelt created the **Office of War Information (OWI)**—*the forerunner of the U.S. Information Agency*—in 1942, under the directorship of Elmer Davis, a veteran journalist. The office had two branches, domestic and overseas. The domestic branch coordinated the release of war news and tried to attract workers to jobs in support of the war effort. Photographers shot pictures of aircraft factories, members of the armed forces, and women in the workforce. The photographs, with emotional captions, were widely published to inspire patriotic fervor in the American public. The overseas branch launched an information and propaganda campaign abroad, aimed at undermining enemy morale. Like the Creel Committee during World War I, the OWI became a training ground for a new generation of public relations practitioners. About 100,000 people were trained as public information officers during the war, and many of them translated their wartime work into professional careers after the war.

The **Ad Council,** *a nonprofit public service advertising organization*, got its start during World War II as the War Advertising Council. Its first campaign was a drive to sell War Bonds. The council created many other ad campaigns to help the war effort, including "Rosie the Riveter" ads to attract women to jobs in offices and factories and the "Loose Lips" campaign to advise American soldiers on what to say and not say when writing home, carrying on a conversation, or if captured during the war.

After the war, Roosevelt urged the council to continue its work. It has created hundreds of ad campaigns, including the "The Toughest Job You'll Ever Love" for the Peace Corps and "A Mind Is a Terrible Thing to Waste" for the United Negro College Fund. Today, the Ad Council remains the leading producer of public service communications in the United States.

The **Voice of America** is another agency that got its start during World War II. The agency began as the U.S. Foreign Information Service (FIS), *created by Roosevelt to spread war propaganda via radio.* The announcer for the first European broadcast on February 24, 1942, opened the program with the words "Here speaks a voice from America," giving the agency its signature. Since then, the Voice of America has expanded to include satellite television broadcasts; distribution of text, audio, and video via the Internet; and a targeted email program to countries where its Internet; site is blocked. Today, about 100 million people tune to the Voice of America on more than 1,400 radio and television stations around the world.

"We Can Do It!" World War II poster. c. 1942 (colour litho). Miller, J. Howard (1918–2004)/Private Collection/Peter Newark American Pictures/The Bridgeman Art Library International

Rosie the Riveter

The Rise of Television: Instant Opinion Making

In the years following World War II, television came of age and became an important force in forming public opinion. Although still a young medium, television had been around for a while. The first broadcast occurred on April 7, 1927, when then Secretary of Commerce Herbert Hoover's remarks were transmitted live over telephone lines from Washington, DC, to New York City: "Today we have, in a sense, the transmission of sight for the first time in the world's history." On September 4, 1951, President Harry S. Truman inaugurated transcontinental television service when AT&T carried his address to the United Nations in San Francisco to viewers as far away as New England.

During the 1950s, as television sets became more affordable and programming more varied, millions of Americans brought television into their homes, making it the dominant mass media. The power of television to sell opinion and products, as well as to entertain, was not lost on American politicians, journalists, and business leaders. Television became a prime medium for molding public opinion.

The Growth of Modern Political Public Relations

While many politicians have had an impact on the development of contemporary political public relations, this section will focus on how three modern U.S. presidents, John F. Kennedy, Richard M. Nixon, and Ronald Reagan, helped to shape the practice. It will look at the interrelationship between politicians and the media and will examine how media coverage of one divisive war, the Vietnam War, led to modern U.S. military public relations policies.

The Kennedy Years: Television, PR, and the Presidency

As *New York Times* columnist Frank Rich has noted, John F. Kennedy did for television what Roosevelt did for radio: made the medium into a "political force." By the time Kennedy was elected president in November 1960, 90 percent of American households owned a television set. Kennedy recognized the power of the medium and became the first president to use television to speak directly to voters.

The first of four televised debates between Kennedy and his opponent, Vice President Richard Nixon—known as the **Great Debates**—was held on Sept. 26, 1960. An estimated 70 million Americans tuned in to the contest, which marked television's entrance into presidential politics. The broadcast highlighted the visual contrast between the two men. Kennedy was at ease and looked tan, confident, and rested. Nixon was pale and underweight, having just spent two weeks in the hospital for a knee injury. He wore an ill-fitting shirt and refused makeup to cover his five-o'clock shadow.

In substance, the men were more evenly matched. In fact, those who listened to the debate on the radio thought Nixon was the winner. But television viewers, who saw a still sickly Nixon, disconcerted by Kennedy's good looks, quickness, and charm, perceived Kennedy to be the winner by a wide margin. The debates raised questions about the influence of television on the democratic process, causing voters to consider the extent to which the presence of the television camera could change the outcome of the debate.

Kennedy held the first live, televised press conference in 1961. His quick wit and skill in handling reporters became a standard against which succeeding presidents would be measured. Kennedy's tragic assassination in Dallas on November 22, 1963, became a watershed in the history of television news. By 1963, according to surveys, Americans were getting more news from television than from newspapers, and television coverage of the assassination and the events that followed drew even more people to their sets as a source of information. Kennedy's funeral was broadcast across the nation and around the world via satellite. These emotional events were indelibly printed on the minds of viewers and expanded the power of broadcast news. During the following decade, television became a dominant source for news information and for molding political opinion.

The Pentagon's PR Nightmare: The First Televised War

In 1965, the Vietnam War became the first war to be televised. Footage of the brutality of the war was broadcast nightly, helping fuel the country's largest anti-war movement and diminish support for the war. The movement became the most successful protest against a war in U.S. history, forcing the U.S. government to accept withdrawal without military victory. But the movement's success led to a military backlash against the press. Believing it had lost the war due to public opposition, the Pentagon adopted a policy in the 1980s of using press pools, which gave the military control over who could talk to troops and under what conditions. The policy was implemented during the U.S. invasions of Grenada in 1983 and of Panama in 1989 and during the two recent Gulf wars against Iraq.

This exercise of virtual censorship, combined with careful public relation campaigns, was intended to ensure that the public saw the military in the best light. By the outset of the first Gulf War in 1991, advances in satellite transmission technology made it possible to broadcast events as they happened. For the first time, the world was able to watch live footage of missiles hitting their targets and fighters taking off from aircraft carriers. All the major networks aired the massive bombing of Iraq's capital city, Baghdad, that opened the war. Print media carried graphic descriptions and illustrations, as well as photos. The Pentagon used the media to showcase its strength, and its management of the news—and the media's acquiescence to it, for the most part—produced a sanitized version of the war. After the war, the heads of large media outlets met with Pentagon officials to

American TV news correspondent Mike Wallace of CBS News reports from a trench during the Vietnam War, 1967.

change the policy. By the second Gulf war in 2003, reporters were allowed to travel with some troops under a policy called "embedding," but military public relations officials still, for the most part, control the message.

Richard Nixon and "Spin Control"

In 1969, the year after Nixon was elected president, Joe McGinniss' book *The Selling of the President 1968* was published. McGinniss, a Philadelphia journalist, described how Nixon's public relations team re-created his image in an effort to achieve his political comeback following his defeats for president in 1960 and for governor of California in 1962. The result was a campaign—and a presidency—that used modern advertising techniques, public relations tactics, and political strategies to manage the media.

During his campaign, Nixon's team created a set of television commercials in which Nixon would brilliantly answer questions from a group of "citizens," all of whom were preselected supporters to ask favorable questions. This "fake town hall," along with other marketing strategies, worked so well that Nixon established the White House Office of Communications to manage his administration's message.

Another of Nixon's methods for managing the media was to use his vice president, Spiro Agnew, as a hatchet man. Agnew was an outspoken politician, whose role became peddling the administration's distrust of the media. Agnew called the press an "effete corps of impudent snobs." He denounced television news broadcasters as a biased "unelected elite." He suggested that the media—"a virtual monopoly"—should be more regulated, a suggestion which newscaster Walter Cronkite saw as "an implied threat to freedom of speech in this country." Ironically, the media, which Nixon so distrusted, became an instrument of his demise, breaking and covering the so-called **Watergate** *scandal, a series of events that began with a botched burglary and ended with Nixon's resignation in 1974.*

Ronald Reagan: The Great Communicator

When she was a young congresswoman, Democrat Patricia Schroeder coined the phrase **"Teflon president"** to describe Ronald Reagan, who served as president from

1980 to 1988. She said she got the idea while fixing eggs for her kids. She noticed that *the president had a Teflon coat, like the pan; no criticism stuck to him.* One reason for his success was his talent and charm. A former actor, Reagan was comfortable in front of the camera. He delivered speeches with sincerity and connected well with his constituents. During his 1980 campaign, he even borrowed a line from *Knute Rockne*, a 1940 movie in which he starred, and asked Americans to "win one for the Gipper." He was an optimist, who—according to his supporters—made America feel good about itself again. More importantly, Reagan's public relations advisors knew how to play up his strengths, downplay his weaknesses, and use a compliant media to get the administration's message out.

ENGAGING ETHICS

Reagan's PR People

According to Mark Hertsgaard, author of *On Bended Knee: The Press and the Reagan Presidency*, Reagan's PR successes can be attributed to both a brilliant public relations staff and self-censorship by the media itself. His carefully orchestrated public relations was planned well in advance and "fine-tuned" daily. Administration spokespersons were well rehearsed in what they should tell reporters. Reagan's public appearances were staged to avoid his having to answer reporters' questions. His staff supplied the press with timely, interesting stories and appealing visuals—often turning journalists into virtual spokespersons for their agenda.

The media, for its part, made the job of managing Reagan's image easier by muzzling some of its reporters. For example, White House correspondent Lesley Stahl was told by CBS to lighten her criticism of Reagan because "ordinary Americans supposedly didn't want to hear it." And ABC News killed the story of the U.S. invasion of Grenada, despite the fact that its camera crew had footage of U.S. troops on their way to the island.

Hertsgaard criticizes the media for failing, in the main, to make the reality, rather than the "spin" of the policies of the Reagan years clear to the public. The fault for this, he claims, lies in the way modern American media works:

> In the United States, the media shape mass opinion but tend to reflect elite opinion, and most of the nation's elite either supported Reagan or were afraid to criticize him. This was true not only of the executives who employed the journalists covering Reagan but also of most Democrats. Because the doctrine of objectivity prevents reporters from saying the sky is blue without citing an official source, they look to the opposition party for quotes and perspectives to counter the White House's claims. The coverage of any President, therefore, tends to be only as critical as the opposition party is. The failure of Democrats to criticize Reagan meant he faced relatively uncritical coverage.

1. Do you agree with Herstgaard's analysis of the interplay among public relations professionals, the media, and politicians? Why, or why not?
2. Find and analyze two current examples of news management by politicians.

SOURCE: Hertzgaard, Mark. "Beloved by the Media," *The Nation*, June 28, 2004

Changing Minds to Change Society: The Growth of Social Public Relations

Public relations for social good has its own long history. In the United States, supporters and opponents of great social reform movements—abolition of slavery, civil rights, suffrage, women's rights, gay rights, consumer's rights, peace, environmental justice—all depended on the media to spread their messages and garner public support. Here we will look briefly at how early abolitionists and 20th century civil rights activists not only used public relations tactics but also helped to create them.

The American Anti-Slavery Society and the Power of Free Speech

While opposition to slavery had been expressed since colonial times, the abolitionist movement formally began with the establishment of the American Anti-Slavery Society in 1833. The society held meetings, arranged the signing of petitions, circulated anti-slavery propaganda, and sponsored lecture tours. By 1840, the society had more than 2,000 local chapters and significant political influence. The abolition of slavery became the policy not only of the Liberal Party (1840–1848), begun as an offshoot of the society, but also of the Free-Soil Party (1848–1854) and Abraham Lincoln's Republican Party, founded in 1854. The society closed down in 1867 after the passage of the 14th Amendment, which required the states to provide equal protection under the law to all persons, regardless of race.

Among the leaders of the society were William Lloyd Garrison, Wendell Phillips, and Frederick Douglass. Garrison was the publisher of an influential weekly anti-slavery newspaper, the *Liberator*, which he began in 1831 and continued publishing until after the end of the Civil War in 1865. As Cutlip states: "He (Garrison) single-mindedly propagandized the wrongs of human slavery and marshaled the forces of discontent of his generation." Phillips, a passionate and skilled orator, traveled the country speaking out against slavery. He also wrote pamphlets and editorials for Garrison's newspaper.

Douglas, a former slave and a brilliant speaker, was asked by the Anti-Slavery Society to give a series of lectures on the immorality of slavery throughout the United States and England. He gained fame with the publication of his autobiography, the *Narrative of the Life of Frederick Douglass*, in 1845. Two years later he began publishing the *North Star*, an anti-slavery newspaper, and later published several other abolitionist papers. During the Civil War, he helped recruit black troops for the Union army, and his friendship with Lincoln helped convince the president to make emancipation a cause of the war. He went on to serve the federal government in several capacities after the war.

Another effective propagandist against slavery was writer Harriet Beecher Stowe, whose novel *Uncle Tom's Cabin* roused the public against the brutality of slavery. Her story—written in reaction to the Fugitive Slave Act of 1850 that required citizens to help in recovering runaway slaves—ran in serial form beginning in 1851 in the *National Era*, an anti-slavery newspaper. It was published in March 1852, and by the end of the year had sold more than 300,000 copies in the United States. The book was so successful that it inspired many spin-offs, including advertisements, poems, and dramatic presentations.

According to historians, the principal achievement of the abolitionists was to make slavery a public issue. They drew the nation's attention to the issue and helped mobilize the North to fight for abolition.

The Modern Civil Rights Movement: Mobilizing the Grassroots

The Civil Rights movement in the 1950s and 1960s is a model for **grassroots** activism. *Mobilizing supporters from the ground up*, the movement fought to eradicate Jim Crow laws, which—particularly in southern states—had legalized segregation, disfranchisement, and discrimination against black Americans. The movement's leaders understood the power of mass media and used every powerful opinion-shifting tool at their disposal: the press, the pulpit, television, public speeches, and organized events, including acts of civil disobedience, to win their fight for equality. Three of the many public events that brought about significant changes were the Montgomery, Alabama, bus boycott in 1955, the Freedom Rides in 1961, and the March on Washington in 1963.

The Montgomery Bus Boycott

For 11 months in 1955 and 1956, black residents of Montgomery, Alabama, boycotted the city's public buses to protest segregation in bus seating. The boycott began after Rosa Parks, a Montgomery seamstress, was arrested on December 1, 1955, for refusing to give up her seat to a white person. After her arrest, leaflets were distributed throughout the black community calling for a one-day boycott. When 90 percent of Montgomery's black citizens stayed off the buses four days later, the city's black leaders mounted a long-term campaign.

The boycott proved effective, causing the city transit system serious financial losses. Boycotters organized carpools, biked, hitchhiked, rode mules, drove horse-drawn buggies, and walked. Across the nation, black churches collected shoes to replace the well-used ones worn by Montgomery's black citizens. When the city pressured local insurance companies to stop insuring cars used in the carpools, the boycott leaders arranged for coverage with Lloyd's of London.

In response to the boycott, opposing whites joined the pro-segregation White Citizens' Council. Boycotters were often physically attacked; Martin Luther King's and fellow civil rights leader Ralph Abernathy's houses were firebombed. Black taxi drivers who lowered their fare to 10 cents a ride, the cost to ride the bus, were fined. City officials obtained injunctions against the boycott in February 1956 and arrested 156 protesters under a 1921 law prohibiting the hindrance of a bus. King was tried and convicted on the charge and ordered to pay $1,000 or serve 386 days in jail. Despite these pressures, the boycott went on.

The wide publicity mounted pressure across the country to resolve the conflict, and on June 4, 1956, the federal district court ruled that Alabama's racial segregation laws for buses were unconstitutional. The ruling was appealed, and then upheld by the U.S. Supreme Court. Montgomery then passed an ordinance allowing black bus passengers to sit wherever they wanted, and the boycott ended December 21, 1956. The boycott gave the civil rights movement one of its first victories and King international attention. The tactic of using mass nonviolent protest became a model for later challenges to segregation in the South.

Freedom Rides

During the spring and summer of 1961, student activists supported by the Congress of Racial Equality (CORE) and the Student Nonviolent Coordinating Committee (SNCC) launched the **Freedom Rides** *to test the 1960 U.S. Supreme Court ruling that declared segregation in interstate bus and rail stations unconstitutional.* Riding from Washington, DC, to Jackson, Mississippi, the riders met violent opposition, got wide media coverage and eventually forced the U.S. Interstate Commerce Commission to issue rules prohibiting segregated transportation facilities. The Freedom Rides are a striking example of how an organized event can raise public awareness and change social conditions.

The first Freedom Ride began on May 4, 1961, when seven black and six white students left Washington, DC, on buses both bound for New Orleans. At first, the freedom riders met only minor hostility. Then one bus was burned outside Anniston, Alabama. When the riders reached Birmingham, Alabama, they were attacked. The group flew to New Orleans, ending the first ride. Then more volunteers took up the challenge, joining some members of the first ride who wanted to go on. When the second group arrived in Birmingham, they were arrested, jailed, and driven out of town. They quickly returned. President Kennedy intervened, and police escorted the bus to Montgomery, Alabama. When they arrived in Montgomery, however, the police disappeared, and the riders were attacked by a mob of more than 1,000 whites.

The violence of the mob and the indifference of local police created national support for the riders. Escorted by national guardsmen, they continued on to Jackson, Mississippi, where they were jailed for using white facilities. The brutal treatment of the riders generated more publicity and inspired dozens more Freedom Rides. By the end of the summer, the protests had spread to train stations and airports across the South. In November, the Interstate Commerce Commission desegregated transportation facilities.

March on Washington

The 1963 March on Washington was the largest political demonstration in U.S. history to that date. Organized by A. Philip Randolph, Martin Luther King Jr., Roy Wilkins, James Farmer, John Lewis, and Whitney Young Jr., the march drew an estimated 250,000 demonstrators, a crowd larger and more diverse than the organizers had ever dreamed. They walked down Constitution and Independence avenues—carrying signs that ranged from the mass-produced to the unique—then gathered at the Lincoln Memorial for speeches, songs, and prayer. The closing speaker was King, who delivered his memorable "I Have a Dream" speech.

Leading newspapers in many countries ran the story on their front pages. The major television networks broadcast the event live to an audience of millions in the United States and abroad, via satellite. The wide press coverage brought attention to the struggle for civil rights. "The March on Washington established visibility in this nation," wrote King's chief aide, Ralph Abernathy. The following year, Congress passed the landmark Civil Rights Act of 1964, banning racial discrimination in public facilities and in voting rights. The march succeeded in its goals of pushing civil rights legislation and raising public awareness. And it became a model for anti-war, women's rights, and many other social issue marches that would follow.

"Astroturfing": A Bad Copy

One measure of the success of the grassroots tactics used by civil right reformers is the extent to which they are mimicked by government and industry groups wanting to affect

Dr. Martin Luther King Jr. addresses crowds during the March On Washington at the Lincoln Memorial, Washington, DC.

Central Press/Getty Images

public opinion. Unlike true grassroots efforts that originate with individuals or local communities, *artificial grassroots efforts*—termed **"astroturfing"**—*are public relations projects that seek to engineer the impression of spontaneous grassroots behavior.* The agency, industry, or company will establish a front group that behaves like a local grassroots campaign to marshal support for its plan or product. The term, said to have been first used by former Senator Lloyd Bentsen, is wordplay based on AstroTurf, the bright green artificial grass used in some sports stadiums.

One classic example of astroturfing is the campaign mounted in 1994 by the Coalition of Health Industry Choices, a front group established by the U.S. health insurance industry, to kill the Clinton administration's healthcare reform plan. The group used direct mail, phoning, "focus groups," and surveys to lobby against the plan. They engaged the media on radio and television, and sponsored TV spots featuring "Harry and Louise," a middle-aged couple who complained about the plan's cost and complexity. *New York Times* reporter Robin Toner wrote at the time: "'Harry and Louise' symbolized everything that went wrong with the great health care struggle of 1994: A powerful advertising campaign, financed by the insurance industry that played on people's fears and helped derail the process." The insurance industry's cynical uses of grassroots tactics help defeat the plan.

The Challenges of Contemporary Corporate Public Relations

The impact of the consumer movement, recent corporate scandals and globalization poses challenges for modern practitioners of public relations. The U.S. consumer movement, which began in 1899 with the formation of the National Consumer's League, matured during the past century to become a powerful voice for buyers. The original league was established to fight for minimum wage laws, safer conditions for workers, and the abolition of sweatshops and child labor. With the start in 1936 of the Consumer's Union, the group that publishes the monthly consumer magazine *Consumer Reports*, the movement's focus shifted toward product testing and evaluation. Other groups, such as Ralph Nader's consumer advocacy group, which began sending consumer statistic tips to Congress in the early 1960s, started exposing shoddy products. In 1972, the Public Relations Society of America (PRSA) set up a task force to examine the effect of consumerism on business.

The movement's impact was so strong that it affected political leaders, as well as corporate ones. In 1962, President Kennedy outlined the four basic rights of consumers: "the right to be informed, the right to safety, the right to choose, and the right to be heard." He established the Consumer Advisory Council to advise the president and Congress on consumer matters. Every president since Kennedy has a consumer advisor on his staff.

A second challenge to public relations practitioners arises out of recent corporate scandals, such as those at Enron, WorldCom, and the mutual funds industry. (See Chapter 7 for a detailed description of some of these scandals.) One significant effect of these scandals was the passage of the **Sarbanes-Oxley Act** *of 2002, also known as the Public Company Accounting Reform and Investor Protection Act of 2002. The wide-ranging bill establishes new or enhanced reporting standards for all U.S. public company boards, management, and public accounting firms.* Among the law's requirements is the setting up of strict mechanisms for documenting all the information in financial disclosures. Any practitioner involved in preparing company reports is affected by the new law.

A third challenge lies in the growth of multicultural marketing and global public relations, both of which make doing business more interesting but require

BRIEF CASE STUDY

Positive Public Relations: Johnson & Johnson and the Tylenol Scare

Historically, this case marks the first known incident of product tampering that resulted in deaths. PR played a major role in crisis management and communication, resulting in restoration of public confidence in a product. In October of 1982, seven people in Chicago died of cyanide poisoning after taking Extra-Strength Tylenol, the over-the-counter pain reliever manufactured by drug giant Johnson & Johnson. Once the connection was made between Tylenol and the deaths, Johnson & Johnson issued public announcements warning consumers not to use Tylenol, recalled the product from shelves across the country, and stopped all advertisements. The recall alone, which totaled about 31 million bottles, cost the company more than $100 million. Although the tampering occurred after the Tylenol had reached the shelves and Johnson & Johnson knew it was not responsible for the tampering, the company assumed responsibility for public safety.

To restore consumer confidence and regain its market, Johnson & Johnson took three steps. First, Tylenol products were repackaged in triple-seal tamper-resistant bottles and in caplet form, which is more resistant to tampering. In so doing, Johnson & Johnson became the first company to comply with the FDA's new mandate for tamper-resistant packaging. Second, they offered a discount coupon on the purchase of Tylenol and lowered the price by up to 25 percent. Third, they implemented a broad marketing campaign, sending more than 2,000 sales people to make presentations to the medical community.

By acting as it did, Johnson & Johnson not only insured the survival of its Tylenol brand but also advanced its reputation as a responsible, trustworthy company.

Working the Case

1. Compare Johnson & Johnson's response to the poisoned Tylenol to Dow Corning's handling of silicone breast implants. (Check the Internet for details of this case.) How did the behavior of each company affect its business?
2. Find and describe another case in which a company reacted positively to a potential crisis.

sensitivity to the needs of people from different backgrounds and ethnic and religious groups. The rapid expansion of the Internet, which draws viewers from different national and cultural beliefs to websites, has also widened the scope of public relations campaigns.

Since the Internet became public in the mid-1990s, it has evolved into a valuable medium for promoting good relationships with clients, the media, the public, and members of the organization. Its impact cannot be understated and has been compared in effect to Gutenberg's invention of the printing press. Corporations, nonprofits, schools, churches, government agencies, libraries, local shops—many organizations now have websites. Public relations practitioners can use organizational sites to post and archive press releases, provide information on the history of the organization and its finances, and promote the organization's goods and services. They can also use the Internet for research, to find information on everything from a competitor's address to its corporate officers, advertising campaigns, and stock price. While the Internet makes doing business faster, it also requires that practitioners become and remain technologically savvy.

YOU'VE COME A LONG WAY, PR

Since the first public relations practitioners hung out their shingles at the turn of the 20th century, the public relations industry has matured into an influential profession. Today, more than 200,000 men and women in the United States practice public relations, and thousands more work in the field overseas. The industry's scope, too, has widened: Press relations, Web relations, employee communications, public relations counseling and research, local community relations, audiovisual communications, contributions, interactive public relations, and numerous other activities all fall under the public relations umbrella.

To meet some of the challenges posed by public relations practice, professional organizations for practitioners have been established. The first such group, the Public Relations Society of America (PRSA), was chartered in 1947 to advance the standards of the profession and to provide members with opportunities for professional development. Today, the PRSA has more than 20,000 members and is the world's largest public relations society. The **International Public Relations Society,** *was founded in London in 1955 to meet the needs and challenges of an increasingly international industry.* In 1970, the **International Association of Business Communicators,** which *provides a professional network for more than 13,000 business communication professionals in more than 60 countries,* was begun. In 1998, the Council of Public Relations Firms was established to advance the public relations industry; its members now include nearly 100 of the top U.S. public relations firms.

As the practice of public relations becomes more widespread and its practitioners are subject to more public scrutiny, many professionals think practitioners should be licensed to guard the industry's reputation and cement its legitimacy as a profession. This is not a new idea. Late in his life, Bernays favored licensing public relations professionals. "Any dumbbell, nitwit or crook can call himself a public relations practitioner," Bernays told an interviewer. "The only way to protect yourself from dumbbells and crooks is to install intellectual and social values that are meaningful and keep out people who only hand out circulars in Harvard Square." Today, licensing remains an open question.

Public relations has also gained legitimacy as a profession as it has become recognized as a field of study at institutions of higher education. The study of public relations had its origins in publicity courses that were offered by some institutions in the 1920s. After World War II, the profession began to be taken more seriously. According to Cutlip: "A 1946 survey identified 30 major institutions offering public relations courses. Ten years later a PRSA survey found that 92 were offering courses designed to prepare students for the work, with 14 schools offering a major. By 1964 . . . 14 institutions offered a bachelor's degree in public relations, 29 had undergraduate sequences and all told, 280 were offering instruction in various courses." Today, more than 200 journalism and communication programs offer concentrated study in public relations.

In 1956, the Association for Education in Journalism formed the Council on Public Relations Education to promote an exchange of ideas among instructors and enlist the help of public relations practitioners in developing the practical application components for academic programs. In 1999, the Commission on Public Relations Education, chartered by the PRSA, recommended a public relations curriculum that emphasized such nontraditional topics as relationship building, societal trends, and multicultural issues.

Over the past 100 years, public relations has become a far-reaching industry and a serious course of study. As Seitel has stated: "(the industry) has become solidly entrenched as an important, influential and professional component of our society."

Only Truth Will Combat PR Stereotypes

Tom Martin wrote this point of view as president of the Arthur W. Page Society and SVP, Corporate Relations, ITT Industries. PRWeek, *January 24, 2005.*

The book contains essays from 23 leading CEOs on issues that relate directly to the Page Principles, including telling the truth, proving it with action, and managing for the future. The book has been well received and has made it onto some 2004 lists of "Best Books for PR Pros."

While this is gratifying, I have encountered another side to the story. As Society president, I've been interviewed on several radio talk shows as part of the book-promotion activity. These interviews have been straightforward for the most part.

Many of the interviewers have seemed genuinely interested in hearing a positive portrayal of how corporate leaders grapple with issues of trust in the business world. But in many such encounters, mostly in drive-time talk-radio slots, the interviewers have been more than surprised that an organization made up of corporate communications and PR leaders would have the nerve to publish a book with the word "trust" in its title. They feel PR is about anything but truth and transparency, and have espoused the common view that PR has more to do with obfuscation, rationalization, and hypocrisy.

In one of these interviews, with a Boston radio station, I was paired with Tom McGarity, an author and professor at the University of Texas School of Law. He is also president of the Center for Progressive Regulation.

In his most recent book, *Sophisticated Sabotage: The Intellectual Games Used to Subvert Responsible Regulation*, McGarity describes what he views as the deceptive tactics some companies use to influence the regulatory environment by employing questionable risk assessment and economic models that favor their positions. He has written other books that explore efforts to undermine the impact of OSHA and EPA regulations.

In our joint interview, McGarity called into question the practice employed over the years by companies and PR firms to create "front" organizations pretending to be independent boards of experts on controversial subjects. As his most potent example, he used the well-catalogued tactics employed by many tobacco companies with the help of their PR firms to use pseudo-science to try and minimize the dangers of smoking, long after they knew these dangers were real.

He pointed me and radio listeners to websites on which the damning evidence documenting these practices is portrayed in unyielding detail.

In response, I noted that having lost my father to cancer and my mother to emphysema (both were smokers) I was not going to defend tobacco companies, their firms, or the tactics he described. I noted that the Page Principles are based on truth-telling and on the conscientious actions of many in our profession and in the business world in general to do the right thing for employees, customers, and shareholders alike.

While none of us profess to be perfect, we do try to counsel our organizations and clients to make good decisions, ones that balance the needs of these different constituents and form the basis for reputation management.

Having said all that, the dialogue with McGarity, and other similar ones with other radio talk-show hosts, left me with some major questions about our profession. How have we earned the reputation we have? Have we done enough to overcome the negative stereotypes about our profession that clearly persist among a significant percentage of the population? Are we destined to be perpetually viewed as empty spinners rather than legitimate business counselors? Can we credibly claim that we are advocates for truth within our organizations?

There are clearly no simple or consistent answers. PR counselors come in many flavors. Some are more comfortable with ambiguity than others. Some view immediate publicity as the ultimate goal, while others take a longer view. Some see nothing wrong with paying experts to advocate a position without disclosing the fact that they are being paid by a stakeholder in the fight. Others feel this practice and others like it undermine credibility. Some have a steady unwavering compass when it comes to matters of veracity, and others . . . well let's just say that others see things differently.

The Page Principles offer a starting point for stating what we believe in and try to practice as professionals. Tell the truth, prove it with action, listen to the customer, manage for the future, conduct PR as if the whole company depends on it, and remain calm, patient, and good-humored. Not a bad prescription for PR. Not a bad prescription for running a business. Not a bad prescription for living.

SOURCE: Tom Martin, *PRWeek*, January 24, 2005

Summary and Review

First Fruits: PR in the Colonies and the Early United States

- Public relations as we know it today is a particularly American phenomenon that had its roots in the early settlement of the country.
- The profession evolved during the 20th century in response to significant historical events: the growth of industry, World War I, the Great Depression, World War II, the postwar economic boom, major advances in communication technology, and social upheaval and change.
- Globalization has led to the profession's growth throughout the world. Public relations practice, which began with individual consultants, has grown to a major industry with large, multinational firms, as well as private consultants.
- The industry's legitimacy is confirmed by its inclusion in the communications curriculum of major colleges and universities.
- The following timeline points to key moments in political, technological, and social history that have shaped the profession of public relations:

1580s   English trading companies begin publishing promotional materials to lure settlers to the American colonies.

1641   First fundraising public relations brochure, *New England's First Fruits*, issued to raise money for Harvard College.

1700s   Early in the century, the *Boston News-Letter* becomes the first regularly published colonial newspaper to carry advertisements.

1730s   Benjamin Franklin uses eye-catching typography to make ads in his *Pennsylvania Gazette* more readable.

1758   King's College, now Columbia University, uses commencement exercises for publicity and fundraising.

1772   Samuel Adams ("press agent" of the American Revolution) sets up Committees of Correspondence to ignite fervor for colonial independence.

1773   Boston Tea Party.

1788   Federalist Papers published to rally support for the new U.S. Constitution.

1830   Baltimore and Ohio Railroad starts publishing train schedules in newspapers and using the press to attract customers; rise of press agentry with the advent of the penny press.

1831   Joseph Henry invents the first electric telegraph.

1835   Samuel Morse invents Morse code.

1835   Amos Kendall becomes Postmaster General under Andrew Jackson and the first person to serve as a presidential press secretary (without the title).

1836   P.T. Barnum, one of the masters of 19th century press agentry, begins his career as a circus showman.

1841   Volney Palmer sets up first ad agency in the United States.

1843   Morse invents the first long distance electric telegraph line.

1850s   Tammany Hall organization in New York uses interviews to cull information about public opinion, marking the beginning of poll taking.

1858   Dairy products manufacturer Borden Co. begins precedent of issuing a financial report to stockholders.

1862   Jay Cooke organizes sale of war bonds during the Civil War to raise money and public support for the Union army, giving rise to the fund drive.

1870   Henry Ward Beecher gives the first celebrity endorsement, in an ad for Waltham watches.

1876   Thomas Edison patents the mimeograph, an office copying machine; Alexander Graham Bell patents the telephone.

1877   Jay Gould opens a "literary bureau" for the Union Pacific Railroad to attract settlers to the West; Edison patents the phonograph.

1879   John Wanamaker, owner of Wanamaker's department store, places the first full-page department store ad in a newspaper.

Late
1800s   Railroads pioneer the use of the press release in an effort to create a favorable public view of the industry.

1884   John and Frank Patterson found National Cash Register; the company uses newsletters, brochures, and flyers in the first direct-mail campaign.

1888   Richard Sears uses a printed mailer to advertise watches and jewelry, beginning the Sears mail-order catalog.

1889   Westinghouse Corp. sets up the first U.S. in-house publicity department.

1892   Joseph Pulitzer writes editorial supporting labor in the Homestead strike, marking the start of the muckraking era.

1897   University of Michigan establishes the first campus public relations office.

1899   Florence Kelley and John Graham Brooks form the National Consumers League, the first national consumer group; Valdemar Poulsen invents the first magnetic recordings.

1900   Publicity Bureau, the first publicity firm, is established.

Early
1900s   Muckrakers Lincoln Steffens, Frank Norris, Ida Tarbell, and Upton Sinclair reveal corruption in industry and politics.

1902   Guglielmo Marconi transmits radio signals across the Atlantic Ocean.

The Evolution of Modern PR

1904   Ivy Ledbetter Lee, the first practitioner of modern public relations, starts his first firm; his theory of public relations is contained in his "Declaration of Principles"; University of Pennsylvania and University of Wisconsin, two major state universities, set up publicity bureaus.

1905   Samuel Hopkins Adams' series "The Great American Fraud" appears in *Colliers Weekly* magazine, exposing patent medicine ads, medicine shows, and other "snake-oil" salesmanship that was popular in the 19th century; U.S. Forest Service establishes the first formal press bureau in a federal government agency.

1909   Samuel Insull, a publicity expert for Chicago Edison Co., is the first to make public relations–related movies.

1910   Edison demonstrated the first talking motion picture.

1914   Ford Motor Co. sets up the first corporate film department; first cross continental telephone call is made.

1917   American Association of College News Bureaus founded (now the Council for Advancement and Support of Education) and American Association of Advertising Agencies are founded.

1917–   Committee for Public Information (Creel Committee) promotes support for
1919   U.S. involvement in World War I; becomes a training ground for many early public relations practitioners.

1919   Edward Bernays, considered by many to be the father of modern public relations, opens his firm; is joined by his wife, Doris Fleischman, in 1922.

1921   NBC radio station in New York broadcasts the first paid radio commercial.

1922   Walter Lippmann's *Public Opinion* is published; coined the phrase "manufacturing consent."

1923   Bernay's *Crystallizing Public Opinion* is published; Vladimir Zworykin invents the cathode-ray tube, enabling the first television camera.

1925   John Logie Baird transmits the first experimental television signal.

1927   NBC starts two radio networks; CBS is founded; Warner Brothers releases *The Jazz Singer*, the first successful talking motion picture.

1927   Arthur W. Page, the first public relations practitioner to serve as an officer and board member for a major corporation, becomes vice president of public relations for the American Telephone and Telegraph Company.

1934   Joseph Begun invents the first magnetic tape recorder for broadcasting.

1936   National Association of Accredited Publicity Directors is founded; becomes National Association of Public Relations Counsel; George Gallup correctly predicts Franklin Roosevelt's defeat of Alfred Landon for the U.S. president, putting the Gallup Poll on the map; The Consumer's Union of the United States, publisher of *Consumer Reports* and an independent product-testing group, is established.

1938   Television broadcasts are taped and edited, rather than produced only live.

1939   American Council on Public Relations is founded.

1939   Scheduled television broadcasts begin.

1942   The Office of War Information, the forerunner of the U.S. Information Agency, is founded to support the war effort; public relations develops as a strong profession during World War II.

1944   Government-owned computers, such as Harvard's Mark I, are put into public service, beginning the information age.

1945   Earl Newson is hired as a public relations counselor for Ford Motor Co., a new role for a public relation practitioner.

1947   The Public Relations Society of America (PRSA), the first professional public relations group, is founded.

1948   Long-playing vinyl record (33 rpm) and the transistor are invented.

1949   Network television starts in the United States.

1951   First commercial computers are sold.

You've Come a Long Way, PR

1953   The International Chamber of Commerce sets up a commission on public relations.

1954   PRSA develops its first code of professional ethics.

1955   The International Public Relations Society is founded.

1958   Chester Carlson invents the photocopier, or "Xerox" machine; the integrated circuit is invented, enabling the further miniaturization of electronic devices and computers.

1966   Xerox invents the telecopier, the first successful fax machine.

1969   The Internet is started with ARPANET.

1970   International Society of Business Communicators is begun.

1971   The computer floppy disc and the microprocessor, a computer on a chip, are invented.

1973   In the Texas Gulf Sulphur case, the U.S. Supreme Court decides that public relations professionals are "insiders," and subject to the same regulations on disclosing a company's financial information as other company members.

1976   First Apple home computer is made.

1979   Cellular phone communication network is started in Japan.

1980   Sony Walkman is invented.

1981   First IBM personal computer (PC) is sold; computer mouse becomes regular part of the computer.

1983   *Time* magazine names the computer as "Man of the Year"; first cellular phone network is started in the United States.

1984 Apple Macintosh is released.

1992 Edward Bernays files bills with the Massachusetts legislature that provide for licensing public relations professionals; the bills fail.

1994 U.S. government releases control of Internet, and the World Wide Web is born.

Key Terms

Ad Council
Arthur W. Page Society
astroturfing
begging mission
Creel Committee
Declaration of Principles
Fireside Chats
Freedom Rides
front group
Gilded Age
grassroots
Great Debates
International Association of Business Communicators
International Public Relations Society
medicine show
muckrakers
Office of War Information (OWI)
patent medicines
photo-op
propaganda
Public Relations Society of America
Sarbanes-Oxley Act
snake-oil salesman
Teflon president
Voice of America
Watergate

Questions for Review and Discussion

1. Describe some modern events that parallel the examples of historical uses of publicity found early in this chapter. Here are some hints: (1) advertising military prowess to advance a political career, (2) shameless self-advertising, (3) promoting military victories to advance a nation's self-image, (4) propagandizing. You can choose examples from any field: politics, business, education, entertainment, and so forth.

2. Many of the American Revolutionists' techniques helped inform modern public relations. As Cutlip has noted, "Today's patterns of public relations practice were shaped by innovations in mobilizing public opinions developed by Adams and his fellow revolutionaries." Using specific examples, describe how the colonists used these public relations techniques: (1) developing an intense public relations campaign, (2) using easily identifiable symbols that roused to action, (3) popularizing slogans that compress complex issues into sound-bites, (4) staging events, (5) getting their side of the story out first, and (6) saturating the market.

3. Find some examples of modern publicity. How do they compare with early efforts? Can you find evidence of modern Barnums and snake-oil salesmen?

4. You are an associate at a public relations firm. One of the firm's clients is a major manufacturer of kids' cereals. Recently, the company's cereal sales have dropped because of parents' concern about the cereal's high sugar content, and your firm has been asked to help turn sales around. How would you handle the campaign if you were Ivy? Bernays? What would be your own professional approach?

5. Think about the growth of the field of public relations. Who are the current leaders in the field? With what issues will future leaders have to contend? How will the increasingly diverse face of America affect the field?

Web Links
Public Relations Society of America
www.prsa.org

International Association of Business Communicators
www.iabc.org

International Public Relations Society
www.iprs.org

Institute for Public Relations
www.instituteforpr.org

Strategy in Public Relations

EVERYDAY STRATEGIES

Strategizing is not an unfamiliar concept to any of you. You plan strategies and make strategic decisions every day. Whenever you identify a desired outcome, consider options for achieving it, and decide on what you believe is the best course of action, you are employing strategy. Take, for example, driving from one place to another. Most of you mentally map out your route. If you're running late, you choose the shortest route. If you are tired, you may pick the route with the fewest construction or streetlight obstacles. If you have the time or want to lift your spirits, you might decide on the most scenic route. Whenever you consciously choose a driving route, whether it's familiar or new, you are creating and executing a strategy.

Strategy is also an integral part of everyday interpersonal communication. For example, when you determine the best time, place, and way to confront a coworker about a problem on the job, you are employing strategy. Imagine that you work in an electronics store, and you have a coworker who consistently interrupts you when you are talking to customers. One day, it happens again, and you have had enough. On the spot, you analyze the situation and determine your options: You could blow up at him right there; you could firmly tell him that you are with a customer and will meet him near the DVD players as soon as possible; or you could just grit your teeth, ignore him, and confront him once and for all in the break room before the end of his shift. If you lose your temper, you run the risk of embarrassing

In strategy, it is important to see distant things as if they were close and to take a distanced view of close things.

—Miyamoto Musashi,
16th century samurai

yourself, your coworker, or your employer. If you ignore your coworker, you might make the customer angry or uncomfortable. So you decide on the second course of action: acknowledging his interruption and directing him to meet you elsewhere in a minute. Determining a solution to such a problem involves employing strategy: You identified a desired outcome, analyzed each option, and chose a course of action. By definition and in practice, then, being strategic involves engaging in a process that includes these essential steps:

1. Identifying a desired outcome or goal
2. Identifying a means of achieving the outcome or goal
3. Evaluating the strengths and weaknesses of the options
4. Making choices

CRITICAL THINKING, REASONING, AND DECISION MAKING IN STRATEGY

In order to complete these steps successfully, in public relations practice as well as in everyday life, you must use critical thinking and decision making. Most likely, throughout your life, your parents, teachers, and others have asked you to go beyond the "face value" of what you read, see, or hear, and analyze the material. In other words, they've asked you to think "critically." **Critical thinking** involves *asking questions and avoiding assumptions, and leads to the discovery of information and insights that lead to better ideas.* Better ideas, when carefully considered and fully developed within the context of a plan, merit being formalized as strategies.

The practice of critical thinking comes from the teaching of Socrates, the Greek philosopher who discovered more than 2,500 years ago that people learn best when they question. Socrates taught by questioning his listeners—the Socratic Method—encouraging them to find deeper truths and understanding. His students, Plato and Aristotle, took his teachings and emphasized the need for a trained mind that reasons and looks below the surface for deeper truths. The method of the ancient Greeks became the foundation for building critical thought in the Western world.

Critical thinkers have at least one trait in common: They never assume or prejudge; instead, they question assumptions. Why? Because things are rarely what they seem at first glance. Critical thinking therefore requires analytical skills. The modern word *analysis* is derived from the Greek word *lysis*, which means "a breaking up." Analyzing something complex involves breaking it up into its constituent parts, considering it from multiple perspectives, and evaluating it in light of related factors or relevant information.

Maintaining a critical, questioning perspective is essential to successful strategic public relations. Making assumptions out of habit, laziness, or prejudice is the opposite of critical thinking. Consider this pair of anti-drug public service announcements (PSAs) produced by the U.S. Office of National Drug Policy for its National Youth Anti-Drug Media Campaign. Each was designed to challenge our assumptions about African Americans. To the steady beep of a cash register scanner, a young black woman asks, "When you scan me, what do you see? Just another futureless, pot-smoking teenager. Like you can just look at me and know what I am, what I'm worth. Well, you're wrong. I'm an artist, a therapist, and the last time I took a hit, I was kickboxing. Drugs aren't me. My life. My decision. I am my anti-drug." In the second ad, a young black man asks the same question, then says, "I see when you scan me.

A new ad by the Partnership for a Drug-Free America emphasizes a similar stereotyping message.

You're sure I'm just another disturbed, pot-smoking teenager. Like you can just look at me and know what I am, what I'm worth. Well, you're wrong. I'm a thinker, an uncle, and the last thing I lit up was a rugby scoreboard. Drugs aren't me. My life. My decision. I am my anti-drug."

Scanning, as the word is described, is a mindless reliance on stereotypes, an absence of real thinking. Scanning can also mean to glance quickly. For example, if you want to get a sense of a topic or subject, you scan a chapter in a book or a web page. If, on the other hand, you need to gather information for a research paper or study for a final exam, you gather facts, organize information, and make judgments—that is, you prepare yourself to think critically.

Here's another scenario: One person watches a local evening news broadcast, while another watches the nightly news, reads a national newspaper or news magazine, visits a reputable news website, checks out a few reliable blogs, and perhaps listens to National Public Radio (NPR). The first does the equivalent of scanning what is going on in the world, getting only a brief, superficial overview. The second finds the meat for critical thinking—analyzing what is going on in the world, digging for story details. As a critical thinker, therefore, you deliberately ask such questions as the following:

- How can I find out if this information is accurate?
- What is the source of this information?
- Can I trust the source?
- What is the fundamental issue presented here?
- From what point of view should I approach this problem?
- Is it reasonable to assume this?
- Looking at these sets of data, what should I deduce?
- What is the basic implication of this illustration?
- If I accept this account, what else might be so?
- What other truths are presented here?
- What is the basic concept here?
- How does this information relate to what I already know?
- Where are the inconsistencies?
- What makes this question complex?

You ask such questions so you can make decisions based on reasoning that you apply to the answers.

STRATEGY WITHIN ORGANIZATIONS

As fundamental and useful as strategy is to everyday life, it is crucial to organizations. Attempting to run an organization, such as a business, without a strategy is folly because organizations must always know where they are headed in order to achieve their goals. Organizations participate in strategic planning to increase their chances for success. It is the process by which organizations determine what they want to achieve and how they intend to achieve it. You will recall that a strategy is a plan—a set of steps that, when followed, lead to accomplishing a goal. The public relations department or an outside public relations firm usually manages an organization's communication planning and implementation. This means that public relations practitioners must be actively involved in an organization's strategic planning both long-term and annually.

Long-term strategic planning sets forth goals and objectives that guide the organization's overall development and business plan. The annual, or short-term, strategic planning sets the objectives that must be accomplished during a fiscal or calendar year in order for the organization to stay on track with its growth and development. Both should be in concert with an organization's written mission statement.

Mission Statements

The mission statement is a brief and clear description of the organization's goal—its *raison d'etre*. This message is directed to the organization's primary target audiences. Mission statements usually appear in the most widely disseminated communication vehicles such as annual reports, websites, and brochures. Some organizations call them statements of commitment. Some mission statements are more direct than others, and corporations tend to include a statement to their competitors or reveal their marketing strategy in their statements. Consider the following mission statements:

Dell: "Dell's commitment to customer value, to team, to being direct, to operating responsibly and, ultimately, to winning continues to differentiate us from other companies."

IBM: "At IBM, we strive to lead in the creation, development and manufacture of the industry's most advanced information technologies, including computer systems, software, networking systems, storage devices and microelectronics. We translate these advanced technologies into value for our customers through our professional solutions and services business worldwide."

Nike: "To bring inspiration and innovation to every athlete" in the world. "If you have a body, you are an athlete."

The Annie E. Casey Foundation: "The primary mission of the Foundation is to foster public policies, human service reforms, and community supports that more effectively meet the needs of today's vulnerable children and families."

Mission statements must be thoughtful and describe the organization's goals.

AARP: "AARP is dedicated to enhancing quality of life for all as we age. We lead positive social change and deliver value to members through information, advocacy and service."

The Coca-Cola Company: It envisions itself as the "world's most inclusive brand": "The Coca-Cola Company exists to benefit and refresh everyone it touches."

Pepsi Cola: "At Pepsi-Cola, quality, taste and consumer satisfaction are our highest priorities."

The Johnson & Johnson mission statement in Figure 4.1 is one of the oldest and most well known.

Figure 4.1
Johnson & Johnson
Credo

SOURCE: Johnson &
Johnson, http://www.jnj
.com/connect/about-jnj/
jnj-credo/

> **Our Credo**
>
> We believe our first responsibility is to the doctors, nurses and patients, to mothers and fathers and all others who use our products and services. In meeting their needs everything we do must be of high quality. We must constantly strive to reduce our costs in order to maintain reasonable prices. Customers' orders must be serviced promptly and accurately. Our suppliers and distributors must have an opportunity to make a fair profit.
>
> We are responsible to our employees, the men and women who work with us throughout the world. Everyone must be considered as an individual. We must respect their dignity and recognize their merit. They must have a sense of security in their jobs. Compensation must be fair and adequate, and working conditions clean, orderly and safe. We must be mindful of ways to help our employees fulfill their family responsibilities. Employees must feel free to make suggestions and complaints. There must be equal opportunity for employment, development and advancement for those qualified. We must provide competent management, and their actions must be just and ethical.
>
> We are responsible to the communities in which we live and work and to the world community as well. We must be good citizens — support good works and charities and bear our fair share of taxes. We must encourage civic improvements and better health and education. We must maintain in good order the property we are privileged to use, protecting the environment and natural resources.
>
> Our final responsibility is to our stockholders. Business must make a sound profit. We must experiment with new ideas. Research must be carried on, innovative programs developed and mistakes paid for. New equipment must be purchased, new facilities provided and new products launched. Reserves must be created to provide for adverse times. When we operate according to these principles, the stockholders should realize a fair return.
>
> Johnson & Johnson

Long-Term and Short-Term Goals

Clearly, an organization's mission statement reflects its long-term goals. But short-term goals are established often to enhance and move the organization along in accomplishing its mission. Communication programs and campaigns are designed to help the organization to attain its mission and meet its goals. Therefore, there must be long-term and short-term communication strategies. When we speak of communication or public relations programs, we are referring to "ongoing" communication activities designed to help accomplish the mission. Programs are usually long-term, with activities taking place over a long period of time and may include many individual campaigns. Communication campaigns are very specific and are usually short-term. Some campaigns such as the "Smokey the Bear" campaign to prevent forest fires and the "Five-a-Day" campaign designed to encourage consumers to eat five fruits and vegetables a day can be long-term. Both programs and campaigns have strategies and tactics. In fact, the Centers for Disease Prevention and Control (CD) updated the "Five-a-Day" campaign to the "Fruits and Veggies Matter" campaign.

Strategic Management

Again, public relations should be a component of the strategic management of an organization. James E. Grunig wrote that public relations must be managed and practiced strategically in order to contribute to an organization's success. He and Todd Hunt added:

> Organizations use strategic management to relate their missions to their environments. They use strategic management to identify opportunities and dangers in the environment; to develop strategies for exploiting the opportunities and minimizing the dangers; and to develop, implement, and evaluate the strategies.

According to Grunig, and other public relations scholars, public relations plays a significant role in moving an organization's mission forward and in helping to solve problems of the organization. At its best, public relations anticipates and identifies problems within and external to an organization to assist management in the problem-solving process, providing sound counsel and strategy. See Chapter 10 for more discussion of the role of PR in problem solving.

Effective, proactive public relations is based on solving a series of problems and taking advantage of every communication opportunity. In this sense, problems do not have to be a bad thing, such as a crisis. Instead, problems can be welcomed as anticipated opportunities.

Let's follow this scenario as an example: The city council of a small town wants to encourage businesses from surrounding areas to move into the town to boost the town's economy. On the face of it, the managers may be making an excellent decision. However, research the PR counsel has been conducting about residents' views on increased industry suggests that the decision might be opposed by the community. The research indicates that community members have concerns about increased traffic congestion, pollution, and the ability of the town's infrastructure to support expanded industry.

If the council managers hold a news conference or issue a news release inviting surrounding businesses to

Courtesy of Jim Collins

Best-selling author Jim Collins

consider moving or expanding into the town, the news might very well elicit strong opposition from the community. However, acting on PR counsel, the council members instead decide to implement a strategy that begins with educating community members about the benefits of bringing in new industry. The education program addresses the concerns of traffic, pollution, and infrastructure. By the time the city council starts its program to attract industry, city managers anticipate full community support.

Taking advantage of every opportunity to interact positively with your key audiences is another proactive and effective way to practice public relations. Opportunities often present themselves during the day-to-day operations of an organization and are uncovered through careful listening to your environment. These occasions can be as small as open houses for volunteers or as large as orchestrated productions for annual meetings. In the previous scenario, the managers in the town might have learned that many of the parents in town wanted the high school to begin offering a more advanced computer class for high school seniors. This is an opportunity for the town manager to provide information to parents about a computer firm in a nearby town interested in offering internships to students as a way of "screening" future employees. Such an opportunity might help the council gain support for the idea of a new business coming to town. There are no PR silver bullets that can be deployed to solve a problem or take advantage of an opportunity, but thinking and planning strategically is always the best beginning.

In *Good to Great—Why Some Companies Make the Leap . . . and Others Don't*, best-selling author Jim Collins explains the importance of asking the right questions about a company. Collins and his team of researchers found that the companies that move from good to great have "The Council," a "strategic thinking group," which helps the company grow and sustain growth by analyzing, asking questions, and engaging in dialogue and debate focused on how to achieve established goals. Strategic thinking goes beyond planning and includes exploring the hard questions about an organization in order to improve its chances for greatness. As a management function within organizations, public relations plays a particularly important role in strategic planning, strategic communication, and integrated communication.

Strategic Planning

All successful organizations participate in strategic planning. General Electric (GE)—often referred to as the best-managed corporation in the world—created its strategic planning grid in the early 1960s. The GE grid took many factors into account, including the company's strengths, product quality, price, knowledge of the customer, relative market share, market size, market growth rate, and profit margin. If General Electric were to make public the updated version of this grid, it would include even more factors, such as employee satisfaction and the corporation's value statement.

The way strategic planning is done varies from organization to organization, but in general **strategic planning** *is the process by which organizations determine what they want to achieve and how they intend to achieve it.* While originally a corporate tool, strategic planning became popular with other types of organizations—government agencies, associations, universities, and nonprofits—in the 1990s to meet the need for better financial accountability. Investors of all types—oversight committees, board directors, employees, members, volunteers, consumers, funding organizations—all demand information about how their capital investment in an organization is being spent and to what end.

Strategic planning requires an organization to examine its internal and external environments and resources and to devise the best approach for taking advantage of its long-range opportunities while minimizing threats to its success. Generally, this process involves top executives and managers from all departments; all those involved should have a deep understanding of the organization and its environment. Strategic plan-

Strategy is built upon making the correct short- and long-term moves.

ning is a process that should never end, because its function is to ask the questions that result from critical thinking in order to keep the organization's success in focus. Most strategic planning groups are convened regularly, not to solve a particular problem but to provide advice and counsel. Organizations also often seek the assistance of outside consultants, such as pollsters, trend watchers, public opinion experts, public relations practitioners, and management consultants to help them with this process.

Strategic Planning Is a Learning Tool

While clearly a management function, strategic planning is also a learning tool. Jim Collins' research suggests that the good-to-great companies had a "deep understanding" of three key elements upon which they built their strategies and that guided their leap from good to great: What they were best at, what drove their economic engines (cash flow and profitability), and what they were most passionate about. Understanding these elements enabled the companies to focus on growth and sustainability, as well as their core competencies.

Strategic Planning Is a Focusing Tool

Given the complexity of today's global economy and organizational environments, managers and employees at every level need help focusing their efforts. Strategic planning provides that assistance, helping members of organizations prioritize what they do each day, how they spend their time and their organizations' money.

Strategic Communication

Vicki Spruill and Lynne Murphy are co-founders and directors of FoundationWorks, an organization that helps foundations work more strategically with their grantees and use communication to advance program goals. They created a model that contrasts what they call FYI communication with strategic communication. According to FoundationWorks, **FYI communication** (literally, "for your information," but what might better be described as "I-need-you-to-know" communication) is *developing a message to inform a specific audience*, while **strategic communication** is *delivering a message to a specific audience to elicit an intended response*. Taking their comparison a step further, FYI communication often fails to inform a specific audience because, if the message is not effective, the intended audience neither hears nor retains it.

Clients and managers often begin conversations about communication with public relations practitioners by telling them what they want, asking for brochures, newsletters, websites, and other items before the practitioner has an opportunity to provide advice. Production of materials is never a first step, and having a tangible product immediately is not always the measure of a job well done. FYI communication emphasizes the production of collateral materials. Collateral materials are the products developed by PR practitioners such as newsletters, brochures, media kits, etc. (These are discussed in depth in Chapters 14, 15, and 16.) Clearly, sometimes practitioners want to show what they have accomplished and, even more often, clients and management want to "see" what they bought. But focusing on materials often overlooks the need to integrate less traditional public relations forms, such as relationship building through interpersonal communication.

To put it bluntly, when you employ FYI communication, you are not being strategic; you are simply sharing knowledge because you have it, believe it to be valuable, and assume that key audiences want to know the information. The other assumption is usually that the key audiences will *do* something with the information. Plans based on assumptions are never strategic, and communication based on assumptions is not effective. Instead, as a practitioner you must conduct appropriate research to avoid making assumptions and you must communicate with the purpose of obtaining a desired response. Let's consider an example.

It is a fact that passengers in an automobile should wear seat belts to protect themselves in the event of an accident. It is not enough to simply say, "Fasten your seat belt because seat belts save lives" or "Buckle up for safety because safety belts saved X number of lives last year." These types of messages rarely elicit the desired response. How do you know that these messages are not effective? Because millions of teenagers do not fasten their seat belts when traveling in an automobile. The leading cause of death among U.S. teens is motor vehicle crashes. According to the National Highway Traffic Safety Administration, two-thirds of those killed are not buckled up.

What would be a good way to reach an audience of teenage drivers? You might guess that PSAs would work well, but that would be only a guess. Getting the attention of teenagers who still do not use seat belts is more complex, requiring research into the best approach. Since teens listen to other teens, the key audience for getting this group to change may be those who have influence over them, their peers. In this case, our message would be directed not at those who don't buckle up, but at *influencers*—those who influence the key audience's behaviors (see Chapter 5). While it is reasonable to conduct additional research to determine why teens don't buckle up, it is highly likely that the best messenger to encourage a behavior change is their peers.

Audience-focused messages are at the heart of strategic communication. These messages are compelling. We create them by developing an understanding of our audiences so that we can use words, symbols, music, and other elements that resonate with their values, ideas, attitudes, norms, and behaviors. Product-focused or organization-oriented messages, on the other hand, are not likely to be strategic. When organizations attempt to communicate solely from the orientation of the product, program, behavior, issue, or organization itself, they cannot reach key audiences effectively. Similarly, raw data or just the facts, even when laced with statistics—mainstays of FYI communication—do not make compelling messages.

The American Diabetes Association (ADA) conducted in-depth research with its members and volunteers before creating a new video to introduce the organization to key audiences. They found that ADA's old video, highlighting what the organization does for members was too focused on the organization and its work. The new video emphasizes the patient and the disease before it attempts to explain ADA's role and how it helps patients. The key audiences—patients, their family, and volunteers—star in the video. They tell the story of their challenges and how the ADA helps them. It is difficult to imagine a more compelling message for the ADA's audience, which is why this video is a stunning example of strategic communication. Table 4.1 highlights the primary differences between FYI and strategic communication.

Elements of Strategic Communication

One of the most important elements of a strategic communication plan is setting *measurable objectives*—that is, stating from the outset what we expect to accomplish and how we will measure the success. (Chapter 6 covers measurement in depth.) FYI communication focuses on measuring *output criteria,* such as how many brochures were disseminated or how many news stories were printed or broadcast. Measurable results, or *outcomes,* are important, but they should not drive a program or campaign to the extent that we do not actively look for less-direct correlations and results. For instance, if one of the objectives of the seat-belt campaign is to increase by 10 percent the number of drivers and passengers who fasten their seat belts, and we accomplish this objective, we are successful. But if we fail to fully analyze the

Table 4.1.   The Differences between FYI and Strategic Communication

FYI Communication	Strategic Communication	Key Difference
Disseminates information	Informs while identifying a specific desirable action	The audience is given an option to "do" something
Hopes the audience will do something	Asks audience to do something specific/change a specific behavior • Write a letter • Visit a website • Make a purchase	Identifies a specific behavior that is doable
Inward perspective • Organization-focused • Focus on product	Outward perspective • Audience-focused • Focus on effect of action	Considers audience needs and not the organization's needs
Ineffective messages • Data-driven • Designed for general public • Created in vacuum	Effective messages • Audience-driven • Targeted audience • Informed by research	Speaks to the audience in ways that resonate
Emphasizes specific collateral	Emphasizes integrated communication	Takes advantage of many ways to reach the audience
Formulaic • Automatically uses same approach	Iterative • Systematically identifies and uses unique opportunities and at unique times	Checks in with the audience to know how, when, and where to communicate
Increases chances for mistakes	Decreases chances for mistakes	Monitors and tracks for pitfalls
Expensive	More expensive	Adds levels of evaluation that require more budget
Evaluation of output	Evaluation of results	Measures effects

SOURCE: Adapted from Vikki Spruill, Ocean Conservancy

campaign, we miss an opportunity. For instance, the additional 10 percent who are using seat belts may have been influenced to do so by an audience we did not see as key to the campaign.

Strategic communication is opportunistic in that it takes advantage of the dynamics of communicating. That is, we continue to learn and our messages to evolve as our programs and campaigns bring us closer to accomplishing our mission. Strategic communication is also somewhat risky. Taking advantage of a dynamic process and allowing risk are key elements of strategic communication. That's why it is not strategic to rely on a plan that predicts outcomes and measures only the end result. When we communicate strategically, we are consistently testing our messages, observing what is taking place, and making adjustments throughout the course of a campaign or program. Taking risks does not mean being irresponsible with your client's or organization's reputation or resources—instead, it means understanding that maintaining the status quo is not always the best avenue to success. Employing strategy and communicating strategically increase our chances for success.

Integrated Communication

The marriage of strategic planning and strategic communication results in what is known as **integrated communication.**

Where does the idea of integrating strategies come from? It comes from an approach known both as integrated marketing communications (IMC) and integrated communications (IC) developed by communication professionals in the 1990s. Inherently strategic, the **integrated approach** *merges the functions of advertising, marketing, promotions, and public relations to ensure that all an organization's communication functions speak as one.* Using public relations and marketing concepts to enhance the exchange between organizations and audiences, it coordinates and sharpens messages into a unified message to increase the organization's effectiveness. Execution and strategy are especially important in IC (see the Brief Case Study on page 81).

STRATEGIC PR IN CONTEXT

Ready, Shoot, Aim! That once described the way public relations was practiced. Armed with a product or emboldened by an idea, practitioners marched off to tell the public what they wanted them to know. Today, most public relations practitioners would agree that the practice requires following more complicated steps than that, and that increasingly their activities must be strategic.

Two origins of the word *strategy* firmly connect strategy and PR practice, as it is derived from the Greek term *strategos*, which means "the art of the general or generalship." In fact, *strategy* is defined by the fourth edition of *Webster's New World College Dictionary* as "the science of planning and directing large-scale military operations (as distinguished from tactics), maneuvering forces into the most advantageous position prior to actual engagement with the enemy." The contemporary definition of *strategy* continues to reveal its military origins: "skill in managing or planning, especially by using stratagem," such as 1) "a military maneuver designed to deceive or surprise an enemy," or 2) "a clever, often underhanded scheme for achieving an objective, stratos, *army,* + agein, *to lead.*"

The use of strategy in military operations is ancient, and sports and computer game fans are familiar with the military-like strategy required by these entertainments.

BRIEF CASE STUDY

Bank One's 140th Anniversary

In 2003 on the occasion of its 140th anniversary, Bank One, Chicago's largest bank, launched a celebration campaign in the form of a communitywide program to salute its hometown of Chicago and its nine million residents. The $15 million program included an advertising campaign designed as a tribute to Chicagoans and significant financial support for programs that enhance the quality of life in the city. The campaign included a series of television, print, radio, and outdoor ads featuring well-known Chicagoans, such as football player and coach Mike Ditka and blues singer Koko Taylor, talking about the things they love about the city.

This message was supported by a public relations community outreach effort that included underwriting a wide range of community programs at popular venues, including Garfield Park Conservatory, the Goodman Theatre, Grant Park, and Ravinia. In support of the city's love affair with biking, the bank launched "Bike One," a program providing complimentary bike valet parking at Chicago events, free summer bike tours, funding for the city's "Bike Chicago," "Bike to Work Day," and "Bike the Drive" programs and distribution of 100,000 free bike maps.

Bank One became a presenting partner of the city's beloved Chicago Bears, entering into the first presenting partnership agreement in NFL history. The 12-year multi-million-dollar corporate partnership committed the bank to working with the Bears at their home stadium—Soldier Field—and in publications, broadcasts, special events, and year-round community outreach.

Working the Case

1. What indicates to you that Bank One used an integrated approach to its celebration?
2. In what ways was this campaign integrated?
3. Do you think this campaign was considered a success? Why or why not?

Not coincidentally, the original "sport of kings" was war-making, an expression that dates back to at least the mid-1600s. Similarly, just as games or other contests have rules, there are "rules of engagement" in war, and generals as well as coaches (and businesspeople) come up with a game plan.

A Closer Look at the Language of PR

A review of public relations jargon shows the field's considerable reliance on military terminology. In addition to *strategy*, the field routinely uses terms such as *campaigns*, *targets*, *tactics*, *execution*, *phase*, *collateral*—all of these are terms with military origins or lingering militaristic connotations. It is very important to note that mentioning PR's language's origins is *not* to suggest that public relations is in practice militaristic, per se, but to put effective public relations practice in its proper context: Like war, PR is complex and high-stakes, and any such endeavor requires strategy. The desire to conclude a process successfully, to, in a word, *win*, prompts us to marshal resources and plot our moves. Wars are won. Political campaigns are won. Contests are won. Games are won. However, in PR, campaigns are *successful*—that is, they achieve desired results. Those results are often more complex than the either/or realities of winning or losing a contest with a clearly defined beginning and ending.

ENGAGING ETHICS

A Whopper and a Pepsi Max, Please . . .

In late 2008 two companies flirted with controversy by creating ads that most people felt the companies knew would be controversial. You may recall that an ad for Pepsi Max featured the drink's only calorie committing suicide in a German publication. A Burger King ad was a "quest" for virgin Whopper eaters in developing countries. The Pepsi ad was a PR nightmare and the company pulled its ad, while Burger King continued its "quest" despite the negative publicity. PR professionals critical of the ads said the companies knew the ads would be played and replayed on YouTube, resulting in expanded publicity. Still other critics pointed to the companies' insensitivity to the seriousness of suicide and to poor countries where many cannot afford a hamburger. Search the Internet and look at criticism of "Whopper Virgins: The World's Purest Taste Test" and the Pepsi Max ad.

1. Do you agree or disagree with the critics?
2. What role could PR have played in avoiding the reactions?
3. What role did PR play in responding to the negative coverage?

Traditional Models of PR Practice

Four- or five-step process models for developing public relations programs and campaigns have been part of public relations practice and education for nearly 30 years, and some would argue that strategy is inherent in each. The Public Relations Society of America (PRSA) encourages the use of these models, requiring that five categories of information be included in case studies entered for the organization's prestigious Silver Anvil professional excellence awards: situation analysis, research, planning, execution, and evaluation. Because it is important that all practitioners be familiar with these approaches, a brief survey of the traditional models follows.

The traditional models are all known by their acronyms, which serve handy mnemonic devices to remember the model's stages.*

- RACE: **R**esearch, **A**ction, **C**ommunication, and **E**valuation: The oldest model and the one from which others were developed; devised by John Marston in 1979
- REPACE: **RE**search, **P**lanning and **A**ction, **C**ommunication and **E**valuation: Devised by Wilcox, Ault, and Agee in 1986
- ROSIE: **O**bjectives, **S**trategies, and **I**mplementation between **R**esearch and **E**valuation: Devised by Sheila Crifasi
- RAISE: **R**esearch, **A**daptation, **I**mplementation, **S**trategy, and **E**valuation: Devised by Robert Kendal in 1992
- ROPE: **R**esearch, **O**bjectives, **P**rogramming, and **E**valuation: Devised by Jerry Hendrix in 1998

While the sequenced steps of these approaches are helpful, they are not adequate for planning and implementing a successful PR program or campaign today. They are useful for *reporting* what happened, but not for *developing* a fully strategic campaign or program. While acronyms are effective for helping us to remember research first and evaluation last, they are not very useful for strategic planning. The public relations

---

*Ronald D. Smith, *Strategic Planning for Public Relations*, Lawrence Erlbaum Associates, Mahwah, NJ, 2002

process is too complicated and dynamic to be contained in the few steps. And research and evaluation should be taking place throughout the campaign or program, so to conduct it at the end of the process is faulty at best.

A more comprehensive model with greater strategic applications is one created by Sharyn Sutton, called the Six Steps, or Six Building Blocks to Communicating: Target, Action, Reward, Support, Image and Openings (TARSIO). This model puts the target audience at the beginning of the process, acknowledging the need to conduct research. It emphasizes the importance of giving the audience an action to take and a reward for taking the action. It asks the practitioner to support his or her claims by making them credible. It directs us to focus on the current or desired image of an organization or a desired action and on where and when the target audience will be open to receive the message.

OVERVIEW OF THE PROCESS OF STRATEGIC PUBLIC RELATIONS

Part Three of this text presents a detailed guide to practicing public relations strategically, one based on a process with four basic stages. Like the traditional PR models described previously, this text's comprehensive guide to strategic public relations practice cannot be considered a panacea, as communication is dynamic and situations and circumstances are always changing. But this guide attempts to anticipate and delineate the steps that most reliably lead to successful PR programs and campaigns. As the Preface of this text states, the model is designed to demonstrate and guide a process that is dynamic. This model acknowledges a key feature of strategic public relations practice: it is recursiveness. A process that is **recursive** is *not linear. Instead it involves backtracking, leapfrogging, and repeating, as well as completing multiple activities simultaneously.*

Each stage of the process of strategic public relations has several steps and does not, in practice, progress linearly from step to step, stage to stage. It is a *recursive process.* That is, it is organized around a formal sequence but ultimately determines its own unique course each time it is undertaken, as the process likely repeats itself in part or in whole, steps are likely taken out of order, and steps are often taken simultaneously.

The strategic public relations process is dynamic and purposeful. Each stage in the process builds on the previous steps taken and anticipates the next, ensuring that each instance of communication has been well planned and has the best chance for success.

Figure 4.2 provides a visual overview of the process of strategic public relations. The audience is at the center of this process (hence our attention to "audience-focused practice"). The audience is surrounded by the environment, which includes factors such as problems and opportunities, people's attitudes, social issues and events, media influences, and organizations' mission, vision, and goals. Research is ongoing, as practitioners are constantly trying to understand the environment. And the process surrounds, contains, helps practitioners manage the complexity within, and achieve desired outcomes.

Stage One: Discovery and Analysis

The activities that comprise the first stage of the strategic public relations process involve gaining a sense of where your organization or issue is positioned in the environment. The specific activities are discovery, problem analysis, and what is called *formative research.*

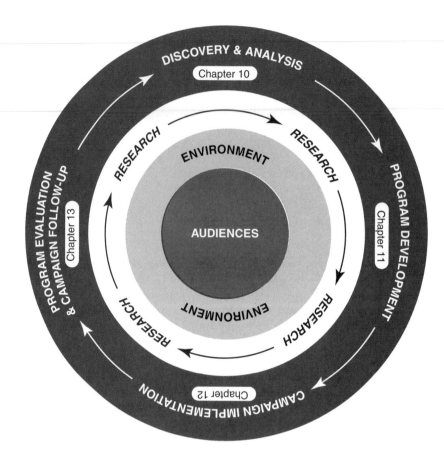

Figure 4.2

The Process of Strategic Public Relations

Discovery

This stage of the process begins with identifying the problem or opportunity that is the impetus for the public relations campaign or program. Once this is understood, the next step is setting goals and indicators for success. To be strategic, communication activities must be a part of the organization's overall strategy. You will recall that a strategy is a plan—a set of steps that when followed lead to accomplishing a goal. Every effective strategy begins with a clear statement of the goal of the effort. As a PR practitioner you must align public relations efforts with the stated mission of the organization to ensure that the PR goals are aligned with the organization's goals. In addition to setting goals, identifying internal and external resources, discovering stakeholders (supporters, opposition, competition), and identifying potential target audiences as specifically as possible are crucial to you at this stage.

As an example, let's use the efforts of the Department of Health and Human Services (DHSS) to put an impending pandemic influenza and its possible consequences on the radar screen of the American public. The department's goal was to have as many Americans as possible be prepared for and survive the epidemic. This goal was directly aligned to the department's mission, which included "protecting the health of all Americans." Interestingly, the department's key audience was "all Americans"—a difficult and unenviable position. The primary problem was the impending disease and the crises that would ensue after it hit the nation. The department identified community leaders in business, faith-based organizations, and community activism as key audiences for a message about pandemic influenza preparedness.

Problem Analysis

In the practice of public relations, analyzing a problem requires varying degrees of research and analysis. The research conducted during this phase is not formal audience research. Instead, informal research methods are used to help answer questions about problems and provide information for building a more formal research strategy. Research methods are discussed in depth in Chapter 6. Environmental scans or situation analyses, tools for determining what is going on outside of the organization and amongst the key audiences, help you to understand the marketplace, while analysis of the organization's internal strengths, and weaknesses and external opportunities and threats inform your understanding of the organization's place in the market.

Formative Research

The research conducted before and during public relations planning is called **formative research** or *developmental research*. This research helps us to form or develop the goals and objectives, strategy, message development, and tactics of a program.

Informal Research   Conducting an environmental analysis to determine what other organizations are involved in the issue, how they have engaged audiences, and how effective their efforts have been is part of the public relations process, also. This process helps you to identify the resources available and assists in determining the barriers to success. It provides a reasonable view of the marketplace, including identifying competitors and potential partners.

DHHS discovered from its tracking of conversations taking place globally about pandemic influenza preparedness that while many conversations among concerned individuals were taking place, community leaders are not in the conversation.

This stage also employs existing data such as demographic data sets (age, income, education, etc.), psychographic lifestyle and values data (what the key audience reads, views, listens to), and public opinion polls. Discovery and problem analysis employ many tools, including interviewing key informants; conducting communication audits; conducting media audits, mystery shopping, and literature review; locating knowledge gaps; listing and prioritizing relevance of what's known about each target audience; formulating research questions based on what information is needed; and prioritizing research questions.

Formal Research   The discovery process does not crystallize the primary audience(s) but provides your best educated guess of who the target audience will be. The formal audience research begins with these audiences and the questions you formulated in the previous step. This step begins with creating a research plan that guides implementation of the research and outlines how the primary formal audience research will proceed. Its primary purpose is to delineate the steps to be taken and why. Research instruments are created based on the type of research method chosen. Quantitative research usually involves surveys for which we create questionnaires with closed-end questions. This method is designed to ask how many and to what extent. Topic guides or moderator guides are the tools of qualitative research that help you ask why, how, and why, during focus groups, in-depth interviews, and many other qualitative methods. The step usually ends with a written report, survey findings, or other analyses and reports presented to the client. The reports include recommendations for communicating and often include reevaluating audiences and formulating core message strategy, as your guesswork is done and you should know your primary audiences. All of these tools and reports are discussed in depth in Chapters 6, 11, and 12.

To return to our example, DHHS conducted a series of focus groups and interviews with the key audiences to learn what they knew and how they reacted to the future crisis caused by pandemic flu. The findings were what you may have guessed. The community leaders had some knowledge about pandemic influenza but wanted to hear from health authorities about the details of the threat of the outbreak *and* wanted evidence that other leaders were taking action toward preparation.

Stage Two: Program Planning

The activities that comprise the second stage of the process focus on planning, specifically strategic planning and program management. The specific activities are considered program planning. Formative research continues during this stage.

Program Planning

The first and most important task in this step is writing the campaign or program plan. A strategic communication plan provides a guide for how the work of the PR effort will unfold. Its major components include the following:

- A precise statement of the opportunity or problem that created the need for the campaign or program
- Goals, statements of the broad outcomes desired, and objectives (the measurable results of the public relations effort)
- The specific and well-defined audience to whom the campaign is directed
- Tactics, major action steps that will take place to implement the strategy
- Monitoring, tracking, and evaluation plans for measuring success of meeting the objectives of the program or campaign
- A time line
- Staffing
- A budget that closely reflects the proposed cost for the program

Anticipating Outcomes

Anticipating outcomes is allied to setting goals, but it is more specific. After all of the formative research is done, you will clearly articulate the desired outcomes. This means establishing measurable objectives.

Identifying the desired results is stating as specifically as possible what you want to achieve. As stated earlier, every effective strategy begins with a clear statement of the goal of the effort.

After the plan is completed and agreed to by the client, the work of developing a creative strategy statement and creative concepts that determine the messages and the message strategy begins. After a core message is developed in copy and visuals, you begin testing them with members of a key audience to be sure they resonate and are effective. The results of the testing reveal if and how the message needs to be "tweaked." At this point in the process, you should deliver message-testing reports to the client and prepare a final implementation plan and schedule for approval.

The implementation plan helps organize the manner in which your communication will transpire. This is another crucial point at which to consult all outside partners involved in the campaign. Planning every step and assigning roles and responsibilities for each necessary step and task is very important. Primarily, you are concerned with production, dissemination, and monitoring of your campaign rollout. Producing campaign materials can be done in-house, externally, or a combination of both. Regardless, your implementation plan must account for production time and glitches, as there is always the possibility of difficulties no matter how well you plan.

The DHHS example provides some detail in terms of the planning process. Clearly, one objective was to provide the science-based evidence community leaders required from credible health authorities, and the other to demonstrate the activities of other leaders toward a national movement for preparation. Ogilvy PR, the firm engaged by DHHS for this initiative, planned two significant events: a high-level, one-day leadership meeting—Pandemic Leadership Forum—and a leadership summit by blog prior to the face-to-face forum.

Stage Three: Program/Campaign Implementation

Implementing a PR program is exciting, especially after so much planning, formative research, analysis, and revisions. Throughout program implementation, strategic practitioners continue researching their audiences and the effectiveness of their plan and materials. This stage's research is called *monitoring research.*

Program Implementation

Launching a campaign requires additional planning, so while this is the phase during which you get to see the fruits of your hard work, planning and a little research are still required. Two things have to happen before implementation can begin. First, depending on your budget and findings during message pretesting, you may still need to test the proposed materials. You will employ the identical principles that you applied to pre-testing messages. The idea, of course, is to make sure your materials adhere to and reflect what you learned in message pretesting. This is a final check to be sure you are on the right track. If you find out the look and feel of your materials are a little off, it is better to garner that information now than later.

Second, you must follow your implementation plan. It is your best tool for this phase of the work. It serves as a guide and a checklist to assist you in dealing with the complexities of the many activities that go on in implementing.

Disseminating materials has its intricacies as well. In addition to tracking the release of information such as news releases and audio and video materials, you may need to manage the warehousing of materials not yet ready for dissemination. Tracking responses and monitoring success are crucial to knowing how you are doing currently, and serve as research for future initiatives. Implementation includes reporting to the client what is going on. You will, of course, report the quantities of materials distributed, but much more information is also required. Your feedback should include a reading on audience response, success and weaknesses of the campaign, requirements for readjusting your plan if and as necessary, and repeating some of the steps you took previously.

Looking at the DHHS example, implementation of the DHHS pandemic flu plan to engage community leaders involved hosting virtual and face-to-face meetings. The virtual forum was the first blog hosted by a Cabinet member, which was conducted to gain interest and to get conversations going online. The face-to-face meeting gave community leaders an opportunity to discuss how to help Americans prepare with key DHHS leaders. Ogilvy conducted media outreach and developed collateral materials, also.

Measuring Results   Measurement of the results of a program or campaign is crucial to delineating success. We discussed earlier the need to demonstrate to management and the client what was accomplished by the campaign or program. You know it is necessary to measure the success of your efforts as you progress, but you must also conduct *evaluative research*. Practitioners have found measuring the success of their efforts more important than in the past, as increasingly clients, executives, and funding organizations are asking for a demonstration of the effectiveness of a communication campaign or program. More and more, clients want to see a return on their investment (ROI). Measuring results should not be limited to the products produced; it must include how you made a difference. It is not helpful alone to indicate how many fashion editors attended the annual Heart Truth campaign Red Dress Collection fashion show during New York's Fashion Week. But attendance statistics combined with the quantified measurement that awareness of heart disease by women has increased during the three years of the campaign from 34 percent to 57 percent is an indication of results. Evaluation tells you how well you planned and what you learned, and it is useful information at the formative phase of new programs or campaigns.

Stage Four: Program Evaluation and Campaign Follow-Up

The activities that comprise the fourth stage of the process focus on strategic program evaluation. The specific activities are program evaluation and results reporting. What is known as *evaluative research* dominates the stage.

Program Evaluation

Just as it is important to monitor and measure the success of implementation, it is important to evaluate when the work is done. You establish effective objectives during the planning phase so that you can determine if you accomplished what you proposed and so that you can analyze them against the overarching client or organizational goals. You assigned objectives to each key audience and created mechanisms for gathering feedback, determining the best design given your resources. In the end, you are trying to ascertain the effects of your program or campaign on the audience. In other words, did you achieve the behavior you desired, and how did the audience react? Program evaluation depends on the complexity of the design and the points at which you will collect data. You can use observation, survey, and qualitative methods, and collect baseline data before the implementation begins, and collect ongoing results. Ideally, you want to find participants that have been exposed to the campaign messages and materials. Also, be aware of not being too simplistic. While you can use qualitative research methods effectively for formative research, evaluative qualitative methods require you to think in terms of analysis and diagnosis of the program effects. It is best to think about evaluation early instead of waiting until the end of implementation. You should be gathering feedback from partners and tracking and monitoring systems.

In the DHHS example, little evaluation of the type we have discussed was conducted, but Ogilvy reported that it "exceeded its year-one goal of recruiting partners and designing substantial partnership roles." This means that community leaders were working together to have Americans prepare for pandemic influenza.

Results Reporting

In the end, evaluative or summative research is used to begin the discovery process for future initiatives. It helps you to use feedback to improve future programs and communication. Ultimately, you want to learn how to improve future campaigns and programs. A formal evaluation report should be prepared for the client, providing a clear statement of the campaign or program results.

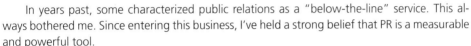

Strategic and Tactical Behavior Shouldn't Be Confused

Bob Wheatley was CEO of Wheatley & Timmon when he wrote this point of view for PRWeek.

In years past, some characterized public relations as a "below-the-line" service. This always bothered me. Since entering this business, I've held a strong belief that PR is a measurable and powerful tool.

In fact, we're witnessing the dawn of an exciting era, with PR claiming its rightful place above the line as a legitimate first-string player in the marketing mix— securing a lead role with other disciplines to draw new customers and keep existing ones from wandering. It's a heady opportunity for us to realize a new and vital responsibility in the building of strong brands. But are we ready for the disciplines and skill sets that this will require? I'd venture to say yes in some cases and no in others. The words "strategic thinking" and "planning" have been thrown together for some time in our field. And I would argue that, in some instances, the users do not know the difference between strategic and tactical behavior. To illustrate, years ago I worked for a Seattle-based division of Ogilvy & Mather called Cole & Weber. Back then, C&W was a great regional powerhouse, a dominant player that counted many of the local blue-chip companies on its roster, from Boeing to Westin Hotels. Even in the late 1970s, cross-disciplinary integration was present within the agency's two principal companies: an ad agency and a PR firm. Both were separate entities and leaders in their respective marketplaces. There was, however, a distinct difference in the processes and skills practiced by each side of the house. The PR agency successfully sold its services and capabilities, and executed programs with great effect and creativity. The ad side, on the other hand, carried a sacrosanct devotion to research and business analysis that preceded any attempt to generate a plan. The approach was not only to study a client's products and brand values, but also to understand the vagaries of how the business operated from the factory floor up through the channels of distribution. From there, significant assets were deployed for research in order to get beneath the skin of consumers and understand their lifestyle interests, media habits, and purchase behaviors and motivators. The ultimate answer was always some sort of ad, but the effort up front was far deeper and [more] demanding than the somewhat cursory overviews we developed in the "situation analysis" sections of our PR plans. While much has certainly changed since those days, time and again in the PR business we've witnessed—perhaps out of expediency or a lack of training—a tendency to fall back on our tactical roots and bypass much of the account planning discipline by leaping over substantive business and audience analysis and heading straight for the creative. Let me posit that this won't fly anymore. Senior management is demanding accountability from virtually all areas of marketing. "If the revenue needle isn't moving, then why are we doing it?" Gone are the days when we could operate in relative comfort under the softer metrics of "awareness" and image. At no other time has public relations been given such a clear opportunity to sit at the table with those who shepherd the growth of great brand reputations—ones that can drive business results and reward the faith of shareholders. Why? Because the strategic paradigm is shifting, due to the seismic change in how consumers consume information and make decisions of brand choice. Pundits are extolling the virtues of media-neutral thinking and the cultivation of word of mouth. Similarly, the buzz-speak lexicon of brand managers is adjusting to recognize that effective solutions are built on a foundation of ideas that offer up authentic, credible communication to the target audience. Does all this mean we just show up for dinner and the rewards are served on the dessert tray? No. The requirements here are significant. If PR is to play at the branding table, then the ability to understand and execute brand-profile studies and other forms of ethnology and consumer anthropology must take root. We must also stop looking at our role as executing PR—that, at its core, is tactical thinking. Rather, a more holistic approach of diagnosis without presumption of cure will lead us toward the right mix of ideas that take brands from point A to B successfully. Said more simply, we need to halt the practice of repackaging essentially the same solution for every problem and answer the call to think differently about how we reach out and persuade. If we're successful in this transition, our industry is going to grow exponentially.

SOURCE: Bob Wheatley, *PRWeek*, February 2004

Summary and Review

Everyday Strategies

- Developing strategy is fundamental to our daily lives. We use it to help ourselves attain personal goals, win games, and navigate some of life's complexities, determining the best course of action after considering our options and the potential outcomes.
- We employ strategy in our communication. We seek to have the best outcomes in our interpersonal interactions and use strategies to be successful.

Critical Thinking, Reasoning, and Decision Making in Strategy

- Critical thinking is fundamental to strategy because critical thinking depends on asking questions, avoiding assumptions and looking closely at situations and ideas.
- A questioning perspective is essential to successful practice of strategic PR.

Strategy within Organizations

- Successful organizations, especially businesses, have employed strategic planning for decades. Within the past two decades, other types of organizations have begun to engage in strategic planning because investors, members, and partners have insisted upon transparency. Public relations, indeed all communication practices, have had to plan strategically and demonstrate a return on investment (ROI).
- Strategic thinking goes beyond planning to exploring the critical questions about an organization that are difficult for internal staff to ask in order to improve and succeed. It is infinite and focuses on growth and sustainability, as well as core competencies.

Strategic PR in Context

- Strategic communication is planned according to a process that results in messages that resonate with the intended key audiences and elicit a desired response. In order to be strategic, practitioners must first listen to the audience and then communicate—always considering the audience's perspective.

- The characteristics of strategic communication differ greatly from communication that is intended to share information. Strategic communication is purposeful, planned, and informed.

Overview of the Process of Strategic Public Relations

- Strategic public relations can be divided into two phases: formative and execution.
- During the formative phase we ask and answer a lot of questions to help us determine to whom we want to communicate, the best way to communicate with them, where to find them, what to say, and under what best set of circumstances. The formative phase ends with recommended tactics and an execution strategy for implementing the tactics.
- The execution phase of public relations employs all of the activities and tactics we devise in the planning or formative phase. Messages are developed and disseminated. Practitioners must be strategic in the manner in which they implement the tactics.
- Media relations strategy, website strategy, product and idea placement strategy, and branding strategy are just a few of the execution strategies that can be used.
- Effective and memorable communication campaigns are often the product of integrating strategies for greater reach, especially in the retail market where products are launched with the help of public relations, marketing, and advertising.
- Integrated communication (IC) or integrated marketing communication (IMC), introduced in the 1990s, merges advertising, marketing, promotions, and public relations.
- Communicating strategically in the field of public relations means adhering to a process that will help the practitioner achieve the best results. The process model should begin with identification and observation, move to research and analysis, close with evaluation, and begin again.

Key Terms

critical thinking	integrated approach	strategic communication
formative research	integrated communication	strategic planning
FYI communication	recursive	

Questions for Review and Discussion

The following questions are among the activities on the book's website, where you can email answers to your instructor, if required.

1. How does critical thinking lead to creating effective strategy?

2. Look at the kind of questions a typical critical thinker asks as presented in this chapter. Now watch one of your favorite television news magazine shows such as *60 Minutes, Dateline NBC,* ESPN's *Outside the Lines,* HBO's *Real Sports with Bryant Gumbel,* or *Entertainment Tonight.* Apply the critical thinking questions and list how differently you are required to watch the shows. List your own questions. What questions would you ask that the shows' interviewers do not ask?

3. Look at the Johnson & Johnson credo on page 74. How would you decrease it to a paragraph or two or three sentences? Explain why you might want to do this if you were the client company.

4. Today, most public relations practitioners use an integrated approach to campaigns. Select a product advertising campaign to which you have been exposed. Try to delineate and discuss the public relations activities associated with that campaign.

5. Compare the traditional models presented in this chapter with the one introduced in this text. What are the similarities and differences?

Web Links

Johnson & Johnson
www.jnj.com

American Diabetes Association
www.diabetes.org

IBM
www.ibm.com

Nike
www.nike.com

Annie E. Casey Foundation
www.aecf.org

American Association of Retired Persons
www.aarp.org

Coca-Cola Company
www.coca-cola.com

PepsiCo
www.pepsi.com

Understanding Audiences

KNOW YOUR AUDIENCE

We described the fundamentals of audiences (sometimes called publics) in Chapter 1 by saying they are the people or organizations most likely to limit or enhance an organization's ability to pursue its mission. In this chapter, we learn more about specific, or targeted, audiences, because this understanding is essential to your being able to create and implement effective public relations programs. We begin by discussing advertising and marketing, because understanding how these disciplines rely on the accurate identification of audiences will help you understand the importance of research in understanding audiences for public relations. We'll start with a few examples.

When the low-carb diet craze hit its peak, fruit growers and bread makers started losing consumers to producers of eggs, cheese, and meat, and new "carb-friendly" solutions started popping up in grocery stores and fast-food restaurants. Nearly everyone in the food and beverage industry scrambled to offer something with fewer carbohydrates; the soft drink industry was no exception. Coca-Cola's and Pepsi's response to the low-carb trend even added a new product category: the "mid-calorie" soda. Coca-Cola's C2 and Pepsi's Edge both offered consumers the taste of a regular cola with fewer calories and carbohydrates. When planning the campaign for C2's launch, Coke created a distinct look and feel with two TV commercials that would be attractive to a key group of people. Not coincidentally, this was the same group of people who they thought would buy their new soda.

I've learned that people will forget what you said, people will forget what you did, but people will never forget how you made them feel.

—Maya Angelou,
American poet

New Coke was an early marketing attempt to bolster cola sales. Unlike C2, New Coke was rejected by consumers and Coca-Cola went back to the original formula.

Al Freni/Time Life Pictures/Getty Images

This first TV ad of the C2 campaign, featuring the Rolling Stone's "You Can't Always Get What You Want" (the second ad featured Queen's "I Want to Break Free"), debuted during the final round of Fox's "American Idol" and on movie screens during previews at theaters.

As Mick Jagger's familiar voice delivered the repeated opening lines, ". . . you can't always get what you want," expressing sympathy for people (mostly young men) encountering frustrating moments of life, short taglines explained each scene: fighting a crowded line at an airport (you can't jump the line); watching an angry girlfriend throw your belongings—even your guitar—out the apartment window (you can't take back what you said); trying to program and master a treadmill (you can't get a break); and scrambling at the beach to pack up after a sudden downpour (you can't change the weather). Midway through the commercial, as the song's line "but you get what you need" rang out, the announcer confirmed, "You can't get what you want…until now," and images of exhilarating moments rolled: skateboarding in a kitchen; driving in a convertible while holding hands with a girlfriend; and sliding down the handrail of an escalator. The commercial ended with the statement that C2 offers the great taste of Coke with half the carbs and calories.

Based on this description, who was Coca-Cola targeting? Young children? Preteen girls? Of course not. Coke spokesman Kelly Brooks described the group as adults in their 20s and 30s (compared with their target of 18- to 24-year-olds for traditional Coke) who were "young enough to be soda drinkers, but old enough to be watching their weight." They were health conscious and might be watching their calories, but disliked the taste of diet soda. Clearly, the TV commercial featured images that would resonate with career-minded, but youthful enough, aspiring hipsters: pulling off a tie while waiting in line at an airport, frolicking on the beach with friends, trying to find time to exercise.

Think about your favorite commercials, the ones that speak directly to you and your understanding of who you are. Others are not even blips on your radar screens, but they may be favorites of your children, your parents or spouse, or younger siblings. There is a good reason for this. Advertisers design commercials to appeal to certain people and not to others. To do so, they make it their business to know everything they can about their audiences. If you don't like a commercial, most likely you are not the audience the advertiser wanted to reach.

Advertisers are expected to spend almost $188 billion in 2010 to get consumers to purchase everything from toothpaste to potato chips, from cars to smartphones. They want to be sure that this money will encourage consumer purchases and brand loyalty. And they understand that, most likely, only a certain segment of the population will buy their particular product or service. To get the most bang for their advertising buck, they rely on **market research,** *the formalized study of various aspects of* *groups of consumers,* to make their marketing and advertising strategy effective. This market research helps to determine advertisers' **target audience**—*people most likely to buy or use their product*—and to create a message that will specifically speak to that group.

In this chapter, we look at what marketing and advertising have learned about knowing and interacting with audiences and how those concepts are translated and manifested in the world of public relations.

Contrast Coke's C2 TV ad with Sprite commercials that were released just a few months prior. The Sprite campaign, which debuted during an NBA All-Star game, introduced a new character: a black action figure named Miles Thirst, outfitted with an Afro, basketball jersey, and some bling. Commercials featuring Thirst showed him interacting with black and Hispanic teenage boys and basketball star Lebron James, in movie theaters and on the front stoops of urban streets. He greeted his friends with street slang, joked about "honeys," and talked about "getting his drink on." Thirst appeared on Sprite's website and even had his own blog where visitors could watch his video clips and download Thirst instant messaging buddy icons. (You can view many of the Miles Sprite ads on youtube.com.)

Quite obviously, the Sprite and C2 commercials targeted different groups of people. How would you describe the Sprite ad's target audience? That's easy based on who's shown in the ad, even if you don't know what Sprite's manufacturer (interestingly, also Coca-Cola) knows: More than half of Sprite drinkers are under 24, 30 percent are African American, and 15 percent are Hispanic. Just as the language and scenarios depicted in the Sprite ad would not likely appeal to a 30-something store manager, a girlfriend throwing her boyfriend's guitar out the window probably won't grab the interest of a 60-year-old tax attorney, nor would a tour that Thirst gives from Lebron James' "crib" probably appeal to a 40-year-old soccer mom or a 27-year-old firefighter.

So, what does successful target marketing look like?

MARKETING 101

To explore why target marketing is such an important concept within marketing, let's stay with the soft drinks industry. In 2007, Coca-Cola undertook its biggest product launch in more than two decades. The beverage giant's consumer research indicated that young adults ages 18–34 were looking for a soft drink they could call their own. The company introduced a new beverage, Coca-Cola Zero and labeled it a "zero-calorie cola." In addition to wanting to reach the demographic, the company wanted the beverage to appeal to young adult men who associated "diet sodas" with older women. "Coca-Cola Zero is exactly what young adults told us they wanted—real Coca-Cola taste, zero calories, and a new brand they can call their own," said Dan Dillon, vice president, Diet Portfolio, Coca-Cola North America.

The company changed its advertising approach in marketing Coke Zero, also. The company usually spends the biggest part of its budget on television spots, but marketing for Coke Zero is different. In addition to television, the product has a website and the company uses email marketing, video clips posted on websites and digital banner advertising in an effort to suggest that its product is a contemporary choice. Is the product successful? Yes. Coca-Cola Zero is available in 100 countries and continues to outsell other company products. What's a main reason the campaign was

Newscom

successful? The solid knowledge Coca-Cola had about how young adults felt about soft drinks—especially how diet drinks were perceived by young adult males—helped them to connect.

Finding and Understanding a Market

Like the Coca-Cola examples, most other successful advertising campaigns are based on effective consumer research, where market researchers have looked at who is likely to buy their (or their client's) product, and then found out everything they can about those people and what appeals to them.

Marketers seek their **market,** *the group of people who have desires and needs (perceived or otherwise) for products and who have the ability, willingness, and authority to purchase those products.* To know and understand their market as specifically as possible, they even break down their audience into smaller groups, known as segmenting. According to the American Marketing Association's *Dictionary of Marketing Terms,* **market segmentation** is *the process of subdividing a market into distinct subsets of customers that behave in the same way or have similar needs.* For example, if you are reading this textbook for an undergraduate class, you are most likely between 18 and 21 years old. You are one of the most lucrative markets for commercial marketers; they call you the college market. Your market can be further segmented according to lifestyles—athletes, Greeks, campus community leaders, and more.

Once you've figured out who your audience is, you need to figure out what to say to them. Most people would agree that to communicate well with someone, you need to know something about the person to whom you're talking. For example, if you just failed an exam, you may have different approaches of breaking the news depending on your intimate knowledge of the person with whom you're talking. You wouldn't have the same type of conversation with your parents, your teacher, your significant other, and your employer. You would probably alter the message, the tone of the message, and the language you use. Why? Because each person has a different interest in the message you're sending, a different background and personality and a different reaction to your message. Each audience has different values, norms, expectations, concerns, and views about your education. Your parents, for instance, may be concerned about your grades and your college scholarship or graduate school admission, and you may know from experience that they may respond best to bad news after they've come home from work and have eaten dinner.

After conducting the proper market research to know about an audience and therefore how to communicate with its members, advertisers begin developing an idea for a commercial or advertisement. They know a lot about their target audience *before* entertaining the development of a single element of a message strategy. For example, research informed Nintendo about what people thought of its game system and knew that, to beat Xbox, it would need to offer something to older teens. It then planned a campaign and commercials that promoted the aspects of its system that appealed to that group.

Interacting with a Market

Marketers are trying to gain what they call the **marketing exchange,** which the American Marketing Association *Dictionary of Marketing Terms* defines as "*all activities associated with receiving something from someone by giving something voluntarily* *in return.*" Essentially, this means that marketers want to create an atmosphere in which the consumer is willing to exchange something (usually money) for a company's product or service because they think it is valuable. Marketing asks what can be offered to our audiences that they want in exchange for the desired action from them. It is very easy to see in commercial marketing.

Facilitating that market exchange is the job of communication. Communication spells out the exchange, though usually very delicately and subtly. It tells the audience what they will gain (popularity, desirability, more leisure time, more fulfillment) and points to what they need to do to achieve those things (use whitening toothpaste, take Viagra, buy the latest Apple product, eat fewer carbohydrates). Research has shown that the most effective communication—the communication with the most impact—is between one sender and one receiver. In other words, it is a highly personal interaction between two people. Marketers think of their audiences as a person, so they develop a profile of that audience. They can then tailor their message to make the most convincing argument for the marketing exchange. C2 commercials targeted young professionals who might be straddling the line of youth (drinking regular soda) and adult discipline (counting calories) and sold them the idea that they could become responsible adults without being boring...along with a can of soda, of course.

Marketers use this principle of personal communication to personalize, or customize, their ads depending on the information they've compiled on their audience. A good example is Frito-Lay, who wanted to reach the teen market. Frito-Lay decided to pull its TV ads from the Super Bowl—an advertiser's dream spot—to do online advertising instead. Their market research said the teens are on the web, so that's where the advertising dollars went.

Chapter 1 highlighted the fact that the practice of public relations involves focusing on the audience and seeking to establish mutually beneficial relationships. Public relations strategies rely on the same principles as marketing—knowing audiences and using that knowledge to interact with them strategically to accomplish goals.

ENGAGING ETHICS

Good Marketing or Bad Decision?

October is National Breast Cancer Awareness Month and in October 2008, Philip Morris announced plans to market Virginia Slims Super Slims Ultra Light and Virginia Slims Super Slim Lights in "sleek pink packets called Purse Pack," emulating the use of pink to demonstrate breast cancer awareness and fundraising. The American Legacy Foundation, which seeks to prevent tobacco use, especially among youth, and the Susan G. Komen for the Cure grassroots network responded with indignation and media relations efforts. Their joint news release said the company's efforts were "an insult to all those struggling to protect women's health and the millions of women who have battled and are battling breast cancer."

1. Search the Internet to learn more about how the foundation and Komen for the Cure responded.
2. What course of action might you take to communicate with young audiences if you work for a nonprofit that seeks to prevent tobacco use?

ADAPTING MARKETING CONCEPTS

Thinking like a marketer and adapting just a few marketing principles to public relations can help us to be more effective communicators. Doing so helps PR practitioners position an organization, person, or issue favorably within the marketplace of ideas, and to affect the attitudes and behaviors of target audiences. Just as advertisers and marketers seek their targeted markets, public relations practitioners must identify and understand those with whom they are concerned. This does not mean we become marketers or that public relations is practiced only in commercial settings. It just means we can adapt principles from the marketing field.

Indeed, the field of public relations seeks to have an interactive and dialogue-based relationship with its audiences. It is the constant talking and feeding back that makes public relations most effective. One thing that marketers and public relations practitioners alike understand is that they are never going after the *general public*, basically anyone who encounters sent messages. Our society is far too large and diverse for there to be any such thing as a general public, and serious, knowledgeable public relations practitioners avoid using the term to describe any group of people, regardless of how big. Marketers and PR specialists can always find common characteristics of a group they're trying to reach, whether it's age, ethnicity, income, habits, or geographic location. Spending time or money to reach everybody is an exercise in futility. Because believing that a campaign will appeal to all people is unrealistic, it is our job to identify the specific people the campaign is targeting. Any successful communication strategy has to be based on a defined target audience. It matters in terms of getting the desired response from the audience you want to reach.

It is possible to list hundreds of audiences, groups of people sharing one or more common characteristic, so understanding which audiences are important and when they are important is the key. In essence, we must be able to identify our priority audiences based on our situation or communication strategy. If a campus sorority or fraternity is seeking additional volunteers to help build a house for Habitat for Humanity, its priority audience would differ greatly from the audience it would want to appeal to help with recruiting new members.

Like marketers who have determined who their market is, public relations researchers view their main role as determining which audiences are pertinent to a particular organization or campaign. Organizations have to communicate with many audiences. Understanding the different types of audiences is useful for narrowing the public that is most influential to your particular need.

Types of Audiences

Some scholars have suggested categorizing audiences as *primary, secondary,* or *marginal.* This thinking acknowledges audiences according to their effect on the organization, with **primary audiences** *having the biggest effect on the organization,* **secondary audiences** *having some effect, and* **marginal audiences** *having little effect.* For example, in a university or college setting, students and prospective students, parents, and alumni can be seen as primary audiences. Their relationship with the school is the most important, as they can have an enormous effect on its success in meeting its mission and goals. Specifically, the school depends upon these groups for revenue, enrollments, and reputation, which means, essentially, that these groups are the school's customers.

The board of trustees, faculty, and staff of a college or university are also important, because they are the groups of people who keep the school functioning. These audiences identify with the school and can be advocates for it in the community and among other audiences. They are not, however, primary audiences. They are a school's secondary audiences because, while they have great impact on the institution's ability to serve its primary audiences, they represent less of a threat to it. They pose less of a threat because they have a vested interest in the school, wanting to ensure its success for reasons different from those of the primary audiences.

Marginal audiences for a university or college include professional member associations and accrediting bodies, state regulatory agencies, and political figures such as mayors, governors, and community leaders in the jurisdiction in which the school is located. These audiences generally have little effect on the school but can move up in priority during certain periods. For instance, an accrediting body for a university can appear to have little impact until it is time to prepare for reaccreditation. This example also makes the important point that audiences are not stagnant. Because a group's audience standing or classification can change from campaign to campaign, and possibly even during a single campaign, PR practitioners must continuously evaluate audiences.

In addition to identifying an audience's degree of importance to a campaign, PR practitioners also classify them based on which of the following subclassifications they fall into: internal/external; traditional/nontraditional/future; and proponents, opponents and the uncommitted.

Internal/External Audiences

Some practitioners refer to internal and external audiences. **Internal audiences** are *usually a part of the organization's structure and are involved in implementing or supporting its mission and assisting in accomplishing its goals.* In its broadest sense, the term refers to an organization's management and staff employees, officers, current and prospective members, investors, and donors. Generally, **external audiences** are *those groups that exist outside of the organization and have the ability to have an impact on the organization and its ability to attain its mission and goals.* External audiences include government and regulatory agencies, consumer advocacy groups, customers, and the news media. Like the term *general public,* internal and external are not useful terms for definitively identifying the audiences for PR practice. Unfortunately, although used in the practice to refer to an organization's audiences, the terms *internal* and *external* are far too broad to assist the public relations practitioner in comprehensively delineating who is important to the organization and how to reach them. As well, the term *internal audience* has become synonymous with employees of an organization and suggests or implies that they are not a part of the overall management of the organization.

Traditional, Nontraditional, and Future Audiences

Scholars also divide an organization's audiences by considering the audience's existing status with the organization. Current customers, members, and employees can be considered an organization's **traditional audiences** *because the organization has had a long and ongoing relationship with them.*

Nontraditional audiences are an opportunity for an organization. These groups *do not have an existing relationship with the organization but present an opening for the organization to study a potential audience.* For example, as society has become more comfortable with the Internet and digital technology, the customers for digital and electronic products has expanded. Grandparents were not a traditional customer base for computer and digital equipment companies, but they now are considered traditional as they have begun to utilize the technology. They are now staying in touch with family members around the globe through email, Facebook and Skyping.

While nontraditional audiences may not have a relationship with a particular organization currently, they are part of a future or potential audience base. Prospective students and potential customers and members can be described as future audiences. Similar to internal and external audiences and primary, secondary, and marginal categories, this manner of dividing audiences is too broad. While it can be used to ensure that an organization acknowledges that there will be new audiences with the passing of time, it is not particularly helpful in establishing a delineation of an organization's audiences.

Proponents, Opponents, and the Uncommitted

Audiences can also be evaluated according to their support or lack of support for an organization's mission and goals. **Proponents** are *those audiences that support the organization.* Often, they have an ongoing and long-term relationship with the organization. Proponents of an organization should be given priority, and require meaningful and regular communication. An audience segment of the proponents is a group that actively supports the organization. Among this group are volunteers, employees, shareholders, and board members. This segment is one of the most important audiences for an organization's growth and success.

For example, the American Diabetes Association (ADA) is a nonprofit organization that enjoys a relationship with millions of volunteers in 800 communities across the country. These volunteers help the organization to raise funds, to solicit other volunteers, and to assist families who are living with this dangerous and debilitating disease. The ADA communication department maintains vigorous two-way conversation with this important segment of its proponents.

Predictably then, **opponents** *of an organization oppose the organization's mission and goals.* In fact, they can have a long-term relationship with the organization as well, though the relationship is adversarial. Like proponents, the opposition can be very active and is usually very vocal. This is an audience that requires constant monitoring and dedicated research. Some opponents can become proponents of an organization, but they should not be the primary or priority target of a campaign to convert them. Other opponents are competitors and must be viewed as such.

The **uncommitted** are *neither proponents nor opponents, and they may be completely unaware of the organization.* The uncommitted should be given particular attention in certain areas of the practice of PR. One of those areas in which the uncommitted are extremely important is politics. When a political candidate or issue is in the hands of the electorate, the uncommitted can make the difference in the outcome. Many political strategies are based on converting the uncommitted.

UNDERSTANDING AUDIENCES

Once an organization has prioritized its audiences and has chosen with whom to communicate, research is how we learn about its characteristics. We know the groups with whom we want to communicate effectively, and in order to do so, we must know more about them in order to create strategies, campaigns, and messages that they understand. Just as you could spend a lifetime getting to know the various facets of a person, there are many different ways to look at audiences. Here are some of the different types of characteristics that PR attempts to capture about its audiences.

Demographics

First, research can determine the basic demographic information about an audience, such as gender, income level, education, ethnic background, political affiliation, and age groupings. This type of information is very useful for getting a handle on what an audience "looks like." These characteristics often shape how a campaign communicates with its audience.

The California Milk Processor Board learned the hard way that one-size-fits-all is not the way to reach a target audience. It had previously tried to reach the Hispanic teen market with a Spanish version of the very American-centric "Got Milk?" commercials. The commercials were ineffective in reaching the target audience, and in fact, research showed that the teens were drinking 12 percent less milk than they had been two years earlier. So the milk board spent more money to develop ads tailored to the target audience, featuring a Hispanic myth about "La Llorona" (the Crying One). According to the Hispanic myth, La Llorona, who has been shunned by her husband, throws her two children into a river. Recognizing what a terrible thing she has done, she jumps into the river to save them but dies trying. Her ghost roams for all eternity looking for her lost children. In the milk commercials, La Llorona is looking for milk. She roves through middle-class homes and to a refrigerator, only to find an empty milk carton. "Got milk?" she asks. The spot won an Ad Age creative award.

These demographics group people in such a way that enables us to shape a message that will resonate with the audience, though determining what that exact demographic is can be tricky. In the 1996 presidential election, pollsters identified a group of voters who could make or break a candidate's campaign. This group was the famous "soccer mom"—defined by the *American Heritage Dictionary, Fourth Edition,* as "An American mother living in the suburbs whose time is often spent transporting her children from one athletic activity or event to another." Using research, the campaigns of presidential hopefuls Bill Clinton and Bob Dole learned about this important group of suburban mothers and targeted much of their campaigning to issues that research indicated were near and dear to this group: education reform, tax cuts, and health care.

Habits

Research also looks at an audience's buying habits, disposable income, and ways audience members spend leisure time. For example, the "soccer mom" of the 2004 presidential election turned out to be the so-called "NASCAR dad." Grouping these men by their leisure time interest captured a unique group of people and pointed to other possible similarities that they shared. The fact that George W. Bush appeared at NASCAR races during pivotal points of the campaign was not a coincidence.

Retail researchers discovered that one of the most lucrative retail markets is a group of spenders who can't drive, don't have a job, and couldn't qualify for a credit card. It's the 'tweens, kids aged 8 to mid-teens, and even though these kids don't have any of their own money, researchers found that they spend $104 per week and visit the mall 40 percent more than any other shopper. Other market researchers have found that these kids and teenagers influence the buying decision of their parents for electronic equipment and even cars. Understanding the power of these kids shapes the way that retailers advertise. The messages and tactics they use appeal to kids instead of to only their parents.

While this basic demographic information is extremely important, it isn't always the most effective. Researchers have found that even though people in a specific demographic category share some common characteristics, their values, motivations, and beliefs are not necessarily the same. For example, within the "soccer mom" category could be married women, divorced women, working mothers, stay-at-home moms, wealthy, religious, Latinas, and more. This group label may give an indication of some commonality between members of this group, but it does not account for all the underlying values and beliefs.

Psychographics

Although people may share age, gender, income, and education demographics, their values and beliefs are not always the same. To make up for this disparity, researchers use what they call *psychographics* to describe audiences.

Psychographics refers to *the emotional and behavioral characteristics of an audience.* It is concerned with the values, beliefs, and attitudes of an audience. It then applies knowledge from social science disciplines like psychology and sociology to this information, as well as marketing information like religious affiliation and political leaning, magazine subscriptions, car ownership, and other basic market research. Many marketing companies maintain huge databases that sort people into groups based on their similarities and create profiles with names like "shooting stars," "guns and trucks," and "struggling singles." These profiles include information on what is important to these groups, their optimism and confidence financially, and how their beliefs shape the way they spend their money. Marketers use this information to predict their future behavior—and with amazing success. A representative from a psychographics research company said that researchers using demographic data only can correctly guess what kind of car a person will buy 18 percent of the time. But combined with psychographic data, marketers can correctly predict the car choice 82 percent of the time.

Beliefs, Attitudes, and Values

Researchers also want to know about their audience's beliefs, attitudes, and values, which are usually defined as a predisposition to think in a certain way about a certain topic. Attitudes are shaped by many factors, ranging from culture, family structure, social class, religion, and education.

When Tide wanted to build brand loyalty in the Hispanic consumer market, it listened to the research. The research said this particular market segment is family-focused and very community-oriented. To build brand loyalty, Tide needed to show specific Hispanic markets that Tide was concerned with their local communities. Tide looked for public relations opportunities to increase its visibility in the community and created a program called "Tide Renueva tus Canchas" (Tide Renews Your Fields), which involved renovating neighborhood soccer fields in Los Angeles, New York, and San Antonio. Tide partnered with local families and soccer leagues to reseed run-down fields, brought in coaches to teach soccer clinics, and sponsored a weekend tournament.

While it is interesting to note that many of the factors that contribute to an audience's attitudes, beliefs, and values are demographic information, it is important to understand that we shouldn't use just demographics to infer an audience's motivations or behaviors. It is more effective to investigate the attitudes within demographic

BRIEF CASE STUDY

U R the Spokesperson

In 2006 the National Highway Traffic Safety Administration reported that automobile accidents remained the number-one killer of American teenagers. The "U R the Spokesperson" campaign is a partnership between the Ad Council and the Coalition of State Attorneys General and Consumer Protection Agencies. The campaign's premise is based on research that indicates youth have little concern about hurting themselves but don't want to hurt their friends. The campaign seeks to reduce youth reckless driving by encouraging passengers ages 15 to 21 to speak up when they feel unsafe in the car with friends. The campaign's objective is to reach media, young drivers, and parents to change teenage driving habits. Ultimately, the audience strategy revolves around passengers, similar to the strategy for the Friends Don't Let Friends Drive Drunk campaign. Partnerships with Students Against Destructive Decisions (SADD), the American Automobile Association (AAA), and National Organizations for Youth Safety (NOYS) helped with the reach of the campaign tactics to teen drivers through online and social media, including a YouTube contest. Other tactics included classroom toolkits, partner web packages, and the website www.urthespokesperson.com.

IF YOUR FRIENDS DRIVE RECKLESSLY, SAY SOMETHING.
SpeakUpOrElse.com

This newer Ad Council campaign, SpeakUpOrElse.com, continues to highlight teens as spokespeople.

Media relations tactics to launch the campaign included a web conference, a *New York Times* exclusive and a *Good Morning America* segment, news releases, op-eds, and letters to the editor.

A study conducted by the Ad Council showed that the number of drivers who reported that a friend spoke up when he or she was driving recklessly increased from 45 to 60 percent during January to October 2007. Television, radio, outdoor, alternative, and interactive public service advertising is valued at $21.8 million. The campaign generated more than 30 million impressions, as the website drew more than 285,000 unique visitors last year.

The campaign budget was $125,000 and the Ad Council partner was Hager Sharp communications firm (Washington, DC).

information than to assume, for example, that all religious people believe that gay marriage is wrong.

Being knowledgeable about an audience's attitudes about, say, nutrition, can make a significant difference in the way that an organization reaches that audience. For example, organizations trying to persuade Americans to eat less may look to the underlying beliefs and values about why we eat "value meals" at fast-food restaurants. Is it that we want or need the extra food that comes in such a meal, or is it that we often seek to get the most for our money? Understanding beliefs and attitudes can make a subtle or not-so-subtle difference in the way we communicate to our audiences.

Using this information is key to developing successful public relations campaigns. Smart practitioners lean on this research and remember that they are rarely the target audience; what the practitioner thinks is irrelevant. For example, if your campaign targets 40-year-old divorced fathers, you wouldn't assume that they like the same things, have the same needs, and share the same concerns as 21-year-old single women. It's easy to think that a message or strategy will be effective simply because you, the practitioner, like it, but we must remember that we're usually not in our target market.

It is also important to continually conduct audience research during the communication campaign so that the campaign can be improved as it moves forward. This research helps us to continue to hone our message, to determine audience reaction to our message, to identify new audiences, to ascertain if our audiences have changed, and to investigate many other variables. It is not unusual for an organization to name its audiences once and only once, and continue to produce messages for that original audience, but environments change, circumstances change, and public opinions change, so organizations should regularly review their audience characteristics and values.

UNDERSTANDING AUDIENCE-FOCUSED PR

Audience research can take many forms, including in-depth interviews, focus groups, anthropological techniques (including observation in natural consumer environments), and surveys, which are all used to identify what our audiences want. The results of this work help us to formulate our communication strategy and message development and assist us in interacting with audiences. Chapter 6 describes in detail research methodologies and how to use them to shape messages and tactics, but it is important to highlight here the crucial role of research as the beginning of any effective communication campaign.

Using initial audience research, public relations practitioners are able to begin strategically developing a communication effort. The research helps us see the world through our audiences' eyes so we know what to say and how to say it to them. We must *want* to know what they want and must listen and give value to their desires. If we want people to eat more fruits and vegetables, it does little good to send them a message to eat more fruits and vegetables just because it's good for them. We need to find out why they don't eat more fruits and vegetables, what they eat instead, and what benefit we can offer them for changing the way they eat. We need to know what our audience wants.

Here's an example of audience-focused PR: The investment corporation Charles Schwab & Co. wanted to position itself—and Carrie Schwab Pomerantz, vice president of consumer education and daughter of the company's founder and chairman—as a company concerned about women's challenges in investing. It also wanted to close the 29-point gap between women's and men's confidence in their investing skills. Existing research showed that women did not visualize themselves as smart investors, and Schwab's own research showed that, while women weren't as knowledgeable about investing, they wanted to learn more. Research also showed that women preferred to learn through seminars and investing clubs for women instead of the books-on-tape and websites that men favored. Research also showed that younger women were just as likely to be intimidated by investing as older women.

Based on these research findings, Schwab and PR firm Patrice Tanaka & Co. developed a program, Women Investing Now (WIN), which was specifically designed to motivate women to learn more about investing and offered expertise and numerous resources to help women educate themselves.

Research not only identified the company's challenge but also provided a framework

Carrie Schwab Pomerantz

for the resulting strategies. For example, the WIN website offered comprehensive resources as well as forums, message boards, and other interactive features that allowed women to communicate with experts and other women, which fit in with women's tendency to seek knowledge from "communities." Schwab also promoted WIN seminars and other community functions where women could learn in environments they considered "comfortable." Schwab also publicized the fact that, unlike many other financial firms, about 40 percent of Schwab's employees are women and more than two-thirds of employees report to a woman. Schwab also initiated a program to encourage these employees to increase their knowledge of investment and become "money mentors" to other women.

The success of this campaign came from Schwab's knowledge of its audience—gained through research—and the implementing of strategy based on that knowledge. Understanding women's perspective on investing and their needs and behaviors shaped the strategies of the campaign so that the tactics they employed resonated with the women they were trying to reach. Just as advertisers seek the "market exchange," PR practitioners also seek a similar exchange, though it may not involve an actual exchange of money for a service. In PR, the exchange often means getting the audience to adopt or change certain behaviors for identified rewards. Successfully making the exchange depends on offering something consumers or audiences want, which means knowing them well enough to know what they want.

A More Targeted Message

PROFESSIONAL
POINT OF VIEW

This point of view is excerpted from an article in PRWeek. *Several professionals are quoted and the information on multicultural audiences is valuable.*

One of the areas where ethnic PR has gained sophistication is in its ability to tailor messages for specific audiences through research. Only a few years ago, clients would have been happy to simply foist a general market campaign on minority audiences after a quick translation of materials, assuming that core ideas would resonate across cultural boundaries. But that leftover mentality has fallen out of favor as ethnic PR pros prove time and again that minority communities have their own values, ideas, and idiosyncrasies that must be addressed.

"In the past we've assumed PR programs that were for general market venues reached everyone. But you can't just translate what you did for the general market. That's not good PR," says Ann Hardison, SVP at Fleishman-Hillard and project director for one of its largest accounts, the Office of National Drug Control Policy's (ONDCP) National Youth Anti-Drug Media Campaign. Hardison points to Fleishman's work with that client as an example of the kind of tailored effort that is becoming common.

One of the campaign's goals was to reach parents of varying ethnicities with strategies to discuss drugs with their kids. While researching the topic, Fleishman quickly found that each community viewed the threat of drugs in a different way.

"The family discussion around drugs is very different in Asian-American households compared to African-American households," she says. Asian parents tended to be "much more in denial about drugs even being a threat or a risk for their kids, whereas with the African-American audience, they get it, they know their children are at risk." Those findings lead Fleishman to craft different messages for each community.

For Asian-American families, the message was that drugs did indeed pose a risk. For African-American parents, "what they need to know is they make a difference in their children's lives, and they shouldn't assume other influences are stronger," explains Hardison. Using targeted messages is also gaining popularity as a way to reach ethnic subgroups, another audience that has gained recognition in recent years.

"A lot of companies lump consumers into this Hispanic group," points out Armando Azarloza, EVP of Weber Shandwick Worldwide's LA office and head of its national Hispanic marketing practice. "It's not a homogeneous group. Cubans are different than Mexicans, and Mexicans are different than Puerto Ricans." The same holds true for Asian and even African-American communities. Companies are realizing that simply targeting Asians or Latinos isn't enough. Campaigns need to work on the micro-level, understanding the needs of specific cultures within those generic labels.

At Ogilvy's LA office, pinpointing exactly what those differences are is part of an upcoming project on teen pregnancy for the California Wellness Foundation. Ogilvy recently completed a year-long survey on minority community attitudes toward the issue, and is now in the planning stages of another project to look at five different Asian subcultures to gain an even deeper understanding of how to target those groups with appropriate messages. "We're finding that we have to do a different approach around different ethnicities. You need specific things for Filipino versus Thai," says Ogilvy SVP Dawn Wilcox.

SOURCE: "Have We Learned How to Reach Ethnic Groups Yet?," *PRWeek*, August 5, 2002

Summary and Review

Know Your Audience
- We understand consumerism and marketing better than we suspect. Because they are integral to our daily lives, advertising and marketing can be illustrative of what it means to *know* your audience.
- Advertisers spend millions of dollars to reach their target audiences. Given the size of the investment, advertisers are strategic in attempting to reach those important audiences.
- The practice of strategic PR incorporates some of the important marketing principles that can help you best reach and interact with your audiences.

Marketing 101

- As a public relations practitioner, you can use some marketing principles and techniques to better understand the key groups you want to reach and therefore create more effective messages that elicit the desired results.
- An audience-focused approach to PR means that practitioners strive to understand things about their audience and its perspective, behaviors, needs, attitudes, beliefs, and norms. Learning about a key audience means going beyond demographics. While demographics are helpful, they must be complemented, and sometimes informed, by qualitative information about our key groups. You must use that knowledge to plan strategies and messages for your PR campaigns.
- When communication is targeted to a specific audience, it will make appropriate appeals to get the necessary "buy-in" from audience members. On the other hand, if you don't know your audience, you're probably talking to the wrong audience. If the right people aren't hearing your message, your effort is a total loss.

Adapting Marketing Concepts

- In the practice of effective PR, there is no such thing as a general public. Messages cannot be effective if they are not directed to specific audiences about which you know a great deal. Any successful communication strategy has to be based on a defined target audience.
- The terms *audience* and *public* can be used interchangeably to identify a key group with whom the public relations practitioner wants to have effective communication.
- The coming chapters are aimed at showing you how to conduct and interpret research, design strategy, and implement plans that make your communication efforts effective.

Understanding Audiences

- Research can get you closer to understanding your audiences. Basics such as demographics can provide some information.
- Additional research can help you understand the attitudes, beliefs, values, and behaviors of your audiences. Conducting research at the beginning your work helps you to best understand how your audiences live and what is important to them as well.

Understanding Audience-Focused PR

- Audience research such as in-depth interviews, focus groups, anthropological techniques, and surveys help you formulate your communication strategy and message development and assist you in interacting with audiences.
- Research is crucial at the beginning of any effective communication campaign. The research helps you see the world through your audiences' eyes.
- Like marketers, you want to see the world through our audiences' eyes so you know what to say and how to say it to them. You want to value their desires and want to interact with them in a way that engages and prompts feedback.

Key Terms

external audiences
internal audiences
marginal audiences
market
market research
market segmentation

marketing exchange
nontraditional
   audiences
opponents
primary audiences
proponents

psychographics
secondary audiences
target audience
traditional audiences
uncommitted

Questions for Review and Discussion

1. The Coca-Cola Company's marketing described earlier in the chapter was successful because they understood their target audience. What is an example of an advertising campaign that appealed to you? Can you explain why?

2. Although market research aims to get many members of a targeted audience to do something, such as buy a product, in order to have the most impact, research shows the most effective strategy is communication between two people. Do you think these two points are contradictory?

3. Why do public relations practitioners avoid using the term *general public?*

4. Audiences can be categorized as primary, secondary, or marginal. Take a community organization, such as a church or volunteer organization you are familiar with, and categorize its various audiences.

5. What is a nontraditional audience? Give an example of one for pharmaceutical products. What are some other audiences that present particular challenges for communication strategies?

6. What are some of the characteristics of audiences that can be explored through research?

7. Why is it important for organizations to continually conduct audience research throughout a campaign? Can you give an example of when changing circumstances dictated a need to do more research?

8. Have you ever used audience research to get a group of people to change their behavior or do something? Explain your response.

Web Links

Susan G. Komen
www.komen.org

Philip Morris
www.philipmoririsusa.com

Coca-cola
www.coca-cola.com

American Marketing Association
www.marketingpower.com

California Milk Board
www.realcaliforniamilk.com

Clariats
www.claritas.com

Speak Up
www.speakuporelse.org

Ad Council
www.adcouncil.org

CHAPTER PREVIEW

- What Is Research?
- Why Conduct Research?
- What Kinds of Research Do PR Practitioners Use?
- Where Should Research Be Conducted?
- How Is Research Conducted?
- Tips for Buying Research Services
- Ethical Considerations in Social Science Research

Researching Effectively

Chapter 6

WHAT IS RESEARCH?

Research is *the careful and systematic study, investigation and collection of data for the purposes of knowing, describing, and understanding.* It is the hallmark of effective public relations strategy—indeed any communication strategy.

Communicating with a target audience involves *knowing and understanding*—and knowing and understanding a target audience obviously involves research. In fact, excellent strategic planning relies on *strategic* research. David B. Rockland, senior vice president and global director of research for Ketchum PR has said, "It is unacceptable today to solely produce a binder of clips, an industry search and some consumer trends data to understand a target audience or a prospective corporate client. Instead, a distillation of this information is needed that is both manageable and plots the course for a strategic and creative approach." [See the "Professional Point of View" on page 134 in this chapter for Dr. Rockland's advice on how to talk to clients about returns on their investment (ROIs).]

As a public relations practitioner, you can profit from well-designed and well-executed research before, during, and at the end of a public relations communication campaign or program. As the field has continued to evolve in terms of increased credibility and perceived corporate value, the head nodding in support of the use of research to plan strategic PR has become more vigorous.

But head nodding is not enough. The amount of actual research conducted by practitioners in the field is still minimal. It is not clear how much formative, iterative and evaluative research is actually conducted by practicing public relations professionals. In fact, scholars continue to rely on the survey findings of

> *Research is formalized curiosity. It is poking and prying with a purpose.*
>
> —Zora Neale Hurston, American author, folklorist

Women participating in a focus group

PRWeek (2001), Schenkein/Sherman and PR News (1995) and Lindenmann (1990). As students and practitioners in the field, you must learn to make an effective argument for resources to support an audience-focused approach that begins with research. Research based on best practices and social science research principles is crucial for effective public relations.

Research plays an important role in the development of effective communication and especially in creating message, but it is not an inexpensive tool. Because it can be costly, you should be able to point to the reasons for conducting research and you should be able to justify the research to those you ask to pay for it—the client. As well, you should present as many inexpensive and creative—but effective—research strategies as possible, demonstrating to the client that you keep costs in mind. This is a strategic approach—it asks you to have a plan for the actions you want to take.

WHY CONDUCT RESEARCH?

Research is one of the best decision-making tools you have at your disposal. Sometimes communication professionals conduct research for the wrong reasons—to support decisions that have already been made or to sustain existing attitudes. Similarly, others conduct research to impress peers, for political gain, or to justify the decisions of another manager. Some research is simply the result of the musing of an executive or program manager, performed for the sake of quelling curiosity. All of these motives cause bias, and none of them is justified.

As a practitioner/researcher, you have ethical responsibilities in conducting research. In order for research to be useful and to bring new insights, it must be unbiased. This means the researchers must be careful with sampling, interviewer influence, and distortion by respondents. Biased research can cause you to make the wrong decisions and waste a lot of money.

Questions to Ask *before* Considering Research

When preparing for research, you should ask yourself a series of questions to determine what you hope to gain from the research you conduct. The answers to these questions help you formulate a strategy for the research.

- *What do I want to accomplish for my client or organization?* This question encourages you to think about the core reason for undertaking a communication campaign or program in the first place and provides information for a statement of the problem or opportunity at hand.
- *Who do I think I want to reach and are there subgroups of that audience?* Here you are getting to the core of the market research approach because you are doing preliminary thinking about your target audience. These answers also

help develop thinking about **segmentation**—*creating subgroups of a target audience*—and whether or not attempting to reach the entire target audience is the best strategy. What do you want to know about them? Thinking about this question helps formulate the design of the research study and begins the listening process.

- *What questions should I ask the audience, and have they answered these questions before?* If so, where are the answers and how will you get them? These questions begin your thinking about research strategy and planning. The answers here are crucial because you may not need *primary* research if there is plenty of *secondary* research to support your efforts. **Primary research** is *that which you conduct* and **secondary research** *is the work of someone else*.

The Benefits of Conducting Research

There are clear and measurable benefits to the communicator who conducts research that is strategically oriented. The first benefit we have discussed briefly—decision making. Research helps you make the best, *informed decisions*. Being strategic means having a plan of action, and planning requires information and data from many directions—within the organization and outside. Research helps to develop strategy.

Again, too, audience-focused research helps you craft messages that resonate with your target audience. Your executions will be effective because you listened to your audience and built the best *message strategy*. This research tells you enough about their attitudes, beliefs, norms, behaviors, and motivation to assist you in talking directly to them.

Properly *identifying a public relations problem or opportunity* and understanding the scope of that problem or opportunity is a key benefit of conducting research. It helps you explain what you know to your clients. You need to have as much information as possible when suggesting a course of action or a particular campaign.

Lastly, good research helps to *save time and money*. Like other managers and professionals, the manager of communication is expected to keep an eye on the bottom line. When you choose to communicate without conducting research before, during, and after, you are gambling with the resources entrusted to you. It is easier to make an argument for the resources to conduct research that will ensure the success of your messages than it is to explain a communication failure. The worse possible scenario for a communication professional is to have to explain to a client or boss why a campaign or program is not working.

WHAT KINDS OF RESEARCH DO PR PRACTITIONERS USE?

The kinds of research PR practitioners use are specific to the stages of a strategic process, and answer the question *When should research be conducted?* The short answer to this question is that savvy, committed public relations practitioners are conducting research all of the time. Long before planning of specific communication efforts is undertaken, you should have an ear to the ground, watching for trends and learning about the issues. The key is to know what people are thinking about, which issues have their attention, and how their perceptions might affect your organization or client. Eventually, this information will be useful in developing strategy and planning messages. Of course, the research for creating a specific public relations plan will be more purposeful. As discussed, research should be conducted before, during, and after planning a program. Specific types of research are described in the sections on informal and formal research methods.

The research conducted before and during public relations planning is called **formative, or developmental, research.** This research helps you form or develop goals and objectives, strategy, message development, and tactics of a program. Here, you are listening to your target audiences to learn as much as possible about them. This listening helps you learn the words and pictures you want to use in your communication, the channels to use, how to encourage the actions or behavior changes you want, the reward or benefit you can offer your target audience, what image you want the actions or behaviors to have, and what evidence you need to provide to support your communication.

Monitoring, or iterative, research is *conducted at significant stages of a public relations program.* Prior to launching a campaign, messages should be pretested with members of the target audience. Pretesting provides information that will allow you to make changes before resources are spent to create and disseminate a message that is not effective with your target audiences or one that is even offensive or condescending. A great deal of time and money can be saved. Also, after a program or campaign begins, you must know if the target audiences are receiving messages and if those messages are effective. This type of research lets you make adjustments to the program or campaign as it is under way. Research at this stage is not designed just to confirm that things are going as planned. Instead, it is listening and tracking and being ready to make changes if any are necessary.

Evaluative research *tells you how well you planned and what you learned.* It is conducted at the close of a campaign or program, or it may be useful as formative research at the discovery stage of new programs or campaigns. It has become increasingly important to the practitioner as clients, executives, and funding organizations are asking them to demonstrate the effectiveness of a communication campaign or program. More and more, clients want to see a return on their investment (ROI). Table 6.1 delineates the general types of PR research.

Table **6.1**	General Types of PR Research		
	Formative (developmental)	**Monitoring (iterative)**	**Evaluative**
Used when	Before and during PR planning	At significant stages of a public relations program (before, during, after)	At the close of a campaign or program
Purpose	Listening to your target audiences to learn as much as possible about them to help you to form or develop goals and objectives, strategy, message development, and tactics of a program	This type of research lets you make adjustments to the program or campaign as it is under way. Research at this stage is not designed just to confirm that things are going as planned. Instead, it is listening and tracking and being ready to make changes if any are necessary.	This research tells you how well you planned and what you learned. It is also useful as formative research at the discovery stage of new programs or campaigns.

WHERE SHOULD RESEARCH BE CONDUCTED?

Research can be conducted inside and outside of an organization. Clearly, audience-focused research is conducted externally among the target audiences, but some internal research is necessary to help an organization to effectively communicate internally and externally.

Most internal research is finding out facts about the organization or client's business. Each has documents on file that will help you understand more about target audiences, historical facts, structure, competition, and the organization's previous communication. This type of information is revealed in publications such as newsletters, brochures, and annual reports of both the client and its competitors. Also helpful are examples of previous media coverage, media lists, correspondence with the news media, and biographical information on the principals of the organization. Of course, the client's website and those of its competitors are a good place to look for facts.

External research is often more formal and requires more sophisticated methods. This research is performed to get an outsider's perspective of the organization and to provide the really important information about audiences. Here, the emphasis is on knowing so that you can create the most effective messages possible. This research should be both *quantitative* and *qualitative*. We will discuss each later in this chapter.

HOW IS RESEARCH CONDUCTED?

Informal Research Methods

When viewed and used as exploratory and for purposes of discovery, **informal research methods** are techniques for identifying and exploring problems and opportunities. These methods can be valuable and help answer questions about problems and can provide information for building a research strategy. As well, if informal research is well planned, it can provide insight into the target audience. Effective informal methods used widely in public relations include, key informant conversations/interviews, community and town meetings, communication audits, environmental scans, and news media audits.

Key Informant Conversations/Interviews

Key informant conversations, *in-depth discussions with subject matter experts (sme) who share their opinions and insights,* can be very informative and revealing. This method requires creating a comprehensive list of experts who are knowledgeable about an industry, problem, issue, or trend. Discussions are then held with the experts who provide their views—and the views of others whom they are perceived to represent—in their own words. Many practitioners use conversations with key informants to try to gauge public opinion. They meet with local elected officials, civic and religious leaders, board of trade and chamber of commerce officials, banking executives, editorial boards, academics, and leaders of special interest groups.

The greatest advantage of conducting key informant research is also the greatest limitation. While you have the time and attention of leaders, they are not always in tune with the people they represent. Therefore, the information may not accurately reflect the feelings of the constituency group. As well, these sessions may be biased. Bias has a great opportunity to creep in unless you are very well aware of a tendency to select leaders who are in your own camp. It is crucial to talk to community leaders who are not in lock step with your client and who may hold opposing views or represent constituents perceived as out of the mainstream.

A woman expresses her opinion in a town hall meeting.

Community and Town Meetings

Unlike key informant conversations, **community and town meetings** *are tantamount to going straight to the target audience.* Many politicians use these meetings successfully. Bill Clinton was exceptionally good at employing this method during both his presidential campaigns. Two things are gained for the researcher/practitioner with this method. First, those who attend are clearly interested in the issue, problem, or trend, as they have invested their time, a valued commodity. Therefore, as interested parties who take the time out to express their opinions, they are likely to be candid in expressing their views. Second, a forum of this type is useful in determining how a community will react to a proposal that will affect the community such as new development. In one example, Sean O'Neill, public relations practitioner seeking feedback from local residents on a proposal to build a power plant in their community, offered to host the annual Christmas dinner for a local grassroots group. At the dinner, he distributed a written survey designed to capture residents' opinions on the proposed project and to gather volunteer information for the grassroots organization.

For the purposes of planning, measuring, and monitoring, it is important to know and understand what target audiences think about your organization or client. Talking directly to constituencies or leaders of constituency groups is a good way to stay on top of public opinion.

Communication Audits

Reviewing the content of communication vehicles such as websites, intranet sites, and publications thoroughly and interviewing audiences to determine the communication effectiveness are the essence of a **communication audit.** The audit is a diagnostic tool that can help identify changes needed to improve the effectiveness of an organization's communication with its internal and external audiences. An internal communication audit can tell you how well the information within an organization is flowing and if the intended messages are reaching employees. Effective external audits of an organization's communication to its target audiences can serve to inform strategies for future communication programs. Both internal and external audits can be used as benchmarks when new communication campaigns are launched. A **benchmark,** sometimes called a **baseline,** is *a metric against which new and succeeding efforts can be measured.*

Communication audits can reveal whether or not a publication should continue in hard copy or become web-based or both. Many government agencies provide health-care content to audiences seeking information about healthy eating, chronic conditions, diseases, and aging. Periodic communication audits help determine whether or not these publications should be discontinued or require new dissemination strategies.

Environmental Scans

The **environmental scan** is *an ongoing research method that feeds information into the organization by continuously monitoring issues, trends, public opinion, and reputation* *among its target audiences.* An environmental scan might incorporate several elements to take a pulse of what is going on around an organization. SWOT analyses, literature reviews, mystery shopping, and industry-specific databases are among the tools of an environmental scan.

The SWOT analysis is one of the most well known elements of an environmental scan, as it is widely used in business and industry. The SWOT analyzes an organization's **S**trengths and **W**eaknesses in responding to the **O**pportunities and **T**hreats in its external environment. The analysis is designed to assist the organization in setting priorities—deciding which among its opportunities and threats are most important, and marshaling its strengths to accommodate the opportunities and battle the threats while attending to its weaknesses.

The literature review is a time-honored scholarly tradition that requires a researcher to search exiting published materials or literature on the topic or issue exhaustively to identify and understand everything that has been written. A **literature review** is exactly what the name suggests: *an exhaustive review of what's been written about a topic or subject.* It should concentrate on academic, professional, and trade publications. The goal is to understand what has been written about the subject and to discover who the *players* are in a topic or subject area.

Mystery shopping *allows the practitioner to test the competition or opposition's strengths and weaknesses by discovering what products and services they offer and to what extent.* A mystery shopper might call or use the Internet to ask if a particular service or product is offered, where it can be found, how to access or acquire it, its cost, benefits and barriers, and many other answers to questions. The person making the inquiry indicates that she is seeking information, guidance, assistance, or a product. Mystery shopping is conducted in all sectors. For example, the federal government's Centers for Medicare and Medicaid Services (CMS) operates healthcare programs for the nation's more than 75 million seniors. The agency uses consumer research to determine how its beneficiaries find healthcare services and products and what is offered to them by providers. In order to provide better services to its members, associations try to discover benefits and costs offered by other associations.

Databases such as Dow Jones Factiva are valuable to environmental scans. In addition to monitoring competitors, audiences, and industries, the service provides customized research for organizations and companies on any issue or topic.

News Media Audits

A **media audit** *analyzes the news media coverage of an organization or client.* It is not as scientific as it sounds, but it can be informative. It can be used for the purposes of benchmarking, serving as a baseline against which to measure program success. It is also valuable in determining how a problem may have been framed in the news media. If nothing else, this type of analysis helps you observe how some target audiences may have been informed about a problem, issue, or trend. Many commercial tracking companies, such as Vocus, have software to assist in conducting this type of research, and the software provides impressive reports. These reports can be expensive but are worth the investment if you are tracking on a national or international basis. If the scope is regional or local, the organization can conduct its own news media analysis by subscribing to a clipping service for newspapers and magazines and a tracking service for television and Internet news. Also, PR professionals in nonprofit organizations, companies, and government are served by database media services such as PRNewswire that distribute PR tactics (see Chapters 14, 15, and 16) such as news releases as well as tracking coverage.

Other informal research can be conducted through the Internet by monitoring online chat and blogs. Call-in lines, hotlines, and correspondence to an organization can also be analyzed to gain insight about a situation or subject.

As helpful as these informal methods can be, when incorporated as part of a strategy, they should never be used alone to develop program and campaign plans. When paired with more formal methods, they create a clear picture of the target audience, and practitioners are better prepared to make informed decisions.

Formal Research Methods

As the name suggests, **formal research methods** are *much more planned and strictly conducted than informal research, involving specific protocols or prescribed ways for collecting the data.* There are two types of formal research—quantitative and qualitative. Both can be used throughout the communication program or campaign.

Qualitative research is *descriptive, providing the how and why.* **Quantitative research** *tells us how many; it measures the numbers and percentages of a particular research question.*

Research designs and techniques of quantitative and qualitative studies are vastly different, as are the costs and time frames needed to accomplish the research. Two factors influence the type of research you should employ. The first is the decisions you need to make, and the second is the information you require in order to make those decisions.

Qualitative Research

At the most simplistic level, qualitative research is questioning people as individuals or in small groups about the *why* of an action or behavior. It provides descriptive information that can help you better understand the feelings of your target audiences. Through qualitative research, you can gain insight into a target audience's perception of reality. This research helps you to listen to and hear how your target audiences actually live their lives and how your client's issues and problems fit into them.

Qualitative research does *not* measure the how many or to what degree, or frequency of the feelings, perceptions, or attitudes. While it does not provide precise numbers that can be projected to a population, it provides contextual information to help you learn about your target audiences as individuals. It allows you to "paint a picture" of the audience you want to reach. This picture is extremely important to creating communication plans that have impact.

What you learn from qualitative research is that there are relationships among attitudes, beliefs, motives, and behaviors of a target audience. The picture you gain from it is a model of how your audiences think, feel, and behave. This type of research results in more depth than just how many. What you gain is an understanding of why your audiences do what they do, what benefit or reward they seek, what barriers they face and must overcome, and what will encourage them to take an action or make a change. Delving into these types of answers is not possible with quantitative research. Often, people find it difficult to express their feelings or they are unable to articulate why they do things or their attitudes about issues and problems. Qualitative research allows researchers who are adept at conducting qualitative research to probe and eventually identify feelings. The open-ended question format (discussed later in this chapter) of most qualitative research invites respondents to be expansive in their responses and permits the researcher to explore many sides of an issue.

Qualitative research methods require relatively small numbers of people, while quantitative methods sample large numbers of people in order to make valid statistical assumptions about a population.

When to Use Qualitative Research   Qualitative research methods should be used when you want to pursue the *feelings* of a key audience. After you have conducted quantitative research, you can use qualitative research to understand the *why* behind what numbers of people feel. For instance, your university may know that 65 percent of its alumni never attend an alumni event. It would be important to the development office to understand why the alumni do not attend. A series of focus groups or in-depth interviews might reveal a recurring theme such as the perception that the events are not of high quality, or the alumni who don't attend do not perceive a benefit from attendance, or something as simple as they cannot afford the events the university plans. You can use qualitative research to help inform questions you use in quantitative research studies to help quantify how many in a population share specific feelings, beliefs, opinions, and behaviors.

Qualitative research is used to test messages and concepts and materials such as brochures, other publications, and websites. It gives the practitioner an opportunity to understand how key audiences may react to copy, images, and themes. Figure 6.1 provides a summary of when to use qualitative research and what it can achieve at each stage.

Advantages of Using Qualitative Research Methods   Qualitative research is exploratory. It is useful when you do not have a thorough understanding of how your target audiences relate to the issue or problem. It enables you to gain insights into behavior, attitudes, motives, and opinions of your target audiences. Qualitative research is helpful when you are unsure of the *why* behind your target audience's behavior. For instance, you can use qualitative research to discover why your university's alumni contribute to the institution or why they do not attend alumni events.

Because it is designed to be in-depth and descriptive, qualitative research allows you to decipher attitudes, motivations, and beliefs. Group interactions of focus groups (discussed later in the chapter) and lengthy discussion techniques stimulate in-depth responses as well as new and valuable thoughts. These methods are helpful when trying to understand complex behaviors, motivations, and decision-making processes.

One of the most appealing characteristics of qualitative research is flexibility. Study design can be modified while the study is in progress because it builds upon what is being learned and allows new questions to be raised. In fact, astute interviewers can follow up right away if a new point or issue is presented during an interview. If alumni mention "prestige" as a factor in deciding to support the university and prestige is not part of the line of questioning in the study, it can be added to the study.

Two additional advantages of qualitative research are that it generally costs less than conducting a quantitative study and takes less time. Not only do data collection and analysis typically take less time in qualitative research than in many quantitative studies, but some qualitative research techniques such as focus groups allow for gathering several opinions at once.

Disadvantages of Using Qualitative Research Methods   The primary disadvantage to qualitative research is that it cannot be projected to the population and a general statement cannot be made about the findings that applies to everyone. No matter

Prior to Message Development:

To explore everything you can about your target audiences and learn who they *really* are

To learn about the daily concerns, desires, and needs of your target audiences

To identify the *language* your target audiences use

To understand how your target audiences see your client or organization issues and problems

To discern what your target audiences are doing now instead of what you want them to do

To garner new ideas

During Message Concept Development:

To examine reactions to message concepts

To garner creative ideas for message execution

To get your target audience impressions of creative concepts, headlines, and copy—getting feedback at this early stage to avoid obvious "red flags"

After Material Development:

To ensure your target audiences understand the creative execution

To assess whether your target audiences take away the intended message

To ensure that the message is appropriate for the intended target audiences

Before Developing a Quantitative Study:

To specify particular information needs for the quantitative study

To help identify variables or attributes to be examined in a quantitative study

To learn the language of the target audience to use in developing questions

To help identify the types of people to be interviewed

To Help Understand the Results of a Quantitative Study:

To explain, expand, and illuminate results from quantitative data

To gain understanding about the reasons for certain trends

To find out why target audiences have specific attitudes

Figure 6.1
Using Qualitative
Research

how many focus groups or interviews you conduct, you cannot use a percentage or number to describe the feelings of the population. While it is flexible, qualitative research is time consuming and labor intense.

Qualitative Research Methods   Qualitative techniques give you direct access to your target audiences, providing the opportunity to view and experience those audiences directly. The in-depth interactions intrinsic to the following methods are invaluable:

- Focus groups
- In-depth interviews

- Observations such as usability studies
- Theatre testing

Let's take a closer look at some of these methods.

Focus Groups   **Focus groups** are *structured group interviews that proceed according to careful research design and with attention to the principles of group dynamics.* They have become a respected research method for social and market research. Like any good thing, they are sometimes overused and misused. Too often when faced with indecision or lack of understanding, practitioners turn to focus groups when they are not the appropriate answer. Focus groups are not just a lot of people chosen arbitrarily to discuss an issue. They are not a gathering of coworkers who talk about their opinions about an issue. They are not designed to help groups reach consensus or to make decisions, but rather to elicit the full range of ideas, attitudes, experiences, and opinions held by selected participants.

Participants are chosen because of characteristics they possess that are of special interest to the client and to research objectives. They are screened for participation in the group through a telephone interview process that determines if the respondent meets the desired characteristics and has not participated in a focus group in the past six months to a year. The best size for focus groups is 8 to 10 participants. Focus groups tend to last one to two hours.

There are very good reasons for conducting focus groups. The group interaction that takes place in a focus group helps to stimulate diverse responses as well as new and valuable thoughts. Participants are encouraged to think for themselves, knowing that there are no right or wrong answers. As a result, participants stimulate each other in an exchange of ideas that may not emerge in individual interviews or surveys. The length of the sessions allows for more in-depth responses than other research methods. The size of a focus group enables the researcher to get the opinions of 8 to 10 people at one time.

A focus group is one of the best ways to discuss concepts prior to message and material development and to pretest and evaluate materials and messages. The group can help identify and define a problem. Very important to the client and practitioner is that focus groups save time because they can be completed and analyzed quickly. And clients, program managers, and practitioners can watch the groups from another room, allowing firsthand observation of members of the target audience.

Of course, there are limitations to this research method. It is crucial for focus groups to be planned scientifically or they can be misleading. Part of that planning is the development of an effective topic guide or moderator's guide. Much like a questionnaire in survey research (discussed later in this chapter), the moderator's guide should be developed with care, building a logical sequence of questions for the discussion. Moderators must be skilled and understand the purpose of the groups to eliminate distortion of the findings because of poor facilitation.

If groups are conducted at a single facility the average cost is $5,000 to $7,000 per group. This fee includes recruiting and screening participants, hosting, moderating, audio- and videorecording, and report writing. This cost does not cover incentives for participants, which usually run around $75 to $100 per person, or transcripts of the discussion, about $700.00. If the studied population is particularly hard to get, the cost can be higher.

Customized Focus Groups   In **telephone focus groups,** *participants dial a toll-free number and use a password provided to them in advance. The participants are all brought on the line and the moderator introduces participants and begins the discussion.*

A telephone focus group follows a course similar to face-to-face focus groups. The duration of the over-the-phone focus group should not exceed one-and-a-half hours, since it is more difficult for participants to maintain concentration without face-to-face contact. The client, program manager, and practitioner can listen in on the group discussion.

Telephone focus groups have the same advantages of the face-to-face focus groups, plus they can sometimes garner more candid responses because the anonymity is higher than in face-to-face encounters.

Also, if needed, a moderator can leave out certain group participants. For example, if some of participants are familiar with a certain issue and others are not and the moderator would like to have opinions of both, the moderator can leave those who are familiar out, while soliciting opinion of those who are not familiar with the issue. Also, telephone focus groups are a cost-effective way to bring together people who are not located in the same area.

Among the drawbacks are that telephone groups eliminate the ability to observe nonverbal cues from the participants, and it is more difficult to keep the group focused on the discussion because people's attention span is shorter.

An hour-and-a-half tape-recorded telephone focus group with 10 participants costs approximately $350 to $420, depending on the telephone provider. This does not include the cost of a moderator, data analysis, report, or participant incentives.

Videoconferencing focus groups merely *use a different medium, video, to conduct a traditional face-to-face focus group.* If the studies are conducted in a number of different locations and the client's budget or schedule does not permit travel to observe the groups, videoconferencing equipment can be used to observe the groups. However, not all facilities have videoconferencing capabilities, and those that do charge additional fees for using the equipment. On average, fees for observing a focus group via videoconferencing are approximately $500 to $650 per hour and $250 for transmission charges.

In-Depth Interviews (IDIs)   **In-depth interviews** are *one-on-one interactions, organized to encourage the respondent to talk freely and to express her ideas on the subject under investigation.* To ensure a range of viewpoints, it is advisable to conduct at least 10 in-depth interviews with each type of respondent. As an example, if the researcher wants parental and teen views on an issue, 10 in-depth interviews should be conducted with parents and 10 should be conducted with teens.

Typically respondents are not compensated for their time when participating in an interview. However, compensation may become necessary when interviewing specialists, especially if they have no stake in the research. For example, physicians are generally paid between $300 and $500 to participate in a half-hour interview—the amount of money they would be compensated if they were with a patient.

In-depth interviews are designed to provide an environment for getting a respondent to reveal motives and attitudes that would not be revealed in other settings. Sometimes individual interviews are the only way to get information from some types of respondents, such as policy makers, doctors, corporate executives, and lawyers.

There is also an advantage to getting in-depth responses from respondents because the answers are likely to differ from first responses. In-depth interviews are preferred for probing sensitive or emotional issues or materials. For material pretesting purposes, in-depths are appropriate for longer and more complex materials. These interviews also allow researchers to learn more about hard-to-reach audiences and individuals who have limited reading and writing skills.

While they are excellent research tools, in-depth interviews can be expensive. They are time consuming to conduct and to analyze. Also, if the researcher goes to the respondent, control of the environment or interview setting inherent in conducting in-depths in the field and the opportunity for program managers or practitioners to observe are lost. If interviews are conducted by telephone, there is opportunity for listening in; or if conducted in a facility, observation of the interview is possible. Both possibilities increase the cost of an already expensive tool.

On average, in-depth interviews cost more than focus groups because they take more research time—both to conduct the interviews and to analyze the findings. The cost depends on the number of interviews conducted, whether incentives to participate are incurred, and how difficult it is to reach the interviewee.

Customized In-Depth Interviews   **Dyads** are *intense discussions between two people guided by a moderator.* The participants are selected based on their relationship, such as husband and wife. **Triads** *consist of interviewing three people simultaneously who have different perspectives on the same topic.* For example, if a practitioner is interested in perceptions of the issue of home healthcare, a triad might include a potential patient, his adult child, and a home healthcare provider.

Perceptual analyzer is *a system that allows test subjects to record their reactions to test materials, such as advertising or new product concepts, using handheld dials with a wireless connection to a computer.* Information directly translates into data and graphic output, and is presented in real-time to both the group moderator and viewing clients. The perceptual analyzer can be used with groups ranging from two to 400 participants.

Perceptual analyzers can be used in a focus group setting. For example, if the purpose of the group is to concept-test several public service advertising executions, prior to the beginning of the discussion, the participants from the groups are gathered in one room. They are shown the advertising spots and are asked to react to them using a perceptual analyzer. Testing using perceptual analyzers minimizes group interaction bias.

Obviously, this kind of technology can be very effective but pricey. The average cost for focus groups with 25 to 30 participants using the perceptual analyzer is $20,000 to $27,000 (including report and moderator).

Central Location Intercept Interviews   **Central location intercept interviews,** also called **mall intercepts,** are a *research technique that involves stationing interviewers at a point, such as shopping malls, frequented by individuals from the target audience.* Interviewers stop, or intercept, consumers and interview them using a survey method. Although a survey method is used, the results of intercept interviews cannot be projected statistically to the population from which participants are drawn.

A typical central location intercept interview begins with the intercept. Potential respondents are stopped and asked whether they are willing to participate and are screened for participation by the answers they provide to a few questions. If they fit the criteria of the target audience, they are taken to an interviewing station (a quiet place) and are asked a set of questions.

Intercept interviews are an excellent way to test program materials to see how your target audiences interpret them. Do they comprehend your communication message? Does it motivate them to take the desired action?

The questionnaire used during intercept interviews is structured containing primarily closed-ended questions (discussed later in this chapter). Open-ended questions are kept to a minimum.

A typical intercept interview study involves 125 to 150 participants and is conducted in five or six different locations (25 interviews per site). The cost for these studies depends heavily on the number of interviewers used.

Intercepts can test many different kinds of material and they are quickly conducted. Generally, it takes about seven days from setting up to receiving the tabulated results, making them less expensive than a focus group study or in-depth interview. However, because they are usually no more than 10 minutes each, there is no opportunity to explore in-depth target audience attitudes and perceptions or to probe. Another drawback of intercept interviews is the sample is restricted to individuals at the location.

Approximately 125 mall intercept interviews in five locations with data analysis and final report averages $12,000 to $15,000.

Usability/Readability Testing   **Usability/readability testing** is a form of using observation as research. It *is used to predict how easy it is for a person to understand written materials and the ease of using certain materials.* For example, you may want to know how user friendly an application form is or what your target audience experiences in using a guidebook. Such testing can help you assess whether the materials are written and organized at a level most of the audience can understand. It also predicts what education level a person should have in order to understand the material.

Observing participants in the study as they use the materials is one way of using the usability test. Participants might be asked to read a document such as a brochure or set of instructions prior to a readability study. A questionnaire designed by the researcher can then test a respondent's level of understanding of information covered in the materials by asking a set of specific questions. The questionnaire also might include questions that test the respondent's ability to find specific terms or to fill out a form. Questionnaires are coded and the answers analyzed statistically.

Such testing can be expensive because of the costs of using participants from the target audience and because conducting the sessions and analyzing results require extensive researcher time. Also, researchers do not know why people do not understand the materials because they cannot probe the respondents. The cost for such testing is approximately $8,000 to $9,000.

Theatre Testing   The **theatre testing** method *brings a large group of respondents into a room that is arranged theatre style for the purpose of getting their responses to audio and audiovisual materials.* It can be used to pretest radio and television public service advertising (PSA). The respondents are told that they are being asked to watch or listen to a program to see if it should air. The program has commercials and PSAs interspersed throughout. Respondents are asked to give general feelings about the program itself. They are asked if they remember the PSAs and are asked specific questions about their responses to the PSAs regarding to whom the ads are focused, relevance, music, spokesperson, music, and more.

The greatest advantage to this method is that it allows you to get very quick responses from a large group of respondents. Also, the presentation is quite natural with commercials throughout as respondents are accustomed to at home. It allows you to see just how likely it is that your target audience will pay attention to the PSAs.

Theatre testing by commercial testing firms is very expensive. The practitioner can conduct theatre testing at other facilities, including schools and universities, libraries, and community centers.

Quantitative Research

There are two kinds of quantitative research—survey and experiments. As a communication professional, you are most likely to use survey methods, but effectiveness of message strategies and promotions can be measured through experimental tests. Both surveys and experiments employ scientific methods and provide results that allow you to make predictions about a larger population based on the results of testing a smaller population.

Survey research is *the systematic gathering of information from respondents for the purpose of understanding and/or predicting some aspect of the behavior of the population of interest.* This research method uses scientific *sampling and questionnaire design* to measure the preferences, activities, and habits of a population with statistical precision. It asks a sample of a population a series of standardized questions and then creates several different charts of the answers for study and comparisons. As a result, the researcher can use the findings to indicate how many people feel a certain way or how often they take a particular action or participate in a particular behavior. Survey research findings enable us to make comparisons between groups as well.

A Closer Look at Samples   A *sample* is exactly what it sounds like: an example of something. In the case of survey research, a **sample** is *an example of a larger group of people*—the population. As we've discussed, it is very advantageous for you as a public relations practitioner to understand as much as possible about your target audiences—but, clearly, you cannot talk to all of them. Survey research talks to a small group—a representative sample—of the population to determine what your larger audiences think. The key in sampling is that it must enable you to generalize from the sample results to the larger population from which the sample was drawn. For example, if your target audience is undergraduate students in the United States, you cannot interview all of them to understand more about their behaviors. But you can select a sample of that population to gain insight into the entire population.

There are many sampling designs, but not all of them are crucial to our discussions about research. Important is the concept that **probability sampling** *has many advantages, chief of which is the ability to calculate* **sampling error.** *This allows you to estimate the degree of discrepancy between the sample results and the population.* Another important advantage of probability sampling is that you know there is a probability of any person in the population being selected in the sample.

It is helpful to look at examples of **nonprobability sampling** to help make the concept of probability sampling easier to grasp. *When people are asked to express their opinions on an issue by calling-in on a radio show, they are a part of a nonprobability sample because the callers may or may not represent the community at large.* Similarly, a candidate for public office might ask members of a town hall meeting to indicate their opinions by a show of hands. Despite the results of the survey, it cannot be generalized to the total population of the town.

Random sampling and systematic sampling are two types of probability sampling. In **random sampling,** *the manner for selecting the participants can vary from a computer-generated list of numbers, to a random number list, to putting all the numbers in a drum, spinning them and then drawing the numbers*—*much like winning lottery numbers are drawn.* Random sampling requires a complete and accurate list of everyone in the population you are studying. With such a list, the researcher can assign a unique number to each person on the list and then select a sample of these numbers.

Systematic sampling *selects every nth name from the list after the first name is selected randomly.* Like random sampling, systematic sampling from a complete and accurate list can be a straightforward way to sample, as long as the names on list are not grouped in any particular fashion. An alphabetical list provides an easy way to do this; however, if a list is organized with alternating names representing a variable, the list is problematic.

In **stratified sampling,** *you divide the population into strata or subgroups that share a particular characteristic in which you are interested.* It is mostly useful when you are interested in particular characteristics of the population. After the population is stratified, it can be randomly or systematically sampled. Important here is the fact that you are guaranteed the sample will be representative with regard to the variables you use to stratify.

Random, systematic, and stratified sampling require a list of all the people or certain types of people in the population. Sometimes an exhaustive list does not exist or is impossible to compile, but there may be groups to which the people you want belong. This form of *sampling based on groupings or clusters from which you then randomly select* is called **cluster sampling.** For example, if you wanted to study elementary teachers in a state, you could start with a list of elementary schools from which you would randomly sample for the study, then contact the selected schools for a list of teachers and contact those teachers.

Using your own judgment about whom you want to interview because of their expertise or experience is called **purposive** or **judgmental sampling.** Similarly, you use **convenience sampling** *when you are aware of a group of people who are available— convenient—to use for study.* This is true on most college campuses where professors ask students to participate in their studies. Mass media efforts to survey readers, listeners, and viewers is another example of convenience sampling.

Sample Sizes   Many people are suspect of survey results because they have never been surveyed about the topic. How many times have you read or heard survey findings with which you do not agree and respond, "Nobody asked me!" Others find it difficult to understand how a small **sample size,** *the number of people surveyed,* can accurately reflect the opinions of the much larger population—when, in fact, if properly constructed, surveys based on 1,500 people can accurately predict the outcome of an election within 3 percent of the actual results. The acceptable **margin of error**—*the percentage of errors the study may contain after which the results are still valid*—is plus or minus 5 percent. Enlarging the sample size can reduce the margin of error.

Statisticians and mathematicians know statistical and probability theory for why small sample sizes are adequate. We will not endeavor to understand them here, but perhaps we can understand based on analogy. While hardly scientific, the best analogy this author has heard for the validity of sample sizes is that of the chef and the soup. A chef preparing a soup for the evening dinner in a restaurant needs to know if more herbs and spices need to be added to the soup in order to reach the chef's idea of perfection. In order to make that determination, the chef tastes a spoonful of the soup. As long as the chef has stirred the soup well at each tasting, the spoonful is representative of the taste of all the soup in the pot.

Questionnaire Design   In addition to a proper sample, a successful survey depends on a well-designed instrument, or questionnaire. The **questionnaire** is *the document containing the questions and onto which the interviewer or interviewee enters a respondent's answers.*

The respondent can complete **self-administered or individually-administered questionnaires** *sent by mail or fax or received by computer.* In a **group-administered questionnaire,** *a researcher has the opportunity to survey respondents at a facility where* *people usually meet and administers the questionnaire to those who are in attendance.* **Computer-administered questionnaires** *can be administered by computer and are helpful because tabulation is easier.* These are the growing trend in the United States, and there are several software packages for delivering surveys online.

Creating an effective questionnaire depends upon a few elements—words, the logical sequence of questions, options for answers, and format. Clear and concise phrasing of questions is crucial. While always important, phrasing is most important if the respondent is not interviewed face-to-face because there are no nonverbal cues from the researcher to assist in understanding. An effective survey instrument should contain close-ended, specific answer questions as much as possible. **Open-ended questions** are *composed without a prescribed manner or limitation to how the questions can be answered and allow respondents to answer as they wish.* They are not helpful for tabulating, and analysis becomes much more complicated, as answers must be coded and the researcher must interpret the answer.

Closed-ended questions are *composed with a predetermined list of possible answers.* They require the respondent to answer by choosing from a list of answer categories. The researcher must be careful in framing both the questions and the answers. The categories must be all-inclusive while eliminating other possible answers. In other words, if a researcher wants one answer to a question, the categories must provide the respondent every possible answer and not overlap into other answers: they must be mutually exclusive. Still, it is possible for a respondent to answer in more than one way. For this reason, the instructions should be clear: Ask the respondent for the *primary reason* or to check the *best answer.*

In the PR business, words are everything. You will spend your professional life making sure you are clear and concise. It is no different with writing a questionnaire. The questions and statements should be worded so that they are unambiguous. The researcher—to be sure the respondents are clear about the instructions and clear as to the attitude about which they are being asked—uses statements. All researchers are susceptible to lack of clarity, especially when it is "your issue." You must make sure to choose words that have clear meaning to your target audience. Remember that the meaning of words changes over time, and words translate differently in different cultures and have different meanings among age groups and generations.

An example of a questionnaire that didn't yield the anticipated results because of its question design is that of practitioner Anya Karavanov, who has conducted survey research on adoption of children in Russia. At the time of the study, in that country, the subject of adoption was sensitive and a secrecy law forbade parents from saying they have adopted children, so the manner in which the questions were developed was crucial to the success of the study. Against Karavanov's advice, the questionnaire asked about income—another sensitive subject. Fully one-third of the respondents refused to answer income questions. Infrastructure in Russia was another concern for questionnaire development. Because the telephone system made it unacceptable to conduct interviews over the telephone and cost prohibitive, all the survey interviews were conducted face-to-face.

Clarity and breadth of questions go hand-in-hand. It takes a skilled practitioner/researcher to form questions into the most logical order. Some questions appear to have only one part when in reality they are several questions in one. The questionnaire should flow logically in breaking down questions into parts and in the manner in which questions flow from one to the other. *Questions that contain more than one question are referred to as* **double-barreled questions.** Avoid double-barreled questions. If asked to agree or disagree to the following, what would your respondent answer? "The United Nations should intervene in any international crisis without need for a full vote." Some can answer yes without reservation. Other respondents can disagree without hesitation. But what about the respondent who feels intervention is the correct course of action but a vote should be used to determine the intervention? Or what about the respondent who feels intervention should depend upon a vote? Clearly, the question should be posed differently. Generally, if *and* is part of a question, the question is double-barreled and should at least be checked.

Intensity of feelings is important to some survey questions. There are ways to present questions so that respondents can express the intensity of their feelings. The **semantic differential technique** is *widely used to help measure intensity*. Depending upon the question, words and their acronyms such as "fair" and "unfair," or "acceptable" and "unacceptable" are used to describe the respondent's feelings. **Summated ratings** *provide statements in a range such as "strongly approve" to "strongly disapprove" with a weight of 1 to 5 attached to each.* As students, you have seen these techniques at work in student evaluations of professors and courses.

The manner in which you request an answer is also crucial to the effectiveness of the questionnaire because it affects the answers. Some questionnaires are mixed formats while others seek to remain true to one format throughout. Respondents are looking for ease in answering the questions and caution is required when you mix formats in one questionnaire.

A quantitative survey questionnaire should be informed by qualitative research. Preliminary qualitative research will reveal areas that need to be measured by the survey. Pretesting questionnaires is an unbreakable rule. It is folly to assume that because you understand the questions and logic of the questionnaire, your target audience will also understand.

Advantages of Using Quantitative Research   The greatest advantage of quantitative survey research is that it is precise, definitive, and standardized. It can answer the "how many" and "how often" of a population at large. It can also measure the extensiveness of attitudes held by people and can measure occurrences, actions, and trends. The results of the survey can be condensed to statistics, ensuring accuracy and allowing for statistical comparison between groups.

For campaign development, surveys can help quantify the number of people who fall into a market segment and can help us select and prioritize audiences. Because they can identify the media outlets your target audience favors, surveys can help you determine the appropriate venues and channels for delivering your message. Surveys can be used to track program and campaign effects by measuring attitudes and behaviors throughout the life of the program or campaign.

Disadvantages of Using Quantitative Research   The primary disadvantage of quantitative research is that issues, concerns, ideas, and opinions are measured only if they are known prior to the beginning of the study. That is to say, you must have the list of questions when you begin the study; most survey research methodology does not allow for inserting questions at the time of the interview. So, for instance, if you return to the university trying to determine why alumni do not attend alumni events the university plans, you would have to know, from qualitative research perhaps, what to ask. If you don't know what to ask, you cannot answer the question of whether or not the events are too costly, not well-timed, or generally unappealing.

When to Use Quantitative Research   Quantitative research methods should be used when you need to get a "number" picture of the population. It identifies population demographics and quantifies different audience segments.

After you have conducted qualitative research, quantitative research can help quantify and verify your results. It is used to quantify opinions, attitudes, and behaviors and to find out how the whole population feels about a certain issue, providing an exact number of people who think a certain way.

For program planning, quantitative research is used to set benchmarks or baselines—measures of consumer attitudes regarding an issue prior to a campaign. To test whether or not a message has reached an intended population, and measure progress, survey research can tell you if target audience attitudes change and if they did, how.

Quantitative Research Methods   Surveys are the primary quantitative research instrument. Within this category, practitioners have several options:

- Personal interviews
- Computer-assisted telephone interviews
- Omnibus surveys
- Self-administered surveys
- Internet and online surveys

Again, survey research is the systematic gathering of information from respondents for the purpose of understanding and/or predicting some aspect of the behavior of the population of interest. Survey research is concerned with sampling, questionnaire design, questionnaire administration, and data analysis. Let's look at these leading types of surveys more closely.

Personal Interviews   **Personal interviews** are *conducted face-to-face with the interviewer asking the questions of the respondent and recording the answers on the questionnaire.* The interview may take place at the respondent's home or at a research facility arranged by the researcher.

These interviews are the most flexible type of the survey methods. They can be used to administer any type of questionnaire—structured questionnaires with specified but variable question sequences, and unstructured questionnaires, requiring a close rapport between the interviewer and the respondent.

If the study involves material testing, personal interviews allow the interviewer to provide the respondent with visual cues on those questions that require them and withhold them on other questions. This method is expensive, as it takes a long time to code and analyze data.

Computer-Assisted Telephone Interviews   **Computer-assisted telephone (CAT) interviews** *require programming a survey questionnaire directly into a computer. The telephone interviewer then reads the questions from a monitor screen and records the answers directly on the terminal keyboard or directly onto the screen with a light pen.*

There are several advantages to computer-assisted interviews, the greatest of which is that data analysis is almost instantaneous. Often the exact set of questions a respondent is to receive will depend on his answers to earlier questions. The computer allows for the creation of an "individualized" questionnaire for each respondent based on answers to prior questions. The computer can present different versions of the same questions, rotating the order in which the alternatives offered by the question are presented.

One disadvantage of computer-assisted interviews is that they are inappropriate for studies that require the respondent to react to the actual product, advertising copy, package design, or other physical characteristics. Another is that the interviewer cannot observe the respondent to ensure the instructions are understood.

Omnibus Surveys   An **omnibus survey** is *a type of telephone survey in which the conducting agency (survey firm) inserts questions of special interest to several clients.* Sometimes referred to as *piggybacking*, the omnibus survey is a shared survey. It can be extremely useful for "pulse taking" (i.e., monitoring opinions and attitudes regarding a certain issue).

Omnibus surveys consist of a minimum of 1,000 interviews (50 percent men and 50 percent women). The survey uses **random-digit-dialing sampling** *of telephone households; the central computer is programmed to select a telephone number at random.* Within each sample household, one adult respondent is randomly selected using a computerized procedure. Usually, interviewing for each omnibus survey is conducted over a five-day period. Up to four attempts are made to a number on various days and at different time periods. Depending on the company used to administer the survey, the response rate is between 30 to 40 percent.

Omnibus surveys have relatively quick turnaround time. A researcher can have analyzed data within a week, and it is fairly inexpensive in comparison to other survey methods. (Prices for a question on an omnibus survey range from $1,000 to $1,500 per question.) Our client or organization is sharing the cost with other clients of the research firm. The response rate is fairly low and, although the sample is drawn randomly, the data cannot be completely generalized to the population in question.

Self-Administered Surveys   Respondents themselves fill out self-administered survey questionnaires, which are generally distributed through the mail. Upon the receipt of the questionnaire, the respondent fills it out and returns it via mail to the researcher. The questionnaires can be also distributed by means of magazine and newspaper inserts or they can be left and/or picked up by the organization conducting the study. Because they are self-administered, this method enables researchers to elicit detailed information from respondents who may not be accessible otherwise, such as homebound or rural respondents.

Also, self-administered questionnaires can be used for pretesting campaign or program materials before execution. In this case the questionnaire is mailed to the respondent along with the pretest materials. However, it is not the best method for pretesting.

This method is inexpensive because it does not require interviewer time. It can be very effective because it allows respondents to maintain their anonymity and reconsider their responses.

Mailed, self-administered questionnaires have a very low response rate and require follow-up with respondents to increase the possibility of responses. As a result, it may take a long time to receive sufficient responses. The chance for bias is increased because respondents self-select. This is not a preferred method for pretesting materials because exposure to the materials is not controlled. As with all uncontrolled situations, this method may not be appropriate if respondents have limited reading and writing skills.

Internet, Intranet, and Online Surveys   As discussed earlier in this chapter, online surveying is becoming quite popular because it is fast and has the advantage of visual and audio for testing messages and concepts (see "Professional Point of View"). Social media communities also offer PR practitioners access to their key audiences for the purposes of research. Facebook, Twitter, and LinkedIn can be used for conducting surveys to engage and garner the opinions of targeted audience segments. For instance, you can send an opinion survey to an online community interested in your issue or product. You must be careful, however. It is important to become an established member of the community before you suggest using it for research. And, just as important, you must be a part of the conversation and share information with the community.

Considering Psychographics   In the mid-1970s SRI International in California devised a research tool called *psychographics*. The Values and Lifestyle Program or (VALS) classifies adult North Americans into eight categories, or profiles, assigning characteristics to each. The characteristics are based on the apparent values and lifestyles. This technique has been useful in some public relations campaigns, especially those using mass media tactics.

The profiles—*Survivors, Sustainers, Belongers, Emulators, Experientials, I-Am-Mes, Achievers,* and *Societally Conscious*—are interesting but cannot be considered all-encompassing, especially in light of the changing demographics in the country. Clearly, survey research could determine how many people fit into these categories at a particular time.

A newer system Claritas Prizm-NE, built on geography and demographics, has 66 demographically and behaviorally distinct types, or "segments," that categorize likes, dislikes, lifestyles, and behaviors of households and neighborhoods. The 66 segments are grouped into social groups based on where people live, and socioeconomic rank and life-stage groups, based on socioeconomic ranks, age, and presence of children in the household. Interesting titles such as Young Digerati, The Cosmopolitans, and Multi-Culti Mosaic are used to label the segments. This technology has been used beyond its commercial marketing application. Based on this segmentation, researchers can now determine how best to communicate with parents about helping their children become reading ready and getting involved in their children's schools.

TIPS FOR BUYING RESEARCH SERVICES

The practitioner/researcher model is not always the best. Many of you will be practitioners and many of you will be researchers. Few of you will be both. While you may master the basics of qualitative and quantitative research methods, it's not likely you will perform most of your formal research.

In the absence of a research department in your organization or firm, the best strategy is to buy research services from a reputable researcher or research firm. Buying research services from professionals is not complicated. The key, of course, is to be an informed consumer.

The first step is to articulate as clearly as possible what decisions need to be made and the information necessary to make the decisions. The practitioner and colleagues who will work on the program or campaign for which the research is needed should collaborate to answer the questions presented in the "Why Conduct Research?" section of this chapter (see page 110). The answers to these questions will help you to be smart about what your needs really are. You should complete this process before shopping for research services.

You should then shop for a researcher as you would any other service. You must become a researcher yourself. A good first source to check is others in the field whose judgment you trust. Find out whom they have used, what their level of confidence is in the researcher, and what is was like to work with the company. If a trusted source in the field is not a possibility, contact a university or college that offers research courses and talk to a professor. It is very likely that you will get help there. Often, practitioners need reputable researchers in other geographic areas where they don't have contacts. Two sources you can consider for hiring a research vendor are *the Green Book* (The International Directory of Marketing Research Companies and Services, published annually by the New York Chapter of the American Marketing Association) *and the Blue Book* (a list of more than 200 research organizations published by the American Association for Public Opinion Research). Of course, checking websites is a good way to find firms, but it is much better to check out the capabilities of a firm that has been recommended to you already.

During a first meeting with a prospective researcher, the practitioner should explain the research needs and how the findings will be used. Try to interview at least two, optimally three if time allows. There are two things to be gained here. First, you can try to get the best price from the best researcher, but even more important, you will learn a lot.

The researcher should respond with a comprehensive proposal and statement of cost. The proposal should be much like the ones you produce for your own clients or organization. It should include a *background* section that demonstrates the researcher understands your needs for the research. The proposal should explain why the researcher is uniquely qualified to conduct the research. This section provides the *capabilities* of the staff that will be assigned to your project.

The proposal must spell out specifically what types of research methods will be employed and with what specific audiences. This section—usually titled *methodology*—is crucial and should be presented in detail. It is important that the number of interviews, surveys, or other methods be outlined here. Sometimes a researcher will propose additional approaches not discussed in the initial meetings. This is acceptable, but read the rationale carefully and, if necessary, contact the researcher to thoroughly understand what is proposed.

Make sure the proposal clearly states that the analysis and report are included in the quote for the services. Also, if you have special needs such as having the researcher present information or findings to your client or executives of your organization, be sure this is reflected in the proposal. A good proposal will present a *timeline* that reflects not only a schedule of when the actual research is to be conducted but also meetings and presentations. Lastly, the proposal should have a comprehensive budget for the services, reflecting a bottom line cost. It is acceptable for the researcher to present daily rates for meetings and presentations rather than a total price.

As you have probably noted, research firms can be pricey, but there are quite a few small companies and freelancers who are reputable and ethical and cost less. Remember when you decide to buy research services, you are buying the reputation of the researcher as well. Research firms are expected to adhere to a code of ethics much like your own. The research conducted for PR and other communication purposes falls into the category of social or social science research.

ETHICAL CONSIDERATIONS IN SOCIAL SCIENCE RESEARCH

Aside from being unbiased in our research, as we discussed earlier in this chapter, we must remember other ethical considerations when we conduct or commission research studies. We all like to think of ourselves as ethical, but as you will learn in the next chapter, what is ethical is not always obvious. For that reason, you would be wise to become familiar with the codes of ethics or agreements that prevail in the social research field. Most universities have Institutional Review Boards (IRBs) to assist in assuring that the research is conducted ethically. The IRB process requires researchers to answer very specific questions about the standards applied to the research study. In order to understand what is expected by ethical researchers and the questions IRBs

BRIEF CASE STUDY

The Robert Wood Johnson Foundation's "Cover the Uninsured Week" Campaign

You will see references to this campaign throughout Part Three: The Process of Strategic Public Relations (Chapters 10, 11, 12, and 13) of this textbook where the stages of strategic PR are explained. This campaign is used as an example during the process for several reasons: 1) it is strategic; 2) it relies on formative, iterative, and evaluative research; 3) it is a decade old and growing; 4) it has demonstrated measurable results; and 5) it has grown from a once-a-year campaign to a social change movement that culminated in a healthcare reform bill signed by the President in 2010 that expands healthcare coverage to all Americans.

The Robert Wood Johnson Foundation (RWJF) has as its mission "improving the health and health care of all Americans." In an effort to continue bringing the plight of uninsured Americans to the national agenda, the foundation hired political consulting and advocacy advertising firm GMMB in 2004 to develop a national education program similar to the successful "Cover the Uninsured Week 2003." This Brief Case Study is a good example of the dynamic quality of the strategic public relations process, as the work and evaluation from "Cover the Uninsured Week 2003" helped inform the planning and strategy development for the 2004 campaign. Research guided the planning, implementation, and evaluation.

Research began with U.S. Census data showing that 40 million Americans were uninsured for healthcare in 1999. With that statistic as fodder, RWJF hired Washington, DC-based research and strategic communication firm Sutton Group to conduct qualitative research such as focus groups and in-depth interviews to determine the attitudes of Americans about the growing number of uninsured Americans. The research found that most had not thought about Americans who did not have healthcare insurance. It was not on their radar screen. The number of uninsured Americans grew from 40 million in 1999 to more than 43 million Americans without healthcare in 2003.

RWJF next began to discover who might be supporters of its overall goal of achieving affordable and stable coverage for all by 2010. In 2000 RWJF convened a meeting in Washington, DC, with eight partner organizations, beginning a conversation on national, regional, and local levels. Partnerships were a very important component of both the 2003 and 2004 campaigns.

Working the Case

1. What type of research is the census data consulted by RWJF? Primary or secondary? Quantitative or qualitative? Explain.
2. How could RWJF have used the qualitative data it obtained from the Sutton Group to determine how many Americans were concerned about the uninsured?
3. What type of research did RWJF conduct in convening the organizations in Washington, DC?

ask, let's look at an ethical code from the education research field and highlight the major areas of ethical consideration.

More than 10,000 researchers belong to the American Educational Research Association (AERA). The association has a code of ethics for researchers to use as guidelines. While it is risky to attempt to excerpt the most cogent content from a code of ethics, it is worth it to provide a strong philosophical and practical set of standards that are well worth adherence. Figure 6.2 presents excerpts from AERA's code foreword and the guiding standards.

Foreword

Educational researchers come from many disciplines, embrace several competing theoretical frameworks, and use a variety of research methodologies. AERA recognizes that its members are already guided by codes in the various disciplines and, also, by organizations such as Institutional Review Boards (IRBs).

A main objective of this code is to remind us, as educational researchers, that we should strive to protect these populations, and to maintain the integrity of our research, of our research community, and of all those with whom we have professional relations.

It is, therefore, essential that we continually reflect on our research to be sure that it is not only sound scientifically but that it makes a positive contribution to the educational enterprise.

II. Guiding Standards: Research Populations, Educational Institutions, and the Public

A. Preamble.

It is of paramount importance that educational researchers respect the rights, privacy, dignity, and sensitivities of their research populations and also the integrity of the institutions within which the research occurs. Educational researchers should be especially careful in working with children and other vulnerable populations.

Standards intended to protect the rights of human subjects should not be interpreted to prohibit teacher research, action research, and/or other forms of practitioner inquiry so long as: the data are those that could be derived from normal teaching/learning processes; confidentiality is maintained; the safety and welfare of participants are protected; informed consent is obtained when appropriate; and the use of the information obtained is primarily intended for the benefit of those receiving instruction in that setting.

B. Standards.

1. Participants, or their guardians, in a research study have the right to be informed about the likely risks involved in the research and of potential consequences for participants, and to give their informed consent before participating in research.
2. Informants and participants normally have a right to confidentiality, which ensures that the source of information will not be disclosed without the express permission of the informant. In some cases, e.g., survey research, it may be appropriate for researchers to ensure participants of anonymity, i.e., that their identity is not known even to the researcher. Anonymity should not be promised to participants when only confidentiality is intended.
3. Honesty should characterize the relationship between researchers and participants and appropriate institutional representatives. Deception is discouraged; it should be used only when clearly necessary for scientific studies, and should then be minimized. After the study, the researcher should explain to the participants and institutional representatives the reasons for the deception.
4. Educational researchers should be sensitive to any locally established institutional policies or guidelines for conducting research.
5. Participants have the right to withdraw from the study at any time, unless otherwise constrained by their official capacities or roles.
6. Educational researchers should exercise caution to ensure that there is no exploitation for personal gain of research populations or of institutional settings of research.
7. Researchers have a responsibility to be mindful of cultural, religious, gender, and other significant differences within the research population in the planning, conduct, and reporting of their research.

Figure 6.2

Excerpt from the American Educational Research Association's Ethical Standards

SOURCE: www.aera.net

8. Researchers should carefully consider and minimize the use of research techniques that might have negative social consequences.
9. Educational researchers should communicate their findings and the practical significance of their research in clear, straightforward, and appropriate language to relevant research populations, institutional representatives, and other stakeholders.
10. Informants and participants have a right to remain anonymous. This right should be respected when no clear understanding to the contrary has been reached.

Figure 6.2
(*continued*)

Integrity and Quality of the Research

Researchers are expected to conduct research that is scientifically sound while respecting the rights of subjects. There are specific standards for developing research plans, instruments, analysis, and findings. The researcher is expected to meet those standards, and Institutional Review Boards are responsible for providing quality control.

Participants Are Volunteers

Research study participants must be volunteers and have the right to withdraw from the study at any time they become uncomfortable. All of us have been asked to participate in a survey, including online surveys regarding customer service, telephone surveys regarding lifestyles and products, and surveys about whether or not you believe in global warming. Responding to the surveys is usually not the way we planned to spend part of an afternoon or the hour before dinner. The norm is that all participants are told that they are not required to respond; the researcher should do everything she can to ameliorate or eliminate any concerns. Generally, participants are willing to participate if there is a benefit or reward. This accounts for the token dollar included in a mailed questionnaire or the 20 percent discount on your next purchase from a retail store.

Researchers must be thorough in measuring the possibility of harm to participants. The IRB process helps the researcher to think through the slightest, most subtle possibility for injuring a participant. Harm and injury do not have to be physical, of course. Psychological harm is far more likely in social science research. Our research often asks people to tell us very personal information, to share their honest opinions about a subject, or reveal behaviors that are embarrassing. Conducting research about race relations or ethical behavior can cause subjects to second guess themselves and others. Researchers are expected to respect participants of different cultures, gender, religions, and abilities, in planning, conducting, and reporting research studies.

Informed Consent

Informed consent is *a practice that assists researchers in explaining to subjects that a study is completely voluntary and inform them of any possible harm that may result from their participation.* The author has conducted many studies using children as subjects. For these, a signed informed consent form is expected from the children and their parents.

Confidentiality

Participants in a research study should be told that anonymity for them and confidentiality of data is ensured. The researcher should give participants some idea of how the data will be handled and who will see it. It is important that the researcher be honest in all matters concerning the study, but it is especially important that he be specific about what happens to the data. Some research interviews are video recorded. If the researchers thinks that the video may be used for the purposes of presentations to the client or outsiders, participants should be informed and asked to sign a consent form.

PROFESSIONAL POINT OF VIEW

Don't Be Scared: Having the ROI Conversation with Clients

This article, by David Rockland, Ph.D., partner and managing director of Global Research and Interactive Communications at Ketchum, and Joanne Puckett, research director at Ketchum, was published in the July 2006 issue of PR Tactics.

Talking about return on investment, or ROI, with your boss, agency, staff, or client can feel like a cross-examination no matter which side of the table you're on. However, it's necessary to understand what ROI means to develop and introduce a measurement plan for your program. And, if you are serious about getting the biggest impact for your PR bucks, ROI is where it's at.

Here's how to be primed for the conversation, whether the person you are talking to is new to ROI or a measurement guru. First, start with some key messages:

- ROI can be measured. Where PR measurement once proved elusive, a variety of tools and methods exist to quantify ROI at the profession's disposal. While a precise mechanism remains a ways off, the profession is closer than ever. The last five years have brought dramatic changes in the ability to measure ROI.
- It doesn't cost a lot. The routine argument has been that measurement costs too much. In most cases, this simply isn't true. In some cases, components of a ROI measurement program can be tacked on to things a client is already doing. Also, some methods are less expensive than one might think.
- Basically, if you are spending $100,000 or more on public relations, ways exist to spend 4 to 7 percent of that amount to measure the program. And, it isn't just about showing it was worth it, but also learning how to improve the program.
- Often, the data already exist. Most organizations usually have some type of measurement program evaluation in place (e.g., many brands routinely conduct awareness, attitude, and usage studies). As a result, findings from these studies can be used with data from PR programs to gauge changes in familiarity, beliefs, and behaviors in the target audience. For example, slight tweaks to an advertising tracker will do the trick.

What Clients May Ask

Clients may have specific questions about how or what to measure, who should do it or costs associated with conducting ROI measurement. Some of the questions we hear most frequently from clients include:

What Do I Get for My Investment?

Clarify what this means. The question may simply relate to anticipated deliverables or expectations about results—a certain number of placements or, more specifically, an appearance on "Ellen." Find out if the client wants to know a dollar figure or some other measure that will show PR's positive impact on the brand or company's bottom line. Often, we interpret this question to mean a hard ROI figure and discover the client really wonders whether their messages were in their media coverage.

How Much Will It Cost to Measure the Program?

While measurement budgets vary based on the nature and sophistication of the work, spending about 4 to 7 percent of the program budget is typical. Also, it doesn't have to come from the PR budget, particularly if the organization has an existing research program.

What If We Just Want to Know How Effective a Tactic Proved? Can You Measure the ROI for That?

It depends, but usually you can measure the effectiveness of one tactic. For example, if a program includes a specific event, it's possible to track media coverage and sales for that event. Sponsorships, traveling road shows, and local market events can be measured.

Is ROI Always Measured Using Dollars?

The equation for ROI is based on dollars—(incremental gain in dollar sales ÷ investment) × 100 percent—but other ways exist to find ROI for a program. For example, you can examine employee retention, loyalty, or productivity.

Should My Agency Measure Its Own Work?

That's a decision to be made by the client. Typically, at the agency level, a group outside the day-to-day account management team is charged with PR measurement. If objectivity is a concern, members of the measurement group tend to be brought in as needed and aren't necessarily members of the core team. Clients might choose to work with other firms to evaluate program success. No matter who does it, a measurement component is a must-have for a PR plan.

If I'm Using Other Forms of Marketing, Is It Possible to Isolate the Effects of Public Relations?

Statistical analysis does allow for isolating the effects of public relations. Generally, understanding the effects of a program is most successful when looking at a snapshot in time, such as changes in sales immediately after a high-quality media placement. In other cases, survey questions can fill in the blanks of the effects of public relations. You can isolate the effects with tracking studies or market-mix modeling.

What's the First Step in Creating a Measurement Program?

Connecting the dots between communication and market research functions is vital. Determine what research is taking place and what data are collected. From there, a conversation with the agency, client, and the client's marketing-research function will go a long way in defining objectives and the roles the agency and market research will play in executing an ROI measurement program.

Clients may have other questions, but, in many cases, an internal discussion about the resources already in place suffices. Once the client knows what's available and what he or she would like to measure, you're ready to begin developing a program.

Don't be scared. Those who shy away from an ROI conversation because they don't think they can measure this or—more often than not—because they fear the results, are the first to lose the client, budget, staff, promotion, etc. If we are serious about treating public relations as a business discipline, we must measure; it doesn't count unless you can count it.

SOURCE: David Rockland, July 2006 issue of *PR Tactics*

Online Research

Maria Ivanci is an assistant professor in the American University School of Communication and a market research consultant.

Because of its importance in helping to guide our public communication plans, it's imperative that the research we conduct provides us with the highest quality, reliable data. Data collection—how we get the information from our audiences—is an important part of the process. If it isn't collected properly, no amount of analysis can make it worthwhile.

Telephone interviewing has been the standard method for collecting data in quantitative research for the past few decades. There have been other techniques (mail, door-to-door), but researchers have relied on the telephone for most of our data collection. But telephone interviewing is facing a challenge—most researchers are now looking to the Internet as a way to conduct research.

The reasons have to do with both methods. Even without the promise of the Internet as a viable new alternative, researchers would be concerned with telephone interviewing. The concerns include:

- *Dropping cooperation rates.* Due to consumers' ability to screen calls (through answering machines, caller ID, and call blocking), busier lifestyles, and annoyance with telemarketers, the general public is less likely to participate in our surveys. Although the Do Not Call registry does not apply to research studies, many people do not make a distinction between research calls and telemarketers who are trying to sell something, and simply don't respond to any calls from someone they don't know.

- *The use of cell phones.* More and more people (primarily younger adults) are relying just on their cell phones and no longer have land lines. Researchers are developing ways to include cell phone only households in our telephone surveys, but potential respondents may be unwilling to give up their minutes to do a survey. Because of the demographic and psychographic differences in those who have cell phones only (now estimated at about a quarter of the total population and increasing), the samples we're using for our telephone research may not be entirely representative of the population.

- *The proliferation of phone numbers.* In the past it was more likely than not that each household had only one phone number associated with it. Now many households have multiple land lines—different family members may have their own numbers, there may be a number for the fax machine, another line for the Internet connection. This has ramifications for sampling—households with more than one number may be more likely to be included in our sample than those who have only one. Again, this may lead to bias in our results because households with more than one line may be different from those who have just one number (e.g., they may be more affluent).

As more and more people turn to the Internet as a way to communicate, researchers are seeing it as an opportunity to collect information. Online research is much less expensive than telephone interviewing. Without the labor costs for interviewers, the costs for an Internet survey can be substantially less than those for telephone interviewing. And, while phone interviewing has always been considered fast, the Internet allows for even faster collection of the information. Online research also allows us to show visuals and play audio. We can show product concepts, message statements, logos, even full ads and ask our respondents to react to them.

But there are still some shortcomings with Internet surveys. The most obvious one is that not everyone has access. While this will likely be less of a problem in the future, right now as many as 20–25 percent of the American public does not use the Internet. Many of these individuals are older or less affluent. So there are still some concerns with covering the entire public in our research.

Another concern is that the samples that are used for most Internet research are convenience samples. Although there are several different methodologies that researchers are looking at for online research, the most common uses a panel or a database of individuals who have signed up to complete surveys from time to time. Most of these panels provide small rewards to respondents and respondents don't volunteer for a specific survey, but have indicated their willingness to complete surveys in general. From a statistical standpoint these are still convenience samples and therefore are nonprobability samples.

Another drawback of online surveys is that they are self-administered. In a telephone interview, which is interviewer-administered, an interviewer can probe responses and clarify some statements that may be vague (especially in open-ended questions). In a self-administered survey, we must rely on the respondent to be as detailed as possible. We may lose some accuracy or detail in the response. On the other hand, some researchers feel that without an interviewer, respondents may be more honest in their responses, eliminating any interviewer bias.

While there are still limitations that need to be considered, the Internet is a promising method and undoubtedly the wave of the future in research. The key to remember is that there is no ideal method of data collection; each has its own advantages and disadvantages. It is important to understand both the strengths and limitations and select the best method for your particular study.

SOURCE: Maria Ivanci, assistant professor, American University School of Communication, ivancin@american.edu, 202-885-2780

Summary and Review

What Is Research?
- Research is the careful and systematic study, investigation, and collection of data for the purposes of knowing, describing, and understanding.
- As a public relations practitioner, you can profit from well-designed and well-executed research before, during, and at the end of a communication campaign or program.
- Because knowing your audiences is crucial to effective communication and interaction, you must learn to make a good and effective argument for an audience-focused approach that begins with research.

Why Conduct Research?
- The role of research in public relations is to help you make good decisions and guide the development and implementation of the PR campaign or program.
- You should answer a series of questions regarding why you are conducting the research. The questions are designed to make sure the research is actually needed and that the research accomplishes specific objectives.
- In addition to helping you make informed decisions, research can help you identify the problem or opportunity at hand, develop strategy, and save time and money.

What Kinds of Research Do PR Practitioners Use?
- As a PR practitioner, you are always conducting some form of research to inform their work.
- Both formal—quantitative and qualitative studies—and informal research methods are used in PR planning and implementation.
- Three broad categories of investigation include formative, monitoring, and evaluative research.

Where Should Research Be Conducted?
- Research should be conducted within an organization. This internal research helps you discover facts about an organization or client. If the PR effort is for internal audiences, research is crucial for the success of an initiative.
- External research is usually conducted among the organization's key external audiences.

How Is Research Conducted?

- Informal and formal research methods are conducted in the practice of PR.
- For exploratory and discovery purposes, informal research methods are valuable. These methods can help answer questions about problems and can provide information for building a research strategy.
- Well-planned informal research provides some insight into the target audiences.
- Informal methods alone should never be used to develop program and campaign plans.
- Effective informal methods used widely in public relations include key informant conversations, community and town meetings, communication audits, environmental scans, news media audits, and general fact finding.
- There are two types of formal research—quantitative and qualitative. Both can be used throughout the communication program or campaign.
- Both quantitative and qualitative studies have advantages and disadvantages.

Tips for Buying Research Services

- You must be clear with an outside research firm as to why the research is being undertaken and what decisions the answers will help inform.
- You must be careful when purchasing services from outside research organizations. It is wise to seek references and recommendations and to talk to more than one research organization.

Ethical Considerations in Social Science Research

- Consideration of ethics in conducting research for PR is crucial. You should be aware of the basic ethical agreements that prevail in the social research field.
- Research studies should meet the highest standards for integrity and quality.
- Study participants are volunteers and must not be coerced or made to feel uncomfortable during research study.
- Standards for informed consent of participants and complete confidentiality must be met.

Key Terms

benchmark or baseline
central location
    intercept interviews
    (popularly called
    mall intercepts)
closed-ended questions
cluster sampling
communication audit
community and town
    meetings
computer-administered
    questionnaire
computer-assisted-
    telephone (CAT)
    interviews
convenience sampling
double-barreled questions
dyads
environmental scan
evaluative research

focus group
formal research
    methods
formative or
    developmental
    research
group-administered
    questionnaire
in-depth interviews
    (IDIs)
informal consent
informal research
    methods
key informant
    conversations
literature review
margin of error
media audit
monitoring or iterative
    research

mystery shopping
nonprobability sampling
omnibus survey
open-ended questions
perceptual analyzer
personal interviews
primary research
probability sampling
purposive (judgmental)
    sampling
qualitative research
quantitative research
questionnaire
random sampling
random-digit-dialing
    sampling
research
sample
sample size
sampling error

secondary research
segmentation
self-administered
    or individually-
    administered
    questionnaire

semantic differential
    technique
stratified sampling
summated ratings
survey research
systematic sampling
telephone focus group

theatre testing
triads
usability/readability
    testing
videoconference
    focus group

Questions for Review and Discussion

1. Select a target audience. Segment that audience and choose one. Do you think secondary research exists for this audience? What kind? Where would you go to find it?

2. Think about an organization or client for which you think you want to practice public relations. What kind of everyday listening and monitoring would you be doing? Where would you learn about trends, issues, or problems?

3. Where might you find additional information?

4. Conduct a SWOT analysis of an organization in which you are an active member or conduct a SWOT analysis of yourself.

5. A university campus on a pleasant afternoon is an excellent place to conduct mall intercepts. What types of target audiences might we find for what types of clients?

6. Write two close-ended questions and rewrite them as open-ended questions.

7. Explain the difference between probability and nonprobability sampling.

Web Links

American Marketing Association
www.marketingpower.com

American Association for Public Opinion Research
www.aapor.org

American Educational Research Association
www.aera.net

Gallup
www.gallup.com

Nielsen
www.nielsen.com

Claritas Prizm
www.claritas.com

Public Relations Society of America
www.prsa.org

Robert Wood Johnson Foundation
www.rwjf.org

Roper Center
www.ropercenter.uconn.edu

U.S. Census Bureau
www.census.gov

Adhering to Ethical Practices and Meeting Professional Standards

WHAT IS ETHICS?

In 1964, in writing his opinion on a landmark obscenity case, U.S. Supreme Court Justice Potter Stewart tried to explain "hard-core" pornography by saying, "I shall not today attempt further to define the kinds of material I understand to be embraced . . . but I know it when I see it. . . ." This quote became a famous summary of the difficulty in trying to define what is obscene. Ironically, we can also apply the quote to the difficulty in trying to define what is ethical. Just as we all intuitively recognize obscenity, we all also understand which actions are ethical, namely those that are truthful, just, and executed with integrity. Defining ethics, on the other hand, is more difficult. Often, it is easier to sense what is ethical than to define it.

One broad definition of **ethics** is *doing what is right and avoiding what is wrong*. But this answer

Character—the willingness to accept responsibility for one's own life—is the source from which self-respect springs.

—Japanese Proverb

seems too easy. Ethical decisions are not always that black and white. What about all the gray areas, the places where it is hard to know what is right, when it is right, and for whom? While this chapter cannot provide solutions for every ethical dilemma you might face, it will provide viewpoints and tools for handling ethical conflicts.

Ethics and Good Stewardship

One useful way to judge whether or not our behavior is ethical is to decide if we are acting as good stewards. Today, we hear a lot of talk about stewardship; we are exhorted to be good stewards of our talents, our environment, and other resources. But what does that mean? To be a good steward is to protect and value that which is entrusted to us by those with whom we enter relationships. We need to look carefully at who we are and what our responsibilities are to our colleagues, our clients, and our community. Let's examine this case involving fresh juice manufacturer Odwalla. The company's reaction to a public health crisis is a good example of how practicing proper public relations and exercising corporate responsibility leads to good stewardship.

In the fall of 1996, Washington State health officials notified Odwalla of a link between its fresh apple juice and several cases of E. coli, bacteria that cause an intestinal infection that can be life threatening to infants and young children. On receiving the notice, Odwalla voluntarily and immediately recalled its apple juice, sending delivery trucks to retrieve its products from retailer's shelves in seven Western states. The company hired Edelman Public Relations of San Francisco to handle the crisis.

A communication crisis team was set up to handle media questions. The team made sure all information was made available to all company spokespersons and that company executives were available to answer questions. Media updates were issued daily. Neither Odwalla nor Edelman made any attempt to hide the truth. Lines of communication were established with consumers through a website and a toll-free 800 number. Business clients were brought into the loop quickly; top executives made personal calls to all 4,600 accounts within 18 hours of the notice.

In addition, Odwalla voluntarily let the U.S. Food and Drug Administration (FDA) into its plant for an inspection. It made a presentation to the FDA on the need for mandatory pasteurization. The company then formed an advisory board to develop safe methods for the industry for processing juice.

Throughout the crisis, Odwalla was a good steward, behaving responsibly toward the public and the industry. The company acted quickly to take any tainted juice off the market and to tell consumers and business associates about the problem in order to protect public health. It then asked the FDA to inspect its processing plants to ensure that its juice was safe to drink and to regain public confidence in its product. Finally, the company engaged the industry in establishing safety standards to try to avert a similar crisis in the future. By acting ethically, Odwalla not only survived the crisis, but also gained public approval. Ninety-seven percent of the public felt the company responded well, according to opinion polls.

Because of Odwalla's good stewardship, the company continues to thrive.

Bonnie Kamin/PhotoEdit

What the Odwalla case shows us is that good stewardship is also good business. Behaving in ways that are truthful, just, and responsible—in other words, acting ethically—may cost organizations in the short term. In Odwalla's case, the company had to pay the costs of recalling the juice; informing the public, the industry, and the government; and improving safety. However, the company also gained public respect and confidence, factors that contributed positively to the juice maker's image and profits in the long term. As PR practitioners, we should always point clients toward the high road, reminding them that ethical behavior improves their bottom line in the long run.

Ethics and the Culture of an Organization

The choices that Odwalla's executives made in reacting to the juice crisis were informed by the company's corporate culture, that is, by the norms and values to which it adheres. Fortunately, in Odwalla's case, the company's values were ethical. Company leaders were forthright, honest, and just, putting the public's health and safety ahead of short-term profits. Not all organizations, however, will do the right thing when faced with a crisis. All too often, an organization's culture encourages denial of a problem and delay in taking proper steps to solve it, resulting in harm to the public and the company.

A 43-state outbreak of salmonella poisoning resulted in the largest-ever food recall in U.S. history in 2009. The Peanut Corporation of America (PCA) was forced to close two of its plants—first in Georgia when outbreaks began and then in Texas after the contamination of food products was investigated and proven. The contamination scare was associated with killing eight people, causing more than 19,000 illnesses, and leading to more than 1,800 separate recalls. The recalls of peanut butter, cookies, crackers, frozen dinners, snack bars, disaster relief meals, and other foods sent peanut butter sales plunging by 25 percent.

Stewart Parnell, president of PCA, served as spokesperson for the company. He apologized for the recall in a company news release and informed the media that the company was working with federal regulators. The FDA, which is responsible for food regulation, eventually determined the Georgia plant had knowingly shipped contaminated products to the nation's largest food makers. The makers of Jif, Skippy, and Peter Pan peanut butter began to run ads with coupons for savings on the products, advising consumers that their products were not contaminated.

It was the American Peanut Council, a private trade association representing the American peanut industry, that worked with PR firms Ogilvy and Argyle Communication to educate consumers about recalled and safe products. The council put a list of products not recalled on its website.

At the time of the Georgia plant closing, the PCA had ceased responding to media inquiries. Unlike Odwalla, PCA responded only to the recall and not to the deaths and illnesses caused by the outbreak of the food-borne disease. And the company did not take responsibility for what happened even after it became clear that it shipped contaminated food knowingly.

As a result of their choices, two PCA plants were forced to close.

AP Photo/Ric Feld/file

Organizational Norms

For better or for worse, we often conduct ourselves according to the expectations of the organization or group with which we are affiliated. When the group's expectations are high, doing right becomes the norm and most members of the group will rise to its standards. When the organization's standards are lax or when we find ourselves in situations where the right choice is not readily apparent, we must take the time to think carefully and clearly and to learn the rules that apply to the situation before we act.

Let's consider this situation. You just landed the internship of your dreams in the office of investor relations for a successful pharmaceutical company. You are familiar with the company because your family owns some of its stock and monitors its progress regularly. This morning at a meeting you learned that the company is going to split its stock in the next few days. You want to give your family a heads-up, so you tell them about the stock split. Should you have told them?

The ethical—and legal—answer to this question is no. As an employee of the company, you became an "insider," someone with access to important, confidential information. The U.S. Securities and Exchange Commission (SEC), which regulates the financial transactions of publicly traded companies, has ruled that it is illegal for "insiders" to share information that could affect a company's stock price before the information is made public. In other words, when, as an intern, you gave your family a "tip" about the upcoming stock split, you became a "tipee" and violated insider trading regulations. As a public relations professional, you will often have access to confidential information and will need to learn company and government regulations regarding disclosing it.

ETHICS AND STANDARDS OF PROFESSIONALISM

As you can see, when it comes to making ethical choices, you are your most important judge. You must understand the rules and challenge yourself to deal honestly, and sometimes courageously, with difficult situations you encounter. "We can't legislate ethics, but we can motivate people to do the right thing," said SEC Cynthia Glassman when speaking about the agency's efforts to reform the mutual fund industry. Since influencing people's opinions and behavior is one of the functions of public relations practitioners, you—as a student of public relations—will need to think seriously about how you will do your job in a responsible manner. What does it mean to deal ethically with the news media, stakeholders—including customers, suppliers, communities, governments, owners, stockholders, employees—and the general public? To whom will you owe primary allegiance—the organization for which you work, the people it serves, or yourself? How will you balance the interests of the organization with those of its key audiences, the general society, the public relations profession, and yourself? In other words, what does it mean to be an ethical and professional public relations practitioner?

One way to sharpen your understanding of professional ethics and standards is to look at the current marketplace. It's a tough environment. Consumer confidence in organizations of all types is low. High-profile scandals, many of which were made worse by attempts at cover-ups, have rocked Wall Street, a number of top businesses, government agencies, and religious institutions. One example is the Enron scandal of 2001, which came to epitomize corporate excess.

A laid-off Enron worker waits for a ride outside the company's headquarters in Houston.

Enron Corporation was a Houston-based energy company, originally involved in transmitting and distributing electricity and gas in the United States and developing, building, and operating power plants, pipelines, and similar infrastructure worldwide. After federal deregulation of the natural gas and the electricity industries in the late 1980s and 1990s, Enron became a broker for buying and selling energy and the nation's largest energy trader. It was named by *Fortune* magazine "America's Most Innovative Company" for six consecutive years. By 2000, the company employed about 21,000 people and had revenues of $101 billion. Then, in 2001, the company filed for what was then the largest U.S. bankruptcy, following the disclosure that it had reported false profits.

Enron's auditing firm, Arthur Andersen, was also involved in the scandal. The firm did not render adequate oversight, partly because providing consulting services for Enron was more profitable than providing auditing services. It was found guilty of obstructing justice for destroying documents in anticipation of SEC investigation. As a result, it lost its major accounts and its position as one of the world's largest accounting firms.

Following Enron's collapse, many of the company's employees lost their jobs and much of their retirement savings, which were invested in Enron stock through 401(k) retirement plans. The scandal also shook investor confidence in U.S. business because Enron had been able to hide its losses for nearly five years. The reputations of some stock analysts—who told investors to buy Enron stock even though they knew the company had reported a $1.1-billion revision in its net worth—were also compromised. People began to wonder whether they could trust businesses, auditors, stock analysts, or the public relations persons who spoke for them.

Company spokespersons, the PR practitioners on the ground dealing with the news media and informing employees, were responsible for briefing and answering questions from reporters. Primary spokesperson, Patrick Dorton, continued to answer media inquiries throughout the crisis, indicating that Arthur Andersen was doing all that it could to help resolve the matters. After Andersen employees admitted destroying documents crucial to the investigation, CEO Joseph Berardino admitted to Congress that "our team made an error in judgment." While none of the firm's spokespersons was charged with violating the law, they were trusted to tell the truth, which raises ethical questions about their behavior. (See the following "Engaging Ethics" section.)

The scandal led to legislation to reform corporate behavior. In 2002, Congress passed the Public Company Accounting Reform and Investor Protection Act of 2002, which provided for stricter government oversight of business financial accounting. The fraud also led to a high-profile federal investigation and trial. Several highly placed Enron executives pleaded guilty to financial crimes. Five years after the company collapsed, former Chairman Kenneth Lay, who has since died, and President Jeffrey Skilling—both of whom had stubbornly maintained their innocence—were found guilty of fraud and conspiracy. From the start, misrepresentation by company spokespersons and executives served only to harm those involved with the company and anger prosecutors and the public.

ENGAGING ETHICS

Arthur Andersen—Accounting and Accountability

As you have read, Arthur Andersen was Enron's auditing firm, responsible for reviewing Enron's financial transactions and verifying the quality of its accounting practices. Arthur Andersen was convicted of obstructing justice for destroying documents in advance of the SEC's investigation into Enron's books. When Enron filed for bankruptcy, spokespersons for Arthur Andersen may or may not have known the extent of the company's culpability in Enron's misconduct.

1. If they were aware of their company's role, what position should Arthur Andersen's spokespersons have taken as the media began to inquire about Enron's financial position and Arthur Andersen's knowledge of its problems?
2. Following Arthur Andersen's conviction, its attorney insisted on the firm's innocence, maintaining the company was being destroyed by the "conduct of a few employees." If Arthur Andersen had been your client, would you have recommended this statement to the attorney?
3. What ethical issue does the attorney's statement raise?

Another Look at a Difficult Marketplace

Given the scandals at Enron and Arthur Andersen, as well at other companies, it is troubling but not unexpected that in today's marketplace many American workers shrug off ethical concerns. Consider these results of a national survey of 1,500 U.S. workers regarding ethical behavior at the workplace: About one-third of respondents said their coworkers condoned questionable business practices by respecting those who achieved success using them. Almost one-fifth said they observed coworkers lying to or withholding needed information from other employees, customers, vendors, or the public. And more than half said that misconduct was more likely in companies where top management only talked about ethics, rather than behaved as ethical role models.

These results are disturbing and beg for a change in the way we do business. One PR agency, Ruder Finn, is trying to tackle this problem by adding a new practice area in the firm to help its clients handle ethical dilemmas. The practice, launched in 2005, has "codes of conduct, risk assessment, training, and internal communication plans" as its core areas of concentration. Ruder Finn's action raises an important question: Can we as practitioners act as the conscience of an organization? Our answer as professionals should be a resounding "yes." To understand the challenges presented by this role, let's look at the ethical problems PR professionals face and the realities of the profession.

ETHICAL CHALLENGES FOR PR PROFESSIONALS

"How can you talk about ethics when you've spent a career in PR being a professional liar?" a leading publicist was asked during an interview on British television. While the question may seem flippant, a survey of PR practitioners conducted by *PRWeek* shows that dishonesty within the profession is a serious concern. Twenty-five percent of the 1,705 practitioners who responded admitted to lying on the job, and 62 percent said they had been compromised in their work by being told a lie. Nearly two-thirds said that they did not always check the validity of what they had been asked to communicate. Forty-four percent expressed uncertainty as to the ethics of tasks they were performing and less than a third believed "ethical boundaries had been clearly defined."

On the positive side, one in five practitioners in the business for less than two years and two-thirds of those in business 12 years or more said they had turned down an account for ethical reasons. Almost 20 percent said that they left a job due to ethical concerns, and nearly 30 percent said they knew someone who had done so. Half supported an ethical charter, despite the risk of being dismissed should they be found guilty of ethical violations.

Another provocative indictment of the profession can be found in the book *Toxic Sludge is Good for You: Lies, Damn Lies and the Public Relations Industry.* As students of public relations, you should become familiar with this important book. Its authors, John Stauber and Sheldon Rampton, are the editors of *PR Watch*, a quarterly newsletter dedicated to protecting the public from misinformation, and the founders of the watchdog group the Center for Media and Democracy. (See Web Links at the end of the chapter.) The group's stated mission is to

> [c]ombat manipulative and misleading PR practices. . . . Whether the issue is health, consumer safety, environmental preservation or democracy and world peace, citizens today find themselves confronted by a bewildering array of hired propagandists paid to convince the public that junk food is nutritious, pollution is harmless, and that what's good for big business and big government is good for the rest of us.

Clearly, having an ethical PR practice is not simplistic, and sometimes, not easy. One challenge lies in making the hard choices while making a living. Sometimes, your sense of what is best may conflict with your ambition to move ahead in your field. Public relations scholar Scott Cutlip warned against making self-serving decisions when he wrote: "The principle behind professional ethics is that one's actions are designed to create the greatest good for both the client and the community as a whole, rather than enhance the position and power of the practitioner." You might also find yourself in a situation where your values differ from those of your client, presenting you with a difficult choice between your conscience and your paycheck. Consider this case at Hill & Knowlton, one of the world's largest PR firms, described in the "Engaging Ethics" box.

Another challenge arises from the fact that your decisions as a PR practitioner may affect several groups who may have conflicting interests. In their book, *This is PR*, Doug Newsom, Judy Van Slyke Turk, and Dean Kruckeberg identify these audiences to which practitioners may be responsible: clients, news media, government agencies, educational institutions, consumers, stockholders, the community, competitors, critics, and fellow practitioners. Considering the needs of your audiences is essential but can make ethical decision making even more complicated.

Let's look at this hypothetical case. You work in the PR department of a large, global energy company that has just discovered a vast oil field deep below the ocean floor. The firm's vice president tells you he wants your announcement to downplay the discovery. What parties will be affected by what you decide to write? First, the company, its board of directors, shareholders, employees, and the financial community at large, all of whom require accurate information regarding the company's financial condition. The second is the SEC, whose regulations would be violated by failure

ENGAGING ETHICS

Hill and Knowlton and the Catholic Bishops

In 1990, Hill & Knowlton mounted an anti-abortion campaign on behalf of the National Conference of Catholic Bishops (U.S.). The firm defended the campaign on First Amendment (free speech) grounds. Trouble arose because the firm did not fully inform all its employees of the campaign. Some left, even though Hill & Knowlton said that those who were morally opposed to the campaign did not have to participate in it. For some employees, the campaign pitted their loyalty to the company against loyalty to their own beliefs.

1. Do you think the firm was right to accept the controversial account without first consulting its employees? Explain your answer.
2. What would you do if the firm for which you were working conducted a campaign that ran counter to your values? Would you leave the firm? Stay, but excuse yourself from working with the client with whom you disagreed? Work on the campaign, rationalizing that it is your job and you need the money?

to fully disclose the discovery. The financial media and the PR profession itself are third, both of which have a stake in preserving the integrity of the communications process. Fourth is the public, who deserve to know the truth. And last but not least, you—the practitioner—who would have to share the responsibility for disseminating deceptive information.

What should you do? After identifying the SEC regulations, federal and state laws, and company policies regarding nondisclosure, you should advise the company against deceptive practices. Deception would be illegal and would poorly serve all the stakeholders. The difficulty with this decision, of course, is that you will have to stand up to the managers who asked you to deceive. As stated earlier, making the ethical choice is not always easy. To practice PR with integrity, you will often have to summon up your courage. But how will you know what to do?

Guidelines for Making Ethical Choices

One guideline that can help you to do right is to recall the advice of Polonius in Shakespeare's Hamlet, "To your own self be true." Ask yourself, "What are my personal values—the principles in which I believe strongly and which I can never violate?" The answer will put you in a position to make wise decisions about your professional conduct and will help mitigate some of the "bad press" that the profession receives.

Another set of guidelines for principled decision making comes from Michael Josephson, founder of the Josephson Institute of Ethics and a consultant to many large companies. He advocates making judgments based on six values, which he calls the *Six Pillars of Character*:

- Trustworthiness
- Respect
- Responsibility
- Fairness
- Caring/good citizenship
- Responsible participation in society

If we look again at Odwalla's response to its tainted juice crisis, we see that the actions of the company's leaders encompassed these values. They took responsibility for their product, acted fairly and respectfully toward consumers and the general public, behaved as a trustworthy member of the industry, and were generally good citizens. The leaders of the Peanut Corporation of America during the peanut butter contamination crisis and Enron during its collapse, on the other hand, did not act in accord with these values. As a result the companies, their consumers' health, employees, and investors were damaged.

A good summary of ethical guidelines can be found in self-tests offered by public relations scholars Kathy Fitzpatrick, and Sherry Baker and David Martinson. Each of them provides a framework for asking yourself how your decision will affect yourself, others, and society at large before you take any action. (See Table 7.1.)

Confronting PR Ethics Violations

The assumption that PR practitioners—given the nature of their jobs—must be dishonest is at the bottom of many negative attitudes toward the profession. Many people think that practitioners who represent companies found guilty of ethics violations are themselves unethical, an accusation that may or may not be true. Baker and Martinson write that "critics insist that public relations has been used as manipulation by powerful political, economic and social interests intent on achieving their own narrow goals at the expense of the greater good." PR practitioners are often labeled "spin doctors" or "spinmeisters"—ruthless liars willing to manipulate their publics for their employer's gain. The difficulty with these criticisms is that they contain some truth.

Table **7.1**	Fitzpatrick's Five Duties and Baker and Martinson's Self-Tests for Ethical Decision-Making
Fitzpatrick's Five Duties	**Baker and Martinson's TARES Test**
Duty to self: Are you willing to compromise your values for the sake of a firm or client?	Truthfulness of the message: Your intention must be to provide others with accurate information that they need, not to deceive them.
Duty to client: Can you represent the client and maintain your peace of mind, knowing what you do about the client and understanding that some of this information is confidential?	Authenticity of the persuader: You must be true to yourself while avoiding or minimizing harm to others; acting with authenticity demands personal integrity, sincerity, loyalty, and independence.
Duty to employer: Are the company's activities harmful to others? Knowingly allowing harmful work to continue violates your duty to the public.	Respect for the people, groups, or organizations you want to persuade: You must take care not to violate the rights of others in order to serve your client or yourself.
Duty to profession: As public relations professionals, you must be responsible to your peers; what would peers whom you respect think of what you are doing?	Equality of the appeal: You must be fair, not unjustly manipulative; one test of equality is to apply the Golden Rule—"Do unto others as you would have them do unto you."
Duty to society: Do your activities serve the public interest?	Social responsibility: You should ask yourself whether your campaign serves the public interest or is motivated solely by self-interest and profit, perhaps at society's expense.

SOURCES: Kathy Fitzpatrick and Philip Seib, *Public Relations Ethics*, Wadsworth 1994; David L. Martinson, "Ethical Decision Making in Public Relations: What Would Aristotle Say?" *Public Relations Quarterly*, Fall 2000, Vol 45, pp 18–20

ENGAGING ETHICS

A Test: What Would You Do?

Suppose you worked for a large, urban developer who is planning a multi-family housing project on a former landfill site. You discover in environmental agency reports that low levels of contaminants are present at the site. You recommend that the developer make the contamination report public but are told there will be no public communication about the issue.

1. Using Fitzgerald's list of duties, decide what the proper decision for you would be.
2. What would be the proper decision using the TARES Test?
3. Are they the same? Explain your response.

Some of the ethical violations for which PR practitioners have been criticized in recent years include the following:

- Establishing front groups, or groups of citizens and so-called "experts" who claim to represent the public interest but are really a cover for promoting the interest of the corporation. The practice is often referred to as *astroturfing*, a term coined by former U.S. Senator Lloyd Bentsen as a wordplay on "grassroots democracy" efforts, which are spontaneous undertakings by individuals. Two examples of front groups: A California-based PR firm that represents SUV manufacturers created Sports Utility Vehicle Owners of America to launch efforts against proposed clean air regulations, and the Center for Consumer Freedom, largely funded by the food industry, was created to publicize what it sees as "greatly exaggerated" reports of obesity morbidity.

- Conflicts of interest, situations in which a professional has competing professional or personal obligations, which would make it difficult to fulfill his or her duties fairly. An example from political PR is illustrative. Mark Penn, then chief strategist for the Hillary Clinton presidential campaign, is also CEO of the global PR firm Burson-Marsteller, which represented the Columbian government. When Penn met with the Columbian government officials during the campaign, despite Clinton's opposition to a free trade agreement with the South American nation, he said his business with Columbia involved only those duties related to his firm. But he admitted that the purpose of the meeting was related to the trade agreement. The result of this conflict of interest was that Penn lost his position with the Clinton campaign and Burson-Marsteller lost its contract with the Columbian government.

- Violating nondisclosure agreements, which are legally binding contracts in which a person or business promises to keep specific information as a trade secret and not disclose it to others without proper authorization. Nondisclosure statements are internal and external documents. PR practitioners sign these contracts when working with proprietary information from clients, and employees of PR firms are often asked to sign these agreements that are intended to keep confidential the creative work of the PR firm. For instance, if a PR practitioner is assisting in the launch of a client organization's major product innovation the practitioner is expected to keep the innovation a secret and not share it with anyone. Similarly, if an employee of a PR firm is involved in a pitch—presentation for new business—to a client that includes a new or creative approach, the PR firm's employee is expected to keep the information confidential. Also, some PR firms ask prospective

ENGAGING ETHICS

European Women for HPV Testing

In 2004, a group called The European Women for HPV Testing launched a campaign in the United Kingdom for national screening for the human papillomavirus (HPV), a leading cause of cervical cancer. Digene, an international biotechnology giant, had developed a test to screen for HPV. If approved by the British National Health Service (HNS), the test could save the lives of thousands of women 30 and older who were most at risk for the disease. High-profile women celebrities were recruited to be group spokespersons and to lobby for the test's approval.

The European Women for HPV Testing group appeared legitimate; it had its own letterhead, sent out its own press releases, and even got mentioned in the *British Medical Journal*. The problem was, the group did not actually exist. As noted in the *Guardian Observer*, a London newspaper, the "group" was a front organization created by Burson-Marsteller, the global PR firm, and funded by Digene.

1. Clearly define the ethical issue here. Is it proper to omit or to fail to fully disclose sponsorship? On what principles do you base your answer?
2. What audiences might be affected by this decision?
3. If Digene were your client, what questions would you ask yourself and what standards would guide your decision?

clients to sign nondisclosure agreements to keep the contents of a PR approach revealed in a pitch confidential.

- Engaging in unfair competition or commercial activity that tends to confuse or deceive the public about the sale of products or services.
- Representing dubious clients, those whose motives or behavior is suspect. An example may be the two PR practitioners who resigned from working for the "Octomom" Nadya Suleman. Suleman is the single mother of six who gave birth to octuplets conceived through in-vitro fertilization in 2009.
- Engaging in deceptive practices, which mislead consumers.
- Giving gifts to the media with the intention of gaining favorable press coverage. This is a major concern for practitioners who work with the news media who cover travel and luxury products because travel to cover quality accommodations and cruises and samples can be misconstrued as gifts. Reporters are usually prohibited from accepting travel or samples by their organizations.
- Failing to safeguard confidential information, resulting in leaks or use of client information.

ORIENTING YOURSELF FOR ETHICAL DECISION MAKING

"'The truth is rarely pure, and never simple,' wrote Oscar Wilde. He should have worked in public relations." This statement by a professor of public relations shows how difficult making the "right" decision can sometimes be. Understanding the ways we instinctively approach making judgments may help you understand where you or your colleagues are coming from as you sort out thorny situations. Generally speaking,

ENGAGING ETHICS

Exploring Front Groups

Your PR firm represents a national industry association of cement and asphalt contractors. The association board asks you to create a group called Citizens for Active Road Expansion that will advocate for the growth of roads and highways throughout the country. You are asked to create a business card that identifies you as the group's executive director but you have no group members or staff. In essence your group is not real. You are to create and implement a media relations campaign that gets the group and its stance on highway and road expansion attention in the news media. A reporter asks you about the group.

1. Begin by identifying and clarifying the dilemma.
2. Now, use the tools described in this chapter to solve the ethical problem presented in this hypothetical case.
3. What choices do you have in responding to the reporter?
4. What ethical principles are involved?
5. What decision would you make? Why?

there are three fundamentally different approaches towards judging moral behavior: absolutist, relativist, and situationalist.

To an **absolutist,** *actions are either right or wrong.* A person whose thinking is oriented this way tends to see things as black or white, rarely as gray. Consider, again, Hill & Knowlton's anti-abortion campaign on behalf of the Catholic bishops. Pro-choice employees of the firm whose approach to problems was absolutist would more than likely have left the firm, judging the campaign to be morally wrong.

Relativists, *on the other hand, believe that values are not absolute, but are molded by a person's culture and background.* To the relativist, different groups could hold different values. Relativists at Hill & Knowlton who were not pro-lifers would probably have stayed at the firm but declined to participate in the campaign. They would have respected the bishops' right to their point of view, but insisted on having their own values acknowledged.

A **situationalist** *will make decisions on a case-by-case basis, choosing the courses of action that he or see thinks will cause the least harm or do the most good.* At Hill & Knowlton, situational ethicists who opposed the bishops would have had to weigh the harm they would do by staying at the firm and, at least nominally, endorsing the campaign or leaving and putting themselves out of work and the firm short an employee.

Theories behind Ethical Thinking

Theoretically speaking, we can be either intuitive or deterministic in our thinking as we make moral judgments. In practice, we often combine these ways of thinking. **Intuitive thinking** is *reasoning based on intuition and logic.* It is based on "deontology," the study of duties, and comes from the Greek words "deontos," or duty, and "logos," or study. It is based on a system of rules or duties and focuses on the intentions or motives of the doer. People who make judgments based on intuitive thinking believe that certain actions are right, in themselves, and should be done regardless of consequences. The American Declaration of Independence (all men are created equal and have inalienable rights), Aristotle's Golden Mean (moderation in all things), "Justice is blind" (all should be judged as equals, regardless of race or ethnicity, sex, class) and the "Customer is always right" (satisfied customers equal profits) are classical examples of intuitive moral thinking. In the minds of extremists or fanatics, intuitive thinking can devolve into "Do what's right, though the world should perish."

Deterministic or **naturalistic thinking** is *reasoning that acknowledges conditions, circumstances, and changes* and is based on *teleology*, the study of ends, and comes from the Greek *telos*, or end. It is results-oriented and focuses on outcomes, or the usefulness of an action. People who make moral decisions based on deterministic thinking believe that the rightness of an action is determined by its consequences. To them, an ethical action is one that creates the greatest good for the greatest number of people. Utilitarianism and "Robin Hood" thinking are good examples of naturalistic thinking. Taken to the extreme, deterministic thinking can lead to believing "the ends justify the means," or that wrongdoing can be justified if the results are good.

TOOLS FOR ETHICAL DECISION MAKING

Whether you usually make judgments based on what you perceive as good intentions or what you perceive as good results, sometimes you will find that there are no clear answers to ethical problems, just different courses of action from which to choose. In Table 7.2 are three well-known decision-making tools. While none of them is a guarantee that PR professionals will make the right choice, they do give you a framework for thinking through an ethical dilemma. Responsibility for making ethical choices ultimately lies with you and the organization with which you work.

Models of Ethical PR Communication

Scholars have created models to describe the way public relation practitioners communicate with their clients and society. None has been adopted by professional public relations organizations, but they present interesting ways for practitioners to look at their practice. Here are some of the pros and cons of using each model as a basis for constructing ethical standards:

- **Attorney–Client:** In the **attorney–client model,** *public relations practitioners are seen as functioning as lawyers do, representing a client.* The potential problem with using this model as an ethical standard is it allows for just one version of truth to be communicated, that of the client. The interests of the public may not be served, especially if important information is withheld. (The Public Relations Society of America has said that this model does not apply to PR.)
- **Enlightened Self-Interest:** Proponents of the **enlightened self-interest model** *believe that if business is conducted with the public interest in mind, the business will profit.* To them, it is good business to behave ethically. While this may be true, enlightened self-interest suffers as an ethical standard because actions are motivated only by profit, ignoring other considerations, such as serving the common good.
- **Social Responsibility:** The **social responsibility model** *holds that companies have a responsibility to society.* Professors Kruckeberg and Stark go even further, suggesting that "... an ethical approach to public relations might be found through an emphasis on the restoration of the community." While social responsibility may be a worthy standard, defining exactly what a company's "social responsibilities" are may be problematic.

Table **7.2**	Three Decision-Making Tools		
Decision-Making Tool	Potter Box	Sims Approach	Navran/Plus
Creator of tool	Four-dimensional model for moral analysis, proposed by Ralph Potter of the Harvard Divinity School	Practical approach to problem solving, suggested by Ronald Sims, professor of business at the College of William and Mary	Decision-making tool developed by Frank Navran, who runs the ethics management consultancy, Navran Associates, and was a consultant to the Ethics Resource Center in Washington, DC
Analyzing the problem	Describe the problem, delineating all the facts	Recognize and clarify the dilemma	Define the problem
Gathering all possible solutions	Define all the values relevant to the situation; they may be positive, negative, or both	List all your options	Identify available solutions
Evaluating possible solutions in light of ethical principles	• Examine the ethical principles—laws, industry codes, and personal codes—that apply to the situation • Determine which individuals, groups, organizations, principles, and laws demand your loyalty	Test each option by asking yourself if it is legal, right, and beneficial	Evaluate the alternatives; ask yourself if the option is consient with the organization's policies and values, if it is legal, and if it satisfies your sense of what is right, good, and fair
Making a decision	Look at each plan, then decide how to move forward, choosing the plan that best reflects your values, principles, and loyalties	Make your decision, then double-check it, asking yourself what would happen if your family found out or if it were printed in the local paper	Make your decision
Implementing the decision	Take action	Take action	Take action
Evaluating your success	Analyze what happened as a result of your decision	Review your decision	Evaluate your decision

SOURCE: The Potter Box and Sims Approach material is from David W. Guth and Charles Marsh, *Public Relations a Value-Driven Approach*, Pearson Education, Second Edition 2003. Navran is from www.navran.com.

- **Partisan and Mutual Values:** According to Professor Fitzgerald, partisan values are commitment, trust, loyalty, and obedience and rest on the practitioner's obligations to his or her client or company. Mutual or "higher" values rest on respect for human rights and also need to be considered when serving the client or company. This **partisan and mutual values model** *highlights the biggest ethical challenge for public relations practitioners, balancing the interests of the client with the interests of those who are affected by the client's actions.* Should public relations practitioners place public interest above the interests of the client or company? If so, when?

- **Two-Way Symmetrical:** Based on a theory of public relations developed by professors Larissa Grunig and James Grunig, the **two-way symmetrical model** *says that if the talks follow ethical rules, the outcome should be ethical.* The problem with this model is that the company, not those who are influenced or affected by the company's actions, usually sets the rules.
- **Professional Responsibility:** The **professional responsibility model** *tries to solve the problem of balancing the interests of the client or company with interests of the public.* It holds that the public relations practitioner's first loyalty is to his or her client or company and that he or she best serves the public interest by avoiding or minimizing harm to all those affected by the client's or company's actions.

Avoiding Questionable Practices

A sure-fire way to get into trouble in your PR practice is to be overzealous and bend the rules. Practitioners have lost their jobs and their credibility by breaking these simple, basic rules:

1. **Never make assumptions about dealing with the news media:** Learn how the news media works and familiarize yourself with the journalist's code of ethics; think of the news media as another audience.
2. **Never indulge in puffery:** Do not exaggerate the truth or omit negatives—an example would be writing a news release that contains only half-truths about a product—in order to promote your client or company; "puff pieces" undermine credibility and can mislead those considering buying or using a product or service, voting for or against an issue, or changing a behavior.
3. **Never invent and attribute quotes:** Make sure any quote you write is approved by the spokesperson to whom it is attributed and that it accurately reflects the institution's position and the spokesperson's views.
4. **Never leave an error uncorrected:** Letting mistakes stay on the record is highly unethical. If you make a mistake, issue a correction quickly by emailing, faxing, and calling all the journalists who received the erroneous information. If the mistake has already been printed or broadcast, you may find an unflattering story with the correction. Correcting the error yourself, however, is always better than having the reporter investigate the misinformation.
5. **Avoid disinformation:** Deliberately releasing information you know is false—lying—is unethical and can lead to dismissal by the client or organization, exclusion by peers and colleagues, and lawsuits.
6. **Never agree to be a funded "front group" or virtual organization:** Acting under the guise of a public interest, grassroots, or expert group to lobby the government and promote corporate interest is unethical. These so-called front groups carry out campaigns with the support of the corporations that fund them. They are organized to accomplish a specific goal and often disbanded when the mission is accomplished.

On the Level: Working with Journalists

Cultivating strong working relationships with reporters is crucial to good news media relations. There are several things you can do as students of public relations to prepare yourselves for working with the media. First, learn how journalists work. If possible, take a course in basic journalism or interview a professor with extensive experience as a reporter to learn about news-gathering techniques. Second, familiarize yourself with the professional codes of ethics for journalists. The American Society of Newspaper Editors has published the codes for regional and national newspaper editors and publishers and for news wire services, such as the Associated Press. (They are available on the society's website.) The codes offer journalists guidelines for working with public relations practitioners, which will provide you with insight into a reporter's ethical concerns when working with media relations professionals.

As a public relations practitioner, you will want to treat reporters with respect. Always provide them with accurate information, and avoid practices that could compromise the journalist. You should not make an offer to a journalist that would make him or her obligated to you. Be wary of giving reporters gifts; most will only accept gifts of nominal value. Many large news organizations prohibit reporters from accepting free travel and will not accept stories from freelancers who have been hired by the companies that own the resorts, accommodations, and transportation that are the subject of the stories. Never hire a journalist without full disclosure to the journalist's employer. And never offer a loan, investment, or advertising to a news organization to obtain preferential treatment.

ENGAGING ETHICS

"The World Breathes Easier": A Quote That Was Never Spoken

In November 1985, U.S. President Ronald Reagan and Soviet President Mikhail Gorbachev met in Geneva for the first of their five summits. At the time, the Soviet Union was undergoing reconstruction, or "perestroika" as it was called in Russian. The Soviet government's hold over its member republics and its satellite nations in Eastern Europe was weakening, The Cold War in which the United States and the Soviet Union had been engaged for the past 40 years was beginning to get a bit less chilly, and both countries were interested in putting a positive spin on the summit. Following the first meeting, Deputy Press Secretary Larry Speakes told reporters that Reagan said, "There is much that divides us, but I believe the world breathes easier because we are here talking together." The dramatic quote made every news report.

In 1988, after leaving the White House, Speakes wrote a memoir, *Speaking Out: The Reagan Presidency from Inside the White House*, in which he admitted that Reagan never made the statement. Because Speakes could not find much to report following the meeting, he invented the statement. Speakes justified the fabrication, saying he was not lying because "I knew those quotes were the way he [Reagan] felt."

PR practitioners write speeches, official statements, and quote for their clients and bosses every day. The protocol is to clear those quotes with the principals involved.

1. Did Speakes cross the line?
2. Define the ethical issue here, and identify the values at stake and the audiences that could be affected by the fabrication.
3. What might have happened had the Soviets said they knew the statement had not been made by Reagan?

PROFESSIONAL CODES OF ETHICS AS GUIDELINES

Members of groups depend upon each other to behave in the manner that the group has established as appropriate—the manner that reflects its norms and values. For instance, when you enroll for courses at a university, you agree to adhere to the school's code of behavior, which holds you to specific expectations of conduct as a scholar. Practicing professionals in most fields have professional norms and conduct of behavior. Physicians, for example, take the Hippocratic Oath, promising to care for their patients and do no harm. When you visit your doctor, you expect her to treat you with respect, administer to your condition to the best of her ability, and keep your health records private. Attorneys must pass bar examinations in the state in which they practice and abide by the rules of practice adopted of the state's courts. When you consult an attorney, you expect him to keep any information you share about the status of your health, your finances, and your lifestyle confidential. As PR practitioners, you will be expected to adhere to the standards of conduct set by the profession. These standards are set out in codes written by companies and various professional associations.

Company Codes

Today, many corporations establish company codes of conduct, which their employees must pledge to follow. Let's look at Texas Instruments, for example. The technology company established a formal ethics code in the 1960s, several years after it said its employees had "placed their personal imprint on the ethics of the company. They chose to conduct themselves to the highest standards of personal integrity, and they demanded the same of others." Today, Texas Instruments has a director-level Office of Ethics. Many other companies, both in the United States and throughout the rest of the world, have institutionalized codes. You can read many of these on company websites.

International Codes

As the business world continues to shrink, international codes of business ethics are evolving to help organizations in different nations do business with each other. One example is the Caux Principles of Business, written by the Caux Round Table, a group of international business leaders seeking to create a world standard of business behavior. The Caux Round Table has sought to begin a process that identifies shared values and reconciles differing values in order to develop a shared perspective on business behavior acceptable to all business people. These principles are rooted in two basic ethical ideals: kyosei and human dignity. The Japanese concept of **kyosei** *means living and working together for the common good, enabling cooperation and mutual prosperity to co-exist with healthy and fair competition. Human dignity* refers to the sacredness or value of each person as a goal in itself, not simply as a means to fulfilling others' purposes.

Professional Codes

Most professions have a set of **codes,** *which reflect the practices and customs of the discipline and provide a set of standards of behavior for members.* Professions that require licenses, such as the medical and legal professions, have legally binding codes to which practitioners must adhere. In other fields—public relations among them—professional organizations have adapted codes of ethics. These codes serve as guidelines but contain no procedures for punishing those who violate them. In the United States, no state laws or regulations enforce standards of behavior for public relations practitioners. Therefore, to have an ethical practice, you must look to your own integrity; you must have the backbone to do what is right.

Many public relations organizations have written professional codes, which may be useful to you in your practice. Presented below in Table 7.3 is a summary of the code of ethics for the Public Relations Society of America (PRSA), the largest professional organization for public relations practitioners in the United States. Codes for the International Association of Business Communicators (IABC), the International Public Relations Association, and the principles of PR management practiced by Arthur W. Page, the first corporate vice president for public relations (see Chapter 3) are in Appendix A. Codes for professional organizations in related fields, the Radio-Television News Directors Association (RTNDA), the Radio-Television Digital News Association (RTDNA), and Society of Professional Journalists (SPJ), can be found online.

Table **7.3**	Summary of PRSA Code of Ethics
Honesty	• Adhere to the highest standards of accuracy and truth in advancing the interests of those you represent and in communicating with the public. • Be honest and accurate in all communications; avoid deceptive practices.
Advocacy/expertise	• Serve the public interest by acting as responsible advocates for those you represent. • Provide a voice in the marketplace of ideas, facts, and viewpoints to aid informed public debate. • Acquire and responsibly use specialized knowledge and experience. Build mutual understanding, credibility, and relationships among a wide array of institutions and audiences.
Independence	• Provide objective counsel to those you represent. • Be accountable for your actions.
Loyalty	• Be faithful to those you represent, while honoring your obligation to serve the public interest.
Fairness	• Deal fairly with clients, employers, competitors, peers, vendors, the media, and the general public.
Free flow of information	• Preserve the integrity of the process of communication. • Act promptly to correct erroneous communications for which you are responsible. • Preserve the free flow of unprejudiced information when giving or receiving gifts by ensuring that gifts are nominal, legal, and infrequent. • Respect all opinions and support the right of free expression.
Competition	• Follow ethical hiring practices designed to respect free and open competition without deliberately undermining a competitor. • Preserve intellectual property rights in the marketplace.
Disclosure of information	• Investigate the truthfulness and accuracy of information released on behalf of those represented. • Reveal the sponsors for causes and interests represented. • Disclose financial interest (such as stock ownership) in a client's organization.

(*continued*)

Table **7.3**	Summary of PRSA Code of Ethics (*continued*)
Confidentiality	• Safeguard the confidences and privacy rights of present, former, and prospective clients and employees. • Protect privileged, confidential, or insider information gained from a client or organization. • Immediately advise an appropriate authority if a member discovers that confidential information is being divulged by an employee of a client company or organization.
Conflicts of interest	• Avoid actions and circumstances that may appear to compromise good business judgment or create a conflict between personal and professional interests. • Disclose promptly any existing or potential conflict of interest to affected clients or organizations. • Encourage clients and customers to determine if a conflict exists after notifying all affected parties. • Act in the best interests of the client or employer, even subordinating the member's personal interests.
Enhancing the profession	• Acknowledge that there is an obligation to protect and enhance the profession. • Keep informed and educated about practices in the profession to ensure ethical conduct. • Advance the profession through continued professional development, research, and education. • Accurately define what public relations activities can accomplish.
Obligation to the code	• Counsel subordinates in proper ethical decision making. • Require that subordinates adhere to the ethical requirements of the Code. • Report ethical violations, whether committed by PRSA members or not, to the appropriate authority. • Decline representation of clients or organizations that urge or require actions contrary to this Code.
Enforcement of the code	• Enforcement replaced by education. The Board retains the right to bar from membership or expel from the Society any individual who is sanctioned by a government agency or convicted in a court of law of an action that is in violation of the Code.

SOURCE: www.prsa.org

THE BOTTOM LINE

As Seib and Fitzpatrick stated in their book, *Public Relations Ethics*, "The keystone of an ethical profession is the individual practitioner." The burden of responsibility for ethical decision making lies with you as a practitioner. Being an ethical person requires maturity, independence, and a sense of obligation to society and the public interest. Engaging in an ethical practice also requires that you be loyal to the standards of the profession, as described in the professional codes. If you make job security, prestige, salary, and recognition from supervisors more important than adhering to professional standards, you may find yourself making ethically questionable choices. Similarly, if you focus only on technique—on preparing technically competent news releases, brochures, newsletters, VNRs, and so forth—and not on what you say in the communications, you may find yourself distributing inaccurate, misleading, or wrong information. To be an ethical and successful PR practitioner, you must remain true to yourself, work hard, and stay smart.

BRIEF CASE STUDY

No Child Left Behind

In 2004, the U. S. Department of Education contracted with the PR firm Ketchum and with African American political pundit Armstrong Williams to help build public support for the Bush administration's education agenda. The deal, worth $1 million to Ketchum, was a campaign to promote the No Child Left Behind (NCLB) education law.

Former President Bush at a "No Child Left Behind" rally

Because the administration was seeking to build support among black families for the law, $240,000 of the Ketchum deal was earmarked for Williams, who hosts The Right Side, a nationally syndicated conservative talk show on television and radio, writes op-ed pieces for newspapers, and heads his own public relations firm, The Graham Williams Group. Williams was to promote the law on his television show, encourage other black journalists to support NCLB, and urge "producers to periodically address" NCLB.

Part of Williams' contract required that he interview then Secretary of Education Roderick R. Paige for television and radio spots. The interviews aired during the show in 2004. Since Congress prohibits lobbying or propaganda efforts to promote government programs, the Ketchum contract may have been illegal. Williams said he understands that critics could find the arrangement unethical, but "I wanted to do it because it's something I believe in." He said he does not recall telling audiences about the contract on the air but told colleagues about it when urging them to promote NCLB.

In addition to working with Williams, Ketchum produced video news releases (VNRs) about NCLB designed to look like news reports. The Bush administration used similar releases to promote its Medicare prescription drug plan, a tactic that the Government Accountability Office has called an illegal use of taxpayers' dollars. (See Chapter 16 for more on the Medicare VNRs.) Early in 2005, Congress began inquiries into the Education Department's public relations spending.

Working the Case

1. Evaluate Ketchum's activities on behalf of the U.S. Department of Education. How well did Ketchum serve all the interests of all the persons involved? On what are you basing your evaluation? Please explain.
2. What ethical principles did the PR firm break or follow? How so?

Communicators Can Shine as the "Conscience" of a Company

PROFESSIONAL
POINT OF VIEW

Lisa Davis consultant, is former communications director for AARP. She wrote this point of view for PRWeek.

The former CEO of a company that had a very public flameout participated in an off-the-record discussion. Asked about the performance of his communication team during the crisis, he—not surprisingly—wasn't kind.

What was surprising was his view of the central communications problem he experienced. He felt his PR counsel should have acted as the company's "conscience."

It's a definite red flag when a CEO needs others to be the conscience of an organization. But there is a truth for PR leaders to absorb. Top communicators should be a conscience by speaking up when good management proposes bad ideas and by resisting the pressure to simply promote the company line.

Being the conscience of an organization means taking positions with senior management that underscore the company's positive values even if the tide is swiftly moving in the other direction. It's not fun, but it's smart.

A top executive for a major investment firm commented that what he wanted most from PR counsel was to provide big ideas just like any other senior executive, and to inform senior management of how potential decisions will be perceived. Rather than being a career-ending mistake, speaking up can be a career-advancing move.

Most executives never intend to violate company values. Business goals and external events can create a "rock and a hard place" scenario, pitting company values against business realities. Communicators are aware of how the media, third-party players, and staff view the company. Share this insight. Detail how actions will be interpreted as either supporting or breaching company morals. Then show the link between reputation and meeting long-term goals.

Don't forget the value of diplomacy and offering options when speaking up. Sometimes a better way to tell the emperor that he has no clothes is to ask if he's feeling a draft and then offer him a coat.

Vada Manager, director of global issues management for Nike, has a good rule when decisions are made that conflict with company values: "Don't defend in public what you don't help define." Personal credibility is as important as organizational integrity. Rather than taking a hard-line approach, establishing this principle early on helps ensure involvement at the appropriate time. The argument to senior management is simple. Having input makes it easier to credibly interpret the decision for others and increases the likelihood of successful delivery. Torie Clark, former assistant secretary of defense for public affairs under Donald Rumsfeld, provides the best advice, especially to CEOs and other executives who propose reputation-busting activities. She writes in her new book, *Lipstick on a Pig*, "Once you figure out you can't put lipstick on a pig, what you've really learned is far more powerful: you've learned not to produce a pig in the first place."

SOURCE: Lisa Davis, *PRWeek*, April 24, 2006

Summary and Review

What Is Ethics?
- Ethics is hard to define and sometimes harder to practice, especially given today's tough business climate.
- Ethics may be broadly defined as doing what is right and avoiding what is wrong.
- Public relations professionals have a unique opportunity to help steer their organizations and clients in proper ethical directions.
- Understanding the philosophical theories behind ethics and applying tools for decision making, such as those presented in this chapter, may help practitioners make ethical choices.

Ethics and Standards of Professionalism
- Ethical codes of professional public relations organizations give practitioners guidelines to follow.
- Practitioners need to follow their own inherent sense of what is just and not let themselves be misled by unscrupulous persons or their own weaknesses.
- While the PR professional and her conscience is really her own best judge of what is ethical, there are professional codes that help guide conduct.

Ethical Challenges for PR Professionals
- PR professionals must look at their work as more than a job. The profession requires that the practitioner put his client and the community first. In other words, we must value our duty above self-gain.
- Ethical decision making is especially complicated because the practitioners has many audiences to consider, including clients, news media, government agencies, educational institutions, consumers, stockholders, the community, competitors, critics, and fellow practitioners.

- Sometimes there is a conflict between the practitioner's personal values and what is required by a client or employer.
- Conflicts of interest, violating agreements, serving as a front group, and making false statements about products are just a few ethical concerns for practitioners.

Orienting Yourself for Ethical Decision Making

- One way to orient yourself is to think about the ways in which people see things and make decisions and look for yourself in those descriptions.
- Absolutists see actions as either right or wrong. Relativists believe that our values are molded over a period of our lifetime, while situationalists make decisions based on the circumstances and one case at a time.
- You can judge based on what you perceive to be good intentions or what you perceive to be good results, but sometimes you will find that there are no clear answers to ethical problems.

Tools for Ethical Decision Making

- Ultimately, you, your client, or the organization with which you are working are responsible for making ethical choices.
- There are several decision-making tools that can give you a framework for thinking through an ethical dilemma.

Professional Codes of Ethics as Guidelines

- Members of groups depend upon each other to behave in the manner that the group has established as appropriate—the manner that reflects its norms and values.
- Professional codes exist for PR practitioners and for many of the audiences with which the practitioner have frequent contact. The Public Relations Society of America (PRSA), National Association of Broadcasters (NAB), International Association of Business Communicators (IABC), Radio-Television News Directors Association (RTNDA), and Society of Professional Journalists (SPJ) have all adopted professional codes with which you should become familiar.

The Bottom Line

- At the end of the day, ethical decision making is your responsibility. As much as it would be nice to have every circumstance and decision codified, that is not the case. You must make the decisions.
- Personal credibility and access to top management are crucial to making the best decisions and providing the best counsel.

Key Terms

absolutist	ethics	relativist
attorney-client model	intuitive thinking	situationalist
codes	kyosei	social responsibility
deterministic or	partisan and mutual	model
naturalistic thinking	values model	two-way symmetrical
enlightened self-interest	professional responsibility	model
model	model	

Questions for Review and Discussion

1. In the everyday practice of public relations, it is not always clear what is the most ethical thing to do. Why is it that people can see the same circumstances but do not agree that there is an ethical dilemma?

2. A practitioner has been working closely with a journalist to get a news story. Following an interview late in the day with one of her company's executives, the practitioner suggests drinks and dinner. Should the practitioner offer to pay for the reporter's meal or suggest a separate bill? Why or why not?

3. A practitioner suspects that a children's toy made by a leading toy company he represents is badly made and may be unsafe. Should he report his suspicion? Defend the product? Do nothing? Explain your response.

4. A practitioner works for a chemical company that makes pesticides and herbicides. She had been asked to promote in foreign markets some brands that are banned in the United States. Should she accept the assignment? Turn it down? Point out the immorality of selling potentially poisonous products in other, probably less developed, countries? Explain your response.

5. A practitioner at a leading public relations firm representing a U.S. tobacco company has been asked to help run a campaign to sell cigarettes in Asia. He finds out that some of his associates are running another campaign for the same tobacco company, encouraging young people in the United States not to smoke. Should he point out the ethical conflict in running these two campaigns? Why or why not? Explain your response.

6. As a spokesperson for a politician accused of improper, and possibly illegal, behavior, she faces a dilemma. Should she try to deflect public attention and criticism from her boss? Explain your response.

7. A practitioner has been asked to represent a construction company; he finds out that the company violates environmental safety and labor regulations. Should he report his findings? Turn down the account? Whitewash the violations? Explain your response.

8. Based on the examples cited in this chapter, compare the activities of Ketchum PR in the No Child Left Behind case and Edelman's activities in the Odwalla case. How well did they serve all the interests of all the persons involved? What ethical principles did they break or follow?

9. The PRSA and IABC codes are standards for the practice. Should these codes be enforced? Why or why not? Explain your response.

10. Both PRSA and IABC have accreditation programs that require practitioners seeking accreditation to take comprehensive examinations. Should all practitioners be required to be accredited? Why or why not? Also, should public relations practitioners have to be licensed in order to practice? Who, if anyone, would benefit from this requirement?

Web Links

International Association of Business Communicators
www.iabc.org

International Public Relations Association
www.ipra.org

PR Watch: Center for Media and Democracy
www.prwatch.org

Public Relations Society of America
www.prsa.org

Radio and Television News Directors Association
www.rtnda.org

Radio Television Digital News Association
www.rtdna.org

SourceWatch
www.sourcewatch.org

Society of Professional Journalists
www.spj.org

Staying within Legal Bounds

AVOIDING HARM

As a public relations professional, you must be careful not to harm others through words or actions. You have a responsibility for maintaining your own and the organization's reputation and credibility, and your communication can have impact on consumers and investors.

CHAPTER PREVIEW

- Avoiding Harm
- Creative Property Protections
- Freedom of Speech
- Regulating Speech
- Working with Lawyers

Libel and Slander

Basically, **libel** means *injuring another's reputation.* Each state has its own laws regarding libel. *Some states make a distinction between libel and slander, considering libel as written or otherwise printed injury and* **slander** *as spoken.* In either case, the term **defamation** *usually includes both terms.* A defamatory statement is one that causes another to be hated, ridiculed, or scorned. Defamatory statements are not merely insulting or offensive, but actually harm another's reputation, putting his or her social or professional life at risk.

For a libel suit to be successful, the defamatory statement must be false—name-calling, hyperbole, or other characterizations that

Congress shall make no law respecting an establishment of religion, or prohibiting the free exercise thereof; or abridging the freedom of speech, or of the press; or the right of the people peaceably to assemble, and to petition the Government for a redress of grievances.

—First Amendment to the U.S. Constitution

cannot be proven true or false cannot be the subject of a libel claim—and the person who made the statement must have intended to cause harm. These conditions were not always required. Two famous cases helped shape American libel laws. The first was the case of John Peter Zenger, a colonial New York publisher who was imprisoned in 1734 for printing political attacks against the state's colonial governor. Zenger's lawyer argued successfully that one could not be guilty of libel if the statements made were true. Until then, it had not mattered whether the allegedly libelous statements were true or false. The Zenger case also established the precedent of trying libel cases under civil law, rather than as criminal cases, heard by a jury.

The second case was *The New York Times Co. v. Sullivan*, ruled on by the U.S. Supreme Court in 1964. The court decided that public officials could not sue successfully for libel unless reporters or editors were guilty of "actual malice" when publishing false statements about the officials. *Malice* in this context is a legal term meaning that the person who made the statement knew it was false or recklessly disregarded its truth or falsity. Later, the Supreme Court later extended the so-called Sullivan rule to cover "public figures," those who are not public officials but are in the public eye. Over the years, this category has come to include well-known writers, entertainers, athletes, and others who often attract media attention. In most states, private individuals must show only that the person who made the allegedly libelous statement was negligent or failed to act with due care.

Trade libel, or **trade disparagement,** is *defamation of a product, rather than the product's manufacturer.* In trade libel, the product's quality or usefulness is defamed. The requirements for a successful trade libel suit are the same as those for suits brought by public figures.

Individuals, corporations, unincorporated businesses, associations, and unions can sue for libel; governmental agencies cannot, but a government official can bring suit for statements made about him or her as an individual. The laws regarding libel suits apply to Internet as they do to more traditional media. However, federal law protects Internet service providers (ISPs) and other interactive computer services from many lawsuits.

What does this mean for public relations professionals? When speaking with the media or producing materials for print or broadcast, take these precautions to avoid libel:

- Check facts and sources thoroughly.
- Back up opinions with facts.
- Avoid innuendo and suggestive implication.
- Be careful not to change the meaning when editing quoted materials and make sure the quote expresses the facts accurately.
- Avoid using clippings or news articles that defame someone.
- Do not link random photos to a story that could be defamatory; for example, do not place a random group photo with a press release about the rise in crime.
- Keep all your notes and tapes from interviews.
- When you finish a story, edit it carefully and remove any potentially libelous material.

Invasion of Privacy

According to scholar Karla K. Gower, privacy—as first clearly defined by Justice Louis Brandeis and his law partner Samuel Warren in an 1890 *Harvard Law Review* article, "The Right to Privacy"—is the right to seclusion and to control overdisclosure of information about one's private life. The idea was expanded in 1960 by legal scholar William Prosser, who defined these four aspects of privacy:

- **Intrusion:** Trespassing on private property or surveillance, the use of electronic or mechanical equipment to gather information
- **Appropriation:** Using the name or likeness of someone without his or her consent for commercial purposes, such as advertisements or promotional pieces (does not include news stories)
- **False light:** Making a nondefamatory false statement that creates a distorted picture of someone and is highly offensive to a reasonable person
- **Public disclosure of private information:** Revealing embarrassing private facts that offend the average person's sensibilities

What does this mean for public relations professionals? Practitioners need to take care not to misappropriate information or violate someone's informational privacy. Be sure to get written consent before using photographs of employees or persons outside the organization in public relations materials. Ask employees before publishing information about them in a company newsletter, an external publication, or on a website. In most states, the only information about employees that can be made public without their consent is confirmation of employment, job title, job description, date hired, and date terminated.

Negligence

Negligence is *professional misconduct or unreasonable lack of skill that results in personal injury.* Although negligence lawsuits are not usually brought against public relations practitioners, you should take reasonable precautions when planning promotional events, plant tours, or open houses to reduce the risk of liability if a visitor is hurt.

ENGAGING ETHICS

Dog and Cat Food Recall

The biggest pet food recall in U.S. history took place in March 2009 and spread worldwide as hundreds, possibly thousands, of cats and dogs fell ill with kidney failure and many others died. The pets ate food products contaminated with melamine, an industrial chemical used to make products such as plastics, cleaning products, glues, inks, and fertilizers and cyanuric acid, used to chlorinate swimming pools. In 2009 two Chinese nationals and the businesses they operate, along with a U.S. company and its president, were indicted in federal court for their role in intentionally manufacturing and distributing melamine-tainted wheat gluten that was used to make dog and cat food. Many major food manufacturing companies in the United States, Canada, and Europe recalled products. One of the largest, MenuFoods, recalled 60 million containers of its pet food during the crisis and settled lawsuits with pet owners in 2008.

1. Aside from being illegal, the actions of the importers were unethical. Explain why?
2. Spokespeople for MenuFoods, Del Monte, and other U.S. manufacturers were straightforward in their interactions with the news media. What were their ethical obligations in keeping the media and consumers informed? What might have made the ethical concerns even more difficult?

NORM BETTS/Landov

A store's bin filled with pet food returned by consumers

Product Liability

Manufacturers and sellers of goods are liable for damages caused by defective products. Most states now have some version of strict liability laws, which impose liability without regard to fault. As a public relations practitioner, you would be wise to ask for product certification before writing news releases or other copy advancing a product. If you should represent a company that has been found to have sold defective goods, you have an ethical responsibility to inform the public honestly. (For detailed information on ethical responsibility, see Chapter 7.)

CREATIVE PROPERTY PROTECTIONS

Creative property—works, trademarks, and inventions—is protected by federal laws that grant the owner exclusive rights to decide who can use the property and how it can be used. Public relations practitioners have an obligation to protect their clients' creative property rights and to respect the rights of others.

Copyright

Copyright *laws give the author or joint authors of creative works the exclusive rights to reproduce, distribute, perform, and display their work and to make derivations of it.* Such works include writings, art, graphics, photos, music, plays, motion pictures, audiovisuals, and other creative works. If an employee does creative work on company time using company resources, the work belongs to the company. The work becomes eligible for copyright once it is produced in "tangible form," which can range from printed materials to films, CDs, and Internet postings.

Generally speaking, facts and ideas are not protected by copyright, but their artistic expression is protected. You are usually free to use the facts and ideas contained in other works as long as you present them in your own original way. If you want to use a quote, song, photo, or other material from a copyrighted work, you must ask for permission unless the use falls under the doctrine of fair use. This allows for the use of copyrighted materials for purposes such as criticism, comment, news reporting, teaching, scholarship, and research. To determine whether the use is fair, the courts consider the purpose of the use, the nature of the work, the amount and substantiality of the portion used in comparison to the work as a whole, and the effect of the use of the work's market value. Once a copyright expires, the work enters the public domain and may be used by anyone.

The work you perform for an organization belongs to the employer, so you cannot copyright what you create while you are hired and under employment by the organization. If your organization seeks to copyright material, it is not necessary to register or publish a copyright but it is helpful in the event of infringement.

If you are not sure if your use of copyrighted material is fair, you should consult with your organization's attorney.

Trademarks and Patents

A **trademark** is *a word, phrase, logo, symbol, color, sound, or smell used by a business to identify a product and distinguish it from those of its competitors.* Federal law prohibits one business from using another's trademark. Ownership of trademarks arises from "first use" of the mark, which can be established by actual use or by applying to the U.S. Patent and Trademark Office. To be considered a trademark, the mark must be used to identify a product, be distinctive, and not be too similar to another organization's mark.

A **patent** *grants an inventor the exclusive right to make, use, or sell his invention for a given period of time.* Patents are similar to copyrights. Once a patent expires, the invention enters public domain and can be used by anyone. To qualify for a patent, an invention must be new, useful, and not easily duplicated.

If you want to use patented material or a trademark, you must check with the patent office and ask the owner's permission. As with copyrighted material, if you are uncertain about the use of a trademark or patented invention, consult your organization's attorney.

FREEDOM OF SPEECH

The First Amendment to the U.S. Constitution protects an individual's right to free speech, regardless of what the government thinks about what is said. However, there are some limits on speech, which are determined by the U.S. Supreme Court and vary depending on the times and the attitude of the court. The following section will examine the ways the courts have defined corporate communication and the regulations they have placed on them.

Corporate Speech

Speech that presents a corporation's views on social or political matters is referred to as **corporate speech.** Public relations practitioners may engage in this kind of speech when they release papers, pamphlets, brochures, or advertisements that present the corporation's position on a public issue. Corporate speech is generally protected by the First Amendment.

The first case to address corporate speech was the *First National Bank of Boston v. the State of Massachusetts,* decided in 1978. The bank wanted to mount a campaign against the state's graduated income tax proposal. A state court ruled that the bank could not use a public relations campaign to tell its customers about its position because corporations do not have First Amendment rights. The U.S. Supreme Court disagreed, saying that whether or not speech is protected depends on the content of the speech, not the speaker. The Supreme Court upheld this position in *Consolidated Edison v. Public Service Commission,* allowing the utility company to insert a pamphlet in its bills to customers, explaining the benefits of nuclear power. In both cases, the court said the public was served by knowing the corporation's views on an important issue.

Commercial Speech

Commercial speech is *communication that is motivated by a desire for profit.* Most communication regarding a company's business, including advertisements, reports, and public relations brochures and pamphlets, is considered commercial speech and, unlike corporate speech, is subject to government regulation.

BRIEF CASE STUDY

Demonstators protest
Nike labor practices.

Kasky v. Nike: Defining Corporate and Commercial Speech

In the 1990s, in response to the accusation that the company used sweatshops to manufacture its products overseas, Nike launched a public relations campaign that included newspaper ads, letters to editors, and correspondence with college and university presidents. Nike's goal was to show that it was improving conditions for overseas workers and to maintain customer loyalty.

Marc Kasky, a California consumer advocate, objected to this campaign and sued Nike in 1998, alleging that the company's claims were misleading. In the spring of 2002, the California Supreme Court ruled in favor of Kasky, a decision that Nike appealed to the U.S. Supreme Court.

The crux of the case was the distinction between corporate speech and commercial speech. Under the U.S. Constitution, corporate speech—speech on public issues—is protected by the First Amendment, but commercial speech is subject to regulations, including truth in advertising laws. The Supreme Court was asked to decide whether Nike's campaign constituted corporate or commercial speech and to clarify the free speech rights of corporations. Unfortunately, the Supreme Court reversed its decision to hear the case.

In September 2003, Kasky and Nike announced a settlement: Nike agreed to pay $1.5 million to the Washington, DC-based Fair Labor Association for a worker development program. The case closed, without a ruling on corporate free speech.

Subsequently, in 2010, the Supreme Court ruled in *Citizens v. Federal Election Commission* that "the government may not ban political spending by corporations in candidate elections. This ruling—5 to 4—demonstrated a deeply divided court and set off a debate about the ruling's effect on government and a slippery slope to political corruption.

Working the Case

Both of these cases are categorized as corporate First Amendment issues. Explain how each is seen as corporate free speech.

REGULATING SPEECH

As a public relations practitioner, you need to be aware of the various federal and state regulations and agencies that can affect your organization and your clients. If you fail to comply with applicable laws and regulations, you and your client may be liable.

Federal Trade Commission (FTC)

The U.S. **Federal Trade Commission (FTC)** was established in 1914 to *protect businesses from one another*. Up to this time, advertising was largely unregulated, and some public officials began to fear that unscrupulous businesses were stealing customers from their competitors. Later, the commission began to focus on protecting consumers from unfair or deceptive advertising.

Today, FTC regulations and surveillance apply to publicity releases, as well. Both the client describing the product or service and the public relations department or agency that writes and distributes the publicity are legally liable if the assertions are false or misleading.

Publicists will also be judged liable if the courts decide that they reasonably should have known the deceptive nature of the publicity. Careful practitioners, then, should verify the claims made about a product or service before publicizing them.

Securities and Exchange Commission (SEC)

The U.S. **Securities and Exchange Commission (SEC)** was established after the stock market crash of 1929, which triggered the Great Depression of the 1930s. *The SEC is tasked with protecting the financial interests of investors in publicly held companies—those whose stock is publicly owned and traded—by overseeing the companies' financial activities and by monitoring financial markets.* To this end, the SEC requires that companies disclose relevant information about their business activities fully and in a timely manner.

The best known of the reports required by the SEC is the annual 10-K report, which provides specific information about a company's financial state and direction. The 10-K forms the basis of the company's annual report, which must be distributed to shareholders no less than 15 days before the company's annual meeting. According to SEC regulation, annual reports must include audited financial statements; additional financial data, such as net sales and gross profits; a description of the company's business; names of directors and officers; an analysis of the company's financial condition; and a description of any lawsuits in which the company or its directors are involved. Companies often use the annual report as a vehicle for promoting the company.

In addition to the 10-K report, companies are required to file financial statements quarterly and to announce important developments or events that are likely to affect stock prices promptly. In addition, they must issue timely news releases to the major media outlets, notifying the public before they release reports.

Public relations practitioners need to be aware of SEC reporting regulations because they are often involved in writing the required reports and press releases. Also, the courts and the SEC hold practitioners accountable for the accuracy of the information in reports. All disclosures must be full and truthful, must not mislead investors, and must not cover up bad news. As with publicity, careful public relations practitioners should verify all facts before releasing reports and press notices.

Because public relations practitioners have access to sensitive financial information, they must be careful to avoid insider trading, long forbidden by the SEC. As described in Chapter 7, insiders are those who have information that is not available to the general public; a company's directors, officers, employees, and agents—such as accountants, lawyers, consultants, and public relations professionals—are all considered insiders. They are prohibited from trading stock based on privileged information they have before the information is known by the general public. This regulation prevents insiders from having an unfair advantage. They are also prohibited from "tipping off" others about the nonpublic information.

One famous insider trading case involving a public relations practitioner was the Anthony Franco case. Franco was a public relations consultant and president-elect of the Public Relations Society of America at the time of the incident. He prepared a news release announcing the intention of his client, Crowley, Milner and Company, to buy another company, then bought shares in Crowley. The SEC argued that Franco bought the shares hoping to make a profit when Crowley's stock prices rose after the announcement. As a result, Franco signed a statement promising to abide by SEC laws in the future and stepped down as president of the PRSA.

Food and Drug Administration (FDA)

One of the tasks of the U.S. Food and Drug Administration (FDA) is to regulate the promotion of prescription drugs through advertising and public relations materials, such as news releases, brochures, pamphlets, and information on company websites. The FDA requires that all materials tell consumers about the risks, as well as the benefits of the drug, state clearly that the drug will not help everyone, and be accompanied by supplementary materials giving the full prescribing information.

If you work as a public relations practitioner for a company or client that manufactures products regulated by the FDA, you should have the FDA screen all promotional materials before you release them.

Other Regulations

Lobbyists

Public relations practitioners who **lobby,** *or contact executive and legislative branch officials on behalf of their organizations or clients,* must register with the government. They must also file statements identifying their clients and listing the issues on which they have lobbied.

Freedom of Information

Enacted in 1966, the Freedom of Information Act (FOIA) is designed to make government documents available to the news media and the public. Many of these documents are filed by corporations that must report to regulatory commissions, agencies, and bureaus. The act seeks to honor the public's "right to know" while providing exemptions that protect sensitive information and personal rights. Exemptions include trade secrets and some financial and commercial documents. Corporate practitioners are informed of documents that are filed and are advised when an FOIA request is made. Citizens often make requests unrelated to corporate matters. Many requests are from news media and interested parties who are seeking Federal Bureau of Investigation (FBI) files.

State "Right to Know" Laws

Some states have enacted laws that are similar to the FOIA. These laws give the public legal access to information about environmental hazards, occupational safety and health, and other social issues.

WORKING WITH LAWYERS

Before the days of 24-hour cable news, Court TV, and the Internet, legal and public relations professionals rarely joined forces. Today, law firms rely more regularly on public relations agencies, and most large agencies have set up litigation public relations practices. Some large law firms have even entered into joint relations with public relations firms to offer clients legal and PR services.

Litigation Public Relations

Litigation public relations *has two meanings in the field. One refers to the practice of public relations in a crisis when an organization becomes a party in a legal procedure and is faced with court proceedings. The other is used to describe the practice by lawyers or* *their public relations representatives of using the media relations to advance their clients' cases and to promote their own reputations and services.*

One of the first high-profile cases to feature public relations experts was the $120 million libel lawsuit brought by retired Gen. William G. Westmoreland, the commander of U.S. forces in Vietnam, against CBS. In 1982, CBS correspondent Mike Wallace reported that Westmoreland had misrepresented enemy troop strength during the Vietnam War and had helped mislead the public. CBS hired public relations expert John Scanlon to help handle the case in the court of public opinion.

One of the best-known defense lawyers to use litigation public relations was Robert Shapiro, who acted as both lawyer and publicist for his client, O.J. Simpson, during his murder trial. In 1993, Shapiro wrote an article, "Using the Media to Your Own Advantage," in which he argued that defense attorneys need to manipulate the news media to counter what he saw as the natural advantage of prosecutors. Prosecutors have also used litigation public relations to try their cases in the media as well as the court. But this practice can jeopardize the defendant's Sixth Amendment rights, which protect one's right to a fair trial.

Litigation PR Vital to Winning in Court of Public Opinion

PROFESSIONAL POINT OF VIEW

Karen Doyne was managing director, Crisis and Issues Management, at Burson-Marsteller in Washington when she wrote this piece for PRWeek, *March 22, 2004.*

When former Vice President Aaron Burr entered a Virginia courtroom to stand trial for treason in 1807, nobody had yet invented the term "pretrial publicity"—but the press was learning on the job. One observer said that the allegations against Burr had "resounded through the newspapers so long and so strongly" that they already had created "the general opinion" that Burr was guilty.

Despite the negative press, Burr beat the rap. But nearly two centuries later, the law and PR professions, which have long inhabited separate planets, seem to be recognizing reality: The playing field for legal action doesn't exist solely behind the courtroom door. In many cases, litigants who ignore the court of public opinion do so at their own peril. Celebrity cases, high-profile murder trials, and the like have always been hot topics in the U.S. media. But over the last decade, two trends have raised the stakes and driven lawyers, albeit reluctantly, into the arms of PR professionals. The first is the increase in high-profile civil corporate litigation, particularly the rise of class-action injury lawsuits. As savvy plaintiff lawyers quickly discovered, these cases are gold mines for attracting media coverage and shaping public opinion well in advance of a trial. They offer numerous human-interest stories and play into the well-worn cultural themes of David versus Goliath, conspiracy, corporate greed, and exploitation of the powerless. Corporate defendants began fighting back with their own PR efforts to support their legal cases and to protect their reputations and bottom line.

The second factor has been the super-charged information environment created by the internet. While television was making litigation a staple of news and newsmagazine programming, the internet's unprecedented speed and reach created a powerful platform for plaintiff law firms, activist groups, and others to recruit plaintiffs and influence opinion at the grassroots level. Nevertheless, the PR–legal courtship has been a rocky one. For a time, joint efforts were more competitive than cooperative. Lawyers typically considered PR to be somewhat distasteful and probably dangerous to their interests. Accustomed to a forum with rules and the ability to exert control over the process, attorneys couldn't wrap their minds around the anarchy, uncertainty, and immediacy of media relations. If lawyers were arrogant, a lot of PR practitioners were just plain ignorant. Relatively few understood the basics of the legal system or the dynamics of communications during litigation. PR people who failed to know and respect the lawyer's mindset found themselves talking to brick walls. In the worst cases, public statements or other actions did real damage to the party's legal position. That learning curve has spiked dramatically. In-house PR people got wise that they needed to work with lawyers if they were to have any influence over communications strategy, and PR firms recognized their clients' growing needs for specialized experience. Over time, litigation PR has become an essential element of crisis and issues management. The Institute for Crisis Management's annual report continues to list class-action lawsuits as the single largest category of business crisis (although its growth rate seems to have slowed somewhat, at last). Lawyers, too, are getting with the program. Many defense attorneys have recognized the importance of managing outside-the-courtroom audiences. Others have decided that keeping an eye on PR is smarter than shutting it out. The best made it a point to learn the rudiments of our world, as we have theirs. If litigation PR has evolved greatly, its next phase is likely to be the most challenging of all. A company's legal exposure has become a key factor to industry analysts on whose opinions stock prices rise and fall. Sensitive documents turn up on websites like thesmokinggun.com long before a judge even considers them. Perhaps most important, PR counselors now have a real opportunity to secure a seat at the table where strategic business and legal decisions are made. There is a growing recognition that, just as communications can play a role in legal strategy, legal actions often have an impact on a firm's reputation and relationships—a factor that is far better examined before the controversy hits than after. When legal and reputational goals collide, no one is better positioned than the communications professional to be sure executives make decisions with their eyes wide open. Earning and keeping that coveted seat will require us to continue educating ourselves, showing attorneys that we "get it" even if we don't always agree, and doing all we can to turn the shotgun marriage between PR and law into a very meaningful relationship.

Law Firms as Clients

In all likelihood, more public relations firms will find themselves advising attorneys on how to deal with the media. Here are some practical tips from journalists:

- Know where the firm would like to see its attorneys' articles published. Encourage the attorneys to read the publication and build a relationship with its editors and reporters, a key to landing stories about the firm in the publication.
- Before you pitch a story to a reporter, know who the reporter is. Read his or her stories to find out what the reporter covers. If an attorney is called by an investigative journalist for questioning, encourage the attorney to do a quick background check on the journalist before talking with him or her.
- Understand timeliness and deadlines. Do not hold on to good stories; send them out to reporters or editors right away. Get back to reporters when you said you would.
- Make sure the client understands the difference between "off the record" and "not for attribution." "Off the record" means the reporter cannot print what the interviewee says, in any context; the information can be printed, however, if it is gotten from other sources or becomes public. "Not for attribution" means the reporter can print the information, but not the source's name.
- Advise the client to answer reporter's questions briefly but truthfully and to disclose all. Do not let reporters find out for themselves information the attorney may not want them to know. Encourage them to act like prosecutors, who will reveal plea-bargains during a trial before the defense has the opportunity to do so.
- Educate legal clients about the value of public relations.

SOURCE: Karen Doyne, *PRWeek*, March 22, 2004

Summary and Review

Avoiding Harm
- A primary objective and responsibility as a PR professional is to ensure that you avoid doing harm to others through the use of words and actions.
- PR professionals must avoid libel.
- Libel and slander are two different grounds for litigation against an organization or individual. Libel is usually written or otherwise printed injury, while slander is spoken. But both usually involve accusations of defamation, a statement that causes another to be hated, ridiculed, or scorned—harming reputation.
- Successful libel lawsuits prove a statement as false, defamatory, and malicious.
- Trade libel involves defamation of product, not the product's manufacturer.
- Privacy rights can be infringed upon through intrusion, appropriation, false light, and public disclosure of private information.
- Negligence, professional misconduct resulting in personal injury, is an important concept for PR professionals to be aware of though not usually a cause for litigation against individuals in our field.
- There are strict state laws regarding product liability and as a PR professional it is incumbent upon you to disclose information regarding defective goods.

Creative Property Protections
- Copyright laws protect authors and joint authors of creative works by giving them exclusive rights to reproduce, distribute, perform, or display their work. The work is protected as soon as it is produced in a tangible form. Facts and ideas do not fall under this category, but artistic expression does.
- It is not necessary to register for a copyright in order for it to be valid, but it is helpful to the copyright owner in case of an infringement allegation. The work a PR professional does for an employer belongs to the employer.
- As a PR professional, you may use facts and ideas from other work as long as it is presented in an original way, but you must seek permission to use any portion of a copyrighted work unless it falls under the doctrine of fair use.
- Trademarks are used to identify a product and distinguish it from its competitors, and patents grant an inventor exclusive rights to make or sell an invention for a period of time. Once the period is passed, a patent expires and the invention is in the public domain.

Freedom of Speech
- Because it is a right guaranteed by the First Amendment of the U.S. Constitution, freedom of speech is guaranteed an individual no matter what the government thinks about it.
- Limitations to freedom of speech have been decided by the U.S. Supreme Court. While corporate speech is generally protected, commercial speech is regulated.

Regulating Speech
- Speech is regulated by various federal and state regulations and agencies. Federal agencies regulating speech include the Federal Trade Commission (FTC), Securities and Exchange Commission (SEC), and the Food and Drug Administration (FDA).
- Many of the duties of a PR practitioner, especially media relations and writing for publications, involve regulated speech. You should familiarize yourself with federal and state regulations that apply to this type of work.

Working with Lawyers

- The thriving practice of litigation PR makes extensive use of media relations and behavior research.
- As it has evolved, litigation PR is a prominent part of dealing with crisis planning and management.

Key Terms

commercial speech	litigation public relations	slander
copyright	lobby	trade libel (trade
corporate speech	negligence	disparagement)
defamation	patent	trademark
Federal Trade	Securities and Exchange	
Commission (FTC)	Commission (SEC)	
libel		

Questions for Review and Discussion

1. As a PR practitioner, why is it crucial that you understand the concept of avoiding harm?

2. What kinds of copyright infringements can confront you as a PR professional?

3. As a PR practitioner, when are you required to register with the U.S. government and what are the personal liabilities you face?

4. With what U.S. government regulatory agencies are you, as a PR practitioner, usually involved and in what ways?

5. Why should corporate PR staff know what information has been filed with government regulatory entities and why might nonprofit practitioners gain from the knowledge of some of the information on file?

Web Links

Fair Labor Association
www.fairlabor.org

Supreme Court of the United States
www.supremecourtus.gov

U.S. Federal Drug Administration
www.fda.gov

U.S. Federal Trade Commission
www.ftc.gov

U.S. Securities and Exchange Commission
www.sec.gov

Understanding Public Relations Theory

WHAT IS THEORY?

Definitions of *theory* abound. Simply put, a **theory** is *an attempt to explain a phenomenon*. It is a series of assumptions that explains how something works and what happens during and as a result of the work or process. It can examine events and situations to explore how variables are related in order to explain and predict. Scholars venture theories and test them to determine if the theory is predictive and supported. Then through observation, a theorist can explain a phenomenon or reject the theory and start over again. Theorizing is formal investigation—you predict, test, and confirm or deny. Postulating, proving, or disproving theories relies heavily on deductive and inductive reasoning.

When you begin with a theory or idea, moving downward or narrowing down toward a specific hypothesis, you are engaging in **deductive reasoning**—*moving from general to more specific*. Observation helps you to narrow down even more, and as you collect data from your observations, you can test the hypothesis and confirm or deny your original theory. This is sometimes called "the top-down approach."

Inductive reasoning is *a "bottom-up" process, during which you move from observations to broad generalizing statements based on patterns or trends upon which we can formulate hypotheses*. As you move through the patterns and trends, you are seeking to validate the hypotheses that lead you to valid theories.

Theory is valuable to the decision-making process during the planning

If you can't explain it simply, you don't understand it well enough.

—Albert Einstein, physicist and philosopher

and implementation of strategic communication campaigns and programs. Learning about theories and applying them to your work is crucial to effective practice. There is no single theory that guides the strategic public relations practice, and you should not think of theories as rules. Instead, multiple theories should guide you and explain why some strategies and tactics are appropriate in some situations and not in others.

Most core textbooks on public relations cover public relations models and theories thoroughly and provide some theoretical background on communication. As discussed in an earlier chapter, strategic public relations relies on knowledge of more than just communication and public relations. This chapter attempts to provide a communication context for public relations practice, explores the major public relations process theories, and reviews theories from the many disciplines that have enriched the practice of strategic communication.

COMMUNICATION PROCESS THEORY

Public relations is very much a communication process. Indeed, effective communication is at the core of strategic public relations practice. Communication is our way of sharing ideas and experiences with other individuals, groups, and institutions. Through communication, we inform, teach, entertain, and persuade. Communication scholars have posited a number of theories about effective communication, but in essence, successful communication takes place when a receiver understands the meaning of the message as intended by the sender and the receiver acts upon the message. Crucial to your understanding of strategic public relations is that one-on-one communication is the most effective communication *if* the two parties share experiences or know one another. The more you know about the person with whom you want to communicate, the more likely you are to have a personal communication experience.

Six Levels of Communication

Communication takes place on six levels or within six different contexts (see Table 9.1):

- intrapersonal
- interpersonal
- small group
- organizational
- face-to-face public communication
- mediated mass communication

Intrapersonal communication is *the thought process we use to communicate with ourselves—one individual talking to himself.* This is the way you reason, ponder, and make decisions. **Interpersonal communication** *takes place between two or three people.* This level or context of communication is the most effective.

Small-group communication is much less powerful than an interpersonal experience. *Group contexts can be as small as a business or committee meetings or as large as board or club meetings.* There is a shared experience, but it is mitigated by many variables such as who is in attendance, how active the participants are in engaging the communication and how large the group gets. **Organizational communication** *takes place within a system of individuals who work together to achieve a set of stated goals.*

BRIEF CASE STUDY

American Humane Society Refreshes Brand

Nonprofits often have a difficult time keeping their causes and profiles in the news, as the news agenda changes constantly. The American Humane Association (AHA) is one of the nation's oldest nonprofits and at the ripe, old age of 130, the organization engaged in strategic planning to revive its image and to meet a major communication challenge. While the AHA is the "foremost expert on preventing cruelty to children and animals," it is often confused with the local pet humane societies.

The association launched its "Advancing Humanity" campaign to realign the organization internally, to revamp its public image, and to raise awareness and funds. Aside from a new brochure celebrating its anniversary and a well-honed elevator speech (a short and snappy description) about the association, the AHA conducted research that resulted in an updated look and feel, including a new logo that connotes "passion and protection." The association's communication team rebranded two of its signature programs and joined forces with a media relations agency that helped the AHA demonstrate its role of expert during news events connected to animal cruelty such as the Michael Vick dog fighting case, natural disasters, and the release of the movie *Evan Almighty*.

AHA sought partnerships with businesses that could help them raise funds while demonstrating their own concern for animal cruelty. These partnerships were good for business and the organization. The association launched a program with dog-food manufacturer Pedigree that allowed the company to gain prestige from aligning itself with the association while driving consumers to both organizations' websites. Pedigree matched a level of the donations received, and the AHA raised more than $1.6 million. Another company, Eggland's Best, joined the AHA in its humane certification program, which ensures humane treatment of food animals, helping to increase its corporate donations by 600 percent in 2007. The AHA communication team won the *PRWeek* 2008 Nonprofit Team of the Year award.

An example of the AHA's "Advancing Humanity" campaign

Courtesy of American Humane Association

Working the Case

1. What theories above apply to the media relations portion of the case?
2. Discuss the business partnerships AHA engaged and the success of the programs using the theories described in this chapter.

This communication is formalized and hierarchical. **Face-to-face public communication** *usually involves a speaker and a live audience such as a speaker delivering a formal speech, a rally, or a concert presentation.*

As you can see, the larger the group, the less likely the communication is to be a personal one. In **mediated mass communication,** *a sender attempts to communicate with a very large audience of receivers through a mass medium.* This is, of course, the least personal of all the levels of communication, as the audiences are millions of people who are not located in the same place and are sometimes in different time zones. To add to the complexity of communicating in this context, the communicator is usually a group of people who develop the communication, and yet another group of people operate a mass medium employed to reach the intended audience.

Table **9.1**	Communication Contexts and Characteristics
Intrapersonal Communication	• An individual talking to himself • Used to reason, ponder, make decisions • Not relevant within public relations communication context
Interpersonal Communication	• Range from one to three people • Focused context; maximal number of sensory channels • Strong impact of nonverbal acts; strong impact on the nature of the communication, providing intentional and unintentional feedback • Little need to prepackage messages • Relatively spontaneous content, allowing interruptions, changes in focus, etc. • Formal or informal roles for speaker and listener • Absence of participants' clearly defined purposes and goals typical
Small-Group Communication	• At least three people • Speaker choice of whom to address in the group • Nonverbal acts possible, providing intentional and unintentional feedback • Possibility for prepackaged messages • Content less spontaneous • Leaders may emerge • Typically, clearly defined goals and purposes • Formal or information roles for speaker and listener
Organizational Communication	• Larger numbers of people • Hierarchical • Limited to nonexistent opportunities for nonverbal acts, requiring more formal and less spontaneous systems for feedback • Feedback less spontaneous and direct—more structured • Highly goal oriented • Roles formalized
Face-to-Face Public Communication	• Speaker to a large number of people at once • Feedback often nonverbal • Structured and planned in advance • Messages prepackaged, not individually tailored • Formal roles
Mediated Mass Communication	• Speaker to millions of people • No direct contact with the audience; speaker transmits message using mechanical or electronic medium • No immediate feedback • No nonverbal cues • Audience consumer of the message • Careful planning and production of a message • Roles highly defined

Awareness and Retention Model

The Shannon and Weaver (1949) model attempts to illustrate the communication process. It was originally developed by Shannon as a new science of information theory with a model that charted the communication process. Intended initially as a model for telephone transmission, it is centered on the message and not the communicators. As a result it illustrates clearly why people have difficulty understanding others. As outlined in Figure 9.1, the source encodes or transmits a message that travels along a channel until it reaches its destination, where it is decoded by a receiver. Any feature not intended by the sender but inadvertently included in the message is noise. Of course, the goal of communication is the transfer of a message from source to receiver with as little noise as possible. Think of it in this way: You call your friend on your cell phone as you are headed through the city in your car to a meeting, forgetting you have the windows down because the weather is great. Your friend answers and you begin talking nonstop. After you finish your introductory monologue, your friend says, "I didn't hear a word you said. Are you in a wind tunnel?"

The extent to which the message retains its integrity at various points along the channel is called **fidelity.** The model works the same way whether the source is a person or a radio because it illustrates the communication process as linear and sequential. That is, the message flows along the channel in a straight line from sender to receiver. If there is interference, the system stops. The result of the model is to depict communication as a process composed of material objects with the message as a "thing" traveling between sender and receiver and separate and apart from them. The communicative response of the receiver is caused by the sender's ability to construct a message and the channel's ability to carry it. But as a strategic PR practitioner, you know that things happen along the way and messages are not always received as you perceive they are. For one thing, human factors can get in the way. This model accounts very little for the human or psychological factors involved in the communication process.

Psychological Perspective

The psychological perspective recognizes that messages do not exist outside the human mind and suggests that any information processed by the human mind is a message. Communication, then, takes place within mental processes of senders and receivers. This perspective sees human beings as organisms who actively seek out and process incoming stimuli and whose behaviors are the result of learned responses.

Figure 9.1

Shannon and Weaver's Model of Communication

SOURCE: Adapted from Shannon, Claude E. and Weaver, Warren (1949)

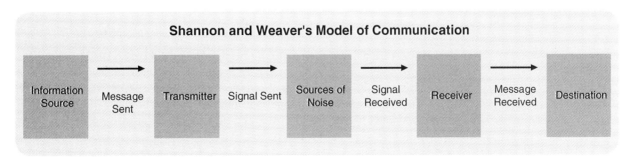

Shannon and Weaver's Model of Communication

In the end, meaning is something "invented," "assigned," "given" rather than something "received" (Barnlund, 1970). People can selectively attend to incoming stimuli and can choose future responses on the basis of both past experience and anticipation of the future. Different responses lead to different consequences, and individuals are simultaneously sender, receiver, channel, message stimuli, internalized responses, and noise. Therefore, human communication is a continuous production and reception of stimuli added to and selected from that which is available in the informational environment.

MEDIATED MASS COMMUNICATION

Mass communication theories explaining the process of communication have evolved during the decades. Scholars in the 1920s became alarmed at what they saw as the impending power of mass media and the effects they could have on society. Their image was that of a hypodermic needle or a magic bullet. The hypodermic needle image suggested that the communicator can simply inject the information into the intended receiver. Similarly misguided, the **magic bullet theory** *proposed that audiences were all submissive and inclined to be affected equally by media messages.*

The media were thought to have the ability to shape public opinion to the extent that they could encourage everyone to think or act as the messenger suggested. Early thinking was that messages were like magic bullets: they struck all members of the audience equally and created uniform effects among them. The underlying premise was that the mass media were so influential that they could manipulate public opinion and American policy. While scholars and practitioners have discounted these theories of *powerful effects,* many public relations campaigns and messages are nonetheless based on a one-size-fits-all theory. This is the mistake made by practitioners who want to educate the "general public" about an important issue, say, a safety issue. Drowning is the second-leading cause of unintentional injury-related deaths for ages 1 to 14. But children under 5 years old drown in many places other than swimming pools. They drown in bathtubs, cleaning buckets, and toilets. And 70 percent of preschoolers drown while in the care of both parents. All of these are important statistics and provide opportunities to discuss prevention, but they will not equally motivate parents, grandparents, caregivers, and other relatives to take preventive steps. Instead, communication is a very intricate and complex process during which many variables such as perceptions, experiences, interference, mediator, influencers affect the success of the communication. As a PR practitioner, you must use knowledge of these variables to interact with audiences more relevantly and to make messages significant and meaningful.

Resonance and Meaning

Renowned mass media scholar and practitioner Tony Schwartz (1973) suggests a **resonance theory** *in which the function of a communicator is to achieve a state of resonance with an audience receiving electronically mediated stimuli* (from TV, radio, or audio). Communicators must present stimuli so that it resonates with information the audience already has stored and thus the new information instigates the desired behavior. Messages must be relevant to resonate.

According to Schwartz, "Resonance takes place when stimuli put into our communication evoke meaning in a listener or viewer" (p. 25). In the resonance theory, the meaning of communication lies with what a person extracts from her previous experience as a result of communication stimuli. Therefore, communicators must understand the types of information and experiences their audiences have stored.

Schwartz argues that the resonance principle is important because communicators and their audiences store similar experiences as a result of a shared media environment. He also suggests that communicators attempt to elicit stored information from audiences in a patterned way instead of directing information into them.

Mass Media and PR Practice

Because the mass media are important to many strategic media relations strategies, the concept of **gatekeeping** is very important to you as a PR practitioner. Scholars such as Lewin (1947) and White (1964) explained it as *the process by which editors, reporters, and producers decide whether or not a news story has potential for coverage, reporting, and eventually publishing or broadcasting.* Public relations products such as news releases have to pass through a series of *gates* kept by editorial staffs that decide the fate of a potential news story.

INFORMATION CAMPAIGN THEORY

Scholars observe and analyze the success and failure of information campaigns in an effort to help the field improve its scholarship and practice. You will note that the following scholars underscored the need to conduct research and to attempt to understand key audiences.

Five Obstacles to Successful Campaigns

While exploring why campaigns succeed and fail, Hyman and Sheatsley (1947) provided five obstacles to campaign success. First, a portion of a population, the chronic "know-nothings," lacks knowledge of particular events. This segment of the population, they theorized, is harder to reach regardless of the level or nature of the information. A second obstacle to the successful information campaign lies with a fact that a gain in information does not guarantee that attitudes will change correspondingly. People interested in the issue are going to respond to the message, while disinterested people will remain apathetic. Therefore, researchers must determine who those disinterested people are and what is the best way to reach them. In accordance with the third factor, selective exposure produced by prior attitudes affects an audience's inclination to attend to messages that are congruous with their beliefs. The fourth factor, selective interpretation following exposure, assumes that people interpret information campaign messages based on their prior attitudes and beliefs. The last factor impeding success of information campaign is differential changes in attitudes after exposure. People change attitudes in light of their prior beliefs. Hyman and Sheatsley suggest that because these factors exist, research is essential in the design of information campaigns.

Working with Researchers to Help Reach Audiences

Mendelsohn's (1973) campaign research findings emphasized the importance of collaboration between researchers and communicators. He believed that communication professionals should work in collaboration with social scientists toward carefully planned goals in order to create more effective information campaigns. Social science principles help target specific audiences, thereby vastly improving the quality and effectiveness of communication efforts. Public information campaigns have relatively high success potentials based on three suggested effectiveness inputs. First, success potential improves when campaigns are planned around the assumptions that most of the audiences to which they will be addressed will be either only mildly interested or not at all interested in what is communicated. Let's apply Mendelsohn's research to the example discussed in Chapter 4 about the Department of Health and Human Services wanting to engage the American public's interest in preparing for a pandemic influenza.

Mendelsohn suggested that it is imperative to create innovative approaches to reaching and getting the attention of target audiences. Second, middle-range goals, which can be reasonably achieved as a consequence of exposure, are set as specific objectives. Within the context of preparing for pandemic flu, perhaps an objective to get all Americans to prepare for it is too extreme. A more moderate objective would be to get all public school administrators to prepare. Third, careful consideration must be given to delineating specific target audiences in terms of demographic and psychological attributes, lifestyles, values and belief systems, and mass media habits. He suggested the use of social science research in combination with communication research as a way of determining the needs and appeals of the target audience. Of course, this means segmenting audiences and perhaps getting those segments to prepare for pandemic influenza based on what we know and understand about them. Mendelsohn contended that the major task facing the communicator is to recognize, understand, and attempt to overcome audience apathy. He also argued that in addition to evaluating what did not work, it is important to also evaluate what did work in communication campaigns.

James Grunig (1989) also argued that information campaigns can succeed only when specific conditions are met. He contended that perhaps the most important of these conditions is the requirement that campaigns be directed to carefully selected segments of the mass audience. He suggested that segmentation of audiences is crucial to the success of an information campaign—and to understanding the effects of mass media. He suggested that segments must be "definable, mutually exclusive, measurable, accessible, pertinent to an organization's mission, reachable with communication in an affordable way, and large enough to be substantial and to service economically."

THEORY ON THE EFFECTIVE PRACTICE OF PUBLIC RELATIONS

We explained earlier that communication is used to entertain, inform, persuade, and teach. These are most certainly the roles mass communication performs around the world. Public relations is one of those things the mass media communicate.

Four Models of Public Relations/ Communication Campaigns

Grunig and Hunt (1984) developed theoretical models to explain public relations practice.

1. **Press Agent Model:** *One-way communication during which the organization tells the audience what it wants it to believe.* The organization has conducted little to no research to determine the audience's needs, interests, or inclinations to agree to the organization's objectives. This is very much a lose–lose model.
2. **Public Information Model:** *A journalistic approach to public relations, offers information about an organization that was truthful and accurate but usually left out damaging or harmful information about the organization.*
3. **Two-Way Asymmetrical Model:** Made popular by Edward Bernays, who had an appreciation for social science research, this model ran short of the ideal for public relations/communication campaigns. This model *emphasizes a change in behavior of audiences only in accord with the objectives and goals of the organization.*
4. **Two-Way Symmetrical Model:** *Uses research to better understand the target audience and resolution of disputes.* Both the organization and the target audience want to further their own interests within the win–win zone.

Public Relations Role in Organizations

David Dozier, Larissa Grunig, and James Grunig conducted a study on excellence in public relations and communication management in 1995 that was the basis for a new model of symmetry and two-way communication. They found that in 321 organizations in three countries, the most effective public relations practices employed both two-way symmetrical and two-way asymmetrical models resulting in the

| Table **9.2** | Characteristics of the Grunig and Hunt Model |

Direction of Communication
- One way
- Two way

Balance of Intended Effects
- Asymmetrical
- Symmetrical

Press Agency Publicity Model
- One-way transfer of information
- No feedback
- Little or no research
- Information is not always accurate
- "All publicity is good publicity"

Public Information Model
- One-way transfer of information
- Some evaluation on effectiveness

- Little or no research on audience
- Used most often by government
- Truthful and accurate information

Two-Way Asymmetrical Model
- Scientific persuasion model
- Two-way transfer of information
- Research is done to persuade the audience
- Spin message to persuade
- Model is tilted in favor of the organization

Two-Way Symmetrical Model
- Behavior change occurs in both sides
- Research is done to understand, not manipulate, the audience
- Tools include, bargaining, negotiation, and compromise
- Best model of communication

SOURCE: *Managing Public Relations.* Grunig, J. E. and Hunt, 1984, New York: Holt, Rinehart, and Winston "the new model of symmetry as two-way practice." The researchers observed that in the best practices, organizations and their outside constituencies sought to persuade each other in public relations situations. The model depicts audiences linearly at opposite ends of a band, where they are clearly asymmetrical, with the organization attempting to force the public to accept the organization's position, or clearly cooperative, with the public trying to force the organization to accept the public's position. Symmetry is depicted in the center as a win–win zone where the two meet and agree so that both sides accept the outcome.

PR's Management Role

Grunig's 1992 excellence research defined four broad roles for communicators, three of which deal with impacting an organization's practice and communication approaches through some degree of a managerial role. At one end is the role of *expert prescriber,* who autonomously manages communication for an organization. While this is a strategic role for the communicator, it separates communication decision making from program decision making. The *communication technician* role at the opposite end of the spectrum also separates communication from program decisions, as it is where tactics and tactical skills are the key strength of the communicator and there is minimal program or management decision making.

The other two public relations practitioner roles are sandwiched between prescriber and technician. The *communication facilitator* has little to no program decision making, while the *problem-solving facilitator* draws on the strengths of the other three, as it is a strategic role, but requires strong technical skills and focuses on organizational goals while considering communication and relationships with audiences.

Behavior Change as a PR Effect

One of the most respected public relations professionals in the United States, Patrick Jackson, contributed many theories to the public relations field, and he believed the most important effect is behavior change. He is probably best known for his five-step process to generate behavior change:

1. Building awareness for the audience through communication (e.g., publicity, advertising, face-to-face communication)
2. Developing a latent readiness, an inclination to make the change, during which public opinion begins to form
3. Creating a triggering event—either natural or planned—that draws public attention and triggers a desire to change
4. Taking advantage of an intermediate behavior during which an individual begins to investigate the new behavior
5. Changing behavior, adopting the new behavior

PERSUASION STRATEGY

Understanding the psychology and persuasion theory applicable to the field is crucial. It represents the conceptual foundations that help you to understand the underpinnings of successful public relations strategy.

Influencing People

Social psychologist Robert B. Cialdini (2001) has written extensively about persuasion and marketing. He spent three years "undercover" applying for jobs and training at used car dealerships, fundraising organizations, and telemarketing firms in order to observe persuasion in action. He defines the following six "weapons of influence":

- **Reciprocation** acknowledges that people are inclined to return a favor, giving power to persuasion through the use of free samples.
- **Commitment and Consistency** results in a behavior that is in concert with **cognitive dissonance theory.** *When people agree to make a commitment to a goal or idea, they are likely to honor that commitment. And if an incentive or motivation is eliminated after they agree, they continue to honor the agreement.*
- **Social Validation** or conformity explains that people do things that they see other people are doing. During one of the Cialdini experiments, traffic was brought to a halt by the number of people who looked up at the sky as a result of the accomplices who were looking up.
- **Authority** figures can get people to obey or perform acts, even if the acts are objectionable.
- **Liking** is a concept many people would like to discount, but it is a very powerful factor in persuasion. People are easily persuaded by other people whom they like, especially if the person is physically attractive or they perceive the person as like themselves.
- **Perceived Scarcity** generates demand among audiences because limited supply or offers for a limited time encourage sales.

Another scholar, Forsdale (1981), researched the role of individual complexity and perceptions. He suggested that every person uses three selective processes to "metabolize" information—selective attention, selective perception, and selective memory. *Selective attention* assumes that a person hears and perceives messages that are relevant to his needs and interests. *Selective perception* describes the tendency that people have for perceiving communication that is salient with their beliefs and assumptions. *Selective memory,* the last process, assumes that people remember things that are relevant to their schema of the world.

Persuasion and Perceived Needs

Vance Packard (1946) discussed eight hidden psychological needs exploited by marketers—emotional security, reassurance of worth, ego gratification, creative outlets, love objects, sense of power, sense of roots, and immortality.

Some products can be sold using an appeal to the need of *emotional security* (e.g., a freezer represents food in the house and food, in turn, represents safety). The second need, *reassurance of worth,* can be capitalized upon when a product is targeted to a particular audience (e.g., doctors, stay-at-home mothers). The product should be positioned so that this audience's self-image is enhanced and reinforced. The next need merchandised is *ego-gratification*. An audience should feel important (e.g., if you are selling machinery, show the consumer operating the machinery as its master).

The fourth need to be sold is *creative outlets*. Marketers can improve sales by urging the prospective customer to add his creative touch. The fifth need merchandisers sell is *love objects* (p. 67), such as the need for long, deep, and sustaining love relationships or love of brother. Exploitation of another need, *personal extension of power,* can increase gasoline sales by using two words: TOTAL POWER. Sales of a product

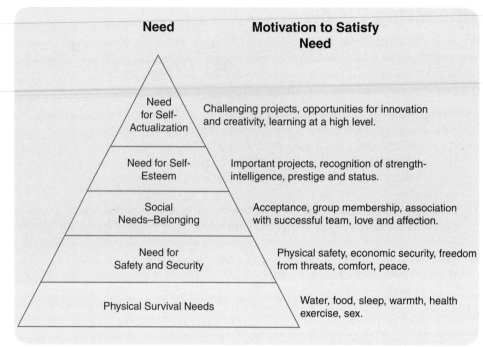

Figure 9.2

Maslow's Hierarchy of Needs

SOURCE: Maslow, Abraham, 1954, *Motivation and Personality*, New York: Harper, p. 236

can skyrocket if marketers sell the seventh need—as a *sense of roots*, an appeal to "the good old days." The final need Packard discusses is *immortality*; selling this need can help, for example, increase sales of life insurance. Packard states that exploiting the previously described needs will help merchandisers increase sales.

Also in the 1940s, psychologist Abraham Maslow developed a hierarchy of needs *based on how the individual views his level of comfort with his environment*, now known as **Maslow's Hierarchy of Needs.** The hierarchy is a primer for students studying human behavior (see Figure 9.2). The needs are *basic* such as food, water, shelter, and even transportation; *security* such as physical and financial; *social* such as acceptance, friendship, love, romance, and sex; *ego* such as status, recognition, accomplishment, and fame; and *self-actualization* such as education, travel, and creative or artistic development.

Persuasion and Words

Hugh Rank (1976) studied persuasion techniques in political speeches. He argued that speakers persuade by intensifying their own "good" and downplaying their own "bad." Likewise, the communicator can choose to intensify the other's bad and downplay the other's good. He observed the three most common techniques in intensifying are association, repetition, and composition. In *association*, the speaker makes a connection between an idea, person, or product and something already loved and desired by the audience. You can see this at work in product advertising that prominently display families, babies, sexual prowess, and religious or national icons. *Repetition* of the message helps the speaker to continue to make the associations and remind the listener, while *composition* pays close attention to word choice and syntax. The "Yes We Can" mantra of the 2008 Obama presidential campaign is an excellent example. Omission, diversion, and confusion are downplaying techniques. Intentionally leaving something out, changing the audience's focus, or complicating messages so that the audience is confused all redirect attention away from the real issues or circumstances.

Persuasion and Values

Steele and Redding (1962) introduce 17 cultural values shared by most Americans. They suggest that concepts of culture and of cultural values are intellectual abstractions that ". . . refer to a type of behavior that any rhetorical theoretician or critic cannot afford to ignore" (p. 91). The concept of cultural values helps communication practitioners better understand human persuasion and communication. Values introduced by Steele and Redding are puritan and pioneer morality; individualism, achievement, and success; change and progress; ethical equality; equality of opportunity; effort and optimism; efficiency, practicality, and pragmatism; rejection of authority; science and secular rationality; sociality; material comfort; qualification; external conformity; humor; generosity and "considerateness"; and finally, patriotism.

Steele and Redding present these values as an effort to portray the vital characteristics of the categories of value orientations as they are described by social scientists. The scholars caution that this is not an exhaustive list of American cultural values and that for every value they describe, there is a conflicting value. The preceding values do not represent entities on their own; rather, they apply to a group of concepts existing in American culture.

According to Steele and Redding, the concept of cultural values helps to explain audience premises. Thus, it helps communicators to improve their understanding of human persuasion.

Ajzen and Fishbein's theory of reasoned action demonstrates that the intention to perform a behavior is a function of attitudes toward engaging in the behavior and the perceived normative pressure to perform the behavior. Actually performing a behavior is a function of a person's intention to perform the behavior. In fact, attitudes don't directly predict behavior; they predict intention. And norms don't directly predict behavior; they predict intention. So, intention predicts behaviors. Depending on the behavior, attitudes may have more influence on intention when the behavior is personally relevant and not very observable such as whether you intend to brush your teeth and wash your face before bed.

Norms may have more influence on intention when the behavior is socially relevant and highly observable such as what you intend to eat in front of your date the first time you go out to dinner.

Bandura's **self-efficacy theory** proposed that people can or cannot perform the necessary behavior to change their environment. People with high self-efficacy believe they have the ability to change their environment to affect a change they desire. People with low self-efficacy believe that they are incapable of changing their environment. The mere belief in one's self can boost the chances of achieving change. *Self-efficacy is acquired and changed through four sources: 1) enactive attainments, 2) vicarious experiences, 3) verbal persuasion, and 4) physiological arousal* (Bandura, 1977).

The first source is *enactive attainments,* which means performance. Successful performance raises self-efficacy, while failures lower self-efficacy. The shift in self-efficacy will also be in proportion to the difficulty of the task. Tasks performed by one's self are more effective than ones performed in a group. In addition, failure will decrease self-efficacy more when people are sure they put forth their best effort.

Vicarious experiences enhance self-efficacy. By observing others succeed, our own self-efficacy can be raised. These vicarious events have the most impact when they are a novel experience to the viewer. Vicarious learning is more effectual when dealing with inefficacy. Watching someone of equal ability fail can have aversive effects on the watcher.

Although *verbal persuasion* has its limits, under the proper conditions it can be very effective. Belief in the persuader is paramount. If we hold no stock in the person speaking to us, we are more likely to disregard the person than listen to her. The source must be credible. In addition, the task being described must be within the listener's repertoire of behavior. It would be impossible to convince people with no gymnastic background that they could execute a double handspring on the first try. The action is not within the person's normal behavioral repertoire.

Behavior change theory (transtheoretical model) proposed by Prochaska and DiClemente (1983) *also holds that individuals pass through five stages toward adopting new behavior: precontemplation, contemplation, preparation, action, and confirmation.* This theory is widely used in social marketing programs.

At the *precontemplation stage,* a consumer is unaware of and not thinking about the behavior. If there is awareness, the consumer doesn't think it is currently appropriate for her. For the practitioner, this is the stage during which information and awareness messages are most effective.

Consumers at the *contemplation stage* are aware and are actually thinking about the behavior. Here consumers may be evaluating the behavior for themselves. At this stage, the practitioners should tout heavily the benefits of the desired action and, if appropriate, look for ways to apply social pressure through messages.

At the *preparation stage,* consumers have made a decision to take the action and are planning and preparing. This is the point at which the practitioners should develop messages that minimize the perceived barriers to the action because this is the stage at which many consumers stop in the progression.

At the *action stage* the individual is doing the action for the first time or returning to the action. This is the stage at which positive reinforcement is crucial because the consumer may find the experience a positive or negative one and need encouragement.

Confirmation is the final stage of the model. Here the consumer is committed to the behavior or product and has no intention of reverting to previous behavior. This stage requires continued reinforcement and tips for maintaining the action.

The chart in Table 9.3 delineates the five stages just described, the characteristics of each stage, and the communication techniques appropriate for audiences at each stage. It includes an additional stage for relapse in behavior.

Theory for Reaching Audiences

It is clear from the theory we have reviewed thus far that audience behavior is crucial to planning and implementing successful strategic public relations programs and campaigns. While we know that mass media are channels for reaching some of our audiences, we know that not everyone uses the mass media in the same way or at the same time. More and more, individuals decide how and when they want to consume newspapers, magazines, radio, television, and the Internet. Some communication techniques bring information to audiences' doorsteps or driveways or via email and still the flyers, weeklies, or emails are completely ignored. This selective process is part of **uses and gratifications theory** which *looks at why consumers use media and for what purposes.* We know that our audiences are active users of media and, at the same time, are selective in the media they employ. As a strategic practitioner, recognize that one size does not fit all and in order to be successful in reaching your audiences, you have to know their habits. Just because you have a message to deliver does not mean

Table **9.3**	Stages of Change Model	
Stage of Change	**Characteristics**	**Communication Techniques**
Precontemplation	• Not currently considering change: "Ignorance is bliss"	• Validate lack of readiness • Clarify: decision is theirs • Encourage reevaluation of current behavior • Encourage self-exploration, not action • Explain and personalize the risk
Contemplation	• Ambivalent about change: "Sitting on the fence" • Not considering change within the next month	• Validate lack of readiness • Clarify: decision is theirs • Encourage evaluation of pros and cons of behavior change • Identify and promote new, positive outcome expectations
Preparation	• Some experience with change and are trying to change: "Testing the waters" • Planning to act within 1 month	• Identify and assist in problem solving regarding obstacles • Help identify social support • Verify that audience has underlying skills for behavior change • Encourage small initial steps
Action	• Practicing new behavior for 3–6 months	• Focus on restructuring cues and social support • Bolster self-efficacy for dealing with obstacles • Combat feelings of loss and reiterate long-term benefits
Confirmation and maintenance	• Continued commitment to sustaining new behavior Post–6 months to 5 years	• Plan for follow-up support • Reinforce internal rewards • Discuss coping with relapse
Relapse	• Resumption of old behaviors: "Fall from grace"	• Evaluate trigger for relapse • Reassess motivation and barriers • Plan stronger coping strategies

SOURCE: Prochaska and DiClemente, "Stages of Change in the Modification of Problem Behaviors." In Hersen, Eisler, Miller (Eds) *Progress in Behavior Modification,* Sycamore Press, 1992

everyone will hear or attend to it. You should also know that audiences are not monolithic and will select and interpret according to their own perceptions and experience.

Sociologist Joseph Klapper's idea is that if media have any impact at all, it is in the direction of reinforcement. His theory is basically in agreement with the uses and gratification theory, as media is not seen as being all-powerful. And he acknowledged many influences upon audiences, of which the media was only one.

Also crucial to reaching your audiences is understanding how innovations or changes in behavior progress through the population from which audiences are selected. Everett Rogers' (1983) **diffusion of innovations theory** introduced still another stage model. In this case, the researcher proposed *the manner in which something new or novel moves through a population.* He suggested that with any new product or behavior, there are those who will adopt early and those who will never adopt. Given a particular innovation, there are those who will accept a new idea, product, or behavior as members of the following groups: innovators, early adopters, early majority adopters, late majority adopters, and laggards. This model suggested that those in the early stages have made decisions to adopt or buy but the latter groups are the more difficult. The late majority adopters and laggards are more easily convinced through opinion leaders and social networks. Therefore, the appropriate spokesperson is crucial to winning over this group, and word-of-mouth marketing is an effective tactic.

Identified by the American psychologist Hovland and Lumsdaine and Sheffield (1949), there can be a **sleeper effect** of a message sent to an audience. This effect occurs *when a message has more impact on attitude change after a long delay than when the message is first heard*.

This theory was devised to describe the latent impact that a mass communication or propaganda message can have on its audience. The attitude change produced by the message is frequently not detectable until a period of time has passed, hence the term *sleeper effect*. As time passes, the persuasion may increase and the connection to the source of the messages weakens. The audience may forget the source but remember the message.

Messages from low-credibility sources (such as a politician) usually have limited impact because of the source's low credibility. But studies show that this can grow over time and can have a delayed effect. The reason is that as time passes, your mind begins to disassociate the information from its source. It's not that you can't remember where the information came from, but the two things (the information and the source) are not kept together in your mind. The message becomes separated from the source in mind of the receiver. So any feeling of "contamination" associated with the information lessens over time. Two variables make it more likely the sleeper effect will occur—a strong persuasive argument and a *discounting cue*—something that makes the listener doubt the accuracy of the message. After enough time passes, the discounting cue and the message become disassociated.

The increasing prominence of negative advertising in election campaigns is driving renewed interest in the sleeper effect. The sleeper effect appears to be a key ingredient in why negative advertising is so effective (Lariscy & Tinkam 1999): "The initial perception that the assailant has low credibility has only a temporary suppressive impact on the effectiveness of the attack ad." However, its impact can emerge over time. When politicians are attacked, they have no choice but to counter-attack, even if there is no immediate impact evident in the opinion polls, sometimes draw greater attention to the original attack. But the first law of political advertising is, once you get punched, you punch back. The best strategy is an explicit rebuttal strategy that calls into question the credibility of the attacker—ads that counter the attack and remind people of the low credibility of the information source. This cycle needs to be kept going, otherwise the sleeper effect could reemerge.

Funkhouser and Shaw (1990) argued that electronic and electric media (such as motion picture, television, and computer) create "synthetic experiences," those that come through the medium and not reality but which shape the audience's perception and interpretation of the depicted physical and social reality.

"Synthetic experiences" are events that occur outside of our sensory capabilities (e.g., seeing a TV ad for flower seeds or televised pro football game). Synthetic experiences are achieved by using background music, instant replay, zooming, and many other techniques. The crucial distinction between real and synthetic experiences is whether a person perceives and stores synthetic experiences as real ones as opposed to an ". . . authentic experiences of viewing unreal depictions" (Funkhouser & Shaw, 1990, p. 27).

Funkhouser and Shaw suggested that there are five reasons that can help explain the prevalence of synthetic experiences in contemporary American life. These reasons are, first, low tolerance for boredom or inactivity; second, heightened expectations of perfection and of high-level performance; third, expectations of quick, effective, neat resolutions of problems; fourth, misperceptions of certain classes of physical and social events, and finally, limited contact with, and a superficial view of, one's own inhabited environment.

Funkhouser and Shaw maintained that mass media, by using synthetic experiences, are able not only to influence audience's opinions on issues but also are capable of distorting cultural world views by presenting images suited to their agendas.

PUBLIC OPINION AND MASS COMMUNICATION THEORY

Noelle-Neumann (1974) introduced the **spiral-of-silence concept theory,** *which implies that the opinion of the majority will dominate and eventually silence the opinion of the minority because nonconformity threatens the minority with isolation.* She argues that the concept is essential in the study of the influence of the mass media on public opinion. Noelle-Neumann maintained that mass media create public opinion by providing the environmental pressure to which people respond with alertness, compliance, or silence.

Davison (1983) presented a concept of the third-person effect. He argued that individuals perceive mass media's persuasive communication as having more influence on other people than on themselves. He also suggested that sometimes such communication elicits action from people not targeted by the message because they think it will affect others.

Davison (1983) supported Noelle-Neumann's spiral-of-silence theory by suggesting that the third person effect concept is involved in that theory. He argued that individuals tend to conform to what they perceive to be the opinion of the majority because they exaggerate the mass media's ability to persuade other people. Davison suggested that such behavior can be explained by the following train of thought: "I don't find much difference between the parties, but the fact that others seem to be persuaded by the arguments or image of Party A probably means that this is the better party" (p.13).

Both Noelle-Neumann (1974) and Davison (1973) emphasized the importance of the mass media role in shaping people's opinions and maintained that this role should not be overlooked in further studies of the subject.

Larson (1994) introduced the quadrant model of cognitive consonance and cognitive dissonance, which applies to a variety of persuasive situations. *Consonance* is a state of psychological equilibrium that is reinforced by situations and circumstances that make people feel comfortable. Persuaders use consonance to reinforce desired behaviors and attitudes. Conversely, they use *dissonance*, a state of psychological imbalance, to plant a question and solicit a change in human behavior as a response to this question. Two quadrants of the model depict persuasion that relies on dissonance and the other two depict persuasion that relies on consonance. The model describes the kind and amount of experienced psychological comfort or discomfort and the dynamics of dissonance and consonance. The application of the model ranges from voting behavior to switching product brands.

Larson also described psychological sources of dissonance and consonance targeted by persuaders. Sources of dissonance are loss of group prestige, economic loss, loss of personal prestige, uncertainty of prediction (fear of unknown), and finally sense of guilt (related to human fear of losing self-respect). Larson named reassurance of security, demonstration of predictability, and use of rewards as sources of consonance. People want to be secure in all areas, from social interactions to making secure investments. Human beings want to know that the world functions in predictable ways. Lastly, persuaders try to make people feel good about themselves in order to elicit desired actions.

Larson presented the model and discusses sources of dissonance and consonance because it is important to realize what puts people in the state of imbalance and makes them susceptible to persuasion.

Robert Entman (1993) argued that salience and selection are essential elements of framing. *Salience* refers to making a piece of information more noticeable, meaningful, or memorable to audiences. He argued that framing is selecting particular aspects of a perceived reality and making them more important in the message "to promote a particular problem definition, casual interpretation, moral evaluation, and or treatment recommendation for the item described" (p. 52). Within the communication process, frames are found with the communicator, the text, the receiver, and the culture. Textual frames are apparent by the presence or absence of certain key words or phrases, stereotyped images, or sources of information that present a collection of facts or opinions in support of the message.

An increase in salience, according to Entman, increases the likelihood that the audience receives the message, perceives it, understands and processes the intended meaning, and remembers it. The public practitioner can increase salience by using repetition and appropriate placement of the text.

Another example of psychological perspective research has focused on the study of news content and the process by which public learning about the world is influenced by mass media news coverage. That is, to what extent does the content individuals read in the newspapers and watch on the television news affect their world view? This research tradition, referred to as **agenda setting theory,** was inspired by the writings of Walter Lippmann (1922), who proposed that *the news media created the "pictures in our heads," providing a view of the world beyond people's limited day-to-day experiences.* The basic hypothesis in such research is that there will be a positive relationship between media coverage of issues and what issues people regard as being important. In the 1960s, researchers extended the hypothesis by arguing that the media focus attention on specific issues, thereby suggesting what people should think, know, and have feelings about (Cohen, 1963; Lang & Lang, 1966).

In order to link mass media and public knowledge, a seminal study compared press coverage of the 1968 presidential campaign with the salience of campaign issues among a sample of undecided voters (McCombs & Shaw, 1972). Finding a significant positive correlation between voter knowledge and press coverage, the authors (Shaw & McCombs, 1977) concluded that the direction of influence was indeed from the press to the audience. McCombs and Shaw (1972) argue that mass media (print and electronic) play an important role in shaping political reality by setting the agenda for people's perceptions of a political campaign. McCombs and Shaw contend that media influence the salience of public's attitudes toward political issues.

In their study of voter perceptions during the 1968 presidential campaign, McCombs and Shaw found that voters not only acquire information about the issue but they also learn how important that issue is from the amount of space, position, and time allowed for it in the news. Voters' attitudes toward the issue were strongly correlated with the media's definition of what is important. Thus, McCombs and Shaw concluded that mass media have an agenda-setting function.

Summary and Review

What Is Theory?

- At the core, public relations practice is communication. Communication process principles and some mass communication theory are important to understanding the practice. Formal investigation is the process by which you produce theory. You predict, test, and confirm or deny. Postulating, proving, or disproving theories rely heavily on deductive and inductive reasoning.

Communication Process Theory

- Communication allows us to share ideas and experiences with other individuals, groups, and institutions, and through it we inform, teach, entertain, and persuade.
- Communication takes place on six levels or within six different *contexts*—intrapersonal, interpersonal, small group, organizational, face-to-face, and mediated mass communication.
- Public relations activities take place within five of the six communication contexts—interpersonal, small group, organizational, face-to-face public communication, and mediated mass communication.

Mediated Mass Communication

- Mass communication theories explaining the process of communication have evolved during the decades moving from the idea that audiences can be *injected* with information and made to think in a particular way.
- The process by which editors, reporters, and producers decide whether or not a news story has potential for coverage, reporting, and eventually publishing or broadcasting is gatekeeping.

Information Campaign Theory

- Early scholars sought to determine what elements or variables affected the success or failure of PR information campaigns.
- Scholars agreed that practitioners must realize that every issue does not resonate with our key audiences and research that reveals audience need and opinions is crucial.

Theory on the Effective Practice of Public Relations

- Public relations theories continue to evolve, but the four models of how public relations is practiced are an excellent starting point for understanding PR activities.

Persuasion Strategy

- Persuasion happens at all levels of communication but most often during interpersonal or face-to-face and mass media communication.
- Theories indicate that audience research is necessary in developing effective persuasive messages.

Public Opinion and Mass Communication Theory

- Many theorists have studied the effects of mass media on public opinion and audience reactions to the media they consumer.
- Also, scholars have tried to determine the agenda-setting effect of political coverage in the news media on voter opinion.

Key Terms

agenda setting theory
behavior change theory
cognitive dissonance
   theory
deductive reasoning
diffusion of innovations
   theory
face-to-face public
   communication
fidelity
gatekeeping
inductive reasoning
interpersonal
   communication

intrapersonal
   communication
magic bullet theory
Maslow's Hierarchy
   of Needs
mediated mass
   communication
organizational
   communication
press agent model
public information model
resonance theory
self-efficacy theory
sleeper effect

small-group
   communication
spiral-of-silence concept
   theory
theory
two-way asymmetrical
   model
two-way symmetrical
   model
uses and gratification
   theory

Questions for Review and Discussion

1. In the six decades that have transpired in American marketing, a lot has changed in consumerism. How would you update Maslow and Packard to reflect today's American society?

2. Cultural values exist beyond our own. If you were public relations director for an American cosmetic and skin care corporation in Japan, to what values would you attempt to appeal?

3. Given the gatekeeper role in the news media, what are the challenges to a practitioner for getting news coverage?

4. Think of a behavior you really need to change. Who is the person who could best encourage you to make that behavior change? Support your idea with a theory.

Web Links

Public Relations Society of America
www.prsa.org

Institute for Public Relations
www.instituteforpublicrelations.com

Association for Education in Journalism and Mass Communication
www.aejmc.net

Journal of Public Relations Research
www.aejmc.net/PR

Discovery and Analysis

THE FIRST STAGE OF THE STRATEGIC PROCESS

The first stage of strategic public relations practice centers on **discovery** and **analysis.** The common definitions of the terms *discover* and *analyze* provide ample insight into the purpose and activities of each step, which together lead to gaining knowledge "*through observation, study, or search*" (discovery) and then separating "*elemental parts or basic principles to determine the nature of the whole*" (analysis). While completing this stage's steps, the you should be looking at the problem or opportunity, trying to pinpoint what might be accomplished toward solving or taking advantage of it by identifying the target audience(s) and gathering background information through preliminary research. Your purpose at this step is threefold: 1) to gain knowledge of the environment, whether that's in an actual market place or the conditions/opinions that dominate an issue, 2) determine what is known about the potential target audience(s), and 3) begin to formulate questions for the formal audience research that will be conducted during the latter part of this stage of the process. While completing the steps at this stage, you will be engaged in the critical *strategic planning* that will guide the resulting program's overall development and influence the details of its campaign's management. After completing the process's initial steps, you may proceed to create the formal research plan, prepare the research instruments, conduct formal audience research, and analyze findings, re-evaluate and segment the target audience(s), prepare initial reports, and begin formulating the core message strategy (which is discussed in Chapter 11).

The real voyage of discovery consists not in seeking new landscapes but in seeing with new eyes.

—Marcel Proust,
French writer

DISCOVERY

Discovery requires varying degrees and types of research. They are covered in detail in Chapter 6. Without research, you have little if anything to analyze. That's why strategic public relations practitioners are conducting research all of the time, throughout the entire process, even before planning a specific communication effort. As a strategic practitioner, you must always have an ear to the ground, monitoring trends and learning about audiences and issues. The key is to know what people are thinking about, which issues have their attention, and how their perceptions might affect the organization or client. Eventually, this information will be useful in developing program strategy and campaign messages. Below are the steps you can take to begin the discovery process.

Identify the Problem or Opportunity

All public relations strategy begins with a clear statement of the problem or opportunity at hand. Regardless of whether the problem or opportunity appears gradually or suddenly, the problem or opportunity statement helps keep you focused on the specific communication campaign's motivating factor.

While some practitioners argue that the problem or opportunity should be self-evident, apparent to all involved, that is rarely the case. As with all things in life, perception is personal and subjective. Your view of the problem or opportunity may differ from the view of both internal and external stakeholders such as managers and community members. After the appropriate preliminary research is completed, the organization—or interested individual(s)—you should have a comprehensive view of audience influence such as behaviors, attitudes, and opinions that will need to be addressed through the campaign. Most importantly, preliminary research should tell you which specific audiences the communication campaign should target.

Write the Problem Statement

The statement of problem or opportunity is an important first step in the planning process. It should be a clear and concise written explanation of the situation and should not exceed two or three sentences. The written **problem statement** functions much like the lead of a newspaper article does for a journalist. You may recall trying to write a lead in your writing for mass media course. You sought to include *all of the crucial and summary information in the first two or three sentences of the story*. Typically, the lead attempts to answer the *who, what, when, where, why, and how* of an event. So it is with problem or opportunity statements, too.

ENGAGING ETHICS

What Would You Do?

Your boss asks you to join a chat room and to participate in discussions about clinical trials for a new vaccine offered by a competitor. Is it ethical for you to participate without disclosing your identity? Why or why not? Explain your response.

To be complete, a well-written problem or opportunity statement should accomplish the following, answering the fundamental questions just listed:

- State *who* is affected by what is happening. Be as specific as possible. Remember it is likely this group includes your target audience(s).
- Explain exactly *what* the problem or opportunity is. Be as concrete as possible in your description and don't think that anything is too obvious to include.
- Explain *when* the situation is a problem or when the opportunity occurs.
- Identify *where* the problem or opportunity is found.
- Explain *why* the problem or opportunity is important to the client or organization. Why is it important to your target audience(s)?
- Identify *how* the problem or opportunity affects the organization and its target audience(s).

Identify Success Indicators

After writing a problem statement, you need to establish an overall goal for the program or campaign. The **goal** *states the indicators of success. It answers the question: How will we know if our work has been successful?* This step is *not* asking you to set the actionable and measurable objectives to be reached as part of the communication messages developed during the second stage of the strategic public relations process (see Chapter 11). Again, the overall goal for a PR program is established in this early stage to provide a clear picture of what a successful program or campaign will look like at its end, what it will accomplish. The overall goal for the program should be aligned with the organization's mission. The goal for the Robert Wood Johnson Foundation (RWJF) in the case below might have been *To highlight the plight of America's uninsured and garner support to help solve the problem.* This goal would be in concert with the stated mission of the foundation, which is *improving the health and health care of all Americans.* It could be argued that, in the case of the RWJF, the goal should be to ensure that all Americans have health insurance. This goal might be a good program, policy, or legislative goal (as stated above) but not a public relations goal, which, as a form of communication, is an element to help reach the goal and is more limited than the broad goal.

Identify Internal and External Resources

A public relations effort can be effective only if there are sufficient resources available to support the initiative. Two kinds of resources are available to PR practitioners: **internal resources** (*those within an organization or possessed by an interested individual*) and **external resources** (*those outside the organization or interested individual*).

Internal resources include crucial financial resources such as travel and printing budgets. However, successful PR initiatives also require many other nonfinancial resources. If an organization intends for its internal public relations team to conduct a campaign or program, there must be enough people in the department to give the effort what it will require. Support from within the organization includes nontangibles such as cooperation across functional areas and "buy-in" from the organization's leadership. You will recall from our discussion of the characteristics of public relations in Chapter 1 that support is an essential management function in any institution. While the public relations function is often to support other divisions of an organization, its input into management strategy and policy is crucial to accomplishing the mission. Managers and executives of the organization need to be briefed and kept abreast of the PR campaign or program so that they are aware of budgets, human resources, messages, and effectiveness of the overall initiative. Corporate chief executive officers and chief operating officers will be looking for a measurable return on investment (see Chapter 17) when they commit money, time, and people to an initiative. As a PR practitioner, you must be clear about how the effort will enhance and help attain the organization's mission. A preliminary meeting with other appropriate members of the management team should be the starting point for an internal project.

If an outside public relations firm or freelancer is hired to undertake the new initiative, your initial interview with the client is used to identify the problem and indicators of success and should be used to glean as much information about resources and internal and external support as possible.

Schedule Initial Meeting

An initial meeting with the client is an excellent way to garner information regarding resources and support. When you are an outside PR practitioner (a freelancer or agency practitioner hired by a client for a project), you should arrange the first meeting with the client at the client's office if at all possible. It is always wise to go to the client if you can, not only for the client's convenience but because you want to know as much about the client as possible. It gives you an opportunity to observe the organization at work, garner the general image and atmosphere, and increases the opportunities for picking up "take-away" materials that will assist you in beginning your background research and developing your campaign plan or proposal. The client is your target audience, and you are always looking for opportunities to meet client needs and to remind the client of the benefits of working with you.

The agenda for an initial client meeting should itself be strategic—planned and developed well and in concert with the client. The idea is to get as much information as possible. The initial meeting agenda would be written on the PR agency or freelancer's letterhead and might look like the sample shown in Figure 10.1.

External resources include the various *stakeholders* involved in the issue. These stakeholders fall into three categories: *supporters*, *opposition* and *competition*. Identifying the stakeholders is crucial to the success of a campaign or program, as they may be able to help you succeed or help cause your failure. Supporters can be used as partners in developing your initiative. In the Robert Wood Johnson Foundation "Cover the Uninsured Week" example, organizing a coalition of supporters was important to the campaign. RWJF was joined by 18 national organizations and foundations to raise awareness of the fact that too many Americans are living without health insurance. In 2009 the original national partners were joined by more than 200 additional organizations.

Identify Potential Target Audiences

Another main activity undertaken while completing the discovery step is identifying, preliminarily, who might be your target audience or audiences. Here, you take a stab at your best educated guess for who would be the appropriate audiences for your campaign. In some cases, you can make very good assumptions based on what you

Client Name
Initial Meeting
Date
AGENDA

    I. Introductions of Principals
   II. Discussion of the Problem or Opportunity
        Scale and magnitude of the problem/opportunity
        Areas of organization that may be affected
        Effects on internal and external audiences
        Relevant background facts and issues
  III. Discussion of Overall Goals and Mission
  IV. Discussion of Internal and External Resources
   V. What Will Success Look Like?
  VI. Next Steps toward Creating a Plan/Proposal

Figure 10.1
Sample Agenda
for Initial Meeting

discover while identifying the problem. More often than not, the audiences you identify in your educated guess need to be modified, added to or, in some cases, thrown out completely. The probability that your initial educated guess will be at least partly incorrect is the reason for conducting the formal audience research in the next stage of the process. This first-pass attempt at identifying potential audiences helps us find out if we have the right audiences and, if not, how to find them.

In the case of the Robert Wood Johnson Foundation, the initial guess was that Americans in the middle- to upper-class demographic might be the right audience to make aware of the plight of the uninsured and that increasing their awareness might help to bring the issue to the national agenda. When formal audience research was conducted, though, the findings were quite different. While the participants in the studies were very concerned about—and even had experience with—being uninsured, they were not moved to action or did not perceive there was an action to take. While in the end the American public gained awareness of the issue during the "Cover the Uninsured Week" activities, the target audiences are Washington, DC-based opinion leaders such as Congress and staff, healthcare policy experts and policy makers, news and entertainment media, national opinion leaders, local opinion leaders, and active citizens.

Gather Preliminary Data about the Problem or Opportunity

When viewed and used as exploratory for purposes of discovery and analysis, informal research has immense value. These methods can help answer questions about the client or organization as well as the problem as it is perceived, and can provide information for building a formal audience research strategy. As well, if informal research is well planned, it can provide insight into the target audience. As mentioned in Chapter 6, planned or not, informal research methods alone should not be used to develop PR programs or campaigns. However, when well-executed informal methods and formal methods are paired to help reveal a clear picture of the target audience, you are better prepared to make informed decisions that result in effective message strategy. The following informal research methods are used widely in public relations for gathering preliminary data for analysis: conversations, communication audits, news media coverage analysis, mystery shopping, literature reviews, and database searches. See Chapter 6 for an in-depth discussion of these techniques.

Gather Preliminary Data about the Audience

The previous steps lead to listing and prioritizing the relevance of what is known about each target audience, or rather our best guess of who will be our target audiences. During this step of the formative or strategic planning phase, existing and readily available data is useful and has many advantages, not the least of which is that it can be very inexpensive. There are many types of available data, but those most useful to the PR practitioner fall into two categories—demographic and psychographic. Although qualitative research helps create vivid profiles of target audiences, using the preliminary audience research tools of demographics and psychographics can be very helpful during this early stage of the process. For more information on these types of research, refer back to Chapter 6.

ANALYZE YOUR INFORMAL RESEARCH

When research begins, most practitioners are concerned with where to find enough information and data. At the end of the initial informal research process, it is likely you are asking what to do with all of the data you have accumulated and how to report it. This is where careful analysis begins and analysis requires organization. If you have conducted key informant interviews, conducted an environmental scan, or other investigation, you usually have received some information that is not useful. The first order of business is to get rid of the extraneous material. Invariably, the research process produces information that is not central to the question at hand. So you should begin by revisiting the original question(s). What were you looking for in the first place? As you look through the data, you begin analysis by synthesizing, identifying gaps, and drawing conclusions.

Identify Knowledge Gaps

Crucial to problem analysis is identifying the knowledge gaps. After you have collected all of the data from the environmental scan and other situational information, it is important to determine what is known and where more research is necessary. You can investigate case studies on situations similar to that of the existing client or organization. This research is best conducted in the library and online journals where books and scholarly journals on public relations and communication can be found. Case studies can be found on websites, too, but this type of online research is not always the most trustworthy, as the information may not have been vetted and may lack critical elements. The books and journals found in libraries and online journals have been through a rigorous publishing process that helps ensure the standard and quality of the reporting, findings, and analysis. It is also helpful to contact communication professionals who have experience in similar situations.

BRIEF CASE STUDY

The Robert Wood Johnson Foundation's "Cover the Uninsured Week"

Think of the Robert Wood Johnson Foundation's "Cover the Uninsured Week" campaign used as a Brief Case Study in Chapter 6. The foundation has as its mission "improving the health and health care of all Americans." Its "Cover the Uninsured Week" campaign has run every March since 2003 with a program goal of affordable and stable health insurance coverage for all Americans by 2010. A first attempt at a problem statement for it could have been *The U.S. Census Bureau estimates that 43 million Americans* [WHO and WHERE] *were without health insurance* [WHAT] *in 2003* [WHEN]." What's missing from this sample problem statement, however, is an explanation of *why* the problem or opportunity is important to the client or organization, *why* is it important to the target audience(s), and *how* the problem or opportunity affects the organization and its target audience(s). To be considered complete, those missing elements would have to be added.

Working the Case

1. Look on the Robert Wood Johnson Foundation, Cover the Uninsured, Let's Get America Covered, and GMMB websites to better understand the problem and campaign.
2. Complete the problem statement above by providing the *why* and *how*.

Synthesize the Data and Draw Conclusions

Synthesizing the data requires looking for trends and information that are germane to the question at hand. Here, you will be looking for consistency in the similarity of information. How often does a viewpoint on an issue emerge? Are there similarities to the media coverage and key informant perceptions? Are they completely divergent, and are the subject matter experts' views on the issue at odds with the way the news media understand and report on the issue? Why? Are there organizations with which you were envisioning a partnership that clearly have contrasting, or less than complementary views on how to address the issue?

Key to the synthesizing process is asking this author's favorite question: So what? What does this mean to the central question(s) you asked and how might it help you make decisions about where to conduct more research? In the end, you are asking, is the problem exactly what you thought? Is there a variation of the problem you envisioned? Who do you want to talk to about it and what will it profit you?

The answers to these questions and others become obvious as you begin to comb through the data, categorize them, and reflect upon them. Reflection leads to drawing conclusions. Conclusions should never be drawn without reflection. When you are in the midst of reviewing information, you are trying to make sense of it all and how it all fits. Stepping back from the data and giving the mind a minute to regroup is crucial to drawing conclusions. Also, drawing conclusions—like many PR processes—is more valid when it is not done alone. This is where colleagues with different perceptions and viewpoints can be helpful. They can help you see more clearly the information before you.

Segment the Audience

The first question to ask yourself is whether or not you really need to segment the audience. Though it is not often, you can sometimes have an audience that is homogeneous enough that you can communicate effectively using the same messages, vehicles, and openings. If segmenting audiences is necessary, you have to conduct a two-pronged process. You first identify the audiences with whom you think you want to communicate and then divide them into smaller subgroups who possess similar characteristics that determine their susceptibility to the message and that indicate they can be reached similarly. As we discussed in Chapter 6, audiences can be divided into subgroups many ways. The most obvious are the following:

- **Demographics:** Age, education, income, gender, occupation, family size, religion, marital status, cultural background, and perceived social class
- **Lifestyles:** Recreational and fitness behaviors, consumer product preferences, political activity, and lifestyle
- **Behaviors:** Knowledge, use, attitude, advocacy, practice, and perceived benefit sought of a particular thing, idea, or issue
- **Geographic:** Country, state, province, region, town, urban, suburban, rural, climate, and population

The best tool for helping you to segment your audiences is a table with columns and rows as shown in Figure 10.2. The first column should be labeled *potential audiences* and the remaining columns should be headed by what you currently guess are the significant differences of the audiences. Then, fill in the rows under differences for each potential audience.

The information you use to segment your audience will allow you to determine with whom you want to conduct research and later to develop strategies for creating messages and reaching the audience.

Brainstorm Formal Research Questions

Brainstorming can be a very rewarding process if the brainstorming sessions remain targeted on the question or problem at hand. As a problem-solving tool, **brainstorming** is *a process through which a small group of about six to eight participants develop as many solutions as possible*. The concept is that there are no wrong ideas during the brainstorming session. Participants should feel free to suggest any ideas that might help solve the problem, even if the ideas may appear to be absurd. When the participants feel have they have exhausted their ideas, they should meet for an additional short period in order to reflect and see if any additional

Figure 10.2

Audience Segmentation Table

Potential Audiences	Demographic Differences	Lifestyle Differences	Behavior Differences	Geographical Differences
1. Audience One				
2. Audience Two				
3. Audience Three				
4. Audience Four				

ideas come to mind. If not, all of the ideas should be weighed for feasibility. The group should ask the tough questions such as, do we have the human and financial capital to implement, what will be the affect of the initiative on other parts of the organization, is this within the mission? Eventually, the solutions, ideas, or questions begin to dwindle until the group has eliminated that which is not useful. Finally, they decide on how many solutions or questions seem appropriate and settle on the remaining best ideas. The results are often built on the ideas of everyone involved.

Brainstorming can be an excellent creative tool. For the purposes of developing research questions, two or three people who have cursory knowledge of the subject is just the right mix. By the time you are ready to start thinking about research questions, you may be too steeped in the background information to be as creative as possible. Having outsiders ensures there will be fresh ideas.

DEVELOPING FORMAL RESEARCH QUESTIONS

After discovering the problem or opportunity and analyzing preliminary research data, you are ready to compose and prioritize formal audience research questions. This step will assist you in creating a **research plan,** which is *central to the second stage of the strategic public relations process, program development* (Chapter 11). The key is to ask what we need and want to know about the audiences we have pinpointed. Understanding the differences between what you want to know and what you need to know will help you discipline yourself to conduct research that meets your *needs only.* Researchers can be very curious people, often, wanting to know more than is necessary in order to discover how to proceed with an effective communication strategy. So, it's fun to formulate every possible relevant question and then the key to success is to eliminate questions that do not lead to relevant answers.

Get Others' Input

At this stage of the strategic process, you should share your list of draft questions with the client exclusively for the purpose of continued brainstorming. These questions will not be the final questions because preparation of the research plan and research instruments must take place in order to complete them, but formulating research questions is difficult to do in a vacuum. You should try to involve others in the process, and revise the questions as appropriate, based on what you've decided is really important to learn. Figure 10.3 is a sample list of broad research questions.

Prioritize the Questions

Prioritizing your questions is both simple and difficult. The key is to discipline yourself and help your clients do the same. Some of the questions that made it through brainstorming and input from others are probably still not completely crucial to the problem or opportunity at hand. So the next step is getting rid of some of the questions and keeping the important ones. This can be done first individually, giving it your best try. Then, you may have to consult your client or someone on the team. But the work has to be done. Qualitative research is more susceptible to superfluous questions than quantitative research is, though both can increase the cost of the research. It is important to

1. Does our target audience know that:
There are working people who do not have healthcare insurance coverage because their employer does not offer it?
There are working people who cannot afford even the minimum and lowest cost coverage?
The uninsured don't get screenings when they use emergency rooms for care?
Children are especially vulnerable because there is no prenatal, postnatal, or well-baby care, and childhood diseases can be dangerous?
People with chronic and life-threatening diseases such as high blood pressure and diabetes do not receive medications to maintain their health?
Some families are not covered even when one member is working because family coverage is not mandatory and workers cannot afford the additional coverage?
Majority of uninsured are part-time workers, low income, low education, Hispanic?
One in 10 Americans is uninsured?

2. Does our target audience perceive:
The uninsured situation as a major issue facing the nation? Where does it rank among issues?
The uninsured situation in America as a crisis?
The uninsured as an average American?
Healthcare insurance as a right or a privilege?

3. What are our target audiences' attitudes about:
Being uninsured personally?
Helping poor children get healthcare insurance despite the costs?
Paying for healthcare for the uninsured?
The government paying for healthcare insurance for the poor? children? seniors? people with disabilities?

4. Does our audience have ideas on how to solve the problem?

5. Is our target audience willing to take an action to solve the problem?

Figure 10.3
Broad Research
Questions

guide the discussion, and outlying questions can change the tone or direction of the conversation. Also, the questions should flow logically. So, get out your red pen and narrow down the questions to cover only the scope of the work at hand.

Once you have a list of research questions that reflects your collaborators' input and is carefully prioritized so that it may serve as a solid foundation for a formal research plan, there are other questions you must ask.

BRIEF CASE STUDY

CTUW Revisited

The Robert Wood Johnson Foundation "Cover the Uninsured Week" campaign introduced in Chapter 6 is serving as a Brief Case Study for the strategic public relations process in Chapters 10, 11, 12, and 13. Let's consider the broad research questions the PR practitioners may have faced.

Working the Case

Look at the draft broad research questions posed for the Robert Wood Johnson Foundation "Cover the Uninsured Week" case. Think of them as falling into five categories as delineated above that can be expanded. Which categories of questions do you see as least relevant to the audience research in this case?

Creating a Research Plan

Because communicating effectively is your fundamental goal, you develop PR research plans based on the answers to a series of questions that help you determine what you hope to gain from the research and formulate a strategy for the research itself. The preliminary research done during the discovery and analysis steps often provides a valuable starting point for answering these key questions:

- **What do I want to accomplish for my client or organization?** This question encourages you to think about the primary reason for undertaking a communication campaign or program in the first place and provides information for a statement of the problem or opportunity at hand.
- **Who do I think I want to reach and are there subgroups of that audience?** Here you are getting to the core of the market research approach because you are doing preliminary thinking about your target audience. These answers also help develop thinking about *segmentation* and whether or not attempting to reach the entire target audience is the best strategy. **Audience segmentation** *allows you to create subgroups of a target audience.* What do you want to know about them? Thinking about this question helps formulate the design of the research study and begins the listening process.
- **What questions should be asked, have these questions been answered before, where are the answers, and how will I get them?** These questions begin your thinking about research strategy and planning. The answers here are crucial because they guide decisions about the kind or kinds of research that may be needed. First and foremost, you do not want to duplicate efforts.

The research plan is essentially an outline or *map* of the how formal audience research will proceed. Its primary purpose is to delineate the steps to be taken and why. The basic components of the research plan are the following:

- A brief statement of what you have learned about the target audience as a result of preliminary informal research
- A brief statement of the research goal that is the overarching reason for conducting the research
- A brief statement of the research objectives that delineates precisely what you expect to identify, to gauge or measure, or to determine
- A description of the approach deemed most appropriate based on what is known about the target audience, indicating the demographics (ethnicity, age, etc.) of the audiences/research participants/respondents and issues such as expected timing and length of interviews
- A listing of the types of research methods you intend to use and why
- A time line for conducting the research, explaining what research will be undertaken and when
- A delineation of the geographic locations of the research. This is crucial in outlining where you will find the type of participants you want to include in the study. When particular audiences are sought, the researcher must be careful to conduct research where they can be found geographically. It is important not to make assumptions here. Know where there is a concentration of a particular special audience and be sure the screening process gets you to the audience you want
- A listing of the deliverables to the client such as protocols/research instruments and reports and presentations of findings

Some research plans also include statements regarding risks to participants; benefits to participants; risk/benefits analysis; statement of confidentiality of the data and participant identity; and protections. The inclusion of these items depends on the client and the nature of the project for which the study is conducted. The research plan itself is a *deliverable* and should be submitted to the client both to share information and receive any necessary approvals. Figure 10.4 is a sample of a research plan.

Preparing Research Instruments

There is a lot of fun to be had at this step, but it is time to be brutally honest. If you know what you are doing as a researcher and trust your in-house research staff, let the games begin! If you hesitate in the least, it is time to hire someone to help you

Figure 10.4
Research Study Plan

Project Number: 1234567
Project Title: The North Castle Education Program Strategic Communication Study
Project Director: Lauren Warner
Agency Office: New York City

1. Target Audience Participants

The target audiences for this study are middle school students and their parents or caregivers. Our preliminary informal research indicates that parents want a tool to help them guide their children through the middle school years in order to increase their success in high school and in careers or college after graduation. Literature indicates that students become less engaged with school as they leave the primary grades and transition into high school. While indicating they want to go to college or want to have technology careers, students do not enroll in the courses that will help them meet their objectives and do not understand how to navigate the public education system to help ensure success.

2. Research Goal

The goal of the research study is to find out more information regarding students' and parents' perception and knowledge of steps involved in getting into a college or university or in gaining employment in a highly technological workplace after high school. The moderator will ask participants questions about their general perceptions and concerns about education and current schools; perceptions as to why some students are not able to enter college; and, steps involved in getting into college. A concept of a guide or checklist, outlining steps students and parents need to take to improve students' chances of entering college will be pretested during the groups and interviews.

3. Research Objectives

The objectives of the research are to delineate 1) parent perceptions about their children's readiness for college-going or the workforce; 2) parent readiness to get involved with teachers and schools to help increase the chances for success; 3) parent understanding of and readiness to use a guide to assist their interaction with teachers, schools, and their students; 4) student perceptions of what college and work force readiness means; and student understanding and readiness to use a guide to assist their navigation through middle school and beyond.

4. Research Study Methods

Qualitative research methods have been selected because the purpose of the study is to determine perceptions of actions and efficacy; attitudes; and understanding of a concept.
The following activities will be carried out as part of this study (see Table 10.1 detailing research design):

- Three focus groups with parents of eighth-grade students attending public schools (8–10 adults ages 18 and older per group). One group will be conducted at each site.
- Three focus groups of eighth-grade students attending public schools (7–8 children per group selected with parental/primary caregiver consent). One group will be conducted at each site. All student participants will have a grade of "B" or below in math and physical sciences disciplines. In New York and Los Angeles the groups will be conducted with girls, and in New Haven focus group participants will be boys.
- Twelve in-depth interviews (IDIs) with eighth-grade students attending public schools. Four interviews per each site.

Figure 10.4
(*continued*)

5. Geographic Locations and Recruit Details
The research project will take place in three cities (Los Angeles, New York, and New Haven, CT), where client projects are under way.

Table 10.1   Research Design

The North Castle Education Program Strategic Communication Study
Qualitative Research Study Design

	New York	New Haven, CT	Los Angeles
Eighth-Grade Students	X (Girls)	X (Boys)	X (Girls)
Parents of Eighth Graders	X	X	X
IDIs with Eighth Graders	4 IDIs Boys & Girls	4 IDIs Boys & Girls	4 IDIs Boys & Girls

An attempt will be made to select a sample of individuals who represent various racial and ethnic groups. For parent focus groups, the focus group facility vendor will be instructed to recruit participants who have varying levels of education (holds no more than one doctorate), and who are of different ages and genders. Students and parents will be comfortable speaking, reading, and listening in English. Research participants will be recruited using the following screening criteria:

- They either have children in the eighth grade attending public schools in the school district or are eighth-grade students attending public schools;
- They have not participated in a focus group in the last six months; and
- Parent participants are not employed by a school district, an advertising or market research agency or client.
- All student participants should be interested in pursuing college education or high technology careers.

Vendors will recruit participants from the local area using their databases and by making phone calls to potential participants. Compensation for study participation will be as follows:

- Students: $75 for participation in the focus groups and $50 for participation in an in-depth interview.
- Parents: $100

The vendor at each site has confirmed this compensation level. Given the difficulty of the recruit, vendors want to make sure that the compensation level is sufficient to ensure a productive recruiting effort and to encourage the participants to attend their scheduled sessions.

6. Consent
Participants will either provide an assent (students) or sign a consent form (parents) before beginning the focus groups/in-depth interviews. Also, any questions will be answered before beginning the focus groups/in-depth interviews. The consent and assent forms tell participants their involvement in the research is voluntary and inform them they can leave at any time or refuse to answer any questions. The forms also inform them they will be audiotaped and videotaped and describe other data to be collected and how data will be used. We will ask participants and students' parents to sign the form. We will never conduct a session without informed consent/assent from participants. Copies of the consent forms and verbal statement of assent for the child are attached.

7. Study Schedule
Los Angeles	Tuesday, February 3, 2011
New York	Tuesday, February 17, 2011
New Haven, CT	Wednesday, February 18, 2011

To accommodate participants' schedules, all research activities will take place in the evening.

8. Deliverables
The client will receive draft and final versions of the screeners, topic guides, interview guides, and concept materials for testing for approval prior to the conduct of research. Following the research, the client will receive a summary report and final research report. All reports will be delivered to the client's office during a one-hour meeting and presentation of findings.

determine how to proceed. This would include reviewing your research plan *before* it reaches your client. Some clients decide ahead of time that they want one company to conduct the research and another to develop message strategy and implement the campaign or program. Regardless, it is time to acknowledge how much you actually know about conducting research and determine if you need additional assistance from someone else or a research firm. If you engage a research company, the research team should present the protocols to you for approval. Having the research instruments or protocol reviewed and approved by the client is a very important step in the process, as it establishes that all parties have agreed to what the thrust of the research should be.

Research instruments—the actual tools used to conduct audience research—include *questionnaires, screeners,* and *moderator's discussion guides.* Preparing the research instruments begins with acknowledging the type of research we are conducting (qualitative or quantitative—see Chapter 6). Again, qualitative research often helps to inform quantitative research ideas and vice versa. Often if we have heard the why of a particular behavior or action from an audience, we want to know how many do it—that's usually when we use quantitative research methods. Similarly, if we know that many people do one behavior or not another, we want to know the how and why for the behavior; that's usually when we use qualitative research methods. Questionnaires are discussed in Chapter 6 under the heading "Quantitative Research" (page 123). The basics of preparing the other two most common research instruments, screeners and moderator discussion guides, are presented here.

Screeners

Screeners are *used to help the participant recruiting process by screening who we want for participants and screening out others.* A screening document includes instructions for what types of participants are wanted and a list of questions to be asked of the potential participant during a very brief telephone interview. The document is much like a script in that it leads the interviewer through the questions, indicating which answers may cause the conversation to be terminated and which help the interviewee remain in the running. The idea is to avoid participants who have participated in a focus group or in-depth interview recently; and who are experts such as market research, advertising, and public relations professionals or persons whose occupations deal directly with the topic of the study. If you are recruiting for focus groups, you want to recruit participants who have similar demographics (e.g., education level, income, age) so that they may feel more comfortable with expressing their views. It is also important to screen for participants who have not participated in research studies, or at least in the past six months. Figure 10.5 is a sample of a screener.

Moderator and Interviewer Guides

Moderator's topic guides and interviewer guides are similar to questionnaires used in quantitative research in that they list questions to be answered by the participants, but there is one major difference. *These guides are designed to encourage participants to talk at length and are made up of open-ended questions.* The guides also provide instruction to the in-depth interviewer or focus group moderator, providing instruction on how to discuss ground rules for the discussion and how to conduct introductions, when to probe for more discussion, when to use props or record answers on paper or a white board for participants to see, and what warm-up exercises to employ.

The guides contain the questions you brainstormed, created, and had approved by the client. Sometimes a client wants every single question asked, while others allow for some discretion by the facilitator. Highly trained facilitators know when to allow conversation to move away from the specific question because the discussion is

Figure 10.5
Screener

Focus Groups with Caucasian Parents and In-Depth Interviews (IDIS) with Caucasian Children

Hello, this is _____. I am calling from _____. We are not selling anything. We are conducting research about diversity in the media. May I please talk to a parent of a school-age child?

[If necessary, reintroduce yourself.]

We are conducting research concerning diversity issues in the media. If you are interested in helping with the project and meet certain requirements, we will invite you and possibly your child to come for a group interview at (LOCATION). It will take about two hours of your time and we will pay you $100 and your child $75 as tokens of our appreciation.

Would you and possibly your child be willing to participate in our research study?

In order to find out if you two are eligible to participate in this study, I'd like to ask you a few questions. Would you like to proceed?

PARENT SCREENER

1. Have you participated in any marketing research group or panel discussion in the past six months?

   Yes   [THANK AND TERMINATE]

   No   [CONTINUE]

2. Do you currently work or have you ever worked for any of the following organizations? [READ and RECORD]

   FedEx   [CONTINUE]

   Wal-Mart   [CONTINUE]

   Starbucks   [CONTINUE]

   Marriott   [CONTINUE]

   Client Name   [TERMINATE]

3. On average, how often would you say you watch TV?

   At least once a day   ____

   Three times a week   ____

   Once a week   ____   [THANK AND TERMINATE]

   Once in a couple of weeks ____   [THANK AND TERMINATE]

4. On average, how often would you say you watch or listen to the news?

   At least once a day   ____

   Three times a week   ____

   Once a week   ____   [THANK AND TERMINATE]

   Once in a couple of weeks ____   [THANK AND TERMINATE]

5. On average, how often would you say you read newspapers/magazines?

   At least once a day   ____

   Three times a week   ____

   Once a week   ____

   Once in a couple of weeks ____   [THANK AND TERMINATE]

(continued)

Figure 10.5

(*continued*)

6. On average, how often would you say you go to or rent movies?

At least once a week	___	
Once every couple of weeks	___	
Once a month	___	
Once every two months	___	[THANK AND TERMINATE]

7. How would you describe your ethnicity?

White	___	[RECRUIT FOR FOCUS GROUP]
African American	___	[THANK AND TERMINATE]
Latino/Hispanic	___	[THANK AND TERMINATE]
Asian American	___	[THANK AND TERMINATE]

8. [RECORD GENDER] If not obvious, ask: Please tell me, what is your gender?

Male	___
Female	___

9. What is the highest level you completed in school?

Less than high school	___
High school graduate	___
Some college	___
College graduate	___
Advanced degree	___

10. What would you say is your annual income?

Below $35,000	___
Between $36,000–$50,000	___
More than $50,000	___

11. Are you available to participate in a focus group on DATE at TIME?

NAME _____

ADDRESS_____

PHONE NUMBER_____

Now I would like to ask you a series of questions to see if your child qualifies to join us in the study.

CHILD SCREENER

1. Has your child participated in an in-depth interview in past six months? In-depth interview is a discussion between a person and a moderator.

YES	___	[THANK AND TERMINATE]
NO	___	

2. Is your child between 10 and 15 years old?

YES	___	
NO	___	[THANK AND TERMINATE]

3. Is your child currently enrolled in school?

    YES   ___

    NO   ___ [THANK AND TERMINATE]

4. What grade does your child attend?

    [RECORD THE GRADE]   ___

5. Would you please identify your child's ethnicity?

    White   ___   [RECRUIT FIVE IDIs]

    African American   ___   [THANK AND TERMINATE]

    Latino/Hispanic   ___   [THANK AND TERMINATE]

    Asian American   ___   [THANK AND TERMINATE]

6. What is your child's gender?

    Male   ___

    Female   ___

    [RECRUIT MIX FOR THE IDIs]

7. Does your child watch TV on a regular basis?

    YES   ___

    NO   ___ [THANK AND TERMINATE]

8. Would your child be available to participate in an in-depth interview on DATE at TIME at LOCATION?

NAME _____

Figure 10.5
(*continued*)

uncovering information the researchers did not anticipate. Figure 10.6 is a sample guide for a focus group and Figure 10.7 is a sample of an in-depth interview guide.

Conduct and Report the Research

Actually conducting the research involves many steps, including coordinating with research facilities and locations, checking logistics, and making sure things move smoothly. When you hire a research company to take care of these matters, the job is simpler. If you are doing this work yourself, it is important to have a checklist of all of the steps that must be taken to make this a successful effort. (See "Tips for Buying Research Services" in Chapter 6.)

If you are considering conducting quantitative research yourself instead of hiring a research company, you must consider the time and effort it will take. It is wise and not too terribly expensive to have basic quantitative research conducted for you. Of course, this depends on the extent of the population you need to sample, the types of questions you want to ask, and the type of analysis you require. Simple and straightforward quantitative research such as surveying an association's membership regarding services members might desire or determining the extent of the diversity of the membership is not complicated. But unless you are a trained researcher, and especially if you need to find correlations among variables or any number of complex analyses, let someone else sit with the data sets and agonize over the precise wording of questionnaires. It is important to the credibility of the data you intend to use and share with others.

If you are not a trained researcher, you can conduct some qualitative research if you are very careful. Qualitative research requires as much precision to conduct as quantitative research, but the analysis is not as scientific. The concerns for conducting your own qualitative research are researcher bias and the ability to find enough staff trained and experienced in interviewing and moderating. In addition to having staff to conduct the research, lists of possible participants, the quality of the screening process and the appropriate facilities for conducting the research are very important.

Figure 10.6

Focus Groups with Parents: Parents' Views on Race Moderator's Guide

A. Introduction

1. Thank you for agreeing to participate in our study.
2. Your thoughts are very important to me.
3. What we about to do is referred to as a focus group. A focus group is a small group of people who get together to discuss a particular topic. I'm here to hear your thoughts and opinions about the topics we'll be discussing.

B. Purpose

1. Today we are going to talk about parents and children relationships, the media, and race.
2. I am interested in all of your ideas, thoughts, comments, and suggestions on each subject.
3. There are no right or wrong answers. All comments—both positive and negative—are welcome. Don't worry about offending me with anything you might say. I am merely a researcher, hired to ask you questions and to carefully record your answers. You should be as open as possible with your answers.

C. Procedure

1. Our session is being recorded because I cannot take notes fast enough with pen and paper so, please allow one another to complete a thought before adding your comments. This way, your comments can be better understood.
2. If at any point you want to add to previous answer or want to make a point, please feel free to do so.
3. Do you have any questions? Let's get started.

D. Warm-up

1. Please tell me your first name and how many children you have. If you could use just one word to describe them, what would that word be?

You and your family (20 minutes)

1. How would you describe communication in your family? How open is it? How much do people speak their minds? How do people resolve conflicts?
2. What do you and your children talk about? What kinds of "stuff" do you talk about? Does he/she ask you a lot of questions about things that he/she sees in his/her life? What kind of questions does your teen ask?
3. Do you talk about events in the news, movies, etc.? When important issues are in the news, do you start conversations about the events and what happened? Or explain movie plots? Who usually initiates conversations of this sort—you or your child?
4. What are some important issues that you worry about when it comes to your children growing up?
   [Probe:] drugs, crime, AIDS. . . .
   [MODERATOR:] Make a list on the chart. Let's rate them.
   What about the war in Iraq and the downturn in the economy? What kind of thoughts/concerns/emotions did they stir up in regard to your children growing up?
   [MODERATOR: If race is not mentioned, *probe*.]
   You did not mention race or diversity issues. Is it a nonissue? Does it ever come up in your conversations with children?

E. Race

1. Where does diversity/race issue in America fall on a scale of 1 to 10 when it comes to raising your children—if 1 is low priority and 10 is high priority? What makes you say that? Why? Has the election of President Obama affected your views on race?
2. If you had to define race, how would you define it? What are some things that come to mind?
3. Do you think you or your children are colorblind? Why? If you had to define colorblind, how would you define it?
4. How would you define racism?

Figure 10.6
(*continued*)

5. Have you ever talked with your child/children about race?
6. Who initiated the conversations about race, you or your child? What prompted it?
7. What did your teen say and how did you respond?
   [Probe:] How do you respond to their questions about race? For example, if he or she asks if a person acts or does something because he/she is black or Asian or Hispanic, how do you respond?
8. What do you think your child thinks about people of other races?
   [Probe:] Why do you say that?
   Where do they get their ideas about it? What's the role of parents and families role in transmitting these ideas?
   Can you give an example of something that you have witnessed or heard that lead them the other way?
9. Would you be willing to initiate conversations about race with your children?
   [Probe:] Do you think it is appropriate to talk to children about race? Do you think your children understand/will understand what you talk about when you discuss race?
10. Do your children talk to you about events at school? Is race ever a topic?
11. Are there white (or black) teachers or administrators in your children's school(s)? How do you know this? [ONLY AFRICAN AMERICAN GROUP]

F. Campaign

1. Do you think America is ready to talk openly about race issues at home and school? Why? Why not?
2. You mentioned the economy and the election of President Obama earlier. Do you think those events have any impact on race issues or our readiness to discuss those issues? What is the impact?
3. If your children have gotten to understand and know people of other races, *who* has benefited from it and *how*? Please list.
4. What are the benefits for children to get to know and understand people of other races? What is great about it? What is unique about it? What is the essence?
5. Can you think of any things that would stand in their way, if they would like to get to know people of other races?
6. Think of your neighbor who you know well. Imagine that I'm that person. How would you convince me of benefits for children to get to know and understand people of other races?
7. Imagine I'm the neighbor who does not believe that this is such a good idea. What would be my reasons for not believing?
8. Imagine we would like to create a generation of kids who do not live their lives and make decisions based on the assumptions and stereotypes about race. How would we do it?
9. We are interested in developing messages that would focus on a way to have an open conversation about race relations in America between parents and children—similar to the "Just Say No" campaign on drugs. What do you think about this idea? *Let's do some role-playing. Half of the group will come up with the reasons for doing the campaign and the other half will come up with reasons for NOT doing the campaign. Please take 10 minutes to discuss your reasons and then we'll report out.*
   If we were to do the campaign ...
   • What should the tone of this campaign be like? (Give me words to describe it.)
   • What shouldn't it be like?
   • What do you think a realistic goal of the campaign should be? Let's brainstorm possible goals (list)
   • If you were to come up with a message for such a campaign what would it be? Think about you and your child— what would you want to say? [MODERATOR: Write down the list.]
10. Here are some ideas that other people came up with. What do you think about them?
    • *"It's cool to have friends from cultures all over the world. In our time we have an opportunity to be friends with people all over the world. You can touch people from all over the world in your back yard."*
    • *"An appreciation of different things is very important. Exposure does not hurt. It benefits everybody."*
    • *"Different is different—not bad. Our way is not the only way."*
    • *"Getting to know each other"*
    • *"We're not as different as we appear to be."*
    • *"God made us all the same on the inside."*
11. Do you have any additional thoughts or comments that you would like to share before we wrap up?

Thank you for your contribution and valuable ideas.

WARM-UP AND EXPLANATION (1 minute)

Introduction
I want to thank you for participating. I'm here to hear your thoughts and opinions about the topics we'll be discussing. I'm interested in all your ideas, thoughts, comments, and suggestions on these subjects.

There are no right or wrong answers—so your answers do not have to be the same and you shouldn't be *afraid to say what's on your mind.*

All comments—both positive and negative—are welcome. Don't worry about offending me with anything you might say. It's important that you express openly and honestly how you feel.

I. Family and Likes (5 minutes)
1. Tell me how old you are and a little about yourself or your family.
   What are some of the things you like to do in your spare time? What are some of your favorite TV shows?
2. What are some of the things that kids your age think about? And what are some of the things that worry or upset you?
3. Think about the friends you hang out with most. How are they like you? How are they different from you? [PROBE for race]

II. Race (20 minutes)
1. Are they of the same race as you? If I were a Martian and never heard of the word "race," how would you describe it to me? What are the names of some different races? How do you know your race or that someone is a member of another race? What does it mean to be a member of a race?
2. Do your parents have friends who are [to the white participant] black? [to the black participant] white? Do you hang out with people who are [to the white participant] black? [to the black participant] white? What do your parents think about your friends who are [to the white participant] black? [to black participant] white?
3. Have you and your parents ever talked about race or about white people and black people? Could you tell me about some of those conversations? Has the election of President Obama caused you and your family to talk more about race?
4. Do you ever talk about race with your friends? Do you talk differently about it with your friends as opposed to your parents?
5. At your school, how much time do people from different races spend together? [If not much, ask:] Is that okay with you?
6. How do your teachers feel about friendships between black kids and white kids?
7. At your school, how much time do people from different races spend together? If not much ask: is that okay with you?

III. The Campaign
1. We are interested in getting your ideas about getting white kids and black kids to want to like each other and want to play with each other. If you had a magic wand—and could wave it to make this happen—what kinds of things would happen? What would your parents or teachers think about it? How can parents and teachers help?
2. We are talking to kids and parents of different races because we'd like to design a campaign like the "just say no to drugs" campaign—but this campaign would try to stop racism, or to encourage kids of all races to want to get to know each other and play together. Can you think of some message for our ad (like a "just say no to drugs" message)?

Figure 10.7
Children's In-Depth Interviewer Guide

As discussed earlier, screening instruments are used to filter out participants who may in some way have experiences that would affect their participation in interviews. Appropriate facilities are crucial to conducting effective qualitative research, as confidentiality, recordings and transcripts of interviews, and efficient management of the participants and researchers while the interviews are transpiring are very important. If you choose to conduct quantitative or qualitative research for a client or your organization, invest in a good research course and a few good research primers.

If you select a research company to collect your data, thorough preliminary and final reports should be a part of the contractual agreement.

If you are writing the report, in order to report the research findings effectively, it is important to receive all qualitative data and analysis from your moderators or interviewers in a format that assists in the analysis. All moderators and interviewers should submit a summary report. The summary report should include the number of participants, trends in the opinions of the participants, the primary concerns, issues, barriers, etc. expressed by the participants, and key findings resulting from the interviews. This will assist you in writing a comprehensive report.

Reporting Research to Clients and Management

Reporting your research to the client or management is a major milestone in the planning process, called a **_Process Milestone,_** and can be a point for billing the client. Your clients have usually waited a long while to discover what their target audiences are thinking, feeling, and doing. Also, it is the point at which you may have to take a step back and regroup. While it is an important point, little is written about how research reports should be organized and presented. There are general formats for presenting academic research, and much of this work is eventually published as articles in scholarly journals. But research conducted for understanding markets and audiences are usually business products, and a very different format and presentation are used. Reports of research findings should follow a format similar to the one outlined below.

- **Cover or Title Page:** Includes the name of the study, for whom it was conducted, by whom it was conducted, and the date of the report.
- **Table of Contents:** Lists the major sections of the report. Many readers know where they want to begin reviewing the study.
- **Executive Summary:** This must be the most clearly written, concise, and organized section of the report. Many reviewers read _only_ the executive summary. It provides a summary or abstract of the entire report.
- **Background and Introduction:** This is a brief situational analysis. Much of this information can be found in the environmental scan and other background information. It explains why the research was undertaken.
- **Objectives:** States specifically what the research sought to accomplish or discover.
- **Review of Literature:** Usually found in academic reports only, this section can be useful if the topic of the research has a rich body of literature. It can set the research into context.
- **Methodology or Study Design and Execution:** Objectives: A complete explanation of the methodology, dates, and geographical locations of the research should appear in this section.
- **Summary of Key Findings:** An in-depth discussion of what the research uncovered, summarizing trends and including direct quotations from participants, is found in the section.
- **Analysis and Interpretation:** Often in qualitative research this section is included in the Summary section.
- **Recommendations:** Discusses the most important next steps in planning and should be justified clearly by the findings.
- **Appendix:** Contains a copy of all screeners, questionnaires, topic guides, consent forms, and other materials related to the research.

Reporting Research to the News Media

Although we are following our process model toward the development of communication for target audiences, it is important to note that survey research is often used by organizations to gain news media coverage. "Research for ink," as it is often called, is an excellent media relations tool. It is important to consider whether or not the research you have conducted is newsworthy. If it is, discuss its PR value with the client to decide if you want to release the findings. If so, the findings should be provided to the media relations team for developing the appropriate tactics.

Survey and research results have become ubiquitous, and editors and reporters have become cautious about reporting results. The Associated Press and other news-gathering organizations have established guidelines for reporting research results. It is wise for you to adhere to these guidelines when releasing the results of research conducted for a client or organization. The following Associated Press guidelines consist of several cautions to reporters and provide several key questions that should be answered in a story on a poll or survey.

Reporting Polls and Surveys

Stories based on public opinion polls must include the basic information for an intelligent evaluation of the results. Such stories must be carefully worded to avoid exaggerating the meaning of the poll results. Information that should be in every story based on a poll includes the answers to these questions:

1. **Who did the poll and who paid for it?** The place to start is the polling firm, media outlet, or other organization that conducted the poll. Be wary of polls paid for by candidates or interest groups. The release of poll results is often a campaign tactic or publicity ploy. Any reporting of such polls must highlight the poll's sponsor, so that readers can be aware of the potential for bias from such sponsorship.

2. **How many people were interviewed? How were they selected?** Only a poll based on a scientific, random sample of a population—in which every member of the population has a known probability of inclusion—can be used as an accurate and reliable measure of that population's opinions. Polls based on submissions to websites or calls to 900-numbers may be good entertainment but have no scientific validity. They should be avoided because the opinions come from people who select themselves to participate. If such unscientific pseudo-polls are reported for entertainment value, they must never be portrayed as accurately reflecting public opinion, and their failings must be highlighted.

3. **Who was interviewed?** A valid poll reflects only the opinions of the population that was sampled. A poll of business executives can represent only the views of businesses executives, not of all adults. Surveys conducted via the Internet—even if attempted in a random manner and not based on self-selection—face special sampling difficulties that limit how the results may be generalized, even to the population of Internet users. Many political polls are based on interviews with only registered voters, since registration is usually required for voting. Close to the election, the polls may be based only on "likely voters." If "likely voters" are used as the base, ask the pollster how that group was identified.

4. **How was the poll conducted, by telephone or some other way?** Avoid polls in which computers conduct telephone interviews using a recorded voice. Among the problems of these surveys are that they do not randomly select respondents within a household, as reliable polls do, and they cannot exclude children from polls in which adults or registered voters are the population of interest.

5. **When was the poll taken?** Opinion can change quickly, especially in response to events.

6. **What are the sampling error margins for the poll and for subgroups mentioned in the story?** The polling organization should provide sampling error margins, which are expressed as "plus or minus X percentage points," not "percent."

The margin varies inversely with sample size; the fewer people interviewed, the larger the sampling error. Although some pollsters state sampling error or even poll results to a tenth of a percentage point, that implies a greater degree of precision than is possible from a sampling; sampling error margins should be rounded to the nearest half point and poll results to the nearest full point. If the opinions of a subgroup—women, for example—are important to the story, the sampling error for that subgroup should be included. Subgroup error margins are always larger than the margin for the entire poll.

7. **What questions were asked and in what order?** Small differences in question wording can cause big differences in results. The exact question text need not be in every poll story unless it is crucial or controversial.

When writing and editing poll stories, do not exaggerate poll results. In particular, with preelection polls, these are the rules for deciding when to write that the poll finds that one candidate is leading another:

- If the difference between the candidates is more than twice the sampling error margin, then the poll says one candidate is leading.
- If the difference is less than the sampling error margin, the poll says that the race is close, that the candidates are "about even." (Do not use the term "statistical dead heat," which is inaccurate if there is any difference between the candidates; if the poll finds the candidates are tied, say they are tied.)
- If the difference is at least equal to the sampling error but no more than twice the sampling error, then one candidate can be said to be "apparently leading" or "slightly ahead" in the race.
- Comparisons with other polls are often newsworthy. Earlier poll results can show changes in public opinion. Be careful comparing polls from different polling organizations. Different poll techniques can cause differing results.
- Sampling error is not the only source of error in a poll, but it is one that can be quantified. Other potential sources of error in surveys include question wording and order, interviewer skill, and refusal to participate by respondents randomly selected for a sample.
- No matter how good the poll, no matter how wide the margin, the poll does not say one candidate will win an election. Polls can be wrong and the voters can change their minds before they cast their ballots.

Reevaluate Target Audiences

At this step, you must determine if your guess at the primary target audiences is correct. Sometimes you must adjust for what you found in our research. For example, in a campaign to increase natural lawn care in Seattle, the communicators assumed their primary target audience would be the men of households. The quantitative research indicated that the men of the household were usually responsible for the lawn care. Additional research verified that although men generally cared for the lawns, the women of the household were the driving force behind the activity. It was soon clear that the message development should target women as the primary target (influencers) and men as the secondary target audience.

The case of the "Give Swordfish a Break" campaign is another good example. Initial thinking and preliminary planning considered restaurant customers as the primary target audience for advocating a reduction in swordfish consumption. Instead, a campaign directed to chefs, encouraging them to give swordfish a break from their menus for a limited time and asking them to influence their colleagues was extremely successful.

The Robert Wood Johnson Foundation "Cover the Uninsured Week" campaign began with preliminary audience research that showed that the average middle- to upper-socioeconomic American was not very concerned about Americans who were uninsured. Because many of them had periods during which they were uninsured or were very familiar with others who had limited periods without health insurance, they were clearly not going to be the primary target audience. So, a campaign that included public awareness was launched, but it was not the primary or sole objective of the campaign.

DISCOVERY AND ANALYSIS: PROCESS GUIDE AND CHECKLIST

Each of the chapters representing the public relations process stages presented in Chapter 4 ends with a guide and checklist created to assist you in monitoring your work strategically, checking in at milestones that indicate progress and assessing the work and deciding where adjustments might be made.

The tasks described thus far in the chapter are time consuming yet essential. The guide and checklist shown in Table 10.2 are designed to guide you through the

Table 10.2 Discovery and Analysis: Process Guide and Checklist

Objectives	Steps	Tools	Outputs/ Deliverables	Process Milestones	TAPs (Typical Assessment Points)
• Identification • Discovery and data collection • Analysis and understanding • Effective research • Effective research reporting • Reevaluate target audiences	1. Identify problem or opportunity 2. Analyze the problem or opportunity 3. Identify internal resources 4. Identify external resources 5. Conduct informal research 6. Gather preliminary audience data 7. Identify knowledge gaps 8. Synthesize info and draw conclusions	• Problem statement • List of success indicators • List of internal resources • List of external resources • Existing benchmarks/ baselines • Conversations • Communication audits • Media audits • Environmental scans • SWOT analyses	• Agenda for initial meeting • Draft of audience research questions • Research analyses and reports	• Initial client meeting • Delivery of research analyses and reports	• Following delivery of research analyses and reports

| Table **10.2** | Discovery and Analysis: Process Guide and Checklist (*continued*) |

Objectives	Steps	Tools	Outputs/ Deliverables	Process Milestones	TAPs (Typical Assessment Points)
	9. Draft formal audience research questions	• Audience data (demographic & psychographic)			
	10. Create a formal audience research plan	• Research plan • Qualitative research methods			
	11. Enact formal audience research plan	• Quantitative research methods			
	12. Analyze research results	• Audience research instruments			
	13. Prepare and deliver research analyses and reports	• Audience observation			
	14. Determine if news media should receive a report	• Instrument usability/ readability testing			
	15. Reevaluate target audience	• Theater testing			

process, help ensure you have covered all of the steps that make sense for your discovery and analysis process, remind you of the tools available, and help you measure your success. Please pay close attention to the last three columns. These are designed to help you think about the process and business of what you do as a PR practitioner. The "Outputs/Deliverables" column tells you the products that should result from the first three columns. These are the products you can deliver to your client. The "Process Milestones" column is designed to encourage you to think about the strategic public relations process and to identify the most important points in your planning and implementation (discussed later in Chapters 11 and 12). Also, these milestones are good points at which to bill the client. The final column, "Typical Assessment Points (TAP) marks when you and your client evaluate how well the work is going. Here you and your client may decide to make changes to the objectives, audiences, and/or tactics.

Throughout Chapters 11, 12, and 13, you will find references to **Process Milestones** and **TYPICAL ASSESSMENT POINT** designed to assist you in observing these important intervals in your work.

Boomers' Shifting Priorities

Tonya Garcia, a senior reporter at PRWeek.

Marketers frequently segment their target audiences by age group, with baby boomers being a common target for outreach efforts.

According to a recent *Wall Street Journal* article, baby boomers, defined as those born between 1946 and 1964, will start turning 65 in 2011. They are expected to spend an additional $50 billion on consumer products in the coming decade, and, by 2030, nearly 20% of the U.S. population, about 71.5 million people, will be 65 or older.

The article also looks at research consumer companies and retailers have been conducting to help determine an aging population's shopping needs. For example, Walgreens plans to install magnifying glasses on store shelves and call buttons near heavy items.

Marketers should take a cue from these organizations. If they haven't begun the task of conducting research to learn more about the needs of this aging demographic and how best to communicate with them, now is the time to start. The baby boomer generation has already transformed marketing. They were the first generation to come of age in a time of television, creating a mass audience for advertising. Now they're poised to do it again.

Baby boomers, as they move into the age of retirement, are unlike the aging population before them. Medicine has advanced, prolonging life span and improving the quality of life. Many are active and still seek to take part in some of their favorite activities, or use their later years to branch out into new ones. A travel video on AARP's website offers alternatives to traditional water sports like scuba diving, suggesting that viewers try "snuba," an amalgam of snorkeling and scuba diving. And, most vital for marketers, boomers have access to social media. In addition to AARP, Boomer Authority, for example, links visitors to a network of social media sites and communities specifically for this age group.

Already, some firms have taken steps to launch practice groups targeting baby boomers. Still, PR firms and in-house pros across the board who are targeting the boomer generation must continue to learn about the communications preferences, lifestyle attributes, and other needs and desires of this group. All of these things will continue to change.

Marketers recognized the spending power of baby boomers years ago. However, as time passes and the boomers take steps into old age, the way they spend their money and their time will shift. PR pros—some of whom may fall into this category and should be tapped as a valuable resource—should keep up with this changing age group as they would a younger demographic.

SOURCE: Tonya Garcia, *PRWeek*, October 2009

Summary and Review

The First Stage of the Strategic Process
- In this stage, you want to gain knowledge about the environment, to gain knowledge of the environment, determine potential target audience(s), and begin to formulate questions for the formal audience research.
- During this phase of the process, you are involved in strategic planning.

Discovery
- The strategic PR process begins with identifying a problem or opportunity and analyzing it. The subsequent steps involve learning as much as possible about the situation and possible audiences surrounding the problem or opportunity.

- Overall goal for a PR program is established to provide a clear picture of what a successful program or campaign will look like at its end, what it will accomplish.
- Internal resources (those within an organization or possessed by an interested individual) and external resources (those outside the organization or interested individual) are crucial to the success of any PR program, project or campaign. Without sufficient resources not only will the initiative fail, but its failure will present new problems for the organization.
- Making a preliminary guess of the identity of the target audiences is an important step in the discovery stage. Often audiences drop from the initial list, but it is necessary to think broadly and then narrow and refine the list through research.
- There are several informal research methods available to assist you in gathering preliminary data for analysis of the problem: key informant conversations, communication audits, environmental scans, SWOT analysis, news media coverage analysis, and general fact-finding are widely used.
- Informal methods for helping you understand possible target audiences include gathering demographic data such as age, education, income, and occupation, and psychographic data such as lifestyle choices.
- You need to determine if audience segmentation is needed. Sometimes a target audience may be homogeneous enough that effective communication may be possible using the same messages, vehicles, and openings.
- Segmenting audiences is a two-pronged process, involving first identifying the audiences and then dividing them into smaller subgroups possessing similar characteristics that determine their susceptibility to the message and that indicate they can be reached similarly.

Analsis Your Informal Research

- At the end of the initial informal research process, you must determine the value of the data you have accumulated and decide how it should be reported.
- Crucial to problem analysis is identifying the knowledge gaps. After you have collected all of the data from the environmental scan and other situational information, it is important to determine what is known and where more research is necessary.
- Synthesizing the data requires looking for trends and information that are germane to the question at hand and for consistency and similarity of information.
- To determine your communication strategy, you first identify the audiences with whom you think you want to communicate and then divide them into smaller subgroups or segments who possess similar characteristics that determine their susceptibility to the message and that indicate they can be reached similarly.
- Audiences can be segmented in many ways such as by demographics, lifestyles, behaviors, and geographic location.

Developing Formal Research Questions

- After a decision is made to conduct audience research, you must decide if the research can be conducted by internal staff or if a research firm should be engaged as a subcontractor.
- Formal research questions and a definitive research plan should be developed with the client so that all parties are aware of the purpose and extent of the audience research.
- All research documents such as screeners and moderator's guides and all research facilities should be approved by the client.

- After audience research is completed, you will prepare reports for the client, and if the findings are newsworthy, prepare reports and news releases for the media.
- Both qualitative and quantitative research shed light on the choice of target audiences and audiences must be reevaluated. After you know with whom you will be communicating, the next stage of the process begins.

Discovery and Analysis: Process Guide and Checklist

- The checklist assists you in monitoring the progress of the project, acknowledging the objectives and ensuring the tasks needed.
- The process guide portion of the tool helps you to remember to observe the varying stages of the process and to make adjustments where necessary.

Key Terms

analysis	goal	research instruments
brainstorming	internal resources	research plan
discovery	moderator's topic guide	screener
external resources	problem statement	

Questions for Review and Discussion

1. Explain why strategic planning is important to all organizations.

2. Look at your university's website. Does it have a mission or vision statement? Does it have a statement of goals or statement of common purpose based on strategic planning? How do they relate to the students?

3. Go to the Claritas website and look at the software it licenses for providing demographic data. What PR applications can you think of for this type of data?

4. Make a list of five Internet search engines and search them for the same set of topics. How similar or dissimilar are the top 10 sites that appear from the search?

5. Use the Internet to discover how Kodak tried to market digital cameras to new moms/expectant couples? What was the demographic and what did Kodak use as a news hook?

Web Links

GMMB
www.gmmb.com

Health insurance coverage site links
www.covertheuninsured.org

Mystery Shoppers Providers Association
www.mysteryshop.org

Nielsen
www.claritas.com

Robert Wood Johnson Foundation
www.rwjf.org

Vocus: On-Demand Software for Public Relations Management
www.vocus.com

Program Planning

DEVELOPING A WRITTEN STRATEGIC PUBLIC RELATIONS PROPOSAL

At this point in the planning stage of the model you have already narrowed down your key audiences and are ready to begin planning. However, this chapter starts by asking you to go back and look at the process of developing a PR proposal first. After all, the success of your PR proposal is what allowed you to work on this program or campaign. Also, you will look at how PR proposals and PR plans differ since some confusion exists among students and new professionals in the field about these concepts.

The main section of this chapter gets you back on track with the planning process—beginning with writing the plan.

At this point in the textbook, you know the character of the profession you've chosen, you've learned the classic communication theories that underlie the effectiveness of good public relations, and you know the important roles strategic planning and research play in developing an effective PR program or campaign. You are now ready to embark on the part of public relations that is visible above the horizon—the actual program or campaign.

Before you can execute your ideas for the program or campaign, however, you will most likely have to write a PR proposal in order to secure approval and funding. New client work

He who every morning plans the transaction of the day and follows out that plan, carries a thread that will guide him through the maze of the most busy life. But where no plan is laid, where the disposal of time is surrendered merely to the chance of incidence, chaos will soon reign.

—Victor Hugo,
19th-century writer

will almost always require a proposal, and even within an organization, a manager or chief executive usually has to approve the concept and funding for new work. Once the project is funded, the actual strategic PR process can begin. In any case, an effective, and therefore winning, public relations proposal for client consideration should be compelling and professional.

The PR proposal is a very important tool in developing new business. In developing new business, you must impress the client twice: first with your presentation at the client meeting, and second when the client reads your proposal. In the case of proposal development, you are asking the client to invest in the future. Whether the benefits of your proposal include expanding the client's business, improving the client's reputation, or motivating your target audience to take a particular action, all these benefits happen in the future. Your proposal must convince the client that this future is achievable and desirable.

There are two types of proposals—solicited and unsolicited. *The solicited one is written in response to a* **request for proposal (RFP)** *distributed by an organization seeking assistance.* An **unsolicited proposal** *is submitted to an organization when you have knowledge about the organization's possible needs or issues facing the organization but an official RFP has not been issued.*

The elements of a **solicited proposal** are *usually very specifically outlined by the requesting organization.* A successful response to an RFP requires paying very close attention to the elements in the RFP and responding to them in a prescribed manner. RFPs require the bidder to demonstrate both understanding of the tasks to be performed and similar experience. Your response to an RFP usually includes the following elements:

1. **Introduction:** A short, perhaps three- or four-paragraph opening that establishes that you are capable and enthusiastic about working with the potential client to solve the problem or take advantage of the opportunity. Avoid using boilerplate language, and personalize the introduction as much as possible.
2. **Statement of the Understanding of the Problem or Opportunity or Client Needs:** A concise, two- or three-sentence description of the circumstances that necessitate the program or campaign and several paragraphs that demonstrate that you understand the client's needs.
3. **Research Approach:** This section is not a complete research plan but it should delineate the specific research methods you intend to employ and how you will report findings, results, and recommendations.
4. **Communication Strategy Approach:** Here you are outlining a bit of guesswork. Your strategies depend upon what you discover about your key audiences. Sometimes you know, but often you will learn, how you will communicate and interact after you are sure of the audiences. If the audiences are delineated by the client or organization, you can be more precise.
5. **Evaluation Approach:** This section describes the evaluative research you propose to undertake during and after the campaign or program is implemented.
6. **Duration of the Work:** This is an estimate of how long it will take to accomplish the work. It is not a specific time line of dates and accomplishments.
7. **Budget:** The cost for the program should be reflected as specifically as possible. The costs should include labor—the people who will conduct the work—and the expenses, or other direct costs (ODCs), required to implement the program.

Because solicited proposals do have to meet the requirements of an RFP, there is little room for including the points that might make the practitioner or agency uniquely qualified for the work. So, it is important to be creative and look for every opportunity to refer to your capabilities and credentials ("capes and creds").

In contrast, the unsolicited proposal has the elements outlined previously but can also include creative ideas, concepts, and themes. These additions should be included in moderation unless you are sure you *know* the target audience—the soliciting organization.

The opportunity to make an in-person presentation of a proposal, or pitch, for new business is a chance not to be squandered. When you have this opportunity, you should be sure to 1) bring members of the team to the presentation so that the client can see a full array of talent available for the work; 2) use visuals and sound to enhance the messages; and 3) demonstrate that you understand the organization's mission, business goals, and its target audiences. The details of the skills and techniques required for making an impressive presentation are beyond the scope of this textbook, so you are encouraged to take a public speaking class or join an organization such as Toastmasters to refine your skills.

DEVELOPING A WRITTEN STRATEGIC PUBLIC RELATIONS PLAN

After an organization agrees to hire a public relations agency or decides to launch a public relations campaign, a plan for the initiative must be developed. Clients expect to see a document that outlines the work to be accomplished and how it will be done.

As stated previously, public relations proposals and plans are two distinctly different documents. A **PR proposal** is *a document developed by a PR practitioner for the purpose of winning the proposed work*. The PR plan is different. Much like the process you are reviewing throughout this part of the book, a **PR plan,** or **strategic communication plan,** is *the document that outlines the work to be accomplished and gives an overview of how that work will be accomplished*. (The shorter term—PR plan—is used throughout this chapter.) Although both proposals and plans contain an introduction and an understanding of the problem or the clients' needs, the PR plan, as you will see next, focuses on specific objectives, strategies, tactics, time lines, and implementation steps.

The PR plan usually follows the following framework, although there can be many variations:

1. **Statement of the Opportunity or Problem:** This section usually explains the circumstances that created the need for the campaign or program, where the organization is located in the marketplace, what the initial research findings indicate, and if additional research is necessary.
2. **Goals and Objectives:** The goals are statements of the broad outcomes desired, while objectives are measurable results (outputs and outcomes) of the public relations effort.
3. **Audience:** Here the practitioner states the specific and well-defined group(s) to whom the campaign is directed.
4. **Tactics:** This section of the plan delineates the specific and major action steps that will take place to implement the various strategies. The specific activities selected will depend upon the tactical strategies. For example, publicity and media relations strategies will include editorial board meetings, news releases, or news conferences while promotion may require email and special events.
5. **Monitoring, Tracking, and Evaluation:** Evaluative research should take place during and after the campaign or program is implemented. The plan should include milestones at which the stated objectives of the program or campaign are measured.

6. **Time Line:** This section plots out as closely as possible the actual timing of each activity of the campaign or program. While adjustments will, no doubt, be made during the process, a carefully formulated time line is crucial because many of the tactics and activities are dependent upon each other and will overlap.

7. **Budget:** The costs for the program should be reflected as closely as possible. The costs should include labor—the people who have to conduct the work—and the expenses, or other direct costs (ODCs), required to implement the program.

Statement of the Problem or Opportunity

As we discussed in Chapter 4, effective, proactive public relations is engaging in communication and relationships with audiences in order to solve a series of problems and to take advantage of opportunities. See that chapter for a full discussion of problems and opportunities.

The statement of problem or opportunity in a plan should be a concise, two- or three-sentence description of the circumstances that necessitate the program or campaign. Our previous example of the Robert Wood Johnson Foundation (RWJF) "Cover the Uninsured Week" (CTUW) is illustrative. Recall the problem that RWJF wanted to help solve is that more than 45 million American men, women, and children have no healthcare insurance and the country currently does not have a plan to cover them. A statement of the problem for the communication or PR plan might have been: The number of uninsured Americans has increased from 40 million in 1999 to 43 million in 2003 and 45 million in 2009, including 9 million children. These Americans have no access to regular medical or dental treatment and cannot have their chronic diseases monitored and cared for, leaving the uninsured at risk of serious illness and death. All the while, the American government does not provide assistance for these citizens. As noted in Chapter 6, an historic healthcare reform bill was signed into law in 2010 that has regulations that assist uninsured Americans.

Goals and Objectives

Now let's take a closer look at establishing goals for the PR program. Goals are established to help you to see what a successful program or campaign will help accomplish at its end. **Goals** are *the broad outcomes desired or descriptions of the future state.* Again, the overall goal of the communication plan should be aligned with the organization's mission because it must reflect the organization's purpose or desired end state and is discussed in greater detail in Chapter 4. If you continue to look at the Robert Wood Johnson Foundation CTUW campaign as the example, you know that a stated goal such as "to highlight the plight of America's uninsured and garner support to help solve the problem of uninsured Americans" is in line with the stated mission of RWJF: "Improving the health and health care of all Americans."

Objectives are *the actionable and measurable statements of the intentions of what is to be accomplished as a result of the communication messages and activities you will develop.* They are somewhat different than goals in that they are created to assist in measuring the success of your communication efforts and are based on what your situational analysis and audience research findings show. Formulating appropriate objectives is crucial to helping you understand what you hope to accomplish and provides the only means by which to measure your success. Objectives should be established for each target audience and should not exceed three objectives per audience.

Goals, Objectives, and the Bottom Line

Knowing the client's business is crucial to your success and that of the PR initiatives. Given the global economy today and expectations for the future, all companies and organizations, for-profit and nonprofit alike, look for their return on investment (ROI) on several levels. As a PR practitioner, you must be able to set objectives that reflect an understanding of that corporate reality. As you begin program development and identify the goals for a program or campaign, you must be steeped in your client's business goals and objectives. You should know the organization's mission and products (commercial or nonprofit) as though you are a member of the staff. The organization's mission, history, key audiences, strategic partners, business goals, and objectives must be a part of your public relations thinking and strategy.

Three Types of Objectives

In general, objectives can be divided into three categories—*informational, behavioral,* and *attitudinal. Informational objectives* state what you want the target audience to know and understand at the end of the communication initiative. *Behavioral objectives* state the exact action you want the target audience to take, while *attitudinal objectives* specify the change in attitude or opinion you want from the target audience.

Informational Objectives   Informational objectives for a campaign can pose a public relations challenge because audiences don't always pay attention to your messages if they are not relevant to their current priorities, lifestyles, and activities. But sometimes, providing information is the only way to get started communicating with an audience and sometimes, telling an audience where it can find actionable messages when they are ready is all that you can do.

As in the example used in an earlier chapter, the U.S. government was trying to help the American public prepare for an influenza pandemic when people have more immediate worries, like a failing economy. So as a communicator, the best you can do is to try to increase awareness of something so that people will know where to get information if a pandemic occurs in their lifetimes. Essentially, informational objectives that require the audience to become aware are found in public awareness campaigns. To be successful, an informational objective would take a particular audience, or percentage of an audience, from unknowing to knowing.

Behavioral Objectives   The second type, behavioral objectives, state specific behavior you want the audience to do; they can also be referred to as action objectives. Behaviors can be both verbal and physical actions in that you may want an audience to express an opinion or move from one place to another. We may want an audience to adopt a new behavior, change an existing one, or eliminate a behavior all together. Behavior change campaigns can be very challenging because it is difficult to get people to change what they are already doing or take on a new behavior. Listening to your audience research is very important here because the benefit to modifying behavior must be crystal clear to the intended audience. Also, audience segmentation is crucial because you need to know who within your audience is most likely to take the action. The Centers for Disease Control and Prevention's (CDC) "America Responds to AIDS" campaign includes messages to bring public attention to key behaviors that reduce the risk of HIV infection. While providing information that HIV primarily is spread by sexual activity and contaminated injection drug needles, the CDC also segmented its audiences and began messages that included prevention through safe sex among many audiences, including men who have sex with men (MSM) and through clean needles for injected drugs. While the development of testing and drugs has been a major turning point in America, behavior change communication has played a major role.

Attitudinal Objectives   Attitudinal objectives are established to identify what you want your target audiences to feel or to think about something. These objectives are usually expressed in results that are positive or negative but can also aim to establish interest or reinforce existing attitudes. These objectives are very important in establishing how you want your audiences to *see* your issue, organization, or client. Here, you are being persuasive and are concerned with more than awareness. Attitudinal objectives are key to crisis and risk communication messages because you are attempting to affect the way an audience perceives the situation and views the response to crises and risks.

Staying with the HIV/AIDS example, the CDC had as one of its biggest challenges public attitudes about people with HIV/AIDS. Its 10-year multimedia campaign helped to change the attitudes of millions of Americans and broke some of the nation's political and religious barriers to understanding the disease and its victims. Thanks to these communication efforts, the days when people were afraid of "catching" the disease from toilet seats or from handshakes or from Ryan White, an HIV-positive young man whose mother had to fight to get him safely enrolled in an Indiana public school, now seem like the Dark Ages.

The Characteristics of Effective Objectives

Public relations communication objectives should be credible and realistic, should be as precise and measurable as possible, and should meet the expectations of the organization or client. Scholars and practitioners alike agree that clear, concise, and measurable objectives are the best metrics for evaluating results and monitoring progress of a communication effort. Well-defined objectives also assist you in evaluating ideas for a program, resulting in eliminating inappropriate ideas and enhancing those remaining.

As a PR practitioner, you should ask a series of questions to help determine if the objective is effective: Does the objective reflect the stated mission and goals of the organization? Does the objective respond to the public relations problem or opportunity that initiated the development of the program or campaign? Is the objective achievable—both its time frame and its intended outcome? Does the objective seek to communicate with a specific audience? Is the objective measurable?

Writing Objectives

There are many roadmaps for writing effective, measurable objectives. One formula that works well uses a very simple rule: An objective begins with an Infinitive (a verb preceded by the particle *to*), states a desired Result, is Measurable, specifies a target Audience, and ends with a Time frame. This mnemonic device is IRMAT.

You can write effective communication objectives if you adhere to the following outline:

1. The result or effect of the communication is to: _____.
   Here is where the infinitive comes in. The result or effect should be, for example, *to create, to affect, to increase, to decrease, to raise, to maintain*, etc. such things as awareness, acceptance, or rejection, etc.
2. The measure of the result: _____
3. This objective is intended for the following target audience: _____
   This is the first question we always ask in audience-focused communication. Who is the audience? List the audience(s) to whom the objective is aimed.
4. The time frame of the result: _____

Let's apply the IRMAT framework to our example of the Robert Wood Johnson Foundation's 2003 "Cover the Uninsured Week" campaign—the first of seven campaigns.

- To increase awareness among voters of the uninsured by 20 percent during the month of March
- To create a partnership of more than 10 national organizations before the campaign launch
- To demonstrate broad support for action on the issue by getting Democratic and Republican formal leadership in the Senate and House to send letters to colleagues, encouraging their support during the "Cover the Uninsured Week" (CTUW)
- To generate national media attention during March

Another Formula to Consider

Another mnemonic device for remembering the characteristics of clear objectives is SMART: Specific, Measurable, Agreed upon, Relevant, and Time specific. For strategic public relations purposes, the SMART mnemonic does not allow for the audience element—a crucial omission. In order to accommodate the SMART formula, we need to add an "A" to create SMAART because objectives should be written for each target audience. Clear and concise public relations objectives must:

- Be specific
- Be measurable
- Be agreed upon by client and staff
- Specify a particular target audience(s)
- Specify a desired outcome (results)
- Include a time frame

ENGAGING ETHICS

Engaging Ethics in Government Contracting

Federal government agencies release hundreds of requests for proposals (RFPs) during the course of a year. Many of them are public relations or strategic communication solicitations (see Chapter 19 for a discussion of government PR). An investigation in 2009 shows that an official of one of those agencies circumvented standard federal procedures by awarding a $300,000 PR contract to an Alaska Native American firm that did not have to compete because it qualified for special "set-asides" for government work. The firm gave the work to still another company, a PR agency based in Washington, DC—the one preferred by the government official. In effect, the government official arranged to go around and violate numerous federal procurement and contracting laws.

1. While it is clear that the investigation uncovered some illegalities, what are the ethical issues raised here?
2. Look at the PRSA Code of Ethics in Chapter 7. What codes are breached in this case?
3. If the Alaska Native American company had not passed the work onto the Washington, DC-based agency, would there have been ethical issues? Explain your response.

DEVELOPING EFFECTIVE MESSAGES AND CONCEPTS

The next step in the planning process after establishing and writing goals and objectives is developing messages for the audiences identified in the research phase. Effective messages are not just clever slogans and themes. Instead, they are the result of clear thinking regarding what our research has told us and knowledge of communication and behavior theory. As you know, it is not easy to get people to enter into relationships (even mutually beneficial relationships), change behaviors, or adopt new ideas, so messages must be well thought out and grounded in behavior science and how audiences think and act.

How Theory Informs Message Development

There are many consumer behavior theories, ranging from those proposed by Ajen to Zimicki. We will briefly review just those theories that help provide a framework for message development. The idea is to understand the theory well enough to better understand your audiences. Remember, when you listen to the audiences and try to understand their beliefs, attitudes, norms, and who influences them, you know better how to speak to them. Therefore, the theory helps to serve as an underpinning for what you hear during your formative research. Remember that these theories often discuss products, but you can think of or substitute any action in trying to understand and use the theories.

While it would appear that audience members behave in very simple ways when deciding to take an action or not, this is not the case. Celsi and Olson (1988) and Laurent and Kapferer (1985) characterized consumer decisions as high and low involvement. Low-involvement decisions, as you may have guessed, are not very important to consumers and they make these decisions rather routinely. The most simplistic of decisions, low-involvement decisions, are not made after intelligence gathering, discussion, and weighing alternatives. Instead, they can be very whimsical and based on nothing more than packaging or convenience or availability of the products. Toiletries, snacks, magazines, and other convenience items fall into this category. Indeed, the creation of the convenience store is likely the result of consumer needs for these types of purchases.

On the other hand, high-involvement decisions are very important and consumers spend a great deal of time and effort seeking advice, gathering information, and thinking about the purchase. These decisions are usually very emotional and take a long time. Purchasing a home, choosing a physician, deciding to lose weight or making lifestyle changes, or taking a vacation all fall into this category.

As we stated earlier, human behavior does not just happen, especially in high-involvement behaviors. Several marketers have explored the notion that consumers progress slowly toward making high-involvement decisions, and scholars have defined various stages of consumer behavior. McGuire (1976), studying the difficulty for advertising in persuading a consumer to prefer one brand over another, postulated six stages consumers follow: 1) message exposure—the consumer is shown or hears the message, 2) attention—the consumer becomes aware of the message, 3) understanding—the consumer comprehends the message, 4) persuasion—the consumer values and is persuaded by the message, 5) retention—the consumer maintains the message, and 6) behavior—the consumer takes the desired action.

Rogers' (1983) **diffusion of innovations theory** introduces still another stage model. In this case, the researcher proposes the manner in which something new or novel moves through a population. He suggests that with any new product or behavior, there are those who will adopt early and those who will never adopt. *Given a particular innovation, there are five categories of those who will accept a new idea, product or behavior: innovators, early adopters, middle majority adopters, late adopters, and laggards.* This model suggests that those in the early stages have made decisions to adopt or buy but the latter groups are the more difficult. The late majority adopters and laggards are more easily convinced through opinion leaders and social networks. Therefore, the appropriate spokesperson is crucial to winning over this group, and word of mouth is an effective tactic.

Silverman (2001) created a matrix to indicate the types of messages that should be created for consumers in each of the Rogers (1983) stages. The matrix to aid in message development when the audience has been segmented in this manner is shown in Table 11.1.

Table 11.1   The Decision Matrix™

The idea is to get your audience to the next stages of the decision process, using the following messages in the right order, from the right sources. So, if you are going after early adopters, read across the early adopter row and create messages that will resonate with that group of potential users.

	Deciding to Decide [What he/she wants to hear in regular type.] [Examples in italics.]	Weighing Information	Trial	Implementing	Expanding Commitment
Innovator Wants to be outstanding	Wants to hear how "far out" the product is. *It's so new and unusual, no one's even heard of it or tried it. It works on a totally new principle. Most people wouldn't even understand it.*	There is little information to gather. He will have to investigate the product firsthand. *It's so far out that there is nothing to compare it to. It's in a different class.*	Wants to be among the first to try. *It is so new that no one has tried it yet. You would be the first.*	Wants to be the pioneer who will lead the way for other people. *Now that you've tried it successfully, you can help others learn about it.*	Wants to push the envelope to the limits. *Have you tried the wild new things it might be used for?*
Early adopter Driven by excellence	Concerned more about possibilities than actualities.	Looking not as much for "hard" information as for a vision of what might be.	Doesn't care that it hasn't been used in his situation, just that it may be applicable.	Knows there will be problems, wants to know what they are, and how they can be handled.	Wants a major advantage for being at the beginning of the curve.

(continued)

Table 11.1	The Decision Matrix™ (continued)				
	Deciding to Decide [What he/she wants to hear in regular type.] [Examples in italics.]	Weighing Information	Trial	Implementing	Expanding Commitment
	Think of the possibilities. If this product really worked in your situation, it would change your life or give you a competitive edge.	*Here's how I envision using the product. The other products are more ordinary. This one has possibilities.*	*This product doesn't work all the time. But when it does, wow!*	*Here is how to get the most out of it and minimize the problems.*	*Here are the additional possibilities that will give you a competitive edge.*
Middle majority Wants to be competent	Concerned with practicalities. *This has been tried and really works in situations like yours, in your industry, etc.*	Wants comparisons about how it's working out in situations similar to his own. *Here is the practical information about how this is working out in the real world.*	Wants to verify that it will work in his situation without investing too much time and trouble. *The bugs have been worked out and it is highly predictable.*	Wants to know that there is an easy way out if it doesn't work out. *Training, support, and guarantees are in place and reliable.*	Wants to know usage is getting pretty standard. *It is rapidly becoming the standard in our industry.*
Late adopter Wants to reduce risk	Promise a good deal on a tried and true product. *It has become virtually a commodity and this product can get you better price, delivery, service, training, etc.*	Wants to "shop around" and get the proven product with the best deal. *I've checked out the pricing and service, etc. and it seems to be the best product.*	Trial tends to be not for product excellence, but centers around the support system. *Check out how wonderful they are to deal with, everyone can fix your problems, etc.*	Wants complete support for rolling out full usage of the product. *They'll come in and do it all for you.*	Wants to use what everyone else is using, in the way that they are using it. *Everybody is using it for everything.*
Laggard Wants to be completely safe	Wants reassurance that it is a safe product where nothing will go wrong. *You'll get in trouble if you aren't using this.*	Wants to find the loopholes, problems, negatives, etc. If he doesn't find some, will keep looking. *Here are the risks and how to render them harmless.*	Basically won't try anything new. Needs reassurance that the product is the standard product used in his industry, situation, etc. Try it, everyone else has and likes it.	Implements only when he has to. *Adopt this product, or else.*	Wants reassurance that he is using it in the standard way. *That's the way we all use it.*

SOURCE: Image courtesy of The Advertising Archives "Secrets of Word-of-Mouth Marketing," American Management Association, 2001

Transtheoretical Model

Another model proposed for consumer behavior is the transtheoretical model, based on Prochaska and DiClemente's (1983) *behavior change theory*, described in Chapter 9. In summary, the stages in this model include precontemplation, contemplation, preparation, action, and confirmation. The communication messages and media recommended in these stages are as follows:

- **Precontemplation Stage:** This is the stage during which information and awareness messages are most effective. For instance, if your objective is to get obese 'tween girls (ages 10 to 14) to exercise, you must think about this stage during which they are not thinking about exercise as a behavior for them, especially if it is not a part of their families' activities. This is the stage during which you might use online social networking as a tool for communicating.
- **Contemplation Stage:** At this stage, consumers are particularly receptive to social pressure through messages. This is the point at which your obese 'tweens may be considering exercise as a result of the messaging. It is the opportune time to move to messages that reinforce the thought process; other 'tween girls might be the best influencers.
- **Preparation Stage:** This is the point at which many individuals stop in the progression, so your messages should minimize the barriers. Your 'tween girls are ready to begin exercising and may have difficulty determining just how to get prepared and may find the logistics of getting to a tennis court, gym, or other location for activities daunting. Messages at this stage should help the key audience with strategies for accomplishing the behavior.
- **Action Stage:** In this stage, when the individual is doing something for the first time, or returning to the action, positive reinforcement and encouragement are crucial. Your obese 'tween girls are exercising and it is not easy. They may be experiencing boredom; it may seem too hard; they may be embarrassed. The girls need messages that reinforce their decision to exercise; influencer messages will help, also.
- **Confirmation Stage:** In this final stage of the model, an individual is committed to the behavior or product and has no intention of reverting to previous behavior. Messages should provide reinforcement and tips for maintaining the action. Messages to your 'tween girls at this stage should be similar to the action stage messages. The online social networking strategies will reinforce the decision to stay with exercising.

The Role of Intention

Itzak Ajzen discusses planned behavior in his 1991 theory. Essentially, if a person *intends* to take an action or make a behavior change under particular circumstances or in a particular situation, it is more likely to occur. He suggests that intention depends upon the individual's beliefs about three things: 1) positive and negative consequences, 2) what significant people in her life think and her motivation to live up to their expectations, and 3) external factors that make it easier or more difficult to take the action.

General Considerations for Developing Messages

After reviewing the consumer behavior theories, you can see that product marketers have given a lot of thought and consideration to the way in which consumers undertake their highly involved decisions. As a PR practitioner, you should think about your audiences, too. Audiences are always weighing the benefits and costs of a particular transaction. You will recall that we discussed the "marketing exchange" concept in Chapter 5. Your target audience asks, what am I going to have to give up in return for what I am going to receive? What will it cost me to exercise an hour every day? What do I have to give up in order to drive sober? What will I lose if I quit smoking?

The average person thinks in these terms every day. When considering whether or not to attend a meeting or ask to call-in and participate by telephone and desktop sharing, you might consider the benefit and cost, weigh them, and make a decision. If your meeting is downtown and you have to drive because there is no public transportation, you might consider the cost of having to find a parking space or garage or taxi fare. You think the telephone sounds easier and a lot less frustrating. On the other hand, the in-person meeting provides a little "face time" with the client, resulting in a better working relationship.

Another consideration for developing messages is the way audiences consider benefits and the cost of the product, service, or behavior. Marketers discovered long ago that a consumer "packages" the benefits and costs, putting them into not-so-neat little bundles. With the previous scenario there may be additional costs traveling downtown for the meeting such as the travel time that could be better spent at your desk and the possibility of getting caught in a much longer than necessary meeting. But the additional benefits create a neat little bundle when you add that you can stop at the barber's to get a trim and because it is a nice day you can grab a bite to eat at an outside bistro.

Lastly, the influence of those who make up an individual's network or social environment—the influencers—cannot be overlooked in considering consumer behavior and ultimately message development. Fishbein and Ajzen (1975) discuss the importance of social influence on the consumer's choices and behaviors. Their work acknowledges the "attitude toward the act"—essentially the consumer's view of the personal consequences—and "normative behavior." Normative behavior is what an individual believes is expected of him, in fact, what others whose opinions he values want from him.

Given this discussion, it is clear that audiences are complicated in their reasoning, and understanding their beliefs and norms, as we discussed earlier in this book, is crucial to our ability to communicate with them effectively.

Writing Messages: Begin with a Message Strategy Statement

In many ways, the message strategy statement reaffirms many of the details we know from our research findings and objectives. And, it is a very important tool for that very reason—it verifies that we are on track with what we have found and where we are headed. The message strategy statement consists of the following elements:

- **Competition:** Create a clear and concise statement of the marketplace in which you are competing. When the audience is not doing, thinking, or buying what you want, figure out what it is doing, thinking, or buying and with or from whom.
- **Audience Profile:** For creative development, you define the key audience in terms of attitudes, lifestyles, norms, beliefs, and/or other findings you garnered from formative research. This profile should be a rich description of a person who becomes real to you and the creative team. If it is an organization, it must be given a personality profile. Work with the creative team to construct an identity for the audience so that he, she, or it is real. Give her a name, an address, a family,

a job to go to in a real location, and feelings about the behavior you want her to take.

- **Promise:** This is a statement of the best argument possible for taking the action you want the audience to take. The promise must state the benefit to the audience.
- **Why:** Here you want to write a statement that directly supports the promise. It must be derived from a fact about the offer. If the action doesn't have a real reason *why*, then what authority can be used to support the promise?
- **Manner, Mood, and Tone:** How will the creative team convey believability and motivate the audience? Describe the voice in which the audience will be addressed.
- **Limitations:** Delineate any restrictions imposed by policy, regulations, cultural differences, etc. that may be necessary or may affect a clear understanding of creative direction.

When the creative director signs off on the message strategy statement, it should be approved by the client. While it is a **Process Milestone,** it is not necessarily an appropriate point to bill the client. Your goal here is to get the approval you need to move forward with your creative ideas.

Creative Concepts Come Next

A campaign must have a plan for the creative work to be developed, and this is when you turn to the creative team for help. Much like the public relations process, the creative process has to evolve using steps that lead from audience understanding to final execution. Creative strategy determines what the message will say or communicate, while creative tactics determine how the message strategy will be executed.

Creative concepts are, of course, creative ideas. These come to the fore during brainstorming sessions with the creative director and the creative team. The team is made up of copywriters, graphic designers, and the PR practitioner. A simple word or phrase accompanied by visuals that the team envisioned should be the goal in developing a creative concept. It should be designed to catch the attention of your audience. All of the audience and formative research should come to bear here.

Of course, the benefit to the key audience is the major attraction. It answers the question, what's in it for me? The creative concept must encompass and revolve around this benefit and it must be illustrated in word and visual. The creative concepts or ideas must help solve the PR problem(s). So if the problem is that Americans are uninsured and suffer because of it, the creative concept needs to depict the problem and the solution.

The creative process follows the PR process in other ways, as well. First the creative staff must think about the audience data and the issue—quantitative and qualitative data, public opinion, what others are saying, etc. Creative concepts are abstracted from concrete particulars. The creative team also uses a technique that researchers and scholars use frequently—it's called "forget it." It means you have to learn to give it a break and not think about it for a short while. It is sometimes referred to as "retreat." Taking a break in whatever way is possible—lunch, another type of task, or checking on other details help the team to escape from what they know. This is usually followed by a sudden thought or illumination that sends the creative team in a particular direction. This process brings you back full circle to evaluating the concept, refining the idea, and developing it for the campaign.

A **unique selling proposition (USP)** should be a part of the creative concept. It is an advertising term but it also can be used in public relations to help delineate the benefit. *It says, buy this product or make this change or care about this or that issue because you will benefit in this fashion or enjoy this reward.* Your benefit must be unique; the competition cannot make the same claims. Lastly, the promise must be powerful; it must encourage the audience to move in order to accomplish your objectives.

Creating Message Concepts

Now that the creative ideas are developed, the message concepts can be written, designed, and tested. Some large public relations agencies have in-house creative teams. Some large organizations with substantial communication or public relations staff also have creative staff. Both are usually headed by a creative director who may also supervise an art director. Smaller organizations may assign the public relations practitioner to contract with designers and copywriters.

Creating message concepts is both creative and managerial. Clearly, the creation of the messages belongs to the creative team, but getting those messages from the creative team and out for approval and testing requires the management skills of the public relations practitioner. As a PR practitioner, you are responsible for working with the creative team to be sure all copy and images are prepared in a timely manner. It is best if the number of concepts to be presented to the client or management is agreed at the outset. Three to four concepts is generous and if the client is kept informed during the creative stage, the concepts should be close to what the client wants or expects. The creative director or vendor should accompany you when the concepts are presented to the client. In the end, the concepts should be submitted as a *mock-up*—a depiction—of the words, tone, images, and visuals that reflect your client's message and credibility. When the client accepts the final concept, she should be required to sign an approval or release so the concept can be tested with the target audience. This is another ***Process Milestone.***

Pretesting Messages and Concepts

Although pretesting is a recommended step, it's only fair to acknowledge that—in the routine practice of public relations, pretesting messages and concepts is not routine. Many clients and organization managers will react incredulously if you suggest pretesting, but it doesn't mean you should not make the suggestion. Such a suggestion will indicate that you take communicating with target audiences seriously. Does pretesting ensure that your campaign or materials will be successful? No. Is pretesting itself foolproof? No, but pre-testing gives you a better chance at communicating effectively. Pretesting messages is a **TYPICAL ASSESSMENT POINT** and is crucial to communicating effectively. The time and funding invested in getting to this point in the process requires that you test the messages. You want to be sure that the selected words and images resonate with the target audience. Hopefully, testing will validate the work you have done so far and your concepts will need just a little "tweaking." You test messages for three specific reasons: 1) to ensure that the target audiences understand the creative execution; 2) to assess whether the target audiences take away the intended message; and 3) to ensure that the message is appropriate for the intended target audiences. This step in the process can help you to become reacquainted with your target audiences. These steps will help determine if the insights you gleaned from your research really resonate with the audiences. Occasionally, you might think you are on target only to learn that an execution is too "cheesy" or a message is too direct or even offensive.

The best method for testing messages is a two-step approach. If you have the time and money, it is wise to pretest the messages and concepts to see which are most effective and then pretest the materials you develop based on the first pretest findings. Messages can be tested in a variety of settings and the budget often dictates to what extent you are able to test. The most appropriate qualitative methods for pretesting messages with audiences are focus groups (the more expensive) and intercept interviews (the least expensive) because they can be completed and analyzed quickly. But there are other methods for pretesting such as review by experts, theatre and observation testing, readability testing, usability testing, and questionnaires. These methods are discussed in Chapter 6.

The criteria we use for developing messages and materials are the very ones you should turn to when pretesting. Use a set of questions similar to the following when creating topic guides or questionnaires designed to pretest:

1. **Are message and materials attractive to the target audience?** Will the intended receiver notice the message in the midst of all of the competing messages? Would the target audience stop to listen, read, or watch?
2. **Does the target audience understand the messages?** Do the target audience members understand the main points? Do they understand the action they are asked to take and how to take it? Is every word recognizable, familiar, culturally acceptable, and friendly?
3. **Are the message and its attending visual and audio elements relevant to the audience members?** Are they pertinent to the audiences' lives? Can they relate to the message? Do they think the message was intended for them?
4. **Is the message credible?** Will the target audience believe the message? Is the spokesperson appropriate, recognizable, and credible? Do members of the target audience see themselves in the spokesperson?
5. **What does the target audience view as the strengths and weaknesses of the message?** If the audience members would make a change in the materials or message, what would they change?

A report of the pretesting findings and recommendations for adjustments to the message and materials should be provided to the client. The report should answer the preceding questions and include a time line for completing the recommended changes. The time line is important because it highlights the effect changes will have on the timing of implementation. Your report should highlight those things that must be changed and the reasons why the changes are needed. These are the elements that your testing demonstrates clearly will not work such as layout, color, fonts, errors, and words, phrases or sentences that are unclear to the target audience. The report should be submitted to the client for approval of changes in direction. This is both a **TYPICAL ASSESSMENT POINT** and a ***Process Milestone;*** it is a billable deliverable to the client.

Again, pretesting does not ensure your program or campaign will be effective. While you can continue to pretest, revise, pretest, and revise some more, you have to recognize when you have pretested enough and move on to implementation.

BRIEF CASE STUDY

"Drink–Drive–Lose" Ad Campaign

An ad from the Drink-Drive-Lose awareness campaign targeting teens

Faced with statistics that indicated alcohol-related fatalities in Connecticut were 4.7 percent higher than the national average and 1.4 percent above the region, the state recognized it needed to take action. In addition, while 54 percent of the drunk drivers at fault in fatal crashes were between the ages of 20 and 39, 12.5 percent were under 21.

The Department of Transportation launched a statewide drinking and driving awareness campaign directed at young drivers. Cronin & Company helped develop a program comprised of a youth-oriented section on a website to raise awareness of the dangers of drinking and driving among teens age 14–20. The key challenge was how to drive them to the site. The answer was the Drink–Drive–Lose Ad Challenge, encouraging the target audience to visit the site to learn about an advertising contest in which they could enter and vote for their favorite entries. This was designed to get teens talking to other teens about a serious problem that was taking their lives.

Other tactics in addition to the website and contest included a radio partner for contest development, awareness, and execution; outreach to administrators and teachers at 320 high schools and colleges and groups like Students Against Drunk Driving and Mothers Against Drunk Driving to support the contest. News media relations included a contest announcement news release, a deadline release, a voting announcement, and a final winner press release.

Website hits increased 4,000 percent and 58 contest entries were evaluated by more than 1,200 online voters.

Working the Case

1. What type of objective was set for the campaign—informational, behavioral, or attitudinal?
2. How would you measure the success of the campaign?
3. Given the information presented, what objective(s) would you write for this target audience?
4. How could Cronin & Company have pretested the campaign message? What are the advantages/disadvantages of the method?

IMPLEMENTATION PLAN AND SCHEDULE

This is another step in the planning process that distinguishes you as a strategic communicator. Strategy dictates that you create a plan and not begin implementation the minute the PSAs are ready or the ink is dry on the materials unless you have a plan.

A plan and schedule drive how the execution will roll out. It is a more elaborate version of the time line you submitted in your public relations plan (see previous sections and Chapter 10). The timing of the campaign itself is something you gave thought to in the planning process as you identified the public relations problem or opportunity, considering what the best timing is for communicating. For instance, increases in oil prices beginning in 2010 sent the cost of gasoline to new heights in the United States. This presented an excellent opportunity for encouraging carpooling and mass transit use among commuters. Or Thanksgiving and Christmas holidays are seasonable opportunities for charitable organizations to increase their public relations efforts to increase charitable giving.

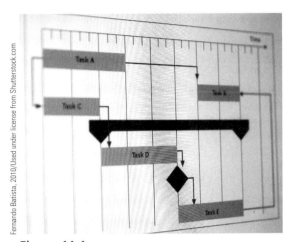

Figure 11.1
Example of Gantt Chart

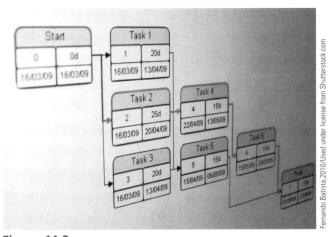

Figure 11.2
Example of Pert Chart

But implementation plans delineate what activities are scheduled to take place and at what point in time. Gantt charts and Pert charts are the most frequently used time lines. Templates for these tools can be easily downloaded for use in spreadsheet software such as Microsoft Excel. *The time line, or* **Gantt chart (time line)** *is a method to show when tasks happen; the* **Pert chart** *illustrates how the tasks will flow.* Figure 11.1 is an example of a typical Gantt chart.

The activities are listed vertically at the right-hand column and the time frames in weeks or months appear above in a horizontal line. This format makes it easy to locate an activity and follow it across the time line to understand when it begins and ends. Figure 11.2 is an example of a Pert chart.

The Pert chart is helpful in indicating where one task ends and another begins. It is particularly helpful in demonstrating the sequence of activities. Some implementation plans are very simple because a campaign or program may be very targeted and involve only one tactic. Other plans are more complex because of the number of tactics involved. An implementation plan and schedule will help you keep up with the activities and the roles and responsibilities of everyone on your team. As a PR practitioner, you must think ahead to make sure that the implementation transpires in the proper and planned sequence.

To develop your implementation plan and schedule, you should prepare a Gantt chart and Pert chart. Before creating your charts, list every major activity associated with the campaign. Under each major activity, create an indented list of the tasks that must be completed in order for each activity to be accomplished. To the right of the indented tasks, list the dates on which the tasks should be accomplished followed by the contact person responsible for accomplishing the task. Now, you have all of the ingredients for your charts. Draw them into your software and check and double-check that you have included every step of the process. You may want to get another team member to review what you propose. You are now ready to implement, *finally.*

Program Development Process Guide and Checklist

Your Program Development Process Guide and Checklist is presented in Table 11.2. Remember. This tool is designed to guide you through the process, help ensure you have covered all of the steps that make sense for your planning process, remind you of the tools available, and help you monitor your progress. Pay close attention to the *Process Milestones* and **TYPICAL ASSESSMENT POINTS** because they mark important items to be observed.

Table 11.2   Program Development Process Guide and Checklist

Objectives	Steps	Tools	Deliverables	Process Milestones	TAPs (Typical Assessment Points)
• To create a core message strategy • To create communication plan (internal practitioner proposal) • To create strategic communication/ PR proposal (external practitioner proposal/job bid) • To create strategic communication/ PR plan (external practitioner plan) • To develop effective messages • To prepare strategy statement for creative team • To develop creative concepts • To produce creatively represented messages • To pretest creatively represented messages	1. Prepare strategic PR/ comm plan 2. Write clear and effective objectives 3. Prepare message strategy statement for creative partners 4. Route strategy statement for approvals 5. Develop creative concepts 6. Manage production of creatively represented messages 7. Pretest message and creative materials 8. Report pretesting results 9. Create implemen- tation plan and schedule	• Communica- tion plan • Strategic communica- tion proposal • Strategic plan • Decision Matrix™ • Message strategy statement for creative team • Brainstorming with creative team • Pretesting methods • Pretesting results report • Time line/ Gantt chart/ Pert chart	• Communica- tion plan (internal) • Strategic communica- tion/PR proposal (external) • Strategic communica- tion/PR plan (external) • Strategy statement for creative team • Pretesting results report • Implemen- tation plan and schedule	• Creative director's approval strategy statement • Client's or management's approval of strategy statement • Client's or management's approval of pretesting results report • Peer's or supervisor's review of implemen- tation plan and schedule	• After drafting implemen- tation plan and schedule

Before Speaking to Latino Market, Listen to What They Say

Andrea Clark was General Motors' general director of communication for diversity and growth markets when she wrote this for PRWeek.

The release of the most recent round of U.S. Census data has shed some timely and much deserved light on the growing influence of the Latino community. "35 million, and with a purchasing power of over $500 billion," read the headlines. But these headlines do not convey the full scope of the Latino experience today, an experience characterized by greater Latino cultural pride and a stronger influence on the American mosaic.

Get weekly news alerts on the consumer, healthcare, or technology industry. Newsletters include news round-ups, features, and jobs tailored to the particular sector.

As more entities seek to engage Latino audiences, PR can play a key role in extending and clarifying your brand's value proposition to this audience, and, in turn, help you build a strong, long-term, culturally-relevant relationship with the Latino community. It all begins with telling a strong, consistent, and relevant story. Your overall positioning should center around what constitutes your brand and its mission for the Latino market. Start this process internally by incorporating all the messages from your organization's teams. Through this function, your communications team will also serve as the "center of expertise" that will communicate internally the full scope of Hispanic activities.

When speaking to the community, you must recognize that perceptions are created by a multitude of messaging signals and sources. In order to communicate effectively, you must identify your audience, understand its mindset, craft the proper messaging, and then tap that community's influencers and leaders in a way to share your story and give it credibility. The most effective communication taps into emotions and establishes a connection with an audience. It's like any human relationship: Before talking about yourself, make sure you understand the individuals you are speaking to.

When reaching out to the Latino community, tap into their strong sense of culture. You'll see this pride in a first-generation immigrant waving his or her flag, or a bilingual, bicultural Latino youth singing and dancing to the latest salsa or Tex-Mex hit. The best way to convey this respect is to identify a spokesperson team that can demonstrate your commitment to the Latino market. They don't have to be Latino (though it's a plus), but they must show a thorough understanding of the culture. Latinos have done an incredible job of creating an extensive network of leaders and organizations to advance their social and economic objectives. Before disseminating your message to this community, you must engage these key audiences. These leaders can provide immensely valuable feedback. Tap into them for counsel as to what your organization is doing right and wrong as it relates to the Hispanic community.

In all PR efforts, there is no stronger third-party endorser for your initiatives than your family of employees. A strong internal communications initiative, including the creation of an internal network of Latinos, will motivate employees to support your overall vision, will encourage them to provide feedback, and ultimately serve as effective spokespeople to communicate the breadth and scope of your efforts. These are the entities that facilitate points of fusion around which the community lives. Research has proven that Latinos will respond most favorably to brands they perceive as caring about their communities. Tap into these groups' leaders to identify areas for collaboration that could favorably impact the host communities, and, in turn, your relationship with them.

Hispanic media is a trusted voice for Latinos as they seek the American dream. They turn to broadcast and print media for information about immigration, education, health, products, services, and other matters that shape their lives and futures. Establish a relationship with Latino media based on respect and adding value beyond sending the press release and cold-calling. Understand their information needs. Tap into them as counselors for feedback on all of your activities. They have the most immediate pulse on the market; learn from them. As more corporations and organizations seek to speak to the Hispanic community, PR can provide them with a great opportunity to differentiate themselves and showcase their Hispanic initiatives. Look for the attribute or focus that sets you apart from the competition. This kind of effort demands a thorough grasp of Latino culture. Understand them, invest in them, communicate to them, and they will thank you.

SOURCE: Andrea Clark, *PRWeek*, Jun 23, 2003

Summary and Review

Developing a Written Strategic Public Relations Proposal
- Public relations proposals and plans are two distinctly different documents. A strategic communication, or PR, proposal is a document developed by an outside practitioner for the purposes of winning the proposed work. A strategic communication, or PR, plan is the document that outlines the work to be accomplished and an overview of how that work will be accomplished.
- A PR proposal is usually written in order to get funding for new client work or even new work within an organization because it is needed by an in-house practitioner to get buy-in from a manager or chief executive.
- A solicited proposal is written in response to a request for proposal (RFP) distributed by an organization seeking assistance.
- An unsolicited proposal is submitted to an organization when you have knowledge about the organization's possible needs or issues facing the organization, but an official RFP has not been issued.

Developing a Written Strategic Public Relations Plan
- The overall goal of the plan should be aligned with the organization's mission.
- The PR plan elements include 1) a statement of the opportunity or problem; 2) goals and objectives; 3) audience; 4) tactics; 5) monitoring, tracking, and evaluation; 6) time line; and 7) budget.
- Objectives are established to assist in measuring the success of your communication efforts and they are based on what your situational analysis and audience research findings reveal.
- There are three types of objectives: informational, behavioral, and attitudinal. Informational objectives state what you want the target audience to know and understand at the end of the communication initiative. Behavioral objectives state the exact action you want the target audience to take, while attitudinal objectives specify the change in attitude or opinion you want from the target audience.
- Public relations communication objectives should be credible and realistic, should be as precise and measurable as possible, and should meet the expectations of the organization or client. They must also be realistic and credible.

Developing Effective Messages and Concepts
- Communication and consumer behavior theories help provide a framework for and assist in the creative work of message development.

- You test messages for three specific reasons: to ensure the target audiences understands the creative execution; to assess whether the target audiences take away the intended message; and to ensure that the message is appropriate for the intended target audiences.
- If you have the time and money, it is wise to pretest the messages and concepts to see which ones are most effective, and then pretest the materials you develop based on the first pretest findings.

Implementation Plan and Schedule
- Implementation plans delineate what activities are scheduled to take place and when, and are accompanied by illustrative charts.
- Templates exist to assist in creating implementation and task flow charts.

Key Terms

Gantt chart (time line)	PR plan (strategic communication plan)	solicited proposal
goals		unique selling proposition (USP)
objectives	PR proposal	
Pert chart	request for proposal (RFP)	unsolicited proposal

Questions for Review and Discussion

1. What is the difference between a communication, or public relations, plan and proposal?

2. What are the major elements of a strategic public relations plan?

3. Discuss informational, behavioral, and attitudinal objectives.

4. What are the five characteristics of effective objectives?

5. How can behavior theory help us to develop effective messages?

6. Discuss the importance of a message strategy statement to PR practitioners.

7. Discuss the importance of a message strategy statement to the creative team.

Web Links

TeamGantt
www.teamgantt.com

Cisco Webex
www.webex.com

Dropbox
www.dropbox.com

JoinMe
www.join.me.com

Campaign Implementation

LAUNCHING A CAMPAIGN

Researching, planning, brainstorming, testing, and replanning bring you to the most exciting phase of the strategic PR process. You can now begin to implement the campaign or program guided by the implementation plan created in the previous phase. Implementing the program or campaign involves doing and applying the selected tactics, paying close attention to the time line and budget, and managing staffing. Along the way, you are also tracking and monitoring success, correcting the course of action or making changes as they arise, and keeping the team up to date on progress. All of this requires a fair amount of multitasking and organization skills, so frequent meetings and updates are crucial to success.

A team meeting of everyone responsible for implementing elements of the campaign or program is the first step in this phase. Sometimes called a **kickoff meeting,** this gathering is convened by the *leader of the team known as the* **account director (AD)** or **project director (PD)** to review the implementation plan and tactical strategy and report on the status of the project. This meeting agenda should include staffing assignments and roles and responsibilities of partner organizations; review of relationships with external team members contracted for the project (e.g., photographers, graphic designers, freelance writers, and meeting or events planners); budget discussion; outline of milestones and client billing; communication protocols; and review of the time line.

Staffing

Staffing depends heavily on how many different organizations are involved in the project. Generally, a client organization working with a public relations firm is likely to have a few staff

> *Anything that is worth doing at all is worth doing well.*
>
> —Philip Dormer Stanhope, Fourth Earl of Chesterfield

members who will work with the PR agency staff. If an organization's internal public relations department is responsible for the project, the staff of that department may work closely with other employees of the organization. Most important, there must be a clear delineation of the roles and responsibilities of everyone on the team. The structure of the staffing assignments can vary greatly and sometimes depends on the culture or idiosyncrasies of the organizations. A simplistic approach is that every major task should have a **task leader** *who is responsible for accomplishing that task within budget and on time.* Task leaders and the project director should meet regularly as a team, and task leaders, as members of the leadership team, should meet individually with the AD or PD to discuss concerns specific to their tasks.

Secondary and tertiary to the task leaders are the members of the teams responsible for executing the many activities that make up the tasks. Staffing assignments can include conducting additional formative research and evaluative research; writing and distributing a host of written tactics such as news releases, brochures, fact sheets, backgrounders, bios, etc.; buying media distribution; and planning news conferences and events. These staff members should be clear on the extent of their responsibilities and from whom they should seek guidance and approval of the products they are charged with delivering.

External Team Members

When campaigns involve partner organizations, the waters are bound to get muddied unless roles and responsibilities are clearly outlined from the very beginning and adhered to until the very end. Also, the protocols for approving materials among organizations should be clear so that issues such as identity (logos, colors, graphics, etc.), clearance and approval of spokespeople, timing, budgets, and logistics are clearly defined. A look at the Robert Wood Johnson Foundation "Cover the Uninsured Week" (CTUW) campaign discussed in previous chapters is a good example. During the past six years, the number of campaign national partners has almost doubled, from 10 to 19, and the campaign now has a national interfaith advisory board, which adds at least another 10 organizations. This part of the campaign strategy likely has a task leader and support by at least one coordinator.

Working with external vendors and/or freelancers is very common in the practice of public relations. Rarely does a company, agency, or organization have the necessary staff to implement every element of a campaign. Vendors are companies that provide services (such as photography, video recording, printing, sound, web development and hosting, graphic design, teleconferencing, media tours, satellite feeds) or products (such as audio and video news releases, giveaway items and novelties, banners, furnishings) needed for the project on a fee basis. Sometimes freelance practitioners are used because of their expertise in a particular subject or practice area. For instance, a person with subject matter knowledge of teens and smoking cessation might be helpful in a teen smoking initiative, or a practitioner with broad experience in communicating with Asian American parents would bring expertise to such a campaign.

Effective management of the vendors and freelancers is a must for a successful project, and team leaders with outside assistance are responsible for review and approval of the scopes of the work to be performed, contract negotiations, approval of invoices for payment, and monitoring progress of activities and final products. Roles and responsibilities may change during the course of a project, and the AD or PD makes sure that these are spelled out so that everyone on the team knows who is responsible for tasks during the life of the project. For instance, an external vendor may complete the initial web development and design, but an internal staff member may take on the responsibilities of monitoring and updating the site.

Budget Tracking

Keeping track of the overall budget is usually the domain of the account director or project director and is one of her most important duties. Monitoring the budget means making sure the project is within the budget guidelines *and* determining how to mitigate costs.

Hopefully, the initial budget negotiations result in funding that can support the activities recommended for the program. Underfunded communication campaigns and programs can fail the most brilliant strategies. When strategies and tactics are chosen based on their costs and not on their effectiveness, the outcome is likely to be less than satisfying for the client, the practitioner, and the audience. If you have never taken an accounting course, consider doing so. It will better equip you to handle the financial side of our business. If taking an accounting course is unrealistic, at least familiarize yourself with accounting principles by consulting a reference guide such as *Accounting for Dummies* or *Business Accounting for Dummies*. If you have never used spreadsheet software such as Excel, familiarize yourself with one and pay close attention to the tutorial. Many agencies, companies, and other organizations have their own computerized accounting systems for which you will be trained if you are an employee. But you will find the training and concepts easier if you are familiar with accounting, and if you are interested in becoming a freelance practitioner, you will need a working knowledge of accounting principles.

While there are many ways to organize or develop a budget, the budget can be divided into three primary areas: 1) labor costs, 2) production costs, and 3) management and administration costs. Clearly, **labor costs** *refer to the cost of personnel required to get the activities accomplished and can run as much as 70 to 80 percent of the budget.* Agencies or freelancers would reflect the labor costs on an hourly basis, with the hourly rates reflecting costs such as benefits and other compensation in their proposals. During the implementation phase, monitoring budget for personnel costs means watching carefully the **burn rate,** *or the speed at which the personnel costs of the budget are being expended.* Agency employees and freelancers should have time recording tools to assist in making sure the practitioners' hours are applied to the proper client or projects. Salaried employees of the communication department of an organization may not have to keep track of the hours. Traditionally, timesheets are the tool for recording hours, and hours are recorded against a charge code associated with the project or client. Task leaders are usually given an estimate of target hours for each team member at the initial kickoff meeting. This helps them to manage hours and know when they are in danger of overspending.

Production costs are *the expenses incurred when working with outside vendors who design and produce many of the campaign or program materials.* These include printers, graphic designers, advertising costs, catering, and event equipment. The **administrative costs** are *those expenses that keep things moving during a project such as travel, shipping, rental cars, office supplies, copying, and almost every cost of conducting an event.* Services provided under this category are paid for by the agency or freelancer and "marked up." The **markup,** *sometimes called handling or service fees, run approximately 15 to 20 percent of the cost.*

Billing the Client

The AD or PD is usually responsible for client billing as well. Providing timely and accurate bills to the client is crucial in the implementation of a campaign. There are several ways to bill a client, and the billing method should be negotiated when the project costs are discussed before contracts are signed. One way of billing is to divide the negotiated cost of the project by the number of months the work is expected to transcend and the result represents the monthly billing amount. A 12-month program cost of $144,000 can be billed to the client at $12,000 per month. Another approach to billing is to negotiate a retainer so that the client pays an amount in advance. For example, as a 12-month project begins, the client would pay a substantial amount of the proposed costs before the work is started, and you or the agency "draws down" on the retainer to get the work accomplished. This approach means you would be less likely to have to finance the work.

Another option is to agree to bill at major "milestones" or deliverables. Under this term, you can determine the costs for producing communication materials and bill for the costs of each deliverable such as research protocols and reports, drafts of particular materials, concepts and message strategy statements; and dissemination of collateral. A very risky and therefore rare arrangement is to agree to complete the project and bill the client after completion. Terms such as this expose you or the agency to greater liability, as you may never be paid.

Cross-Project Communication

Another important role of the PD, AD, and team leaders is communication. No matter the size of the project, the lead public relations practitioner is responsible for keeping everyone informed about what is going on as an initiative is implemented. In addition to the regularly scheduled meetings, written communication and telephone calls are important to ensuring everyone is on the same page. This includes the client and others within the organization or agency. There are many who may not have a direct role in the project but who are expected to have at least tacit knowledge of progress, success, and challenges such as vice presidents of the practice area, members of the board in nonprofits and foundations, financial officers, etc.

The Time Line

Finally, everyone should leave the kickoff meeting with an understanding of the time line. The idea is for everyone to visualize what must be accomplished by him in order to get the project in on time. See our previous discussion on time lines in Chapters 10 and 11.

CAMPAIGN MATERIALS

Let's take a step back to recall how you got to the step of creating campaign materials. You conducted formative audience research at the beginning so that you could develop messages and materials to which your audiences will pay attention, understand, and act upon. You know that your messages are competing with the many messages that barrage your audiences every day, so you used what you learned to create audience profiles. You profiled the key audiences as instructed by the formative research you conducted. Part of the profiling helped you select the best openings and channels for reaching those audiences.

As a result, you outlined a tactics strategy in the PR plan (see Chapter 11), delineating the specific tactics and how they should be implemented because the tactics selected to communicate the campaign messages depend on the objectives stated for the target audiences. Your strategic thinking assisted you in the selection of each medium for the message. Now you can have confidence in your materials.

Controlled and Uncontrolled Media

Campaign materials known as **collateral material** and tactics can be categorized as *controlled* and *uncontrolled media* or products. In this case we are talking about public relations media and not mass media. **Controlled media** are *those products and messages that you create and over which you have the most control.* Newsletters, brochures, web pages, presentations, annual reports, and paid advertising are all controlled media. Content, timing, and distribution of these media depend completely upon you as the PR practitioner.

Uncontrolled media are *those products you cannot control after they are sent.* After a release, media kit, or feature story is sent to a news-gathering organization, you have no control over how, when, where, or even in what context it will be used by producers, reporters, and editors. The news release in all of its forms—print, video, electronic, interactive, and audio—is a perfect example of uncontrolled public relations media. You carefully choose all of the words, images, and sounds of the news release, and you tell the story perfectly from the client's point of view. However, a news release can be used as it is received or it can be used as the start of or part of a new journalistic endeavor, can be edited, and can be rearranged to suit the editors. In fact, B-roll—a series of rough video images that incorporate a variety of different camera angles with natural sound—and audiotape can be used many times over. See Chapters 14, 15, and 16 for a discussion of these and other PR media.

Tactical Strategies

Campaign materials must be created to accommodate your tactical strategies. Tactical strategies include news media relations, websites, including social media, email, events and exhibitions, advertising, publications, grassroots, partnerships, direct mail, speeches and meetings, and film and video. Each of these strategies is a well-thought-out plan for how to use the various tactics. The list of possibilities is exhaustive and all are not appropriate to every campaign. Thought must be given to what strategies best suit a campaign message and audience(s). As we discussed previously, public relations practitioners think in terms of an integrated communication approach, when appropriate combining more than one strategy for the most effective communication.

If we look at the Robert Wood Johnson Foundation "Cover the Uninsured Week" example from previous discussions, we see a very integrated approach to reaching the primary audiences targeted for the campaign messages. RWJF's public relations agency, GMMB, used a partnership or constituency-building strategy to gain the support of national, regional, and local organizations. The RWJF relationship with 19 national partners helped increase funding and exposure through almost 900 events in 50 states. GMMB combined bought media with earned media, advertising in major newspapers and on television while garnering national news media coverage. An arts and entertainment media strategy was pursued to encourage network executives, writers, and producers to include the topic of the uninsured in television scripts. Of course, with policy makers and influencers among the primary audiences, it did not hurt to have two former presidents as spokespersons.

MATERIALS PRODUCTION PROCESS

Managing the Process

The actual production of collateral materials developed from the message strategy is a multitiered process and a **Process Milestone.** The idea is that the PD or AD monitors progress through continual contact with the task leaders responsible for materials. This is where a well-delineated Gantt chart comes in handy (see Chapter 11 for an example of a Gantt chart.) The PD should have regularly scheduled meetings with the task leaders to review time lines and status of materials production. The task leaders are responsible for monitoring the progress of everyone involved in the project. The task leaders must coordinate with graphic artists, website developers, writers, printers, and others responsible for the production of collateral products. They conduct reviews with internal and external sources to monitor progress and in preparation for reviews with the PD.

The task leader responsible for coordinating and monitoring partner involvement must be a good manager of relationships. This team member has to walk a veritable tightrope to keep the project moving and to keep all parties invested in the relationship. This means being sure all agreements are in writing and that every organization is aware of its responsibilities. As regards the production of materials, the task leader has to stay in constant contact to be sure the responsible organization is on track with development and production without appearing to micro-manage the work. This is a task that profits greatly from weekly conference calls because they allow all parties to discuss status and the task leader can ferret out any possible complications or concerns.

All materials are submitted in final draft or mock-up form to the PD for client approval and pretesting if approved.

Pretesting

The practitioner learns a great deal about the effectiveness of her messages during the message and concept testing processes described in Chapter 11. Testing materials during the implementation phase is another important **TYPICAL ASSESSMENT POINT** and should be budgeted in any proposal, but it is important to recognize that another round of testing may not be valued by the client or management. The argument to make is that testing materials allows you to talk to the primary audience and get a reaction to materials *and* it is an opportunity to talk to target audiences about more than just the message. With materials testing, you can determine if the many elements—graphics, photographs, fonts, logos, icons, taglines, and others— actually resonate with the target audience. The test is to ensure that your key audiences understand the creative execution, to assess whether or not the audiences take away the intended message, and to ensure that the message is appropriate.

This research can be conducted in many ways such as focus groups, usability studies, cognitive interviews, and mall intercept interviews. The least expensive and still effective methodology is the mall intercept interview, a research technique that involves stationing interviewers at a point frequented by individuals from the target audience such as shopping malls (see Chapter 6 for a discussion of research techniques). Interviewers stop, or intercept, respondents and interview them using a list of qualitative research questions.

Study participants are asked to read or look at the materials and answer a set of questions similar to those used in pretesting to determine that the materials:

1. Are credible.
2. Are attractive to the target audience and will be noticed amongst competing messages.
3. Appear to be intended for the target audience.
4. Would be attended to by target audience.
5. Are understood by target audience—main points, action to take, and how every word is recognizable, familiar, culturally acceptable, and friendly.
6. Are visually and aurally relevant to the audience members.

In some cases pilot testing is possible, but is rare. A pilot test allows practitioners to conduct a "dry run" or "dress rehearsal" of campaigns if it is national or even statewide in scope. Essentially, it is like conducting an experiment by rolling the campaign materials out in selected cities that have the characteristics and demographics of the target audience and market. The primary advantage is that the findings can be projected onto the entire population to be reached, and quantifying results can measure success. The primary disadvantage is that it takes additional time and means a slower rollout. Pilot testing can help save money in the long run but it is an added cost. Most important is to be sure the sites selected for any pretesting are representative of the demographics, relevant to the problem the campaign addressed, possess the resources necessary for audiences to take the desired action, and represent the geographic and political environment sought. Again, as in most cases, caution must be given in dealing with cultural differences. We cannot assume that because we are trying to test success with Asian, Hispanic, or African-American cultures, that San Antonio, Miami, Los Angeles, New York, Oakland, and Chicago cultural communities will be identical.

Finalizing Materials

Hopefully, the materials pass the test with the key audiences. If the materials require more adjustments, you have to determine the degree to which you are confident about making changes and make the best recommendations for improving the materials to the client. After complete approval of all materials, a **Process Milestone,** the concluding stage of materials development begins—finalizing the products for distribution. This step involves following up on some of the steps taken during the planning stage. You now know the final specifications and standards, design, graphics, colors, quantities, and distribution needs for each collateral product. Orders can now be placed with the printers and production houses contacted during the planning stage. Most practitioners have worked with vendors previously and like to use those with whom they have had satisfying experiences. However, it is always wise to

ENGAGING ETHICS

To Release or Not Release?

You have spent the past three months moving a new brochure through the process for a very important client. During the process you selected photographs that include a shot that basically "defines" your message. The photograph includes an image of an employee of your company. When the employee was photographed, she agreed to sign a release letter, allowing you to use her image. She has left the company for a new position and did not sign the release. Later you learn that she is a professional model and voiceover talent on a part-time basis. It is time for the brochure to go into production and you do not have a release letter. What do you do?

get bids from new vendors who can expand a list of "go to" companies and checking with colleagues who might share vendor names and contact information is always good. The rule of thumb is to acquire bids from three vendors in order to make the best and most affordable choice. Of course, the cheapest is not always the best choice. Consider requiring references from vendors in order to increase the opportunity for getting quality jobs accomplished on deadline. It is impossible to say too much about planning ahead for the production of collateral materials. Unfortunately, not everyone can meet the deadlines they promise. Allowing an abundance of time for production is the key to success.

All products must be carefully checked during this stage of production. Printers and production houses provide "proofs" to approve along the way of the process. The key is reviewing everything before final production. You should take sufficient time and enlist another pair of eyes to be sure the materials are accurate and meet the standards and specifications established in collaboration with the vendor. The vendor should keep you informed of the progress of the projects and advise of any changes that must be made.

Collateral materials are *made of many components, including quotations, photographs, video, audio, and testimonials.* **Release letters** are *required in order to give you complete and unrestricted use of these elements, which grant you permission to use materials as you indicate are appropriate* (see Figure 12.1). Usually, this is not a problem, especially if it is made clear from the outset. The important thing is to be sure the releases are signed and kept as part of your files. If actors have been employed for the material, they should be asked to sign the releases at the time of the photo shoot. Sometimes the release is difficult to accomplish because of union concerns. If this is the case, you can negotiate a "buyout," which means the residual value is paid in a lump sum amount as opposed to having to pay for each use. Such is the case also with stock photography royalties. You can buy stock photos for a flat fee or pay for each use.

Many things can go wrong and many problems arise during the production of materials from small mistakes such as typos to very big mistakes such as inaccuracies and wrong photographs, to even bigger problems such as unavailability of everything from the paper for a brochure to a spokesperson backing out at the last minute. As the PR practitioner, you are the final decision maker and arbiter when Murphy's Law, "What can go wrong, will go wrong," takes effect. In some cases, creative staff is able to assist in review. In other circumstances, you are on your own. After materials are checked and triple-checked and the client or management has approved, the dissemination plan for each collateral product can be implemented.

Client Name

Project Title

Talent and Consent Waiver

I agree to the use of my likeness or voice, or both, by the Client Name and its employees, agents, assigns, partners, and affiliates in audio or visual materials. Such materials may include, but are not limited to, still photography (film or digital), motion pictures or videotape, and voice recordings. These materials may be used in forms such as print media (for example, newspapers, magazine, and brochures), electronic media (for example, television, video, and audio), the Internet or Client Name's internal website.

Any of these materials may be used with information including, but not limited to, my age, job, employment, and relationship to Client Name. Client Name may use these materials in their entirety or in part.

I understand that I am supplying my likeness or voice, or both to Client Name without limit on their use and that Client Name does not need my approval each time my likeness, voice, or both are used. I also understand that I will not be compensated (that is, paid in cash or kind) for use of my information, likeness, or voice.

I state that I am at least 18 years of age or, if I am younger than 18 years of age, I understand that my parent or guardian, if he or she agrees to these terms, must provide consent for the release and use of the materials detailed in this form.

Dated this _____ day of _____, 20_____.

_____

Print Full Name   _Signature_

Address:_____

Email Address: _____

Home Phone: _____

Parent or Guardian Consent

I, the undersigned, being the parent and/or guardian of the above named minor, do hereby consent to the above authorization and general release.

Dated this _____ day of _____, 20_____.

_____

Print Child's Full Name (if under 18 years old)

_____

Print Parent's Full Name   _Signature_

Figure 12.1

Sample of Release
Letter

DISSEMINATING MATERIALS AND MONITORING IMPLEMENTATION

Dissemination

Dissemination of collateral material depends, of course, on the product itself. For instance, a public service announcement is usually developed for television or radio and sometimes online, while an ad is developed for print media. Also, a single collateral piece can be delivered in many ways. For instance, a brochure can be disseminated through USPS mail, email, on a website, or at point of contact such as a doctor's office or grocery store. Decisions such as these are made when the dissemination plan is written. A discussion of the various public relations tactics are outlined in several dissemination strategies for several controlled and uncontrolled media products in Chapters 14, 15, and 16. For convenience of this discussion, a dissemination plan answering the following questions should be presented to the client:

1. Who are the primary and secondary audiences? Be specific in describing each.
2. State the objective for each audience.
3. Are there intermediary audiences? That is, are there audiences and organizations who will assist you in disseminating your media products?
4. What is the quantity of materials to be distributed?
5. How will you distribute? What specific vehicles will you employ?
6. What specific assumptions will you make in terms of quantities and markets reached?
7. What are the expectations for your partner organizations in distribution and dissemination?
8. What additional materials may be needed to accompany the products (e.g., cover letters, packaging, email templates, PowerPoint presentations, and advertising)?

Monitoring the Rollout

Monitoring actually takes the pulse of the several activities that are taking place during the implementation phase. Monitoring, which is both ***Process Milestone*** and a **TYPICAL ASSESSMENT POINT,** is designed to retrieve feedback, to track problems and to inform campaign adjustments and alterations. It can help the practitioner to check quality, to address and anticipate problems, to know that implementation is taking place as planned, to begin early assessment, and to determine where new efforts or additional materials may be needed. In essence, effective monitoring is the way to stay in tune and on top of what is transpiring in the implementation of the project.

Monitoring the rollout of the campaign or program is actually the first step in the evaluation process, but it is helpful to include it in this chapter so that it is incorporated in your thoughts as you implement. In fact, this step of implementation is actually evaluating the process and progress of everything designed for implementation. Here, you watch closely the day-to-day process in order to understand what is happening and what may need changing. The monitoring and tracking process helps you begin to see the effects of the campaign along the way instead of waiting until the end to look at outcomes. If you look at the Robert Wood Johnson Foundation CTUW campaign, you can delineate the questions that tracking activities may have answered. As a reminder, in Chapter 11 we stated the overall objectives of the CTUW campaign might have been:

- To increase awareness among voters of the uninsured by 20 percent during the month of March
- To increase public awareness of the issue by 10 percent during March

- To create a partnership of more than ten national organizations before the campaign launch
- To demonstrate broad support for action on the issue by getting Democratic and Republican formal leadership in the Senate and House to send letters to colleagues, encouraging their support during the CTUW
- To generate national media attention during March

We know that GMMB used an integrated communication approach in its campaign, employing public communication tactics such as town hall meetings and regional conferences; a national advertising campaign; partnership development; media relations to garner news media attention; and collateral materials. During the implementation phase, GMMB needed to answer a number of questions as the campaign progressed such as:

1. How many people attended the planned town hall meetings and conferences?
2. How many organizations participated as partners for CTUW?
3. How many materials were distributed to the target audiences?
4. Did the partner organizations distribute the collateral materials and how many?
5. How many media hits did the campaign efforts generate?
6. How many members of the target audience were reached through the paid advertising? Was it executed on time?
7. Did the campaign stay on budget?
8. Were all activities conducted on time? Was the overall time line adhered to throughout the campaign?
9. How many people have taken the action—telephone calls, visited website, etc.?
10. Have all organizations responded to inquiries appropriately?

It is helpful to understand what should be monitored and why before putting measuring structures into place. You should ask a series of questions to determine monitoring objectives and why they are important to measuring the success of the campaign or program. Campaign or program objectives and tactic objectives can inform development of monitoring objectives.

Let's use the Robert Wood Johnson Foundation's CTUW campaign as an example, again. We know that one of the objectives was to generate national media attention and to create public awareness of the plight of the uninsured in the United States. The campaign employed several tactics to accomplish these objectives. They employed two strategies that could be monitored—paid advertising and media relations. Stated objectives for measuring overall media exposure during implementation might be "to determine if paid and public service advertising ran as planned and scheduled, if media relations tactics resulted in media coverage, and how many of our target audiences were reached."

Another objective of the CTUW campaign was to increase awareness of the plight of the uninsured among Washington, DC opinion leaders and opinion elites. During implementation, the campaign staff might want "to determine if more of the DC opinion leaders and elites were becoming aware of the issue."

Tracking Systems

Monitoring requires an ongoing structure or manner for keeping track of all of the campaign activities. This system ensures that you are aware of how things are progressing and assists you in making changes in the midst of the implementation. Some activities lend themselves to simply counting actions such as how many telephone calls or website hits occurred during a particular period, how callers or visitors found out about the initiative, or how many people attended an event or watched a show. This counting can be monitored by programming the website to count hits, tracking calls, counting tickets, or counting brochures disseminated. Some activities may be tracked every day while others may require weekly or monthly tracking.

More sophisticated monitoring systems may be needed to track other activities. Political campaigns and highly sensitive issues may require tracking such as overnight surveys and quarterly surveys to measure the effects of activities. For instance, some clients want to know if the target audiences understand the desired action and if the action is taken. This requires a research plan that will allow measurement of communication success and indicate precisely what changes need to be made to the communication in order to get the desired action from the audience. The research will require omnibus surveys that deliver fast turnaround times, and you will be using "panels" of previously screened and "opted-in" participants who will respond by Internet within a matter of a few hours.

Media Exposure

Tracking overall media exposure for a campaign requires a few different tracking mechanisms. Publications in which you purchased advertising space will provide tear sheets or copies of the pages on which your advertisement ran. Similarly, if you purchased television and/or radio time, the stations will provide a list of when each announcement ran and a list of additional times donated by the station as public service advertising. If you worked with a public service director or community relations manager at a station or publication to get public service time or space, you can provide a feedback, or "bounce-back," postage-paid card with a few questions. Earned media is tracked in a variety of ways. Tracking services that monitor news wires, newspapers

BRIEF CASE STUDY

Getting Boomers on the Move

With obesity among American adults climbing to an astounding 65 percent, the American Heart Association (AHA) focused on adult inactivity to key audiences. The "Start!" campaign is an awareness strategy designed to raise funds and to encourage adults to engage in healthy behavior. The campaign's focus is baby boomers (adults 45 to 64 in 2009) and seeks to reach them where they spend most of their time—at work. The primary objective is to get the boomers to build walking into their daily routines. Other objectives are to get employers to include walking as a part of organization culture and to raise funds for research.

An opening event for the campaign was held in Manhattan's Financial District and featured the CEOs of American Hospital Association, Subway, ConAgra, and AstraZeneca ringing the NYSE opening bell to emphasize business involvement. The integrated communication strategy uses media relations, events, advertising, celebrity appearances, and promotions to generate awareness. A PSA campaign strategy led up to the launch and national and local sponsors were involved during the year-long campaign.

Minneapolis-St. Paul International Airport employees encourage airline passengers to "start!"

Working the Case

1. What staffing needs would you need to run this campaign for its first 52 weeks?
2. What methods would you use to track the activities of the campaign?
3. What social media tactics could the campaign have used?

and magazines, and television and radio news are the most popular tracking mechanisms. They provide clippings and transcripts of news coverage on your issue, event, or organization. This coverage includes mentions as well as complete stories.

To track whether or not more opinion leaders and opinion elites became aware of an issue during the course of implementation, a baseline survey taken before the implementation of the campaign would have to be conducted. During the implementation, other surveys must be conducted to see if the campaign messages move the needle. In the case of CTUW, tracking polls were used to see if the issue and ads were recalled among these key audiences during the implementation period.

Tracking the efficiency of the distribution of collateral materials is another implementation process evaluation. Its objective is to evaluate whether the manner and quantities of distribution are progressing as planned. Tracking methods can include using forms to assist in counting the number of materials going out, helping to determine if new materials need to be ordered. This is referred to as inventory tracking. It is also wise to keep track of the collateral materials distributed to partner organizations and to monitor whether the materials are being displayed, distributed, or placed as agreed. Simply visiting the partners' sites and creating distribution lists can assist in this monitoring.

Tracking Databases

Many research and public relations firms have sophisticated computer databases that allow them to track news coverage for clients. Research companies offer customized tracking and analysis of media coverage. For example, LatinClips provides both bilingual and English analysis of print media coverage and online Hispanic forums, including verification and assessment of a campaign's key messages and audience demographics for each source. Table 12.1 is a listing of features and database offerings.

Table 12.1

Types of Tracking

Scanned or text version of the article or streaming broadcast/television/radio clip: For many PR pros, seeing the actual story is still important, although the story's placement has become less of an issue.

Impressions/opportunities to see: Show how many people were exposed to a particular article or televison or radio clip.

Share of voice/discussion: Shows how much an organization's coverage comprises the entire amount of coverage about the industry or subject.

Tone: Shows if the slant of coverage is positive or negative. Many measurement companies use this to determine an overall score for coverage.

Competitor tracking: Measures your organization's media coverage against that of similar organizations or competitors to see if it differs in quantity or quality.

Spokesperson messaging: Helps you to determine if a company's spokesperson is "on message." This is important to the overall strategy.

Third-party commentary: Helps you to monitor and analyze what third-party experts, customers, and competitors say about a client.

Table 12.1   *(continued)*

The Measurement Menu

The following is a sample of some of the measurement and monitoring firms and the clip-book solutions that they offer:

Biz360: Its Media Insights product aggregates and analyzes content from print, broadcast, online, and blog media. It offers a variety of metrics that can then be used to generate reports about a company's media coverage. It also offers in-depth campaign tracking reports prepared by Biz360's research team.

BurrellesLuce: Provides a full range of media monitoring services and tracks 5,000 print publications and wire services delivered through email and web reporting.

CARMA International: Its CARMA Online product allows users to search press coverage by subject, time frame, publication type, company, circulation type, and country. The software then generates a chart showing the volume of stories and favorability rating, which can be printed or downloaded onto a spreadsheet. In addition, users can obtain information on their coverage in the news media. Other functions include the ability to search by journalist and spokesperson.

Cision: Provides press clippings, media monitoring services, and media coverage evaluation.

Cymfony: Offers a suite of products, including Cymfony Dashboard, which offers analysis and reporting capabilities; Digital Consumer Insight, which does the same for consumer-generated media; and Orchestra, one of its newer products, which offers a convergence of traditional and consumer-generated media. It also offers reports prepared by the Cymfony research team.

Delahaye: Its MediaCompass product is a web-based media monitoring and analysis tool. The company also offers detailed measurement on a quarterly, monthly, or even daily basis.

Dow Jones Factiva: Offers several products and services including business news monitoring and tracking.

KD Paine & Partners: Offers the Do-it-Yourself and FYI Dashboard solutions, both customized products that allow users to view information about media coverage, including opportunities to see share of positioning on key issues and share of positive and negative coverage. It also allows users to generate charts and graphs.

Lone Buffalo: The company offers a web-based product that monitors news and allows users to search by topic, product, competitor, publication, journalist, and date range. Users can track coverage of certain issues or business goals, as well. The product is also optimized for real-time updates.

VMS: Offers Insight, which allows users to monitor and analyze broadcast, print, and online content, as well as generate graphs and charts. Its Broadcast Center product does the same for broadcast content. The company recently acquired PRTrak, which offers a do-it-yourself web-based measurement solution for clients, as well as in-depth analysis that can be incorporated into VMS' other products.

Vocus: Their Analytics software product analyzes print, broadcast, and online media coverage in real time. The product also allows users to create and electronically distribute media coverage analysis.

Reporting Results and Adjusting the Plan

Regardless of your choice of monitoring mechanisms, the tracking process requires that you diligently report to your client or management. Reporting the results of the implementation can take several forms from conference calls to emails to in-person meetings. You should provide updates and feedback to your client at regular intervals, noting the status of every activity. You can use your Gantt and Pert charts to create a simple dashboard. The dashboard should be color coded to indicate the status of the activities. For instance, add to the Gantt chart the colors green, yellow, and red; green

Table **12.2**	Campaign Implementation Process Guide and Checklist

Objectives	Steps	Tools	Deliverables	Process Milestones	TAPs (Typical Assessment Points)
• To implement strategies and tactics successfully to accomplish the established objectives.	1. Launch campaign 2. Produce campaign materials 3. Pretest materials 4. Disseminate materials 5. Track & measure success 6. Report results 7. Readjust the plan	• Tracking documents • Implementation plan • Tactical strategy plan • Status report • Budget & budget guidelines • Timesheets • Audience profiles • Audience research strategies for materials pretesting • Vendor agreements • Delivery channels • Bounce-backs, clipping services, polls, & surveys • Evaluative research methods	• Kick-off meeting agenda • Milestones & billing schedule • Campaign time line • Staff assignments • Tactics/ collateral materials (proofs, preliminary, final) • Vendor agreements • Dissemination plan • Distribution lists	• Kick-off meeting • Preliminary tactics/ collateral materials for pretesting • Finalized tactics/ collateral materials for distribution • Pretesting results report • Monitoring report	• Upon receiving pretesting results report • Upon receiving monitoring report(s)

to indicate successful, yellow to signify that an activity warrants closer monitoring, and red to alert you to a need for change.

If there are problems with the rollout such as materials are not being distributed by your partners or your organization lacks the staff necessary to execute your social media strategy, you can adjust your plan in time to improve execution. See Table 12.2 for the Campaign Implementation Process Guide and Checklist.

PROFESSIONAL POINT OF VIEW

Measurement of Outcomes Is Integral to the Future of PR

Lou Capozzi was CEO of MS&L and chairman of the Council of PR Firms when he wrote this for PRWeek.

Several respected senior PR counselors have been speaking out lately about the reasons PR can't be measured accurately. The problem is, they're looking at a dated model for PR measurement—oriented around output, rather than outcomes.

Business is like football—you either score or you don't. And like football, we all ought to be accountable for the outcomes of our business efforts—money in, results out. PR is no exception.

Other communications disciplines have blazed this path before us, and we should follow their trail. In advertising, where the financial stakes are high and accountability has been an implicit part of the business for many years, the measure falls into two categories: impact and influence. Let's look at the opportunity for measuring PR work in these two arenas.

First, impact. If we set out to deliver a message to an audience, we should be willing to be measured on how effectively and efficiently we delivered that message. There's little point in counting clips if we don't also take into account who the clips reached, how often we reached them, and how many of our messages were conveyed. We must subject our coverage to an analysis of reach and frequency, which any advertising media firm can do for a small amount of money. Simple stuff, but critical to turning the corner on one of our profession's Achilles' heels.

Second, influence. Most large firms and major brands have tracking studies in place to measure key brand attributes like familiarity, favorability, and audience intentions to act. PR needs to engage in this effort and take responsibility—and credit—for its role in the outcomes.

These measures can apply to every facet of our work, from marketing PR programs to CEO counseling to crisis avoidance. They're not esoteric number crunching exercises. They're straightforward, tried and true techniques for understanding the outcomes created by communications.

The classic example of PR advice that can't be quantified is the immeasurable value of a crisis avoided. The problem is, if the crisis had happened despite our advice (let's say the lawyers' advice prevailed!), we certainly would be moaning about the negative impact on the company's reputation. So we ought to be able to celebrate the value of steady positive feedback from the marketplace when the reverse is true.

Stressing the importance of judgment or trust in our relationship with management begs the issue. Of course we need that. But until PR people are willing to be evaluated on the impact and influence of our advice and our work, we won't earn that "seat at the table" with other executives who understand the importance of results.

We've spent many years building the reputation and credibility of our industry. The education of what PR can and can't do is still ongoing, and we shouldn't hang our hats on any one tool or technique. But measurement is vital to the future success of our industry. Our challenge now is to agree on the most effective methodology for measuring our work.

Measurement isn't only for the benefit of convincing management of our value or gaining a bigger budget for the next launch. By holding ourselves accountable for the work that we do, we can learn how to do it better. That's how we have advanced our profession and its goals, and how we'll continue to do so.

Unquestionably PR has a unique value proposition. But its value can and should be measured. So, what can we do from here?

One, come together as an industry and embrace a consistent methodology for measurement. Two, champion measurement to demonstrate the value of our work. Three, continue to push our profession to embrace their role as business—not just communications—counselors.

As business counselors, we should recognize that PR is both an art and a science. When your strategic counsel helps a CEO recover from a worldwide crisis with limited damage to the corporation's reputation, that's art. But if you can raise the awareness and relevance of a cleaning product to college students through audience insights, third-party alignments, and a targeted grassroots campaign, that's science. The effect of both can and should be measured.

We shouldn't be afraid to embrace the left and right sides of our PR "brain." Measurement should be an integral part of the profession's culture—hand in hand with research and strategic planning.

I respectfully agree with my professional colleagues that there is a time and place for measurement in our profession. The time and place is now.

SOURCE: Lou Capossi for *PRWeek*, February 23, 2004

Summary and Review

Launching a Campaign

- A well-planned implementation stands to gain the most success for a communication campaign or program. It increases your chances of reaching your audience with the right message, at the right time, and in the most effective manner.
- While it is the most exciting phase, implementation can be the most stressful because during this time everything you have developed is now in process and there is much to monitor, track, manage, and communicate.
- Managing an effective implementation requires multitasking items such as staffing, budgeting, contracting with vendors, watching the time line, communicating with internal team members and external partners, and monitoring and tracking results.

Campaign Materials

- Tactical strategies include news media relations, website and email, events and exhibitions, advertising, publications, grassroots, partnerships, direct mail, speeches and meetings, and film and video.
- Testing materials is a **TYPICAL ASSESSMENT POINT** at which you can learn a lot about the possible effectiveness from members of the primary audience. You can find out if the materials are credible, attractive, relevant, and understandable. Findings can assist you in avoiding costly mistakes in materials development.

Materials Production Process

- Production of collateral materials is an important point in the implementation phase and is a ***Process Milestone.*** It must be managed tightly, reviewing time lines, watching status of products, meeting with task leaders, and working with internal and external teams.
- Pretesting during the implementation phase is not typical in the practice but it is an excellent opportunity to assess the effectiveness of collateral materials. It allows you to have direct interaction with your primary audiences and garner their reactions to many elements that make up your message.
- Testing is effective but can be expensive. Mall intercept interviews remain the least expensive and still effective methodology to determine the credibility, appeal and understanding of the message and its elements.
- Finalizing materials means moving the production process to the stage at which vendors can begin to provide proofs and final products. After materials are reviewed and approved by clients or management, the distribution plan for each product can be implemented.

Disseminating Materials and Monitoring Implementation

- Dissemination during the implementation stage must be tightly managed and a dissemination plan is an effective tool for assisting the practitioner in monitoring dissemination.
- The public relations practitioner is responsible for checking all materials as they move from the development phase and enter the production phase and securing all the necessary client approvals, copyright permissions and releases from models, artists, photographers, and others involved or featured in collateral materials.
- Monitoring and tracking during the implementation stage provides feedback on exactly what is transpiring with each of the activities and helps the practitioner to problem solve during the campaign rollout.

- Reporting the results of the implementation can take several forms. You should provide updates and feedback to your client at regular intervals, noting the status of every activity.
- You should use your Gantt and Pert Charts to create a simple dashboard. The dashboard should be color coded to indicate status of the activities. If there are problems with the rollout such as materials are not being distributed by your partners or your organization lacks the capacity to execute your social media strategy, you can adjust your plan in time to improve execution.

Key Terms

account director (AD) or project director (PD)	controlled media	release letters
	kickoff meeting	task leader
administrative costs	labor costs	uncontrolled media
burn rate	markup	
collateral materials	production costs	

Questions for Review and Discussion

1. What argument would you make to persuade a client to include materials testing as a step in the development of a campaign?

2. Make a list of the skills and characteristics you think are necessary to be a good project or account director. Do you possess these skills? If so, how can you hone them, and if not, how can you develop them?

3. Look at a public relations campaign case study submitted for a PRSA Silver Anvil award that has multiple strategies. If you were the project or account director, how would you staff and organize the implementation?

4. What are the many costs that must be monitored and managed in a campaign? How do you do that?

Web Links

Advertising Age
www.adage.com

AdWeek
www.adweek.com

Biz360
www.biz360.com

BrandWeek
www.brandweek.com

Cision
www.cision.com

PRWeek
www.prweek.com

Public Relations Society of America
www.prsa.org

Vocus
Vocus.com

Program Evaluation and Campaign Follow-Up

EVALUATION

Evaluation assesses the effectiveness of a program or campaign in achieving its objectives. While evaluation is at the final stage of the process, it is not the final step. You have conducted evaluative steps and provided feedback to assist throughout the process, but you cannot measure whether your objectives were achieved until you have implemented the initiative. In fact, the evaluation phase of the strategic public relations process brings you full circle to the beginning of the process. Indeed, you are at a discovery phase, again because evaluation is research and is used at the beginning. Conducting and communicating during the evaluation phase is crucial to the strategic practice.

Evaluate what you want—because what gets measured gets produced.

—Dr. James A. Belasco,
professor and author

Those who cannot remember the past are condemned to repeat it.

—George Santayana,
philosopher and essayist

Posing and Answering Overarching Evaluation Questions

Campaign and program evaluation examines and measures the particular outcomes and results of a strategic public relations project. The evaluation should be based completely on the objectives that were set in the planning process. You set clear, specific, and agreed-upon objectives at the outset so that everyone involved knows how you will measure success (see Chapter 11).

Measuring the results of a program or campaign is crucial to delineating accomplishments. It is imperative for you to demonstrate to the client what was accomplished by the campaign or program. You know it is necessary to measure the success of your efforts as you progress, and you must also conduct *evaluative research*. You will find that measuring the success of your efforts to be more important than in the past, as increasingly clients, executives, and funding organizations are asking PR practitioners to demonstrate the effectiveness of communication campaigns or programs.

More and more, clients want to see a return on their investment (ROI). And measuring results should not be limited to output—the products you produced; it must include how you made a difference. It is not helpful alone to indicate how many fashion editors attended the annual "Heart Truth" campaign Red Dress Collection fashion show during New York's Fashion Week for example. But combined with the statistic that awareness of heart disease by women has increased during the five years of the campaign from 34 percent to 57 percent is an indication of results. **Evaluation** *tells us how well we planned and what we learned,* and it is useful information at the formative phase of new programs or campaigns.

As we discussed in Chapter 6, evaluation of strategic public relations efforts takes place at three distinct stages—formative evaluation, process evaluation, and summative evaluation. George Balch and Sharyn Sutton (1997) wrote that evaluation of strategic communication plans should answer three overarching questions. Their approach to evaluation research is not easy but they do have a way of phrasing it simply. "What should we do?" is answered by the formative evaluation you conduct at the beginning. It helps you plan strategy, target your audiences, and create and test messages and materials.

During implementation, evaluation is valuable in helping you answer the question "How are we doing?" Called process evaluation, this stage tells you what is going on in the implementation phase—is everything going as planned, should you make changes while implementation is in process, what should you do the next time? It measures effort and indicates how much has been accomplished.

Finally, summative evaluation answers the question "Did we do it?" It examines the extent to which you accomplished your objectives and had an effect on your key audience. This is the outcome measure that tells you the effect or changes that have taken place during the campaign. It answers questions about individual behavior change, policy change, and changes that come about within the community.

Answering "Did we do it?" is difficult in this field, not because it cannot be done but because it is still rarely done. There are a few reasons. First, it is an expense many clients and organizations don't want to incur. Research is not an inexpensive item. Second, when the campaign or program is completed, practitioners are well on their way to another project and are often pulled away from the existing project. Last, many practitioners are not evaluation savvy and have not planned the project with reasonable and measurable objectives. This is unfortunate, as more and more funding sources, organizations, and clients are clamoring for demonstration of the ROI from public relations activities. As a result, practitioners talk a lot about evaluation but practice it less. A study by Dr. Walter K. Lindenmann, former head of Ketchum Communications' research unit independent consultant specializing in measurement, found that less than 3 percent of public relations campaign total budgets go to evaluation.

Is this discussion an indication that evaluative research is easy or that it should be written off as never happening? Of course not. Practitioners should continue to emphasize its value and continue to encourage clients to invest in evaluation. At the end of the day, evaluation is the beginning of formative research—back to the beginning of the process.

Basic Evaluation Rules

You will recognize some of the basic principles of public relations evaluation from the discovery and planning phases of the process. This is because you have used formative and process or iterative evaluation throughout to ensure that your communication with key audiences is on track.

1. There is no single right way to evaluate a public relations initiative. Evaluation design depends on the purpose of the research and campaign or program objectives. Researchers do not rely on a single method of evaluation but use triangulation—providing the results of several research methods to avoid weaknesses of findings—to be sure results are not skewed.
2. It takes several research methodologies to evaluate the effectiveness of public relations efforts. Usually, you must combine several methods to evaluate your results. And the findings from each method must be analyzed in light of each other.
3. It is crucial from the outset to establish clear and measurable objectives for each target audience that are in concert with the goals and objectives of the organization or the client.
4. You must know the difference between measuring output such as collateral or products disseminated and results or impact such as whether the key audience actually understood and retained the message and took the action or behavior you sought.
5. While every practitioner points to it and all clients like to see it, mass media coverage is not the pinnacle of public relations evaluation. It really tells you very little about the success or effectiveness of the message you sent because it cannot tell you if your target audiences attended to the message and took the action promoted.
6. Remember that most public relations initiatives take place among other efforts on behalf of the client or organization. You must be sure that evaluation takes into account all current activities. It is difficult to isolate the effects of each individual campaign.
7. Ask only the necessary and relevant questions. Researchers often get carried away with formulating questions, becoming intrigued by interesting questions but not necessarily helpful ones.

Evaluation Study Design

Like our programs and campaigns, evaluation requires a clear plan. Much of the evaluation plan is put forth in the communication plan discussed in Chapter 10. Now that you are at the evaluation stage, you should pull it out for guiding your evaluation design. The **evaluation design** *should include at least the following elements:*

- **Statement of goals and objectives:** You are certain why you included these in the planning stage. Use them now to explain what is being measured and how they indicate if you accomplished your stated purpose.
- **A list of research questions that guide the evaluation work:** See a discussion of research questions in Chapters 6 and 10.
- **A delineation of data you are collecting:** Be specific in outlining the data you intend to collect to measure the accomplished objectives.
- **An outline of the methodology:** This section explains how the research will be conducted, specifically *how* the data will be collected. It should include the specific research methods to be employed (e.g., type of survey, focus groups, one-on-one interviews), the data collection protocols (e.g., screeners, questionnaires, topic guides) and how they will be tested, recruiting plans, specific participants to be recruited, the sample size, and the timing of the data collection.
- **Analysis procedure:** Here you outline what happens to the data after they are collected. This step explains to the client and field researchers how the data will be analyzed. The analysis procedure affects the design and implementation of the data collection. For instance, if a content analysis is to be conducted, the plan should indicate that a coding system will be used or not. If a survey is to be conducted, the plan should indicate what variables will be studied and what correlations are being made. In conducting qualitative research, you want to explain what trends, similarities and dissimilarities, and real differences exist.
- **Research report:** Indicate how and when the evaluation will be reported to the client or executives of the organization and how the evaluation will be used.

While it is a **_Process Milestone,_** the evaluation design is not necessarily an appropriate point at which to bill the client.

The significance of measuring against agreed-upon, clear objectives cannot be overemphasized. Evaluators like to think in terms of indicators—those things you are looking at to indicate change—and it is prudent for you to consider them as well. The key indicators must change in order to claim success of the campaign or program. For example, the number of voters who wrote letters, the percentage of teens who say they ask friends to drive carefully, or the projected number of partnership organizations garnered in a year can be all indicators used in stated objectives. Evaluation indicators are linked to the stated objectives and must be measurable. Remember when we explored developing objectives during the planning phase, we discussed three different types of objectives—informational, behavioral, and attitudinal. Individual evaluation indicators match these objectives, as they represent data for particular individuals that can be combined and analyzed. These indicators are measures of behaviors, attitudes, awareness, and demographics. While it is not always within the purview of public relations campaigns, many strategic communication and social marketing campaigns include community-based indicators such as changes in the environment or government policies and regulations. But these indicators do not tell you about the attitudes, behavior, or awareness of individuals within the community.

EVALUATION RESEARCH METHODS: A REVIEW

Recall that there are two types of primary research (see Chapter 6)—qualitative and quantitative. **Qualitative research** *such as focus groups, in-depth interviews, and mall intercept interviews usually involve the use of open-ended questions to which a respondent may answer in an unstructured manner.* This type of research seeks to answer questions like what, why, and how. Qualitative findings from this research cannot be generalized or projected onto the general population. On the other hand, **quantitative research** *methods such as polls and surveys are highly structured, usually employing all close-ended questions. The results of this research can be statistically analyzed and projected onto the population from which the study was drawn. Quantitative studies usually answer the question of how many.*

Quantitative Methods

Surveys are the most tried and true method of testing campaign results. A comparative analysis from a *before* and *after* survey is usually required to determine whether there have been any changes in audience awareness, comprehension levels, attitudes, and behaviors. It is probably the most used and least expensive method used to measure possible change from a period of time before the message was disseminated to another period of time after the message was sent. It can also be used at midpoint to measure progress. The after survey should use the same questions in your evaluation questionnaire that you used in the before survey, or baseline survey, used to measure knowledge, behaviors, and attitudes during the formative stages of the process.

You may add questions to determine if the respondents were actually exposed to the campaign messages and what actions they took as a result. Surveys can be conducted by mail, telephone, in person, through the Internet, and by fax. "Test" and "control" group studies, during which one segment of a target audience is exposed to the message or concept and a second target audience deliberately is not, can be used for this purpose. Research conducted among the groups helps determine if one group is more aware or is better informed about the issue than the other.

GMMB used this method, also called *recall and retention measures,* to evaluate the effectiveness of the Robert Wood Johnson Foundation "Cover the Uninsured Week" (CTUW) campaign activities discussed in previous chapters. Traditionally, recall and retention measurement are the domain of the advertising industry. These measures are conducted first, after a series of ads has appeared to determine if the target audiences, aided and unaided, recall the messages and again after several weeks to see if the target audiences remember the primary messages, concepts, and themes. One of the campaign objectives for the CTUW campaign was to reach "opinion elites"—members of Congress, the executive branch of government, and organizations that affect policy—with the key messages. For evaluation, GMMB used a tracking survey to determine if the target audiences were exposed to and remembered the campaign messages.

Garnering an audience's opinion or what it says about an issue or organization or product can be accomplished through polling during which respondents are asked a series of very direct, close-ended questions to gather what they think. Opinion polling is something you hear reported in the news media every day. Measuring an audience's attitude is much more complex. Attitude is what people say *and* what they think or are predisposed to; how they feel and are inclined to act; and what they perceive as barriers and drivers, things that impede or encourage the adoption of a behavior or taking an action. A series of straightforward, close-ended questions will not get the answers to these types of questions. It is easier to garner someone's position on racial prejudice by asking a few simple questions than it is to ask if that individual is racially prejudiced. This takes a lot more work. Conducting focus groups, dyads, and in-depth interviews in order to gather how parents and children feel about racial discussions requires asking many questions subtly and indirectly to determine what a target audience feels, values, believes, and prefers. This is the work of qualitative methods.

Qualitative Methods

Qualitative methods play a very important role in both the formative and implementation stages of the strategic public relations process. In the planning stage they are used in shaping and forming the campaign or program and to test strategies, messages, and materials. During implementation, process evaluation assists in knowing how things are going with the initiative. In the summative or final stages, qualitative research can be used similarly to tell you how you did with the target audiences.

In-depth interviews and **focus group interviews** with the target audiences can be used to determine if the elements of the campaign were effective. In-depth interviews are *one-on-one interactions, organized to encourage the respondent to talk freely and to express her ideas on the subject under investigation.* Focus groups are *structured group interviews that proceed according to careful research design and with attention to the principles of group dynamics.* While you cannot project these findings onto the population, these studies can provide information that will help you in the future. Using these methods can give you the opportunity to explore the responses with the target audiences, providing more context and ideas for improvement. These methods allow you to ask respondents:

- The extent to which you were exposed to the campaign and where, when, and how the exposure took place.
- Do you think the campaign message(s) were designed for you? If not you, who were the messages designed to reach? What do you think about what you saw and heard?
- What do you think about the campaign?
- What did you like about the campaign and its messages?
- What did you dislike about the campaign and its messages?
- If you could change the campaign or its messages, what would you do?
- Do you know anyone else who saw the campaign? Do you know where they saw it? Did they agree with your thoughts about the campaign? If not, why?
- Who would we want to talk to if we wanted to talk to people like you? Who are they? Where would we find them?
- Did you take the action the campaign suggested you take? Why or why not?
- Is there something the campaign could have said to make you consider taking the action? To make you take the action?

Although GMMB did not use qualitative research such as in-depth interviews or focus groups with the opinion leaders and elites who made up one of their target audiences for the CTUW campaign, they could have.

Observations, also known as **ethnographic studies,** *provide an eyewitness account of what respondents actually do as opposed to what they claim.* The researcher can

ENGAGING ETHICS

Michael Newman/PhotoEdit

Crossing the Line

You recently monitored two focus group sessions of teenage women for a client who launched a new product for this audience segment recently. The focus groups were designed to garner participant reaction to the product. Several of the participants expressed interest in learning more about the product and becoming involved in special events and asked you for more information. As a monitor of the groups, you know you should not interact with the participants.

You know the small public relations agency you work for could use some help with getting crowds and volunteers for the events. How should you handle their interest?

observe how subjects behave or if they have the skills necessary to perform specific tasks. Observing people as they navigate in their own environments can tell you a lot about whether they have adopted a behavior or can complete a form or a web task. The caution for researchers is maintaining the voluntary and anonymous participation of participants—one of the guiding principles for conducting research.

EVALUATION RESULTS

Claiming Behavior and Action as Results

Nirvana for the strategic communicator is when the target audience takes the action or performs the desired behavior. It is the premier praise and the most difficult to measure because you must prove the public relations message caused the effect. There are many variables that can influence the actions that people take and often we are not aware of them all. This is where writing clear and specific objectives for a specific target audience and a specific activity assist in your effectiveness. As a scenario, if the CTUW had encouraged registered voters to support public funding for covering the uninsured, the cause-and-effect argument might be easy to make. Clearly, GMMB can draw a cause-and-effect correlation for the actions they wanted if 85 percent of voters agreed to support the public funding.

Measuring changes in behavior and action requires a combination of research methods, including quantitative such as benchmark and follow-up surveys, and qualitative such as interviews and ethnographic and observation studies. And even then, you may not be able to claim cause and effect.

Gathering Feedback from Partners and Staff

In spite of what may be program or campaign fatigue, a strategic public relations summative evaluation is not complete until everyone involved in implementing the project has been debriefed and interviewed. As we discussed earlier, the evaluation phase is often the beginning of the next public relations effort. You know that the strategic public relations process is dynamic, and research and evaluation take place at every step of the process, overlapping at many of the stages. Therefore, it is crucial to ascertain staff and strategic partner reactions to the campaign or program. This can be accomplished using most of the methods we discussed earlier.

You conduct evaluation of partners and staff during the planning and implementation of the campaign or program. Meetings and continued correspondence with both groups keep the initiative on track until this stage of the process. However, conducting a formal evaluation helps develop best practices and provides information you will need for your future projects.

The foundation of good PR is gathering feedback and data.

Reporting Results

Of course, you can't wait until the end of the campaign or program to report to the client's management. Instead, reporting has been going on in many ways as the project has progressed through the strategic public relations process. You have conducted meetings, written briefings, made presentations, reported research findings, reported process evaluation, and remained in constant contact. At this point in the process it is time to report what the summative evaluation has found. This reporting should take place in the form of a formal in-person presentation and a final summative evaluation report. The in-person presentation should be conducted in a small-group meeting of the principals, involve a brief 20-minute talk that comes primarily from the executive summary of the written report, and provide a question-and-answer session.

Like all of the written reports we have discussed throughout the process, the evaluation report is designed to communicate to the client or organization executives precisely what you found. In outlining your findings and organizing your report, you must consider your target audience. As we discussed earlier, organizations of all types are acutely interested in the bottom line. Whether nonprofit, government, or for-profit, organizations and the people who run them are successful when there is accountability. As a public relations practitioner, you have a more difficult time demonstrating the ROI primarily because you look at different measures than many of the other departments or components of an organization. Rarely can you claim an uptick in sales figures, increase in market share, or increase in productivity. That said, knowing that the primary audience for your evaluation reports are the same eyes that are looking for accountability, you should develop and write a document that is meaningful to them, employing metrics and demonstrating benefits. An outline of a summative evaluation report includes components you used in your research findings plus a few additional:

- **Background and Introduction:** This is a brief situational analysis. Much of this information can be found in the environmental scan and other background information. It can be taken from the formative audience research finding report.
- **Objectives:** States specifically the strategic public relations objectives and the objectives for each audience and tactic.
- **Review of Literature:** Usually found in academic reports only, this section can be useful if the topic of the research has a rich body of literature. It can set the research into context.
- **Methodology:** Includes the evaluation design; a complete explanation of the methodology, dates, and geographical locations of where the research was conducted; participants; and a description of the research protocols and instruments.

- **Summary of Key Evaluation Findings:** An in-depth discussion of research results, summarizing trends and including direct quotations from participants and a delineation of the strengths and weaknesses, are found in the section.
- **Recommendations:** Discusses the most important recommendations for retaining and enhancing elements of the campaign, eliminating elements and opportunities for future initiatives.
- **Appendix:** Contains a copy of all screeners, questionnaires, topic guides, consent forms, and other materials related to the research.

Because it is a **Process Milestone** the research report is a billable deliverable to the client.

Feedback for Improvement and Future Campaigns

Like evaluation, feedback is not something you offer only at the end of the program or campaign or only after summative evaluation is complete. Feedback has been an active and iterative part of the process—informing efforts along the way and providing the opportunity to improve the initiative as activities unfolded. But it is important also to acknowledge lessons learned; delineate best practices; and document where you can apply them to improve your programs and to enhance your future initiatives.

BRIEF CASE STUDY

CDC Reaches Obese Youth Successfully

A CDV Verb campaign ad

In answer to the growing crisis of obesity in children in the United States, the Centers for Disease Control and Prevention (CDC) launched a national youth media campaign in 2002 that ran through 2006. The award-winning multicultural campaign known as VERB was designed to increase free-time physical activity sessions for "'tweens," youth ages 9 to 13. Formally known as "VERB. It's what you do," the campaign seeks to engage children of all socioeconomic and ethnic backgrounds—including African Americans, Native Americans, Asian Americans/Pacific Islanders, and Hispanics/Latinos in a language that children understand.

The campaign encouraged 'tweens to find a verb or several verbs that fit their personalities and interests and to use them as a launching pad to better health and making regular physical activity a lifetime pursuit. Campaign strategies included advertising, partnership activities, events, websites, and media relations.

As a benchmark, a telephone survey of 6,000 youth and their parents was conducted in 2002 prior to the beginning of the campaign. The survey was conducted among the same families in 2003 and annually through 2006. A rigorous analysis of the data collected made it possible to measure changes in physical activity attributed to the VERB campaign indicating a 34 percent increase in weekly free-time physical activity sessions among children ages 9–10.

Working the Case

1. What other methods would you use to evaluate the effectiveness of this campaign?
2. How would you use the evaluation provided to begin a new public relations initiative?

The question you must answer at this stage is: What would I have done differently? The answer to this question is manifold and will provide direction and knowledge for the future. Answering the question means looking at several things:

- Is there a component that should not have existed and could have been eliminated?
- Is there something you need to add to ensure more success?
- What did you learn about the issue, target audience, or environment that affected the success of the campaign?
- Has anything changed with the issue, audiences, or environment that affects the way in which you view existing objectives?
- What did this effort accomplish on behalf of the organization? Did it enhance a relationship, gain a strategic partner, enhance the earning power of the organization, increase interest in the organization, reveal a new funding opportunity, or uncover a new customer base?

If the summative evaluation points to lessons learned and best practices, you should write a case study and distribute it so that staff, partners, and other organizations can benefit from the experience.

Future initiatives are often seeded by evaluation from previous campaigns or programs. Because it is a dynamic process, strategic public relations loops back to help inform future decisions and projects. Table 13.1 below is your Program Evaluation

Table 13.1   Program Evaluation and Campaign Follow-Up Guide and Checklist

Objectives	Steps	Tools	Deliverables	Process Milestones	TAPs (Typical Assessment Points)
• To measure the effectiveness of the initiative as outlined in the objectives	1. Posing & answering overarching evaluation questions 2. Reviewing evaluation methods 3. Gathering feedback from partners & staff 4. Reporting results 5. Putting evaluation feedback to work	• Campaign objectives • Basic principles of evaluating PR efforts • Evaluative research methods (quantitative & qualitative)	• Evaluation design/plan • Summative evaluation report	• Completing evaluation design/plan • Delivering summative evaluation report	• Upon delivering summative evaluation report • Preparing a case study of the program and its campaign

and Campaign Follow-Up Guide and Checklist designed to assist you through the evaluation process. Please note that it asks you to use the objectives you set in planning and evaluative research methods to guide your work.

PROFESSIONAL POINT OF VIEW

The Cost of Research and Evaluation Is Not Pre-Determined Percentage

Mark Weiner wrote this point of view for PRWeek *as he was president of the research firm Delahaye.*

One of the biggest myths in research and evaluation—be it in PR, advertising, or any other marcomms [marketing/communication] area—is the one that says there ought to be a predetermined percentage of overall budget allocated to research and evaluation.

The flat-rate figure heard most often is 10%, but it just doesn't stand up to scrutiny. In fact, there should not be any fixed relationship between the PR budget and the PR research budget. It must vary with the brand's needs at a given time. For example, is the company's objective to build the brand or milk the brand?

For example, if you were the PR manager for a dying brand, would you allocate the same amount of research as you would if you were overseeing the launch of a new product that could redefine a category?

All things being equal, the answer is "no." Sometimes 10% is the right amount, but sometimes it's too much or too little. For the blockbuster product launch, you might need to spend 20% of your budget on preliminary research and weekly tracking for the first six months before cutting back to 10% over the next six months and then 5% in the second year.

If you manage a dying brand with no support from the top, even 1% may be too much. (This isn't to suggest that you wouldn't measure at all. You'd just spend less as you work to improve brand performance at which time you might call for a bigger budget, some of which you'd allocate to research.)

I run Delahaye, a research and evaluation company, so it could be said that I have a vested interest in generating as much revenue as I can. Flat 10% research budgets would provide my firm with explosive growth, but not for very long. You see, I also have a vested interest in providing counsel and fair value so that clients will remain with us long-term. Once clients realize that the "flat rate 10%" logic just doesn't hold up, they don't stay with us for long.

Ironically, this myth actually holds some people back from using PR research and evaluation at all, as they wrestle with how they can squeeze money out of this year's budget to "do it right." Inevitably, those who focus on a flat rate will either get it wrong or not do it at all for fear that they'll get it wrong.

Instead of concentrating on the appropriate fixed amount of research spending, the focus should be on "what needs to be done" and take it from there. Similarly, people who read this magazine would view with suspicion anyone saying that research is a total waste of money, so you should be suspicious of someone who advocates a flat rate of research and evaluation investment…regardless of whether it's 1% or 20%.

The right level of expenditure depends on your current situation, your business goals, and your PR strategy objectives. The best advice for investing in research and evaluation is consistent with any investment advice: Do so wisely and with a long-term view. That logic will yield the returns you seek.

SOURCE: Mark Weiner, *PRWeek*, April 24, 2006

Summary and Review

Evaluation
- Two very important things to remember: 1) Evaluation planning is an important component of the planning process and is highlighted as a section in any first-rate communication proposal or plan; and 2) The target audiences and objectives established in your communication plan must be measured in the summative evaluation.
- Evaluation requires careful planning and design and should be conceptualized at the beginning of the process and not added on at the end. As part of the overall plan, evaluation planning assures that you have the right things to measure during the process and at the end of the initiative.
- Formative evaluation is conducted at the beginning and it assists planning strategy, identifying your target audiences, and creating and testing messages and materials.
- Process evaluation monitors what is going on in the implementation phase. It answers questions such as, is everything going as planned, do changes need to be made in progress, or what should change the next time? It measures effort and indicates how much has been accomplished.
- Summative evaluation examines the extent to which you accomplished your objectives and had an effect on the target audience.

Evaluation Research Methods: A Review
- Both quantitative and qualitative research methods are appropriate for evaluation of public relations campaigns.
- The most widely used quantitative methods are surveys.
- While observations are used to evaluate public relations campaigns, the most widely used qualitative methods are in-depth interviews and focus groups.

Evaluation Results
- Evaluative studies must be designed carefully using the objectives set at the beginning of the initiative.
- While you may see changes in audience behavior at the end of a PR effort, it is crucial to be sure of cause and effect. Many variables can come to bear on the actions that people take and often you are not aware of them all.
- Feedback from partner organizations and internal team members is important to improving the quality of the next PR project.

Key Terms

evaluation
evaluation design
focus group interviews

in-depth interview
observations and
    ethnographic studies

qualitative research
quantitative research

Questions for Review and Discussion

1. Explain the importance of program or campaign objectives in the evaluation process.

2. Public relations practitioners often assess the value of news stories about the product or issue by converting the space or time into advertising costs as a manner of equating the value of earned media. Do you think this is an effective measure? Why?

3. Find a case study for the "Tobacco-Free Kids" initiative and look at its communication campaigns. How has evaluation fueled new initiatives?

Web Links

Centers for Disease Control and Prevention: Youth Media Campaign (VERB)
www.cdc.gov/YouthCampaign

Institute for Public Relations
www.instituteforpr.com

Written Tactics

UNDERSTANDING WRITTEN TACTICS

The written word remains one of the most powerful forms of communication. And some of the oldest and most-proven written tactics such as news releases, brochures, and fact sheets (in their many forms)—continue to be widely employed in PR programs and campaigns. Use of the written word in the field has changed dramatically as technology continues to change. There was a time when practitioners wrote primarily news releases, brochures, and speeches. Today you must be more versatile, writing for the web and understanding what each medium requires. Writing a news release for delivery to a reporter differs greatly from writing for an organization's website. You need to understand how the writing differs for each medium (consider text messaging versus tweeting) while appealing to the target audience at the same time.

You may write for many audiences as well as many media. This is where all of the strategic thinking and research become useful as you begin to create messages aimed at the particular audience and its

Say all you have to say in the fewest possible words, or your reader will be sure to skip them; and in the plainest possible words or he will certainly misunderstand them.

—John Ruskin,
author and artist

The difficulty of literature is not to write, but to write what you mean; not to affect your reader, but to affect him precisely as you wish.

—Robert Louis Stevenson,
author

275

interests. Interestingly, because technology allows us the ability to communicate with audiences the world over—including audiences with whom we do not intend to communicate—your job as a PR writer is a little more difficult and complex. It has always been necessary to choose words carefully and to be as precise as possible in communicating with audiences, but given the reach of the Internet, it is crucial. Unintended audiences are more likely to be exposed to your messages and you must have a heightened sense of the meanings of words and phrases and how they may be understood or misunderstood.

ASKING STRATEGIC QUESTIONS

Strategy before tactics! Before writing a single word, you must ask and answer a series of questions about a proposed written tactic and its key audience. As we discussed in Chapter 10, many of the questions should be asked and answered during program planning, the formative stage. But there are similar questions with slightly different answers that need to be asked before developing any type of tactic:

1. What do you want to happen? If your message is communicated effectively, what will the reader, viewer, or listener do?
2. List your key audience(s).
3. What are the beliefs, norms, needs, concerns, interests, attitudes of your key audience(s)?
4. Can you frame your story from your audience's point of view?
5. Can you state the specific action you want the audience to take?
6. What benefit can you offer your audience(s)?
7. Who should offer the benefit and request the action? Spokesperson?
8. What do you know about the controlled or uncontrolled medium you intend to use?

HOW TO PREPARE WRITTEN TACTICS

Substance before form is an old adage, but like most adages it doesn't always apply. As a public relations practitioner, you know that your messages must have *substance* to communicate effectively. Appropriate research and effective strategic planning help you create persuasive messages that resonate with your target audiences. But when you know what you want to say, to whom you want to say it, and the best opening and medium for saying it, form is everything. Learning to choose how to present a message—in the best form and style—is important. In the following pages of this chapter, we are going to explore the use and proper formats for the most well-known PR written tactics. The Image Gallery beginning on page 298 contains examples of well-executed formats of some of the written tactics.

The News Release

Only the ubiquitous brochure is better known than the news release. Many still call it the press release, as its first use was dissemination to reporters whose newspapers were published on a printing press. And reporters or journalists are still often referred to as members of the press. Practitioners prefer *news release* because the words keep us focused on the word *news* and there is a plethora of news media other than print.

The news release is a very straightforward and uncomplicated written tactic. When used appropriately, it is the preferred and primary tool for disseminating newsworthy information to members of the news media. Unfortunately, it is often used, misused, and abused in the field. Because of its dominance as a media relations tool and its frequent misuse, this chapter will give the news release more space than any other written tactic. And because every entry-level practitioner must write them, you should learn how to write a good news release.

An example of what *not* to do

Who Is the Target Audience of a News Release? You must answer this question *before* you begin to write. While the ultimate key audience is among the readers, viewers, and listeners of the news, the news media are an audience as well. What we know about news media people is that they are very busy, always on deadline, and must be quick studies of information. While they cannot be experts on all the subjects they cover, they have to "get smart" enough to write about them. This means they value their time and want to use it wisely. Editors must make good decisions quickly when presented with a news release. They must first decide if the subject of the release is newsworthy. The second decision is whether it is worth assigning a reporter to follow up and to begin trying to develop a story. It is expensive to send a reporter to cover a story. News releases that don't generate a *yes* answer on these two questions are immediately discarded.

What Is the Benefit of the News Release to the Media? If the news release is prepared properly, an editor or journalist can use the information in developing an original story. The news release can help guide them in reporting a story by providing quotations and other sources, including the name and contact information of the person sending the release. In the end, good news releases can save the news media time, money, and effort. News releases must have newsworthiness, conform to structural conventions, be presented in a standard format, and adhere to style guidelines.

Newsworthiness
There are specific elements that help us to determine if a story is newsworthy. At least one—preferably more than one—of these elements must be in the story:

- *Timeliness:* relevance to current events or issues or relatedness to an important event that has just taken place
- *Magnitude:* the degree to which the story or issue affects a great many people, large sums of money, valued commodities, etc.
- *Impact:* the effect the story could have on the public
- *Human interest:* an appeal to readers' emotions
- *Celebrity:* the involvement of a well-known person, or of someone in the public eye, in the story
- *Proximity:* when a story hits close to the local coverage area and has relevance for people in a specific community or industry
- *Novelty:* an interesting angle that makes a story significant or unique

Structure

A news release should be written in the traditional journalistic **inverted pyramid structure,** *with the most important or interesting information appearing in the first paragraphs, followed by quotations, details, and less important information in the descending paragraphs.* It should be short and you should put the news in the first paragraph, known as the *lead.*

The basic news release is designed to provide information. Using the journalistic formula for the release does not mean the writer should seek to write the release just like a news story or try to develop the angle of the story. This is the job of the reporter who may be assigned to gather additional information and rewrite the information you provide into the framework of the publication, radio, television, or web news. Instead, the news release should provide accurate and dependable information as concisely and clearly as possible. The news release writer's job is to get the editor to read the information. Given the competition for the editor's time, this is no easy feat.

Format

Remember that as part of a strategy, good media relations resulting in news coverage is very valuable. In effect, news coverage increases credibility because the news media provide *third-party credibility.* It is important that a news release look as though it is credible. Its physical appearance might gain the release a few seconds longer in the hands of an editor, news director, or journalist.

It is amazing how many different formats exist for a news release; many are confusing and add to the likelihood of reaching an editor's trash can before the headline is read. The following is the proper format for a news release, and with it you cannot go wrong. Understand that the use of news media software tracking services provided by companies such as Vocus, BurrellsLuce, and Cision allow you to build your media lists and insert a news release directly into the system so that the release can be disseminated by email. For this reason, you may choose to simply use an organization's logo and pop in the body of the release. The following tips will add to the professional look of your work. (See Figure 14.1 in the Image Gallery on pages 289–300 for an example).

- Use the organization's letterhead. A sheet of plain white 8½-by-11-inch paper is not enough. Remember, your information gains credibility by its appearance and a letterhead is a must. You can use even the most basic word processing software to create a professional looking letterhead. Or as indicated previously, create a template in the database of your media tracking service. The letterhead should include the organization's name, telephone and fax numbers, and email address.
- Write NEWS RELEASE in the top left-hand corner followed by the date and FOR IMMEDIATE RELEASE. "Immediate Release" can be replaced with an embargo date if necessary. An **embargo** *puts a hold on a release and states a future date and time the news media may release the information.* A word of caution is needed here. All journalists do not honor embargo dates and the inclination to embargo information should be well examined. Typically, journalists understand an embargoed release that refers to a speech yet to be delivered and will honor the embargo as a courtesy. Similarly, embargoed information can work to help journalists. A good example is complicated scientific data that editors and journalists are being given advance opportunity to study. If the release date is one other than the date of distribution, write FOR RELEASE and the release date. Some public relations practitioners also include the word embargo; for example EMBARGO RELEASE DATE, April 3, 2011.
- On the right-hand side of the paper across from the date should be the contact information. The name, telephone and fax numbers, and email address of the

person available to the news media for additional information are crucial. This person must be well informed and readily available.

- Following this information should be a headline and a subheadline centered in the middle of the page. Write the headline bolded, underlined, and in all upper-case letters. It must effectively summarize the news written in the text to follow. The subhead provides additional information and appears directly below with headline in upper and lowercase italicized letters. This is a great opportunity to grab the editor's attention, so try to get the news into the headlines. A good way to look at the head and subhead is to think of the subject line in a memorandum or email; write the essence of the information. Many public relations practitioners attempt to make their headlines short but complete sentences.
- Follow the headlines with a **dateline,** *the city and state where the information originated*, in all uppercase letters. The dateline is flush left of the page and appears to be the first sentence of the lead; it is not and should have a dash to indicate so. For example, WASHINGTON, DC – is followed by the first word of the lead paragraph. All of the paragraphs that follow are indented.
- All copy following the heads should be double-spaced.
- A 1.5-inch margin provides space for edits and notes.
- If a release exceeds one page, the first and other continuing pages must indicate there is additional copy. Insert *-more-* at the end of the first page.
- Following the first page, place a **page slug** at the top, flush left of each continuing page. For example, some practitioners use *page 2 of 2* while others use identifying phrase and repeat a page number *Student Wins Lottery/2-2-2.*
- Insert an *end mark* (-30-, ###, or -end-) at the bottom of the final page.

ENGAGING ETHICS

The *Journal of the American Medical Association* (JAMA) is one of the nation's most prestigious and credible medical journals. Physicians, policymakers, journalists, health-care and pharmaceutical industry leaders, and many more key audiences depend on its release to learn about major medical breakthroughs and issues. The nature of scientific research is slow and arduous, as well it should be. Often study announcements require many levels of approval before release and accurate and effective reporting on the stories require time for journalistic study and research. For this reason, it is not unusual for JAMA and other journals to send out an embargoed release announcing findings before the magazine subscribers receive them. Sometimes journalists have an inside track on what is coming or have interviews that seem to lean toward possible findings. The problem is that early reports can cause patients to panic and physicians to react negatively.

1. Why is it unethical for a reporter to ask a PR practitioner about information that is currently embargoed?
2. If a reporter approaches a practitioner regarding embargoed information, indicating she has previous knowledge of the information your organization will release, is it appropriate to acknowledge the embargoed information and answer the reporter's questions? Why?
3. Is an embargoed release a request from the PR practitioner and an obligation for the news media? Explain.
4. What ethical code protects embargoes?

Style

Just as there are rules for structure and format, there are rules for composing the copy that is the body of the release. As indicated previously, the main information appears in the first paragraphs and the less significant facts follow.

- The first paragraph or *graph* of a release is the **lead.** *Always write the lead to include who, what, when, where, and why (sometimes how). This summarizes the most important news of the release.* Two cautions: The name of the organization does not have to be in the first sentence of the lead, and never bury the lead. Of course you want your organization to get credit for an initiative or your company's product to be highlighted, but a lead can have more than one sentence. The key point of the story appears in the lead; make sure you haven't buried it in the second or third graph. This first graph should have a maximum of four or five lines.

- Localize the news the organization or company is releasing. Localizing means making the news relevant to the city, state, or region of the news media. This takes advantage of *proximity* delineated in the elements mentioned earlier. Media use of a news release is substantially higher when the release includes information pertinent to the community. Localizing is especially effective in reporting statistics. When an organization releases a national survey or a national company releases statistics regarding it products, services, or employees, a local angle, such as how many people in the area work for the company or the number of people in the area that have benefited from a community service, in the news release is paramount. You should get the local angle into the lead, expressing the relevance to local readers and viewers.

- The importance of accuracy cannot be overstated. Everything written in a news release is subject to scrutiny. In fact, when you send a document to an editor or producer in hopes a reporter is assigned to develop the story, you are essentially asking to be scrutinized. You must check and double-check the claims and facts in the release and be sure there is no question of truth. Avoid grammatical and spelling errors. Verify the accuracy of the spelling of every word, especially names, titles, and other proper nouns. Finally, errors are embarrassing and unprofessional, so be a vigilant writer. Giving attention and time to the work will win respect from the news media and friends in the organization because they quickly learn to trust your work.

- Clear and concise writing is the basic principle. Edit and re-edit until you are certain you have phrased the information so that it is easily understood with as few words as possible. Speaking of words, avoid all jargon, technical language, clichés, puns, and *puff.* Be careful not to take credit or pat the organization on the back excessively. The point is communication, not persuasion or obfuscation. State the facts as succinctly as possible and let the editors decide if a reporter should try to get more information. Only feature releases—also referred to as "soft" news—tend to exceed two pages because they are generally written to add texture and perspective to a larger news story and are often human interest stories. Finally, the oldest trick in the trade is to read the copy aloud. It helps to find where the writing is superfluous.

- Use a **boilerplate** at the end. *Boilerplate language is a very brief, one-paragraph description of an organization, its mission and, if appropriate, how it was founded and funded.*

- When a news release has global reach, it should be translated into the language of the reporters you want to reach. While most journalists abroad speak English, written material is preferred in the native language. But be careful. Some of the worse blunders in communication happen when translation is involved. Translations must be made with knowledge of both words and cultures. Companies such as Business Wire that specialize in translating and distributing news releases are good resources and far superior to taking a chance on someone who can translate words but not culture.

After the Release Is Written

A few steps need to be taken before the release is ready for dissemination through the preferred channel of distribution. First, someone has to approve it. Most public relations firms and company or organization public relations departments have a sign-off process to help verify content, approve attribution of quotes, and prevent errors. Independent or freelance PR counselors who work for themselves and not an agency or organization maintain client files with signed copies of all text, including news releases. And all quotes should be checked and cleared by the person to whom the quote is attributed.

The news release is one of the most useful tools of an effective media relations strategy, but it must have the proper follow-up if it is to be effective. As stated earlier, the purpose of the tactic is to get reporters to cover your news, but reporters must be able to conduct additional fact finding. To help make this process convenient (a key benefit to reporters), knowledgeable people must be available to answer the reporters' telephone or email queries. Finding the contact person *out of contact* for long periods of time is not acceptable. And failing to return messages from journalists is failing at media relations.

If an organization chooses not to answer news media questions, it is choosing not to have effective media relations. Sometimes the news media initiate contact with a company or organization. Not answering these inquiries is not the key to staying out of the news. The news media will ask questions—like it or not—if an organization is making news. It is wise to answer the queries as promptly and forthrightly as possible. The key to good media relations is not to evade or obfuscate when confronted with difficult news, but to plan and respond professionally. An organization's credibility can ride on how well it handles news media coverage.

Delivering News Releases

Strategy is the key, again. During the campaign research and planning stages, you determine who your key audiences are and the best openings for reaching them. You have learned enough about your audiences to know where to find them. If you determine that your key audiences can be reached through the news media, you plan a media relations plan. A good media relations strategy sets a clear objective and predetermines where news releases will be sent, making strategic decisions about who is likely to use the news. There is no need for guesswork or to "blast" or use "macrodistribution" to disseminate news releases. For example, if a company is launching a new computer product that will significantly reduce system security risks, the objectives might be to introduce the new product to buyers and to tout the positive financial impact the new technology will have on the company. A news release would be targeted worldwide to the editors and reporters of the computer trade media and business and financial editors who cover technology, but not to every newspaper editor in the world.

So how do you get your releases to the editors and reporters you target? You are back to asking what you know about them. You know they receive literally thousands of news releases a week. The releases arrive in various ways, and because the journalists are overwhelmed with them, success might depend on how you send your release.

Practitioners who build media lists from software can query reporters and learn how they prefer to receive news releases. Without that information, first-class mail is the best way to send a release to local media and, in fact, is the way most local reporters prefer to receive it. Faxing a local release is an option, but there are variables that work against the release getting into the right hand. You cannot depend upon a newsroom fax machine to be available and in working order; you cannot be sure the news release will get to the intended journalist, and faxed releases add to the clutter. Deliveries by messenger or overnight mail are better options. Avoid sending local releases by email unless there is a crisis situation and/or reporters are being kept up to date on a specific and evolving situation. If you are using a database to build a media list for a release, you can find out how the reporter or editor prefers to receive releases by looking at the reporter's/editor's profile. These profiles indicate other important details such as deadlines, best time of day to contact by telephone, and beat covered.

Accurate and thorough media lists are the key to the dissemination of news releases regionally, nationally, and globally. When a news story has possibilities for national and international coverage, it is best to depend on a firm that specializes in distribution and maintains mailing lists. Companies such as PR Newswire, Business Wire, Market Wire, Black PR Wire, Vocus, and U.S. Wire offer an array of media contacts. The practitioner writes the release and submits it to the distribution company, and all of the media list headaches are gone. Some of these companies offer electronic delivery of news releases. The news releases are sent out on an electronic wire service and are printed in the newsrooms on a special printer. Others offer the option of sending the release to newsrooms by computer through the Internet. Speaking of the Internet, be sure to post your news releases to your website newsroom so that reporters can find them without having to contact you directly.

Feature Releases

Akin to the news release is the **feature release** or **news feature.** Another media relations tool, the feature release can get the interest of editors and reporters and result in coverage. Whereas a news release should report on serious, formal topics or events—*hard* news—*a feature release* softens *the news by adding texture or highlighting topics of*

BRIEF CASE STUDY

News Releases

StarKist Seafood created a new product that was probably the most innovative in canned tuna history. StarKist offered tuna in a pouch, providing a more convenient package for a popular product.

Working the Case

1. Is this newsworthy? Why?
2. What should be the headline, subheadline, and lead for the news release?
3. Who should receive the release and why?
4. The company's tuna spokesperson is Charlie the Tuna. Should the company use its animated spokesperson? How?

interest. For instance, a release that may have announced the White House stimulus package—hard news—provided the facts surrounding a very serious event. An article in a local newspaper explaining what the package means to local industry is hard news. But an article that looks at how a local family will be affected by the state or local application of funds is a feature or soft news. The feature is based on news, but uses feature writing to develop a short article. Small newspapers, especially small weeklies, and small magazines are receptive to receiving these feature pieces because they generally have small staffs and cannot provide support for reporters to write interesting feature articles.

Consumer features and new or improved product features gain a fair amount of coverage for an organization or company. Television and radio news editors and newspaper and magazine section editors are usually open to stories in these two categories. Consumer features should be directed to the Lifestyle, Business and Money, Food, Travel, Real Estate, and Home sections of newspapers and magazines. Feature releases related to recipes, restaurants, vacation destinations, shopping, family care, home improvement and decorating, gardening, and many other topics are actually in demand in small markets. Also, consumer advocacy articles receive some attention in television and radio news segments and in print when they are seen as a service to the consumer, providing useful information such as comparison shopping, veracity of claims, and dependability of products and services.

News features on business and finance are becoming increasingly popular with radio and television audiences as well as newspapers and magazines. Larger news media outlets have reporters who regularly cover these subjects. The smaller newsrooms can use well-written and easily accessible features. These features may gain coverage for a company or organization that will increase knowledge and trust with investor audiences.

Professionally developed and ready-to-print feature releases can be delivered to newspaper editors ready for publishing. Some distribution services offer news editors "camera-ready copy" or matte articles, including photos or graphics for publications. The public relations professional writes a feature piece and submits it to the distribution company where editors decide if the material is newsworthy and written journalistically. If the release is accepted for distribution, it is laid out in newspaper style—including captioned photographs if provided—and sent to newsrooms. Newspapers use these types of news features in the special sections mentioned earlier and also for holiday special sections.

Op-Eds

An **op-ed** is *a form of opinion writing that addresses current issues and public policies*. Sometimes called *opinion-editorials*, op-eds actually got their name from the position they occupy in the newspaper—opposite the editorial page. Unlike an editorial, which expresses the views of the publication, op-eds are vehicles that allow writers who are not employees of the publication to have their views on a particular subject published and shared with the public. Clearly, if your key audiences are readers of the editorial and op-ed pages and your op-ed is published, the organization's viewpoint will be heard in one of the most credible venues in the marketplace of ideas.

Usually, op-eds are written by experts on the subject. The topics can be local, regional, national, or global in scope. If you are working for an organization that represents a particular view on a current issue, you may be asked to write an op-ed to be bylined or credited to an expert member of the organization or its executive director, president, or CEO. Independent public relations practitioners and public relations firms write op-eds for clients every day. (See Figure 14.2 in the Image Gallery on page 301 for an example.)

Unlike typical news reporting, the op-ed is subjective writing. It is designed to influence opinion leaders, sway public opinion, and influence change in society. In general, it is an essay that takes a stand or position on a particular issue and sometimes provides solutions to the problem.

To avoid writing misleading and manipulative op-eds—something the op-ed editor will be able to detect immediately—you must be clear and concise, getting to the point at the outset, advocating a point of view, supporting the point of view with facts and figures, and suggesting a call to action. Op-eds must be well researched, balanced, and anticipate readers' questions and provide answers. They should stimulate the reader, explain issues, and advocate a position or solution. In short, they should be persuasive and informative. An op-ed should not be shopped around. It can be offered to only one publication at a time and that publication will want exclusive rights to it.

Letters to the Editor

This written tactic is often overlooked by public relations practitioners, but it is a good way to get an organization mentioned in newspapers or magazines. Most publications feel obligated to allow readers to respond to their reporting. **Letters to the editor** are *always in response to an article that appeared in the publication. Often, they take exception to the journalist's view or correct the article in one way or another, but they can also be letters of support.* Letters to the editor can respond to articles, editorials, or an op-ed.

These tools should always be brief. Long letters are rarely used. The letter should highlight and stick to the most important point. Some publications offer email addresses or fax numbers for sending letters to the editor. Take advantage of these because timeliness is very important. Also, many readers respond to the editor, and all letters to the editor regarding the same article are not used. Editors comb through and print a "balanced" representation. As with all that the practitioner writes for publication, the letter to the editor must be accurate and check all the facts. The letter must be signed! It is appropriate to get the most senior officer of the organization to sign. Unsigned letters will not be used.

Pitch and Confirmation Letters

The **pitch letter** is another important media relations tool. *It is directed to print and broadcast news editors and broadcast news producers, inviting them to cover an event or offering them a news interview with a spokesperson.* Pitch letters are sometimes used as cover letters for a news media kit—a tool used to generate news coverage that is a compilation of materials for reporters to use to cover a story. Media kits are discussed in depth on page 287 of this chapter. This often is determined by whether the kit was requested or is mailed from a media list. For example, if a reporter or editor received a news release and expressed interest in covering an event and could not, the practitioner can send a media kit from the event, but not send a pitch letter with the kit. A personal handwritten note will do. If the kit is sent as part of distribution to a media list, a pitch letter can be sent as a cover. If you can avoid it, do not send a media kit with a pitch letter that offers a client or spokesperson for an interview not associated with an event.

Considering your target audience, you must write pitch letters that are personal, short (no longer than one page) and attention grabbing. Editors and producers receive hundreds of letters a week; they have no time to try to discern the point of the letter. A pitch letter must get to the point right away and be interesting. Remember, there is a lot of competition for this audience's attention, so it is effective to offer a benefit. Here are a few tips for writing a good pitch letter. (See Figure 14.3 in the Image Gallery on page 302 for an example.)

- Be sure you know the name of the *current* editor or producer and address your salutation and envelope to that person.
- Let the editor or producer know you've done your homework and have some knowledge of who their viewers, listeners, or readers are. For example, "I know that your listeners depend on you to bring them the most up-to-date information on government waste."
- Be as creative or novel as possible, "Government Watch has a 'waste-ometer' and we want to discuss money squandered in building Route 1."
- Provide the benefit to the editor or producer. Why should they provide news coverage or conduct an interview? See this event or interview opportunity through the editor's or producer's eyes. Be specific about why it will be a benefit.
- Remember that visuals are important to television, and sound is important to radio. In our example, a money-guzzling "waste-ometer" might be a good visual and provide sound.
- Provide specific details about the event and logistics for covering the event.
- Be sure to indicate that someone will call to follow up on the letter. If the pitch is for an interview, let the producer or editor know he will call in a few days, by the end of the week, or next week.

There are only two reasons for sending a pitch letter by fax or email. If it involves a breaking news story, time is of the essence and this is the quickest way possible to offer a spokesperson for an interview. Again, stating the benefit is very important because it is taking license by offering an interview in this manner. Second, if you work regularly with a producer, editor, or even a reporter who covers your beat regularly, you have an existing working relationship. It is then appropriate to send information by email or fax, but always ask or indicate your intentions. In these cases, it is most likely you will have called the pitch before sending correspondence. (See Figure 14.3 in the Image Gallery on page 302 for an example.)

If a pitch letter and follow-up call are successful and result in an interview, you will want to send a letter confirming the details right away. You should indicate that a confirmation letter will follow and ask if there is a preference for fax or email. The confirmation letter is an important media relations tool. It is both tactical and strategic. A **confirmation letter** *confirms the logistics and details of the scheduled interview and provides the opportunity to review the subject and areas of interest to the news outlet.* It's an excellent time to gently remind the producer, editor, or reporter of the primary message by providing a brief summary of the original pitch letter. Caution: Don't try to provide a road map for how the interview should proceed because news people do not want to be told how to approach a story or interview. Instead, gently leading with information that is helpful to the editor, producer, or reporter and reinforcing the primary message you want your spokesperson to deliver are appropriate.

A confirmation letter should begin by confirming the specific day, date, time, and location of the interview, include every detail of the scheduling, who will meet you and your spokesperson, best entrances to use (if the spokesperson is going to the reporter), and details for contact should changes occur. The letter should close with a thank you and remind the editor or producer of why this interview is such a good idea and how it will engage the audience. The confirmation letter should be kept in the practitioner's files, and copies should be sent to anyone who is responsible for the spokesperson's schedule and public appearances such as executive or administrative assistants, schedulers, political advance staffers, and press secretaries.

Best Practices: Reaching Out to Bloggers

Blogs, or **web logs,** are *diaries or news forums that are regularly updated by the person who owns the site, known as a blogger.* Most blogs are updated with new postings every day. In this way, they are much like daily newspapers. But that is where the similarity ends. The whole notion of having a news blog is to free the blogger from the restrictions of editors who control content. Reaching out to blogs or bloggers can be a valuable media relations tactic, but please note the term "reaching out" and not "pitching." The creators of blogs tend to be very independent sorts who reject any notion of spreading a message for someone else. In fact, that is why they become bloggers in the first place. They want to provide a personal or individual view on the topics they cover or discuss on their sites. (See washingtonpost.com/blogs/campus-overload for an example.)

Blogs are usually good sources for reaching a key audience. Most blogs are dedicated to a particular topic, issue, or industry. Like trade magazines, blogs appeal to a narrowly defined, and usually dedicated, audience. Approaching a blogger to offer information requires a few steps. First, as is the case with all audiences we approach, the practitioner should learn as much about a blog as possible. The key is to read the blogger's site and become familiar with her views, interests, and style. Second, forget the idea of a news release or pitch letter. Bloggers are web fans and spend a lot of time at their computers. The best way to reach out to a blogger is through a straightforward and to-the-point email that includes a link to the story or item the blogger may find interesting. Being straightforward and to the point includes disclosing immediately who you represent and why you are contacting the blogger. Don't attempt to be clever in approaching a blogger; the typical pitch letter would be considered offensive.

Finally, bloggers read other blogs and have many links on their sites to blogs similar to their own. If a client or organization is featured on a blog, it may mean additional coverage on other blogs. Of course, the links or URLs on the blog you are pitching will provide other sites to target. Caution: Never ask a blogger to provide a link to your organization or client.

Media Alerts, Fact Sheets, and Backgrounders

The **media alert,** also called a **media advisory,** *makes the news media aware of special coverage opportunities during an event.* It takes a brief, bulleted format and provides a list of who is available for group or one-on-one interviews, exact times, and locations. It also lists who or what is available for photo or video opportunities (photo-ops). It should clearly explain who, what, when, where, and how. This kind of accurate and factual information is important to editors who are deciding what resources should be deployed to cover an event.

Fact sheets *provide details about an issue, study, survey or organization.* They are designed to give a reporter details that help set the context for covering an event and to provide a quick reference tool. Fact sheets can be bulleted or take the short paragraph format. Fact sheets should follow some identifiable order and should not be a mere list of things you think the reporter will want to know. It can be organized in a topical arrangement so that it explains the evolution, chronology, or stages of a situation or event. (Examples are shown in Figures 14.4 and 14.5 in the Image Gallery on pages 303 and 304.)

Special events fact sheets, usually found in the news media kit, include a description of the activities, date, time, location, and duration of each activity, important participants and sponsors, and contact information.

Backgrounders are *lengthier than advisories and fact sheets* and can be used in a variety of ways. Some backgrounders are expanded versions of the history, mission, goals, and purpose of an organization. When used in this way, the backgrounder should anticipate questions the news media may have about the organization and should fully define what the organization does or the company produces. If a new product, services, or merger of two companies are announced, backgrounders can be used to provide a view of the way in which an organization or company division is managed. When short one- to two-paragraph biographies (bios) are written as one document, they are often referred to as backgrounders. (See Figure 14.6 in the Image Gallery on page 305 for an example.)

Media Kits/Press Kits

Media kits are the preferred terminology for this media relations tool, but it is still commonly called the press kit. While *media kit* or *news media kit* is appropriate, it can be confusing if the public relations practitioner is unfamiliar with the meaning of the term as it is used in advertising. An advertising media kit includes the rates, demographics, production specification, and other details provided to media buyers seeking to buy advertising time and space.

In the practice of public relations, a **media kit** is *a tool used to generate news stories about an organization's newsworthy initiative, campaign, special event, major announcement, product launch, or trade show.* While you know news editors are the key audience for this tool, like the other media relations tools, the gatekeeper you target varies based on the news you have to share—business editor, food editor, metro reporter, television or radio news or talk-show producer—to name a few. Also, reporters expect to receive an informative media kit during a crisis and when covering a news conference for a major announcement.

The three most widely used media kits are:

- **Special-event media kits** are used to provide the activities and logistics of an event. They are not focused on the organization or company but on the event itself. Of course, background material in the kit does lay out the relationship of the event to the organization. The materials for a special-event media kit may be produced with special letterhead and logos developed for the event. (See Figures 14.7A and 14.7B in the Image Gallery on pages 306 and 307 for examples.)
- **Promotional media kits** are used primarily by companies and the entertainment industry to introduce, support, and encourage consumer interest in a product or performance. Usually, a new product, new business relationship, new exhibit, or

performance and new technology are the types of subjects for these kits. In addition to news releases and factual information, promotional kits contain materials such as brochures, sample advertisements, quotes from critics and reviews from media critics. In some circumstances, clips from previous media coverage are included in these kits as well.

- **Crisis media kits** are among the most effective tools of crisis communication. They give journalists covering breaking news up-to-date information about the crisis and are distributed during news conferences and periodic media briefings.

Public relations practitioners have to decide the proper amount of material to include in a news media kit. Again, strategic thinking asks what useful information looks like through the eyes of the journalist. Remember to think of the kit as a benefit. The idea is not to make the fattest kit possible but to provide reporters with what they need to write their stories. Another option is to provide media kits online, as shown in Figure 14.8 in the Image Gallery on page 308. Again, your key audience is inundated with public relations materials every day. Your job is to make their jobs easier so that they can cover your news.

BRIEF CASE STUDY

Media Kits

Sylvan Learning Centers remains the largest company dedicated to meeting the education needs of the K through 12 market. With 950 centers throughout the United States and Canada, it boasts that its programs have helped more than one million students experience "the joy of learning." Recently research indicated that fewer than 20 percent of U.S. elementary and secondary school students write at a "proficient" level. Studies also showed that parents feel ill prepared to help improve their children's writing skills. Prompted by the research, Sylvan created an academic writing program. Budgetary restraints prevented a mention of the new program in its paid television advertising, so a public relations launch was undertaken.

Sylvan's PR firm created a broad media relations plan directed to local media. Its objectives were to increase traffic to its website by 5 percent and to gain 10,000 inquiries within three months. The target audience was parents age 25–54, and local media were the chosen vehicles. Among the local media relations tools employed was a media kit delivered to local journalists and packaged in a child's backpack with these instructions: "In Case of Writer's Block, Open Backpack." The packs contained a writing journal with "thought starters" such as "I'm happy when…" and "My fear is…" designed to help students avoid blank page syndrome, writing tools, toys, and a dictionary or thesaurus. The media coverage was excellent and the public relations objectives were met.

Working the Case

1. What written media relations information should have been in the media kits to assist journalists in covering the program launch? Why?
2. What editors or journalists should be key audiences for the media relations efforts of Sylvan Learning?

Format

A standard media kit consists of a shell, a large folder with two pockets, containing news releases, fact sheets, backgrounders, and visuals such as black-and-white captioned photographs, color slides, and line drawings. The content of the media kit depends heavily on the purpose of the kit. Media kits can be sent by first-class or overnight mail, messenger, and the Internet, where they are posted to the organization's website newsroom.

Brochures

Everyone recognizes a brochure, and public relations practitioners usually write and monitor the production of many of these tools of the practice. **Brochures** *can take the form of leaflets or pamphlets, booklets, or can be posted to the web. Organizations use brochures to provide information, persuade, or educate a well-defined target audience.* Some organizations produce brochures tailored to the prospective client's needs and send them in PDF format as an attachment to an email. *Leaflets and pamphlets are formatted on a single piece of paper folded into sections called* **panels.** A booklet is two or more pieces of paper bound together. Booklets are longer in length and have more content than leaflets. All the pages are printed on both sides and are often bound together with centerfold staples.

Although digital printing has helped cut down on the costs, brochures can be expensive products for an organization, making strategic planning of the production crucial. The first question for you to answer is what is to be accomplished with the brochure. The second, and equally important, question you must answer is who is your key audience and what do you want that audience to do. Effective brochures always point the way to additional information and give the intended audience an action to take. They should supply names, addresses, telephone numbers, and other contact information to help the audience act. Lastly, you need to know how long the brochure will be needed; the shelf life of the brochure is important to determining budget. It is not cost-effective to create brochures that need updating within months of production. Some practitioners try to create *evergreen* brochures, keeping updates to a specific time phase.

As is so with all public relations controlled media, brochures must be written and designed with the audience in mind. Both the language and design must speak directly to the audience. Practitioners have to strike a balance between the amount of information and the design in order to create an effective, easy-to-read, and attractive brochure. Knowing the audience helps make many of the language and design decisions. For instance, a heavy paper stock and color make a brochure appear to be important and impressive. Some brochures are printed on stock that is environmentally safe. Look at the brochure shown in Figure 14.9 of the Image Gallery on page 309, created as an evergreen on special stock. This brochure was created to appeal to the nonprofit sector whose members are very concerned about the environment.

A brochure should focus on one clear message. If the goal is to persuade an audience, we use language that is expressive, compares and contrasts, and is personal—sometimes emotional—for the reader. The reader is looking for personal benefits, so it is best to outline these benefits in language that is meaningful to the target audience.

Brochures designed to inform or educate attempt to convey the importance of an issue or idea. The language for these tends to be more authoritative and fact oriented than persuasive because the purpose is to convince the audience that the information is important to them.

Brochure copy should be able to pass the "scanability" test (people tend to scan brochure copy for key information rather than read in depth). Scanability is accomplished by writing headlines that create bold statements and quick summaries. Bullets bring clarity to facts and figures that can be used to support the primary message. Although scanability is important, a brochure should be written so that the reader can garner the information in a sequenced manner. This is especially true if the brochure gives instructions or explains rules.

Newsletters

How many newsletters do you receive at school or at home either through the post or email? Audiences receive newsletters from many of the organizations they encounter in daily life. Nearby hospitals send newsletters that provide health tips and explain the latest technology and other accomplishments they have acquired. Grade schools and high schools send newsletters to keep parents in touch with what is new and exciting. Professional association newsletters are chock full of information. Neighborhood associations send both hand-delivered and email newsletters. Health insurance providers send regular newsletters that provide information about treatments and about how to keep costs down, and the list goes on and on.

Why the proliferation in newsletters? They are targeted to a highly defined audience. During the mid-1990s, it appeared that complimentary newsletters were decreasing while subscriber newsletters were on the rise. The cost of postage and the competition of other communication messages were factors in the decline in numbers of complimentary newsletters. But organizations and associations with large employee and membership bases continue to publish newsletters regularly in order to maintain an active and interested audience, and delivery of newsletters on the web continues to grow.

In *Public Relations Writing: Form and Style* textbook authors Doug Newsom and Bob Carrell list six criteria that affect the success of a newsletter:

- It must fill an unmet need.
- It must convey information in some unique way so people will pay attention to it.
- It must be distributed in a way that is efficient and regularly reaches its intended audience.
- It must be able to do things for its audience other media can't.
- There must be a person or staff of people interested in and skilled enough to produce it and with time committed solely to its production.
- It must be a serial publication (Vol., No.) issued with enough frequency that its contents remain timely in the eyes of the readers.

These criteria can be very daunting in the eyes of a PR director who already has more work than is possible to accomplish, but they represent the kind of strategic planning that must go into a newsletter if it is to meet its goals. Newsletters cannot be successful if they are hastily and carelessly produced—every detail of a newsletter must be carefully planned and well in advance. Organizations with successful newsletters have editorial meetings in which they plan messages, concepts, and production for each quarter of the year and a year in advance.

The newsletter is very much a niche publication, so it is clear that the publisher of a newsletter already knows a lot about his audience. Both organizational and subscriber newsletters speak directly to the target audience. Newsletters are published on topics of special interest to the key audience. They are designed to provide information that is both important and useful to the reader. Also, newsletters are designed to maintain a lengthy relationship with an audience. Therefore, newsletters are serial publications. They are produced and distributed with consistent frequency, whether it is weekly, monthly, quarterly, or yearly.

Employee, member, community, special-interest subscriber, and advocacy newsletters are among the most popular types.

- *Employee newsletters* directly address employees in a fairly informal and conversational tone. They usually take the appearance of a short newspaper and include brief articles and features. Unlike internal office memoranda and organizational briefs, these publications disseminate information with a human-interest tone and quality. The job of the public relations writer is to give employees a sense of belonging while informing them about the inner workings of the organization. These newsletters cover a wide range of topics, including company finances, client and customer information, new program initiatives, employee accomplishments, and more general news from within the organization. (See Figure 14.10 in the Image Gallery on page 310 for an example.)

- *Member newsletters* help to keep members of clubs, organizations, and associations informed about important news, upcoming events, educational opportunities, elections, and other important membership information. They encourage member participation and introduce new members into the network.

- *Community newsletters* are usually geared toward people who live in the same towns, neighborhood, development, or buildings. The primary goal of these publications is to foster a sense of community and involvement among neighbors and to better their quality of living. Articles usually highlight important news that may affect the neighborhood, include a calendar of events, and provide other neighborhood information.

- *Advocacy newsletters* present information about a specific topic or point of view. While this type of newsletter can be produced as a single publication, it can be published in conjunction with employee, member, or community newsletters. The primary purpose is to promote a specific opinion and to gain and maintain public support and activism.

- *Special-interest subscriber newsletters* are designed for groups whose connections are based on common interests. These tend to be produced for very highly segmented audiences. These publications can be related to hobbies, trades, financial interests, professions, and political or religious affiliation. They often provide information on such topics as health, travel, economics, and computers. Special-interest newsletters are primarily purchased by the audience and should contain enough useful information for readers to feel the publication is well worth the money spent.

Format

Newsletters are produced in a variety of sizes. For organizations that want to encourage readers to maintain a reference file, the 8½-by-11-inch paper size is preferable because the sheets can be three-hole punched in order to archive copies in binders. Hole-punching the newsletter prior to distribution can also send the message that the document is important enough to preserve. Longer newsletters are often formatted in the 11-by-17-inch paper size, also known as tabloid. The tabloid size lends itself best to long articles, artwork, and photos.

Newsletters may be either horizontal or vertical in their direction, and they may use a two-, three-, or four-column format. Column choice is as much a nonverbal message as color or font size. Justified columns are more formal while wider columns tend to give the newsletter a more relaxed feel. Photographs and other visuals within the columns need to fit the style of those columns and the theme of the overall newsletter. Other format and style concerns such as number of pages, recurring features, the banner or nameplate, paper stock, color, and more should be decided at the outset. As a public relations practitioner, you should make recommendations, remembering that a newsletter is another tool that has a purpose in the organization's overall communication plan.

Another important decision is whether the organization wants to produce and distribute a hard copy newsletter or an e-newsletter. Many newsletters are now developed and distributed via the computer through the Internet or an intranet. Electronic publication has many appealing characteristics. Besides having the immediacy that goes along with posting something on the web or sending it via email, the costs of printing and postage are saved.

Style

The editor of a newsletter has to be a good writer and a good reporter. It is important to look for news throughout the organization. While some of the news can come from existing reports and initiatives, other news will come from interviews and talking to people who are in the know. Complete adherence to journalistic writing styles is not required, but newsletter writers should borrow heavily from this genre. For instance, to avoid overwhelming the reader with a lot of type, short sentences and short paragraphs are used. This type of writing requires the KISS (keep it short and simple) method. It is important to use active voice and strong nouns and verbs—and to avoid excessive use of adjectives, adverbs, and redundant phrases.

Newsletter articles, like news releases (see page 276), also borrow the *inverted pyramid structure* from journalism. As described earlier, this structure puts key points in the lead, which is the opening one- or two-sentence paragraph. This allows for easy reading and editing. But this rule is not set in stone. Feature articles often use a delayed lead for effect. Newsletter editors should strive for a balance between news articles and feature articles in each issue to help create a well-rounded publication. Most articles are between 100 and 600 words.

Magazines

Magazines serve some of the same purposes as newsletters. Like newsletters, these publications are usually published to maintain long relationships and have narrowly defined audiences. They are used widely for corporations to communicate with employees and stockholders, for associations to provide information to members, for companies to keep in touch with consumers, for universities to impress their alums, and for manufacturers to motivate and educate distributors and marketing and sales teams. Magazines take many formats and styles and have clearly developed objectives. They also vary in terms of the use of color, paper stock, graphics, photos, and distribution. More expensive to produce than the newsletter, the magazine requires a large budget and even more long-range planning. Corporations distribute magazines domestically and on a global basis, depending on the audience and purpose. (See Figure 14.11 in the Image Gallery on page 311.)

Annual Reports

The annual report is a challenging project that is a large undertaking and a highly collaborative process, requiring input from many parts of an organization. Strategic planning for this publication is complicated by the number of audiences who read them.

Depending on the organization, the audiences can include government regulators, stockholders, potential stockholders, financial analysts, customers, potential customers, employees, community leaders, granting organizations, donors, legislators, and the media. And each of these audiences is reading the report for a different reason.

An **annual report** is, *as the name suggests, a yearly reporting of an organization's activities.* But today's annual reports do a lot more than that. The traditional goal of annual reports was to report a company's financial performance to stockholders. By law, all public companies must submit annual reports to the Securities and Exchange Commission (SEC). Now, annual reports are less reportorial and much more promotional due, in part, to two dramatic changes during the last decade.

First, annual reports are no longer the exclusive domain of public corporations. Nonprofit organizations and private companies produce them to share their activities with key audiences. Though private corporations and nonprofits are not required to report to the SEC, many of them realize the benefits of producing annual reports as evidenced by their availability. A controlled medium, the annual report can be used to communicate and promote an organization's image among its most important audiences.

The second major change is the way in which the information is presented. When the SEC changed its rules in 1995, allowing companies to submit shorter, less technical reports to stockholders, the annual report became a summary annual report (SAR)—a more concise document. So, summary reports became less technical and more reader friendly. Still it is the public relations practitioner's job to keep the reports simple and clear.

As a public relations practitioner, you will play a major role in the construction of your organizations' annual report, crafting the messages and ensuring that the design enhances the function of the report. An important component of an organization's overall strategic communication plan, the annual report should promote an organization to its key audiences. Along with other marketing and public relations materials, it plays an important role in creating the organization's public image and should serve as much more than just a means to convey financial status. Used to their full advantage, annual reports provide financial, historical, human interest, and philanthropic work for an organization. (See Figure 14.12 in the Image Gallery on pages 312–314 for examples.)

Corporate Advertising and Public Service Advertising

Advertising has attained a level of sophistication in reaching audiences that surpasses imagination. It is everywhere people can be found—in the movie theatre before a film is screened, on digital billboards, at the gas pump, on the Internet, on telephone recordings while you are on hold, on NASCARs, and bumper stickers. As we discussed in Chapter 2, it is an effective part of an integrated communication strategy. Public relations practitioners or writers often draft or approve copy for several different types of advertising.

For the most part, you will work with the creative staff of advertising firms who will create the copy for product and services advertising and promotion, but the public relations writing for corporate and nonprofit ads that sell ideas, positions, or stances on issues and alliances is likely to be the PR practitioner's charge. Corporate-image advertising, advocacy advertising, and advertorials are placed when a company pays for time or space in the mass media. Public service ads, public service announcements, and internal and external house ads are placed in free time and space.

Corporate-Image Advertising

The major corporations in America have come to understand the importance of good corporate citizenship. Americans have made it clear that company policies about important social issues such as the environment, labor and workforce abuse, children, and values affect their decision on what products to purchase. As a result, corporations purchase **corporate-image advertising,** also known as *institutional* and *identity* advertising. *This advertising is designed to increase the public's positive opinion of the company while enhancing the image of its products or services.* The ad shown in Figure 14.13 in the Image Gallery on page 315 is a good example.

Advocacy advertising *attempts to affect public opinion about an issue.* When a local company wanted to explain its stance on funding for a new road corridor connecting two important metropolitan areas, it used this newspaper advertisement. The objective was to get local residents to support the corridor and ultimately the local government funding necessary in order to make it possible.

Advertorial

Most controversial of the three corporate idea advertisements is the **advertorial,** *which is so named because this is often laid out to appear as editorial material. Special advertising sections that look like a series of feature articles with photographs and other visual material are actually ads.* Many readers do not readily identify these as ads and are often confused by them. Although usually clearly labeled as ads by the publisher, advertorials subtly sell the product or service to the reader.

Public Service Advertising

Public service advertising is *donated time and space provided to nonprofit organizations.* It is added to nonprofit communication campaign strategy because costs for production and advertising time and space are high. When placed in print media, they are called public service ads, but when they run on radio or television, they are called public service announcements (PSAs). Both can be very powerful tools when positioned in the right time and space, but because the time and space is donated by the media, positioning is difficult.

Executed well, public service ads and PSAs persuade, inform, or advocate for the public good. And they can boost an organization's visibility and create awareness about issues, events, and programs. But therein is the challenge: Because they are placed at no cost, the competition is high and it requires well-written advertising copy and visuals that are interesting, attention-getting, and suited to the medium. If this is not done, the PSA will not be placed.

Aside from costs considerations, the primary difference between PSAs and paid spot advertisements is that PSAs contain information that is intended to benefit the key audience. Messages conveyed in PSAs must include information that is beneficial to the community without being self-serving, and they should *not* contain a controversial or political slant. (See example Figure 14.14 in the Image Gallery on page 316.)

For years, communicators in the nonprofit sector were less strategic about their advertising messages than commercial advertisers. Now, many nonprofit organizations use the proper research to identify and understand their key audiences and to design a communication campaign strategy. Audiences include donors, volunteers, teenage-smokers, populations at risk for many physical and mental diseases, the senior population, immigrants, and students. The topics for PSAs are as varied as is the nonprofit sector itself—health and fitness, mental health, safety, environmental issues, quality-of-life issues for the poor and underemployed, the uninsured, community events, and, of course, nonprofit fundraising and volunteer and relief efforts. There are many, many more audiences and topics.

Internal and External House Ads

PR practitioners employed in large organizations are likely to gain some experience with creating **internal and external house ads.** *Internal house ads are placed in an organization's own publications such as the magazines and newsletters we discussed earlier in this chapter.* Usually, internal house ads encourage internal audiences such as employees, retirees, members, or other internal audiences to volunteer or take some other act to benefit the community.

Traditionally, *external house ads appear in newspapers and magazines that run house ads in their own publications to promote their publications to potential subscribers.* These usually describe the advantages of advertising with the publication, and the promotion department prepares these ads and has them available when space is made available. (See an example in Figure 14.15 in the Image Gallery on page 317.)

Web Pages

As a PR practitioner, the Internet is yet another medium for which you will write. Even if you are not responsible for the day-to-day updating of an organization's site, you will be asked to contribute articles, news releases, biographical sketches, condensed versions of remarks given by principals, and other written pieces.

Integral to an organization's comprehensive public relations strategy, the website must be considered during the planning stages. The site helps introduce an organization and its key messages to the public by providing a variety of financial, promotional, marketing, and educational information in one central location. While the design and architecture of the website is not your job as a public relations practitioner, you should be consulted during its development for any major changes.

A website's key audiences are determined by the organization's goals and objectives. Many companies and organizations drive their audiences to the web because they have been designed to answer almost any question an audience may have. Others use websites to help audiences find them so that they can provide resources to assist the audiences.

Often reporters will check websites for up-to-date information when writing stories. If an organization's website is current and well organized, reporters will consult it regularly. Press releases, speeches, and other information posted for the purposes of working journalists should be written and presented in the usual accepted format and style and should be posted in a site newsroom. Remember that all the rules of writing for the news media should be observed when posting material to a website for reporters.

In a crisis situation, a website can serve two purposes. It can help keep reporters abreast of events and circumstances and it can serve as an organization's direct communication link to your key audiences. Two celebrity trials are good examples. The problems for lifestyle mogul Martha Stewart revolved around accusations and eventual conviction for improper stock trading. She was very slow to use the web as a tool to communicate with her audiences and supporters. When she finally adopted an aggressive web presence, including video statements, her public relations firm twice posted early versions of documents not ready for distribution. The late Michael Jackson, on the other hand, used his website early to mount direct communication with fans and supporters during his prosecution for child molestation.

When members of an organization want to find out news or information about the organization, they consult the website.

Writing for the web is much like writing for a brochure. In fact, some of the material on the web is called *brochureware*. This includes the basic information about the organization such as the mission, goals, philosophy, size, location, and major programs, usually found in the "about us" pages. Unlike brochures, websites can expand significantly using pages for case studies, sound and video, and even virtual tours of organization sites. Like brochures, websites are self-contained, but brochures remain stagnant until reproduced while websites can retain format and change content continually. The key to writing for web pages is to write clearly and concisely material that is organized around a central concept. Writing for the web is a definite skill set and one worth developing, and working with web designers is a good way to hone that skill. Designers understand the aesthetics of the medium and how people read on the web. The format and design formula for creating a website are identical to those for planning a brochure.

When the primary audience is employees, an organization's intranet can be used to communicate effectively. Studies show that employees are more productive and organizations run more smoothly when employees are well informed about the organization and the marketplace. Poor internal communication can adversely affect employee morale and leave employees guessing about their value to the organization. Consider that more than 40 percent of new managers fail in the workplace within the first year of a new assignment and 60 percent of all mergers fail. The lack of effective internal communication is a factor in both.

Electronic communication with employees can be almost immediate and very informative. Employees can learn about new projects, products, policy, and job opportunities and they can receive instruction for performing their work better without leaving their desks. PR practitioners in large organizations often write for the intranet. Of course, knowing the audience and having crystal-clear objectives will help present information in an interesting and compelling manner. Remember, the objectives must meet the needs of management as well as that of employees. It is important that the information provided to employees through the intranet not be complex or too detailed. Instead, the data should be simple and straightforward and provide a source for additional information if it is needed.

When research showed that a leading shipping company's attempts at rebranding itself were coming under criticism from the employees, the communication staff used an intranet to get employees to better understand the strategy and act as positive communicators about the company. Likewise, two large pharmaceutical corporations used their intranets to keep employees aware at every step of an impending merger of the two giants.

PROFESSIONAL POINT OF VIEW

Making Sure That Your Opinion Gets Heard

This point of view was written by Tanya Lewis for PRWeek.

Last November, the Treasury Department announced it was considering a new program for investing Troubled Asset Relief Program (TARP) funds. The following day, Porter Novelli (PN) offered *American Banker*, a top publication for financial services executives, an Op-Ed piece about opportunities and potential dangers for private equity investments in banks, written by its law firm client Goodwin Procter. The piece was accepted, and the *New York Times'* DealBook blog also ran a story about the Op-Ed content after it was published.

"Goodwin Procter has...content that adds knowledge and value to the conversation— the partners live and breathe financial service and M&A," says Albie Jarvis, SVP at PN.

"That's...pivotal. Experts need to add value to the conversation about an issue and not just restate the facts."

Jarvis adds that timing is also important. "The issue [must be] timely and relevant, and [you must be] timely in providing the Op-Ed to the outlet," he says. "[One reason *American Banker*] accepted the article was because we committed to get it to them while this issue was very fresh."

Bob Brody, SVP and media specialist at Weber Shandwick, says Op-Eds must offer tangible solutions to a problem, an insight, or a call to action. He also notes that fielding Op-Ed ideas to editors in advance of submission gives "tremendous advantage" in distinguishing your piece from the many other submissions.

"It also helps to take a somewhat contrarian position if you can, instead of aligning with traditional wisdom [on a given topic]," he adds. "For example, instead of saying, 'We need healthcare reform, and here are 10 reasons why,' you could say, 'We need healthcare reform, but [I don't think] we need it to the extent everybody seems to believe.' That type of approach may get more notice because it stands out from the pack."

Jarvis advises getting to the point quickly, as most Op-Eds are only 500 to 700 words long: "[Don't] dance around an issue."

Brody says writing self-serving Op-Eds is the biggest mistake clients tend to make. "An Op-Ed...pegged to a new product or a survey...is a tough sell," he notes. "Look above and beyond...the sphere of your own interest."

Elizabeth Romanaux, VP of communications at Liberty Science Center, a New Jersey museum supported by state funding, says she "had a bit of a learning curve" last year after submitting Op-Eds to *The Star-Ledger*, *The New York Times*, and *The Wall Street Journal* that were considered too self-serving. She notes that it's important for PR pros to help CEOs understand that Op-Eds must balance what they want to address with media outlet needs and requirements.

"We submitted Op-Eds that talked about the need for...science centers and their role," Romanaux says. "We shouldn't talk about ourselves at all—we should talk about the topic of science education."

After *The Star-Ledger* pointed out this mistake, Romanaux regrouped and the paper accepted an Op-Ed last November that addressed the economic meltdown and the role of science education going forward.

Jarvis explains that it's important to use good Op-Ed placements to extend coverage. "You have control of content, and you know when it's coming out," he says. "That gives you the luxury of thinking about who [else] will be interested in the story. Identify commentators, particularly bloggers, and flag that story to them. [They can] link to it and, ideally, add more commentary.

"For this topic, we had a very focused audience and our goal was to drive it toward very specific outlets," he adds. "It isn't a consumer topic; you'd want to go broader for a consumer-oriented topic. Know your audience and what outlets are important for them."

Technique Tips

Do

Address issues in a timely manner.
Add new knowledge and value to a topic.
Make your point quickly and clearly.

Don't

Submit Op-Eds that are self-serving.
Miss chances to extend play online.
Submit before fielding ideas to editors.

IMAGE GALLERY

National Gallery of Art

Office of Press and Public Information
Fourth Street and Constitution Avenue NW
Washington, DC
Phone: 202-842-6353   Fax: 202-789-3044
www.nga.gov/press

Chief Press Officer
Deborah Ziska
ds-ziska@nga.gov
(202) 842-6353

FOR IMMEDIATE RELEASE
Updated: January 9, 2006

For images and more information,
www.nga.gov/press

"CÉZANNE IN PROVENCE" AT THE
NATIONAL GALLERY OF ART, WASHINGTON, AND THE
MUSÉE GRANET, AIX-EN-PROVENCE, IN 2006,
MARKS CENTENARY AND EXPLORES GREAT ARTIST'S TIES TO BIRTHPLACE

WASHINGTON, D.C.—The year 2006 marks the centenary of the death of Paul Cézanne (1839–1906), a founding father of modern art who created some of the most powerful and innovative paintings of the late-19th and early 20th centuries. His achievement will be celebrated in a major international exhibition of 117 of his greatest oil paintings and watercolors of Provence, its people, and its surrounding countryside. Cézanne in Provence is the first exhibition to explore the artist's complex emotional engagement with his birthplace through some of his most original and compelling landscapes; penetrating portraits of friends, employees, and family members; and the monumental series known as the Bathers.

Cézanne in Provence will be shown in the National Gallery of Art's West Building, in Washington, D.C., from January 29 through May 7, 2006, and the Musée Granet in Aix-en-Provence, from June 9 through September 17, 2006, where it will inaugurate a series of events in honor of the artist to mark the reopening of the Musée Granet, one of France's premier regional museums, after a major renovation. The exhibition was organized by the National Gallery of Art, Washington, the Musée Granet and the Communauté du Pays d'Aix, Aix-en-Provence, and the Réunion des musées nationaux, Paris.

"Paul Cézanne was one of the greatest post-impressionist painters and has influenced generations of artists to the present. This landmark exhibition will focus on the sense he had of his own achievement, as a celebrant of the very particular and characteristic landscape around Aix-en-Provence," said Earl A. Powell III, director, National Gallery of Art. "The Gallery is deeply grateful for the cooperation of the many lenders worldwide and our museum partners in France, as well as the generosity of DaimlerChrysler in making this landmark exhibition possible."

Exhibition Support

The exhibition is made possible by a generous grant from the DaimlerChrysler Corporation Fund, which also sponsored Art Nouveau, 1890-1914, at the National Gallery of Art in 2000-2001.

"We are pleased to play a part in bringing Cézanne in Provence to the National Gallery," said Robert Liberatore, group senior vice president, DaimlerChrysler. "We have a strong commitment to making a positive impact in the communities in which we do business, and this exhibition at the National Gallery will demonstrate that commitment to visitors from around the world."

-more-

Figure 14.1

National Gallery of Art Press Release

SOURCE: National Gallery of Art, Email: ds-ziska@nga.gov, Web site: www.nga.gov/press, Telephone: (202) 842-6353 Fax: (202) 789-3044

Cézanne in Provence...2-2-2

The exhibition is supported by an indemnity from the Federal Council on the Arts and the Humanities.

Paul Cézanne and Provence

The son of a banker in Aix-en-Provence, Cézanne along with his friends spent idyllic days of childhood lying under great pine trees; exploring the ruins of a Roman aqueduct; swimming and fishing in the River Arc; or climbing the rocky canyons to the Zola Dam and the foothills of Montagne Sainte-Victoire. The ancient history and natural beauty of the land became part of the artist's persona.

Cézanne pursued his passionate desire to become an artist despite paternal disapproval. After studying drawing and flirting with a career in law, he made several trips to Paris in the 1860s. There he studied the work of old masters such as Veronese, Tintoretto, and Rubens, and the modern giants Eugène Delacroix and Gustave Courbet, and met young impressionist painters, such as Edouard Manet, Claude Monet, and Camille Pissarro. Under Pissarro's influence, Cézanne learned to use a lighter range of color, to vary his brushwork, and paint outdoors. When his father died in 1886, leaving him a legacy, Cézanne returned to his native Aix, where he spent most of his last twenty years.

Although he experimented with impressionist techniques in the 1870s, he soon grew impatient with them and reached instead for a more formal, structured style. An emotional man, he found stability in the painted depiction of nature, especially in the familiar countryside around his native Aix-en-Provence. In 1886 Cézanne referred to his birthplace as "this country, which has not yet found an interpreter worthy of the riches it offers."

At the end of his life Cézanne built a studio on the outskirts of Aix, where he painted a series of Bathers, considered by many to be his crowning achievement. From Aix, Cézanne wrote to fellow artist Emile Bernard, "I have sworn to die painting," a vow he fulfilled, for he was found outdoors after a cold autumn rainstorm, lying unconscious beside his easel. He died a few days later, in October 1906, at the age of 67.

The Exhibition

Cézanne in Provence includes 86 oil paintings, 29 watercolors, and two lithographs that are presented primarily by theme. The exhibition begins with the artist's family estate, the Jas de Bouffan, which is represented by views in its park, such as Chestnut Trees at the Jas de Bouffan in Winter (1885–1886) from the Minneapolis Institute of Arts; portraits of family members, including The Artist's Father, Reading "L'Événement" (1866), from the National Gallery of Art, Washington, and Madame Cézanne (Hortense Fiquet, 1850–1922) in the Conservatory (1891–1892) from The Metropolitan Museum of Art, New York; and estate employees, such as Cardplayers (1893–1896) from the Musée d'Orsay, Paris. The dazzling light of the Mediterranean coast is revealed in various views of the viaduct, rocky hillsides, and gulf of Marseille at L'Estaque, where Cézanne took a house in 1870.

From the coast, the exhibition will take the visitor inland to the old Provençal village of Gardanne where Cézanne studied the angular forms of its buildings that climbed up the hillsides, and Bellevue, where he found vantage points for his most clearly articulated and classical views of Montagne Sainte-Victoire presiding over the verdant valley of the River Arc. Lush paintings and sketchy watercolors, many from the 1890s, depict some of Cézanne's most personal landscape motifs in the abandoned stone quarry of Bibémus; the rocky, overgrown estate of Château Noir, where Cézanne rented space; and the village of Le Tholonet.

-more-

Figure 14.1
National Gallery of Art Press Release (*continued*)

Cézanne in Provence...3-3-3

Cézanne's studio at Les Lauves will be commemorated with many of the late works executed there, including the still lifes, such as Still Life with Statuette (1894–1895) from the Nationalmuseum, Stockholm, and the bathers, including the monumental Large Bathers (1894-1905) from the National Gallery in London, and related earlier figurative works. Cézanne's last great series of panoramic views of the Montagne Sainte-Victoire are included in the last gallery of the exhibition that is devoted to the dramatic gray limestone formation that presides over the valley of the River Arc.

The exhibition is also a tribute to the memory of the late, preeminent Cézanne scholar John Rewald. In the study of the sites in Provence and their significance for Cézanne, the exhibition organizers have been aided by the presence of the original site photographs in the National Gallery of Art Library Image Collections and Rewald's Cézanne papers in the Gallery Archives.

Curators, Catalogue, and Related Activities

The principal curators of the exhibition are Philip Conisbee, senior curator of European paintings, National Gallery of Art, and Denis Coutagne, director of the Musée Granet, Aix-en-Provence. They are also the authors of the exhibition catalogue, which celebrates the artist's remarkable and varied depictions of his native Provence. While Cézanne is recognized as one of the fathers of the modern movement, this book focuses on his own sense of achievement in capturing the landscapes in and around his hometown of Aix-en-Provence. In addition to essays by Conisbee and Coutagne, the catalogue features contributions by Françoise Cachin, Isabelle Cahn, Bruno Ely, Benedict Leca, Véronique Serrano, and Paul Smith. Published by the National Gallery of Art in association with Yale University Press, New Haven and London, the catalogue will be available in early January 2006 for $60 in hardcover and $45 in softcover. To order call 1-(800)-697-9350 or (202) 842-6002; fax (202) 789-3047; or e-mail mailorder@nga.gov (368 pp., 330 color and 34 black-and-white).

The National Gallery of Art is planning a full program of related lectures, tours, and concerts. Please see "Related Activities" in this press kit.

General Information

The National Gallery of Art and its Sculpture Garden, located on the National Mall between 3rd and 9th Streets at Constitution Avenue, NW, are open Monday through Saturday from 10 a.m. to 5 p.m. and Sunday from 11 a.m. to 6 p.m. Admission is free. For general information, call (202) 737-4215 or the Telecommunications Device for the Deaf (TDD) at (202) 842-6176.

Visitors are asked to present all carried items for inspection upon entering. Checkrooms are free of charge and located at each entrance. Luggage and other oversized bags must be presented at the 4th Street entrance of the East or West Building to permit X-ray screening and must be checked in the checkrooms at those entrances. Any items larger than 17" x 26" cannot be accepted by the Gallery or its checkrooms. For the safety of the art work and visitors, nothing may be carried on the back. Any bag or other item that cannot be carried reasonably and safely in some other manner must be checked.

# # #

Figure 14.1
National Gallery of Art Press Release (*continued*)

THE GAZETTE **SUNDAY OPINION** SUNDAY, OCTOBER 16, 2011

By Esme Serrano Sigala

Why Go Green?

REDUCE, REUSE, AND RECYCLE. I heard this snappy little phrase more times than I care to remember when my 10-year-old daughter chose topic as her science fair project. While trying to support her efforts to go green, I helped her with her research and discovered that, much to my surprise, I, too, had turned at least a slight shade of turquoise. One week later I gave up buying bottled water and purchased my very own bright purple, stainless steel water bottle. It came with a mesh strap that allows me to carry it over my shoulder, and it has a guarantee to keep my water cold for up to four hours.

In the past few weeks I have dropped plastic bags off a my local grocery store for recycling, dragged two blue bins filled to the brim out to the curb for Wednesday morning pickup, and sat in line in my car for forty-five minutes while waiting to turn over six empty paint cans and two partially used containers of motor oil.

I have purchased eight reusable shopping bags—four for each of our cars—and I have opted out of receiving catalogs and credit card offers. I began a compost pile in our backyard and have inspected each bag of garbage to be sure my husband did not throw away any compostable items. (He will never again toss his orange peels in the trash can without hearing my new mantra of "Not the trash can--the compost bucket!"

I no longer buy note pads, but make my own by using the backs of manuscript pages that I've put in the recycle bin, and I've started using the backs of my grocery receipts to write down the list of groceries for my next shopping trip. To top it off, I realized just how green I had become when I chose to buy one brand of juice over another based on the recycle number on the bottom of bottle.

When asked recently by a friend why I bother going to such lengths, I am proud to say I shocked her by reciting some of the latest figures gathered by my daughter for her science fair project:

The average person in our state generates nearly five pounds of solid waste per day--over 1,700 pounds per year.

3% of the energy generated in America's is used for producing packaging.

Just one pound of recycled steel saves 26 hours of a 60-watt bulb.

As Americans, we throw away enough paper every year that we could build a 12 feet high wall from Los Angeles to New York.

Before she could say one word, I continued by telling her that if she recycled just one of her soda cans, she could save enough energy to power her computer for 3 hours, and that was the least she could do!

STEP 1:

COLLECTION AND PROCESSING

Collecting recyclables varies from community to community, but there are four primary methods: curbside, drop-off centers, buy-back centers, and deposit/refund programs.

Regardless of the method used to collect the recyclables, the next leg of their journey is usually the same. Recyclables are sent to a materials recovery facility to be sorted and prepared into marketable commodities for manufacturing. Recyclables are bought and sold just like any other commodity, and prices for the materials change and fluctuate with the market.

STEP 2:

MANUFACTURING

Once cleaned and separated, the recyclables are ready to undergo the second part of the recycling loop. More and more of today's products are being manufactured with total or partial recycled content. Common household items that contain recycled materials include newspapers and paper towels; aluminum, plastic, and glass soft drink containers; steel cans; and plastic laundry detergent bottles. Recycled materials also are used in innovative applications such as recovered glass in roadway asphalt (glassphalt) or recovered plastic in carpeting, park benches, and pedestrian bridges.

STEP 3:

PURCHASING RECYCLED PRODUCTS

Purchasing recycled products completes the recycling loop. By "buying recycled," governments, as well as businesses and individual consumers, each play an important role in making the recycling process a success. As consumers demand more environmentally sound products, manufacturers will continue to meet that demand by producing high-quality recycled products. Learn more about recycling terminology and to find tips on identifying recycled products.

Figure 14.2

Why Go Green? Op-ed

EachOneTeachOne
1836 Jefferson Square, NW / Washington, DC 20036

Each One Teach One
1836 Jefferson Square, NW
Our Town 20036

September 1, 2011

Dear Ann Hall,

National Help Educate a Student Day is October 1, and the theme is *All Aboard the 2011 Express for a Quality Education for All Students.* When you're choosing stories for October, will this topic be important to you? Is it important to your readers? If you think it is a given that all students are on track to enter the workforce or go to college in America, you don't have the whole story. Consider the following statistics:
Three out of 10 students in America's public schools fail to complete school with a diploma. In Our Town, the statistics are compelling – 40 percent.

Today, U. S. students rank 25th out of the 29 developed nations for preparedness in math and science. Our Town public school students ranked lowest in the state.

The United States produces only 70,000 graduates in engineering versus 500,000 engineering graduates in China. Our Town's largest manufacturer had only three applications for 10 open positions for engineers.

How can we provide a better education for our children? How can we ensure they receive a world-class curriculum taught by master teachers? What will happen if we don't?

Created in 1999 with funding from the Presidential Safe Schools/Healthy Students Initiative, Each One Teach One provides mentoring, tutoring and financial assistance to Our Town public schools.

Each One Teach One has several spokespeople available to talk with you about children and public school education. We may also be able to introduce you to some of the teachers, families and students who have benefited from Each One Teach One's services, including tutoring and programs that provide one-on-one sessions with scientists and students.

Please give me a call if you would like more information or want to set up an interview. I hope that you will help spread the word about the importance of assistance to our schools, students and families.

Sincerely,

Sarah Woods, Communication Director
Each One Teach One
202.555.3377 (V)
202.555.3366 (F)
202.555.3355 (C)

Figure 14.3
Pitch Letter

Facts and Stats

Elementary Initiative (EI) refers to the CPS initiative to turn around its low-performing elementary schools. *Turnaround Schools* are the 16 schools that are currently the focus of the Elementary Initiative. In this document, the terms are interchangeable.

Five CPS Turnaround schools have jumped two categories in State of Ohio rankings, from "Academic Emergency," the lowest state ranking, to "Continuous improvement." They are Rockdale Academy, Roll Hill Academy, Rothenberg Preparatory Academy, Ethel M. Taylor Academy, William H. Taft School.

This is the first time any of the five schools have emerged from "Academic Emergency," the lowest state ranking.

Frederick M. Douglass School also moved up one category, from "academic watch" to "continuous improvement."

All six schools met federal accountability standards for Adequate Yearly Progress under the No Child Left Behind Act.

Several other Turnaround Schools are expected to have moved up at least one category, when the state releases all rankings on August 27.

From 2009 to 2010, significantly more Turnaround Schools/EI students tested "proficient" in reading and math. Sample data:
- Math performance of third-graders in EI schools improved by 4.4% compared to state averages showing a drop, at -5 %.
- Math performance of sixth-graders in EI schools improved by 14.8% compared to state average improvement of 3%.
- Reading performance of fourth-graders in EI schools improved by 9.6% compared to the state average change showing a drop, at -1%.
- Reading performance of sixth-graders in EI schools improved by 15.1% compared to the state average improvement of 3%.
- Reading performance of fifth-graders in EI schools improved by 5.2% compared to the state average showing no change, 0%.

From 2008 to 2010, 75%, or 12 of 16 of the Turnaround Schools achieved improved performance index (PI).
- Seven of the schools (Chase, Oyler, Rockdale, Roll Hill, Rothenberg, Taylor, Taft) improved by 5 or more points.
- Rockdale's PI improved by 13.7 points, followed by Taylor improving by 8.6 points, and Rothenberg improving by 8.3 points.

The Performance Index for the district overall improved by almost 3 points, in large part due to improvements made by the EI schools.

CPS' Elementary Initiative school gains in reading and math surpassed the state average at every grade level.

Data show progress toward closing the achievement gap. In math, for example, from 2009 to 2010, the gap between the low-performing schools and those that were not part of the Elementary Initiative — most of which serve schools in relatively more affluent neighborhoods that were already meeting proficiency requirements — closed by nearly 7 percentage points.

Figure 14.4

Fact Sheet for Cincinnati Public Schools

SOURCE: Janet Walsh, Director of Public Affairs, Cincinnati Public Schools, P O Box 5381, Cincinnati, Ohio 45201-5381

Reading Performance

Elementary Initiative Schools

% Proficient or above

Grade Level	2009	2010	Change from 2009-2010
3	42.0	48.0	+5.9
4	39.3	48.9	+9.6
5	26.4	31.6	+5.2
6	39.6	54.8	+15.1
7	34.2	43.6	+9.3
8	34.7	50.6	+15.9

Figure 14.5

Turnaround Schools/Cincinnati Public Schools Reading Performance Fact Sheet

SOURCE: Cincinnati Public Schools

National Gallery of Art

Office of Press and Public Information
Fourth Street and Constitution Avenue, NW
Washington, D.C. 20565
Phone: 202-842-6353 Fax: 202-789-3044
Web: www.nga.gov/press

BACKGROUNDER: *CÉZANNE IN PROVENCE* AND "CÉZANNE 2006"

The year 2006 marks the centenary of the death of Paul Cézanne (1839–1906), and the exhibition *Cézanne in Provence* is a commemoration and celebration of the artist's achievement. It is universally recognized that Cézanne was one of the greatest and most influential artists of the late 19th and early 20th centuries: one hundred years after his death, most modern artists would name Cézanne among their most significant predecessors.

Cézanne in Provence marks the first time the artist's engagement with his home in the town of Aix-en-Provence and the surrounding countryside, known as the *pays d'Aix*, has been examined in an exhibition. The last major Cézanne exhibition in the United States took place 10 years ago at the Philadelphia Museum of Art in 1996.

Each year a committee appointed by the French Ministry of Culture and Communication designates a number of national celebrations: cultural icons recently honored include Victor Hugo (2002) and Jules Verne (2005). Paul Cézanne has been chosen for 2006. To mark the celebration, Cézanne's hometown of Aix-en-Provence has been nominated to organize a season of special events, known as "Cézanne 2006." The season will be constructed around the *Cézanne in Provence* exhibition, which has been designated "an exhibition of national significance" by the ministry.

The exhibition owes its conception to cocurators Philip Conisbee, senior curator of European paintings and curator of French painting at the National Gallery of Art, and Denis Coutagne, conservateur en chef du patrimonoine and directeur de Musée Granet, Aix-en-Provence. In 2000 Conisbee and Coutagne had initial discussions with Henri Loyrette (now président-directeur of the Musée du Louvre) and Françoise Cachin (now director honoraire of the Musées de France). The Réunion des musées nationaux, Paris, under the director of Administrateur Général Thomas Grenon, has greatly facilitated the organization of the exhibition in France. The Musée Granet has been closed for renovations for more than four years, but will reopen in advance to host *Cézanne in Provence* from June 9 through September 17, 2006.

Both the National Gallery of Art and the Musée Granet have mounted compelling exhibitions devoted to Cézanne. Aix, which held its first Cézanne exhibition at the Musée Granet in 1953, celebrated the 50th anniversary of the artist's death in 1956 with an exhibition of 70 of his canvases at the Pavillon Vendôme. In 1990 the Musée Granet presented an exhibition focusing on Cézanne's depictions of Montagne Sainte-Victoire. At the National Gallery of Art, Cézanne is richly represented in the permanent collection, which includes 22 oil paintings and 88 works on paper by the artist. In 1989 National Gallery of Art presented the exhibition *Cézanne: The Early Years, 1859–1872,* which was also on view at the Royal Academy of Arts, London, and the Musée d'Orsay, Paris.

Backgrounder: *Cézanne in Provence* and "Cézanne 2006"..2-2-2

The ties between the United States, the National Gallery of Art, and Aix extend even further. The great Cézanne specialist and author of the catalogues raisonnés of the artist's oil paintings and watercolors, the American John Rewald, bequeathed his Cézanne archive to the National Gallery of Art. It was Rewald and the American writer James Lord who successfully gathered the necessary funds from American admirers of Cézanne to purchase the artist's studio, the Atelier des Lauves. Thanks to this American intervention, the studio became the property of the University of Aix in 1954 and was ceded to the city of Aix in 1969; it has been open to the public ever since. (See backgrounder in this press kit on *John Rewald, Cézanne, and the National Gallery of Art* for further information on Rewald's contributions to Cézanne scholarship.)

Cézanne in Provence has been organized by the National Gallery of Art, Washington, the Musée Granet and Communauté du Pays d'Aix, Aix-en-Provence, and the Reunion des musées nationaux, Paris.

The exhibition is made possible in Washington by a generous grant from the Daimler-Chrysler Corporation Fund. The exhibition is also supported by an indemnity from the Federal Council on the Arts and the Humanities.

# # #

Figure 14.6
Backgrounder from The National Gallery of Art (Cezanne Exhibit)

SOURCE: National Gallery of Art, Email: ds-ziska@nga.gov, Web site: www.nga.gov/press, Telephone: (202) 842-6353 Fax: (202) 789-3044

Figure 14.7A
National Gallery of Art Media Kit Cover

SOURCE: National Gallery of Art, Email: ds-ziska@nga.gov, Web site: www.nga.gov/press, Telephone:
(202) 842-6353 Fax: (202) 789-3044

Figure 14.7B
Cincinnati Public Schools Media Kit Cover

SOURCE: Cincinnati Public Schools

National Gallery of Art | Press Office

GENERAL INFORMATION • EXHIBITIONS • IMAGE LISTS • RECENT ANNOUNCEMENTS • PRESS ARCHIVES • CONTACT US

Online Press Kit

Extended Hours

Press Release

Related Activities

Exhibition Origins

Cézanne in Washington

Local Student Art
Inspired by Cézanne

Checklist

DaimlerChrysler
Sponsor Statement

John Rewald

Curator Philip Conisbee

Curator Denis Coutagne
French | English

Cafe Provençal

Acoustiguide Press
Release

Online Resources

Cézanne 2006

For Press Inquiries Only:
Mary Jane McKinven
Senior Publicist
(202) 842-6358
mj-mckinven@nga.gov

Deborah Ziska
Chief Press Officer
(202) 842-6353
ds-ziska@nga.gov

Release Date: June 29, 2005

"CÉZANNE IN PROVENCE" AT THE NATIONAL GALLERY OF ART, WASHINGTON, AND THE MUSÉE GRANET, AIX-EN-PROVENCE, IN 2006, MARKS CENTENARY AND EXPLORES GREAT ARTIST'S TIES TO BIRTHPLACE

Paul Cézanne
Houses in Provence: The Riaux Valley near L'Estaque, c. 1883
oil
65 x 81.3 cm (25 5/8 x 32 in.) framed: 84.4 x 100.3 x 5.7 cm (33 1/4 x 39 1/2 x 2 1/4 in.)
National Gallery of Art, Washington, Collection of Mr. and Mrs. Paul Mellon, 1973.68.1

Washington, DC—The year 2006 marks the centenary of the death of Paul Cézanne (1839–1906), a founding father of modern art who created some of the most powerful and innovative paintings of the late-19th and early 20th centuries. His achievement will be celebrated in a major international exhibition of 117 of his greatest oil paintings and watercolors of Provence, its people, and its surrounding countryside. **Cézanne in Provence** is the first exhibition to explore the artist's complex emotional engagement with his birthplace through some of

http://www.nga.gov/press/exh/194/index.shtm[5/26/2011 3:00:02 PM]

Figure 14.8
Online Media Kit

SOURCE: National Gallery of Art, Email: ds-ziska@nga.gov, Web site: www.nga.gov/press, Telephone: (202) 842-6353 Fax: (202) 789-3044

The GE Foundation

Developing Futures™ in Education

| Advancing the National Education Reform Initiative

JULY 2010

GE Foundation

Figure 14.9
GE Brochure Cover
SOURCE: General Electric Company

The GE Foundation Developing Futures™ in Education Program

SPRING 2010

In 2007, Erie School District received a five-year, $15 million grant from the GE Foundation Developing Futures™ in Education program. Erie is one of six school districts, along with Louisville, KY, Cincinnati, OH, Atlanta, GA, Stamford, CT, and New York, NY, to receive a grant. All of these cities have close ties to local GE businesses. In addition, they all demonstrated the potential to benefit from exploring and implementing new ways to educate students in math and science. The total investment in this project by the GE Foundation is close to $150 million.

The ultimate goal of the grant is to improve students' achievement in math and science—fostering the leaders of tomorrow. School districts use their grants to develop rigorous, system-wide math and science curricula and to help teachers increase their skills through professional development. In addition, the GE Foundation stresses that school districts should strive to improve the way they work with their partners in the community to improve students' educational experiences.

In Erie, the District identified another challenge that needed to be addressed. The District was not benefiting from technological advances. One of the major goals identified by the District was to enhance the information technology (IT) system.

Better Technology

Through the grant, the District invested $4 million towards the implementation of a new IT system, with the help of GE IT staff. GE staff was also instrumental in identifying cost-saving measures, which ultimately reduced the cost of the project by $1 million.

The new system puts student data in the hands of teachers and administrators so that they can track student progress and make better decisions. In addition, it is a timesaver. All teachers K-12 now take attendance using the new system. While it used to take teachers 90 minutes per week to perform their attendance duties, they can now do it in 15 minutes, which means more time for teaching. Wireless Internet access is now available in all District schools, which makes e-mailing and accessing online resources easier.

The District has also launched a new web site that is designed to be a creative, user-friendly way to communicate with students,

parents, employees, and the community. This web site provides students with instructional resources, access to local and national educational sites, and valuable information to help them in their daily academic lives. Parents have access to important information that includes dates, times, and locations of District events, daily school lunch menus, messages from the superintendent, and other essential news about what is happening in the District. Teachers have easy access to instructional resources. As a "one-stop shop" for District information, the new web site (www.eriesd.org) delivers easy-to-access phone numbers, e-mail, instructional resources, and media presentations. Coming soon will be the Parent Portal, which will allow parents and students to check assignments, progress, and grades online.

MATH
New Math Curricula Add Up to Big Changes in the Classroom
page 2

SCIENCE
Science Curriculum Is Evolving
page 3

A Conversation with Dr. Jim Barker and Carol Laskowski
page 4

GE Foundation

Sharing highlights of the GE Foundation Developing Futures™ in Education Grant
This publication was made possible through a grant from the GE Foundation.

The School District, City of Erie, PA
148 West 21st Street
Erie, Pennsylvania 16502

Non-Profit Organization
U.S. Postage
PAID
Erie, PA
Permit No. 207

Superintendent Spotlight
Dr. Jim Barker, President of Schools

Why is Developing Futures™ significant for the District?

Developing Futures™ is a game-changing intervention. It is done in a collaborative way where the GE Foundation is not telling the District what to do but working with the District to find solutions specific to the data and needs in the community. It is a great formula for success. This funding constitutes a commitment to improve education for all children in an urban setting. The way this is accomplished is by creating a collaborative culture among boards, teachers, and administrators to put adult issues on the back burner and to move student issues to the forefront.

What has been the impact of the funding?

The funding has served as a lever to ensure that resources are focused on teaching and learning math and science. The impact has been dramatic in improving teaching skills and student performance. Professionals now talk about inquiry-based learning and other innovative approaches. Students are developing higher-order thinking skills that will allow them to become great problem solvers, not just in math and science but across all areas.

What were the major accomplishments this year?

We will be expanding programs in both math and science across grade levels. We will also be reaching out to parents through science and math nights and developing a link to our IT system through Parent and Student Portals. Parents and

students will have access to course content and associated learning activities around science and math at any time, 24/7.

As you move ahead with planned activities, what are the challenges you will face?

Education is a bullet train—every day 13,000 students show up and are ready to be educated. At the same time, we have to increase the competence of our teachers and integrate new curricula. This year, the math and science curricula in grades K-8 will be better implemented across the District. There will be a flurry of activity to improve teacher and student performance. On a long-term basis, it is not just the materials and equipment that we have acquired through the grant that are important, but the significant amount of professional development and support for teachers that has resulted. The challenge will be how we sustain the level of interest, attention, and accomplishment over time.

What is the role for parents in improving math and science education?

You don't have to be a scientist or a mathematician to help a child be successful in math and science. Dr. Benjamin Carson grew up in poverty in a Detroit housing project and became a successful and pioneering neurosurgeon. His mom followed his school work and communicated with his teachers – she was involved and motivated him. Parents should work closely with the school to support their children.

Teacher Perspective
Carol Laskowski, President, Erie Education Association

Why is Developing Futures™ significant for the District?

The funding has supported new professional development opportunities for teachers. It is helping to improve the teaching of science and math and has resulted in subject areas. In addition to the extra training, teachers have been brought into the decision-making process. They have become involved in so many different areas where they previously did not have a voice.

What has been the impact of the funding at the classroom level?

The math and science programs have changed. The District is focusing on an inquiry-based approach, which stresses asking questions and thinking creatively. Teachers no longer stand in front of the class and lecture. This is a different approach and teachers have been provided with the necessary professional development to successfully implement the new curricula.

What challenges do teachers face as we move forward with planned activities?

The challenge is that everything is new—it is a different way of teaching. We were not trained to teach this way when we went to school. It has also been challenging because both the math and science programs have changed. This makes it twice as difficult because the content is new in two areas.

What is being done to support teachers as they make these changes in the classroom?

In addition to a variety of training activities to support the implementation of the new curricula, the Developing Futures™ program has supported a new coaching program for teachers. Coaches are available to work with teachers in the classroom. What is important is that the coaches come into the classroom to help, not to evaluate performance. They can tailor their advice to the needs of each teacher.

Coaches work on a full-time basis with several schools. They are available to teachers by phone and e-mail, in addition to coming into the classroom to provide guidance. The coaches were recruited from within the District and teachers were involved in the interview and selection process.

Developing Futures™ is a GE Foundation program created to raise student achievement through improved math and science curricula and management capacity at the schools. For questions or comments, please contact Sidney Potter, District Project Manager, GE Foundation Developing Futures in Education at 874-4966, spotter@eriesd.org or Jim Rutkowski, Teacher Program Manager, 874-4060, j.rutkowski@eriesd.org.

PAGE 4 ERIE PUBLIC SCHOOLS

To learn more about the GE Foundation grant visit: www.ge.com/foundation/developing_futures_in_education and www.eriesd.org

Figure 14.10
GE Foundation Sample Newsletter Pages

SOURCE: General Electric Company

ideas:

AN AED PERIODICAL ABOUT LASTING SOLUTIONS

June 2010
Premiere
Issue

www.aed.org/ideas

What Works When
Treating Acute
Malnutrition

Fellowship Program
Prepares
Future
Principals

FORECAST:
Strengthening
Institutions
with Systemic
Approaches

Building a
Better Future
through Improved
Teaching in
Equatorial Guinea

More Help to
More People:
The Story of
Capable Partners

 AED   HEALTH   EDUCATION   SOCIAL AND ECONOMIC DEVELOPMENT
Ideas Changing Lives

PROFICIENCY +
PRODUCTIVITY
Helping People Strengthen Capacity

Figure 14.11

Ideas Magazine Cover and Tech Nation Magazine Cover

SOURCES: Academy for Educational Development and Tech Nation Media; Jack Hornady, Artist

Figure 14.12

AED "It's Possible" Annual Report

SOURCE: mmaguire@aed.org

*Letter from the Chairman
and Vice Chairman*

AED continues to thrive and make a difference in people's lives. Enterprise and economic development, youth programs both in the United States and internationally, and global preparation for pandemic flu are just a few of the key areas in which we are expanding our work.

The worldwide financial crisis has made it even more important for AED to be a careful steward of the donations and grants entrusted to us. In addition to assuring financial accountability, we have strengthened our intellectual capital in order to address expanded and new programmatic areas. New officers with expertise in health, HIV/AIDS, and finance have joined us and we have welcomed three new board members.

Dr. Barry R. Bloom is Joan L. and Julius H. Jacobson Professor of Public Health at Harvard and former dean of the Harvard School of Public Health. Gail A. Galuppo is executive vice president and chief marketing officer, Western Union. Allen J. Weltmann is former partner, Pricewaterhouse Coopers and chairman of the Libraries Development Advisory Board at Pennsylvania State University.

Their diverse perspectives, added to the great strength that already exists on the board, will be invaluable as we move forward. Diversity of staff, portfolio, and funding—public and private—has always enabled AED to better serve the communities in which we work throughout the world. We greatly appreciate the trust of our donors in supporting AED's efforts.

Edward W. Russell
Chairman of the Board

Roberta N. Clarke
Vice Chairman of the Board

Figure 14.12
AED "It's Possible" Annual Report (*continued*)

It's possible.

The cell phone in your pocket can stop a disease outbreak and improve a child's education. ⚕📖

GATHER™ is a new **technology platform** AED created to turn any cellular phone or other mobile computing device, such as a PDA, into a tool that can collect and transmit large amounts of data to a computer in a matter of hours. The open-source technology performed well in an initial pilot for **disease surveillance** in Uganda.

"The collection and transfer of accurate, real-time data is essential to effective development, regardless of the sector," said Holly Ladd, vice president and director of the AED-SATELLIFE Center for Health Information and Technology. "Now that half of all people in the world have access to cell phones, GATHER™ has even greater potential to be a valuable tool for monitoring and evaluation."

GATHER™ is currently being piloted in a **school reform** project in Mali, **food security** efforts in Haiti, and **family planning** in Mexico, Bolivia, Sri Lanka, and Uganda. It will be widely available once the pilot phase is complete.

DONOR: Rockefeller Foundation, AED Incubation Fund

Health workers in Tanzania exchange data using handheld devices.

Figure 14.12
AED "It's Possible" Annual Report (*continued*)

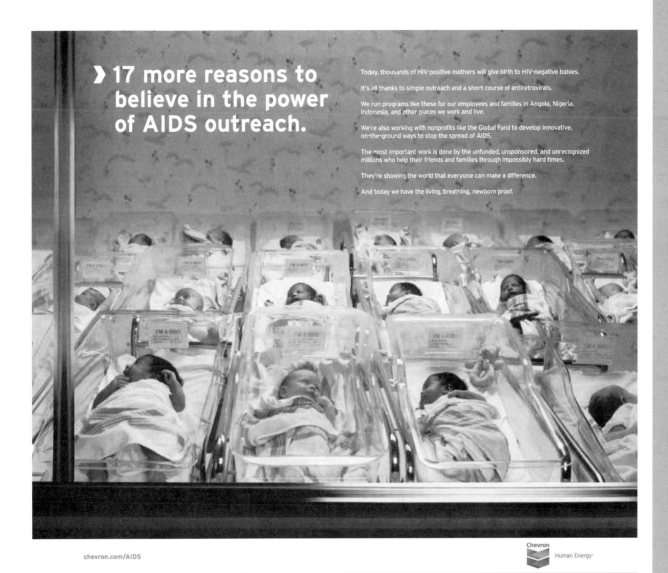

Figure 14.13

Corporate-image Ad

"Twelve Reasons to Celebrate World AIDS Day" *Financial Times* Ad

SOURCE: Chevron Corporate

Figure 14.14
PSA for The Partnership for a Drug-Free America
SOURCE: The Partnership at Drugfree.org

Figure 14.15

USA Today Internal House Ad

SOURCE: USA Today

Summary and Review

Understanding Written Tactics
- The PR practice takes advantage of many written tactics including news releases, feature releases, op-eds and letters to the editor, pitch and confirmation letters, media kits, brochures, newsletters, magazines, corporate and public service advertising, and internal and external web pages.

Asking Strategic Questions
- Like planning, employing tactics must begin with strategy. A good public relations plan includes how particular tactics will be used. You must ask and answer questions such as the identity of the key audience, the goal of the message, what action you want the audience to take, and the benefits to the audiences.

Preparing Written Tactics
- All of the preceding media require particular formats and styles. They must be written concisely and accurately.
- The news release is a tool used in media relations for the purposes of disseminating newsworthy information to the news media. It should be written in a straightforward and concise style, delivered in a direct and timely fashion, and organized in the appropriate format.
- The newsletter is a serial publication and must be published regularly. The most commonly published newsletters are employee, community, advocacy, member, and special-interest subscriber newsletters.
- While paid advertising is sometimes part of a tactics plan, free public service advertising (PSA) is usually associated with PR. The competition for free time and space has become very intense and the cost of production quite high, so practitioners who hope to use PSAs must plan well ahead and work with community service directors in the media to get placements.
- The Internet and intranets have become powerful communication tools for reaching internal and external audiences. Web pages can be used to deliver many of the media products discussed in this chapter.

Key Terms

advertorial
advocacy advertising
annual report
backgrounders
blogs (web logs)
boilerplate
brochures
confirmation letter
corporate-image
    advertising

dateline
embargo
fact sheets
feature release (news
    feature)
internal and external
    house ads
inverted pyramid
    structure
lead

letters to the editor
media alert (media
    advisory)
media kit
op-ed
page slug
panels
pitch letter
public service
    advertising

Questions for Review and Discussion

1. Discuss how the answers to the questions at the beginning of the chapter (p. 276) might affect how you would begin writing.

2. How do the members of the news media use a news release?

3. Discuss the criteria of newsworthiness. Look at daily newspaper articles and investigate whether or not one or more of the criteria exist.

4. How can a practitioner localize a national story in order to interest reporters and editors?

5. Explain how news releases and feature releases differ.

6. Why is follow-up to a news release important?

7. What are the advantages of using companies such as PR Newswire, Business Wire, Market Wire, Black PR Wire, and U.S. Wire to distribute releases?

8. How do op-eds and letters to the editor differ?

9. Why are confirmation letters valuable media relations tools?

10. Discuss the best way to reach bloggers and why.

11. Name the three most widely used media kits and explain the purpose of each.

12. What is "scanability" in a brochure?

13. Why is producing a newsletter time-consuming?

14. Why do for-profit and nonprofit organizations publish annual reports?

15. Name two differences between PSAs and paid advertising.

16. Why are websites useful tools during crisis situations?

Web Links

Fenton
www.fenton.com

Ketchum
www.ketchum.com

Public Relations Society of America
www.prsa.org

PR Newswire
www.prnewswire.com

PR Web
www.prweb.com

Asian News Wire
www.asianprwire.com

Business Wire
www.businesswire.com

Hispanic PR Wire
www.hispanicprwire.com

Market Wire
www.marketwire.com

Black PR Wire
www.blackpr.com

Vocus
www.vocus.com

U.S. PR Wire
www.usprwire.com

Spoken Tactics

COMMUNICATION CONTEXTS

Public relations spoken tactics can be used in all four contexts of communication—interpersonal, small group, public, and mass. The spoken word bolstered by credibility remains one of the most powerful tools of persuasion.

SPOKEN TACTICS OF INTERPERSONAL COMMUNICATION

In Chapter 1, we said that one-on-one communication is the most effective type of communication. Therefore, we try to learn as much as we can about our key audiences, so that we can speak to them directly and personally. Political candidates still board buses and trains to travel around and meet with people because they want the advantage and power of personal influence on another person. For example, interpersonal communication is the hallmark of political caucuses during presidential primary elections. Neighbors and friends who are committed to a particular candidate invite others into their homes to explain why the candidate is best for the party's nomination and to try to talk them into voting for the candidate. The benefit for the candidate is third-party credibility and popularity.

The spoken tactics most closely affiliated with interpersonal communication are the one-on-one interview and word of mouth.

Speak clearly, if you speak at all; carve every word before you let it fall.

—Oliver Wendell Holmes, Supreme Court Justice

Preparing the right spokesperson for media interviews is crucial.

Gino's Premium Images/Alamy

News Media

One-on-One Interviews

The **one-on-one interview,** which is *communication between a spokesperson and a reporter*, is one of the most widely used spoken opportunities for communicating with the news media in person. Preparation is the clarion call for this media relations tool. When the public relations practitioner has prepared well for a one-on-one interview with an organization's spokesperson—the person selected to speak on behalf of your organization—these interviews can be very effective. But when you have not been thorough, one-on-one interviews can be a tragedy. Your role in a one-on-one interview is to act as a liaison between the reporter and your organization. After a spokesperson is assigned, there are a few things you should complete before the interview takes place.

1. Check and double-check the agreed-to day, time, and location of the interview. If the interview is to be conducted by telephone, check and double-check who is calling whom. Please don't forget time zones. Sometimes it is easy to forget at the time of arranging the interview that the spokesperson and journalist are not in the same time zone. This is especially important if the call is international. Also, you should arrange a three-way conference call for you, your spokesperson, and the reporter if possible because speakerphones can be uncomfortable for both parties: it is difficult to hear, delayed voice transmission can cause interviewer and spokesperson to talk over each other, people are generally uncomfortable when they know they may be overheard, and the three of you should be able to hear both sides of the interview. Skyping can be used for one-on-one interviews but the technology is not perfect and images are not good.

2. Determine as early as possible if the reporter will be accompanied by a photographer. Of course, if it is a television interview, plans should be made to accommodate a television crew. Let the spokesperson know that it takes time to set up for photography if the interview is going to take place in his or her office. If possible, another location would be more convenient for the reporter and the spokesperson.

3. If the interview is the result of a pitch (see Chapter 14 for a discussion of pitch letters, although the pitch can be made by telephone or in person) made to the reporter, you want to be sure that you both understand the nature of the interview. When the story is pitched, it is easier to get a clear idea of the direction in which the reporter is headed. If the interview is in response to a reporter's call to the organization, it is a little harder to get clarity about the interview's direction. But you are wise to take time to find out as much as possible about what the reporter wants. Does the reporter want specific information about the organization's corporate objectives, how it intends to position an idea or product, or quotes about a particular issue or direction of the organization? Interviews that concentrate on the industry, issues, or trends tend to help position the spokesperson and organization as thought leaders.

4. Ask the reporter to indicate the type of article expected to result from the interview. Is the story about the organization alone such as a new product or program? Is the interview to provide texture for a larger article about the industry or a local angle on a national or international story? Does the reporter appear to have a specific point of view?

5. Begin to prepare background information and materials right away, to brief both the reporter and the spokesperson. If the reporter covers the organization regularly, a review of the most recent coverage of the organization or the industry is crucial, and time updating the reporter on any significant changes or events is very important. If the reporter is new to the organization or the industry or issue, you should volunteer to provide information to help bring the reporter up to speed.

6. Preparing the spokesperson is just as important as preparing the reporter. You should tell the spokesperson what you know about the reporter if you have worked with the reporter previously, and provide coverage the reporter has done. If this is the first experience with this reporter, you should tell the spokesperson that the reporter may not be familiar with the scope of the business or organization or may be unfamiliar with terminology or the "players" who weigh in on a particular issue.

7. At least two meetings or telephone calls between you and the spokesperson before the interview are recommended. Two things should be accomplished in these meetings. First, the spokesperson and you should establish two key messages or points to be made. This is an important first step designed to give time to agree on those messages. The second meeting is just as important as the first. During this session you two should discuss the questions you both anticipate the reporter will ask. This preparation should be grounded in reality. If the reporter arranges the interview to discuss the details of new government policies that will affect delivery of services to seniors or at-risk youth, the spokesperson should be prepared to respond to those issues. But it is unwise for the spokesperson to be in denial about other issues. If controversy exists or surfaces prior to the interview, you must anticipate the reporter will ask questions about that controversy. The spokesperson should be prepared to answer. The rule is that the spokesperson is being interviewed. You do not answer the questions unless they are directed to you or if clarification is sought.

Instruct the spokesperson that he or she should never suggest or agree to answer a question off the record. Once the words have been spoken or written, it's possible they will be used regardless of what the spokesperson believed (or was told) were the conditions.

During and Following the Interview   While you have a major role to play in preparing for the interview, your role is just as important during and following the interview. In its simplest form, the one-on-one interview is a question and answer session between the reporter and the spokesperson. However, it is much more complicated than that, because you must help facilitate a successful interview—one that accomplishes something positive for the organization.

In further facilitating the interview, you should accompany the spokesperson. Your role at this point is to introduce the reporter and the spokesperson and to take notes. Most reporters will take notes and use a tape or digital recorder. If you want to tape the interview, you should discuss this with the reporter before the interview begins. You must remain in the background during the interview, and not interject unless verification or clarification is sought or the spokesperson promises to provide additional information. It is not your role to get quoted or to end up at the center of the session. An exceptionally painful situation occurred when former Secretary of State Colin Powell was being interviewed on NBC News *Meet the Press*. The interview was running particularly long and the Secretary's press aide became quite upset. She called for a halt to the interview and said, "You're off." The Secretary disagreed with her and asked her to please "get out of the way." Unfortunately, it was all captured on videotape and host Tim Russert showed the videotape of the incident in its entirety. While it is understandable that the press aide was annoyed, interjecting was completely unacceptable.

You should give the reporter all additional information requested. Timely responses to requests for additional information are very important so you must be sure to ask for the reporter's deadline. Your availability is vital to this process. Agreeing to an interview means agreeing to assist the journalist until the article or news segment is complete. That means being available for clarification and additional information.

You are expected to talk to the reporter and the spokesperson following the interview. Escorting the reporter from the interview location provides for a quick debrief to try to get a feel for the reporter's impressions. Sometimes reporters will let on as to whether they felt the interview accomplished what they wanted or was a waste of time. You should talk to the spokesperson as soon as she is free from escorting the reporter. This is an opportunity to give the spokesperson honest feedback on the interview. Understand that this type of feedback is important for the next time the spokesperson is chosen to be interviewed. When the article is published or the interview is aired, you should review it well, looking for accuracy in quotations and facts. Copies of the article or copies of the tapes from the station or the organization's media monitoring company will assist in preparing you and the spokesperson. The spokesperson should receive copies for her review. It is important for the spokesperson to get feedback quickly and when possible, *before* others in the organization are aware.

Word of Mouth

Malcolm Gladwell's internationally acclaimed bestseller, *The Tipping Point: How Little Things Can Make a Big Difference*, quickly became the centerpiece for a new marketing movement, *influencer marketing*. With this book, Gladwell explained how ideas, trends, and behaviors unfold and proliferate, creating experiences like bestsellers, fashion trends, and even drops in crime waves. He included a discussion on the affect of **word of mouth**, *consumers talking to friends, family, and acquaintances about their experience with a particular product, service, or company.* He describes the unexplained resurgence of the popularity of Hush Puppies—yes, Hush Puppies—the crepe-soled, unattractive "old people's shoes." It seemed that there was no accounting for the fact that these shoes suddenly became very popular with a group of fashion-savvy New Yorkers in the early 1990s. Soon the brand, scheduled for demise, was enjoying a renewed vitality and by the mid-1990s sales were in the hundreds of thousands. This was all due, it appeared, to the strength of word of mouth of a few influential New Yorkers.

Gladwell's book got the marketing types thinking about this phenomenon and its impact on selling products and ideas. Before we knew it, books applying his concept began to appear. Roper ASW CEO Ed Keller wrote *The Influential: One American in 10 Tells the Other Nine How to Vote, Where to Eat, and What to Buy*, using Roper research to demonstrate how significant word of mouth has become in the decisions consumers make. Important for public relations practitioners is that while acknowledging the way that technology has enhanced the speed and precision with which we reach key audiences, we must recognize that the ever-increasing message overload for most audiences means we must be more and more strategic in the ways in which we try to reach them. We must think in terms of the influencing audience as well as the primary audience.

Studies show that friends and family influence people more than advertising or editorial content does. Increasingly, studies demonstrate that word-of-mouth communication is an important factor for people considering the adoption of innovation. Scholars also suggest that word-of-mouth communication is very effective when it is difficult to reach certain cultural audiences. Indeed, the theory applies whenever we try to reach an audience, because being culturally aware is part of being strategic. Again, we have to ask our key audiences how we can best reach them and what is important to them. Increasingly, family and friends are part of the answer.

As we discussed in the planning process presented in Part Three of this text, those who influence a key audience are called influencers. Influencers can be categorized as follows:

- Decisive influencers such as friends, peers, family members, physicians, and coworkers who have intimate, personal relationships to the key audience.
- Primary influencers who "exert influence over the ultimate influencers" and/or key audience such as experts, celebrities, news media, and online and community leaders.
- Detractors such as competitors or activist groups.

Reflecting on his work Gladwell wrote, "What is now obvious to me—but was not at the time I wrote *The Tipping Point* is that we are about to enter the age of word of mouth, and that, paradoxically, all of the sophistication and wizardry and limitless access to information of the New Economy is going to lead us to rely more and more on very primitive kinds of social contacts." Of course, social networking, enhanced by technology has brought us to the time he described.

Influencer marketing, also referred to as viral marketing, word of mouth, or creating buzz tactics, can play a part in strategic public relations. The use of influencers as strategy holds a lot of promise for social change efforts in nonprofit and health communication. Sustainability of awareness and change can be heightened through the creation of a network of groups of highly motivated key audiences that keep the buzz going through grassroots efforts.

SPOKEN TACTICS OF SMALL-GROUP COMMUNICATION

Small-group communication is the next tier of human communication. Small group occurs when 3 to 15 people participate in a discussion or gather for the express purpose of solving a problem or accomplishing a specific goal or objective. In the field of strategic communication, meetings are the most common type of small groups employed in public relations settings.

Meetings as Part of the PR Practice

Public relations professionals the world over spend a lot of time in meetings. While the face-to-face encounters that practitioners call meetings can happen on a dyadic—two people talking—basis, they are more likely to be *small group*s. The major advantage of **meetings**—*gatherings of people who come together to share ideas and work together*— is that they provide an opportunity for small numbers of people to get clarity and provide immediate feedback on a subject. Usually, a meeting is the first forum in which communication strategy begins to take shape. The inquiry and brainstorming that take place during meetings are often the source of some of the best thinking on a campaign or program. With that said, meetings can be the bane of your existence if they are not conducted properly, or if they waste time, energy, and goodwill. Productive meetings with colleagues begin with a written agenda, a list of goals to be met, and a specified length of time for the meeting. They should start and conclude on time.

Media Relations Meetings

Editorial meetings and media or deskside briefings—are widely used in the field. Securing these meetings can be sometimes difficult depending upon the frequency with which the organization has legitimate news or the possibility for news.

Editorial board meetings—*meetings in which newsmaker meets with the members of a news organization's editorial writers (and sometimes issue-specific reporters), usually to explore a particular issue in-depth or to attempt to understand the direction or scope of an initiative or policy*—are powerful tools of the media relations practice. There are a few ways to meet with the editorial staffs of the news media. First, you can pitch the possibility of a telephone or face-to-face meeting with an editor to explain an upcoming initiative or your organization's stance on an issue. You would attend such a meeting and be responsible for the content.

Secondly, you can arrange a similar meeting for a spokesperson of an organization. Traditionally, these are referred to as editorial board meetings and involve arranging a meeting with the editorial staff of one news-gathering organization. The purpose of these meetings is to provide background and not hard news. These sessions tend to be informal and are usually held at the news media offices. For instance, a domestic affairs Cabinet secretary, such as Housing, Transportation or Health and Human Services, traveling to Chicago or Los Angeles might ask to meet with editorial staff of the major daily newspapers to provide an overview of the previous year's accomplishments and to discuss topics of specific interest to the residents of these cities. Editorial board meetings may also be used to present an organization's plans for the upcoming year, to discuss current status of various negotiations, or to explain the organization's stance on an issue.

Still operating on a small-group level, practitioners can call together five to 10 reporters from various news media for an informal meeting sometimes called news media briefings. Like the editorial board meeting discussed previously, **news media briefings** are *not for hard news but are for the purpose of updating media periodically when a briefing has not been scheduled for some time.* Reporters should be invited to briefings, but it must be made clear that the briefing will not involve hard news. This will ensure that reporters may choose to attend or not without fear of missing news.

Pharmaceutical manufacturer Eli Lilly organized such meetings and called them the "Monthly Health Forum for Reporters." The idea was to be proactive in establishing news media relationships and to provide reporters with stories. The forums offered experts in medicine, research, health, policy, and regulation who provided insight into important issues. The topic of each monthly forum was announced through a public relations news wire service. The Monthly Health Forum format consisted of 30- to 40-minute discussions followed by questions and answers.

Media briefings for reporters covering crises, important breaking news, and military operations are quite different. They are designed to keep reporters up to date on situations and changing circumstances and to present the newest and most important information. These types of briefings are usually regularly scheduled during the crisis or breaking news period.

SPOKEN TACTICS OF PUBLIC COMMUNICATION

Public communication is the third context in which human communication transpires. Its communication is usually more formal than the previous levels of communication and usually involves one person communicating with a large group of up to hundreds of people.

Meetings or conferences on a larger scale are widely used as a public relations tool. Organizations such as professional and industry associations, government entities, community coalitions, city councils, unions, and advocacy groups conduct meetings to share data and information, to discuss topics, to create strategy to address common concerns, and to generate news media interest in a particular subject.

When meetings are held on this level, they must be highly organized, requiring particular attention to detail, time lines, and checklists. Today, there are many companies that specialize in the organization and management of meetings. They are responsible for the myriad of tasks including securing the venue, invitations, responses of attendees, various vendors, onsite supervision, news media contact, and evaluation.

The most widely used meetings on this scale include news conferences, news media showings, press parties, media events, and speeches.

News Conferences

Inviting the news media in to make an important announcement and provide information is one of the most well known news media opportunities because the public has seen **news conferences** in session so often. Most common in the United States, Canada, and the United Kingdom, news conferences are frequently used by heads of state to discuss important matters and to give the news media an opportunity to pose questions about the general state of affairs in the country. Less often seen in other parts of the world, the news conference is used to make major announcements and to react to crises. It is wise for you to study presidential news conferences to observe how they are conducted.

As a public relations practitioner, you will do well to caution your clients about the use and abuse of news conferences. Again, this is an opportunity to remember the target audience—journalists. Attending a news conference can be very expensive for news media representatives. Generally, attendance involves changing schedules, dedicating staff time and committing expensive photographers and camera crews. The rule of thumb regarding a decision to hold a news conference is: *hold a news conference only in the case of a major news event and if the media cannot get the information or visuals, in-depth exploration of the subject, or access to the newsmaker in any other way.*

Organizations can also organize news conferences for editorial writers to discuss very important issues in which the organization may have some stake. Many large nonprofits

White House Press Secretary Jay Carney holds press briefing in the White House briefing room.

in Washington, DC, have these opportunities when the legislation relevant to their issue is pending or when the federal budget threatens to cut social programs and services.

Some situations that by their very nature automatically require a news conference, such as keeping the public and media informed during crises and emergencies such as a devastating accident, unexpected death of a prominent figure, or extreme destruction resulting from natural disasters. Major medical breakthroughs, mergers and acquisitions, economic changes, prominent awards, or legislative or court decisions merit news conferences as well, but the emphasis here is on the word *major*. Any other circumstances should be weighed and debated heavily. Remember that the news media have scarce time and resources. You must ask yourself, is this something you can advise the news media about through a news release and some well-timed video and photos? If the answer is yes, spare the organization from embarrassment and disgruntled reporters.

There are many positive and genuinely newsworthy circumstances under which a news conference can be held locally. For instance, two manufacturers might hold a news conference to announce their intentions to build a new plant together in order to create a new product. The move will create new jobs and will bring a new facility to a blighted part of town. First, such an idea is novel and second, the manufacturers have good news for the community. Or working with the mayor's office, a local union might have decided to begin a new program to motivate young people to stay in school by offering them paid apprenticeships starting in ninth grade as long as they continue high school and graduate. Again, it is good news for the community and bringing together the mayor, the first youth to participate, a youth advocacy group leader, and union officials benefits the news media because there is an opportunity for questions and answers from all of these participants.

Planning and Organizing a News Conference

The planning and organizing of a news conference is your domain as a public relations practitioner. It is highly unlikely that one of the first tasks in your career will be to plan a news conference, but one never knows. It has happened! It is possible to land a position with a small nonprofit or land a client with real news. The particular circumstances notwithstanding, there are many tasks to undertake to have a successful news conference.

After it is determined that a news conference is needed, follow these steps to ensure a successful event:

Step 1:   Decide who to invite and how to notify them. Invitations to a news conference and related information should be extended to all news-gathering organizations that might be interested in the story. These can include newswire services, newspapers, radio and television stations, magazines, trade publications, online news outlets, and even some newsletters.

Notification depends heavily on the type of news. If the news conference is called because of *spot news*, or hard news that is happening, the news conference should be called right away. In these cases, direct telephone calls, email, fax, and wire services are appropriate.

In all other instances, the news media should be notified on a longer-term basis. The decision for how much lead time needs to be determined is based on a few facts. First, check the community calendar to select a date and time that does not compete with another event. Second, learn as much as possible about the news media you intend to invite—deadlines, lead time, location, times of their news segments and publication, and similar information is important.

Deciding the right amount of time for notification varies. If only local media are invited, you should give them enough time to assign coverage of the conference but not so much time that the story leaks. Three or four days in advance are substantial if the work outlined previously is complete. If the location is a major news media market or if news media from outside the immediate area are invited, a month may be more prudent. The rules for distributing news releases discussed in Chapter 14 apply here regarding to format and delivery system. You may contact editors by regular mail, overnight mail, fax, or email. It is important to provide all of the information necessary for an editor to make a coverage decision. Of course, information about the newsmaker and the choice of spokesperson are important to this decision. The invitation can be an advisory, news release, or even a letter.

Step 2: **Decide where the news conference will take place.** This decision depends heavily on the purpose of the conference. To announce a new product, it is likely wise to hold the news conference at the plant or manufacturer's headquarters. Ribbon-cutting, dedication, or groundbreaking ceremonies are held on site. If the location is particularly remote or journalists from around the region or nation are covering, it may be necessary to offer to provide transportation. Announcements of mergers or partnerships are often best held at a facility such as a hotel or hall equipped to handle the physical and electronic needs of the expected number of attendees.

While news media representatives are accustomed to traveling to locations to cover stories, making it convenient for them is a good strategy.

Step 3: **Decide what time to hold the news conference.** This important decision should be made with the media representatives in mind. Editors are well aware of the desire for television coverage, and you run the risk of alienating the newspaper editors if you set a time that favors the evening television local news above the newspapers. Again, become familiar with the deadlines of your local media. Generally, before 2:00 P.M. is good for morning newspapers, earlier times are better for afternoon newspapers to allow time to leave an event and get a story written for an early afternoon deadline, and evening television coverage requires before 1:00 P.M. Late morning is a time that generally accommodates everyone. Radio news time-of-day preferences are much more flexible because radio carries news segments most of the time it is on the air. Monday through Thursday are the best days while Fridays and holidays should be avoided.

BRIEF CASE STUDY

A News Conference

Aircraft with the new
SkyTeam service logo

Ketchum Communication, a global PR agency, arranged a news conference in New York when Delta Air Lines, Korean Air, Aeromexico, and Air France announced the launch of SkyTeam, an airline service aimed at business and global travelers. It is an example of a global announcement, requiring news media materials that met the cultural demands of each member airline. The news conference drew 170 members of the media from all over the world.

Each of the four airline CEOs made a statement and used a puzzle piece to put together the logo of the new service. Their speeches and the question and answer session were translated and offered through wireless headphones in Spanish, French, Korean, and English. A few years later, Continental, KLM, Northwest, Czech Airlines, and Alitalia joined the alliance and China South Airlines signed an agreement with SkyTeam, marking the first step toward joining the alliance.

Working the Case

1. What are some of the spoken media relations tactics you would recommend for an announcement if China South joins the alliance?
2. Where should these tactics take place?
3. Who should be the spokesperson(s)?

Step 4: **Prepare the spokesperson.** This step begins with writing a statement for the spokesperson, reviewing it, and having it approved. Rehearsal is very important in preparing the spokesperson. Both the statement and questions and answers should be rehearsed. Anticipating the questions reporters will ask and being prepared with a complete answer are important. The rules for preparing for a news conference are similar to those for the one-on-one interview. Like everything we do in media relations, to call a news conference is to ask for scrutiny. The spokesperson must practice answering forthrightly. A news conference is not the occasion to shun attention. Also, it is legitimate for the spokesperson to indicate he does not have the answer to the question. The question can be "taken" and an answer provided expeditiously. The most important rules to remember from the one-on-one interview are, don't lie or obfuscate, and never suggest or agree to answer a question off the record.

Step 5: **Prepare the news media kit.** Use the format and criteria presented in Chapter 14 for preparing a kit for a news conference. At the minimum, there should be a release that repeats the spokesperson's announcement and visuals associated with the news. There may be additional releases, fact sheets, bios, and backgrounders depending upon the complexity of the information provided.

Step 6: **Establish a cutoff time.** Just as executives have pressing schedules, so do reporters. When the questions and answers become repetitive, it is time to stop the news conference. Doing this with aplomb is not easy, so you need to think about it. You do not want to act like the State Department press aide mentioned previously who interrupted and tried to end an interview. Most journalists recognize that a news conference is handled like a business engagement. It is supposed to be informative, beneficial to all concerned, and time efficient. White House news conferences last approximately 30 minutes and the senior White House news service correspondent is responsible for helping to bring it to an end by saying, "Thank you, Mr. President." Short of such protocol, the spokesperson should be trained to know when to say something gracious such as, "Thank you all for coming today." This cannot be done to cut the questioning off. It must be done when the question and answer exchange appears to have ended. If the spokesperson lacks the experience to sense when the news conference is no longer beneficial to all involved, you can agree to offer a signal to the spokesperson, indicating it is time for the gracious remark to bring the session to a close.

Selecting, Preparing, and Using Spokespersons

Key to the success and power of the spoken word is who speaks it and how it is spoken. Selecting the proper spokesperson can greatly affect the way in which messages are received by key audiences. Making messages credible includes the credibility of the reward, the accuracy of the facts, and the image of the spokesperson. But there is more. There are three types of spokespersons—corporate, technical or expert, and celebrity.

The *corporate spokesperson* is usually the CEO and/or president of a company, or executive director and/or president of an organization, or a politician. These spokespersons have a grasp of the broad policies of the organization and can speak with ease and authority about organizational direction, strategy, and goals. The corporate spokesperson should make speeches before industry, national, regional, state, and local audiences, serve as spokesperson for editorial board meetings or other higher-level media occasions, and is the *only* appropriate lead spokesperson during crises, change, and transitions such as mergers, acquisitions, or leadership changes.

The *technical or expert spokesperson* is usually well versed in a particular area of the organization and should act as spokesperson during technical conferences and board of directors meetings and with the news media when the organization is announcing a new product, program, project, or other innovation or when a particular issue needs to be addressed. These spokespersons are technically or professionally knowledgeable about the specifics about technology, product or program development, and other processes.

The *celebrity spokesperson* is hard to acquire and can be even more difficult to manage. New product launches, fundraising, and other major news media events are the domains of the celebrity spokesperson. Politicians, of course, represent their campaigns and the political districts they represent.

The best type of spokesperson is the one who is informed about the subject for which you need him to speak. Quite often, public relations practitioners do not choose and have very little control over who the organization's spokesperson will be. Under these circumstances, you have to hope the spokesperson is cooperative and wants to work with you. Usually, if someone has accepted the assignment of talking to reporters or making a speech, he wants the experience to be as painless and successful as possible. Thankfully, most people don't sign up to be publicly humiliated, and being unprepared in public can be humiliating.

In addition to the broad steps discussed earlier about preparing the spokesperson, the following additional pointers will help your spokesperson feel more confident prior to a public appearance.

ENGAGING ETHICS

Answering Honestly

The executive director of the small nonprofit organization for which you work has a legitimate reason to hold a news conference. Part of a recent federal stimulus package, money promised to your state will result in funding for your cause. Your executive director is delighted to know that both innovation funding and stop-gap measure funding will likely be passed along to your nonprofit. At the least, your organization will be asked to assist in organizing and implementing the funding. You and your executive director have rehearsed possible questions and answers. One of them involves possible redistricting of the public school districts and ceasing the current practice of "tracking" students. Tracking is a touchy subject in your area, as wealthy parents tend to have students in the better tracks while poor parents do not, resulting in *de facto* segregation and unequal education. A reporter asks about this issue and your executive director "takes" the question as though there has been no discussion of this topic, and you know better. You and your boss know the non-profit has agreed to help oppose de-tracking. In effect, your boss is not answering honestly.

1. Is it ethical for you to say something during the news conference or wait until it is over and discuss the situation with your executive director? What is your ethical responsibility as a PR professional?
2. What are your options in dealing with your executive director and news media?
3. What should be the nature of a conversation between you and your executive director?

1. **Study the company or organization.** If the spokesperson is chosen for his technical or professional knowledge, he should study information regarding the organization's most recent overall goals and direction. This overall knowledge is excellent for helping the spokesperson with the context of his specific area in the organization and gives him a sense of confidence in speaking for the organization.

2. **Translate.** The spokesperson should think about what he wants to communicate to a reporter and to an ultimate audience. He should be able to translate what he is selling into language that can be easily understood and simplify data without being condescending.

3. **Be enthusiastic.** It is important that a spokesperson wants to be spokesperson and exudes enthusiasm for the job. Volunteers for the assignment are better representatives than draftees.

4. **Work on presence.** The spokesperson should talk about his presentation style and level of confidence. If he has a personable demeanor, he can work additionally on how to increase confidence level and poise.

5. **Dress appropriately.** Above all else, a spokesperson wants to perform well. Mentioning the apparel that is most appropriate for the occasion is an appropriate subject. There are many ways to tactfully suggest what the spokesperson should wear. The earlier this conversation takes place, the better, and a discussion about attire before a television interview is crucial.

6. **Rehearse, rehearse, and rehearse.** A spokesperson should practice what he intends to say during a news media interaction and should rehearse a speech several times. Spokespersons have to be comfortable with the words they intend to use.

7. **State the benefits.** The spokesperson cannot be reminded too many times of who the ultimate audience is and the importance of stating the benefits to that audience.
8. **Stay on message.** The spokesperson should always remain on message, enumerating the two or three key points and shaping them as answers to most of the questions.
9. **I don't know.** A spokesperson should practice using this simple sentence and use it when it is the honest answer to the question. Work with your spokesperson to help him learn to utter these words followed by a very gracious and businesslike "question taken."
10. **That is a hypothetical question.** The spokesperson should never answer the hypothetical questions. Instead, acknowledge that it is hypothetical and be helpful with an answer from a similar situation.

News Media Showings

The spoken tactic called a **news media showing** is also known as a *press or media tour, press demonstration, press trip, familiarization or "fam" (commonly FAM) trip and press party.* The terminology usually depends on the purpose of the gathering. Regardless of the name, these are social occasions designed to entertain the news media as they become more familiar with an organization, a product, an exhibition or a politician. The gatherings can take place during the day for lunch, but they are usually conducted in the evening when the news media representatives are free to spend an extended period of time.

Press tours and FAM trips are arranged to provide journalists the opportunity to cover events that are usually away from their hometowns. PR professionals in the travel and tourism industries arrange these trips for journalists often. Journalists are asked to attend tours of new resorts, maiden voyages of cruise liners, and openings of theme parks with all expenses paid. Similar all-expense-paid trips are offered to journalists to see products demonstrated or unveiled, especially automobiles.

Press Parties

The press party is held to provide an opportunity for a host to get to know the invited guests. Generally, the host of a press party is expected to make an announcement or unveil a product or idea for the journalists to consider. This is usually done at the end of the party. If the statement is a position on an issue or topic, the journalists are given time for questions. The guests are usually reporters and editors and should be given information in a form similar to a news media kit containing information beneficial to reporters for providing news coverage.

Contact with the news media through tours and parties raise ethical issues, which are seen differently throughout the world. See Chapter 7 for a full discussion.

Media Events

Like all other events planned for the news media, this event requires organization and particular attention to detail. In *On Deadline: Managing Media Relations*, Carole M. Howard and Wilma K. Mathews lay out a 37-point guideline for planning media events.[*] Please note that this is a *general* list and all steps will not pertain to every media event.

---

[*]Carole M. Howard and Wilma K. Mathews, *On Deadline: Managing Media Relations*

Planning the Event

1. Make sure the objective and theme for your information effort is supportive of your organization's goals and your overall media relations plan and is agreed to by everyone involved.
2. It sometimes is good politics as well as good media relations to invite the governor of the state, or the mayor or chief county official to make a few brief remarks.
3. Choose your speakers and spokespersons very carefully.
4. Do not let yourself be distracted by time-consuming tasks.

Implementing the Event

5. If a site or facility tour is part of your program, time it with a manageable-sized group that can move around easily on the big day, rather than your walking the planned path alone.
6. Severely limit the number of officials introduced individually or allowed to speak as part of the news conference.
7. Use still photography (black-and-white and color) and videotape to document each stage of a new facility from architectural drawings through construction and official opening.
8. Review and update your checklist often.
9. Keep track of your expenditures.
10. If you decide to give a memento to the media or to guests, personalize it with your logo so that recipients are reminded of your organization when they use it.
11. Arrange for photography—still and video or film—of the news conference and announcement ceremony.
12. You can have a first-class press kit folder and also save money by showing a photograph or drawing of the new facility along with your organization's name on the cover. By not including the date of the event, you can use the cover at other times as well.
13. Target your press kits so that each reporter has the right information for his audience—hometown angle for the plant site's local paper, long-term growth for the business and financial media, relationship to industry trends for the trade press, etc.
14. Well in advance, circulate a proposed invitation list to key people who can provide counsel on who should be included.
15. Just before the event, write out a final, detailed chronology of every activity related to announcement day.
16. Supervise all aspects of the news conference personally.
17. If there will be a meal after the news conference, put "Reserved for press" cards on tables nearest the podium or head table.
18. If you are having a meal, review the schedule with the catering person in minute detail.
19. If possible, arrange for a separate room for individual private interviews between your CEO and selected reporters after the news conference.
20. Try to have a separate "working room."
21. Have plenty of copies of your business card to give to the media.
22. Understand that the primary focus of local reporters' questions will be on the economic advantages of the community in terms of jobs, taxes, and related support services.
23. Make sure the head table and news conference setup photograph well so that you get maximum exposure for your organization's message.

24. Provide three or four phones for the media's use.
25. Have a reception table where at least one person stays to direct guests to coatrooms and bathrooms, control access to private phones, take messages, and provide other logistics support.
26. Set up a separate table with another dedicated person who will help you handle the news media.
27. Prepare a separate package of materials for your key executives involved in the program.
28. Coordinate the agenda and schedule closely with the press secretary or chief aide of government officials and celebrities who are participating in the program.
29. Arrange for setup time and personally inspect all the facilities the night before and the day of the event.
30. Arrange a separate distribution of the press kit to reporters not attending the event, and put it on your website.

Following Up and Evaluating the Event
31. Monitor that evening's television news programs.
32. Promptly after the event write thank-you letters for the CEO's signature.
33. Set up a system to handle the inevitable queries generated by the news coverage of your announcement.
34. A month or so after the event, when all the news coverage has been gathered, put together a summary that includes objectives and a brief analysis of how they were met.
35. Consider putting together a formal scrapbook and video to commemorate the event.
36. Conduct a post-event performance review.
37. Put together a complete file including everything connected with the occasion, from your private memos and checklists to the press kits, official announcement speech, and overall evaluation.

Speeches

Even with all of the technologically advanced tools available to communicators today, the ancient art of public speaking is still an extremely effective way to evoke emotion and to motivate and inspire an audience. Speeches can also be used as a platform for an individual to voice concerns, promote causes, and influence public opinion.

A **speech** is *a carefully prepared monologue designed to have a specific effect on an audience assembled to listen to a speaker.* Listening to a speech can be one of the most boring experiences or one of the most exhilarating. The success of a speech depends on three things: the speechwriter's ability to capture the speaker's persona and to anticipate the audience's reaction and the speaker's ability to connect with the audience. Speechwriting is an art. Therefore, it is the most difficult assignment you can undertake, requiring not only research on the target audience but also research on the speaker. It is no wonder that many career politicians keep the same speechwriter for years.

Unlike most public relations tools, a speech receives immediate feedback through nonverbal and verbal cues such as applause, facial expressions, body language, gestures, and a wide range of vocalizations. The audiences for a speech are varied and can be both internal and external. For the writer, the most important thing to remember is to write with the specific target audience in mind. Speechwriting and delivery require knowledge of the audience's attitudes, beliefs, and values. A good speechwriter conducts extensive, comprehensive research on the audience and the speaker.

When key audiences listen to a speech, they are participating in a personal communication with the speaker without the advantage of a one-on-one context. When a speaker delivers a speech, the audience immediately interprets the speaker's words, tone, rate of speech, and body language, all of which add meaning to the communication. Remember that audiences are highly sensitive to what is "happening" with the speaker—gestures, facial expressions, friendliness (perceived), personality or lack thereof, eye contact, and emotion. The ultimate success of a speech depends greatly on the speaker's delivery. A speechwriter may write a speech perfect for the occasion and the audience, but the speaker may lack the training necessary to be effective. Training is key to the success of any speech. As well, the speaker must have credibility. If the speaker does not have intrinsic authority with an established reputation, then credibility must be earned. This can occur via a third-party introduction or even through the content and delivery of the speech. If credibility fails to be established, the purpose or goal of the speech can be lost.

There are many reasons to speak in public, but speeches have three main functions. Speeches primarily aim to inform, persuade, and/or celebrate occasions. The audience and occasion generally determine the purpose of the speech. While each type of speech has its own style and purpose, all should convey a specific theme and leave a lasting positive impression.

The *informative speech* is designed to increase an audience's understanding and awareness of the speech's subject, requiring the speechwriter to assess the knowledge base of the audience before constructing this type of speech. The relevance of the subject should be demonstrated early in the speech, and terms unfamiliar to the audience need to be clearly defined throughout the body of the speech. It is important to define, describe, explain, and demonstrate the topic in the appropriate amount of detail. This type of speech can be a state of the organization speech delivered by the executive officer to an internal or external audience, or it could be a speech from a public relations practitioner to explain a new community relations plan to a group of civic leaders.

The purpose of the *persuasive speech* is to get an audience to "buy something"—a person, thing, or an action. This sometimes requires a change in the audience's attitudes, values, behavior, or beliefs about something. The key theme or message should be personally relevant to the audience and demonstrate how a behavior change, product purchase, or vote benefits them. If the speaker is promoting a change, it is crucial to encourage only a small change. An emotional appeal that does not arouse fear or anxiety can help move the audience to take action.

Many different types of special occasions warrant a speech. In fact, most special occasions are an opportunity for the principal of an organization or company to deliver a desired message. The speechwriter identifies the purpose of the special occasion and acknowledges the tone of the event in the speech. Depending on the occasion, the objective of the special occasion speech can be to entertain, celebrate, commemorate, motivate, persuade, or inspire.

The research for writing a speech begins the minute the writer receives the assignment. The questions to be answered include: for whom, to whom, for what purpose, when, where, and how long. Who, what, when, where, and how—sound familiar? The next task is learning as much as possible about the speaker and then meeting her.

Most speechwriters use a résumé, biography, and articles or books the speaker has written, and how long she has been with the organization or, if she's a client, how long in her profession. These things prepare the writer to meet the speaker.

A writer must also find out as much as possible from the speaker. Let's work with a scenario to help you think through the many steps and things you, as a speechwriter, would consider to ensure a successful speech.

It turns out that your speaker is the CEO of your company. She was a successful lawyer for many years at a prominent law firm. She has been your CEO for one year. She has been asked to address a group of business students at a local university. Your CEO wants to take this public relations opportunity to talk about ethics in business. By the way, your company is a small but highly successful record label. You know this is a tough assignment for you. You know that your company has had to deal with piracy as a major issue, and you know this group represents the "enemy." In fact, after the Recording Industry Association of America (RIAA) delivered hundreds of prelitigation letters to university campuses for students illegally downloading music in late 2000, the public began to believe the issue went away. But the issue and damage done to artists and producers persists and RIAA continues to press lawsuits. While the four founders of The Pirate Bay were found guilty in Sweden and sentenced to one year and assessed $3.6 million in criminal damages in April 2009, tens of millions of their users were downloading—pirating—music and movies through their website. The good news is, you've seen your CEO in action putting reporters and stockholders at ease, but this will not be a breeze.

After talking with your CEO, you are prepared to begin the research needed for this 20-minute speech. The research starts with the target audience. It is clear this will be a speech designed to inform, not to persuade. You call the business department at the college and find out this group is larger than you expected—100 juniors and seniors. They are already taking their major courses and they will all soon be looking for jobs in the corporate world. Next you check out the college's website to find out what has been going on at the campus recently. You find two important things. The campus business club, of which some of these students are members, just sponsored a live band. They are music lovers who know your artists.

Your next step is to email this information to your CEO and suggest approaches to the speech. You give her three possibilities and she likes the one that uses a conversation with one of her label's artists as the central theme. All that is left for you is the hardest part—to begin the writing.

Anatomy of a Speech

A speech has three specific sections—introduction, body, and conclusion—that must be developed and honed over the writing and revising process. At the center of an effective speech is adherence to this structural format that keeps the speaker on track and gives the audience a sense of where the speaker is in the speech. Without this structure, a speech can divert in infinite directions without accomplishing its intended goal.

Introduction   The first job of the introduction is to grab the attention of the audience and to establish rapport. This can be done in many ways but the tried-and-true options tend to work best: an anecdote; a relevant well-known quote or brief story—everyone loves a story; a factual statement that will have an effect on the audience; a surprise question or remark that will get the audience thinking; or the blunt announcement of the speech's topic. In the case of the example of the record label CEO, you choose music lyrics that are so well known every student will recognize them.

If the purpose of the speech is not used initially in the speech, it must be presented now. The balance of the introduction (about three minutes) is used to make that statement. You have the CEO state bluntly that she had a conversation with Jam Master Man when she was invited to speak today and she wants to tell the audience how illegal downloading is hurting him, his producer, and his band and explain how it relates to ethics. She adds—almost parenthetically—that she wants to make a major announcement as well.

Body   The body of the speech is where the theme begins to develop, making the two or three major points the speaker wants to make. The CEO talks about the damage to the artist when music is downloaded illegally and how it might affect his career and his ability to remain an artist. A speech should never have more than two or three supporting points. As well, a speech should have only one or two themes. In the CEO's case there is another theme. She continues to talk about the ethical decisions people make when they decide to download music illegally, talking also about the lack of ethics in the business world today and its affects on business. The body of the speech should restate the major theme as it approaches the conclusion. Here, the CEO nicely ties ethics, business, and illegally downloading together before approaching the conclusion.

Conclusion   It's not possible for all speeches to end with a major announcement. Here, you were very lucky. But don't rush to the announcement. Include a few anecdotes for the audience. In the CEO's case, talk about two more artists or decisions the CEO has had to make. This should provide "thinking material" that the audience will take away or an action that the audience can take such as writing letters, volunteering, or making a donation. The conclusion should be quick and never boring. Your CEO announces that through the generosity of an anonymous donor, all of the students on the audience's campus will be given free subscriptions to Napster's authorized library, allowing them access to hundreds of thousands of tracks and turning their computers into jukeboxes. The applause is thunderous.

Few speeches end without questions and answers. Sometimes a speaker plans for an intentional Q and A session, and other times they happen spontaneously. A good speechwriter anticipates questions and prepares the speaker for the most difficult.

Speakers Bureaus

Practitioners can use a speakers bureau as a tactic to reach specific audiences. When the American Association of Motor Vehicle Administrators (AAMVA) engaged Trone Public Relations, it wanted to "improve highway safety and decrease fatalities among older drivers." The key target audience was senior drivers in the United States and the campaign was to educate the key audience about the effects of aging on driving. One of the tactics was to create a speakers bureau consisting of an internationally known expert on aging, Dr. Robert N. Butler, and AAMVA and DMV staff. They visited the target audiences at senior citizens centers and other civic associations in the Washington, DC, metropolitan area where the "GrandDriver" campaign was launched. The campaign saw its greatest success in the community outreach efforts with the greatest response from those who attended a community gathering for a speakers bureau event.

BRIEF CASE STUDY

More than 25 Years of the Right Spokespersons

Research showed the Texas Department of Transportation that the majority of its highway litter problem was being caused by young men between the ages of 15 and 24 years. This target audience was perfect for a campaign that appealed to "cool and macho." When the campaign began in 1985, the right spokesperson—guitarist Stevie Ray Vaughn—spoke the right words: "Don't Mess with Texas." With that launch and theme, the Texas DOT began a very successful anti-litter campaign. Within one year, Texas highway litter decreased 29 percent statewide. Today the campaign has a website featured on "Coolest Site of the Day," has had a road tour through 15 cities, and litter has decreased by 52 percent. The list of spokespersons who have uttered the famous slogan now includes Willie Nelson, Johnnie Dee, and Jerry Jeff Walker. An updated ad campaign, "I Wouldn't Do It," featured (more cool and more macho) Matthew McConoughey and Jennifer Love Hewitt. The campaign returned to "Don't Mess with Texas" with country music icon George Strait as the spokesperson. The Litter Force for kids was launched in 2010.

This campaign had two great appeals: cool and macho for young men and a slogan that fit the Texas personality—proud and boastful.

A "Don't Mess with Texas" sign on a Texas highway

Working the Case

1. Go to the "Don't Mess with Texas" web site www.dontmesswithtexas.org. Who else might make an effective spokesperson for this campaign? Why?
2. What vehicles would you select for spoken tactics?
3. Conduct a little research on "The Litter Force." Who is the target audience? What are the spoken tactics and what vehicles are used?

SPOKEN TACTICS OF MASS COMMUNICATION

The fourth context for human communication is mass communication. This is the context in which messages are sent to thousands and even millions of people at one time. While mass communication can reach large numbers of people in many geographic locations, it is the least personal communication. Although the mass media employ audience segmentation and, therefore, attempt to target their messages, it is not always easy to hone messages. The audiences are likely more heterogeneous than for other types of communication, but good audience research is used to find the right audience for the right message. The mass media for spoken tactics are film, television, and radio. The ubiquitous television (see Chapter 16) is one of the two most widely-consumed messengers in mass communication. But the most often used vehicle for spoken tactics in mass communication is radio. While public service announcements (PSAs) are still read on radio, audio news releases are a widely used PR tactic for that medium.

Audio News Releases

Radio is one of the most effective vehicles for reaching target audiences. Because of its ubiquity in the American home and automobile, radio is an ideal medium for gaining publicity and creating awareness. In fact, 99 percent of all American households have at least one radio, most average five radios per household, and Americans listen to radio by satellite and through the Internet. As well, in many countries in the world radio is the medium from which citizens receive most of their information and news. It remains the most personal of all news media. Radio audiences are inclined to feel a personal relationship and to become addicted to their favorite radio personalities. For this reason, radio is a valuable medium and the audio news release is an excellent tactic.

An **audio news release (ANR)**—*sometimes called a radio news release—is the radio counterpart to the video news release* (VNRs are discussed in Chapter 16). But it is important to note that production and writing styles differ for ANRs and VNRs. Most audio news releases are dependent on actualities—sound bites from newsmakers such as organization executives, celebrities, or experts.

Like a written news release, an ANR is designed to generate media coverage that will ultimately reach a specific audience through radio news. ANR producers accomplish this by planning, writing, and then creating a news release that suits a specific radio station format and audience. Because radio stations have individualized formats designed to attract and keep listeners with particular demographics, the producer can tailor the release to capture the attention of a station's distinct audience. ANRs must be as timely, newsworthy, and relevant to the geography of the key audience as possible. Also, a news director will not use any part of an ANR if it is clearly advertising for an organization, its products, or services. But radio stations do not use reporters to cover a story as often as they once did, because of the expense. Instead, most have television *partners* from whom they receive news stories, so an ANR can help get coverage for your news story.

Many organizations choose to hire broadcast public relations firms to produce their ANRs and to guide them through the process. For a full range of ANR services, it is best to contract with an ANR company. Companies like Medialink Worldwide, MultiVu, and News Generations supply prerecorded background information to news outlets, which construct original stories from this information. As a PR practitioner, you need to understand the process and the unique elements that make up an ANR.

Practitioners who are well versed in media relations pitch ANRs to the news media. As with any news release, you should know the appropriate contact person at the radio station and the opportune time to call. As we have discussed, good media relations means knowing the news cycles and understanding the news director's job. Some ANR producers offer localized interviews, making the chances for putting a story together even greater for editors. These elements greatly enhance the practitioner's ability to get the ANR aired.

Not surprisingly, there are times when you can take advantage of having a good piece of tape in your possession and create an ANR. When Joan Cear, SVP with G. S. Schwartz & Co. in New York found herself with a VNR containing an excellent sound bite from a country music star, she decided to let the VNR do "double duty" in her campaign. She took the VNR to a recording studio nearby and had the sound bite converted to an MP3 file. She distributed the sound bite to the ABC Radio Network that offers "American Country Countdown" to 600 stations and to Westwood One with 7,700 affiliates nationwide. Her cost was negligible—$200 instead of $2,000—and the ROI was great; she added another dimension to her campaign. But remember: She was in a unique situation and took advantage of good fortune. She already had a high-quality sound bite and she needed only limited distribution. You should always be on the lookout for opportunities.

Distribution

When a radio station agrees to use the ANR, it can be distributed to the news director through a number of different means—satellite transmission, telephone calls, hard copies, and the Internet.

Using satellites makes the distribution process both fast and successful. The ANR is uplinked to a satellite by the organization and then downlinked by the radio station. This method is possible only if the news station has the time, staff, and accessibility to receive information by satellite.

An audio news release can also be sent via telephone lines. To do this, the person pitching the piece calls a radio station. If the news director is interested, the ANR can be immediately played over the telephone and recorded by the news station.

Hard-copy releases are sent with both the CD and the script by mail, or they can be hand delivered to the studio by courier. Finally, the Internet delivers MP3 files. These files allow for global reach, allowing radio stations all over the world to download and then play the ANR over both the Internet and traditional radio. Many of the ANR production companies now offer the MP3 format but not to the exclusion of CDs, magnetic tape, or telephone.

Constructing an ANR

A typical audio news release is approximately 60 to 90 seconds long. The overall tone of an ANR is less formal than that of its video and print counterparts. Remember that writing for the ear is different from writing for print. Unlike a traditional news release, ANRs often utilize creative methods to highlight the news—an approach that complements the relaxed and very personal tone of the radio medium.

Short and concise sentences are important because radio audiences cannot follow long, complicated sentences and complex information. As well, maintaining a simple format makes it easier for an announcer to sustain a consistent style of delivery. The writing style and tone of an ANR are not the only unique elements of the medium. Within the composition of an ANR is an element known as the *actuality*. The actuality portion of the release includes the voice(s) of one or more newsmakers, experts, or spokesperson for the featured organization. Whereas the narrator/announcer employed for the introductions and various transitions within the story is often a voice professional or communication professional, the newsmaker is almost always someone qualified to talk about the topic. You should avoid using a publicity spokesperson with little or no connection to the story because it decreases the credibility of the ANR and editors will be less likely to use it.

After all the news is collected and the newsmakers are ready to offer *a recorded quote*—**sound bite**—questions must be developed to obtain an effective quote. As the public relations practitioner, you are responsible for preparing the questions. Time constraints, distance, and expense are all problems for getting flawless sound. It is usually impossible to get a newsmaker into a recording studio, so on-location recordings or even telephone-line recordings are more the norm. Following the approval of a finalized script, a professional narrator or announcer records the script. This usually highlights background information on the topic, introduces the actuality and newsmaker, and provides details of how to obtain further information on the topic. A producer edits the final ANR, incorporating the most effective sound bites along with the ideal narration recordings and blends them for a seamless 60- to 90-second ANR.

ANRs can be important resources to smaller radio stations that cannot send a reporter to cover a story. But some news directors are wary of prepackaged broadcast news pieces including ANRs because they are concerned that the information is biased. Most news directors edit the story in order to fit a particular time frame or to create a more obvious connection to their audiences.

In any type of mass communication, it is important to remember that you do not have as much control in audience selection as you do in other types of communication. Your challenge is to develop strategies and tactics that are suitable to a wider audience.

PROFESSIONAL POINT OF VIEW

Radio Still a Strong Medium to Connect with Consumers

Julia Hood wrote this point of view while publishing director of PRWeek.

Almost every weekday morning I listen to Joe Connolly's morning radio broadcast at 5:55 a.m. Connolly is a news editor and anchor for The Wall Street Journal Radio Network. Even though I read two newspapers on the train and breaking news through my handheld, I don't feel quite right if I miss hearing Connolly's unique take on the business headlines.

The reason he is compulsive listening is twofold: First, and functionally, he digests the key business headlines of the day, with an emphasis on clarifying sometimes incredibly complex details for an audience that is still finding its way through the early-morning fog. Second, and most addictively, is Connolly's way of getting at the sentiment of the business owners and customers that he covers. The *PRWeek*/PRNewswire Media Survey last year found that reporters read blogs to assess public sentiment on key issues. In the same way, I tune in to Connolly, who somehow gets under the skin of business facts and finds a heartbeat.

Connolly says that as many people listen to him in their cars, their needs are very specific to the medium. "I think the sentiment or feeling part of it is particular to radio," he told me. "You are talking to them one-on-one. You are invited into that car. And if you're not honest, you're not a very good carpool partner."

Connolly says he arms his listeners with insight they can redeploy at the water cooler. "The goal is to give the listener something to say when the topic turns to, for instance, nationalizing the banks—to give them something to say at work that nobody else knows," he says.

There is an intimacy to radio that we often overlook in all of our media analysis and focus on the digital world, and a true master of the medium can own your heart and mind like no other. I was recently talking with an industry leader who told me that he regularly listens to radio of a particular political slant, opposite to his personal views. He considers himself better educated about the world because of it, and I suspect it's not simply because he is learning about perspectives that he doesn't embrace. There is an authenticity to the great radio voice that tells the listener, "I am saying this because I believe it to be true." Politically polarized radio is a particularly persuasive example of the genre, and it's all the more apparent when you don't agree with the views.

I'm sure, therefore, that I'm not the only Connolly fan out there, tuning in each morning to hear from him if things are going to get better out there. When he tells me it is so, I will believe it.

Summary and Review

Spoken Tactics of Interpersonal Communication

- Being prepared and getting the spokesperson prepared are the most important things you can do when it comes to a meeting with the news media.
- One-on-one interviews, editorial board meetings, news media briefings, and news conferences are the most common encounters between a spokesperson and journalists. These meetings can take place in person, by telephone, and by satellite.
- You should keep a checklist of tasks that should be accomplished before, during, and after a news media interview. Following up with additional materials and being available to the journalist after an interview are very critical.
- Word-of-mouth communication greatly affects the effectiveness of your message. Studies show that the opinions of friends and family are more important to consumers than advertising and editorial content. Before people adopt new products or ideas, they check with the sources they know and trust the most—their own personal network.

Spoken Tactics of Small-Group Communication

- PR practitioners use small-group meetings extensively in their work. These meeting are where much of the planning, strategies, and tactics for communicating are discussed and agreed upon. When used effectively, meetings can accomplish a great deal.
- Generally, the newsmaker or spokesperson requests an editorial board meeting or news media briefing. If a high-ranking government or international figure is visiting a city, major newspapers will request such meetings.

Spoken Tactics of Public Communication

- You should be cautious about the use of news conferences. They should be reserved for extremely important breaking news when visuals, in-depth exploration of the subject, or access to the newsmaker cannot be accomplished in any other way.
- Special events and media parties and trips should be carefully planned and should in no way suggest or present compromising situations for members of the news media.
- Speeches remain one of the most effective spoken tactics. When the speech is well researched and written and delivered by the right spokesperson, it can persuade, inform and move audiences to take action.
- Meetings or conferences attended by many participants are widely used as a public relations tool. Organizations such as professional and industry associations, government entities, community coalitions, city councils, unions, and advocacy groups conduct meetings to share data and information, to discuss topics, to create strategy to address common concerns, and to generate news media interest in a particular subject.
- Deciding who will represent an organization as spokesperson is a serious consideration. The spokesperson becomes the face of the organization to all key audiences. The decision should not be taken lightly.
- A spokesperson must be well-informed about the subject he will discuss and the organization. Just as important, the spokesperson should be enthusiastic about the role.

Spoken Tactics of Mass Communication

- Mass communication is the least personal of the four communication contexts. While it can reach millions of people at one time in many different locations, its effectiveness depends heavily on audience segmentation.
- Both television and radio are widely-consumed vehicles of mass communication, but radio appears to be the most effective for public relations efforts.

- Radio is a very important and accessible vehicle for reaching key audiences. Because radio is everywhere, tends to be very personal, and has well-defined audiences, it is an excellent vehicle for generating awareness. The audio news release (ANR) is a highly professional way to get radio time.

Key Terms

audio news release (ANR)	news media briefings	speeches
editorial board meetings	news media showings	word of mouth
meetings	one-on-one interviews	
news conference	sound bite	

Questions for Review and Discussion

1. Name the four contexts of human communication.
2. Define word-of-mouth communication.
3. In what context does this spoken tactic occur?
4. Name at least two spoken tactics that occur in small-group communication.
5. Discuss preparing for and conducting news conferences.
6. Under what circumstances should a news conference be held?
7. How do you garner immediate feedback from audiences who hear a speech?
8. How do you select and prepare spokespeople?
9. What is an ANR and how is it used?
10. Why is an ANR effective for generating awareness of an audience?

Web Links

American Speakers Bureau
www.speakersbureau.com

National Heart and Blood Institute
www.nhlbi.nih.gov

News Generation Inc.
www.newsgeneration.com

U.S. Census Bureau
www.2010.census.gov

U.S. Department of Labor
www.dol.gov

U.S. Postal Service
www.usps.com

Visual Media and Interactive Media Tactics

THE POWER OF THE VISUAL IMAGE

Today's 24-hour news cycle and message overload for most consumers have increased the value of a picture beyond a thousand words. It can be worth more when it tells a story without a single word. Most of the people in the world who had access to television at certain points in history can tell a story about a single picture. A Chinese student standing in front of a moving military tank, a spaceship afire, a crowded street with everyone wearing white medical masks, a commercial airliner crashing into a skyscraper, hooded prisoners, flag-draped coffins, a wall crumbling under the battering of citizens are all memorable images. Add audio and motion to a memorable visual image and you have something worth much more. Studies show that the more senses engaged in a communication message and the blend of sight and sound result in enhanced memory of the event or materials presented. You can use visual and multimedia tactics to increase the effectiveness of your messages as long as you are aware of what the images mean to your key audiences.

Seeing comes before words. The child looks and recognizes before it can speak.... It is seeing which establishes our place in the surrounding world; we explain that world with words but words can never undo the fact that we are surrounded by it.

—John Berger,
art critic and writer

The ubiquitous and powerful television now gives us more than ever before. It not only sends pictures and sounds, it beeps and scrolls text along the bottom of the screen and it offers more than one screen at a time. And thanks to computer technology it can make time stand still briefly with a digital video recorder, providing the opportunity for an instant replay of any television show. Because television is everywhere and cable has expanded its accessibility and reach, it is still one of the most powerful, and often allusive, tools for public relations practitioners. Getting your clients on the morning and evening news or a popular talk show or in a commercial is still considered prime exposure and almost instant credibility.

CATALOG OF TACTICS

The magazine *Communication Arts* conducts juried competitions in advertising, design, interactive, illustration, and photographic work annually. You need look at only one of its annual books to understand the power of the visual image. You can look at a visual image and tell a story of your own without text. But when the visual image accompanies text, the message is powerful.

Video News Releases and Electronic Press Kits

The video news release (VNR) and electronic press kit (EPK) are tools you can use to get an organization and its viewpoint on television. The VNR is not the video equivalent of a print news release, as the EPK is not a video equivalent of a news media kit. Recall the discussion in Chapter 14: Traditional written news releases and news media kits are sent to television, radio, and print news editors so that they can decide how to cover a news story. In fact, the video news release *is* the video equivalent of the audio news release (ANR) discussed in Chapter 15, but it, of course, has elements not found in an ANR.

The **video news release (VNR)** is *a 90-second to three-minute news story of carefully constructed images and sound bites that allows an organization to get television news coverage of newsworthy material while maintaining some of its control over the message.* An **electronic press kit (EPK)** is *usually a somewhat longer version of a VNR—closer to 15 minutes in length—and often supplies more extensive information related to an event.* EPKs are generally targeted to entertainment-related shows or programs. Effective VNRs and EPKs result in news stories that ultimately give the sponsoring organization third-party credibility and exposure to the key audience. News outlets are encouraged to incorporate the supplied footage into their own news stories and programming.

VNRs and EPKs should not be confused with printed news releases and news media kits developed primarily for distribution to broadcast news outlets for their use as source materials to cover an event. Instead, VNRs and EPKs supply footage so that individual news stations can construct news stories that reflect their own styles and formatting.

Video news releases and electronic press kits generally include background information slates (information slides that provide background on the organization or issue or introduction of terms with no sound), **b-roll** (a series of rough video images that incorporate a variety of different camera angles with natural sound), *sound bites*

(7- to 15-second audio of quotes from an individual), and sometimes a pre-edited narrated news story. Caution: While including a finished news package is *not* recommended, because it does not allow news outlets to develop their own news stories, many VNR and EPK producers choose to include them as guidelines for news directors and editors. It remains an unwise choice.

It is crucial for both VNRs and EPKs to be newsworthy, but some VNRs can have longer shelf life. There are two types of video news releases—timely and evergreen. A *timely VNR* takes advantage of a recent newsworthy event. It is much like having the opportunity to comment on a news story for a journalist covering the event. The advantage of a timely VNR is obvious. It is most likely to be used by television news producers who are looking for additional information or viewpoint on a story or just looking for filler. The disadvantage of a timely VNR is that its relevance is fleeting. On the other hand, an *evergreen VNR* is designed to have a longer life span and is more likely to be a feature or human interest piece.

Although a VNR or EPK is produced by an organization with a specific message in mind, too many mentions or references to the organization can make the material appear more like a paid advertising piece, guaranteeing it will not be used. Most news departments consider themselves fair and neutral, and they will not provide free time to advertise a message, product, or organization in a biased manner.

Again, knowing the target audience is important. Getting your message to your ultimate audience—television news viewers—depends on knowing a little about what news producers and directors need. You should be looking for the benefit you can provide key groups at all times. First, know that television news directors are always looking for footage. Television news is heavily dependent upon good visuals. If you have *real* news, develop an angle, incorporate footage and sound, and send the finished product to specific television media outlets, you increase the possibility that your message will reach the key audiences.

Visuals can often tell stories that words cannot. Pepsi distributed a widely used VNR to help tell its story when some of its customers claimed to have found syringes in their Pepsi cans. The Pepsi VNR highlighted the bottling process and viewers could see for themselves how unlikely it was for a syringe to get into a can during Pepsi's high-speed process. The customer claims turned out to be fraudulent.

Cost

The rising costs of covering the news and decreasing news department budgets continue to limit the news director's ability to cover stories independently. As a result, VNRs and EPKs are being used more frequently and are becoming a vital part of television news. If the news director can accommodate the news angle, some of the visual material is usually used. Reporters tend to use the raw B-roll and create additional visuals so that they can do the voice-over themselves. VNRs and EPKs have extended shelf life because they are offered free of charge and for unrestricted use; television producers and news directors can use the images again and again without requesting permission. Typically, television producers pay for rights to use some of the footage made available to them by video resource warehouses

BRIEF CASE STUDY

The Pepsi Classic

Pepsi cans during a high-speed process at a local bottling company

There are some cases that represent the best practices in the use of a particular tactic. Earlier we discussed Pepsi's use of a VNR during a crisis. The case merits an in-depth look. In early summer and just one month prior to the July Fourth holiday, a Seattle television station reported that a syringe had been discovered in a can of Diet Pepsi by a local consumer. Soon, a second complaint in Seattle surfaced. The U.S. Food and Drug Administration issued an advisory to consumers encouraging them to empty the contents of their Diet Pepsi cans into a glass before drinking. The national media began covering the story and within 24 hours, reports of syringes in Diet Pepsi cans around the country began.

While Pepsi employed some of the best practices in crisis management, the VNR it released is legendary for its effectiveness. The still photograph from the VNR provided here helps just a little to explain the strength of the moving visuals. Pepsi's longtime video producer and media consultant Robert Chang Productions assembled the compelling video footage that illustrated Pepsi's message: It was illogical for syringes to have been placed in Pepsi cans during the canning process as charged. "Those images, transmitted nationally via satellite, brought consumers into a Pepsi plant to show them the speed and safety of the manufacturing process and the illogic of so many complaints occurring in so many different locations at the same time," Chang said.

Working the Case

1. Why do you think television news producers used the Pepsi VNR?
2. Was there a better way for television news to tell the story than with the VNR?

and catalogs, while VNRs and EPKs can supply visuals without charge. Estimates of the number of VNRs distributed in any given week in the U.S. range between 20 and 40.

The cost of producing a VNR or an EPK varies a great deal depending upon the elements, time constraints, and complexity. Many cost factors must be considered for either a VNR or an EPK when planning a budget. Elements such as preproduction planning, location shoot(s), postproduction editing, graphic composition, distribution, and monitoring of use affect the cost. Once these components have been determined and priced, an overall cost can be estimated. In general, an average VNR runs between $20,000 and $50,000, while an EPK can run upward of $75,000. While this is not a nominal cost, the news story has the potential of reaching millions of people at once, making VNRs and EPKs very cost effective. A mere 30-second spot commercial can cost hundreds of thousands of dollars to produce, excluding the additional expense of purchasing the television time. It is clear that news producers will not give time to VNRs that are clearly commercials for a product. This requires that you be creative in developing ideas for a VNR.

VNRs and EPKs are produced by professional video production firms such as DS Simon Productions, Medialink, and Pathfire. But you should still be aware of the elements of a VNR and EPK and understand how to work with a production company. More importantly, the VNRs and EPKs must have the best in media relations strategy and tactics behind them in order to have a chance of use. As a media relations expert, you must pitch the stories professionally and to the right person at news stations the first time. Because the competition is great, the first pitch is probably the only opportunity for success.

Distribution

The newest development in the VNR and EPK business is distribution. Just as technology has revamped television in the past decades with videotape, satellite transmission, digital editing, and high definition television (HDTV), it has affected the way in which VNRs and EPKs are received. In the not-so-distant past, hard copy videotapes were distributed through the mail to television stations. While hard copies of VNRs are still used by many stations, today they can be delivered in other ways that are convenient for news stations. But hard copies are still the standard of EPKs because they are often planned far enough in advance and generally are sent with additional printed material.

At this writing, the most common method of distribution for VNRs is by satellite transmission. Producers send media advisories and scripts to news directors and show producers by fax or email or make telephone calls to pitch the stories and to advise the stations of the satellite window time for the feed. The media advisories contain a detailed summary, headline, keywords, satellite time and coordinates, and editorial and technical contacts for additional information. The stations then have a technician on hand to download the transmission at the appointed time.

Digital distribution is now the newest way to distribute VNRs and EPKs. Internet applications and websites with video that can be downloaded provide immediate access to VNRs. One of the greatest benefits is that these systems allow reporters to receive the information and tools they need for a story via email. The most interesting digital development for distribution of VNRs is a system created by Pathfire in Atlanta. It is an interesting development for a couple of reasons. First, Pathfire stores and delivers footage on an ongoing basis. As a result, stations can have access for extended periods of time and are not limited to a window of time such as is the case with satellite transmission. This means the material can be captured at times that might be more convenient for the stations, and if the video is suitable for feature pieces, it can be captured at a later date. The other reason Pathfire is an interesting development is that CNN is a stakeholder in the company. Most CNN affiliates have the Pathfire digital system and the company has distribution agreements with CNN, ABC, WB, and CBS affiliates, according to *PRWeek*.

Questions of ethical use of VNRs and EPKs are important to the public relations practitioner and newsgathering organizations. News editors have a code of ethics as do practitioners (Chapter 7 discusses these codes). Many editors refuse to use a finished-package VNR because the stories are clearly designed to place the producing organization in the most favorable light. As you read in Chapter 7 and will see in the Engaging Ethics and Professional Point of View boxes, the argument regarding the use of VNRs is ongoing.

ENGAGING ETHICS

Who Is Really Reporting?

A government cabinet agency, Health and Human Services (HHS), distributed a VNR to promote a new Medicare law that included a very familiar manner of ending a news story, "This is Karen Ryan reporting." The General Accounting Office ruled that the VNRs violated federal statutes because they were not identified as productions of the federal government. The ruling suggested the VNRs were "covert propaganda." Viewers often do not know who is sponsoring the story they are seeing. It is important for news stations to include a reference to the source of the footage or information used in a news story. Chapter 7 discusses ethics in the practice of public relations.

1. Consider that some small daily newspapers use print news releases as stories. They just cut and paste. Why is using a VNR an ethical issue for news producers?
2. Why is the use of this particular VNR, or any government VNR, an ethical issue?

Multimedia News Release

The multimedia news release (MNR) is an online-only tactic that is used more for direct consumer consumption than the news media. These releases are interactive and combine text, video, photographs, and audio to give consumers product experiences online.

Television Talk Shows

Pitching an organization or client to a talk show is not as formidable as you might think. Essentially, television and radio talk shows need guests. Producers who must fill the same time slot week after week or day after day are always looking for something interesting and unusual to capture the attention of their audiences. What producers think is interesting depends upon the audience they are trying to reach. The idea is to know enough about the show to know what will be of interest. For some shows, the possible subjects are endless. For example, a morning "talk of the town" show following the news might have the arts, civic affairs, education, sports, finance, and health as topics. And television talk shows use hard news and feature segments. The key to television is visuals, so you must find a way to make your clients, products, and company visually interesting. Talking heads are deadly anywhere but most surely on television.

If a client or organization representative is asked to appear on a television show, preparation is crucial to success. The "rehearse, rehearse, and rehearse again" mantra is never more appropriate than in the case of a television show appearance. As a society, we become so accustomed to seeing people interviewed on television that we begin to think it is simple. It is anything but simple. When one sits in a chair and looks into a television camera, the world takes on a different look. The "green room," the location where guests are usually asked to wait before an appearance, can be helpful if the show has a makeup artist available. If not, your spokesperson has to get it right alone. Women should apply the makeup they are accustomed to wearing in a business situation, but might consider adding a blot powder. Men who do not wear makeup ordinarily should not use a television appearance as a foray into that fine art, but a blot powder would serve them well.

Television talk show guests should wear business attire. For a man, a business suit, shirt, and tie are appropriate. He should avoid ties and jackets with bold stripes or busy patterns. A woman guest should wear a dress or suit, avoiding ruffles and frills. Jewelry should be understated for both women and men. The guest should remember to sit on the tail of her suit jacket so that it does not bunch at the neck and shoulders. Color is not as important as it was when television was black and white. Color television allows guests to wear any color as long as extremes are avoided; solid colors are always best.

Hints about remaining on message and repeating the major or key points are presented in the previous chapter, but there are nonverbal messages with which to be concerned in a television appearance. The spokesperson should always look at the interviewer and engage her in a normal conversation unless the television camera is directed to the spokesperson only. At that point, the spokesperson should talk to the camera as though it is another person involved in the conversation. Gestures are helpful only if they can be seen. Otherwise, the head and torso are moving about and the guest can look a little ridiculous. It is difficult to tell what kind of shot a camera is in, so the guest should limit gesturing to the area that makes up the width of her shoulders. As is the case for preparation for all appearances, you and the guest should watch the show a few times before appearing. Also, watching anchors and actors on talk shows is helpful.

There can be frustrating and aggravating matters associated with television talk show appearances. One is breaking news if the spokesperson's interview is live. If hard news takes place during the time segment of the show for which the guest is booked, the safe bet is he will be "bumped." Sometimes being bumped means one-half or a full hour, but sometimes it can mean days. One client waited in New York two days to finally get her segment on the *Today Show* on the third day. Of course, she was willing to wait, but all shows are not the *Today Show*. If the show is going to be taped to appear later in the schedule, being bumped is unlikely. Another frustration is the news day cannot be controlled and a guest may lead or follow a segment that is not complimentary. For instance, a spokesperson waiting to talk about the advantages of refinancing home mortgages may follow a story about interest rates increasing.

Sponsored and Commercial Films

Organizations frequently use film and video to inform and persuade their audiences. Although **sponsored films and videos** are rarely seen by paying audiences in theatre settings like feature films, millions of viewers among public relations target audiences see them very often. Companies use them to *introduce employees to new operating procedures and to demonstrate product improvements to investors.* Corporations that market to children and teens sponsor educational films in order to reach their target audiences in schools and with the help of teachers. Nonprofit organizations use them frequently to encourage audiences to support their cause or to train volunteers.

Producing a film is expensive, involving costs associated with shooting on location, hiring actors, and postproduction editing. Usually, when we think of film production, we think of Hollywood, but Washington, DC, has the largest sponsored-film industry in the United States. With hundreds of associations and nonprofit organizations located there, Washington, DC, is home to lucrative film-makers of sponsored films.

Using **commercial films and videos** as public relations tactics is rare but certainly happens. Sometimes referred to as product placement, many manu-facturers have their products placed in television and feature films. This ar-rangement is usually the work of the public relations practitioner and the film's producer. Products and services such as motor vehicles, airlines, soft drinks, and food are highly visible in some films. The first *Home Alone* movie was a lesson in product placement with all of the above visible throughout the film. The story of Reese's Pieces and the film *ET, The Extra-Terrestrial* is a classic and often told. The makers of M&Ms were offered an opportunity to be featured in the film and turned it down. Hershey Food Company, the makers of Reese's Pieces, not only took the opportunity but reported a 65 percent increase in sales of the product. And while not a film, the television show *24 Hours* is replete with product placements.

Of course, these placements are paid publicity and therefore are little more than commercials within a film or show, even if audiences don't necessarily think of them in those terms. Government and nonprofit health organizations have been successful in getting message placement in some films and entertainment tele-vision shows. Notice how often you observe actors buckling their seatbelts and providing an antidrug message in television programs and entertainment films. In February 2009, all the ABC daytime soap operas began promoting American Heart Association's "Go Red for Women" movement by writing women's heart disease issues into their story lines.

Still Photography

Words can help create effective communication, but words are never as clear as when they are accompanied by a good picture. You should use still photos in controlled and uncontrolled media. Sometimes you will provide photos to the news media, at other times you will set up a good shot or photo opportunity that journalists will shoot themselves, and at still other times you will use photos for your own publications and other media.

Still photography is a great asset when working with newspapers and maga-zines if the photos are submitted in the proper format. *Newspapers print both color and black-and-white photography and use them to help enhance a story or as a stand-alone with only a caption.* Photography use in magazines and trade publications varies greatly. You should conduct a little research to determine the publication's preference for color and/or black and white.

Most newspapers use at least one photograph above the fold on the front page and sometimes one or two below the fold as well. *USA Today* uses photos on the front page in its banner, above and below the fold, and in the left column, serving as eye candy to attract readers. Cover photos usually accompany hard news unless there is an unusual feature. Rarely is a front page photo the product of a public relations effort. More often than not, these photos are shot by a staff photographer or provided by a news service such as Reuters or the Associated Press. But you can offer newspapers still photography with news releases in hopes of enhancing the chances for getting the story and photo published on other pages in the newspaper. Head shots or head-and-shoulder shots of a client or newsmaker are the most common still photos distributed by practitioners and used by newspapers.

If you look at a newspaper today, you will find many of this photo style used throughout in a full-column format or smaller. The *mug shot*, as it is called, helps to identify and humanize the news-maker while breaking up the copy in the newspaper. You can submit these photos in a standard 8 by 10 black and white with a caption, on the Internet, or as a part of a media kit. Like feature releases (Chapter 14), photos are used in the interior pages of every section of the newspaper. In fact, the opportunities for getting photographs used is greatly increased in sections such as Lifestyle, Business and Money, Food, Travel, Real Estate, and Home. Editors need photos to accompany articles on recipes, restaurants, vacation destinations, shopping, family care, home improvement and decorating, gardening, and many other topics.

A Texas Association Against Sexual Assault ad featuring the photo of a real victim

While most color photography published in newspapers is shot by staff, color photos for features can be submitted to newspapers in color. These are usually pictures of food, travel destinations, newly decorated rooms, rooms from real estate models, new products, and the latest in trendy fashion. When submitting color photos to newspapers, you should contact the photo editor to ascertain the best format. While color slides have been the standard, digital formats have become very popular and some newspapers now download JPG and PDF files of photographs from websites and email attachments. You should never submit a color print.

Still photographs are important to the media products that you create yourself. They complement the messages you develop for controlled media such as brochures, newsletters, ads, annual reports, and websites.

Nonprofit organizations find that putting a face on their cause makes the issue more personal and easier to imagine. The Texas Association Against Sexual Assault (TAASA) has two top priorities—"raising awareness of victims' service programs

BRIEF CASE STUDY

Pimples and Bellies

The Children's Defense Fund (CDF) became alarmed at the rate of teen pregnancies in the United States and looked for a message that would resonate with teens, especially girls. After significant research on teenage lifestyles and values, messages were developed that were relevant and resonated with teens, emphasizing how pregnancy makes a young woman look and how it limits her ability to party. When it was time to select the right images, the CDF staff was partial to concepts with the message: "It's like being grounded for 18 years" and an accompanying visual of a young woman holding an infant child. When all concepts were tested with the target audience, another concept prevailed. The concept that tested best? A close-up picture of a pregnant stomach was accompanied by the message, "If You're Embarrassed by a Pimple, Try Explaining This."

A Children's Defense Fund ad with the caption "It's like being grounded for eighteen years."

Working the Case

1. Do you think this concept would work with 'tweens also? Why?
2. How does the image amplify the text?

and eliminating the taboo against discussing rape." With the help of a $2 million grant, the 22-year-old TAASA launched its first statewide awareness campaign, using photographs of victims to "raise political support for tougher laws and boost public awareness."

Because photographs are essential to public relations work, you should take heed of the following tips.

- Take a photography class so that you can take advantage of photo opportunities that are not covered by the media or for which you do not have a photography budget.
- Working successfully with a photographer means being prepared before the occasion. Know the shots you want and if possible give the photographer a shot list.
- Avoid offering the news media photographs that are either deadly boring or have poses that are overused such as those usually associated with groundbreakings and ribbon-cuttings.
- Look for ways to get creative and interesting photographs.
- Keep a still photograph file, organizing the shots by topic and content. Remember to date the photographs.
- Remember that newspapers and trade publications keep photo files, too. So be sure to update your photos with editors.
- Remember your internal partners and keep them up to date regarding photographs. This will help to keep your publications, posters, and website fresh and interesting.

Tactics for Improving Presentations

Internal and external presentations are a major part of your job. Sometimes you will create presentations for clients and organization leaders to use and sometimes for your colleagues. There are many tools available to you for engaging an audience— but engaging the audience is the key. The first thing you must do is to research the audience and create a relevant and interesting message. After you know exactly what you want to say, you have to look for the best way to present the message. There are many **presentation aids** *available to help illustrate, inform, and clarify points made by speakers, including DVDs, film, animation, music, stills, and PowerPoint.* All can be used as standalones or in different combinations to create an interesting presentation. Presentation aids should be used to help the audience better understand and recall the most important points made during the remarks.

Presentation aids can also help entertain the audience if needed. Aids to presentations should be chosen because they are appropriate for the occasion and the venue and not because they are seen as impressive or high tech. In fact, some presentations are ruined by the latest in software or lasers because the "magic" can be distracting to the speaker and the audience. They are called "aids" for a reason and should help make points clearer and help draw correlations between points and concepts. They should not dominate or distract. The aid chosen must be in context with the subject or topic being discussed. It is important to remember that using presentation aids should increase the credibility of the speaker, but if the aids are not well prepared the speaker can lose credibility with the audience.

Studies indicate we remember more than twice as much of what we hear and see (50 percent) than what we hear only (20 percent), making the addition of presentation aids a good idea. Using video is a good way to build interest and increase the saliency of a message. DVDs and films produced by sponsoring organizations are excellent for presentations as well. For instance, your client may want to increase the number of employees who volunteer. A speech from your CEO or client might be augmented with one or two short DVDs about volunteering opportunities, about organizations that need volunteers, or "success stories" that highlight volunteers.

PowerPoint by Microsoft, as an example, has made it possible to create slides on the computer and project them using computerized projection such as LCD (liquid crystal diode) projectors. The software makes it possible to create interesting slides with graphics, photographs, video, audio, and movement. PowerPoint presentations can be very effective when you are making a pitch to a client because they can help demonstrate some of the products and results produced for other clients. While a good PowerPoint presentation can be helpful, you must be sure not to overuse slides, especially text slides, and not to hide behind the technology. There is nothing worse than sitting through a mind-numbing presentation of slides.

Graphic Design

The number of ways to incorporate graphics and illustrations into public relations products is endless. The written and spoken word is greatly enhanced by just the right symbol or representation of a message or idea. You are reminded of this fact often when you travel abroad and recognize the language of international symbols or icons. There is no mistaking the right direction for ground transportation, airlines, taxis, and rest rooms. It is generally clear when you should not enter, eat, drink, or smoke in a location. And you know what golden arches, a red cross, and an apple denote. You receive the communication without a single word.

Graphic design is best left to the artists and crafters who have learned to take sometimes disparate elements and create a visual message with impact. *Graphic designers use space, words, photographs, and illustrations to depict and explain.* Public relations practitioners work with graphic designers to help form finished products such as newsletters, brochures, websites, even storyboards for television and film. Working with a graphic designer successfully begins with knowing where the work of the designer begins and yours ends. You want to express as clearly as possible what you are looking for in terms of tone, image, emotion, and culture. After a designer is asked to take on a project, you should step out of the way. The designer will provide feedback in the form of concepts or thumbnails that he feels *says* what you have in mind.

If you do not have a graphic design department, you must be sure to interview more than one designer before agreeing to enter a contract. Research and asking colleagues for the names of firms or freelancers with whom they have had successful experiences are crucial. Ask designers for samples of their work. Also, be sure to discuss budget at the outset. This helps to set expectations at the right level, saving time and energy for both you and the designer.

Often, graphic designers are asked to create a logo for an organization. As we discuss in Chapter 4, the integration of all communication from an organization is important to the success of the message. This is true, too, of the graphic portrayal of an organization. Corporations have long known the importance of creating a logo that catches an audience's attention quickly, resonates with the audience in a positive manner, and is easily understood by the audience.

Not long ago, one might have referred to an organization's corporate logo as its *brand*, but branding is much more than just a graphic representation. An organization's

Three well-known logos

brand is *now seen as almost everything an organization does and how it is viewed by its most important audiences.* (Branding is discussed in more depth in Chapter 17.) But branding strategies are developed for public relations campaigns, too. The agency Crispin Porter + Bogusky helped Florida launch the first anti-tobacco pilot program in 1998, developing a brand that evolved from "rage" to "truth." The truth campaign offered a brand benefit: "Our brand is the truth. Their brand is lies." This strategy helped brand the tobacco companies as liars and juxtaposed against the truth campaign—a clear fight of good against evil.

Final Tips for Using Multimedia Tactics

The term *multimedia* is overused and prone to creating confusion because it is used in many different ways by organizations. As technology advances, the term continues to change. The *New York Times* has a multimedia page on its website that allows access to photos, slide shows, audio clips, and the tried-and-true written article. In essence, it allows visitors to experience more than one message offered in more than one form. A similar offering was created by a joint venture between Business Wire and Medialink. Newstream.com offers journalists, producers, and editors news from the United States and Europe in several media formats.

When major corporations, nonprofits, political parties, and manufacturers hold meetings, conventions, and trade shows, they produce major multimedia shows to engage attendees and to bring additional excitement to the event. These venues have multiple video screens with familiar or exciting pictures such as rally and assembly line scenes, animation, and other visuals with pulsating graphics and music and audio from familiar voices of the event itself or previous events.

Simply put, using **multimedia tactics** means *employing several media tactics at one time.* This is not the same as integrated communication strategy as discussed in previous chapters; instead, it is using more than one medium to engage as many of the audience's senses as possible. For example, with today's web technology, multimedia involves numerous software applications that allow developers to use music, video, animation, and interactivity to create enhanced viewer engagement.

You can use multimedia productions in a variety of ways. In addition to commissioning large complex shows developed by production companies, you can use internal computer staff or contract with multimedia experts to help develop multimedia events. Using laptop computers and several software applications, video, and audio clips can be added to presentation files similar to Microsoft PowerPoint. Please remember that using technology can be tricky and you need a tech assistant whenever you attempt to use multimedia. Before you embark on a project such as this away from the office, be sure to check out the availability of power sources ahead of time; bring extra extension cords; make sure windows can be covered; that seats are set up such that the audience can see the screens (and not be blocked by pillars); and even with a tech along, you need to know how to use the projectors with a computer.

Interactive Media

An entirely new vocabulary has grown from the use of the web for interactive activities. User-generated content (UGC) or consumer-generated media (CGM) are two of those terms. They refer to any content or material created by an amateur and uploaded onto the Internet. That content can be as simple as a comment about a book or movie posted on Amazon or a newspaper site to a profile on Facebook or a video on YouTube. UGC along with social networking are changing the landscape for advertisers and PR professionals who are scrambling to find the right mix and opportunities for using this technology.

Social Media

According to the Pew Research Center 2010 survey, 79 percent of American adults use the Internet. The study found that 32 percent of active online users have read a blog and 14 percent have started their own blogs. These users go online to get news (75 percent) and 61 percent use social networks like Facebook or MySpace. More than 45 percent have uploaded photos and 27 percent have downloaded video clips online. Teens, 12 to 17, are the leading users of the Internet at 93 percent. They report social network use at 73 percent and only 8 percent use Twitter or other status-update services.

Social media is *the term used to describe the activities that result from the integration of technology and social interaction in the creation and combination of words, images, video, and audio.* In fact the things people refer to as social media—blogs (Chapter 14), RSS feeds, message boards, online chats, podcasts, wikis and widgets, social networks, Twitter, and virtual worlds—are digital applications or tools that allow users to generate and exchange information and resources. They are the result of social interaction through the Internet. While there is a wide variety among the activities, they are all possible because of digital technology and were not possible before the introduction of high-speed Internet access and search technology. Prior to this high-speed, wireless Internet access, content online, for the most part, mimicked traditional media, sending one-way communication to audiences. Today, it is common for social media to play an important role in PR activities.

Some of the virtual communities online are excellent opportunities to interact with PR audiences. Wikipedia, the online encyclopedia written by almost anyone who wants to make or edit an entry, now has more than four million articles in 253 languages. Tens of thousands of videos are added to YouTube daily. There are 100 million available for online viewing. There are 200 million blogs and more than one-and-a-half million residents of virtual worlds. Facebook has a staggering 100 million users, a third of whom are ages 34–55, in the United States alone.

According to a projection from the Interactive Advertising Bureau, 101 million users in the United States are expected to be attracted to user-generated content (UGC) sites in 2011, earning the sites $4.3 billion in ad revenue. Millenials/GenYers have $350 billion in direct spending power and 96 percent of them have joined a social network. Studies suggest they will continue networking until 2020.

What is important to you as a public relations practitioner is that your products, issues, causes, political candidates, and organizations are already being discussed on UGC sites. The challenge is for you to engage in the discussion. In 2007, a Nielsen study reported that 75 percent of consumers around the world rated consumer recommendations as trusted. As far back as 1993, review websites were created for consumers to go online and discuss their brand experiences. So, consumers were sharing what they liked, disliked, or encountered with electronics, appliances, and automobiles—and changing the jobs of PR practitioners forever. Almost every campaign these days includes a social media component whether it is

Facebook pages, Twitter feeds, video on YouTube, or photos on Flickr. The use of digital technology is growing in the PR field, and employers are looking for practitioners who can think about strategy. While it is helpful to know the technology and how it works, you are most likely to succeed if you understand social media and the audiences that use it.

The key to success with social media is to provide users information and products and services they need. Some public transit systems use Twitter to keep commuters up to date, and Jetblue is on Twitter with special flight offers for its followers. The makers of Nasonex, whose consumers are mostly women between 25 to 50 years, used an online game as part of various PR tactics to remind users that allergies are a year-round problem. The game was introduced at the beginning of the spring allergy season in 2009. The game's links and widgets allowed players to click through to Nasonex.com or share the game through Facebook.

Everyone wants fans on Facebook and followers on Twitter, and marketers are not the only sector using social media strategies effectively. Government agencies are using social networking as well. The Office of National Drug Control Policy (ONDCP) launched the "National Youth Anti-Drug" media campaign to educate children and parents about drug prevention. It is one of the largest social marketing programs on the web. The federal government has Gov.Twit, the government social media directory with more than 400 government agencies, and Gov.Twit has its own Facebook page.

Social media as a PR tool is growing in the nonprofit sector as well. Through "Share Your Story," the March of Dimes has helped to empower its supporters who are on its online community by giving up some of the control. Groups of people on the online community find ways to fundraise and raise awareness on their own. The Red Cross began listening online as it became concerned with criticism of the organization. Now listening has become a component of its marketing strategy.

Critical for the practitioner is knowing the audience, knowing what social media they use, and what a network community wants and providing it. Thinking strategically is crucial. You must identify the right sites for the message you want to communicate in order to connect and build relationships.

Wikis

Wikis are *websites built through collaboration. Individuals contribute to and update the content of the site using their own browsers.* This is enabled by the software that runs on the web server. All wikis are not open to everyone; some require membership or specific qualifications in order to contribute. Others such as Wikipedia are publicly edited, although only registered users are allowed to create new articles, and volunteer editors can delete or correct content.

Microsites

Microsites are *websites that focus on a single event, cause, product, or service.* They usually consist of one or two pages or three to five very short pages. The sites provide all the information a visitor needs to know in order to take an action and can have interactive text to amplify the text. Microsites can be used to keep journalists up to date such as the one created by BP during the oil spill crisis in the Gulf of

Mexico in 2010. Or the sites can be used to drive visitors to other social media for additional information or the opportunity to take an action such as donate to a cause or tweet a member of Congress or other official. Microsites are also popular with freelance writers, artists, and designers because they can demonstrate their projects, portfolios, and capabilities.

A screen shot from the BP microsite during the company's response to the oil spill in the Gulf of Mexico

Courtesy of BP America

Social Networks

Social network sites (SNS) have very special purposes. They are where users socialize with their friends and others who share their interests or, in the case of LinkedIn, where people network for career reasons. Using SNS as public relations tools requires knowing when and where you can interrupt users who are not on their Facebook pages to hear from you. Social networks such as Bebo, Facebook, LinkedIn, and MySpace are among the most well-known online networks. Users on these sites can *network* based on their interests, professional goals, and friends and acquaintances. This section does not outline how users enter or navigate on a social network site because it is likely that everyone reading this book is a user of a social networking site and has a profile online. If not, your next assignment is to become a user on the networking site of your choice. There you will learn what personal information you are encouraged to include on your page and the options you have for confidentiality. This author has peers who have at least 45 online peers and college students who have more than 700. Get online! And it is important to stress that students are not the only members of these networks. More than 50 percent of MySpace users are more than 35 years old, and LinkedIn reports an average user age of 39 years with $139,000 as an annual income.

Sharing content is a major activity of UGC sites. YouTube provides the opportunity for users to upload and view video while sites like Flickr serve the same purpose for photos.

Widgets

Using **widgets** is *more allied to traditional media in that the content is controlled by the publisher, but the user can put the content or her own page—blog or social network profile—or pass it along to a friend.* Technically, widgets are a form of content syndication. They are used extensively as a popular form of news distribution.

Twitter

Twitter is *an online and blogging service that allows fellow twitters to tweet and read each other's tweets, keeping each other updated on "events in their lives."* Tweets are 140-character messages that are available for twitters to access. The public relations applications for this technology are obviously consumer based, as it can be used to update consumers about events and latest changes in products. But Twitter has been very active on Capitol Hill with members of Congress using Twitter to update constituents. During a recent State of the Union address, members were busy tweeting their reactions and updating audiences on what was going on in the Capitol chamber.

Interacting with Audiences through Their Content

Here is a unique offering you can make as a public relations practitioner. Instead of getting online target audiences to enter into the conversation you are having on behalf of your client, you can enter theirs. While it is both tricky and risky, it can also be very rewarding and you need to consult with experts in UGC. UGC is unique because the organization that chooses to use it is entering into dialogue with existing content that is initiated and owned by consumers.

Some companies have already had marketing success using UGC sites, targeting online audiences they are after. You should consider the following: There are two ways to engage in UGC and social networking. One, the organization can place commercial advertising when budgets allow, or two, organizations can become part of the content. The latter is more in line with the budgets PR practitioners are given. When advertising dollars are unavailable and when the strategy does not include buying space, the following options make it possible to become a part of a UGC and enter a conversation with users:

- As a PR practitioner, you are always conducting research to better understand your audiences and to continue to be aware of your environment. Releasing study findings to blogs and adding to wikis may be a good way to enter the conversation. Many blogs talk about products, brands, health and education, and other interests. Harlequin, the romance novel publisher, failed to get the public attention it wanted from a survey on public views about dating and love. The company hired SEO-PR and Buzzlogic to find UGC sites that have interest in the subject. Harlequin re-released the study to 80 bloggers and the study was soon a major topic of conversation. The leading romance blog, Pink Heart Society, eventually ran a four-part series on the survey.
- Custom communities are another way to get public on the web. An organization can launch its own page on a website, such as Adidas did on MySpace in 2006, and drive traffic to the site through the use of other media. The communities can offer interesting content, games, polls, quizzes, or contests to entice users to come. The best part is that not only will users participate when they find content they consider valuable, but they will pass it along to friends and acquaintances.
- The most common method for most organizations to have presence on social networking sites is to create a profile much as any individual would. The organizations can use the page to pass on materials and information, including graphics,

video, and audio. Users can become fans, pass along materials, decorate their own pages with what you provide, and include the page in their own friend network.

- Users can download widgets onto their desktops or embed them into their blogs or profile pages. Widgets import some form of live content to the user's page.

UGC has its own particular culture, and it must be respected as you would respect the culture of any of our audiences. Entering the UGC conversation means you must be transparent and there cannot be the slightest hint of trying to pass yourself and your content as real UGC. The following cases are useful.

Ray-Ban on YouTube

Ray-Ban uploaded a video onto YouTube in 2007 titled "Guy Catches Glasses with Face." The video had a grainy, amateur appearance and featured a guy catching a pair of sunglasses with his face each time his friend threw them. The friend increased the height and velocity of the toss and the guy continued to catch. Users were fascinated by the brief one-and-a-half-minute video, and conversation ensued about how the feat was accomplished, so everyone passed the video onto friends for their opinions. Eventually, the video was viewed more than 1.7 million times in its first week. Ray-Ban became part of the conversation without trying to pretend it was something else. Everyone watching knew that the source of the video was Ray-Ban and its ad agency Cutwater. Of course, viewers wanted to know if they were being tricked and so they watched the video repeatedly and sought the opinion of several others. Soon viewers began to create their own videos, adding to the conversation. This was word of mouth at its best.

The Burger King and P. Diddy Channel

Just as one company can get it right, others can manage to alienate their audiences. When Burger King and Sean P. Diddy launched their own channel on YouTube, Diddy TV, there was a great opportunity to get involved in the UGC conversation, but in one of its earliest videos, P. Diddy referred to Burger King as "buying" the channel. The video received derogatory comments, referring to Burger King and P. Diddy as clueless. Users were feeling used by advertisers.

Coca-Cola and Mentos Explosions

Coca-Cola had a similar experience, rebounded from it, and perhaps learned a lot during its foray into the UGC, social networking world. Two performers, not associated with either product, created a video featuring a series of geysers caused by the chemical reaction of Mentos dropped into bottles of Diet Coke. They used music, choreography, and timely positioned explosions to create the experience. The video became very popular on YouTube, generating a great deal of media coverage. But the two companies had very different reactions. Mentos reacted positively to the video and encouraged consumers, suggesting they make videos of their best Mentos and Diet Coke explosions. Coca-Cola had a more stodgy reaction, suggesting that the video did not fit its "brand personality." Eventually, Coca-Cola got with the program and generated viral distribution of the video and helped with television and other media exposure.

The arena of social networking holds great opportunity for public relations practitioners, and it is essential that you understand the potential and the idiosyncrasies of the various types in order for your client to benefit from them.

Content Blurring Not VNRs' Fault

George David Drucker was CMO of RF/Binder Partners when he wrote this point of view for PRWeek.

Let me get this straight: A reporter for *The New York Times* writes about this unsavory plot by corporations and their strategic communications representatives to provide news and information via their own paid-for VNRs.

And based on this incredibly incisive "discovery," the Federal Communications Commission (FCC) is now looking into why and how TV stations use these materials. In addition, it's researching whether such material must be labeled by the stations.

Hmmm. Well, I wonder if what's good for the proverbial goose is good for the gander.

So, let's see if this works equitably—at least in television media.

Good Morning America is doing an interview with the star of a major film produced by the Disney Co. The star talks about his role, the plot, a clip of the film is shown... and then there is a wonderful light banter between him and Diane Sawyer—and viewers are urged, "Don't miss this film."

Now, because the Disney Co. owns ABC, ABC owns *GMA*, and the star is appearing in a movie produced by Disney... do you suppose there will be a label of some sort, while the interview is taking place, which states, "This interview and guest were provided by Disney to promote its film—and this segment is being aired on *GMA*, which Disney also owns"?

Somehow I don't think so.

ESPN decided to do a multi-part series on Barry Bonds as he pursued breaking both Babe Ruth's and Hank Aaron's highly vaunted home-run records. The segments focus on Bonds the man—his daily trials and tribulations—as he travels to baseball stadiums across America. Pretty exciting stuff! One slight caveat, though: ESPN was PAYING Bonds for this insightful series—much like you'd pay any actor who appears in a TV series or movie. And, perhaps even more important, Bonds, as part of his agreement with the network, had the right to review all content before airing.

So, if we were to apply potential FCC regulations to this scenario, would ESPN have offered, at the beginning of the show, "ESPN has paid Barry Bonds for the right to interview, follow, and videotape him as he pursues two of the greatest milestones in baseball history—and the show you are about to see was approved by Mr. Bonds prior to airing"?

Nope. Didn't happen. The good news is, though, "his" show was canceled anyway.

The examples are endless... and no one ever says "boo."

So what's my point in all this? Well, as we see the various marketing disciplines melding together as never before, and as "content" gets more blurred between what's original and what's been provided, please don't use PR pros as convenient "whipping boys" for what some media "purists" may consider to be *the* malady.

Truth is, this has been going on for eons in one shape or another. And given the economics of marketing today, necessity is the mother of invention. If it's convenient for a TV station or network to use materials provided by a third party, so be it. They've been doing it to promote themselves and their content since the beginning.

So just don't beat up on us. If the FCC is going to investigate content, why don't they look at a much broader, colloquial "picture"?

Summary and Review

The Power of the Visual Image
- The more senses that are engaged in a communication message, the more memorable it is to the receiver.
- Television dominates all other visual experiences in the world. Because of its ubiquity and 24-hour news cycle, you can easily imagine that many people experience message overload.

Catalog of Tactics
- There are a few ways to contact television news editors and producers. In addition to written news releases discussed in Chapter 14, the video news release (VNR) and the electronic press kit (EPK) are two useful tools. Both require professional production and distribution to the news media for the greatest success.
- Organizations can use television in other ways as well. Television talk shows are accessible in some markets when the guest and information are interesting and grasp the attention of the target audience. The television talk show requires pitching to the producer of the show.
- Companies can buy product placement opportunities in feature-length commercial films as a means of promoting a product or idea.
- Aside from the still photograph, graphic designs and illustrations are the most commonly used visuals of the public relations practice. Graphic designers create the logos that make up your organization's identity, incorporated into everything from letterhead and business cards to product packaging.
- With today's web technology, multimedia involves numerous software applications that allow developers to use music, video, animation, and interactivity to create enhanced viewer engagement.
- User-generated content (UGC) websites and the popularity of social networking have opened new vehicles and opportunities for public relations and its practitioners.

Key Terms

brand	microsites	still photography
B-roll	multimedia tactics	Twitter
commercial films and videos	presentation aids	video news release (VNR)
	social media	widgets
electronic press kit (EPK)	sponsored films and videos	wikis
graphic design		

Questions for Review and Discussion

1. How do video news releases and news releases for print media differ?
2. How do electronic press kits and print media kits differ?
3. How can you justify the cost of a VNR if it gets play in a news market?
4. What is the most common method of distribution for VNRs?
5. How do organizations use sponsored films to reach their target audiences?

6. In what sections of the newspaper are you most likely to get a photograph run?

7. Why is using presentation aids a good idea when you want audiences to remember content?

8. In what ways can graphic designers assist you?

9. How can you take advantage of user-generated content (UGC) websites and the popularity of social networking to reach its audiences?

Web Links

Mashable
www.mashable.com

GovTwit—The Government Social Media Directory
www.govtwit.com

March of Dimes
www.marchofdimes.com

AntiDrug.com
www.antidrug.com

Corporate Sector

CORPORATIONS TODAY

It appears the leaders of corporations had lost perspective during the end of the 20th century through the early 2000s. Caveat emptor, "buyer beware," an old and highly contemptible way of doing business, had apparently returned. Junk bonds, questionable accounting, employee abuse, negligent financiers, shaky secondary mortgages, and plain old cheating sent many CEOs to prison and caused consumers worldwide to be wary and weary of corporations. It is a time reminiscent of the early days of business in America when the robber barons reigned in the 19th century.

Corporations are trying to reinvent themselves and convince consumers that they are good neighbors and good corporate citizens. This is a tough job for corporate public relations and communicators. Surveys show that the public is distrustful of corporations, beginning with a downward spiral in the mid-'80s when American public trust in business fell from 70 percent to less than 20 percent. And distrust of corporations is not uniquely American, as Japanese enterprise is threatened by eroding public trust as a result of continued corporate scandals in early 2000. And the era of multinationals and corporate globalization has made it possible for consumers all over the globe to distrust the very same corporations.

As we have discussed, perception plays a major role in public opinion. It is difficult for the average consumer to understand corporations because they are ubiquitous and enormous. Many of the world's major corporations dwarf the economies of some of the world's countries. In fact, one study released in 2000 indicates that of the world's 100 largest economies, 51 are corporations and 49 are countries. The

All business begins with the public permission and exists by public approval.

—Arthur W. Page,
Vice President of PR for AT&T, 1927–1946

sheer size of an organization can be a deterrent to creating understanding and building relationships. It is likely that everyone who reads this chapter can remember going to a specialty store where he visited often enough to recognize someone behind the counter or cash register—the closest fast-food restaurant, deli, coffee shop, or bakery. We are very comfortable in those situations. Imagine those recognizable faces disappearing and a vast "bigbox" store like Walmart and a legion of faces taking their place.

It's pretty difficult to get personal attention and interpersonal satisfaction under these circumstances. Enormity and anonymity reduce the possibility for effective communication—the goal of strategic public relations.

PR in the Corporate Context

Strategic public relations is practiced in many corporate or for-profit contexts, including small and midsize business, large and multinational corporations, and law. During almost a full century, as technology has advanced and globalization has emerged, corporate practice has helped move the field of public relations from mere press agentry to an important management function. It can be argued that the principles developed and lessons learned in corporate practice have served as the foundation for strategic practice in the other contexts: nonprofit (Chapter 18), politics and government (Chapter 19), and international (Chapter 20).

Your job as a corporate public relations practitioner is twofold: you must counsel the company to operate responsibly and in the public interest while valuing and respecting its employees, and you must work with external audiences to ensure the company's actions are communicated clearly and effectively. The public relations job has not become any easier over the decades, but it has evolved as corporations and the business environment have changed.

CORPORATE PUBLIC RELATIONS EVOLUTION

In its nascent years, corporate public relations was no more than a tool for helping business make sales and generating publicity. In the early 1900s, corporations began to take advantage of publicity as a way to court public favor while also attracting consumers and investors. The railroads, the first major industry in the United States, also comprised the first industry to use advertising and depend on public relations. In the early days, they used public speeches, conventions, pamphlets, and newspaper articles to convince the public that railroad travel was better than other means, such as stagecoach and steamboat, and to attract investors.

The decades surrounding the turn of the 20th century—the so-called Gilded Age—saw the rapid growth of railroads, utilities, and other industries whose owners amassed significant power and wealth, often at the expense of the public and their own employees. Trade unions emerged to fight for decent wages, hours, and working conditions for laborers. The press agent model dominated the practice, with former newspapermen acting as publicists who circulated news favorable to the companies and unfavorable to their competitors. From the turn of the 20th century forward, the battle for the public mind was on, as companies fought for marketing advantage and media attention. The result was the creation of a new corporate strategy to capture the American public. Companies used public relations to convince the public that companies and the average citizen held much in common (see Chapter 3 on history for a comprehensive discussion). As consumers have become more sophisticated and as technology has delivered greater volumes of information in shorter time frames, corporations have had to listen to public relations counsel that advises them to not only act in the consumer's and their mutual best interest but to actively communicate how they are doing so.

Today businesses marry marketing and public relations to tell a story to increase sales. In fact, the terms **marketing communication** and **integrated marketing communication**—*used two decades ago to describe the process of public relations and marketing working together to create customer interest and trust in a product while selling the product*—are making a strong comeback primarily because PR is seen as a major component of the marketing mix. Marketing and advertising executives believe that public relations is lending credibility to their messages. While the marketing and public relations silos still exist in many companies, other companies are smashing down the walls and clients are asking for those walls to fall. Volkswagen's launch of its new GTI model and relaunch of the Rabbit is an excellent example of PR's role in the marketing mix. The company wanted to generate buzz about the return of the Rabbit and position the GTI as the "original hot-hatch." They invited the news media for test drives and arranged test drives for consumers at Volkswagen-owner festivals. A web strategy offered consumers the ability to configure and test drive a car online and to receive electronic brochures.

The MWW Group, 2006 *PRWeek* Agency of the Year, finds companies such as Starbucks and Nike are beginning to merge their corporate and branding functions because effective company communication means managing the brand. And managing the brand means more than marketing and advertising; it means telling a credible story over and over again. Strategic PR does this well and helps prepare the landscape for the marketing and advertising efforts to follow. Joining forces for the most effective strategy means having both internal corporate teams and agency teams working together to manage the brand.

In Chapter 1 we discussed the management function of public relations within an organization. The effective practice of public relations for corporations demonstrates this role. The corporate practitioner assists and counsels management with an eye on the effects of policy decisions, courses of action, and communication. As a PR practitioner, you are responsible for helping management understand the effects of its actions on the public and reminding the corporation of its social or citizenship responsibilities. As a member of management, you must continually assist the company in building, monitoring, and maintaining its many public relationships.

Understanding how corporate PR is practiced begins with understanding the contexts in which it can be practiced. There are three ways to work in corporate public relations—as an employee of the company, as a practitioner in the corporate practice of an agency, and, of course, as a self-employed counselor.

Levels of Employment in Internal Corporate Public Relations

There are four distinct posistion levels of employment within corporate PR and communication departments—entry, mid-level, senior mid-level, and senior. Each is distinguished primarily by the years of experience in the corporate practice. While practice in other areas can be seen as experience toward corporate levels, it is important to understand that career advancement in the internal corporate practice requires experience in working inside corporate communication. Figure 17.1 illustrates levels of public relations employment in internal corporate practices.

Entry level: Administrative assistant, PR specialist, or PR coordinator

Salary range: $32K–$48K

Most individuals who join the PR team at a top company will not come right out of college. Instead, many employers prefer candidates with two to five years of agency or other relevant experience and/or an advanced degree. A minimum of three relevant internships during college is also desirable.

Responsibilities:

- Support activities of the PR department using writing, planning, and organizational skills.
- Learn various disciplines, including employee communications, media relations, and investor relations.
- Gain familiarity with the tools and techniques of communication, including new media platforms, VNRs, SMTs, newswires, measurement tools, databases and all internal platforms.
- Channel requests or inquiries from journalists to the appropriate person.
- Ascertain perceptions from a stakeholder point of view.
- Facilitate internal requests/inquiries from other departments.
- Gather press clippings; monitor media for company news.
- Prepare documents, PowerPoint presentations, and spreadsheets.
- Provide support for events, shareholder meetings, journalist briefings, and press conferences.
- Maintain media lists.
- Coordinate efforts with PR agency counterparts.
- Coordinate/merchandise media clips on the company.

Insider's tip: Make an effort to understand how the company works as a whole, rather than just the PR department. Ask questions and engage people across the organization, including contacts in other marketing disciplines. Interest in the business objectives and the full company environment is important. Don't pretend to know more than you do—executives will respect your eagerness to learn, listen, and contribute. Interpersonal skills are needed, and energy and enthusiasm are essential.

Mid level: PR associate or PR manager

Salary range: $49K–$90K

Individuals will have five to seven years of experience with a greater role in writing, developing plans, and managing various communications efforts. Technical skills should be well-developed, including familiarity with PR industry tools and techniques. An ability to assess key trends that impact your company is vital. An understanding of audience perceptions and how to influence their behavior through communications is helpful. Demonstrate confidence in dealing with senior executives and press, as well as a willingness to take initiative and assume responsibility beyond those listed below. Specialization may occur at this level, leading to roles dedicated to employee comms, media relations, IR, events, and community relations.

Responsibilities:

Give ongoing support to senior management, including setting up interviews, providing message points, writing speeches, and organizing events.

- Write press releases, op-eds, annual report sections, speeches, and internal communications, for traditional and new-media channels.
- Engage with other marketing disciplines to coordinate efforts.
- Develop communications plans to support corporate/product strategy.
- Respond to media inquires, serving as spokesperson on certain issues.
- Provide direction to vendors for services such as newswires, printers, VNRs, SMTs, and measurement tools.
- Serve as primary contact for the PR agency.
- Supervise work of administrative/coordinator level.

Insider's tip: Take advantage of greater senior-level access. Offer opinions and perspective, and demonstrate knowledge of both the industry and how communication relates to business goals. But be warned: know when to listen and when to talk. Also, learn how to connect and integrate all communications pieces together to maximize effectiveness. Knowledge of audience needs and wants is powerful in developing business logic to sell programs and ideas. Network with colleagues at your level throughout the company to build relationships and gain knowledge on other departments, including other marketing disciplines—sensitivity to the environment is key to the job.

Figure 17.1

Levels of Employment in Corporate PR

Mid-senior level: PR director

Salary range: $80K–$160K

At the upper-middle level, you will engage with senior executives on a regular basis, including the CEO and CMO, and frequently be called on to develop and present plans to members of the senior leadership team along with how those plans fit into the overall achievement of corporate objectives. With a mastery of the tactical elements of the job, the focus becomes more strategic. Even if there is a functional responsibility over an area of communication, generally skills and knowledge become more broadly drawn, extending across PR specialties and general business units.

Responsibilities:

Functional responsibility for a key area of communication, such as media relations, internal communication, IR, and community relations.

- Supervise managers, including defining metrics to evaluate performance.
- Serve as number two, sometimes standing in for VP.
- Engage in strategic planning with other marketing disciplines.
- Apply business logic and knowledge of stakeholder needs to sell programs.
- Act as spokesperson on key issues or products.
- Provide front-line engagement on issues and crises.
- Provide counsel to senior management outside of communication.
- Take responsibility for areas outside of the communications function.

Insider's tip: This is when careful consideration is given to career options. The "job for life" is no longer assumed, and many individuals will hop from this level to the top job at another company. Recruiters keep watch over individuals at the director stage for possible opportunities with other organizations. PR agencies will welcome individuals at this level, usually to help run a practice area related to their industry. Thorough execution of the communications function—combined with the ability to build consensus across marketing and other business disciplines—stands out. How you handle stress and manage challenging situations will be viewed critically and determine whether you are viewed as "high potential" or "next in line" for the top communications slot. Superior skills in team building, task management, and leadership are also critical

Senior level: VP of communication, SVP or VP of marketing, external affairs, corporate affairs

Salary range: $190K–$1M

The top post requires the individual to provide high-level counsel to the most senior levels of the organization. Cross-pollination with other marketing and business disciplines, even if not under the VP's purview, is especially critical, as is a thorough understanding of the company's business objectives, its markets, as well as the broader economic and political landscape. Application of fact-based business logic is important to gain consensus for plans and programs. More and more, the role is global in nature and includes responsibilities for marketing, image, or reputation efforts.

Responsibilities:

- Provide senior counsel to the CEO, Chief Management officer (CMO), CFO, Chief Legal Officer (CLO), and board of directors.
- Develop communication strategies across divisions and regions.
- Engage business leadership to project business ideas across divisions.
- Take ownership of brand development and corporate reputation.

Insider's tip: The most effective senior communicator in an organization is a high-level counselor to the CEO and to other senior executives, and an influential player throughout the organization. They also identify ways they can add value to the business and facilitate linkages between the communication function and other areas. Therefore, even if one reaches the top role in his or her company, there are always new responsibilities to assume. Successful leaders never stop learning about their organizations, nor do they ever lose touch with developing their value externally and the fundamentals of the profession. Some PR leaders will also head up marketing, but it still takes a lot of work to prove that a communication professional is best suited to lead this area. Finding ways throughout a career to maximize experience across disciplines while displaying an understanding of customer needs increases the likelihood this will happen.

Figure 17.1
(*continued*)

Corporate Practice in Agencies

In addition to the public relations practice within a company, PR agencies have corporate practices that serve client companies. See Chapter 2 for a discussion of agency practices. It is not unusual for a large company to have more than one—sometimes several—PR firms working for it at one time. Agency corporate practice areas continued to increase during 2005 and beyond. Agencies with global practices are working for more multinational corporations and agency corporate practices are working to take advantage of the economic expansion of nations like India and China. As well, advertising budgets took a turn for the worse in the early 2000s and as advertising waned, public relations practices saw an increase. While the economic downturn of 2009 resulted in reduction of PR agency staff, corporate practices remained healthy.

Reputation management has driven a lot of the corporate practice growth. This is no doubt true because of the recent corporate scandals, recalls, and such incidents as the BP oil spill. Companies with reputation problems look to PR practices to assist them in reputation repair, and others use these professionals to keep their reputations clean. Today, it appears that public relations in the corporate sector is more highly respected than it has been in its more than 100-year history.

THE ROLE OF CONSUMERISM

As reported in Chapter 3, when asked by a Chicago reporter in 1882 if railroads should be run as a public trust, railroad magnate William H. Vanderbilt famously retorted, "The public be damned." During that age and into the turn of the century, consumers were at the mercy of corporations and industrialists. The corporate attitude demonstrated by Vanderbilt's angry reply led to reform and government regulation of industry in the early 1900s.

Much later, the 1960s saw a new consumer rights era led by advocates like Ralph Nader, best known for his work toward creation of car safety legislation in the United States. The mission of the consumer advocacy movement was to ensure safe and quality products under honest terms without misleading and deceptive claims at costs that were financially fair and competitive. This was no easy task, but the era pioneered and won consumer rights that are viewed as mundane today. Today consumer rights are protected by government and advocacy groups that help support boycotts—refusal to buy products or services of a particular company—to demonstrate their disappointment or unhappiness with company conduct and policies. Consumer advocacy and reform efforts are diverse, covering issues such as the environment, healthcare, insurance, pension, and disability. The public relations professional's translation of the company to consumers is more important than ever before. It is the practitioner's job to provide guidance and counsel to a company as it faces consumerism to help it navigate the environment and maintain positive public opinion toward the company. Corporate social responsibility and philanthropy are two ways of demonstrating corporate goodwill and commitment beyond the bottom line of profits.

PHILANTHROPY AND CORPORATE SOCIAL RESPONSIBILITY

While it may not be remembered by most, it was Dow Chemical that outlined the precept of corporate social responsibility when it declared that it recognized the "human element" and that it valued listening to its communities and seeking to be not just "a good neighbor, but a global corporate citizen." The philosophy purports that a company's long-term profit growth is enhanced by its reputation in the community. **Corporate social responsibility,** *sometimes called corporate citizenship, is a company's sense of responsibility or obligation to give back to society through support of social programs, philanthropy, volunteerism, and more in the community and environment in which it operates.* Essentially, social responsibility must be good business and good citizenship.

A recent survey of consumers reveals something that should not be too surprising. Many consumers have different definitions of what dictates whether a company is acting responsibly. As you know, individuals see everything from their own perspectives—their own values, circumstances, beliefs, and feelings—so it makes sense that their views of *acting responsibly* differ. In 2006, public relations firm Fleishman-Hillard and the National Consumers League conducted a benchmark survey of 800 American adults to determine consumer "attitudes toward and behaviors regarding corporate social responsibility (CSR), as well as the role media and technology play in informing people about what companies are doing to be socially responsible." Respondents were allowed to define CSR for the purposes of the survey, and survey participants provided more than 12 unprompted definitions for CSR. Among the most popular: commitment to employees, 27 percent; commitment to communities, 23 percent; provide quality products, 16 percent; and responsibility to the environment, 12 percent.

Turns out consumers are not impressed with the CSR records of U.S. companies in recent years. Using a 5-point scale where 5 is excellent and 1 is poor, "less than, or just over, one-third" (21 percent) rate U.S. corporations at 5 or 4. Corporations were seen as doing "a lot better" or "somewhat better" at being socially responsible compared with two to three years ago by 30 percent of the respondents. Yet, for 35 percent, "being socially responsible" was the factor most likely to make them loyal followers of a particular brand or company. And a whopping 63 percent believe that a company's record of being socially responsible would be "influential to their decision regarding whether to invest in a company." A major finding for companies: 52 percent of the respondents say they seek out information about a company's social responsibility record "all of the time" or "sometimes."

CSR in the United States is a part of corporate philanthropic efforts. Companies make as much in profits as they can and donate a predetermined portion of the profits to charities or causes. The European corporate model concentrates on ensuring business operations are socially responsible *and* on investing in communities. Clearly, in different countries, different priorities and different values shape how business acts. What is clear is that the pressure for business to play a major role in social issues is growing. As corporations operate more within a global sphere than governments, and as countries grapple with difficult economic and social issues, companies, like nongovernmental organizations (NGOs), are able to operate more effectively. As a result, there is growing activity and interest in companies seeking social solutions that governments cannot. This is not to say that CSR is a panacea, but the future holds opportunities for companies to play greater roles in helping to solve global problems.

Unilever's support of sustainable fisheries may be a prime example. According to Corporate Watch, U.S. consumer product giant and maker of frozen foods, Unilever, operates in 150 countries and has committed to buying all of its fish from sustainable fisheries. The impact this will have on the depletion of fish stock is vast and it's something governments throughout the world cannot do. Also, CSR that is built into the corporate business model, such as this one, is likely to survive while other choices for philanthropy may wane or lose to other corporate choices when it is time to cut back on costs.

Cause-Related Marketing

Clearly, businesses participate in activities that are designed to enhance their image. The same is true with corporate philanthropy, as companies adopt and enter into mutually beneficial relationships with organizations representing charities, causes, or social efforts to market their products or services. This is called cause-related marketing. According to the Chicago-based consultant firm IEG, private sector businesses spent more than 13 billion dollars supporting nonprofit causes in 2006.

Ideally, corporate relationships with charitable organizations are designed to be mutually beneficial. The charity or cause receives funding and support and companies receive promotional value. As a result, nonprofits expand their message beyond their usual target audiences and gain insight on additional audiences to pitch. Corporations know it is good business to participate in these activities because studies show that consumers like and are loyal to companies that are committed to doing *good* and supporting worthy causes. Studies show that with all other things equal, consumers would rather do business with a good corporate citizen. In one study, Cone Cause Evolution Study in 2010, 83 percent of the respondents "still want to see more brands, products, and companies support worthy causes." Another study by *PRWeek* and Barkley Public Relations found that the women responding to the survey agreed at the rate of 96 percent that it is "important for companies to support causes and charities." As with politics, perception of doing the right thing is a local matter. The study of 225 adults indicated that while "making a difference on big problems" that may impact society globally is good, most prefer to support local community programs that make a "tangible and noticeable" difference. Of course, Microsoft, Target, and Walmart topped the list of "top-of-mind" corporations that try to make a difference. Target and Walmart are known for their local and community programs.

The *PRWeek* survey results show that consumers make purchases based on what they know about a company's philanthropy with about two-thirds of Gen X and Gen Y consumers purchasing one brand over another because they know "that it supports a cause they believe in." The survey also shows "Generation X is much more skeptical" of corporations' cause-related marketing motivations. And while nearly half of boomers (45 percent) believe that most companies follow ethical business practices, only 24 percent of Gen Xers agree.

During 13 years of corporate cause marketing, Lee Jeans has raised more than $75 million for the Susan G. Komen Breast Cancer Foundation for breast cancer research. What started as a cause marketing initiative to encourage employers to allow employees to wear jeans to work has evolved into a year-round communication strategy. Initially, Lee Jeans was looking for a way in which to engage its key target audience—women. It toyed with the notion of jeans at work and looked for a nonprofit partner to benefit from the effort. The Komen Foundation was a "perfect fit." Lee National Denim Day encouraged employers to give employees permission to wear jeans to work on the designated day in October if they "paid" $5 to do so. Proceeds went to the Komen Foundation.

Today, the Lee National Denim Day still occurs in the month of October. But many companies offer employees the opportunity to wear jeans year-round and the proceeds continue to assist the foundation in finding a cure.

Nike's corporate partnership with the Lance Armstrong Foundation, the cancer research and educational organization, made a great deal of news in 2005. The "Just Do It" manufacturer of sport shoes and clothing continued to support Armstrong after the cyclist learned he had testicular cancer that had spread to his lungs and brain. Against the odds that Armstrong would not live and certainly never compete again, Nike continued its backing. While other sponsors were pulling the plug on deals, Nike agreed to continue backing Armstrong. Of course, Armstrong survived— recovering from cancer and winning a record number of Tour de France victories. Now Nike backs

The "LiveStrong yellow wristbands

the "Wear Yellow LiveStrong" campaign, touted as one of the most outstanding cases of nonprofit fundraising. And the Nike–Armstrong partnership has resulted in the sale of more than 50 million yellow wristbands.

COMMUNITY RELATIONS

The members of the community in which an organization lives make up one of an organization's most important audiences. Being a good corporate citizen is a dual relationship. It means participating in the life of the community and serving where possible to make it a good place to live, but it also means realizing that a company needs the goodwill of the community in order to do business. Local government, community organizations, faith-based organizations, schools and universities, and other businesses all affect the viability of local business. Usually, community relations involves participating in and supporting community activities, such as helping to support health fairs through presence or in-kind services, meeting with community leaders, and serving on community councils or advisory boards. But community relations can also go much further than that. It can also mean inviting the community in, providing opportunities such as open houses, sponsoring community development and revitalization initiatives such as adopting a park or a neighborhood, or initiating efforts to assist the community's less fortunate such as renovating housing. The key, of course, is knowing the community itself and its target audiences.

Developing a dialogue and relationship with the community requires management to think strategically about what it wants to get out of the relationship and determining the benefits to the community. Like any other corporate effort, the return on investment (ROI) has be considered and justified to management. As a PR practitioner, you must analyze the answers to several questions:

- What has been the corporate involvement with the community to date?
- What are the reasons for wanting to create or enhance the company's relationship with the community?
- Are there clear and precise situations where the company can get involved in the community?
- What are competitors or other business entities doing in the community?
- What is the company's current image in the community?
- Does the community consider the company credible?
- What has been the company's stance with community organizations? Has the company run afoul of any community organizations?

After these questions have been answered and the answers considered, if the company decides to initiate a community relations effort, a community relations plan must be developed for implementation. A community relations plan includes many of the elements found in any strategic PR plan.

Recently, company community relations has begun to pay more attention to the schools in the areas in which the companies conduct business. Some adopt schools or provide resources needed in some of the classrooms in their communities. Other corporations have taken a larger role in improving public education in the United States. Corporations spend about $2 billion annually on education in America—some with little success and others with more.

- The GE Foundation, the philanthropic arm of the General Electric Company, has committed almost $200 million to date to a program that supports system-wide change in five school districts to improve student achievement. The program "Developing Futures," continues to fund those districts and two others that were added in 2010 and 2011. GE Foundation supports the work with not only grants but volunteers and pro bono assistance that has resulted in millions of dollars in savings and high-tech and innovative improvements for the districts.
- The Broad Foundation, the major philanthropic organization of Fortune 500 giant Eli Broad, created a 10-month program to train experienced leaders from business, the military, and education to run troubled school districts. This is one part of its continuing support resulting in a $370 million investment since 1999 to improve student learning.
- Walmart's Walton family spent $150 million on charter schools and scholarships for poor children to attend private schools. The Walton Family Foundation continues to support school choice through its scholarships.
- In 1999 the Bill and Melinda Gates Foundation began a now $1.6 billion scholarship program, Gates Millennium Scholars Program (GMS), to assist African American, American Indian/Alaska Native, Asian Pacific Islander American, and Hispanic American students with high academic and leadership promise in ameliorating financial barriers to attaining bachelor's and advanced degrees. The program celebrated its 11th graduating class in 2010.

INTERNAL COMMUNICATION

A company's external reputation often hinges on the messages its internal audiences convey about the organization. It is difficult to overestimate the importance of a company's internal audiences. They are the organization's best salespeople. Internal communication can be segmented into two distinct audiences—employees and members. Employee relations and member relations help to shore up the most important sales team a company can have—the people who work there or who are members. Membership organizations have an additional internal audience—members. Member relations is much more common in organizations such as trade or professional organizations. We will focus on employee relations in this chapter and discuss membership relations when we discuss nonprofit PR (see Chapter 18).

Employee Relations

Smart corporations recognize that communicating effectively with employees is simply good business. After all, employees are the single greatest sales force an organization can have, as they tell the story of the company beyond the product or services provided. Through their very personal experiences, they help to tell the story of the company as a caring employer and as a good neighbor. They are corporate ambassadors. But in order for employees to be ambassadors for the company, they must respect the company they serve. Otherwise, they tell a very different story. Employees who feel valued by their company, believing they are being treated fairly and that they are a part of an institution that is providing value and quality to its customers while managing the business wisely, make the best ambassadors.

A company must communicate with employees to understand them and to give them a sense of ownership in the company's future. In today's corporate environment, employees are more distant from the company's principals, making employees more concerned about how the business decisions are made and how the executives are running the business. Why? Because they are not likely to encounter the CEO or board chair on the elevator anymore. And, again, the average worker now knows that the impact of poor management can result in financial difficulty for her. Given the number of consumers who say they consider a company's commitment to its employees when deciding to buy its product, an emphasis on employee relations is crucial.

Sometimes referred to as internal communication, employee relations is really a category of internal relations. Employees are not to be ignored, as they are crucial to the success of a company. Interestingly, many companies overlook the opportunity to communicate with this audience as effectively as it does with its consumers, often failing to apply the strategic practices they use with consumers. But, like most effective communication, communicating with employees should begin with talking to the target audience. Employee satisfaction surveys are excellent data collection strategies for communicating with employees. These surveys often reveal the workplace issues employees would most like to see addressed, but companies often conduct perfunctory communication efforts focusing on human resources, compensation and benefits, personnel changes, major corporate plans and changes, and new product offerings. This information is delivered through traditional vehicles such as brochures, newsletters, and company magazines. Today's savvy corporations are more sophisticated in determining what and how best to communicate with employees, going well beyond employee satisfaction with the company and workplace. Some companies conduct consumer research with employees to discover how they prefer to receive news and information, advertising, and other forms of communication in their daily lives. This information helps companies determine how best to communicate with an employee beyond the traditional forms. Intranets and videos or film have become the vehicles of preference for many companies.

EDS, an IT services and outsourcing company, has a nine-person employee communication team. Repurposing broadcast news has become a very popular employee communication tool, as VNRs and b-roll are broadcast on the intranet, also. The company considers what is working outside of the workplace, bringing pop culture and trends inside to help communicate with employees. The communication team knew that staff considered news reports as credible sources of information, so they developed "The EDS Minute," a 90-second video news broadcast on the intranet that delivers timely company information. "By Request" broadcasts feature executives answering real-time unscripted questions from global employees. Other proposed EDS employee communication tactics include a news "widget" on the intranet's home page that will provide news from within the company and industry, and link to relevant articles and broadcasts.

BUSINESS-TO-BUSINESS PUBLIC RELATIONS

Many businesses have other businesses as clients and key audiences. For instance, airlines provide travel to passengers—their primary audience. But the airlines must buy airplanes from someone in the airplane-selling business. The airlines are among the engine manufacturers' primary clients. And airplane manufacturers don't make engines and cockpit instruments. They buy them from other businesses. And the airplane manufacturers are their clients. As you can see, like most business, business to business, or B2B, is very competitive and complex. Of course, the market B2B can be even more complex because consumers or clients range from small office/home office small businesses (SOHO) to multinational corporations, and communicating and fostering relationships are crucial to success. While a lot of literature on business-to-business marketing exists, the importance of strategic PR to generating and maintaining business-to-business relationships is often overlooked. Practitioners who specialize in this area of the practice are in high demand by agencies, as they have usually spent some years in the business world and know how businesses communicate with each other. In the end, the strategies differ because the

BRIEF CASE STUDY

Visa Focuses on SOHOs

When Visa recognized that its primary reputation was that of a consumer credit card provider and that it had fallen behind American Express with its Blue Card and MasterCard in the small business market, it turned to Ketchum Communication. Data showed that the SOHOs—companies with fewer than 25 employees—were an estimated $100 billion market, and additional research indicated that a new business started in the United States every 30 seconds. Research also showed that small-business spending was contracted with cash or checks at a whopping 81 percent. Ketchum conducted a campaign to promote Visa as "a multi-faceted financial resource to companies trying to get started. The idea was built on the business incubator concept—organizations that help accelerate the growth and success of start-up companies through providing an array of business support resources and services until the business is strong enough to operate on its own. Visa was to be seen not just as a financial tool but as a one-stop source for information, financing, and business education, linking the Visa brand to the SOHO community. The focus of the launch was a national business plan competition, the Visa Start-Up 2000, attracting 530 small businesses. The three winning companies received cash and participated in an incubation for one year, including advice from some of Visa's business partners, including Compaq, Office Depot, and the Kauffman Center for Entrepreneurial Leadership. Reaching the small-business entrepreneurs was a challenge, as they were not consumers of the usual business news media. Ketchum developed a website, a toll-free number, direct mail, email, and a radio tour to reach its target audience.

Working the Case

1. What primary research could Ketchum have conducted with start-up audiences? Given the information presented, what objective(s) would you write for this target audience?
2. What type of objectives would you have set for the campaign—informational, behavioral, or attitudinal?
3. How would you measure the success of the campaign?
4. How could Ketchum have pretested the campaign message?

audiences are different, but the available tactics are much the same. B2B practice is highly focused on thought-leader strategy for clients. Positioning the brand or business as being forward-thinking about the industry is often the appropriate strategy for the right audience. For instance, a landscape equipment manufacturer can probably maintain a robust business if it is among the best in its industry, but if it wants to grow and stave off the competition, it might want to conduct a survey of its customers and find out what they want besides equipment. It may be that clients want more, such as advice on solving business problems that involve the equipment. If research supports such a need or another, the landscape equipment company just might offer its clients value-added services and position itself as a thought-leader for the industry. Maintenance repair and operations, travel services, jet engines, plastic, food-service equipment and supplies, information and other asset security, and preassembled vehicle dashboards are all products and services delivered from businesses to other businesses.

GOVERNMENT RELATIONS AND PUBLIC AFFAIRS

Corporate public relations practitioners who help their companies communicate and build relationships with government and legislative audiences operate in a complex and complicated arena. Large corporations have staff whose specialty is understanding, monitoring, and influencing legislative action. While sometimes thought to be the exclusive domain of lobbyists, legislative influence occurs through other strategies and tactics that include partnership building, political action coalitions, communication and education campaigns, and government relations activities. These activities are often the job of PR practitioners. In addition to having an impact on legislation, corporations have to be concerned with the existing government rules and regulatory requirements that affect their ability to do business. If you work in government relations, you must maintain relationships with government employees, including staff of members of Congress and the many government agencies that regulate business.

As a government relations PR practitioner active in public or government affairs, you have audiences in local, state, and federal government offices, depending upon the size of your client or organization. See Figure 17.2 for PR case studies textbook author Jerry Hendrix's list of government and ancillary publics, or audiences.

The public relations strategist who practices in this area has often worked in politics and government before joining a corporation, bringing experience with dealing with the government and specialized media. It is difficult to conduct direct audience research with these audiences, as very few of them allow themselves to be interviewed for surveys and rarely do they consent to responding to interviews even as experts. Instead, secondary informal research is usually the best way to find out about legislators and government executives. The news media, public records, and industry publications are excellent sources for discovering how they voted on an issue, the views they've outlined in speeches, and committee reports that delineate the proceeding at hearings. Government staff can be just as elusive when it comes to collecting data although they are willing to share information considered in the public domain. For these reasons, former executive and legislative staff are highly recruited by corporations and agencies after they leave public service.

Generally, affecting legislation has two major objectives: to increase a legislator's or legislative committee's awareness of and favorable attitude toward the company and its position in the marketplace; and to sway favorable votes on a

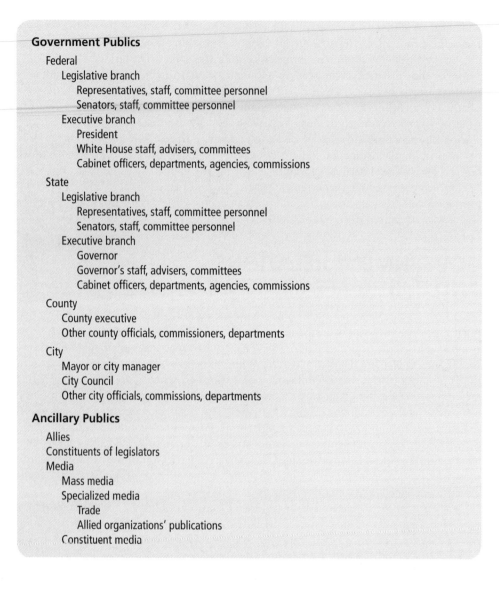

Figure 17.2

Government and Ancillary Audiences

bill. The relationship between government and companies is crucial to business success, as actions taken by local, state, and federal government can greatly influence business operations and latitude within industry. Government relations and lobbying are similar though lobbyists are perceived as having more insight and personal influence among the legislative and executive branches of government. A lobbyist acts as an agent of a group or organization to influence legislators or government officers or executives. Government relations practitioners can conduct many more activities for a company.

Lobbyists

The Lobbying Disclosure Act of 1995 requires anyone who lobbies the federal government to register with the Secretary of the Senate and the Clerk of the House. As of September 2005 there were 32,890 lobbyists registered. While this number represents all who have registered since 1996 and is not an indication of those who may no longer lobby, it is still an astounding number. And the Center for Responsive Politics (opensecrets.org) reported the number of lobbyists in May 2011 alone is 10,458. Thanks to the likes of "superlobbyist" and convicted felon Jack Abramoff, who brought us the corruption scandal of 2006, the public perception of lobbyists is at an all-time low. Abramoff, a well-connected lobbyist in Washington, DC, was convicted of defrauding several Native American tribes of tens of millions of dollars on issues regarding casinos and gaming and corruption of federal officials by trading expensive gifts, meals, and sports tours. But public perception of lobbyists was never high. It appears the term was coined in the early 1800s but its origin is not clear. Some say it refers to the lobby of the Willard Hotel in Washington, DC, that became the meeting place for legislators and those who sought to influence them. The scene that comes to mind involves portly gentlemen with big cigars and snifters of alcohol. Despite the origin, it is a practice as ancient as government itself, and lobbying involves more than a dinner with the rich and famous.

Interestingly, everyone lobbies—for to lobby is to advocate a view, to make a case, and to try to influence. Groups and organizations use more organized and sophisticated techniques to make their petitions to affect legislation than individuals would to block construction of an office building or the closing of a neighborhood library. To be sure, the Washington, DC, and state capitol lobbyists are usually well-connected, influential people who use their contacts—usually through previous employment as a public servant—to gain entrée for their clients and friends. The American League of Lobbyists describes its major components as follows:

> Its principal elements include researching and analyzing legislation or regulatory proposals; monitoring and reporting on developments; attending congressional or regulatory hearings; working with coalitions interested in the same issues; and then educating not only government officials but also employees and corporate officers as to the implications of various changes. What most lay people regard as lobbying—the actual communication with government officials—represents the smallest portion of a lobbyist's time; a far greater proportion is devoted to the other aspects of preparation, information gathering, and communication.*

ENGAGING ETHICS

Lobbying as a Family Affair

In its perennial act of trying to reform itself, the U.S. Congress is attempting to adopt a new ethics package for each chamber—the House of Representatives and the Senate. The Senate enacted its ethics package in early January 2006. It includes an amendment that bans spouses from lobbying the Senate "unless they were registered to lobby for at least one year before their husband or wife was elected." While this ban is specific to the Senate, it has to be approved by the House because it is part of a larger legislative action.

1. Do you think the wife, husband, or partner of a Senator should be allowed to lobby? Why or why not?
2. What about the other relatives of a Senator? Should any officer of the public—legislator or executive of government—be allowed to lobby?

*American League of Lobbyists, P O Box 30005, Alexandria, VA 22310, 703.960.3011 alldc.org@erols.com

Like most practices of influence and communication, lobbyists have a code of ethics by which they are to conduct themselves and their work on behalf of clients. The Code of the American League of Lobbyists, approved by the board of the American League of Lobbyists in 2000, can be found in the Appendix.

INVESTOR RELATIONS

The corporate takeovers and mergers of the 1980s through early 2000 marked the beginning of a new working relationship between CEOs and strategic PR practitioners who specialize in investor relations. Investor relations (IR) PR professionals became more crucial to the stability of these companies, because they were dealing with the international financial news media, communicating with company investors to explain cicumstances, staying within the government requirements and limits for disclosure, and providing information to employees whose jobs and lives were affected by these distant yet ubiquitous circumstances. The IR practice has three very straightforward objectives: to persuade potential shareholders to buy company stock, to encourage shareholders to hold onto stock, and to maintain the interest of counselors, analysts, and influential media.

The growth in the stock market in the 1990s fueled another rise in the importance of investor relations, as even the novice began buying and selling stock. This increased interest in investing fueled the growth of *syndicated research*—subscription newsletters, magazines or newspapers in which analysts, not journalists, report and provide analysis and recommendations—and investor-specific journalism. The year 2000 saw the mega-billion-dollar merger when AOL announced it would merge with Time Warner, creating a huge media company representing a $120 billion investment and great expectations for its investors. Of course, the early 2000s saw corporate CEOs going to court and to jail for their improprieties. Investors grew tired and untrusting of the companies in which they had entrusted their hard-earned cash. Relationships with shareholders needed repair.

IR began as a practice when the federal government passed the Securities Act of 1933 and the Securities Exchange Act of 1934. Both acts were designed to protect investors from stock and security abuses by requiring reporting and disclosure of the value of corporate shares that are publicly traded. Unlike other corporate public relations activities, IR practice is affected by government regulations, and tactics are far less proactive. Effective IR relies on building and maintaining corporate credibility among a very distinct audience base of current and potential stockholders, investment counselors and stock market analysts, the Securities and Exchange Commission (SEC), and the financial media. The overarching goal is to sustain stable shareholders, ensuring the stability of the company and positioning it to grow. Steady investment and managed growth are the hallmark of capital enterprise.

Media relations is a major part of the IR practitioner's responsibilities. No less important than the release of corporate developments and creating media access to the CEO through news releases and interviews, is monitoring the media. Financial news and information regarding a corporation's reputation is now available on blogs, list-servs, and chat rooms, as well as traditional media. IR must know the buzz as well as what the news media are reporting, as these stories have a direct impact on the value of a company's shares. Misinformation is dangerous to a company and its shareholders, so the monitoring process must be diligent and broad, including Internet financial websites, chat rooms, and blogs.

Investment counselors and stock analysts are important financial audiences for IR. Employed by stock brokers, Wall Street analysts look at the value of stock on the market and inform that valuation with what they see as possible earnings for the company in the future. The brokerage firms use this intelligence to recommend stock to investors for buying, selling, and holding. Again, as it cannot be overstated, the IR relationship to analysts is not a proactive, aggressive one, but contact with brokers is important to the practitioners. Due diligence is particularly important in this case. Analysts oftentimes bring their own particular bias to discussions regarding a company's business plan, market sector, and external factors that could affect a company's viability. Research, anticipating tough questions, and building relationships with industry analysts is crucial to successful IR.

There are two primary products of the investor relations group—quarterly and annual reports and the annual meeting. Both require many hours of work for the investor relations team. The quartely or interim report serves as an update to investors between annual reports. Because the SEC is concerned with full disclosure of financial information of companies with publicly held stock, it scrutinizes how this information is distributed and to whom. One of a company's most important publications, the annual report, is discussed in detail in Chapter 14. The Securities Exchange Act of 1934 first required annual reports for publicly held companies and the reports have barely changed over the years with the exception of some innovative covers and size formats. Most comprise a one-way communication effort during which a company conducts a one-way communication with its shareholders and other stakeholders. Many are on company websites on the investor relations web pages and, as a result, are more accessible to shareholders and others than they have been in the past. But experts ask, why limit the Internet's use to little more than an electronic bulletin board for the traditionally bound document? They envision a future where shareholders can go to a company's annual report online for clarification or additional information on a particular point in that annual report. Currently, shareholders can submit questions to a company's investor relations department by mail, email, or telephone. However, a hyperlinked query area of an annual report facilitates stronger communication with shareholders. Investor relations through the company's website and through monitoring financial websites is growing work for IR practice. Just Google *investor relations*. You will find the web pages of thousands of companies, from Adobe to Zebra Technologies, indicating the importance of communicating with the investors of a company through the Internet.

Since companies are owned by the owners of their stock, the senior management is required to meet with the stockholders annually. This meeting is designed for shareholders to ask difficult questions to which management is obligated to provide answers. The meetings serve as a forum for the CEO to explain new developments and practices within the company that might affect the bottom line. IR staff sends "proxy statements" to the shareholders in advance, explaining issues upon which they may be required to vote during the meeting. For young companies, the investor "road show," where top executives travel the globe making presentations to potential investors, has become a burgeoning field. This is not only an opportunity for companies to put their best foot forward, but warrants a serious review of a company's business plan. Among a host of other things, analysts and potential investors will want to know how the company intends to build its market share, protect its intellectual property, and adjust to market conditions, including such factors as exit strategies and product refinement.

CRISIS MANAGEMENT AND COMMUNICATION

Crisis communication is not the explicit domain of the corporate sector. Indeed, all types of organizations in all sectors experience crises, and all organizations should be prepared to meet and respond to crisis situations. For the purposes of this chapter, we will discuss only business crisis preparation. Handling crises in other sectors will be discussed later. Crisis planning requires two very important tools—the crisis management plan and the crisis communication plan. The *crisis management plan* is concerned with how the organization will navigate and negotiate the crisis and its repercussions to minimize loss of financial and human resources. The *crisis communication plan* delineates how the company will communicate with its primary audiences such as employees, customers, investors, the media, the community and government agencies, and the news media during the various stages of the crisis. Your emphasis as a PR practitioner is the crisis communication plan.

Crises happen in all types of organizations, at various levels of severity, always at inopportune times, with varying degrees of impact. A crisis is any situation that threatens the financial stability, veracity, credibility, and/or reputation of an organization. Many practitioners would add that the crisis arises when the public is made aware of the situation by negative media attention. Sometimes the crisis becomes a negative media story because your client does not react to a crisis situation in a manner that the public views as appropriate or proper. For example, while Goldman Sachs was in the midst of being investigated by the Securities and Exchange Commission in 2010 for possibly defrauding its investors during the 2008 subprime mortgage crisis, it managed to report earnings of nearly $5 billion in the fourth quarter of 2009. Thousands of Americans were adversely affected by that crisis. To add insult to injury, Goldman, the most profitable bank on Wall Street, was rumored to be considering a $16 billion end-of-year bonus to its executives. Crises can be caused by financial misconduct and ensuing scandals or other business misconduct such as discrimination against employees or customers, and legal disputes. The Bernard Madoff investment scandal in 2009 is an example of a crisis caused by financial misconduct. Madoff swindled his nearly 5,000 investors of more than $64 billion. A crisis can be accidents, natural and manmade disasters, terrorism, and environmental catastrophes that are caused by your client or for which it is blamed. It can also be a situation where in the eyes of the media or general public your company did not react to one of the previous situations in the appropriate manner. The

BP CEO Tony Hayward answers questions from the media on an oil-stained beach on May 24, 2010 at Port Fourchon, Louisiana. Hayward said that BP was doing everything possible to clean up the massive oil spill still gushing into the Gulf of Mexico.

Photo by John Moore/Getty Images

2010 BP oil spill in the Gulf of Mexico and Toyota's 2.3 million recall of vehicles with sticking accelerator pedals are perfect examples of both.

In order to minimize the effects of a crisis, companies should have written crisis communication plans that are accessible to all of senior management and that are regularly reviewed and updated. The components of a basic crisis communication plan include the plan itself, the crisis communication team, and appropriate spokespersons. Every company is different and must prepare and rehearse for its own contingencies, but the following sections provide information upon which a comprehensive plan can be developed. The components described reflect these four basic tenets of effective crisis communication:

1. When a crisis occurs, the senior manager first made aware of the situation should contact the company CEO and public relations vice president or director.
2. The CEO is the ultimate decision maker and primary spokesperson backed by subject matter and technical experts.
3. Minimizing the effects of a crisis relies on full disclosure—tell the truth as quickly and completely as possible, including what you don't know.
4. Every action taken should seek to protect brand, integrity, reputation, and market value.

Crisis Communication Plan

The crisis communication plan is the road map for communicating in time of crisis. It should be a thorough document that begins with what a crisis is in your company. Use the plan to describe and define a crisis in your company. It is not sufficient to assume that a crisis will be obvious to everyone in the organization. To the contrary, a new or inexperienced employee may not be able to define the qualities of a crisis in your company. You must do so as clearly and broadly as possible; because nothing is obvious, you should err on the side of too much definition. Describe explicitly what crisis scenarios might look like.

Crisis Communication Team

Taking the right actions as soon as possible is critical following the onset of a crisis. The beginning stage of a crisis is not the time to begin determining who is needed to approve and implement next steps. A crisis communication team should be established long before. At the least, the team is made up of the chief executive of the company, the chief public relations officer, the senior attorney for the company, the safety officer, and the chief of security. The members of the crisis communication team and all contact information should be listed in the plan. Do not forget mobile telephone numbers, pagers, PDAs, and email addresses. In addition to assuring the team members have pagers and mobile telephones *now*, be sure they have chargers that do not require the electrical power in your building or in nearby buildings. While they may appear antiquated, car chargers are a must.

A copy of the management recall roster, that is the list of those who should be recalled to duty, should be attached and should include cellular phone numbers and beeper numbers if each team member has one (either one or the other should be issued to the primary team members at least). The plan should include a complete list of the crisis team and it should be updated periodically to be sure it is current.

This team determines what should happen immediately following a crisis event. The job of this team is to come up with a plan of action. It should also identify other executives and managers who should be contacted by the crisis communication team almost immediately. A listing of all of the organization's management and contact information is important, as you cannot guess now who may be needed later.

Appropriate Spokespersons

The person designated as the primary spokesperson representing the company should be the senior-most official who is trained and capable of making company statements and answering questions posed by the media throughout the crisis—usually the CEO. A backup to the designated spokesperson should also be identified to fill the position in the event that the primary spokesperson is unavailable. In addition to the primary spokesperson and the backup spokesperson, individuals who will serve as technical experts or advisors should be designated. These resources might include a financial expert, an engineer, a leader in the community, or anyone your company deems necessary during a specific kind of crisis. Just as crucial to designating spokespersons is identifying the people who will answer the telephone during a crisis. While some will obviously be employees of the media office or communication department, others may need to provide relief for the more seasoned employees.

The Media Center's Location

A media center should be identified that is not too close to the operations center and not too far away from the site if the crisis involves an accident such as a fire, explosion, or flood. The idea is to have a central location to which reporters can report for news conferences and briefings, receive additional written statements, and have access to telephones and the Internet.

Codified Media Policy

Following September 11, 2001, companies began to think in terms of what needs to happen to maintain continuity, yet putting in writing how to handle such matters is often overlooked. A professional public relations practice will have written the basic procedures and policies it uses under normal circumstances. These procedures and policies should form the foundation from which the crisis plan will operate. One of the worst ways to deal with the news media is to change the rules, and a crisis situation is not one during which negotiations with reporters should take place. If the company public relations director is not usually involved in interviews, a crisis is not the time to add a monitor for interviews. If reporters usually find their way to offices or plants, allow them to continue to do so. If reporters need to be escorted because of safety concerns, let that be known at the beginning of the briefing or question and answer session. Establish guidelines and stick to them.

Two Classic Corporate Crisis Cases

Public relations and crisis communication literature is replete with theories and what to do and not to do during an organizational crisis. Suggested readings are provided at the end of this chapter. Meanwhile, the field has several corporate classic

BRIEF CASE STUDY

Two Classic Crisis Cases That Still Teach Us Lessons

Johnson & Johnson

During the fall of 1982 seven people in the Chicago area died from poisoning as a result of taking Tylenol Extra-Strength capsules laced with cyanide. Suddenly, Johnson & Johnson was in the position of explaining why one of America's leading painkillers and most trusted products was killing consumers. With more than one hundred million users and a 37 percent market share, Tylenol was the leading OTC drug in the United States. In the wake of this crisis, Johnson & Johnson did quite a few right things:

- Chairman of the Board James Burke formed a seven-member strategy team to determine how to protect consumers and how to save the product.
- Alerted consumers immediately to stop taking any Tylenol product until the company had determined the extent of the tampering.
- Withdrew the product from the shelves in Chicago and ultimately nationally, again indicating concern for the consumer.
- Established a 1-800 hotline for consumers to call concerning safety of Tylenol.
- Established a toll-free line for news organizations to call and receive pretaped daily messages with updated statements about the crisis.
- Instituted live television feed via satellite to allow national press conferences.
- Burke appeared on *60 Minutes* and the *Donahue Show*.

Johnson & Johnson completely recovered from the Tylenol crisis, returning Tylenol to the status of a highly trusted OTC product. In the process, Johnson & Johnson pioneered "tamper-resistant" packaging that consumers have come to expect as the industry standard.

Exxon Valdez

The Exxon Valdez oil tanker entered the pristine waters of the Prince William Sound, on its way toward California on March 24, 1989. The tanker ran aground of the Bligh Reef and began spilling almost 250,000 barrels of oil into the water. As details unfolded, the public became aware that the third mate of the ship was at the helm. He was not certified to have taken the ship into those waters and apparently, the captain and other members of the crew were under the influence of alcohol at the moment of impact.

Exxon's reaction to the spill was poor in two ways: The existing procedures for containing the spill were woefully ineffective, and the Exxon chairman, Lawrence Rawl, refused to talk to the news media. Within two days, the spillage covered 12 square miles. Rawl continued to refuse news media interviews and Exxon's Shipping Director, Frank Iarossi, finally flew to Valdez to hold a news conference. His assurances and depiction of the circumstances were contradicted by journalists and fishermen on the scene. The mayor of Valdez eventually made a statement of disappointment in the Exxon response.

When Rawl finally met the news media, he was unable to discuss the current cleanup plans, as he had not read them, and blamed the media for the crisis situation. The cost to the environment was immeasurable and the cleanup costs ran into billions of dollars. Exxon lost market share, falling to third, and the public came to see the company as the icon for corporate arrogance.

Working the Case

1. Compare the Exxon and Johnson & Johnson Tylenol case.
2. What could Exxon have done differently to handle its crisis more effectively? What basic crisis communication principles did Exxon ignore?

cases—Johnson & Johnson Tylenol (discussed briefly in Chapter 3), Pepsi hypodermic needles (discussed briefly in Chapter 16), Exxon Valdez, Gerber glass shards, and Firestone tires to name a few. No doubt, scholars are currently writing case studies of the 2010 BP oil spill for our future study. Classic among the success cases is Johnson & Johnson and classic among the failures is Exxon Valdez—perhaps now joined by BP. While it may be history, this history served as the basis for scholarship in crisis communication.

A Word about BP

Although BP was slow at the start of the oil spill crisis in the Gulf of Mexico, it began responding with a variety of PR tactics designed to focus on containment and cleanup of the spill and not to improving its reputation or that of the oil industry. Following the explosion of the Deepwater Horizon rig, a BP-owned well, thousands of gallons of oil began to spill into the Gulf and eventually the coastline, ruining lives and livelihoods. After faltering briefly, BP began communicating openly with the public, using hourly posts to a microsite, Facebook page, and Twitter—each created specifically for the crisis. The company set up a crisis center in Houston, flew in communication professionals from its offices around the world, and hired a PR firm. BP began taking full responsibility for the spill and recovery as indicated in the *Washington Post* full-page ad shown here. Now that the spill has been sealed the work of addressing public perception is underway.

We will get it done.
We will make this right.

The Gulf oil spill is a tragedy that never should have happened.

And while we were deeply disappointed that the recent "top kill" operation was unsuccessful, we were also prepared. The best engineers in the world are now working around the clock to contain and collect most of the leak.

As they do that, BP will continue to take full responsibility for cleaning up the spill.

We have organized the largest environmental response in this country's history. More than three million feet of boom, 30 planes and over 1,300 boats are working to protect the shoreline. When oil reaches the shore, thousands of people are ready to clean it up.

Thirty teams of specialists are combing the shore along with US Fish and Wildlife, NOAA and Louisiana Wildlife and Fisheries. If wildlife is affected, rescue stations have been set up to take care of them. Experts have been flown in from around the country. And BP has dedicated $500 million to watch over the long-term impact on marine life and shoreline.

We will honor all legitimate claims. We will continue working for as long as it takes. And our efforts will not come at any cost to taxpayers.

We understand that it is our responsibility to keep you informed. And to do everything we can so this never happens again.

We will get this done. We will make this right.

www.bp.com
www.deepwaterhorizonresponse.com

For assistance or information, please call the following 24/7 hotlines:
To report oil on the shoreline: (866) 448-5816
To report impacted wildlife: (866) 557-1401
To make spill-related claims: (800) 440-0858

bp

BP America

BP Exploration & Production Inc.

Role of CEOs in Rebuilding Trust and Credibility in Corporations

This article is excerpted from a speech by David Drobis, president and CEO emeritus, Ketchum Communication.

Early in January 2003, the Page Society was instrumental in bringing together the leaders of 19 communications organizations in the U.S. for a summit to focus on the issues of trust and credibility. Most of the discussion of that meeting focused not so much on the issue of trust, but the lack of trust among key stakeholders as a consequence of the corporate scandals that rocked the business community for much of last year. What we hoped to accomplish at that meeting was to reach consensus on actionable models that the public relations community could use to help rebuild trust and credibility in corporations.

Three fundamental issues were discussed: ethics, disclosure and trust—with specific recommendations for our corporate leadership in each area—as a result of the meeting. The first recommendation: Corporate leaders should articulate a set of ethical principles. Clearly this isn't as simple as it may appear. Ethical decisions are frequently complex decisions that fall between competing goals in deciding how you deploy corporate values and ethics. There is also the problem of distinguishing between ethical and legal considerations. The line between the two is not always clear-cut. There is also a problem when expectations are set from top to bottom and the communications of those expectations is not clear and precise.

As you might imagine, the name of Enron comes up frequently as a corporation that lost its way when it comes to ethical decision making. At Enron, it appears there was no internal transparency around the decision-making processes; that there was little room for discussion and dissent, and a general lack of honesty within the Enron corporate culture. Ethical problems, we know, generally begin internally. Too often, it is the result of a fixation on stock price, the pressure to meet quarterly earnings forecasts and the fact that executive compensation is focused on short-term profitability. When these things drive the business, it's hard to take a broad view and manage the business so that the needs of all stakeholders are addressed. Obviously, the CEO is a key player in all of this. And a key recommendation from our meeting is that CEOs need to take more responsibility for ethics and that they should be insisting that ethics become part of organizational behavior. That's the main thrust of the first recommendation. Simply writing down the standards for ethical behavior will not do the job. The standards have to become part of the culture of the organization and the mindset of every employee. There should be ethics training for all levels of management. And those who don't comply with the rules should be penalized. Although this recommendation comes from a public relations and investor relations coalition that is concerned about the public's perception of their businesses, it's really a challenge for the entire corporate leadership. If we are going to restore trust in corporate leadership, we must be able to communicate evidence of a visible, concrete and measurable commitment to ethical behavior.

The second recommendation: Corporate leaders must create a process for transparency— is a little more cut-and-dried because it is backed by the force of law, in this case the new disclosure requirements resulting from legislation and regulation coming from our Securities and Exchange Commission. And, of course, there are some gray areas here. While most people at the summit believe greater transparency will build trust, a number had concerns. How much transparency is required? "You can't let all the competitive secrets out," as one participant said. It was also pointed out that transparency is not the same in every case. These are issues that are going to have to be worked out over time. The bottom line here, though, is that disclosure is here to stay. You can't turn back the clock. Indeed, the bar for transparency will probably rise with new regulations. Furthermore, the public is becoming used to seamless information because information access is getting easier and easier.

So how do you get out in front of the movement towards more transparency? You do it by creating a process that defines a transparency policy for the environment you're operating in and that identifies what you need to fix. The process should include a governance committee for oversight and a "culture audit" that would ask stakeholders, starting with employees, what they think about your actions and behaviors as they relate to transparency. Although I think CEOs understand the need for transparency better than most, all corporate leaders have to be involved in this process. The important thing is that management realizes the value of transparency—and the rewards. Transparency and disclosure can be a critical factor in building trust and credibility.

And finally on the issue of trust: Corporate leadership should make trust and ethics a board-level corporate governance issue. CEOs need to demonstrate their involvement in championing ethical behavior. But there must also be some level of board buy-in. And beyond that, there must be willingness by everybody to put organizational interests above personal interests. We believe that trust brings a lot of benefits to an organization. For one thing, it improves your ability to affect change. Being trusted means there will be less resistance to change from stakeholders of all types. Another trust outcome is increased brand and reputation value since trust can create goodwill and stakeholder approval. Still other outcomes are greater employee and customer satisfaction and loyalty, increased productivity, a better alignment between business and social objectives and fewer adversarial relationships.

SOURCE: David Drobis, CEO Emeritus, Ketchum Communication, Ketchum Communication 205 North Michigan Ave 34, Chicago, IL 60601-5927

Summary and Review

Corporations Today
- In the wake of the corporate scandals of the late '90s and early 21st century and with revenues that dwarf those of some nations, corporations are trying to reconnect with consumers who have become very skeptical of them, their leaders, and their motives.
- Companies are finding that public relations is important to both their product marketing and to reengineering their credibility.
- There are many public relations audiences for business and industry, and of course, the audiences depend on the organization. Strategic public relations can be performed in many practice areas for corporations, including internal, community, business-to-business, government and public affairs, and investor relations.

Corporate Public Relations Evolution
- Corporate public relations is practiced within company departments of communication and public relations and within PR agencies that have public relations practices representing corporate clients.
- There are four levels at which practitioners perform in corporations—entry, mid, mid-senior, and senior levels with varying position titles.

The Role of Consumerism
- The age of consumerism made corporations pay attention to the manner in which they treated customers. Consumer advocates such as Ralph Nader fought for safe and competitive products.

- Today, the government and consumer advocacy groups assist in protecting the rights of consumers.
- PR agencies saw a growth in reputation management for corporations following the corporate scandals of early 2000.

Philanthropy and Corporate Social Responsibility

- In an effort to assist the communities in which they live and to build and maintain their relationships with consumers, businesses engage in corporate philanthropy.
- Two ways that companies demonstrate corporate goodwill and commitment beyond the bottom line of profits are corporate social responsibility and corporate philanthropy.
- Most companies decide what portions of their income they would like to spend for social good and decide what causes or charities they want to serve.
- A company's reputation as a good citizen in the community and among its consumers is crucial to sustained business and growth.
- Studies show that consumers look for companies to exhibit commitment to employees and communities; to provide quality products; and show evidence of responsibility to the environment.
- Cause-related marketing, supporting a charity or social cause to market products and services, is one tool used by companies to demonstrate social concern.
- Studies show that consumers purchase one brand over another because they know "that it supports a cause they believe in."

Community Relations

- Corporations realize that a company needs the goodwill of the community (local government, community organizations, faith-based organizations, schools and universities, and other businesses) in order to succeed.
- Community relations means participating in and supporting community activities and providing opportunities such as open houses, community development, and revitalization initiatives.
- Companies should take an in-depth look at their communities and make strategic decisions about how they will participate with the community.

Internal Communication

- A company's internal audiences are just as crucial as their external audiences. The employees of a corporation are essentially the best ambassadors and sales force.
- Employees should be studied like any other audience of a company. Understanding employee concerns and preferences is important to communicating effectively internally.
- Many companies communicate with employees through intranet and others include video and film into the employee communication mix.

Business-to Business Public Relations

- Many businesses have other businesses as clients and key audiences.
- Practitioners who specialize in this area of the practice are in high demand by agencies, as they have usually spent some years in the business world and know how businesses communicate with each other.
- While strategies may differ with business audiences, the familiar PR tactics are often used in effective communication among business audiences.

Government Relations and Public Affairs

- Large corporations engage in partnership building, political action coalitions, communication and education campaigns, and government relations activities that are often the purview of the PR practitioner.
- Also, because many types of businesses are regulated by government and because businesses want to be abreast of legislation that affects them, PR practitioners maintain relationships with government employees, including staff of members of Congress and the many government agencies that regulate business.
- PR practitioners who work in government relations and public affairs usually have experience in government service.
- Affecting legislation has two major objectives: to increase a legislator's or legislative committee's awareness of and favorable attitude toward the company and its position in the marketplace; and to sway favorable votes on a bill.
- Lobbying means to advocate a view, to make a case, and to try to influence.
- The activities of a lobbyist are many and varied and require critical thinking, analysis, and strategy.
- Lobbyists must be registered with the Secretary of the Senate and the Clerk of the House and operate under a code of ethics.

Investor Relations

- The investor relations (IR) practice has three very straightforward objectives: to persuade potential shareholders to buy company stock, to encourage shareholders to hold onto stock, and to maintain the interest of counselors, analysts, and influential media.
- Effective IR relies on building and maintaining corporate credibility among a very distinct audience base of current and potential stockholders, investment counselors and stock market analysts, the Securities and Exchange Commission (SEC), and the financial media.
- The primary goal of IR is to sustain stable shareholders.
- Media relations, quarterly and annual reports, and company annual meetings are the products of the IR practice.

Crisis Management and Communication

- A crisis is any situation that threatens the financial stability, veracity, credibility, and/or reputation of an organization.
- Communication for companies in crisis situations requires detailed preliminary planning.
- Crisis planning requires two very important tools—the crisis management plan and the crisis communication plan. The PR practitioner is primarily concerned with the communication plan.
- Companies must have management and communication plans in place that are reviewed and updated regularly to ensure readiness for unforeseen situations.
- Among other details, the crisis communication plan delineates the members of the crisis communication team, roles and responsibilities, procedure for communicating within the team, and protocol for dealing with the media.

Key Terms

corporate social responsibility	integrated marketing communication	marketing communication

Questions for Review and Discussion

1. Why have consumers become more wary of corporations around the world?

2. Define a crisis that could take place at your university. List the key target audiences its office of public relations would have to address.

3. What are the key components of a crisis communication plan?

4. Why has corporate social responsibility become more important to companies?

5. How might the roles of government relations practitioners and lobbyists differ?

Web Links

Reuters
www.reuters.com

The Center for Responsive Politics
www.opensecrets.org

CNN Money
www.money.cnn.com

Dow Jones
www.dj.com

Market Watch (a *Wall Street Journal* site)
www.marketwatch.com/

Merrill Lynch
www.ml.com

MorganStanley SmithBarney
www.smithbarney.com

MSN Money
www.moneycentral.msn.com

Nasdaq
www.nasdaq.com

National Investor Relations Institute
www.niri.org

THE REALITIES OF THE NONPROFIT MARKETPLACE

The nonprofit sector is one of the most challenging environments for the practice of strategic public relations. Nonprofits are held to higher standards than most organizations because of their "do good" missions. Larger and older nonprofits have budgets and resources to ensure proper public relations practice but often are big targets for criticism, while the small nonprofits suffer from a lack of resources to get the job done, as budgets are small and within the organization the comprehension of the value of communication can be even smaller.

Today's marketplace is a difficult one for the nonprofit sector, sometimes called the independent sector. First, the economic downturn of 2009 caused many businesses and individuals to give less in support of nonprofits. Unlike government or the private sector organizations, nonprofits exist to serve society or causes that help to better the quality of life for individuals and society. When the economy is bad, nonprofits suffer financially as well. Lastly, like the for-profit sector or market sector, there is enormous competition. There are products and services for almost every person who

Each time a man stands up for an ideal, or acts to improve the lot of others, or strikes out against injustice, he sends forth a tiny ripple of hope . . . and crossing each other from a million different centers of energy and daring those ripples build a current that can sweep down the mightiest walls of oppression and resistance.

—Robert F. Kennedy,
U.S. Attorney General and Senator

needs or supports a nonprofit, from relief efforts to assist after tragedies like hurricanes, tsunamis, and civil war, to environmental issues such as global warming and sustaining forestry, from emergency preparedness for terrorism attacks, to health epidemics such as obesity and pandemic flu.

Keen Competition

Competition for the attention of already message-beleaguered audiences is fierce in a market where consumers are also selecting for themselves where and how they receive their messages. And the crowded market of social causes is teeming with fierce competitors seeking the same funding from government and private donors to do good works and serve the public good. More than the for-profit sector, the nonprofit sector needs to be strategic in its public relations efforts because it is not enough to be passionate. One person's passion is another's yawn. Often, the nonprofit sector practitioner thinks it is effective to merely inform audiences about threats to their health and that of their families, or good nutrition, or taking care of the environment and their communities because it is important for them to know. Not so. You must talk to them about what is relevant to them and their lives if you want to be successful in reaching them and giving them something to do. Some nonprofit causes have had success with glitzy celebrities, high-profile events, and trendy causes, but in the end, good strategic public relations is the only answer to reaching key audiences most effectively.

NONPROFITS DEFINED

Nonprofit organizations are *incorporated entities that serve a public good.* They play an important role in our global society. Unlike government or the private sector organizations, nonprofits exist to serve society or causes that help to better the quality of life for individuals and society. They seek to serve the public good without the motivation of profit. Many seek to educate the public and mobilize support for social or behavioral change. While their missions are lofty, all nonprofits are not small, grassroots "do-gooders"; many are major businesses with corporate concerns. Yet, it is not always easy to identify nonprofits anymore, as many nonprofits act as consultants winning huge contracts to provide government services. Other nonprofits own for-profit arms of their organizations, while many for-profits organizations run nonprofits.

You may be a member of or a volunteer for a nonprofit such as a sorority or fraternity or an organization such as Amnesty International, Habitat for Humanity, National Public Radio, People for the Ethical Treatment of Animals (PETA), or Young Democrats (or Republicans) of America. Essentially, a nonprofit organization is one that does not make a profit.

In **for-profit organizations,** *the goal is to make a profit on products and services sold and pay it to those who own the company.* A nonprofit organization, on the other hand, does not, and legally cannot, distribute revenues to its owners, board members, or founders. Instead, any excess revenues in a nonprofit are maintained in the organization and used to help keep the organization and its mission sustained. Sustainability is one of the major challenges for the nonprofit sector. The ability of an organization to develop a strategy of growth and development that enables it to continue to function indefinitely is essential yet difficult to achieve, and many nonprofits are unable to stay afloat.

According to the Independent Sector, a coalition of corporations, foundations, individuals, and private voluntary organizations that works to strengthen America's nonprofit organizations, there were 1.9 million nonprofit organizations operating in the United States in 2007. The National Center for Charitable Statistics (NCCS) estimates that almost 1.4 million are *independent sector* organizations. That is, they are public charities, private foundations, and religious congregations, and social welfare/advocacy organizations. Nearly 60 percent of them are public charities that receive the billions of dollars contributed by nine out of 10 American households. They had a reported income of $ 2.4 trillion (public charities $1.3 trillion), which amounts to more than 6 percent of the total U.S. income. The estimated number of nonprofit organizations internationally exceeds two million. Most nonprofits are small. More than 73 percent of reporting public charities have expenses less than $500,000. Less than 4 percent of reporting public charities had expenses greater than $10 million. See Table 18.1 for demographic data about U.S. nonprofits.

Table **18.1**	Quick Facts about U.S. Nonprofits, 2008
501(c)(3) Public Charities and Private Foundations	
Public charities	997,579
Private foundations	118,423
Revenues	$1.4 trillion
Total expenses	$1.3 trillion
Total assets	$2.6 trillion
501(c)(3) Private Foundations	
Private foundations	103,880
Reporting private foundations	75,478
Revenues	$61 billion
Assets	$455 billion
Other Nonprofit Organizations	
Nonprofits	453,570
Reporting nonprofits	112,471
Revenues	$250 billion
Assets	$692 billion
Giving	
Annual, from private sources	$260 billion
From individuals and households	$227.41 billion
As a % of annual income	1.9
Average, from households that itemize deductions	$3,576
Average, from households that do not itemize deductions	$551
Volunteering	
Volunteers	65 million

SOURCES: Facts and Figures from the Nonprofit Almanac 2008: Public Charities, Giving, and Volunteering; IRS Business Master Files, Exempt Organizations (2009); Giving USA Foundation (2010); NCCS Core File (2007); NCCS National Nonprofit Research Database, Special Research Version (2008).

Like the private sector, nonprofits want to manage their organizations well with effective systems, prudent financial management, and ethical practices. As well, public scrutiny is a major concern of the nonprofit sector, which has had its share of financial scandals in which CEOs pay themselves exorbitant salaries, employ their family members, abscond with funds, and generally misuse the organizations' funds. Others have been criticized for the tactics they employ and for becoming too politically involved. Congressional investigations of the nonprofit sector began after *The Washington Post* published a series of articles in May 2003 about the Nature Conservancy's business and governance practices. And in 2006, Congress began its examination of charitable and nonprofit organizations with hearings in both Houses. The Senate Finance Subcommittee on Social Security and Family Policy held a hearing on how charities meet the needs of their communities; the Senate Finance Committee held two hearings on the federal tax code and land conservation proposals for reform; and the House Ways and Means Committee held a hearing on the tax-exempt sector, including its legal history, size, scope, impact on the economy, need for Congressional and IRS oversight, and what the IRS is doing to improve compliance with the law. Senate Finance Committee 2010 requested the Internal Revenue Service begin investigations of "issue advocacy" organizations and business leagues or associations for what was described as political activity.

TYPES OF NONPROFIT ORGANIZATIONS

Organizations seeking nonprofit status in the United States must apply to and register with the Internal Revenue Service (IRS). Because nonprofit organizations do not pay taxes on revenues, they are required to file an application with the IRS to receive tax-exempt status. The nonprofit organizations that receive tax-exempt status are often referred to by their IRS tax-exempt status, 501(c)(3)s. The 501(c)(3) organizations must benefit a broad public and contributions to these organizations are tax deductible. Nonprofits such as religious institutions, private schools, hospitals, foundations, public television and radio, and service organizations such as the Salvation Army, American Red Cross, Goodwill, and YMCA/YWCA represent this category. (See Table 18.2 for more information about the 10 largest charities ranked by revenue.)

Other nonprofits exist to benefit their membership and Congress does not consider contributions to these organizations to be tax deductible. Institutions in this 501(c)(4) category include those with whom members are affiliated or have an affinity, such as the National Rifle Association, MoveOn.org, the Civil Liberties Union, and the AARP.

Categories of Nonprofit Organizations

The Independent Sector delineates the following eight major categories of 501(c)(3) charitable organizations:

- *Arts, culture, and humanities,* such as museums, symphonies and orchestras, and community theatres; 11 percent of public charities
- *Education and research,* such as private colleges and universities, independent elementary and secondary schools, and noncommercial research institutions; 18 percent of public charities
- *Environmental and animals,* such as zoos, bird sanctuaries, wildlife organizations, and land protection groups; almost 4 percent

Table **18.2**   Ten Largest Charities Ranked by Total Revenue

Rank	Name	Website	Category	Total Income in Millions 2007	Public Support in Millions	Salary Benefits Highest-Paid Official
1	YMCA USA	ymca.net	Social Services	$6,053.3	$1,004.3	$412,788
2	Catholic Charities USA	catholiccharitiesusa.org	Social Services	3,884.7	801.0	194,082
3	Salvation Army	salvationarmyusa.org	Social Services	3,709.8	1,998.4	190,092
4	Goodwill Industries International	goodwill.org	Social Services	3,168.4	490.4	342,484
5	American Red Cross	redcross.org	Social Services	3,155.3	606.3	684,615
6	Boys and Girls Clubs of America	bgca.org	Youth	1,501.6	697.1	557,013
7	Habitat for Humanity International	habitat.org	Social Services	1,426.2	700.6	249,231
8	Easter Seals	easterseals.com	Health	1,183.5	176.9	654,800
9	American Cancer Society	cancer.org	Health	1,151.4	1,039.3	616,136
10	Food for the Poor	foodforthepoor.org	Relief Development	1,034.9	1,016.6	301,200

SOURCE: Forbes.com

- *Health services,* such as hospitals, public clinics, and nursing facilities; 13 percent of public charities
- *Human services,* such as housing and shelter, organizers of sport and recreation programs, and youth programs; 35 percent of public charities
- *International and foreign affairs,* such as overseas relief and development assistance; almost 2 percent of public charities
- *Public and societal benefit,* such as private and community foundations, civil rights organizations, civic, social, and fraternal organizations; 12 percent
- *Religion,* such as houses of worship and their related auxiliary services; 6 percent

The professional and trade associations with which you are most familiar, such as the National Medical Association, the American Bar Association, the Association of Association Executives, and the American Association of Automobile Manufacturers make up the lion's share of the membership associations with which the public is aware. These 501(c)(4) organizations are tax exempt, but contributions to their causes are not tax deductible.

THE ROLE OF PUBLIC RELATIONS IN THE NONPROFIT SECTOR

While many small nonprofits cannot afford staff dedicated to public relations or any form of communication, large nonprofits have public relations departments and often engage public relations agencies to develop and implement campaigns. Small nonprofits make up a large part of the sector, providing services at local community and grassroots levels. The executive director of these organizations often serves as the primary spokesperson and also performs the public relations functions and acts as development or advancement directors, raising funds for the organizations.

Historically, it has been difficult for small and medium-sized nonprofit organizations to find funding or resources to support the public relations role. As a result, building the capacity to maintain a vigorous PR program is almost nonexistent and the nonprofits, their causes, and the people they serve suffer from a lack of strategic public relations assistance. Other organizations, such as the American University School of Communication Institute for Strategic Communication for Nonprofits and coalitions such as the Independent Sector, SPIN Network, and Communications Consortium Media Center, seek to assist nonprofits with resources and training in public relations. A few foundations attempt to increase communication capacity for their grantees by providing resources through their existing grants or supporting training programs.

The Surdna Foundation provides grants to support strategic communication training for its grantees, while the California Wellness Foundation (TCWF) uses its own communication department to promote and to gain media coverage for its grantees. CWF has awarded 6,213 grants totaling almost $780 million since its inception in 1991 and is one of California's largest foundations, making about $50 million in grants each year.

The roles and responsibilities of public relations practitioners in the nonprofit sector are similar to those of practitioners in the corporate sector. Both sectors seek to promote their products and services while establishing and sustaining mutually beneficial relationships, interacting with their key audiences, and maintaining a positive public image. But the nonprofit sector's challenges are greater. Although some nonprofits hire core staff, much of the nonprofit sector is dependent upon volunteers to help them accomplish their missions.

When professional communicators are hired, either full-time or part-time, tactics tend to dominate the practice, as there is often an emphasis and passion for getting out the information. These circumstances make it difficult for the nonprofit sector to accomplish its communication objectives. Nonprofits also have two key audiences that are not found in many of the other sectors: volunteers and benefactors. The care and feeding of volunteers is an art in and of itself, as good volunteers are to be treasured and maintaining a committed cadre is important to the work of most nonprofits. While those who contribute to nonprofit organizations can be seen as investors, their motives, and therefore the messages required to reach them, are quite different.

Nonprofit Sector Practice

PR practitioners work for membership organizations and in all of the eight categories of nonprofit institutions mentioned previously as employees or outside counsel. As a PR practitioner in a nonprofit, you serve a management role in assisting organizations in accomplishing their goals, missions, and objectives. Like practitioners in the other sectors, you seek to guide management in the best strategies for making policy decisions and taking actions that affect external audiences. You employ the same strategies and tactics found in the other sectors, but often with the oversight of a board of directors whose primary concerns are external audiences that make up the organization's volunteer and financial base. In other words, you are always concerned with voluntary and charitable giving efforts.

As with other entities, you must develop and maintain effective communication with your audiences in order to promote, gain, and sustain support for the organization's mission, and maintain beneficial relationships, and in nonprofits you must also enhance fundraising. The key audiences for PR in nonprofit organizations include the population the organization serves such as patients and families, social welfare recipients, and students and parents; external audiences that affect the environment in which the nonprofit operates such as policy makers and regulators; internal audiences such as employees and volunteers; and the audiences that provide financial contributions such as government (grants and contracts), and benefactors such as foundations and individuals. Again, your PR activities in the nonprofit sector differ depending upon the size, resources, and sophistication of the nonprofit organization. See Table 18.3 for several familiar nonprofit campaigns and symbols.

Membership Organizations

Membership organizations allow groups of people with similar interests and goals to benefit from the advantages of a network and from the strength of numbers. There are several types of membership organizations, the most common of which are professional, trade, business, and union. Professional associations represent lawyers, physicians, teachers, and many others. The Conference of Mayors represents local executives while the National Governors Conference is an association of the country's state executives. Some public relations professionals join associations such as the Public Relations Society of America (PRSA) and the International Association of Business Communicators (IABC). Membership association executives and staff have their own association, the American Society of Association Executives.

Members of associations join forces to increase the benefits to the whole field, trade, or industry and the benefits often include education and training and legislative action. The American Veterinary Medical Association (AVMA) mission is twofold—to improve animal and human health and to advance the veterinary medical profession. Interestingly, the association lists public relations as one of the benefits of membership—supporting "activities and projects to improve relationships between the veterinary profession and the public and educat[ing] the public on the diverse and important role of veterinarians in animal and human health and safety." The number and kinds of benefits vary depending upon the mission of the organization. Some member associations have very broad reasons for existing while others have quite a limited raison d'être.

The sheer numbers of members can make associations very powerful forces to be reckoned with when government legislation, regulation, or policy lies in the balance. For example, AARP (formerly the American Association of Retired Persons) represents Americans 50 years of age and older. AARP boasts a membership base

Table 18.3   Familiar Nonprofit Campaigns and Symbols

Farm Aid

Organization: Farm Aid
Year of launch: 1985
Symbol: Tractor
PR firm: Vanguard Communications
Cause: Family farms
Money raised: $37 million
Description: Concert venue changes each year

Heart Truth

Organization: National Heart, Lung, and Blood Institute
Year of launch: 2002
Symbol: Red dress
PR firm: Ogilvy PR
Cause: Women and heart disease
Money raised: Millions in corporate in-kind donations
Description: Partners with New York Fashion Week

Susan G. Komen Race for the Cure®

Organization: Susan G. Komen for the Cure®
Year of launch: 1983
Symbol: Pink ribbon
PR firm: In-house
Cause: Breast cancer
Money raised: $1.4 billion as of March 31, 2010
Description: Races occur in more than 100 cities year-round

Livestrong

Organization: Lance Armstrong Foundation
Year of launch: 2004
Symbol: Yellow wristband
PR firm: SS&K
Cause: Cancer
Money raised: $325 million
Description: Nike-developed campaign

LIVESTRONG®

of 39 million in 2009. The *Washington Post* estimates it is "10 times the size of the National Rifle Association's (membership)" and its $1 billion budget is more than five times that of the U.S. Chamber of Commerce, the country's biggest business association. "In number of members," the *Post* reported, "AARP is surpassed only by the Roman Catholic Church." Opensecrets.org estimates that AARP expenditures for legislation and research in 2009 were more than $58 million. As a result, AARP was an active player in the healthcare reform debate in 2009 and has been a formidable foe in legislative actions to restructure Social Security and an exuberant advocate for medical drug benefits for Medicare/Medicaid recipients.

The image and reputation of union organizations have suffered greatly in the United States during recent decades. Historically, unions were respected for their work in advocating for safe workplaces and decent pay for the average worker. Today, they are often viewed as rigid and dishonest, owing to the scandals and disputes that have characterized their recent history.

The primary target audiences for membership associations can vary as much as the missions that drive them and the benefits they offer. But often the primary audience is the members themselves. Like AARP, practitioners in other membership organizations publish electronic and hard-copy newspapers, journals, newsletters, and magazines to reach members.

Arts, Culture, and Humanities Organizations

Most arts, culture, and humanities nonprofit organizations are local entities, operating on a community or metropolitan area basis. Their primary concern is to keep arts, cultural, and humanities activities alive and vibrant in the community while making them accessible to all members of the community. They are usually heavily involved in fundraising in order to secure the capital needed to maintain an arts and cultural presence. While public relations and fundraising are intricately intertwined in all nonprofit organizations, the local level requires more PR involvement to help secure financial success.

In addition to fundraising activities, public relations practitioners in these organizations are often very involved in media relations and special events efforts. While most of these organizations seek new audiences, they often serve those who are already participating in the arts and cultural experiences. Partnership development is an important public relations function for these agencies.

The Arts and Education Council is a nonprofit organization that raises funds from the private sector to support the arts and arts education activities in the St. Louis metropolitan area. The council has raised more than 2 million dollars a year—$100 million total, in support of arts and arts education organizations in its 45-year history, an astronomical amount given the competition for arts funding. Such funding resources are not the norm for most small nonprofits; most struggle to stay afloat as the arts and humanities are the primary targets of downsizing and government budget cutting.

Education and Research Organizations

You seldom think of public schools as nonprofits, but they are. Public schools are a challenging environment for the practice of public relations. Issues such as the revolving door of school superintendents, mayors threatening to take over school districts, parental concerns regarding student safety, underfunding and bond issues; curriculum, standards and standardized testing, and teacher credentials and pay keep practitioners busy. Because public schools hold a unique position in the community, they have audiences that reach well beyond the typical day-to-day operations of the schools. Local businesses are concerned with the quality of education in the public schools because many draw their workforce from the public school systems and an entire town can take pride in the sports accomplishments of a single secondary school. Public schools also serve as meeting places for the community and partners for other nonprofit efforts such as anti-drug and anti-violence programs, sources for troops of Girl Scouts of America and Boy Scouts of America, and many other extra-curricular activities.

The quality of American public education is hotly debated and many school districts find they must explain decisions and policies that the public may view as integral to increasing or decreasing educational excellence. The public relations professional is called upon to assist management in developing strategy and messages to communicate with the public schools and their audiences. As with all schools, public and private alike, many audiences overlap, increasing the need to practice strategically and understand these audiences. Teachers, staff, parents, and administrators may be alumni, and parents and board members may be former teacher union representatives or hold positions such as teachers' aides.

As with public schools, we rarely think of colleges, universities, and private schools as nonprofit organizations but, indeed, they comprise almost 18 percent of the United States public charities. The audience segments for these organizations are many and varied. Depending upon their size and scope of services, audiences include consumers, that is, parents and students; faculty and staff; alumni; clients, including government and other educational institutions; research funding sources; accrediting organizations and regulatory agencies; and donors. The group that represents PR practitioners in colleges and universities is the Council for Advancement and Support of Education.

Environmental and Animal Causes

Advocacy to protect and preserve the environment and animal safety gained increased public attention in the early 1970s with the first proclamation of international Earth Day, celebrating life on earth and bringing the message of conservation and protection of our air and water to the average citizen. Nonprofit organizations such as Greenpeace International (founded in 1971) and Earthtrust in Hawaii (founded in the late 1970s) and the Nature Conservancy (founded in 1951) are among the oldest. They have created campaigns and on-the-ground initiatives in support of the earth and wildlife, from the oil flames of Kuwait to the Puget Sound, from the rhinos in Africa and Asia to dolphins and puppies in the North Pacific, and from birds and tigers to the trees and habitats in which they live. Formerly a hard sell for most Americans, concern for the earth and animals has reached new heights with the release of documentaries such as Al Gore's *An Inconvenient Truth* and feature films that highlight the dangers the earth and its inhabitants face in the wake of global warming. In 2006, the United States acknowledged the effects of global warming on polar bears in the Arctic areas and proposed listing the cold-weather mammal as a threatened species. This was a major accomplishment for the communicators who have fought to tell this story to a resistant crowd of legislators and

BRIEF CASE STUDY

Dartmouth College

In 2006 Dartmouth College began a capital campaign that would be seen as ambitious in anyone's eyes—$1.3 billion. By all accounts, it would not have been possible a few years before. But Dartmouth set out to improve its communication efforts domestically and internationally beginning with a strategic plan that involved collaboration across the campus. The collaboration was infused by a campuswide communication committee of all the schools' PR staff and a recognition that all of the marketing areas—admissions, fundraising, and alumni relations—had to work together. The school installed satellite technology so that faculty could appear on national and international television without leaving the remote New Hampshire campus. Media tracking was accomplished with a real system that tracked numbers and content. The school maintained alumni relations through interactive webcasts and electronic newsletters. Media relations highlighted students as well. *The Christian Science Monitor* accompanied a group of students to Biloxi, Mississippi, to cover their relief assistance to Katrina rebuilding.

With pro bono help from the parent of an alumnus, Andy Plesser of Plesser Holland Associates, Dartmouth initiated a few efforts. The agency booked TV and radio spots in major media markets, highlighting faculty, arranged tours, and dinners with faculty and journalists and arranged media trips to the campus for events and lectures.

Working the Case

1. Who do you think were the primary target audiences for Dartmouth?
2. Why was the campuswide committee important? Why did all of the marketing areas need to work together?
3. How might the constituents of each of the marketing areas be the same and different?
4. Do you think any of the activities described above could happen on your campus? Does your campus have these and other activities? Interview your university relations officer to find out.

---

their constituents. Strategic media relations and public affairs are the most effective tools for these nonprofit organizations. Industry is often the most formidable opponent of advocacy for animals and the environment, and well-placed news stories that force legislators and their constituents to pay attention are often successful in creating debate.

Health and Human Services

The delivery of health and human services represents the largest component of the independent sector with 13 percent and 35 percent, respectively. Health services agencies such as public health clinics and hospitals deliver crucial medical care and social services to patients, provide health information to patients and the community, conduct research and prevention programs, and assist communities in emergency preparedness. Hospitals are seldom seen as nonprofits because the rising costs of hospital care and services are often in the public discourse. Yet, even with stories of $5-a-pill aspirin and $20,000 heart attack treatments and charges and collections to the uninsured, many hospitals lose money while seeking to assist underserved communities in rural and urban areas. Some hospitals are supported by taxes, while others are nonprofit or for-profit institutions. Hospitals have marketed directly to consumers for decades primarily through advertising. But just advertising is not enough, as research indicates that patients have strong preferences for the hospitals or medical centers they choose. This indicates a need for public relations efforts that speak to audiences beyond the hospital's offerings and that build and maintain brand, and PR work for hospitals is growing.

The health sector has two tools that help differentiate public relations practice in this area of the sector: 1) health marketing and communication and 2) social marketing. Unfortunately, none of the practitioners of health marketing and communication or social marketing would like to be identified with public relations, as they see themselves as behavior change social scientists but many PR agencies conduct campaigns for nonprofits promoting health.

Health marketing and communication *integrates consumer marketing research with public health science, theory, and research to create consumer-based and science-based communication strategies to protect and promote health and healthy behavior.* The Centers for Disease Control and Prevention is one of the federal government agencies that adheres to the strictest of principles as outlined. Its campaigns are developed by PR agencies.

Social marketing *is the application of consumer marketing principles to social issues to accomplish social change.* It seeks to promote social change through campaigns that encourage individual behavior change and/or to encourage public action that results in policy change. Both approaches have been very successful in encouraging and sustaining social change throughout the world. A few of the more well-known campaigns are listed here and can be researched through the websites listed at the end of this chapter:

- Don't Call Me Street Kid
- Five-a-Day
- Heart Truth
- Once-a-Year for Life
- Team Nutrition
- Tobacco-Free Kids
- VERB . . . It's What You Do

Other types of organizations that make up this segment of the sector include those whose missions are to bring attention to and to eliminate illnesses through advocacy, research, and prevention. These groups usually have large national outreach and include the American Diabetes Association, American Cancer Society, American Heart Association, and the Muscular Dystrophy Association. Others are very small such as the Aplastic Anemia & MDS International Foundation, owing to the lack of public awareness of the devastation of the diseases.

In line with the enormity of the human services sector is its complexity; organizations in this particular sector are as varied in size and scope as the Salvation Army and Meals on Wheels. They meet every imaginable human need in communities around the world and often support smaller charities such as soup kitchens and thrift stores. Partnership development and volunteer relations play a very important role in the PR strategies of these types of organizations.

International and Foreign Affairs

International and foreign affairs nonprofits represent the fastest growing segment in the sector. They are engaged in relief efforts and initiatives to assist the economies of developing nations. Agencies like the Inter-American Development Bank, working in economic and social development efforts in Latin America and the Caribbean, and the World Bank, active in 100 countries, are integral to the successful creation and sustainability of business and improvement of living conditions for the poor in developing nations. These agencies require strategic media relations strategies to explain their important roles in society and to have their work understood.

Public and Societal Benefit

Organizations like the Anti-Defamation League (ADL), American Civil Liberties Union (ACLU), and the National Association for the Advancement of Colored People (NAACP) provide legal, human, and civil rights assistance and advocate for legislation and policy to protect these rights. While defending the rights of citizens is seen as the job of government, nonprofits such as ADL, ACLU, and the NAACP sometimes defend citizens' rights that are perceived as threatened *by* government authority. Organizations such as these depend heavily on fundraising, as their services are expensive and client base expansive.

FUNDRAISING

Fundraising *relies on public relations to increase awareness of the mission and goals of the organization among donor audiences.* PR takes a lead role in delivering the message to donors, potential donors, and other key audiences. This area is similar to that of investor relations in the corporate world where the annual meeting and annual report are important to the practice. PR professionals in the nonprofit sector often support fundraising efforts through writing and producing collateral material, including the annual report, and by creating and implementing fundraising events. Success of fundraising efforts depends on a strategic approach to PR, as the image presented in the fundraising materials must be in sync with the overall brand of the organization. It's critically important that the manner in which the fundraising is conducted be in line with the values of the organization and the highest ethical standards.

When you think of fundraising, you probably think of the highly publicized donations that make national news such as Warren Buffett's gift of the major portion of his life's fortune—$40 billion dollars—to the Bill and Melinda Gates Foundation. Or the gifts of celebrities such as Oprah Winfrey and the late Paul Newman and his wife, Joanne Woodward. But fundraising in nonprofits involves much more modest gifts from those who believe in the cause or mission of an organization and give amounts from $50 to $50,000.

Fundraising has become more sophisticated as competition for funding has increased, and practitioners are often involved in any number of grant or proposal writing initiatives. Sources of funding include individuals, corporations, government, and foundations. In 2009 individual Americans gave more than $303 billion, down 3.6 percent from more than $303 billion in 2008, reflecting the effects of the economic downturn.

Corporations give to nonprofits in a variety of ways and usually expect a return on investment such as publicity for the company and to gain and maintain consumer trust and credibility. (See an in-depth discussion on corporate giving in Chapter 17.) Federal, state, and local government fund projects for the particular services provided by the nonprofit, or to conduct projects and programs the government wants to achieve such as studies and public awareness campaigns. Foundations provide grants for many reasons including research studies, program or project implementation, and communication initiatives.

Ongoing Fundraising and Special Initiatives

Nonprofit fundraising usually falls into two categories—ongoing and special projects fundraising. Ongoing fundraising is usually annual, often known as the annual campaign. The annual fundraiser is cyclical and usually takes place at the same time each year. This fundraising appeals to the base or core group of donors and represents the basis of the nonprofit's annual income. For instance, you are probably familiar with PBS fundraising activities that interrupt its programming each year to make appeals for support. The current listeners and viewers represent its base. Special initiatives are capital campaigns, special events, and planned giving. Capital campaigns are designed to fund specific projects such as increasing the size of an endowment, financing new building projects, or funding a particular research project. Special events are opportunities to connect or reconnect with key audiences. While they do not raise a great deal of funds for institutions, they do provide occasions for donors of like mind to meet and to keep the nonprofit's mission in the mind of its donors. Lastly, planned giving allows a donor to bequeath a gift at her death or to begin to confer the gift during her lifetime.

Fundraising Ethics

Strict ethics guide fundraising, as they do the public relations profession as a whole. Demonstrative of these values and guidelines are the codes established by the Association of Fundraising Professionals (AFP) as written in 1964 and amended in 2007 (see Figure 18.1).

ENGAGING ETHICS

Fallout from 9/11

Americans pledged or gave a record $1 billion for the families and victims of the events of September 11, 2001. The American Red Cross was one of the organizations collecting funds and came under harsh criticism from the news media and questioning by donors when reports indicated that only $200 million of the $529 million raised by a special fund of the Red Cross was allocated for direct emergency services and direct payments to victims' families. The organization was criticized also for TV ads featuring smoldering images of the World Trade Center with Hollywood celebrities encouraging audiences to give. Misuse of funds and hype during a crisis such as disaster relief are two pitfalls for nonprofit organizations. Are either of the examples cited above unethical? Why? What might have been the dilemma for Red Cross executives?

AFP Code of Ethical Principles and Standards

ETHICAL PRINCIPLES • Adopted 1964; amended Sept. 2007

The Association of Fundraising Professionals (AFP) exists to foster the development and growth of fundraising professionals and the profession, to promote high ethical behavior in the fundraising profession and to preserve and enhance philanthropy and volunteerism. Members of AFP are motivated by an inner drive to improve the quality of life through the causes they serve. They serve the ideal of philanthropy, are committed to the preservation and enhancement of volunteerism; and hold stewardship of these concepts as the overriding direction of their professional life. They recognize their responsibility to ensure that needed resources are vigorously and ethically sought and that the intent of the donor is honestly fulfilled. To these ends, AFP members, both individual and business, embrace certain values that they strive to uphold in performing their responsibilities for generating philanthropic support. AFP business members strive to promote and protect the work and mission of their client organizations.

AFP members both individual and business aspire to:

- practice their profession with integrity, honesty, truthfulness and adherence to the absolute obligation to safeguard the public trust
- act according to the highest goals and visions of their organizations, professions, clients and consciences
- put philanthropic mission above personal gain;
- inspire others through their own sense of dedication and high purpose
- improve their professional knowledge and skills, so that their performance will better serve others
- demonstrate concern for the interests and well-being of individuals affected by their actions
- value the privacy, freedom of choice and interests of all those affected by their actions
- foster cultural diversity and pluralistic values and treat all people with dignity and respect
- affirm, through personal giving, a commitment to philanthropy and its role in society
- adhere to the spirit as well as the letter of all applicable laws and regulations
- advocate within their organizations adherence to all applicable laws and regulations
- avoid even the appearance of any criminal offense or professional misconduct
- bring credit to the fundraising profession by their public demeanor
- encourage colleagues to embrace and practice these ethical principles and standards
- be aware of the codes of ethics promulgated by other professional organizations that serve philanthropy

ETHICAL STANDARDS

Furthermore, while striving to act according to the above values, AFP members, both individual and business, agree to abide (and to ensure, to the best of their ability, that all members of their staff abide) by the AFP standards. Violation of the standards may subject the member to disciplinary sanctions, including expulsion, as provided in the AFP Ethics Enforcement Procedures.

MEMBER OBLIGATIONS

1. Members shall not engage in activities that harm the members' organizations, clients or profession.
2. Members shall not engage in activities that conflict with their fiduciary, ethical and legal obligations to their organizations, clients or profession.
3. Members shall effectively disclose all potential and actual conflicts of interest; such disclosure does not preclude or imply ethical impropriety.
4. Members shall not exploit any relationship with a donor, prospect, volunteer, client or employee for the benefit of the members or the members' organizations.
5. Members shall comply with all applicable local, state, provincial and federal civil and criminal laws.
6. Members recognize their individual boundaries of competence and are forthcoming and truthful about their professional experience and qualifications and will represent their achievements accurately and without exaggeration.
7. Members shall present and supply products and/or services honestly and without misrepresentation and will clearly identify the details of those products, such as availability of the products and/or services and other factors that may affect the suitability of the products and/or services for donors, clients or nonprofit organizations.
8. Members shall establish the nature and purpose of any contractual relationship at the outset and will be responsive and available to organizations and their employing organizations before, during and after any sale of materials and/or services. Members will comply with all fair and reasonable obligations created by the contract.

9. Members shall refrain from knowingly infringing the intellectual property rights of other parties at all times. Members shall address and rectify any inadvertent infringement that may occur.
10. Members shall protect the confidentiality of all privileged information relating to the provider/client relationships.
11. Members shall refrain from any activity designed to disparage competitors untruthfully.

SOLICITATION AND USE OF PHILANTHROPIC FUNDS

12. Members shall take care to ensure that all solicitation and communication materials are accurate and correctly reflect their organizations' mission and use of solicited funds.
13. Members shall take care to ensure that donors receive informed, accurate and ethical advice about the value and tax implications of contributions.
14. Members shall take care to ensure that contributions are used in accordance with donors' intentions.
15. Members shall take care to ensure proper stewardship of all revenue sources, including timely reports on the use and management of such funds.
16. Members shall obtain explicit consent by donors before altering the conditions of financial transactions.

PRESENTATION OF INFORMATION

17. Members shall not disclose privileged or confidential information to unauthorized parties.
18. Members shall adhere to the principle that all donor and prospect information created by, or on behalf of, an organization or a client is the property of that organization or client and shall not be transferred or utilized except on behalf of that organization or client.
19. Members shall give donors and clients the opportunity to have their names removed from lists that are sold to, rented to or exchanged with other organizations.
20. Members shall, when stating fundraising results, use accurate and consistent accounting methods that conform to the appropriate guidelines adopted by the American Institute of Certified Public Accountants (AICPA)* for the type of organization involved. (* In countries outside of the United States, comparable authority should be utilized.)

COMPENSATION AND CONTRACTS

21. Members shall not accept compensation or enter into a contract that is based on a percentage of contributions; nor shall members accept finder's fees or contingent fees. Business members must refrain from receiving compensation from third parties derived from products or services for a client without disclosing that third-party compensation to the client (for example, volume rebates from vendors to business members).
22. Members may accept performance-based compensation, such as bonuses, provided such bonuses are in accord with prevailing practices within the members' own organizations and are not based on a percentage of contributions.
23. Members shall neither offer nor accept payments or special considerations for the purpose of influencing the selection of products or services.
24. Members shall not pay finder's fees, commissions or percentage compensation based on contributions, and shall take care to discourage their organizations from making such payments.
25. Any member receiving funds on behalf of a donor or client must meet the legal requirements for the disbursement of those funds. Any interest or income earned on the funds should be fully disclosed.

10/07

Figure 18.1
Association of Fundraising Professionals (AFP) Code

SOURCE: Association of Fundraising Professionals, www.afpnet.org/

Fundraising is affected by the many variables that affect the nonprofit sector. When the economy is good and when a nonprofit can demonstrate its value to the community, fundraising has greater opportunities than during poor economic times and periods of poor or no reputation. When budgets allow, the raising of money—strategy and tactics—for a nonprofit is best left to development or advancement professionals who have the experience and skills. These professionals can be hired to design and implement effective fundraising programs.

7 RULES FOR SUCCEEDING IN PUBLIC RELATIONS

PROFESSIONAL POINT OF VIEW

Emily Tynes was communication director for the American Civil Liberties Union when she delivered this address to the American University School of Communication Institute for Strategic Communication for Nonprofits.

- Innovate.
- Educate your colleagues.
- Study the media.
- Raise money.
- Raise your professional profile.

I know what you're up against. You have the skills, the job, and the drive—but your organization has fundraising problems and expects you to use media to solve them; or to work miracles without a budget. Or you're the only communication person in your organization—and the boss doesn't think communication is important. Or a competing organization makes national news and suddenly you're under attack; or the key players won't take the time to do interviews. There are lots of frustrated strategists out there. To succeed, you have to prepare for the long haul.

Here are some golden rules to get you there, and keep you going:

First, money matters. Some new nonprofit communication professionals make the mistake of not asking to see the organization's budget. They're so glad to have a job they don't even find out whether or not they're going to have the resources to get the job done. To quote Julia Roberts in one of her great cinematic moments: "Big mistake. Huge!" An organization's budget will quickly tell you whether or not communication is a priority.

Second, don't go it alone. If there's not enough support inside your organization, seek outside support. At the Communications Consortium Media Center, the organization I co-founded to promote and provide strategic communication for nonprofits, Kathy Bonk and I ran a "therapy group" for women in communication. We met over wine once a month with the press secretaries and communication directors of women's organizations to share our problems and get advice. We would leave re-charged for the next challenge.

Third, innovate. You've got to keep up. And you can't afford to be arrogant about who you learn from. Recently, while interviewing a young job applicant, I realized that there were whole worlds I knew nothing about. She talked about using text messaging to bridge the technological divide in communities of color. Many people who don't have access to computers may own beepers or cell phones. You don't have to be a technology expert to realize this kind of innovation, but you do have to understand how to apply appropriate technologies as they continue to emerge and create opportunities.

Fourth, educate your colleagues. Talk to them. Explain how you and others have made things happen. Give them some training in strategic communications. You may have to swallow your pride and bring somebody in from outside, to say what you've been saying all along. The better they understand what's involved, the easier your work becomes.

Fifth, study the media. Study all the media, not just the Times and NPR. And don't dismiss the impact of popular culture on your issues. TV, movies and teen magazines can be very important when you're trying to reach specific audiences. You don't have to watch everything, but you should be aware of what's out there. I work with a lot of people who look down on commercial television. At the ACLU we deal with serious, tough issues, but I know that when the organization is mentioned in a new movie, or an episode of *The West Wing*, we reach a people that we might not otherwise.

Sixth, raise money. If you are trying to influence public policy in your work but find it hard to influence the decision makers in your own organization, focus on how you can raise money for the organization. If you're successful they will listen to you. I speak from experience. Early in my career I didn't get the connection. I was making $25,000 a year and felt like I had no power. Yet I had an account that billed $200,000 to $250,000 a month and I had good ideas. So I had something that would make people listen. But I didn't realize it, so I was afraid to open my mouth.

You also have to think strategically about how you can use money to achieve your communications goal. A development director at NARAL taught me this. After I had run a successful earned media campaign that included a particularly positive magazine article, instead of congratulating me the development director said, "Why didn't you tell me about that magazine article? I could have raised $100,000 off that article!"

Seventh, raise your profile in the profession. A demonstrated ability to raise funds for your projects also makes you more marketable, more valuable to other organizations. You are attractive to future employers not just because of your craft, but because you can affect the bottom line.

SOURCE: Emily Tynes, Communications Director, ACLU, 19th Floor, 125 Broad Street, NY, NY 10004

Summary and Review

The Realities of the Nonprofit Marketplace

- The nonprofit sector operates in a highly competitive marketplace where it must be heard above the cacophony of communication messages directed at its target audiences.
- Nonprofit organizations exist to serve society or specific causes that better the quality of life and serve the public good.
- There is a proliferation of nonprofit organizations with 1.9 million operating in the United States and more than two million internationally.

Nonprofits Defined

- Your roles and responsibilities as a public relations practitioner in the nonprofit sector are much like that of the corporate sector. But the nonprofit sector has two key audiences that are rarely found in business—volunteers and benefactors.
- The challenges for PR in nonprofit organizations include a lack of adequate resources and sustaining the work of the organization and thereby its PR activities.
- Unlike government or the private sector organizations, nonprofits exist to serve society or causes that help to better the quality of life for individuals and society.
- Nonprofits are closely scrutinized because of their purpose in society and because most receive public financial support.

Types of Nonprofit Organizations

- Most nonprofits are tax exempt with the permission of the Internal Revenue Service.
- Nonprofit organizations fall into the major eight categories within the sector—arts, culture, and humanities; education and research; environmental and animal causes; health services; human services; international and foreign affairs; public and societal; and religion.

The Role of Public Relations in the Nonprofit Sector

- When professional communicators are hired, either full-time or part-time, tactics tend to dominate the practice, as there is often an emphasis and passion for getting out the information.
- Like practitioners in the other sectors, your role in a nonprofit is to guide management in the best strategies for making policy decisions and taking actions that affect external audiences.
- As a PR practitioner in the nonprofit sector, you will often report to an executive director and a board of directors whose primary concerns are external audiences that make up their volunteer and financial base.
- Membership organizations are a major segment of the nonprofit sector, employing core PR staff. Professional, trade, business, and union organizations are the most common.

Fundraising

- Fundraising is one of the most important activities of a nonprofit organization and is assisted by PR efforts.
- A major role for PR in nonprofits is increasing awareness in order to increase donations.
- Usually, fundraising occurs on an ongoing basis but also during special initiatives designed to meet a particular need of the organization.
- There are professional and ethical codes of conduct for practitioners who participate in fundraising.

Key Terms

for-profit organization	health marketing and	nonprofit organizations
fundraising	communication	social marketing

Questions for Review and Discussion

1. How is the nonprofit marketplace difficult for organizations today?

2. Why has it become more difficult to identify nonprofits?

3. What criteria must a group meet to be classified as a nonprofit and who grants this classification?

4. What are the categories of nonprofit organizations as outlined by the Independent Sector coalition?

5. Why are nonprofits under greater scrutiny than they used to be? Why would Congress want to mount investigations of nonprofits?

6. Why are alumni an important constituency for colleges and universities?

Web Links

Campaign for Tobacco-Free Kids
www.tobaccofreekids.org

Fruits and Veggies: More Matters
www.5aday.com

Inter-American Development Bank
www.iadb.org

National Heart Lung and Blood Institute
www.nhlbi.nih.gov/health/hearttruth

U.S. Department of Agriculture: Food and Nutrition Service
www.fns.usda.gov

VERB
www.cdc.gov/**you**thcampaign

Politics and Government

DEMOCRATIC GOVERNMENT

It is interesting to compare democratic government and business. To be successful, both need public consent. Both need to operate openly and with integrity in order for consumers and citizens to support and tolerate business and government enterprises. That said, both business and government in the United States and abroad are currently viewed with jaundiced eyes, as their ubiquity in society, inaccessibility to the average citizen, and fiscal and moral misconduct make them suspect. Unlike the mission of industry in America, government is designed of, by, and for the people, but it is highly unlikely that the average American citizen feels that such is true. In fact, some polls indicate that the average American distrusts most of government's leaders. A February 2011 Gallup poll showed President Barak Obama's approval rating at 46 percent and his disapproval rating at 46 percent. Americans' approval rating of the job the Democrats in Congress were doing was at the lowest Gallup has measured for the party in September 2010 at 33 percent, and, Americans' views of the Republicans in Congress were not great either, with 32 percent

> *The government being the people's business, it necessarily follows that its operations should be at all times open to the public view. Publicity is therefore as essential to honest administration as freedom of speech is to representative government.*
>
> —William Jennings Bryan,
> politician

approving. In November 2010, Congressional approval rating was 17 percent, just above its all-time low of 14 percent.

If you want to work in the areas of government and politics in the United States, you will be well served by a crash course in democratic governance. It is a good idea to enroll in a basic government course because the departments and agencies of government are myriad and the ways in which the three branches operate are quite different. Chapter 17 outlines the audiences in government that are of particular concern to the practitioner in the corporate sector. In this chapter, you are concerned with government as an organization that must communicate with *its* priority audiences. It is important to understand how government—in this case democratic government—is organized and how it works.

Three Levels of Government

American democratic government operates at three major levels—federal, state, and local with executive, legislative, and judicial branches at each level. In the federal government, the **executive branch** is *composed of the Executive Office of the President and cabinet departments and agencies such as the Department of Defense, the Office of the United States Trade Representative, the Council of Economic Advisors, and many others.* The **legislative branch** *of the federal government consists of the House of Representatives and Senate, together referred to as Congress. This body makes the laws while the executive branch approves or vetoes the proposed laws. The U.S. Supreme Court, U.S. Courts of Appeals, U.S. District Courts, and U.S. Bankruptcy Courts comprise the federal* **judicial branch.** The federal courts protect and interpret the laws; they are considered the guardians of the Constitution, as their rulings ultimately protect citizens' rights. The state and local governments have complementing systems and purposes, for instance with mayors and governors serving as executives, city councils and state legislatures as the legislative bodies, and state courts as judicial.

Politics and the administration of government are completely interrelated. It is difficult to separate them because the political candidate who is elected to office begins to govern and appoints many of the top- or executive-level administrators who affect the manner in which the government functions. Plus, elected officials must present their ideas and work products to the public for approval. Politics and public relations play a strong role in how officials will present that information to the public in order to garner the most support.

THE ROLE OF PUBLIC RELATIONS IN POLITICS

As you would guess, the role of public relations is crucial to the successful operations of political organizations, candidacies, and to elected officials. If you think of politics as a process by which people and groups make decisions, then you are aware that politics takes place in all types of institutions. For the purposes of this chapter, we are discussing **politics** *as the art, science or process of getting officials elected and reelected to government.* In the American democratic process, the art and science of getting candidates elected involves communicating with registered voters. And getting the most votes on Election Day is often the result of how effectively the candidate has conducted research among the electorate, crafted and communicated effective messages, and raised funds.

Audience Research

Political communication is perhaps the most two-way, asymmetrical of all public relations practice. During campaigns and after election to office, politicians are very scientific about understanding their audiences, constantly testing the communication vehicle, message, and messenger. In fact, audience research is paramount in politics. Opposition research, overnight polling, focus groups, and image and message testing inform and measure every step and decision the candidate and her team make. But while the communication is often two-way because the politician requires feedback from the potential voters, the resulting communication is usually imbalanced, and mutual understanding is usually not the purpose or the outcome.

Today's interactive media have made it possible for the candidate and politician to communicate with voters and constituents more directly and quicker than ever before. This direct communication can result in immediate and unfiltered feedback. While the traditional news media—radio, television, magazines, and newspapers—are still important, blogs, websites, social networks like Facebook, Twitter, YouTube, and RSS feeds have helped them talk more directly to the audience and for the audience to talk back to the candidate in virtual real time.

In 2003 Howard Dean, the former governor of Massachusetts who was running for president of the United States, reinvented political fundraising and communication by utilizing the web. He reached out to young, inexperienced voters through email and an interactive campaign website through which visitors could make suggestions and donate online. Use of the web in such a varied way had not been attempted by other campaigns in such a significant fashion. His field campaign offices and organizers encouraged supporters to gather in their cities and towns using websites like MeetUp.com to find other supporters hosting events at homes and coffee shops. His message of better healthcare and an end to the Iraq War resonated in the ears of young Democrats.

These web-savvy voters sent him money, staffed his offices and supported him, and proved that the message can come from untraditional means as long as the message is on target.

The Well-Crafted Message

While communication strategists David Axelrod and David Plouffe probably would not refer to themselves as PR professionals, they would agree that a well-honed message built from well-executed audience research is a hallmark of effective PR. President Barack Obama and his political campaign team were considered by political pundits as masters at communicating a crafted message based on a clear understanding of the candidate's strengths and weaknesses and the electorate's opinions and attitudes. For example, Obama's opponents often painted him as a young, untested outsider. He analyzed that characterization and recrafted it into

Obama supporter holds up "Yes We Can" sign during President-elect Barack Obama's victory speech in Grant Park in Chicago, IL on election night November 4, 2008.

a message of newness and change. In return, the "Yes We Can" mantra empowered voters, giving them a sense of self-efficacy. His staff paid close attention to the outcomes of the 2006 midterm elections and learned. In 2006 voters ousted many local and national career politicians. They wanted new and younger leadership. By painting Obama as an outsider and using his opponents' attacks as his own weapon, he handily won possibly the most historic election in the nation's history in November 2008.

Politics and the Fundraiser

A campaign's communication team works tirelessly to receive earned media—press coverage—of their candidate. This generally occurs at an event at which the candidate will visit and probably speak or shake hands with voters. The news media cover the event and hopefully include positive press for the candidate. In essence, the campaign does not have to pay for the candidate's face to appear on television or her words to appear in print.

However, no campaign can rely on earned media alone. A candidate must control his message by paying for opportunities to reach the public, usually through campaign ads, commercials, direct mail, yard signs, t-shirts, buttons, and billboards. In order to increase name recognition, a campaign must literally inundate the electorate with the name, picture, and slogan of the candidate.

For a national campaign (and for those in larger states) this is an expensive undertaking. So from where do they get the money? According to the Federal Election Commission (FEC) the 2008 presidential campaigns for Democratic and Republican candidates combined raised a record $1.8 billion, with Obama raising more than $745 million and McCain raising $347 million. Combined spending totaled nearly $1.572 billion. Compare that to total presidential campaign and party fundraising amounts in 2004 ($1.016 billion), 2000 ($649 million), and 1996 ($478 million).

Tantamount to any political campaign, especially in the United States, is the fundraiser. On every level—local, state, and national—the fundraiser reigns because political campaigning is a very expensive venture. **Fundraisers** *allow candidates to raise the money they need to support a vast amount of media spending for these campaigns.*

Fundraisers can take many forms but they usually involve a meal and a drink served at a breakfast, luncheon, dinner, or reception. They take place year-round in Washington, DC, and are most visible throughout the country during an election cycle. But eating and drinking are not the only forms of fundraising. There are consultants who specialize in direct marketing campaigns that reach contributors through mail, telephone, email, and the web. The 2008 presidential election revolutionized the use of websites, both those owned by candidates or parties and by social networking sites like Facebook and Twitter. Databases and mailing lists help candidates reach millions of people to solicit contributions. Of course, even with reform efforts, business and industry remain major contributors to the legislators who can assist them in conducting successful business through political access.

Where Do PR Practitioners Work in Politics?

The PR practitioner involved in the political process can represent a client or a political organization. PR practitioners who represent political candidates or politicians are well-versed in the candidate's position on various issues and concerns that face the citizens of the jurisdiction the candidate seeks to represent. They must also be very familiar with the geography and demographics of the jurisdiction and be acutely aware of public opinion. For instance, a candidate for the House of Representatives must be well aware of everything that is going on in her district while a candidate for the Senate must be aware of all that happens in the entire state.

As a political communication strategist or PR practitioner in politics, you would usually serve as counsel to the candidate, providing strategy and managing implementation. Some PR practitioners provide strategy and are directly involved in the political campaign. Other PR practitioners can work in the district or local office, can work for an elected official in one of the houses of Congress, or can work for the local, state, or national political party during a campaign. Campaigns are usually a good place to gain experience if you are interested in politics and government. The primary spokesperson for a campaign is the press secretary, who usually has a cadre of volunteers and entry-level staff to help carry out the many communication needs of a campaign.

The public relations tactics for a campaign run the gamut from news releases to satellite media tours to coordinating special events to canvassing and even assisting in advance work to arrange logistics and to build crowds for a candidate's visit. Elected officials are served by public relations practitioners before and during their terms in office. Some PR practitioners work for a candidate during a campaign and then join the political staff of the elected official in government service. Others remain outside of government after a campaign but continue to advise the politician. Those who join the political staff are employees of the government but "serve at the pleasure" of the elected official. Their positions are specially designated as political public service and they are not counted among the traditional government employees. Some public relations practitioners seek federal, state, and local government service as careers and find permanent positions among the many public relations positions in the government.

POLITICAL CAMPAIGNING

Message development for news media coverage, speeches, and advertising are major components in political PR campaigning and are usually produced by agencies that specialize in politics. Politicians hire these consultants to keep abreast of public opinion and to try to determine what is important and relevant to voters. Staying on message is the mantra for any political campaign. The message—amplified by news media coverage—helps to reinforce the image of the political candidate and helps to maintain a consistent image, the gold standard of a successful campaign—win or lose. Scholars Kathleen Hall Jamieson and Karlyn Kohrs Campbell contend that campaign staff attempts to do five things to accomplish and maintain the consistent image:

> To accomplish these ends, the campaign staff attempts to: (1) control news coverage by controlling media access, setting the media's agenda, and creating credible pseudo-events; (2) blur the distinction between news and commercials in order to increase the credibility of the commercial's message; (3) exploit the linguistic categories reflecting the criteria for newsworthiness and the conventions of news presentations through which journalists view campaigns; (4) insulate the candidate from attack; and (5) enlist the help of journalists in responding to attacks.

As a public relations practitioner, you perform the role of gatekeeper when you control media access. The news media usually must come to you for news conferences, one-on-one interviews, photo opportunities, and the like. As we discussed, the news media have a powerful agenda-setting role, often affecting what the public pays

CBS/Landov

Vice presidential nominee Sarah Palin is interviewed on the CBS Evening News with Katie Couric on September 29, 2008 during a campaign stop in Ohio.

attention to and what it ignores, but your role as a PR practitioner is to seek to help set the media's agenda, attempting to get the media to cover one topic above another, while creating events and opportunities for earned media that serve their needs in terms of access, good visuals, and convenience.

For example, John McCain has long been called a friend of the media. He often complained that the journalists, though, supported the democratic candidates during the 2008 election by devoting more time to Senators Clinton and Obama, especially during the primary and during the few months before the general election. "The Liberal Media" became a common nickname for journalists among Republican voters, especially after Senator McCain announced his running mate, the governor of Alaska, Sarah Palin, in August 2008. Palin was a new face that had not been fully vetted and never scrutinized by the national media. She slowly gave a set of major news interviews, some of which did not portray her in a positive light. The media strategy for the McCain campaign turned from using the media to its advantage to demonizing the media under allegations of blatant bias. This tactic galvanized much of their base.

On the other side of the political coin, both Clinton and Obama used the media at different times to persuade the voters. Early in the primary season, the Clinton campaign invited the media to an event at a local New Hampshire coffee shop at which the senator had a discussion with a group of women about her plan for the presidency. During the discussion, the senator became emotional while answering a question about her passion for the job. Senator Clinton had gained a reputation as First Lady and as senator of being hard and independent, which often translated into masculine. Whether planned or not, her display of emotion and passion for the job debunked the myth that she was not feminine and showed that she was willing to fight for her supporters at all costs. The next day, after the clip was aired and discussed all across the country on the nightly news shows, Senator Clinton won the New Hampshire primary, starting a long back-and-forth battle between her and Senator Obama.

The ability to make a commercial look like the news currently being reported is an advertising production art. While rarely a PR function, public relations helps guide the creative efforts. Understanding newsworthiness (see Chapter 14 for an in-depth discussion of newsworthiness) is fundamental to knowing how to work with the news media, including getting journalists to act as buffers for attacks by reporting the *other side* of the issue.

While most people think of national campaigns during which the president is elected when they think of political campaigning, congressional races are opportunities to watch political campaigning and tactics at their best. One of the most interesting case studies in political messaging and tactics is the 1994 midterm elections during which the Republican candidates promised to enter into a *contract* with America if they were elected to office. While viewed by most serious scholars as a political ploy—and often called one of the biggest bits of "political polemic" in American history—the *Republican Contract with America* was the result of acute study of the electorate.

Seen as a triumph for American conservatism, the contract focused on "60 percent issues," avoiding any controversy or divisive issues. Launched by Newt Gingrich six weeks prior to the election, this document outlined promises to the American people. Only two Republican candidates for Senate and the House of Representatives failed to sign the document and the Republicans retook the House of Representatives for the first time in 40 years, delivering a critical political blow to Bill Clinton's White House and an almost mortal wound to the Democratic Party.

Americans, Morals, and Values

Chapter 9 discusses the theories of persuasion that explain why messages that appeal to values work. You can see the effective use of that kind of appeal in political campaigns. American values were the Republican theme in 2004, the election year in which the Democrats continued to lose miserably in both the presidential and Congressional races. Again, Republicans had a message that resonated with voters. And, real or imagined, voters said they reelected George Bush and returned Republicans to power in the Congress based on values. The voters said this was their vote for *moral values* in America and, not surprisingly, the Republicans had hammered the Democrats on moral values or the lack thereof.

Karl Rove, the strategist and special advisor responsible for crafting the messages and blueprint for President George W. Bush's successful gubernatorial and presidential races, understood the landscape of the national political map and the state of the Republican Party. By focusing on conservative social issues, like gay marriage, abortion, and stem cell research, the campaign rallied the conservative base, especially voters who had become apathetic and had not voted in previous elections. In any election, a candidate needs to receive 50 percent of the votes, plus one more. The 2000 presidential election split the voters almost exactly in half.

In order to prevent that in 2004, Rove crafted a message about morals and values, targeting the voters most opposed to gay marriage, stem cell research, and abortion—the staunch conservative base. Understanding that those most likely to vote in 2004 were the same people who voted in 2000 (and thus leaving the electorate split in half once again), the Republicans needed to bring an additional set of voters to the polls. Rather than target new voters, they targeted those who had not voted in many elections, but who had a strong opposition to these issues. Rove targeted and communicated brilliantly with his "plus one" voters and led President Bush to reelection.

While widely debated (and amid much finger-pointing regarding poorly framed questions), exit polls indicated more than 25 percent of voters cast ballots for moral value issues. From the strategic public relations point of view, it is clear the Republicans were in touch with what more Americans who voted wanted, and the Democrats were not. Findings from a 2004 study conducted by the Pew Research Center for the People and the Press paralleled the exit polls, "showing that moral values was a major top-tier issue for voters."

Of course, you know that audience research tries to identify what audiences really mean and feel about words and images. The Pew Center made some interesting findings about how the voters defined moral values; this research would have been invaluable as the campaign unfolded. Those who cited moral values as a major factor in their voting preference had differing interpretations of the concept. Almost half (44 percent) of those who chose moral values said the term relates to specific concerns over social issues, such as abortion and gay marriage, while almost a quarter (23 percent) associated with the candidates' personal qualities including integrity, religion, and personal values.

Turns out the 2006 midterm elections may have been the most exciting of all and a prime example of the importance of monitoring public opinion. The Democrats were mounting a fight to regain the majority in the House and Senate, and they targeted their message to an American public that was divided and sickened by the Bush

Administration's response to the city of New Orleans following Hurricane Katrina's slam to the Gulf and the war in Iraq. It could be said that "It's the war, stupid"* should have been the 2006 mantra. Most pundits believe the war and the lack of success in Iraq drove the Democrats to victory on Tuesday, November 7, 2006. They took over the House with a large majority, making Nancy Pelosi the first female speaker of the House, and also a narrow edge in the Senate, giving the Democrats full control of Congress.

As if the 2006 midterms were not enough excitement, 2007 began the onslaught of declarations for the 2008 presidential elections. By February 2007 the most diverse group of major candidates in history began to line up in earnest. The need for strategic thinking in communicating with the vast audiences resulting from this political campaign field was crucial in the outcomes of the election. One by one, candidates dropped out of the race, mostly because their message did not resonate strongly enough with the electorate. By the summer of 2008, three candidates who used the media most effectively remained: Hilary Clinton and Barack Obama for the Democrats and John McCain for the Republicans.

Midterm elections of 2010 saw a re-energized Republican Party and the emergence of something called the Tea Party. Initially, bruised by the loss of the White House in 2008, the Republicans looked unorganized (highly unusual for the Republican Party) and divided following the presidential election. But in 2010 the Republicans had a new contract with America—a 21-page legislative agenda called "Pledge America." Dozens of insurgents supported by the tea party movement were elected to the House in 2010, giving the Republicans the majority. Of course, monitoring public opinion and understanding the voters mindset during the 2010 midterms is the work for strategists as they prepare for the 2012 presidential campaign.

GOVERNMENT PUBLIC RELATIONS

The opening quote to this chapter frames the debate that plagues the practice of PR in government. On the one hand, the business of the government is the business of its citizens, and the news media expect open access in order to inform the people. On the other hand, the government maintains that some government information should remain confidential such as national security issues and ongoing criminal investigations. The government and news media have a symbiotic, if sometimes adversarial, relationship. The government wants to inform the public to the extent it wishes, and the news media need to report on the government.

Public relations is the function in government that helps to ensure that democracy remains effective and accountable to the people through effective communication. As the form of government that is of, for, and by the people, a democracy requires effective two-way communication. Once elected, the politicians must attempt to govern. Unfortunately, the ability of government to respond to the needs of citizenry has eroded as society has changed and needs have increased and diversified. Given the size and number of agencies of the federal government and their various mandates, the need for the dissemination of information to its constituencies is enormous. With 15 cabinet-level departments and hundreds of agencies and offices operating domestically and globally, the federal government has an enormous communication challenge.

---

*James Carville, one of President Bill Clinton's campaign strategists, coined the phrase, "It's the economy, stupid," during the 1992 presidential campaign to point out the recession as the main weakness of his opponent, President George H. W. Bush. It became a popular slogan that many say led to Clinton's victory.

The U.S. federal government itself has been in a conundrum for almost a century as it relates to the role of PR. President Obama and his administration promote transparency in government and are attempting to converse with the American people through interactive meetings, town hall meetings, and an expanded website. However, only time will tell if this experiment will meet the tenets of effective PR and if it will be effective. While it is the responsibility of the government to keep citizenry informed, the government does not approve of the use of publicity for government programs and executives.

In fact, Congress passed laws in 1913 and 1919 prohibiting the use of appropriated funds to pay "a publicity expert" except in the cases where that is the specific reason for the appropriation. The 1919 law forbade the use of appropriation for the purpose of persuading a member of Congress. By the early 1970s, the legislative prohibitions were more explicit, including a statement that no appropriated funds may be used "for publicity or propaganda purposes, for the preparation, distribution, or use of any kit, pamphlet, booklet, publication, radio, television, or film presentation designed to support or defeat legislation pending before Congress, except for the presentation to Congress itself."

Following the scandals of 2005 during which political commentators were paid by the Bush administration to make positive statements and write positive op-eds on the administration's initiatives, Congress called for Government Office of Accountability (GAO) rulings on the practice. In 2006 a GAO study indicated that the executive branch of the federal government spent at least $1.6 billion in communication contracts, including 54 contracts with PR firms worth $197 million.

Public Relations, Public Affairs, or Public Information

A rose by any other name . . . In the 1980s the government insisted that the term *public information*, describing the PR function, be changed to *public affairs*. The Government Printing Office (GPO) is the preferred printer for all government materials so that the publications can be closely monitored. Public relations practitioners

ENGAGING ETHICS

Pay for Play?

In 2005 the Department of Education (ED) hired television commentator Armstrong Williams to promote the No Child Left Behind Act. Williams received $241,000 from the department, through Ketchum Communication. Columnist Doug Bandow resigned for accepting as much as $2,000 from lobbyist Jack Abramoff for each favorable op-ed he wrote about one of the lobbyist's clients. Also that year, two other syndicated columnists, Maggie Gallagher and Michael McManus, were found to have received money to promote Bush administration initiatives without disclosing the funding.

The PRSA code of ethics includes provisions for disclosure, conflict of interests, and enhancing the profession. What are they and why are they germane?

DON WILLIAMSON/Newscom

Armstrong Williams, TV and radio talk-show host and columnist

in the federal sector are now called public affairs officers or specialists except in the legislative branch, where they are called press secretaries. PR professionals are employed in all of the branches of government, including the judicial branches and at all levels of government—local, state, and federal. Most state PR practitioners are referred to as public information specialists, or PIOs. The jobs and responsibilities of government practitioners cover a myriad of areas, and their positions span the pay scale, from assistant secretary, which is equivalent to a senior VP, to lower government services grades.

Despite its penchant for eschewing the term, in fact, the government conducts many public relations activities, ranging from news releases to public service announcements to full-fledged campaigns. PR practitioners in the government are responsible for many of the same tasks undertaken by their counterparts in the for-profit and nonprofit sectors. They run comprehensive news bureaus from which they conduct media relations activities, including writing and disseminating news releases and communicating with reporters. Others write speeches for their agency principals or coordinate, write and disseminate publications, while some provide public relations counsel. They provide crisis management, internal communication, and intergovernmental communication.

On Capitol Hill

One of the best examples of the use of PR in government can be found in the U.S. Congress. Members of the House of Representatives serve two-year terms, and members of the Senate serve six-year terms. As mentioned earlier, campaigns are expensive, and a hotly contested race can last for nearly a year. That means a member of the House must essentially consider her reelection campaign almost from the moment she is sworn into office. And because the member of Congress must be in Washington for the majority of the week, she cannot campaign effectively in person in the same way a candidate living in the district or state would. Her best weapon is demonstrating all of the great things her votes or her legislation will do for residents of the home district. A congressperson's office communicates with the voters back home by writing letters and sending photos from Washington, DC, to individuals, sending flags flown over the Capitol to folks like veterans and Boy Scouts, and by sending a colorful newsletter filled with information about the goings-on in Congress to registered voters.

Communicating with constituents by mail would be very expensive, if not for the franking privilege. The **franking privilege** *allows members of Congress (and some other elected officials, like the president) to mail official business without postage, but instead with a frank, or the member's signature, in the area where a stamp would normally be located.* The member's unofficial PR team—the chief of staff, communication director, press secretary, and any senior staff—would craft the message and layout of the mailings, representing their boss in the most positive and effective light, hopefully leading to reelection and positive poll numbers.

Federal Departments and Agencies

The departments, agencies, bureaus, and commissions that make up the executive branch have PR functions as well. Obviously, cabinet-level departments change leadership with the changes in executive administration. As a result, public relations initiatives reflect agenda of the new leadership. The U.S. Department of Transportation (DOT) launched a multiyear PR initiative in 2004 to remind Americans of how important the country's modes of transportation are to "their lives and wallets." Interestingly, these efforts began under the tutelage of a new head of public affairs who believed in a "one department, one message" policy.

As a result of the policy, the public affairs heads of all of DOT's agencies participated in daily news briefings, helping to coordinate the department's media relations. The stated goal was "to enhance the public's understanding, knowledge, and appreciation of transportation's role in supporting the economy and moving people and products safely." Among the activities was a partnership with ExxonMobil to promote the nation's scenic roads and a Transportation Services Index (TSI), a statistic designed to measure the economic strength based on transportation support such as trucks on the highway.

The extent to which this message resonated with American travelers as gas and oil prices rose to unprecedented levels from 2006 to 2008 is unclear. However, the Obama Administration targeted transportation as one of the focal points of the 2009 stimulus package. Time will tell how this PR plan will affect the Department of Transportation's goals.

The National Space and Aeronautics Administration, known to the world as NASA, arguably has the most nimble public affairs staff in government. The practitioners responsible for announcing, postponing, and announcing again the scheduled and rescheduled space launches must have agility, knowledge of highly complex technical information, and nerves of steel. One example is a series of several unscheduled news conferences between August 26 and 27, 2006, during an attempt to launch a mission to deliver new solar panels to the International Space Station. The launch, scheduled for late afternoon of August 27, was delayed 24 hours because lightning struck the Cape Canaveral launch pad on August 25. Continuing poor weather conditions—rainstorms and a hurricane developing in the Caribbean—continued to make the exact launch date and time unpredictable. Primarily, the weather prevented the engineers from identifying damage and repair needs to the shuttle and launch pad. Suddenly, the path of the tropical storm Ernesto forced NASA to remove the shuttle—STS-115—from the launch pad, further delaying the launch. Four press conferences and three delays later, the shuttle launch preparation had to begin all over again.

Most states and large cities have governmental affairs offices that work to maintain relationships with the various federal government departments that impact their jurisdictions. City governments often depend on their states and the federal government to assist them with major projects so they must know who to contact and how to work with the various governmental systems. The mayor's office and city council can work together to solve some of a city's problems, but adequate funding often depends on seeking assistance from other levels of government for strong appropriations for necessary projects and programs.

Often the government takes advantage of research findings that indicate a public relations effort is needed. For example, a 2006 study released by the Global Attitudes Project and the Pew Research Center found that favorable opinions of the United States in many countries had declined during the previous year. In an effort to improve its image and foster cultural diplomacy, the U.S. State Department created a partnership in 2006 with the Kennedy Center, the American Film Institute, the National Endowment for the Arts, the National Endowment for the Humanities, and others. The Global Cultural Initiative is designed to educate Americans and other nations about other cultures.

Outside PR Firms

While the government has its internal PR workforce, it contracts with PR agencies to conduct communication and public relations on its behalf, also. Outside contractors receive multiyear contracts to provide consultation and guidance in developing long-term strategic communication planning, design, and implementation. The services include formative research, message and creative strategy development and testing, implementation and dissemination planning, materials development, implementation and dissemination, process and outcome evaluation, electronic and web-based strategies, graphic design, and project management. In addition to these tasks, contractors develop complete PR campaigns for local, state and federal government agencies. Heart Truth's Red Dress campaign and the successful Centers for Communicative Disease and Prevention (CDC) VERB campaign were developed by Ogilvy PR.

The largest federal department with the biggest budget is the Department of Defense. It spends more than $305 billion recruiting and maintaining the country's armed forces. "Army Strong" is the tagline for the U.S. Army's recruiting program launched in 2006 with television advertising. Since Congress mandated a volunteer

BRIEF CASE STUDY

Enjoying the Beach, Hating the Traffic

Fort Myers Beach, Florida, like many small beach towns, has one main road and bridge that allows visitors and residents to enter and exit the island. Tourism is brisk and the town has a growing number of travelers who contribute to traffic congestion—decreasing the quality of life for the visitors and year-round residents. To minimize the traffic problems, the city partnered with a local transit company to provide a park-and-ride service to reduce the number of cars on the road, traveling on and off the island. The service was underutilized because beachgoers needed cars to carry their beach gear, tourists were unaware of the service, and trolley schedules were inconsistent because the trolleys were caught in the traffic, too. During the height of tourist season, locals could not get on and off the island to get to work, school, and medical facilities, or attend to a whole host of daily activities while the trolleys they were paying for remained empty. An anti-tourism sentiment was growing in town.

Fort Myers engaged Above Water Public Relations to assist them with a campaign to increase passengers on the trolleys and reduce the number of cars. The town had the following other objectives as well:

- Gain funding to improve the trolley system and pay for the PR campaign
- Gain the support of year-round residents
- Add a traffic lane dedicated for trolley traffic

The campaign included media relations, advertising and promotion, and special events. The number of riders increased 120 percent during the four-month campaign with park-and-ride lots filling to capacity.

Working the Case

1. What primary research do you think Above Water conducted and with what audiences?
2. Are the objectives informational, behavioral, or attitudinal? Explain your response.
3. Are the objectives measurable as stated? How can they be measured?

force in 1973, PR efforts for recruitment have been very important to the Army's efforts to highlight the advantages to volunteering. Two PR agencies are handling the multiyear, multimillion dollar projects. The balance of the public relations efforts will include peer-to-peer online opportunities for prospective recruits to connect with current soldiers, sponsorship of NASCAR races and rodeos, and updating the Army website.

In the early 2000s mobile fatalities among African Americans under 15 and ages 15 to 24 prompted the automobile National Highway Traffic Safety Administration (NHTSA), an agency of the U.S. Department of Transportation (DOT), to award a five-year, $1 million contract to Miami-based Sonshine Communications. The firm targeted the African-American community with a campaign to address drunk driving and seatbelt use. The primary target audiences are 'tweens and adults driving children.

In 2006 the Centers for Medicare and Medicaid Services (CMS) selected four public relations agencies—Ketchum, Ogilvy, Porter Novelli, and Weber Shandwick— to serve for five years as its primary communicators as it began an effort to overhaul its image and outreach efforts. The Indefinite Delivery Indefinite Quantity (IDIQ) contract puts the firms in a position to compete against one another for task orders

BRIEF CASE STUDY

The Smokey Bear Campaign

Created in 1944, the Smokey Bear campaign is the longest running public service campaign in history. Smokey's first forest fire prevention message remained unchanged for 50 years until April 2001, when the Ad Council updated his message to address the increasing number of wildfires in the nation's wildlands. At age 65 in 2008, Smokey returned with a new look in a new series of ads designed to inform Americans about their role in causing wildfires. Research studies indicate that Americans believe lightning starts most wildfires. In fact, 88 percent of the fires are started by humans, and most by accident.

The new public service series gives Smokey a new look to appeal to young adults and the message includes a call to action. It calls for young adults to practice fire safety habits and to intervene when they see others act carelessly. The well-known message "Only You Can Prevent Wildfires" is joined by "Get Your Smokey On."

As one of the world's most recognizable fictional characters, Smokey's image is protected by federal law and is administered by the USDA Forest Service, the National Association of State Foresters, and the Ad Council.

Working the Case

1. Go to the Ad Council, Draftfcb, and National Association of State Foresters websites to study the new campaign.
2. Conduct a case study consisting of a short description of the situation, the research, and strategy for the campaign.

issued by CMS, a division of the Department of Health and Human Services (HHS), when work is needed. The value of the combined contracts for the work done by all of the firms is more than $300 million. Actual contracts will depend on congressional funding. CMS has focused its messages to reach Medicare beneficiaries and their caregivers; now, the agency is refocusing that message toward adult children of beneficiaries and the people who are approaching Medicare age. Previously highly focused on media relations, the agency is now concerned with developing partners at the local level. CMS has developed partnerships over the past two years with more than 50,000 local community groups, including senior service organizations, faith-based organizations with senior health ministries, and state health insurance programs, to create awareness on the local level.

NEWS MEDIA'S RELATIONSHIP TO POLITICAL AND GOVERNMENTAL PR

Though some might argue the point, the news media and government need each other. While perhaps too dependent on the news media at times, the government must communicate to the public regarding issues of public interest and it must know what the public is thinking. Similarly, the news media must have something to report, and the work of the government—local, regional, state, and national—is a major news beat for reporters. Historically, the news media have served two roles in reporting the business of government. First, the government wants to inform the people of the actions it takes on behalf of the citizenry, and the news media serve as a vehicle for such information. Second, the news media are seen as the watchdog of government, assuring that the government of the people remains accountable for its actions and is ethical and honest in its conduct of business by reporting its activities. The former is sometimes accomplished with the cooperation and consent of the government while the latter highlights the almost adversarial relationship between the two.

The agenda-setting role of the news media (see Chapters 9 and 10 for discussion) is another major concern for the news media–government relationship. Politicians and government administrators alike understand the power of the news media to get public attention, set public debate, and affect what the public thinks and talks about. This role and power of the media cannot be underestimated. Studies show that voters not only acquire information about an issue but they also learn the importance of that issue from the amount of space, position, and time allowed for it in the news. Voters' attitudes toward the issue are strongly correlated with what the news media defines as important.

Scandal and Sensationalism

The need to inform the public has made the government somewhat reliant on the news media. But what the government and the news media define as news is often very different. As our previous discussion of news values would indicate, the news media are interested in news stories that meet several criteria. The stories must have at least one of the following:

- *Timeliness:* relevance to current events or issues or relatedness to an important event that has just taken place
- *Magnitude:* the degree to which the story or issue affects a great many people, large sums of money, valued commodities, etc.

- *Impact:* the effect the story could have on the public
- *Human interest:* an appeal to readers' emotions
- *Celebrity:* the involvement of a well-known person, or of someone in the public eye, in the story
- *Proximity:* when a story hits close to the local coverage area and has relevance for people in a specific community or industry
- *Novelty:* an interesting angle that makes a story significant or unique

In the case of government, *conflict* is another important criteria. There needs to be a good guy and a bad guy or at least the suggestion of adversity. These being the criteria, the news stories that find the government in a "difficult position" such as issues of funding, abuse of authority, or downright incompetence are bound to get more coverage than the more mundane issues such as improving the highway system or opening additional government offices for processing some obscure paperwork. Of course, the government public relations machine churns out totally unuseful information that burdens the news media and often obscures the more useful and newsworthy stories coming out of government. An episode of the former television series *The West Wing* demonstrated an example of how enhancing or downplaying the spin of stories can be an intentional, strategic decision. In the "Take Out the Trash Day" episode, the press secretary releases information about several sensitive stories simultaneously during a Friday afternoon press briefing. As the character explains, not only do fewer people read the newspaper on Saturday than any other day of the week, but the newspaper will have to fit all the stories into one column, therefore reducing the probability that the news will get major play. Had the stories been released little by little throughout the week, chances are they would have received more physical coverage.

Need for Transparency Boosts PR's Import

Helen Ostrowksi was CEO of Porter Novelli and chair of the Council of PR Firms when she wrote this point of view for PRWeek.

Coverage of the Pentagon's purported placement of articles in the Iraqi press continues the dialogue which erupted earlier this year about the use of PR by both the government and other entities.

Recent stories in *The New York Times*, the *Los Angeles Times*, and other media outlets accuse the government and one of its consultant firms of paying journalists in Iraq to write articles favoring the administration's position in their country.

This coverage underscores the imperative for us, as agencies, to be clear about the role of PR in serving public and private sector clients and in furthering the public discourse that our clients engage in. It also emphasizes what is critical to the success of PR in achieving organizational objectives: transparency.

PR is designed to build relationships between an organization and its most critical audiences. As with any credible and trusted relationship, whether personal or professional, the ability to influence is based on being transparent about who you are and for what you stand. Much of what we do relies on an editorial system in which journalists need to be free to write and make editorial decisions that are not influenced by political and business interests.

In much of the recent coverage, PR is used to describe practices that we would more often associate with advertising or other forms of communications for which organizations pay to place messages. Obviously, that's misleading and requires that we not only correct these misinterpretations, but that we also reinforce our practices in ensuring the transparency that is so critical to our clients' success.

Earlier this year, the Council of PR Firms released a Statement of Principles. These tenets aren't new, but writing them was a way to codify the expected best practices in the working relations among clients, firms, and the channels of communications we tap, especially the media.

The tenets reinforce the overriding principle that openness and transparency serve the public interest and are necessary for accomplishing one's communications goals. The professionalism and objectivity of PR firms help clients engage in that discourse, as clients turn to us for counsel and assistance to pursue their organizational goals in educating or persuading audiences that matter most. To date, the Statement has been downloaded more than 6,000 times from the Council's website.

Three principles, in particular, are key to this transparency. First is the highest possible standards for ethical behavior. Second is accuracy of information. Third is disclosure.

While there may be different points of view represented, we are committed to factual accuracy. Our clients and the public are best served when audiences receiving information—and the channels that convey it, such as the media or the internet—know the source and can trust it, whether that source is a PR pro, a spokesperson associated with the organization, or a PR firm representing the client. Thus, when we engage with journalists or other organizations, we disclose whom we represent. Our bias in counseling clients is toward disclosure, which we feel is an appropriate and effective communication tool. These principles are essential for the public discourse that helps people make informed decisions in a complex world.

Along with the Statement of Principles, the Council, through its affiliation in the International Communications Consultancy Organization, the international forum for country trade associations to discuss practice guidelines, adopted the IPRA Charter on Media Transparency this year, which states: "Editorial appears as a result of the editorial judgment of the journalists involved, and not as a result of any payment in cash or in kind, or barter by a third party. Editorial which appears as a result of a payment in cash or in kind, or barter by a third party, will be clearly identified as advertising or a paid promotion."

Council members embrace our responsibilities to be the stewards of open, transparent dialogue. While the Council represents the US PR agency business, we support reliable, consistent standards around the world. The issue of transparency is of global importance as we seek to develop trusted relationships around the world.

PR, not simply through media relations, but also employee and community relations, advocacy, and reputation management, has a more vital role than ever. Let's respect the channels and work to keep them pristine.

Summary and Review

Democratic Government
- Governing in the United States gets more difficult with every passing year, as the governed grow less trusting and more cynical of those who govern.
- To perform effectively as a practitioner in government and politics, you must understand how the government works.
- American democratic government operates at three major levels—federal, state, and local—with executive, legislative, and judicial branches at each level.

The Role of Public Relations in Politics
- It is difficult to separate politics and government because the political candidate who is elected to office begins to govern and appoints many of the top- or executive-level administrators that affect the manner in which the government functions.

Conducting a multitude of surveys to measure the public's opinion, developing messages, and advertising are major components of political communication work.

Political Campaigning

- Political campaigns depend on well honed messages used in media coverage, speeches and advertising. The purpose of the message—especially when amplified by the media—is to maintain a consistent image of the candidate.
- The public relations professional is the gatekeeper to the media seeking access to the political candidate and should take advantage of that role, employing clear strategy to stay on message. As much as possible, the political campaign needs to let the media tell its story.
- Persuasion theory can be seen at work in campaigns that appeal to their audiences' moral values. Studies indicate that different voters have differing definitions of moral values.

Government Public Relations

- Government public relations takes place at all levels of government—local, state, and federal.
- With the growing responsibilities of government and the many issues it confronts, communicating with the public grows in scope and importance every year.
- PR practitioners in government perform the same kind of work found in other sectors of the practice.
- The government contracts with public relations agencies to create campaigns, but it also employs PR practitioners under the title of public affairs officer.

News Media's Relationship to Political and Governmental PR

- Communicating with the news media is another major function for the government because it relies on the news media to make the public aware of issues, events, and policies that affect them.

Key Terms

executive branch	fundraiser	legislative branch
franking privilege	judicial branch	politics

Questions for Review and Discussion

1. Compare and contrast political PR and government PR practices. How do their audiences and objectives differ?
2. What do politicians do to raise money? What are the pros and cons to politicians accepting money?
3. Compare and contrast the roles of the primary spokespersons for political campaigns and government.
4. What are the primary communication elements of a political campaign?
5. How would you describe the symbiotic relationship between the government and the news media?
6. What are some of the complications and complexities of government PR practice?
7. What laws affect the practice of public relations in the government? What are they designed to accomplish?

Web Links

American League of Lobbyists
www.alldc.org

International City/County Management Association
www.icma.org

Gallup
www.gallup.com

Federal Election Commission
www.fec.gov

MoveOn.org
www.moveon.org.

OpenSecrets.org
www.opensecrets.org

SourceWatch
www.sourcewatch.org

Contract with America
www.the contract.org

The Tea Party
www.theteaparty.net

Tea Party Patriots
Teapartypatriots.org

International Public Relations

GLOBAL AUDIENCES

American business has operated abroad for decades, so marketing, advertising, and public relations activities on behalf of corporations internationally have taken place for a long time as well. Coca-Cola opened its first bottling plants away from American soil more than 100 years ago with plants in Cuba, Canada, and the Philippines. Its first European foray was into Paris, France, in 1919. Multinational manufacturer Procter & Gamble, offering nearly 300 brands from Bounty to Tide, is located across the world with locations from Albania to Yugoslavia. And McDonald's—the largest restaurant chain in the world with operations in 100 countries—began its international operations in British Columbia in 1967. The International Red Cross and Red Crescent Movement, Greenpeace International, Amnesty International, and the U.S. Department of State Fulbright scholars program all represent contexts in which PR is practiced internationally.

Thanks to technological advances during the past two decades, the long-anticipated "global village" arrived without much fanfare on the part of the average villager, but commercial and nonprofit organizations have

When you start to think of the world as flat, a lot of things make sense in ways they did not before. . . . because what the flattening of the world means is that we are now connecting all of the knowledge centers on the planet together into a single global network, which—if politics and terrorism do not get in the way—could usher in an amazing era of prosperity and innovation.

—Thomas L. Friedman from *The World Is Flat*

vigorously participated in its arrival. The ubiquity of the Internet has made communicating across miles, oceans, and time zones much less complicated than it used to be, as both conversations and documents are exchanged easily at all times of the day. Similarly, the evolution of a 24-hour news cycle brought on by satellite publishing, cable television, and the development of all-day financial markets sustained by other communication phenomena such as social networking has resulted in a 24-hour information feeding frenzy and commerce that never sleeps. As a result, international public relations practice has grown as the world has shrunk and the global village is communicating and sharing information about everything.

PR in the International Context

The term *international public relations* is a bit limiting and can be confusing when describing the practice. Often referred to as global public relations, international PR covers almost every possible context of the practice of public relations. To practice internationally one can be involved in corporate or nonprofit, consumer or business, financial or government, politics or law, communicating with every audience imaginable. In addition, international public relations can be practiced in three different ways—the practitioner in one country can work for an organization that has presence in other countries, such as Pepsi or the Red Cross; a practitioner can work for an agency that is located in another country and has clients in the United States and in other countries, such as Burson-Marsteller and Hill and Knowlton; or a U.S. practitioner can represent the government of another country. Scholars Robert Heath and Timothy Coombs (2006) define international public relations as "simply public relations practiced between countries and cultures." That is, it is multicultural public relations practiced between countries. Regardless of the nature of the opportunity or problem, it is an exciting practice fraught with challenges and pitfalls, as practitioners seek to navigate cultures, customs, time zones, languages, images, and meaning on a global scale.

COMMUNICATING ACROSS CULTURES

Americans tend to have an ethnocentric perspective that can often be a barrier to effective communication across cultures. **Ethnocentrism** is *the tendency to view the world through the lens of one's own culture.* We think of ideas or issues, develop opinions and views, and take actions based on our own experiences. Finding the way through the streets of a global village and being a good neighbor requires knowing something about the villagers and learning to live, work, and play with them. It means using another, broader lens. It means knowing, understanding, and respecting the cultures and customs of the villagers. And guess what? They are not always congruent with ours. Students interested in an international practice should learn another language and take cross-cultural communication courses; the following discussion is designed to stimulate your thinking about differences and how those differences can affect public relations practice.

An important part of international PR is following the customs of other cultures.

Many scholars have spent years seeking to understand human culture and developing theories to explain it. For our purposes, **culture** *refers to behaviors and values within a particular society.*

It differs from a **custom,** *which is a particular practice of a group of people.* There are customs that are a part of some cultures. For instance, the practice of bowing from the waist when greeting another individual is a custom in many countries, while the value of honoring elders in some societies is cultural.

Obviously, communicating across cultures effectively involves more than understanding a language because even when the language is the same—English, Spanish, or Mandarin—the context and nuance may be different. British philosopher Bertrand Russell expressed this when he said, "Britain and America are two nations divided by a common language." While translators, even software, can help us receive written communication in many languages, it is tough—and antithetical to the strategic practice of public relations—to practice without interpersonal, two-way communication. Merely translating a phrase to another language does not always impart the meaning we intend, especially since words have different meanings even within cultures. Remember that even within the same culture, people have different experiences that shape their perceptions and the meaning they take from a message or circumstance. And you will recall from our earlier discussions in Chapter 5 that behavior, values, and perceptions are important to understanding audiences. In order to understand the complexities of communicating with audiences in other countries, it is important to understand the complexities of cross-cultural situations. Strategic practice requires that we spend a little time reviewing the work of scholars who study how culture affects communication. This is a component of understanding audiences—both nations and individuals.

Differences in How We View Time and Space

The scholarship of anthropologist Edward T. Hall (1966 and 1976) has enriched the work of communication scholars and practitioners. Hall's most well-known works help us to understand the effects of culture on communication. As you will see, it is not just the written word that affects our practices abroad. Hall's work on **proxemics**— *the human use of space within the cultural context*—helps us to understand that people within different cultures use space differently. Hall argued that humans have different perceptions of space that are shaped by cultural dynamics, and he defined three areas of human space: intimate, social, and public.

Intimate space is *the closest space around us, usually reserved for those with whom we are most personal such as closest friends and family.* **Social space** *refers to the area around us in which we are comfortable conducting our more everyday interactions with both acquaintances and strangers.* We regard **public spaces** *as places in which interaction is anonymous and not personal.* Social distance, then, is very different among cultures. Americans are often shocked by how close a colleague from France stands when we are not intimately involved. People in the United States presume a social distance is about four to seven feet while for our French colleagues the distance is more like two to three feet—much more like the distance we reserve for interaction with intimates. Unlike the French, the British, like Americans, expect a wide physical space during conversation. Japanese business people cherish their close space and do not expect strangers to be too near, while Chinese often converse while standing close.

Time and how we use it is also cultural. Hall (1976) explained it as monochronic and polychronic time. In a **monochronic time**—*one thing at a time*—culture such as the United States, things take place in a scheduled, linear fashion. The scheduling of appointments, being prompt for them,

U.S. President George W. Bush (L) walks hand-in-hand with Saudi Arabia's Crown Prince Abdullah (R) on his ranch in Crawford, Texas, April 25, 2005.

JASON REED/Reuters/Landov

and using the time in a preconstructed manner with the help of an agenda are all based on a culture that uses monochronic time. **Polychronic time** cultures are just the opposite; *members of these cultures view relationships and interactions with others as more important than schedules and appointments.* In these cultures, many things happen at one time and many people are involved in many things at one time. Polychronic time is full of interruptions, and decision making on many subjects takes place simultaneously. The manner in which we practice PR in the United States adheres to very specific time tables, as we are often dependent on the mass media, which operate on tight schedules and deadlines for many of our activities. Special events are another example; the events manager, political advance person, and producers are tied to their timelines and watches. This is not the case with the practices in some other cultures.

Punctuality and its importance vary throughout the world. It is necessary to be on time for German business and social appointments, as it is considered an insult to be just a few minutes late, and German business people expect all deadlines to be honored. Being on time is vital in England and China and being a few minutes early to ensure promptness is acceptable. While business guests are expected to be punctual in Argentina, and Argentineans expect meetings to be confirmed one week in advance, business executives can be as much as 30 minutes late and meetings can go on longer than intended. Guests are expected to rearrange subsequent appointments. Russians expect guests to be on time, but one can expect to wait as long as an hour for a Russian executive. Being on time in France is a casual affair.

Differences in How We Decipher Meaning

Hall (1976) is also helpful in assisting us in understanding that different cultures have different ways of determining meaning in a message. Previously, we discussed that the most effective communication is likely to be the most personal communication. In other words, the more a sender and receiver have in common, the more likely the success of the communication—which is understood meaning. Hall argued that there are "high-context" and "low-context" systems of communication. In **high-context communication,** *the message is beyond the spoken or written word; it is contained in the person or physical context in which it is delivered, also.* In a **low-context communication,** *the information is explicit in the word or code.* In low-context cultures such as the United States, words are very important to the message, and messages are detailed and explicit. In high-context cultures such as Asian or Arab cultures, other elements are more important and the listener is expected to provide the meaning of the messages. High-context messages sound vague to low-context audiences, and high-context audiences are often left looking for clues to provide meaning to low-context messages (Zaharna, 2001).

It appears that high-context cultures are more polychronic while low-context cultures are monochronic. Ihator (2000) argues: "in high-context societies, social and natural harmony takes precedence over strict time control in communication transaction. The future is to shape itself without human intervention." Public relations practitioners then must understand these correlations and build them into interpersonal strategies with audiences and practitioners in and from other cultures.

Message Development across Cultures

Multinational companies have been affecting business management and human resources development for decades. You can learn a great deal about developing messages from scholars who studied these companies. Geert Hofstede (1980, 1988) conducted extensive research on how employee culture affects workplace values. He studied IBM employee values data covering more than 70 countries collected between 1967 and 1973. Initially, he used data from 40 countries, later adding another 10 countries and grouping the balance into three regions—East Africa, West Africa, and Arab-speaking. Hofstede's work resulted in a comparative analysis of 53 cultures. The study results revealed that these cultures differed along four dimensions: individualism–collectivism, power distance, masculinity–femininity, and uncertainty avoidance.

Individualism–Collectivism   According to Hofstede (1991), **individualism** *"stands for a society in which the ties between individuals are loose: everyone is expected to look after himself or herself and his or her immediate family only."* On the other hand, **collectivism** *"stands for a society in which people from birth onwards are integrated into strong, cohesive in-groups which throughout people's lifetime continue to protect them in exchange for unquestioning loyalty."* Further, an individualist society acknowledges the goals, desires, and achievements of the individual while a collectivist society strives for group interests because the individual sees himself as the group.

Western countries such as the United States, Germany, Italy, Australia, and Canada are individualistic and value the work and ambition of the individual. Collectivistic countries such as Argentina, China, Japan, and Taiwan value the success of the group and expect loyalty. Collectivistic cultures seek consensus. In order to preserve harmony, all must agree. In developing public relations strategies, the practitioner should create messages that state the advantages to the group and should emphasize relationship-building tactics. In individualistic cultures, appeal to self are most effective, and messages should emphasize the benefit by stating specifically what is in it for the audience taking the action or making a change.

Power Distance   Understanding where power lies in a society is crucial to understanding how to communicate to audiences. Hofstede and Bond (1988) defined **power distance** *as "the extent to which the less powerful members of organizations and institutions (like the family) accept and expect that power is distributed unequally."* Messages that suggest women are empowered to make decisions are inappropriate in many societies.

Masculine–Feminine   The third dimension is masculinity versus femininity is important as well. In **masculine culture** *societies, men are supposed to be tough, assertive, and focused on material success while women are supposed to be more tender, modest, and concerned with the quality of life* (Hofstede, 1991). Japan, Venezuela, and Australia are high masculine cultures and are more concerned with money and economic growth. **Feminine cultures,** on the other hand, *stress that both men and women are supposed to be modest, tender, and concerned with the quality of life.* According to Andersen (1994), masculine cultures value strength, assertiveness, competitiveness, and ambitiousness, while feminine cultures value affection, compassion, nurturing, and emotion. High feminine cultures such as Sweden and the Netherlands value the environment over economic growth.

Uncertainty Avoidance   Finally, **uncertainty avoidance** *refers to the extent to which the members of a culture "feel threatened by uncertain or unknown situations"* (Hofstede, 1991). According to Ellis (1998), high uncertainty avoidance cultures try to avoid uncertainty by eliminating ambiguity, providing stability, establishing rules, believing in absolute truths, seeking consensus, and valuing the attainment of expertise. Businesspeople in countries such as France, Italy, and Argentina are very concerned with rules, regulations, and controls. For this reason, contracts in Argentina are very lengthy and detailed and every element must be agreed to and signed before negotiations are complete. In contrast, low uncertainty avoidance cultures tend to be more tolerant of uncertainty, are not threatened by deviance, are more flexible, and believe that there should be as few rules as possible. Messages for high uncertainty avoidance cultures must be low-context, and low uncertainty avoidance cultures require messages that are high in context.

The Global Alliance for Public Relations and Communication Management (see Web Links at the end of this chapter) has an interesting resource called PR Landscapes that discusses these cultural values for 16 countries. While basic cultural value orientations provide lenses through which we view our own actions, and the actions of others and can help us communicate, interpret, and evaluate appropriately with others, they are just orientations. They speak generally about *tendencies* in different cultures and help us to communicate across cultures, but we must remember that as guidelines they are not prescriptive and not all members of a culture share the general tendencies of their culture. We could safely say that most people in the United States have individualistic tendencies, but some people in our culture actually have collectivistic tendencies. Cultural dimensions do not predict the behavior of all individual members of a culture, and in order to understand individual behavior, we must study individual characteristics.

THE COMPLEXITIES OF INTERNATIONAL PRACTICE

Counseling domestic clients in implementing their programs and campaigns for audiences abroad and assisting foreign clients, including foreign governments, in their efforts to meet and to communicate effectively with U.S. audiences are the two most important roles of international or global PR. Many PR practitioners agree to assist clients in meeting their global goals without understanding completely the challenges of practicing around the world. Even large PR agencies must be concerned with being effective on a global basis. Many clients are genuinely concerned with the effectiveness of a firm's global network. While web intranets provide quick and easy access to market experts and contracts, and planning and implementation details, personal interactions are difficult. Email and telephone conversations can go only so far and maintaining team attitudes and concerns for the budgets of others across the world can wear thin.

Underestimating the complexity of providing international counsel can be dangerous. It is poor practice to assume you can just pull together a few colleagues living around the globe and become international practitioners. Very large PR firms—owned by parent companies such as Omnicom—address these concerns and avoid problems by acquiring foreign firms or opening offices abroad that work in partnership with native PR companies in other countries.

Research Is Again the Watchword

International practice, as with all strategic PR practice, begins with research. The PR practitioner's research efforts must be as thorough, if not more thorough, than that conducted for communicating with domestic audiences. It should begin with secondary research, involving an environmental scan to determine the client's existing image, reputation, or status in the view of the country's target audience.

Source credibility is important in practicing globally. The audience must know that their country is important to the organization or company operating there so that the international presence is not seen as a foreign convenience brought on by business advantages such as cheap labor, decreased production costs, and fewer environmental restrictions.

A thorough overview of PR practices in the country is crucial to understanding how to operate *in-country* or understanding how to communicate when working with public relations agencies located in the target audience country. The watch phrase is a familiar one: "Think global, act local."

When planning for strategic execution of public relations activities internationally, you must be aware of the country's infrastructure, as your success depends heavily on your awareness of the strengths and weaknesses of infrastructure to support PR programs. There are parts of the world where a web strategy or even a media relations strategy make little or no sense. Despite the ever-growing tendency toward democratic government and open market economies, mass media and media relations are not the same all over the world. You must be aware of the different media models and customs in countries where you expect to practice.

Depending upon the problem or opportunity the client is addressing, you must discover the verbal and nonverbal communication styles and cues in society and business. Government and education systems, politics, laws, and economics of each target audience country can be crucial to the success of a PR initiative, as can social structure, history, and heritage, and business practices of a given audience.

All of the audience research you conduct for domestic practice is relevant to international practice and should be conducted on primary and secondary levels. Ascertaining as much information about attitudes and behaviors relevant to the product or services, understanding the demographics, and analyzing media use are all important to success. You need to investigate and to understand the news and entertainment media, discover who the community and national leaders and influencers are, and learn the major organizations in the country. PR audiences abroad include those you find in domestic practice, depending upon the problem or opportunity and the context. In addition to the audiences you would identify domestically, the following additional audiences must be considered when operating on an international level:

1. Embassy staff and diplomats are a special audience for PR programming and planning but also for research about your target audiences, protocol in relating to the governments and organizations of other nations, and for information regarding current events, trade situations, and relations with the U.S. government or other governments with whom you may be interacting.
2. Other expatriates who work in your organization or your client's organization can be very useful in helping you understand the culture and audiences.
3. The U.S. Department of State is an important partner and resource for assisting in working with organizations abroad and assisting in navigating the social and business nuances.

While different cultures and customs affect your practice, official languages and dialects and how they are used are major concerns, also. As we previously discussed regarding language in domestic practice, mere translations and generalities do not make for effective communication. The written and spoken French of Canada, Haiti, and France can be as different from each other as the Spanish of Cuba, El Salvador, and Spain. Native speakers and writers are the best resources for communicating in other countries.

Tactically, we must decrease the incessant use of mass media or other one-way communication and stress the two-way communication we know is most effective wherever we practice. Overuse of print is especially a problem in some cultures, and sensitivity to opinion leaders and understanding group influence are of special concern.

INTERNATIONAL PUBLIC AFFAIRS: REPRESENTING OTHER GOVERNMENTS

The nations of the world spend a great deal of government time and money communicating with audiences in other countries. Sometimes they want to reach consumers who are interested in international travel or business, and therefore commerce is the driving factor. For instance, vying for the privilege of hosting the Olympic Games has become an enormous and expensive task with governments contributing millions of dollars to execute their campaigns. At other times countries want to affect the legislation and policies of other countries.

For example, the U.S. government has a long and rich history of communicating with the people of foreign countries. The United States Information Agency (USIA), a federal government agency from 1953 to 1999, broadcast and published American news to foreign audiences. According to its archived website, the USIA mission was to explain and support American foreign policy and to promote "U.S. national interests through a wide range of overseas information programs." In 1999 USIA had operations in 142 countries. In addition to the commercial broadcasting of America's broadcast giants, the U.S. government has broadcast through the Voice of America (VOA) for more than 60 years. Currently operating under the International Broadcasting Bureau (IBB), which was formed after USIA was disbanded, VOA is one of several broadcast operations supported by the U.S. government. Others are Radio Sawa, an Arab-language station offering pop music and news, and Radio and TV Marti, programming for Cuban audiences, Radio Free Europe (Eastern Europe), and Radio Liberty (the former Soviet Union). VOA alone broadcasts more than 1,000 hours every week to an international audience estimated at 115 million people in 44 languages through radio, television, and the Internet. Created in 1942, its mission is "to broadcast accurate, balanced and comprehensive news and information to an international audience," and it was created to provide unbiased and reliable news to citizens of countries where either war or policy prevented their access.

Nations abroad often seek public relations counsel to assist them in taking advantage of opportunities or solving problems in the United States. In February 2006 a national security debate ensued in the United States over the sale of a port management business with operations in six major seaports (a total of 16 American ports in all) previously owned by a UK company, P&O Ports. The sale of the port terminals to the United Arab Emirates state-owned company Dubai Ports World was approved by the Committee on Foreign Investment in the United States (**CFIUS**), an interagency committee of the United States Government (chaired by the Secretary of the Treasury) that reviews the national security implications of foreign investments in U.S. companies or operations, and the president but opposed by Congress. DP World postponed its takeover plans. At least two American public relations firms worked with DP World to try to secure deal approval. After Congress killed the purchase, DP World eventually sold P&O's American operations to American International Group. While in the midst of this debacle, the embassy of the United Arab Emirates was working with still another U.S. firm to attempt to get a free trade agreement on other issues.

Following some research and looking toward its 60th birthday, Israel began planning a campaign to rebrand itself. Research findings suggested that the Israeli-Palestinian conflict had become the country's brand. A project of Israel's prime minister and ministers of defense and foreign affairs, the campaign was to highlight the country's technological, pharmaceutical, and cultural contributions and change its image to "a land of achievement." The London-based Acanchi, known for its work in branding countries, was given the contract. Of course, many countries hire PR practitioners to promote their images abroad. Pakistan and the Philippines have hired U.S. firms to work on their reputations among U.S. audiences. It is rumored that following the attacks on the World Trade Center in New York, Saudi Arabia spent almost $15 million in less than six months with U.S. firms to publicize its work in helping to combat terrorism.

U.S. firm Weber Shandwick was engaged by Paris 2012 to help bring the 2012 Summer and Paralympic Games to Paris (London won), and by Sochi 2014 to lure the 2014 Olympic and Paralympic Winter Games to Russia. Weber Shandwick is getting a reputation for its success with this kind of international work, having assisted three other cities in securing host status: Sydney, Australia (2000 Summer Games), Turin, Italy (2006 Winter Games), and Beijing, China (2008 Summer Games).

Clearly, counseling foreign governments is not the venue for the inexperienced and unsophisticated. But some of the world's best and biggest international practices have been burned doing international work.

ENGAGING ETHICS

Citizens for a Free Kuwait

Believe it or not, the Iraqi leader Saddam Hussein was an ally of the U.S. government for nearly a decade when his troops entered the oil-rich nation Kuwait in August 1990, invading the small country and creating an international incident. To help Kuwait secure assistance from the U.S. government against Iraq, PR giant Hill and Knowlton was engaged by Citizens for a Free Kuwait, an organization of citizens concerned about the tiny nation's fate. Hill and Knowlton's media relations strategy targeted American public opinion and government, depicting Kuwait as a striving young democracy. As it turns out, Hill and Knowlton's client was not an independently funded organization but an organization that later admitted that it was almost entirely funded by the Kuwaiti government. With Hill and Knowlton's fees of almost $12 million coming from the Kuwaiti government, it seems fair to characterize it as a "front group."

As part of its public relations efforts, Hill and Knowlton arranged to have a young woman testify in a public hearing before the Congressional Human Rights Caucus in October 1990. "I saw the Iraqi soldiers come into the hospital with guns. They took the babies out of the incubators... and left the children to die on the cold floor." Her name was "Nayirah," a 15-year-old Kuwaiti young woman. American debate over how to react to Iraq's invasion was at a fever pitch and her testimony shocked the committee and the American people. Hill and Knowlton sent a camera crew to the hearing and compiled a VNR that later scored in the *Columbia Journalism Review*'s top 10 VNRs. More eyewitness atrocities were provided in testimony before the United Nations and Congress and were reported by the news media. By January 1991 the atrocities reported by the news media had escalated and U.S. bombing of Iraq began. Later and after the war, Americans learned that Nayirah was not just a hospital worker but the daughter of Kuwait's ambassador to the United States. This campaign has been called the largest foreign-funded campaign aimed at influencing American public opinion.

How do the International Public Relations Association (IPRA) and PRSA codes of ethics apply to this case?

BRIEF CASE STUDY

Why Not Bosnia?

A Bosnian soldier runs through a destroyed building while on counter sniper patrol in the Sarajevo suburb of Grbavica on Friday, June 25, 1993.

When democratically elected governments in the Republics of Slovenia and Croatia declared their independence in June 1991, the Socialist Federal Republic of Yugoslavia began breaking apart. In response, Serbia invaded both the two republics. In February 1992 Bosnia-Herzegovina, too, voted for independence. The United States extended diplomatic recognition in April and Serbia began shelling of Sarajevo. One month later, the Bosnia-Herzegovina government engaged Ruder-Finn (RF) to help it gain world attention on its plight and its plea for U.N. peacekeeping forces to enter the country and put an end to ethnic cleansing. RF already had 10 months of experience and research on the Balkans as a result of a previous engagement with the government of Croatia.

RF mounted a major media relations and public affairs campaign targeted at the U.S. Congress, Bush administration, Clinton Transition Team, ethnic groups in America, Bosnian-American leaders, selected foreign embassies in Washington, selected U.N. missions, the 15-member U.N. Security Council, and international news media.

Ruder-Finn stated that its "role during the crisis was to increase the flow of supportive information, build understanding and support among target audiences, and advise and counsel Bosnian government officials on communication strategy, messages and tactics to help end the bloodshed by energizing world public opinion and involvement."

RF designed a short-term plan to react to the immediate crisis and a long-term plan "to build strong international support for Bosnia as a victim of Serbian aggression." The plan involved four phases, running from spring 1992 through winter 1993.

The tactics RF undertook are too numerous to list here. Briefly, they pitched the story to television and cable producers to encourage them to send crews and correspondents to Sarajevo and convinced the Bosnian government to create a media communication center in Sarajevo from which satellite up-link facilities could send interviews and footage. The foreign minister spoke English fluently and was made the primary spokesperson on television talk shows and public affairs programs. "Bosnia Fax Updates"—brief summaries of events in Bosnia—were sent to the news media and 300 contacts throughout the world, and longer messages, Congressional Communiques were sent to Congress. RF arranged and conducted several emergency conferences and wrote speeches for the participants.

The results of these efforts are impressive. The Senate passed five resolutions in support of Bosnia, and Congress appropriated $50 million for Bosnia and Kosovo humanitarian aid. The Bush administration declared Serbian leaders war criminals and the newly-elected Clinton administration created a peace plan for Bosnia and lead a multinational food and medicine airdrop. The U.N. deployed 7,000 peacekeeping troops to Bosnia, passed 20 resolutions condemning Serbia, established a war crimes commission to prosecute Serbian and other war criminals while approving a no-fly zone over Bosnia and extremely tight economic sanctions against former Yugoslavia.

Working the Case

1. Using the description of Ruder-Finn's self-described role, how would you state the measurable objectives for the campaign?
2. What research do you think Ruder-Finn conducted before launching the short-term and long-term plans?
3. What additional tactics do you think Ruder-Finn used?

You can read more about this Ruder-Finn Silver-Anvil winning campaign at the Public Relations Society of America web site.

INTERNATIONAL NONPROFIT PUBLIC RELATIONS

Many international organizations other than governments and corporations employ public relations to promote their causes and deliver their services around the world. Their efforts include disaster relief assistance, international understanding and development, and foreign affairs. Their missions cover the gamut from human and women's rights to global health issues, from study abroad and cultural exchange programs to environmental protection. Agencies such as the International Red Cross, the International Olympic Committee, Amnesty International, UNICEF, countless foundations, associations, and other organizations maintain international strategic public relations planning and programs as they seek to preserve their reputations, protect their brands, and react to crises.

The March of Dimes recently took a more global view of its work and opened an office of Global Programs, initiating an international campaign to draw attention to the plight of children born with birth defects around the world. March of Dimes (MoD) has fought these health problems for decades in the United States, but recognizing that 80 percent of the estimated eight million children born with serious birth defects of genetic or partially genetic origin are in developing nations, MoD expanded its initiatives. Its first public relations initiative was to launch an international media relations campaign for publication of *March of Dimes Global Report on Birth Defects,* the first world analysis of birth defects. The 84-page report was created by a team of international experts that collected information about birth defects from 190 countries. The pitch, news release, media kit, and B-roll included graphics, and resulted in global coverage from AP, BBC World Service Radio, and the *Wall Street Journal.*

PUBLIC RELATIONS PRACTICE AROUND THE GLOBE

The practice of public relations in other countries is both interesting and informative. It is important that you know how public relations is practiced abroad and that you understand the practices and challenges practitioners face in other countries.

India

Public relations is a growing industry in India, one of the world's two biggest nations and one of its fastest growing economies. U.S. PR practitioners say that communicating in India right now is unique, for three reasons. First, unlike the United States and many other countries where the Internet and other technology have led to decreased newspaper readership, increased literacy rates in India have led to increased readership. According to *PRWeek,* "Newspapers' power varies widely across the country; among English-language titles, *The Times of India* rules in the North and West, and *The Hindu* in the South" (Sudhaman 2011).

Second, papers in Hindi and other native languages dwarf English papers' circulations across the board, meaning that all media relations programs must be multilingual, multiethnic, and tailored for specific geographies. But when it comes to high-level international business coverage, wire services like Reuters and Dow Jones are still deemed most important.

Third, corporate communication in India is moving toward a global framework rather than national. This means that Indian industry is looking for well-experienced agencies to represent them and their programs abroad, significantly raising the bar for small agencies. But, while business is booming, two market conditions affect public relations firms—India maintains its own firms rather than selling to multinationals, and it has a dearth of trained practitioners because PR education has not kept pace. However, two American PR giants—have bought presence in India. Burson Marsteller bought one of the country's biggest firms, Genesis, and Edelman purchased Roger Pereira Ltd.

BRIEF CASE STUDY

Procter & Gamble India

Procter & Gamble India had more than $68 billion in net sales for the fiscal year that ended June 30, 2006. To support the PR work of the company, its corporate practitioners, headquartered in Mumbai, work closely with Indian agencies to develop campaigns that are unique to the country. One such campaign grew out of a claim that 80 percent of the country's most beautiful women prefer P&G's Pantene hair-care products. P&G commissioned an independent survey that, in fact, confirmed the claim. Additional research discovered that Indian women believe shine is the most desirable attribute for beautiful hair. Of course, P&G's research indicated that healthy hair has the most shine and touted the ingredients of its line of Pantene shampoos with "unique Pro Vitamin B formula strengthens hair, smoothens roughness and leaves hair looking shiny from morning to night." With help from Madison PR, an independent Indian PR agency, the "Shine in the Morning" public relations campaign was launched. The Pantene Shine Meters appeared in 30 Indian cities on Pantene Mobile Vans and Pantene Shine Booths at more than 1,100 leading retail stores. Pantene healthy-hair specialists at the booths helped consumers measure the level of hair shine in their hair and recommended the right Pantene shampoo. Neha Dhupia, Miss India–Universe 2002, was one of the campaign's spokespeople. The MTV "Shine Your Soul" contest provided consumers with the opportunity to win a diamond necklace by submitting answers to the following questions: "What gives you a Shining personality": (a) Wealthy mind and Wealthy body, (b) Healthy mind and Healthy body, and (c) Stealthy mind and Stealthy body?"

Working the Case

1. Would this campaign have succeeded in the United States? Why or why not? What changes would have to be made to make it successful with U.S. audiences?
2. Are there any cultural aspects that make this campaign different from one in the United States?
3. Do you think Miss India–Universe was a good choice for a spokesperson for the campaign? Explain why?
4. Leading dermatologists were used as spokespersons as well. Explain why that choice would or would not work in the United States.
5. What do you think is the connection between diamonds and the campaign? Explain why that connection would or would not be successful in the United States.

Russia

Global corporate chiefs have been looking at Russia as a potential market for the past decade. The country has more than 140 million consumers who purchase soft drinks, buy household and personal products, and smoke cigarettes. Two events have brought the Russian market even greater attention: Russia held the presidency of the G8 summit in 2006, and created Sochi 2014—the Russian successful bid to host the 2014 Olympic and Paralympic Winter Games.

The practice of public relations is very new to Russia—less than 15 years old and in some ways reminiscent of corporate PR practice in the United States long ago. Many of the public relations duties are relegated to human resources and marketing staff. Of course, like most things Russian, PR is based on relationships, thereby reducing the opportunities for entrepreneurship or success for foreigners in the practice. Interestingly, the political climate in Russia is having an impact on political and corporate practices, as Russian corporations are growing, and former President Vladimir Putin's authoritarian leadership no longer strangles the country's freedoms.

As is true of many world capitals, English language–based newspapers in Russia are consumed by business leaders, English-speaking natives, and expatriates from major corporations around the globe. The *Moscow Times* was the first daily English-language newspaper in Russia. While it is published by Independent Media, the *Russian Journal* is an English weekly written primarily by Russians. Russian television is government owned, so competition for getting news on television is difficult at best. And, of course, Russia, like most burgeoning economies, has its share of entertainment and tabloid media. All international PR firms have offices in Russia and most multinational corporations have in-house PR staff operating there. While Moscow is the largest of the cities, there are many cities in Russia where the population exceeds one million, such as St. Petersburg, Novosibirsk, Samara, and Omsk.

According to practitioner and scholar Anya Karavanov, the practice of corporate social responsibility is beginning to take hold in Russian corporations. For years, the U.S. Agency for International Development (USAID) has assisted Russia in social welfare initiatives. Now, Russian businesses are getting involved with nonprofits in the country to help solve issues such as adoption and teenage health problems.

China

Public relations is a young industry in this, the second of the world's two largest nations. PR is about 20 years old with about 2,000 agencies employing 30,000 people. It is one of the country's top five careers. With years of experience in China, experienced international firms that served multinationals doing business there are now expanding their business models to work for Chinese businesses in China, as well. China is an excellent example of how cultures can differ within the different regions of a particular country. It is easy to see how marketers would salivate at the prospect of 1.3 billion consumers, but the communication work is certainly not easy. With so many regions and dialects in China, you need to be aware of the cross-cultural concerns discussed earlier. The public relations practices and strategies successful in Beijing and Shanghai may fail miserably in other parts of the country. Interestingly, the country is considering changing its national symbol—the dragon—to something that better depicts its country's desire for harmony and better reflects its diverse culture and geography.

U.S. companies doing business in China often find it difficult to deal with the country's media policies. Businesses still pay journalists to attend their news conferences and write about their products and services. Payment and censorship are a long-standing tradition in China, where the government owns the newspapers and censors other media.

Japan

With 127 million people, Japan has the ninth largest population in the world. Although its population is one-half that of the United States, its economy is second to the United States, and its democratic government is similar to ours. The country has a large number of public relations firms, as PR is a well-established profession and the practice exists in all of the major context areas, with U.S. firms in Japan and with Japanese firms in the United States.

With the world's highest literacy rate, in stark contrast to the United States, 99 percent of the Japanese households receive newspapers every day. Television is highly consumed in the country and 99 percent of all households have color televisions. The Internet rules as a source for news and information, as Japan has the world's greatest and least expensive access to broadband. Most of Japan's newspapers are fighting the competition by joining it and starting news websites.

As a PR practitioner, you are wise to study and understand the Japanese kisha "press" club system if you are to be successful in practicing in Japan. The kisha club system is a centuries-old tradition that helps news organizations to gain access to news from government and industry in Japan. There are hundreds—estimates up to 1,500—of these clubs that have space inside the offices of the National Diet (Japanese houses of national government), local government, local police, the Tokyo Stock Exchange, etc. Clearly the complaint of foreign media is that it is difficult to gain access to the news and the news is controlled. According to the UCLA Asia Institute, Asia Media News Daily, in order to gain membership to one of the clubs, the news organization must be a member of the Japan Newspaper Publishers and Editors Association or similar institution, be recommended by at least two existing members of the club, and pay a membership fee for each employee of the company.

ETHICAL ISSUES

Understanding the culture, politics, and media landscapes of other nations is crucial to effective communication and public relations abroad. To assume that the Western manner of doing things is the only *right* way is to not recognize that a U.S. philosophy is just that—a U.S. philosophy. It is not the philosophy of China or that of Kenya or India. You must be careful to be sensitive to other nations if you are to communicate with their populous. Similarly, as you practice globally, you must think globally about ethics. It can be very tricky because ethics can look very different in different parts of the world. You must keep abreast of international issues that may conflict with your personal and corporate ethics while ensuring that you do not insult the countries that allow you to practice as a guest. The Global Alliance for Public Relations and Communication Management has sought to create a global code of ethics for all practitioners to abide by, but there will always be media and political practices that differ from your own.

Pay-for-Coverage

One of the important issues that PR professionals in the United States and many other countries are concerned about is called journalism-for-pay. Journalists in some parts of the world expect to be paid for covering stories. In fact, many see reporting as paid advertising and expect remuneration. They view it as a business relationship. Chinese businesses actually pay journalists to attend news conferences with promises of real stories resulting only from their presence.

The International Public Relations Association (IPRA) has been active in trying to eliminate this practice. In addition to its professional code of conduct, international code of ethics, and the charter of environmental communication, IPRA has adopted the following policy regarding editorial content:

1. **Editorial.** Editorial or news appears as a result of the editorial judgment of the journalists involved, and not as a result of any payment in cash or in kind, or barter by a third party.
2. **Identification.** Editorial which appears as a result of a payment in cash or in kind, or barter by a third party will be clearly identified as advertising or a paid promotion.
3. **Solicitation.** There should be no suggestion by any journalist or members of staff of an editorial provider, that editorial can be obtained in any way other than through editorial merit.
4. **Sampling.** Third parties may provide samples or loans of products or services to journalists where it is necessary for such journalists to test, use, taste or sample the product or service in order to articulate an objective opinion about the product or service. The length of time required for sampling should be agreed in advance and all loaned products or services should be returned after sampling. All resulting published reports should state clearly that the product or service was provided for the purpose of the test.
5. **Policy statement.** Editorial providers should prepare a policy statement regarding the receipt of gifts or discounted products and services from third parties by their journalists and other staff. Journalists and other staff should be required to read and sign acceptance of the policy. The policy should be available for public inspection.*

Code of Ethics

Currently, there is not an international code of ethics for international business. Differing perceptions, cultures, and values make a universal code almost impossible. What is a bribe in one country is a gift in another and what can be seen as a threat in one culture might be only an incentive in another. The International Public Relations Association (IPRA) has adopted a code for professional conduct that has been translated into 20 languages and is based on the United Nations charter. Referred to as the Code of Athens, it was adopted in 1968. (The Code of Athens can be found in the Appendix.)

Members of IPRA subscribe to a code of ethics adopted in Venice in 1961 that covers personal and professional integrity and conduct for practitioners (also found in the Appendix).

---

*International Public Relations Association, www.ipra.org

Reaping the Benefits from International Teamwork

Josef Blumenfeld was a consultant on global PR management and founder of Tradewind Strategies when he wrote this point of view for PRWeek.

Ever since *Schoolhouse Rock* taught many of us the preamble to the Constitution, we have come to celebrate the US' freedom of the press.

As PR pros, we are acutely aware of the power and freedom of the American media. It is true that there is no other place on earth with a press that is as free, robust, rich, diverse, and independent as America's Fourth Estate. Unfortunately, this view of the press often puts the US PR pro at a marked disadvantage in the global arena. We naturally assume that all press is a free press—particularly English-language media. Even if that press is "free," it seldom has the freedoms of the US media. In effect, the filter with which Americans have been trained to view the world creates a gap between the expectations that we—and our clients and/or executives—have of the global media stage, and reality.

The best bridge over that global gap is a partner agency, office, or team in a foreign market. But working with a global team presents many challenges. I hear repeatedly that foreign agencies are not as strong as those in the US. While PR as a trade is not as mature in many markets as it is here, learning to recognize the value that our foreign counterparts bring to any global effort is a crucial element in fielding the global PR campaigns that so many of our clients/companies are now dependent upon.

How can US PR pros become better international partners? As PR pros, we are acutely aware of the power and freedom of the American media. It is true that there is no other place on earth with a press that is as free, robust, rich, diverse, and independent as America's Fourth Estate. Unfortunately, this view of the press often puts the US PR pro at a marked disadvantage in the global arena. We naturally assume that all press is a free press—particularly English-language media. Even if that press is "free," it seldom has the freedoms of the US media. In effect, the filter with which Americans have been trained to view the world creates a gap between the expectations that we—and our clients and/or executives—have of the global media stage, and reality.

How can US PR pros become better international partners?

- Listen to foreign market counsel. PR pros in international markets are every bit as professional as those in the US. While standards of excellence may vary (and the US does not necessarily adhere to the highest standards, despite our presumptions to the contrary), PR pros in foreign markets play the same role with their media that we play here.
- Working with an American client is often difficult or awkward for an international partner. Being an American is not often the "plus" that it once was. Depend on international counsel to help overcome this.
- We often cite the irony that poor communication riddles the communications industry. When crossing cultures and boundaries, weak communication can doom any PR effort. The importance of clearly written messages cannot be overstated—do not rely on conference calls or e-mail, which many cultures consider to be informal and "unofficial" in establishing communication parameters for an international PR effort. Get on a plane and meet face-to-face.
- Take advantage of experienced and knowledgeable resources. Seek outside counsel to identify strong international partners; utilize global management expertise to maximize worldwide investment.
- The US agency or office need not always take the lead. If your audience is Eastern Europe, a German partner might be more effective. If Southeast Asia is your goal, Sydney, Australia-based PR counsel might be key.
- Understand that international partners are often keen to work with and learn from their US counterparts—in many cases, their markets are in their infancy. The PR sector in the

Arab Middle East, for example, yields only $25 million a year, but this amount multiplies year over year.

Just as Americans do not understand much of the rest of the world, the world fails to understand the US. The famous cover of the November 4 UK *Daily Mirror* asking, "How can 59,054,087 people be so dumb?" illustrated the dissonance between this country and much of the world's perception of it.

Before the presidential election (2004), John Kerry polled 72% in France, according to *Le Monde*, and a *Guardian* poll showed British voters supporting Kerry over Bush by a 2-to-1 margin. In many markets, consumers—particularly those under 30—actively reject US brands. The worsening situation in Iraq only increases this gap.

It is against this backdrop that corporate America now does business in the global marketplace. And it is because of this that the US PR industry must increasingly rely on our counterparts in international markets.

For many US companies, international markets are the strongest—and sometimes the only—avenues of revenue growth. At a time when penetrating international markets is crucial, many companies lack the in-house talent and know-how to drive programs that will reach global consumers. Successful PR pros will learn how to partner with their international counterparts, step back from presumptive leadership, and work hand-in-hand across borders and cultures to drive multinational PR programs...or, as they'd say outside the US, "programmes."

Summary and Review

Global Audiences
- Whether we call it international or global, the practice of public relations is everywhere in the world today.
- The technological innovations of the past decade and increased access to the Internet have created a smaller world. As a result, organizations must be even more strategic in how they communicate with audiences and attempt to foster relationships around the globe.
- Practicing public relations abroad or for clients from other nations is an exciting way to make a living. But it is not all glamour. It can be challenging and fraught with pitfalls.

Communicating across Cultures
- Communicating effectively across cultures involves more than just the translation of words into other languages and adapting visual images to reflect the new environment. And even when these are important to a communication, no language translates without regional and geographical differences.
- As a global PR practitioner, you must be aware of the cultures and customs of the nations and regions in which you are attempting to communicate. The study of theories regarding human behavior within cultures is important. While you should not make assumptions about individuals without studying their behavior, it is important to understand cultural contexts.
- Understanding how people from different cultures understand and react to space, time, context, and power are important to operating in different countries. All things Western do not govern the world.

- Different cultures see personal, business, and public communication and interactions differently. It is important for you to understand your weaknesses in a particular part of the world and to look for local partners. You should be sure to consider all of the local aspects of a community, cultural, or country.

The Complexities of International Practice

- Even global PR agencies are concerned about effective practice abroad. They often acquire or partner with native PR agencies.
- Research begins with understanding how an organization is perceived in the country of interest, making a thorough environmental scan crucial.
- The organization must be seen as credible, working in the interest of the host country and not exploiting it.
- Additional research includes understanding the country's PR practices and ensuring the existing infrastructure can support your PR activities.

International Public Affairs: Representing Other Governments

- All countries invest in communicating with key audiences in other nations. And nations abroad often seek PR counsel in helping them take advantage of opportunities or solve problems in the United States.
- Many U.S. PR agencies assist other nations in vying to host the Olympics.

International Nonprofit Public Relations

- Many global nonprofits employ public relations to promote their causes and deliver their services around the world.
- As nonprofits seek to provide disaster relief assistance, promote international understanding and development, and affect foreign affairs, they must be strategic in planning and execution.

Public Relations Practice around the Globe

- The practice of public relations in other nations runs the gamut from nascent to experienced but the field is growing abroad.
- The primary challenges to the practice abroad are finding experienced talent and maintaining the entrepreneurial spirit in a market that is saturated with multinational companies and international firms based in the United States.

Ethical Issues

- You must be mindful of the philosophy and culture of other nations when you work in countries other than the United States.
- PR professionals in the United States and abroad are concerned about journalism-for-pay—journalists expecting to be paid for news coverage.
- The International Public Relations Association (IPRA) code of ethics and conduct describes the manner in which international PR should be practiced.

Key Terms

collectivism	individualism	power distance
culture	intimate space	proxemics
customs	low-context	public space
ethnocentrism	communication	social space
feminine cultures	masculine culture	uncertainty avoidance
high-context	monochronic time	
communication	polychronic time	

Questions for Review and Discussion

1. Why has the practice of international public relations grown in the recent decade?

2. How would you define international public relations?

3. Compare monochromic and polychromic time. How does it help you understand cultural differences?

4. Explain high-context communication and low-context communication.

5. How can understanding the difference between individualism and collectivism assist you in message development?

6. Why is it important to understand cultural differences when practicing in another country or representing the government of another country?

7. Why is it dangerous for you to assume you can apply all communication and public relations theory globally?

8. Why is eliminating pay-for-play important?

9. Why does the IPRA have both a code of professional conduct and a code of ethics? How do they differ?

10. Josef Blumenfeld, global PR consultant, wrote, "If your audience is Eastern Europe, a German partner might be more effective. If Southeast Asia is your goal, Sydney, Australia based PR counsel might be key." Why do you think he made these suggestions?

Web Links

Geert-Hofstede
Geert-hofstede.com

Global Alliance for Public Relations and Communication
www.globalalliancepr.org
www.globalpr.org

International Public Relations Association
www.ipra.org

Kyodo Public Relations Co. Ltd.
http://www.kyodopr.co.uk

Tokyo Doko
www.tokyodoko.com
www.dev@bharatsamachar.com (Communication Society of India)

Radio Station World
www.tvradioworld.com

Kiss, Bow, or Shake Hands—for various countries, McGraw-Hill
www.getcustoms.com

Codes of Ethics Related to the Practice of Public Relations

CODE OF THE AMERICAN LEAGUE OF LOBBYISTS

Article I—Honesty & Integrity

A lobbyist should conduct lobbying activities with honesty and integrity.

1.1. A lobbyist should be truthful in communicating with public officials and with other interested persons and should seek to provide factually correct, current and accurate information.

1.2. If a lobbyist determines that the lobbyist has provided a public official or other interested person with factually inaccurate information of a significant, relevant, and material nature, the lobbyist should promptly provide the factually accurate information to the interested person.

1.3. If a material change in factual information that the lobbyist provided previously to a public official causes the information to become inaccurate and the lobbyist knows the public official may still be relying upon the information, the lobbyist should provide accurate and updated information to the public official.

Article II—Compliance with Applicable Laws, Regulations & Rules

A lobbyist should seek to comply fully with all laws, regulations and rules applicable to the lobbyist.

2.1. A lobbyist should be familiar with laws, regulations and rules applicable to the lobbying profession and should not engage in any violation of such laws, regulations and rules.

2.2. A lobbyist should not cause a public official to violate any law, regulation or rule applicable to such public official.

Article III—Professionalism

A lobbyist should conduct lobbying activities in a fair and professional manner.

3.1. A lobbyist should have a basic understanding of the legislative and governmental process and such specialized knowledge as is necessary to represent clients or an employer in a competent, professional manner.
3.2. A lobbyist should maintain the lobbyist's understanding of governmental processes and specialized knowledge through appropriate methods such as continuing study, seminars and similar sessions in order to represent clients or an employer in a competent, professional manner.
3.3. A lobbyist should treat others—both allies and adversaries—with respect and civility.

Article IV—Conflicts of Interest

A lobbyist should not continue or undertake representations that may create conflicts of interest without the informed consent of the client or potential client involved.

4.1. A lobbyist should avoid advocating a position on an issue if the lobbyist is also representing another client on the same issue with a conflicting position.
4.2. If a lobbyist's work for one client on an issue may have a significant adverse impact on another client's interests, the lobbyist should inform and obtain consent from the other client whose interests may be affected of this fact even if the lobbyist is not representing the other client on the same issue.
4.3. A lobbyist should disclose all potential conflicts to the client or prospective client and discuss and resolve the conflict issues promptly.
4.4. A lobbyist should inform the client if any other person is receiving a direct or indirect referral or consulting fee from the lobbyist due to or in connection with the client's work and the amount of such fee or payment.

Article V—Due Diligence & Best Efforts

A lobbyist should vigorously and diligently advance and advocate the client's or employer's interests.

5.1. A lobbyist should devote adequate time, attention, and resources to the client's or employer's interests.
5.2. A lobbyist should exercise loyalty to the client's or employer's interests.
5.3. A lobbyist should keep the client or employer informed regarding the work that the lobbyist is undertaking and, to the extent possible, should give the client the opportunity to choose between various options and strategies.

Article VI—Compensation and Engagement Terms

An independent lobbyist who is retained by a client should have a written agreement with the client regarding the terms and conditions for the lobbyist's services, including the amount of and basis for compensation.

Article VII—Confidentiality

A lobbyist should maintain appropriate confidentiality of client or employer information.

7.1. A lobbyist should not disclose confidential information without the client's or employer's informed consent.

7.2. A lobbyist should not use confidential client information against the interests of a client or employer or for any purpose not contemplated by the engagement or terms of employment.

Article VIII—Public Education

A lobbyist should seek to ensure better public understanding and appreciation of the nature, legitimacy and necessity of lobbying in our democratic governmental process. This includes the First Amendment right to "petition the government for redress of grievances."

Article IX—Duty to Governmental Institutions

In addition to fulfilling duties and responsibilities to the client or employer, a lobbyist should exhibit proper respect for the governmental institutions before which the lobbyist represents and advocates clients' interests.

9.1. A lobbyist should not act in any manner that will undermine public confidence and trust in the democratic governmental process.

9.2. A lobbyist should not act in a manner that shows disrespect for government institutions.

PUBLIC RELATIONS SOCIETY OF AMERICA (PRSA) CODE OF ETHICS
(Revised 2000)

A comprehensive document, this code for PRSA members discusses the principles of advocacy, honesty, fairness, expertise, independence, loyalty and fairness.

This statement presents the core values of PRSA members and, more broadly, of the public relations profession. These values provide the foundation for the Member Code of Ethics and set the industry standard for the professional practice of public relations. These values are the fundamental beliefs that guide our behaviors and decision-making process. We believe our professional values are vital to the integrity of the profession as a whole.

Advocacy

We serve the public interest by acting as responsible advocates for those we represent. We provide a voice in the marketplace of ideas, facts, and viewpoints to aid informed public debate.

Honesty

We adhere to the highest standards of accuracy and truth in advancing the interests of those we represent and in communicating with the public.

Expertise

We acquire and responsibly use specialized knowledge and experience. We advance the profession through continued professional development, research, and education. We build mutual understanding, credibility, and relationships among a wide array of institutions and audiences.

Independence

We provide objective counsel to those we represent. We are accountable for our actions.

Loyalty

We are faithful to those we represent, while honoring our obligation to serve the public interest.

Fairness

We deal fairly with clients, employers, competitors, peers, vendors, the media, and the general public. We respect all opinions and support the right of free expression.

PRSA Code Provisions

Free Flow of Information

Core Principle: Protecting and advancing the free flow of accurate and truthful information is essential to serving the public interest and contributing to informed decision making in a democratic society.

Intent:

To maintain the integrity of relationships with the media, government officials, and the public.

To aid informed decision making.

Guidelines:

A member shall:

Preserve the integrity of the process of communication.

Be honest and accurate in all communications.

Act promptly to correct erroneous communications for which the practitioner is responsible.

Preserve the free flow of unprejudiced information when giving or receiving gifts by ensuring that gifts are nominal, legal, and infrequent.

Examples of Improper Conduct under This Provision:

A member representing a ski manufacturer gives a pair of expensive racing skis to a sports magazine columnist, to influence the columnist to write favorable articles about the product.

A member entertains a government official beyond legal limits and/or in violation of government reporting requirements.

Competition

Core Principle: Promoting healthy and fair competition among professionals preserves an ethical climate while fostering a robust business environment.

Intent:

To promote respect and fair competition among public relations professionals.

To serve the public interest by providing the widest choice of practitioner options.

Guidelines:

A member shall:

Follow ethical hiring practices designed to respect free and open competition without deliberately undermining a competitor.

Preserve intellectual property rights in the marketplace.

Examples of Improper Conduct under This Provision:

A member employed by a "client organization" shares helpful information with a counseling firm that is competing with others for the organization's business.

A member spreads malicious and unfounded rumors about a competitor in order to alienate the competitor's clients and employees in a ploy to recruit people and business.

Disclosure of Information

Core Principle: Open communication fosters informed decision making in a democratic society.

Intent:

To build trust with the public by revealing all information needed for responsible decision making.

Guidelines:

A member shall:

Be honest and accurate in all communications.

Act promptly to correct erroneous communications for which the member is responsible.

Investigate the truthfulness and accuracy of information released on behalf of those represented.

Reveal the sponsors for causes and interests represented.

Disclose financial interest (such as stock ownership) in a client's organization.

Avoid deceptive practices.

Examples of Improper Conduct under This Provision:

Front groups: A member implements "grass roots" campaigns or letter-writing campaigns to legislators on behalf of undisclosed interest groups.

Lying by omission: A practitioner for a corporation knowingly fails to release financial information, giving a misleading impression of the corporation's performance.

A member discovers inaccurate information disseminated via a website or media kit and does not correct the information.

A member deceives the public by employing people to pose as volunteers to speak at public hearings and participate in "grass roots" campaigns.

Safeguarding Confidences

Core Principle: Client trust requires appropriate protection of confidential and private information.

Intent:

To protect the privacy rights of clients, organizations, and individuals by safeguarding confidential information.

Guidelines:

A member shall: Safeguard the confidences and privacy rights of present, former, and prospective clients and employees.

Protect privileged, confidential, or insider information gained from a client or organization.

Immediately advise an appropriate authority if a member discovers that confidential information is being divulged by an employee of a client company or organization.

Examples of Improper Conduct under This Provision:

A member changes jobs, takes confidential information, and uses that information in the new position to the detriment of the former employer.

A member intentionally leaks proprietary information to the detriment of some other party.

Conflicts of Interest

Core Principle: Avoiding real, potential or perceived conflicts of interest builds the trust of clients, employers, and the publics.

Intent:

To earn trust and mutual respect with clients or employers.

To build trust with the public by avoiding or ending situations that put one's personal or professional interests in conflict with society's interests.

Guidelines:

A member shall:

Act in the best interests of the client or employer, even subordinating the member's personal interests.

Avoid actions and circumstances that may appear to compromise good business judgment or create a conflict between personal and professional interests.

Disclose promptly any existing or potential conflict of interest to affected clients or organizations.

Encourage clients and customers to determine if a conflict exists after notifying all affected parties.

Examples of Improper Conduct under This Provision:

The member fails to disclose that he or she has a strong financial interest in a client's chief competitor.

The member represents a "competitor company" or a "conflicting interest" without informing a prospective client.

Enhancing the Profession

Core Principle: Public relations professionals work constantly to strengthen the public's trust in the profession.

Intent:

To build respect and credibility with the public for the profession of public relations.

To improve, adapt and expand professional practices.

Guidelines:

A member shall: Acknowledge that there is an obligation to protect and enhance the profession.

Keep informed and educated about practices in the profession to ensure ethical conduct.

Actively pursue personal professional development.

Decline representation of clients or organizations that urge or require actions contrary to this Code.

Accurately define what public relations activities can accomplish.

Counsel subordinates in proper ethical decision making.

Require that subordinates adhere to the ethical requirements of the Code.

Report ethical violations, whether committed by PRSA members or not, to the appropriate authority.

Examples of Improper Conduct under This Provision:

A PRSA member declares publicly that a product the client sells is safe, without disclosing evidence to the contrary.

A member initially assigns some questionable client work to a non-member practitioner to avoid the ethical obligation of PRSA membership.

INTERNATIONAL ASSOCIATION OF BUSINESS COMMUNICATORS (IABC)

Code of Ethics for Professional Communicators is for members and discusses the principles of human rights, rule of law, sensitivity to cultural norms, truthfulness, accuracy, fairness, respect and mutual understanding.

Preface: Because hundreds of thousands of business communicators worldwide engage in activities that affect the lives of millions of people, and because this power carries with it significant social responsibilities, the International Association of Business Communicators developed the Code of Ethics for Professional Communicators. The Code is based on three different yet interrelated principles of professional communication that apply throughout the world. These principles assume that just societies are governed by a profound respect for human rights and the rule of law; that ethics, the criteria for determining what is right and wrong, can be agreed upon by members of an organization; and, that understanding matters of taste requires sensitivity to cultural norms.

These principles are essential:

- Professional communication is legal
- Professional communication is ethical
- Professional communication is in good taste

Recognizing these principles, members of IABC will

- Engage in communication that is not only legal but also ethical and sensitive to cultural values and beliefs
- Engage in truthful, accurate and fair communication that facilitates respect and mutual understanding; and
- Adhere to the following articles of the IABC Code of Ethics for Professional Communicators

Because conditions in the world are constantly changing, members of IABC will work to improve their individual competence and to increase the body of knowledge in the field with research and education.

Articles:

1. Professional communicators uphold the credibility and dignity of their profession by practicing honest, candid and timely communication and by fostering the free flow of essential information in accord with the public interest
2. Professional communicators disseminate accurate information and promptly correct any erroneous communication for which they may be responsible
3. Professional communicators understand and support the principles of free speech, freedom of assembly, and access to an open marketplace of ideas; and, act accordingly

4. Professional communicators are sensitive to cultural values and beliefs and engage in fair and balanced communication activities that foster and encourage mutual understanding

5. Professional communicators refrain from taking part in any undertaking which the communicator considers to be unethical

6. Professional communicators obey laws and public policies governing their professional activities and are sensitive to the spirit of all laws and regulations and, should any law or public policy be violated, for whatever reason, act promptly to correct the situation

7. Professional communicators give credit for unique expressions borrowed from others and identify the sources and purposes of all information disseminated to the public

8. Professional communicators protect confidential information and, at the same time, comply with all legal requirements for the disclosure of information affecting the welfare of others

9. Professional communicators do not use confidential information gained as a result of professional activities for personal benefit and do not represent conflicting or competing interests without written consent of those involved

10. Professional communicators do not accept undisclosed gifts or payments for professional services from anyone other than a client or employer

11. Professional communicators do not guarantee results that are beyond the power of the practitioner to deliver

12. Professional communicators are honest not only with others but also, and most importantly, with themselves as individuals; for a professional communicator seeks the truth and speaks that truth first to the self

Enforcement and Communication of the IABC Code for Professional Communicators

IABC fosters compliance with its Code by engaging in global communication campaigns rather than through negative sanctions. However, in keeping with the sixth article of the IABC Code, members of IABC who are found guilty by an appropriate governmental agency or judicial body of violating laws and public policies governing their professional activities may have their membership terminated by the IABC executive board following procedures set forth in the association's bylaws.

IABC encourages the widest possible communication about its Code.

The IABC Code of Ethics for Professional Communicators is published in several languages and is freely available to all: Permission is hereby granted to any individual or organization wishing to copy and incorporate all or part of the IABC Code into personal and corporate codes, with the understanding that appropriate credit be given to IABC in any publication of such codes.

The IABC Code is published in the association's annual directory, The World Book of IABC Communicators. The association's monthly magazine, Communication World, publishes periodic articles dealing with ethical issues. At least one session at the association's annual conference is devoted to ethics. The international headquarters of IABC, through its professional development activities, encourages and supports efforts by IABC student chapters, professional chapters, and districts/regions to conduct meetings and workshops devoted to the topic of ethics and the IABC Code. New and renewing members of IABC sign the following statement as part of their application: "I have reviewed and understand the IABC Code of Ethics for Professional Communicators."

THE CODE OF ATHENS

INTERNATIONAL CODE OF ETHICS OF THE INTERNATIONAL PUBLIC RELATIONS ASSOCIATION (IPRA)

The Code of Athens was adopted by the International Public Relations Association General Assembly, which was held in Athens on May 12, 1965, and modified at Teheran on April 17, 1968. The author of this code is Lucien Matrat, Emeritus Member (France) of IPRA.

CONSIDERING that all Member countries of the United Nations Organization have agreed to abide by its Charter which reaffirms "its faith in fundamental human rights, in the dignity and worth of the human person" and that having regard to the very nature of the profession, Public Relations practitioners in these countries should undertake to ascertain and observe the principles set out in this Charter;

CONSIDERING that, apart from "rights," human beings have not only physical or material needs but also intellectual, moral and social needs, and that their rights are of real benefit to them only in-so-far as these needs are essentially met;

CONSIDERING that, in the course of their professional duties and depending on how these duties are performed, Public Relations practitioners can substantially help to meet these intellectual, moral and social needs;

And lastly, CONSIDERING that the use of the techniques enabling them to come simultaneously into contact with millions of people gives Public Relations practitioners a power that has to be restrained by the observance of a strict moral code.

On all these grounds, all members of the International Public Relations Association agree to abide by this International Code of Ethics, and if, in the light of evidence submitted to the Council, a member should be found to have infringed this Code in the course of his/her professional duties, he/she will be deemed to be guilty of serious misconduct calling for an appropriate penalty.

Accordingly, each member:

Shall Endeavour

- To contribute to the achievement of the moral and cultural conditions enabling human beings to reach their full stature and enjoy the indefeasible rights to which they are entitled under the "Universal Declaration of Human Rights"
- To establish communications patterns and channels which, by fostering the free flow of essential information, will make each member of the group feel that he/she is being kept informed, and also give him/her an awareness of his/her own personal involvement and responsibility, and of his/her solidarity with other members
- To conduct himself/herself always and in all circumstances in such a manner as to deserve and secure the confidence of those with whom he/she comes into contact
- To bear in mind that, because of the relationship between his/her profession and the public, his/her conduct—even in private—will have an impact on the way in which the profession as a whole is appraised

Shall Undertake

- To observe, in the course of his/her professional duties, the moral principles and rules of the "Universal Declaration of Human Rights"

- To pay due regard to, and uphold, human dignity, and to recognize the right of each individual to judge for himself/herself;
- To establish the moral, psychological and intellectual conditions for dialogue in the true sense, and to recognize the right of these parties involved to state their case and express their views
- To act, in all circumstances, in such a manner as to take account of the respective interests of the parties involved: both the interests of the organization which he/she serves and the interests of the publics concerned
- To carry out his/her undertakings and commitments which shall always be so worded as to avoid any misunderstanding, and to show loyalty and integrity in all circumstances so as to keep the confidence of his/her clients or employers, past or present, and of all the publics that are affected by his/her actions

Shall Refrain from

- Subordinating the truth to other requirements
- Circulating information which is not based on established and ascertainable facts
- Taking part in any venture or undertaking which is unethical or dishonest or capable of impairing human dignity and integrity
- Using any "manipulative" methods or techniques designed to create subconscious motivations which the individual cannot control of his/her own free will and so cannot be held accountable for the action taken on them

CODE OF VENICE
Adopted in Venice—May 1961

INTERNATIONAL CODE OF ETHICS OF THE INTERNATIONAL PUBLIC RELATIONS ASSOCIATION (IPRA)

A. Personal and Professional Integrity
   1. It is understood that by personal integrity is meant the maintenance of both high moral standards and a sound reputation. By professional integrity is meant observance of the Constitution rules and, particularly, the Code as adopted by IPRA.
B. Conduct towards Clients and Employers
   1. A member has a general duty of fair dealing towards his/her clients or employers, past and present.
   2. A member shall not represent conflicting or competing interests without the express consent of those concerned.
   3. A member shall safeguard the confidences of both present and former clients or employers.
   4. A member shall not employ methods tending to be derogatory of another member's client or employer.
   5. In performing services for a client or employer a member shall not accept fees, commission or any other valuable consideration in connection with those services from anyone other than his/her client or employer without the express consent of his/her client or employer, given after a full disclosure of the facts.

6. A member shall not propose to a prospective client that his/her fees or other compensation be contingent on the achievement of certain results; nor shall he/she enter into any fee agreement to the same effect.

C. Conduct towards the Public and the Media

1. A member shall conduct his/her professional activities with respect to the public interest and for the dignity of the individual.
2. A member shall not engage in practice which tends to corrupt the integrity of channels of public communication.
3. A member shall not intentionally disseminate false or misleading information.
4. A member shall at all times seek to give a faithful representation of the organisation (sic) which he/she serves.
5. A member shall not create any organisation to serve some announced cause but actually to serve an undisclosed special or private interest of a member or his/her client or employer, nor shall he/she make use of it or any such existing organisation.

D. Conduct towards Colleagues

1. A member shall not intentionally injure the professional reputation or practice of another member. However, if a member has evidence that another member has been guilty of unethical, illegal or unfair practices, including practices in violation of this Code, he/she should present the information to the Council of IPRA.
2. A member shall not seek to supplant another member with his employer or client.
3. A member shall co-operate with fellow members in upholding and enforcing this Code.

THE PAGE PRINCIPLES

In addition to the codes of professional organizations, pioneers in the field have delineated standards of behavior for public relations professionals. Arthur Page, the first corporate vice president for public relations, outlined this set of principles:

- Tell the truth. Let the public know what's happening and provide an accurate picture of the company's character, ideals and practices
- Prove it with action. Ninety percent of the public's perception of an organization is determined by what it does, 10 percent by talking
- Listen to the customer. To serve the company well, understand what the public wants and needs. Keep top decision makers and other employees informed about public reaction to company products, policies and practices
- Manage for tomorrow. Anticipate public reaction and eliminate practices that create difficulties; generate goodwill
- Conduct public relations as if the whole company depends on it. Corporate relations is a management function. No corporate strategy should be implemented without considering its impact on the public. The public relations professional is a policymaker capable of handling a wide range of corporate communications activities
- Remain calm, patient and good-humored. Lay the groundwork for public relations miracles with consistent, calm and reasoned attention to information and contacts. When a crisis arises, remember that cool heads communicate best.

Guidelines for Using the Internet

The Arthur W. Page Society published ethical standards and practices for public relations on the Internet that have been endorsed by major public relations organizations

1. Present fact-based content
   - Tell the truth at all times
   - Ensure timely delivery of information
   - Tell the full story, adhering to accepted standards for accuracy of information
2. Be an objective advocate
   - Act as a credible information source, providing round-the-clock access
   - Know your subject
   - Rely on credible sources for expert advice
3. Offer opportunities for dialogue and direct interaction with expert sources
   - Reveal the background of experts, disclosing any potential conflicts of interest or anonymous economic support of web content
4. Earn the public's trust
   - Simultaneously contact multiple stakeholders with relevant and accurate information
   - Disclose all participation in online chat rooms and conferences
   - Correct information that is online
   - Provide counsel on privacy, security and other online trust issues
5. Educate the public relations profession on best practices
   - Compile case studies on the best use of the new media
   - Advance and encourage industry-wide adoption of best practices on the Internet
   - Practice principled leadership in the digital world, adhering to the highest standards.

Comparison Table of PRSA, IABC, IPRA, and Page

	PRSA	IABC	IPRA	Page
Honesty	Adhere to the highest standards of accuracy and truth in advancing the interests of those you represent and in communicating with the public. Be honest and accurate in all communications; avoid deceptive practices.	Refrain from taking part in any undertaking which the communicator considers to be unethical. Be honest not only with others but also, and most importantly, with yourselves as individuals. Seek the truth and speak that truth first to yourself.	Refrain from subordinating the truth to other requirements.	Tell the truth. Let the public know what's happening and provide an accurate picture of the company's character, ideals, and practices.
Advocacy/ expertise	Serve the public interest by acting as responsible advocates for those you represent. Provide a voice in the marketplace of ideas, facts and viewpoints to aid informed public debate. Acquire and responsibly use specialized knowledge and experience. Build mutual understanding, credibility, and relationships among a wide array of institutions and audiences.	Be sensitive to cultural values and beliefs and engage in fair and balanced communication activities that foster and encourage mutual understanding. Understand and support the principles of free speech, freedom of assembly, and access to an open marketplace of ideas; and, act accordingly.	Contribute to the achievement of the moral and cultural conditions enabling human beings to reach their full stature and enjoy the indefeasible rights to which they are entitled.	Manage for tomorrow. Anticipate public reaction and eliminate practices that create difficulties. Generate goodwill. Support each employee's capacity to be an honest, knowledgeable ambassador to customers, friends, share owners and public officials. Conduct public relations as if the whole company depends on it. No strategy should be implemented without considering its impact on the public. Be a policy maker capable of handling a wide range of corporate communications activities.
Independence	Provide objective counsel to those you represent. Be accountable for your actions.			
Loyalty	Be faithful to those you represent, while honoring your obligation to serve the public interest.			Listen to the customer. Understand what the public wants and needs. Keep top decision makers and other employees informed about public reaction to company products, policies, and practices.

(*continued*)

Comparison Table of PRSA, IABC, IPRA, and Page (*continued*)

	PRSA	IABC	IPRA	Page
Fairness	Deal fairly with clients, employers, competitors, peers, vendors, the media, and the general public.			
Free flow of information	Preserve the integrity of the process of communication. Act promptly to correct erroneous communications for which you are responsible. Preserve the free flow of unprejudiced information when giving or receiving gifts by ensuring that gifts are nominal, legal, and infrequent. Respect all opinions and support the right of free expression.	Uphold the credibility of the profession by practicing honest, candid, and timely communication and by fostering the free flow of essential information in accord with the public interest. Disseminate accurate information and promptly correct any erroneous communication for which you may be responsible. Obey laws and policies governing professional activities; be sensitive to the spirit of laws and regulations; should any law or policy be violated, act promptly to correct the situation.	Establish communications patterns and channels which, by fostering the free flow of essential information, will make each member of the group feel that he/she is being kept informed. Avoid manipulative methods or techniques designed to create sub-conscious motivations which the individual cannot control and so cannot be held accountable for the action taken on them.	
Competition	Follow ethical hiring practices designed to respect free and open competition without deliberately undermining a competitor. Preserve intellectual property rights in the marketplace.	Give credit for unique expressions borrowed from others and identify the sources and purposes of all information disseminated to the public.	Establish the moral, psychological and intellectual conditions for dialogue in the true sense, and to recognize the right of these parties involved to state their case and express their views.	

(*continued*)

	PRSA	IABC	IPRA	Page
			Act in such a manner as to take account of the respective interests of the parties involved: both the interests of the organization which he/she serves and the interests of the publics concerned.	
Disclosure of information	Investigate the truthfulness and accuracy of information released on behalf of those represented. Reveal the sponsors for causes and interests represented. Disclose financial interest (such as stock ownership) in a client's organization.	Comply with all legal requirements for the disclosure of information affecting the welfare of others.	Refrain from circulating information which is not based on established and ascertainable facts.	
Confidentiality	Safeguard the confidences and privacy rights of present, former, and prospective clients and employees. Protect privileged, confidential, or insider information gained from a client or organization. Immediately advise an appropriate authority if a member discovers that confidential information is being divulged by an employee of a client company or organization.	Protect confidential information. Professional communicators do not use confidential data gained as a result of professional activities for personal benefit and do not represent conflicting or competing interests without written consent.		

(continued)

Comparison Table of PRSA, IABC, IPRA, and Page (*continued*)

	PRSA	IABC	IPRA	Page
Conflicts of interest	Avoid actions and circumstances that may appear to compromise good business judgment or create a conflict between personal and professional interests. Disclose promptly any existing or potential conflict of interest to affected clients or organizations. Encourage clients and customers to determine if a conflict exists after notifying all affected parties. Act in the best interests of the client or employer, even subordinating the member's personal interests.	Do not accept undisclosed gifts or payments for professional services from anyone other than a client or employer.		
Enhancing the profession	Acknowledge that there is an obligation to protect and enhance the profession. Keep informed and educated about practices in the profession to ensure ethical conduct. Advance the profession through continued professional development, research, and education. Accurately define what public relations activities can accomplish.	Engage in communication that is not only legal but also ethical and sensitive to cultural values and beliefs. Engage in truthful, accurate and fair communication that facilitates respect and mutual understanding.	Refrain from taking part in any venture or undertaking which is unethical or dishonest or capable of impairing human dignity and integrity. Bear in mind that, because of the relationship between the profession and the public, conduct—even in private—will have an impact on the way in which the profession as a whole is appraised.	

(*continued*)

	PRSA	IABC	IPRA	Page
Obligation to the code	Counsel subordinates in proper ethical decision making. Require that subordinates adhere to the ethical requirements of the Code. Report ethical violations, whether committed by PRSA members or not, to the appropriate authority. Decline representation of clients or organizations that urge or require actions contrary to this Code.	Adhere to the articles of the IABC Code of Ethics for Professional Communicators.	Public Relations practitioners in U.N. member countries should undertake to ascertain and observe the principles set out in this Charter.	
Enforcement of the code	Enforcement replaced by education.	Communication campaigns rather than negative sanctions.	Members agree to abide by the code; if a member is found to have infringed this code in the course of professional duties, he/she will be deemed to be guilty of serious misconduct calling for an appropriate penalty.	

Glossary

Absolutist In ethics, one who thinks that truth is absolute and not relative to individual differences.

Account director (AD) or project director (PD) The leader of a team of staff working on a project, usually the client contact person.

Ad Council Nonprofit public service advertising organization; began as the War Advertising Council during World War II.

Administrative costs Expenses that support conducting a project or event, such as travel, shipping, rental cars, office supplies, copying, etc. These costs are usually "marked up" by the agency or freelancer.

Advertorial An advertisement presented in such a way as to resemble an editorial.

Advocacy advertising A company's attempt to affect public opinion about an issue.

Agenda setting theory A theory that suggests that the agenda of topics or issues for public discourse is set by the news media.

Analysis A careful and intentional look at elemental parts or basic principles to determine the nature of the whole.

Annual report A yearly reporting of an organization's activities, including initiatives, program performance, sales, and financial performance to stockholders and members.

Arthur W. Page Society Professional organization for public relations professionals formed to honor Arthur Page, the first corporate vice president for public relations.

Astroturfing Public relations projects that seek to engineer the impression of spontaneous grassroots behavior; creation of front groups; name borrowed from artificial grass called AstroTurf.

Attorney-client model A model to describe the way public relation practitioners communicate with their clients; public relations practitioners are seen as functioning as lawyers do, representing a client.

Audience focused Focused on the client's audiences; attempts to understand the audiences' attitudes, beliefs, norms, values, desires, and actions.

Audience Key group of people with whom an organization or individual wants to communicate in order to ensure success in reaching goals and overall mission.

Audience segmentation Audience subgroups who possess similar characteristics.

Audio news release (ANR) A 60–90-second audio production designed to meet the news formats of radio stations and distributed by an organization to encourage coverage of a newsworthy story.

Backgrounder An expanded version of the history, mission, goals, and purpose of an organization; one- to two-paragraph biography (bio) is often referred to as a backgrounder.

Baseline *See* Benchmark.

Begging mission Early American fundraising campaign.

Behavior change theory The collection of studies that explore individual behavior modification and the variables that affect it.

Benchmark A metric against which new and succeeding efforts can be measured. Also known as *baseline*.

Billable hours The hours of the work day that can be charged to a client account.

Blog A diary or news forum that is regularly updated by the person who owns the site, known as a blogger; fiercely independent of editorial control. Also known as *web log*.

Boilerplate Copy used at the end of a news release that provides a very brief, one-paragraph description of an organization, its mission and, if appropriate, how it was founded and funded.

Bought media Vehicles used to attract public attention that is purchased, such as TV commercials, magazine ads, or banner and pop-up ads.

Brainstorming A problem-solving process through which a small group of about six to eight participants develop as many solutions as possible.

Brand An organization's identity; involves everything the organization does, from graphic identity to philanthropy to customer service.

Brochure An informational or persuasive publication that is produced in varying sizes and formats; usually created to have a long shelf life.

B-roll Video shot to augment a news story that can be enhanced by voice-overs from reporters.

Burn rate The pace at which the personnel costs of the budget are expended.

Central location intercept interviews *See* Mall intercepts.

Close-ended question Questions found on survey questionnaires that are designed to elicit short answers that can be quantified.

Cluster sampling A random sampling plan that allows the population is divided into subgroups called clusters.

Code A set of professional standards of behavior to which members of the profession should adhere; reflects the practices and customs within the discipline and provides a set of standards for performing professionally.

Cognitive dissonance theory A theory that suggests that audiences tend to ignore messages that are inconsistent with their previously held beliefs.

Collateral materials Items created to support a public relations campaign or program such as brochures, websites, newsletters, etc.

Collectivism A society behavior and standard in which people are united by shared bonds of values and customs that make them a cohesive group.

Commercial film or video A visual tool created by organizations that can afford the high costs of product or idea placement.

Commercial speech Speech that is motivated by a desire for profit.

Communication audit An assessment of an organization's communication effectiveness with internal or external audiences.

Communication plan *See* PR plan.

Community and town meeting Citizens who live in the same community gather to hear views on particular issues and ask questions.

Computer-administered questionnaire Used to conduct surveys via the Internet.

Computer-assisted telephone (CAT) interview A telephone survey technique that uses an interactive system to assist interviewers asking questions over the telephone.

Confirmation letter Restates the logistics and details of a scheduled interview and reviews the subject and areas of interest to remind the producer, editor, or reporter of the summary of the original pitch letter.

Controlled media Products and messages over which PR practitioners have the most control of content, timing, and distribution. Examples include newsletters, brochures, web pages, presentations, annual reports, and paid advertising.

Convenience sampling Sampling method used when you are aware of a group of people who are available for a study.

Copyright Exclusive rights to creative work.

Corporate-image advertising Advertising designed to increase the public's positive opinion of a company while enhancing the image of its products or services. Also known as *institutional* or *identity advertising*.

Corporate social responsibility A form of corporate philanthropy; includes the role of business in social issues.

Corporate speech Refers to the right of a corporation to present its views on social or political matters.

Creel Committee The propaganda arm of the U.S. government during World War I, where many early PR practitioners got their start; formally called the Committee for Public Information.

Crisis Any situation that threatens the financial stability, veracity, credibility, and/or reputation of an organization.

Crisis communication A set of planned actions and policies adopted and carried out by organizations when an emergency situation involves the public.

Critical thinking Taking a close and questioning look at an idea, situation, or question; involves analyzing or reducing a question to smaller parts that can be further investigated.

Culture The pattern of human behavior and values within a given society.

Customs Particular practices of a group of people.

Dateline Information shown on a news release that indicates the city and state where the information originated.

Declaration of Principles Public relations trailblazer Ivy Lee's idea that practitioners have a responsibility to the public.

Deductive reasoning Developing an argument from the general to the specific; using observation to create an idea or theory.

Defamation Damaging another person's reputation, putting his social or professional life at risk; includes libel and slander.

Deterministic thinking A basic philosophical theory of decision making that says the rightness of actions is determined by consequences. Also known as *naturalistic thinking*.

Developmental research *See* Formative research.

Diffusion of innovations theory A theory that identifies awareness, interest, trial, evaluation, and adoption as the five stages individuals pass through on the way to accepting a new product or idea.

Disclosure To divulge, make evident, or reveal information otherwise not necessarily known.

Discovery Gaining knowledge through observation, study, or search.

Discovery and analysis The first stage in the strategic public relations process during which a sense of the environment of an organization is gained through research and analysis. Also, the stage at which goals, resources and stakeholders are identified.

Double-barreled questions Contain two questions in one and can elicit two different answers.

Dyads Intense discussions between two people guided by a moderator.

Earned media Public attention accorded to an event, person or organization based on intentional efforts to bring its newsworthiness to light, as opposed to paying for advertising.

Editorial board meeting A session during which a newsmaker meets with the members of a news organization's editorial writers, usually to explore a particular issue in-depth or to attempt to understand the direction or scope of an initiative or policy.

Electronic press kit (EPK) Lengthier version than a video news release (VNR)—usually 15 minutes—that provides more extensive information about an event; generally targeted to entertainment-oriented news media.

Embargo A date and time at which information in a news release may be used; always later than the dated release.

Enlightened self-interest model A philosophy that says it is good business to behave ethically; that if business is conducted with the public interest in mind, the businessperson will profit.

Environmental analysis *See* Environmental scan.

Environmental scan An informal research technique used to explore what is going on inside and outside of an organization to detect threats and opportunities for planning; identifies resources, strengths, weaknesses, and competition. Also known as *environmental scan* or *situational analysis.*

Ethics Doing what is right and avoiding what is wrong as delineated by a set of personal, organizational, and societal values.

Ethnocentrism The tendency to view the world through the lens of one's own culture.

Evaluation The assessment of the effectiveness of an intervention, program, or campaign in achieving its objectives.

Evaluation design A detailed outline of how and why research will be conducted.

Evaluative research Determines the extent to which the goals and objectives of a program or plan have been achieved.

Events Planned occasions and experiences designed to bring a specific message to a target audience.

Executive branch The branch of federal government that is composed of the office of the president and its cabinet departments and agencies; state and local equivalents are the governor, county executive, and mayor.

External audiences Audiences other than employees and associates; include government and regulatory agencies, consumer advocacy groups, customers, and the news media.

External house ads Ads that appear in newspapers and magazine that run house ads in their own publications to promote their publications to potential subscribers.

External resources Various assets and support available from outside of the organization such as funding, in-kind services, and partnerships.

Face-to-face public communication Communication that usually involves a speaker and a live audience such as a speaker delivering a formal speech, a rally, or a concert presentation

Fact sheets Documents that provide details about an issue, study, survey, or organization; designed to give a reporter details that help set the context for covering an issue or event and to provide a quick reference tool.

Feature release An article length story provided to news media usually focused on the human interest or local side of a larger news story. Also known as a *news feature.*

Federal judiciary *See* Judicial branch.

Federal Trade Commission (FTC) A federal agency that protects consumers from unfair or deceptive advertising and promotional campaigns.

Feminine culture A culture in which modesty, tenderness, and concern for the quality of life are prized by both men and women.

Fidelty The state of being accurate or exact in details, correspondence, and speech.

Fireside chats President Franklin Roosevelt's series of radio addresses to the nation; introduced radio as a medium for political public relations.

Focus group A market research technique in which a small group of people is led by a moderator, and specific questions are discussed about a topic.

Focus group interview A structured group interview that proceeds according to careful research design with attention to the principles of group dynamics.

Formal research methods Planned and rigorous data collection methods that involve specific protocols or prescribed ways for collecting data.

Formative research Research that is conducted before and during public relations planning to help develop goals and objectives, strategy, messages, and tactics of a program. Also known as *developmental research.*

For-profit organization An entity whose express purpose is to sell products and services at a profit and distribute its profits to its shareholders.

Franking privileges A privilege that allows members of Congress to send mail using their signatures instead of a stamp.

Freedom rides Activists who rode buses to the South in the 1960s to end segregation on U.S. transportation facilities.

Front group A group structured to look like a voluntary association that is set up to act on behalf of its parent group; often set up by companies that are "astroturfing."

Fundraiser The process by which people, groups, or organizations solicit and gather donations of money or in-kind gifts from individuals, businesses, or foundations.

FYI communication Developing a message to inform a specific audience.

Gantt chart A graphic that illustrates when tasks, tactics, and activities will happen. Also known as a *time line.*

Gatekeeping The editorial roles and processes that determine whether or not potential news stories are covered and/or published or aired in the news media; the process of screening out items that are not chosen.

Gilded Age Decades surrounding the turn of the 20th century that saw the rapid growth of industry.

Goal A statement of the broad outcomes desired.

Graphic design A visual message with impact; space, words, photographs, and illustrations used to depict and explain.

Grassroots Activist groups that mobilize support from the ground up.

Great Debates Debates between presidential candidates John F. Kennedy and Richard M. Nixon in 1960; the first televised presidential debates.

Group-administered questionnaire A set of specific survey questions designed to be administered to a specific population in a group setting.

Health marketing and communication The integration of consumer marketing research with public health science, theory, and research to create consumer-based and science-based communication strategies to protect and promote health and healthy behavior.

High-context communication Communication in which the message is beyond the spoken or written word; it is contained in the person or physical context in which it is delivered.

IC or IMC The merger of advertising, marketing, promotions, and public relations. *See* Integrated marketing communication.

In-depth interview A one-on-one interaction, organized to encourage the respondent to talk freely and to express her ideas on the subject under investigation.

Individualism A philosophy that says each individual is expected to look after himself or herself and his or her immediate family only.

Individually-administered questionnaires. *See* self-administered questionnaires.

Inductive reasoning The application of an idea or theory to a situation often for the purpose of testing the theory or idea.

Informal research methods Exploratory research for purposes of discovery; less planned than formal research methods.

Informed consent A practice that assists researchers in explaining to subjects that a study is completely voluntary and inform them of any possible harm that may result from their participation.

Integrated approach Merging the functions of advertising, marketing, promotions, and public relations to ensure that all an organization's communication functions speak as one.

Integrated communication The marriage of strategic planning and strategic communication.

Integrated marketing communication The process of public relations and marketing working together to create customer interest and trust in a product or new behavior change. *See* IC or IMC.

Internal audiences Audiences that are a part of the organization's structure and are involved in implementing or supporting its mission and assisting in accomplishing its goals.

Internal house ad An ad placed in an organization's own publications such as magazines and newsletters; usually encourages employees, retirees, members, or other internal audiences to volunteer or take some other act to benefit the community.

Internal resources Various assets and support available from inside the organization such as staff, capital, and buy-in from management.

International Association of Business Communicators Professional network for business communication professionals founded in 1970.

International Public Relations Society International professional association founded in 1955.

Interpersonal communication Communication that transpires between one or more people that is usually one-on-one or smaller than 15 people; usually friends and family.

Intimate space The closest space around a person, usually reserved for those with whom a person is intimate such as closest friends and family.

Intrapersonal communication The thought process we use to communicate with ourselves—one individual talking to himself or herself.

Intuitive thinking A basic philosophical theory of ethical decision making that holds that certain actions are, in themselves, right and ought to be done regardless of consequences.

Inverted pyramid structure A writing style that puts the most important information in the beginning and leaves less important details for subsequent paragraphs; usually employed in news writing.

Iterative research Research conducted at significant stages of a public relations program to determine if adjustments need to be made to messages or tactics. Also known as *monitoring research.*

Judicial branch A branch of federal government made up of the U.S. Supreme Court, U.S. Courts of Appeals, U.S. District Courts, and U.S. Bankruptcy Courts. Also known as *federal judiciary.*

Key informant conversation An interview with a subject matter expert or other sources who are well versed in a subject, topic, or issue.

Kick-off meeting The first meeting convened by the project director with all of the members of the program or campaign team typically during which roles and responsibilities are discussed and strategies and implementation are reviewed.

Kyosei A Japanese concept that means living and working together for the common good, enabling cooperation and mutual prosperity to coexist with healthy and fair competition.

Labor costs Expenses required for personnel to staff a project.

Lead The first paragraph or first few lines of a news release or news story.

Legislative branch The branch of federal government that consists of the House of Representatives and Senate, together referred to as Congress. These two Houses make the laws and the executive branch approves them or vetoes them.

Letter to the editor A letter in response to an article that appeared in a publication; it may take exception to the journalist's view or correct the article in one way or another, but it could also be a letter of support.

Libel An action that injures another's reputation; sometimes limited to written injury.

Literature review An exhaustive review of what has been written about a topic or subject.

Litigation public relations The practice by lawyers or their public relations representatives of using the media to advance their clients' cases and to promote their own reputations and services.

Lobby To contact executive or legislative branch officials on behalf of organizations or individuals.

Lobbyist One who acts as an agent of a group or organization to influence legislators or government officers or executives.

Low-context communication Communication in which the information is explicit in the word or code.

Magic bullet theory A theory that holds that mass media are so influential that they can manipulate public opinion and American policy with their messages; a theory most scholars have discounted.

Mall intercepts A research technique that involves stationing interviewers at a point, such as shopping malls, frequented by individuals from the target audience.

Margin of error The statistic that indicates the accuracy of a survey. The larger the margin of error, the more likely a survey has error.

Marginal audiences Audiences that have little effect on an organization.

Market The group of people who has needs for products and who have the ability, willingness, and authority to purchase those products.

Market research The formalized study of various aspects of groups of consumers.

Market segmentation The process of subdividing a market into distinct subsets of people that behave in the same way or have similar needs.

Marketing communication Communication that is used to describe the process of public relations and marketing working together to create customer interest and trust in a product.

Marketing exchange All activities associated with receiving something from someone by giving something voluntarily in return.

Mark up The handling or service fee agencies and freelancers add to some administrative and production costs.

Masculine culture A culture in which social gender roles are clearly distinct and in which men are supposed to be tough, assertive, and focused on material success while women are supposed to be more tender, modest, and concerned with the quality of life.

Maslow's Hierarchy of Needs A model proposed by psychologist Abraham Maslow in 1943 that attempted to explain how messages can be devised to appeal to human needs: basic (food, water, shelter, and transportation), physical and financial security, social (acceptance, friendship, love, romance, and sex), ego (status, recognition, accomplishment, and fame), and self-actualization (education, travel, recreation, and development of artistic or creative talent).

Media alert Advises the news media of special coverage opportunities during an event, clearly explaining who, what, when, where, and how. Also known as *media advisory.*

Media audit The analysis of the news media coverage of an organization or client.

Media kit A tool sent to editors and journalists to generate news stories about an organization's newsworthy initiative, campaign, special event, major announcement, product launch, or trade show; can be folders with news releases, fact sheets, photos, slides, backgrounders; often distributed on websites or CDs.

Media relations A specialty in which practitioners attempt to generate and maintain good relationships with the news media to gain positive news media coverage.

Mediated mass communication Communication to mass audiences through media such as print, television and radio media.

Medicine show Promotional show that combined vaudeville acts with sales pitches.

Meetings Gatherings of people who come together to share or exchange information or work together on a project or issue.

Message and materials development The creation of the campaign messages and collateral materials of a campaign. Messages are often taglines, headlines, slogans; and lyrics; materials can be brochures, billboards, giveaways, or other products.

Microsites A website within a website usually dedicated to an event or major issue.

Moderator's topic guide A document that assists a moderator in facilitating a group discussion.

Monitoring research *See* Iterative research.

Monochronic time Things take place in a scheduled, linear fashion.

Muckrakers Group of American journalists, novelists, and critics whose writings exposed corporate abuse and political corruption in the early 20th century; named by President Theodore Roosevelt.

Multimedia tactics The use of several media tactics at one time to create an experience.

Mystery shopping Allows the practitioner to test the competition or opposition's strengths and weaknesses by discovering what products and services they offer and to what extent.

Naturalistic thinking *See* Deterministic thinking.

Negligence Professional misconduct or unreasonable lack of skill that results in personal injury.

News conference A forum in which many journalists are invited to ask questions of a spokesperson or newsmaker, usually following an opening statement.

News feature *See* Feature release.

News media briefing A briefing hosted by an organization in which small groups of four to five journalists are updated on its activities.

News media showing A planned event that gathers journalists to introduce them to new products or services. Also known as *press* or *media tours, familiarization* or *"fam" trips*, and *press parties.*

Nonprobability sampling A survey sampling technique that does not involve random selection. It is considered less accurate or rigorous and may not represent the population well.

Nonprofit organization An entity that does not make a profit and operates to serve a public good.

Nontraditional audiences Audiences that do not have an existing relationship with the organization but present an opening for the organization to study a potential audience.

Objective A statement of measurable results within a stated time frame.

Observations or ethnographic studies Studies conducted by a researcher who can observe how subjects behave or if they have the skills necessary to perform specific tasks.

Office of War Information (OWI) Forerunner of today's U.S. Information Agency; established by Roosevelt as a propaganda machine during World War II; a training ground for early public relations practitioners.

Omnibus survey A method of market research covering a wide variety of topics for several clients who share the expense.

One-on-one interview A meeting with one journalist and a spokesperson usually requested by the reporter and attended by the PR practitioner.

Op-ed A form of opinion writing usually found opposite the editorial page when in a newspaper that addresses current issues and public policies. Writers who are not employees of the publication voice their views on a particular subject; byline usually an expert on the subject or an executive director, president, or CEO; may be found in other media.

Open-ended question A questionnaire question that allows the respondent to respond in her own words without selecting answers provided by the research instrument.

Opponent Someone who is against an organization's goals and mission.

Organizational communication A system through which messages pass through an organization; patterns of interaction among the members of an organization.

Page slug An identifier inserted at the top, flush left of each continuing page of a news release that includes a phrase or page number such as *Student Wins Lottery/2–2–2* or *Page 2 of 2.*

Panel A page or section of a brochure, leaflet, or pamphlet.

Partisan and mutual values model A model in which the focus lies at the point where partisan and mutual values intersect; highlights the ethical challenge of balancing the interests of the client with the interests of those who are affected by the client's actions.

Partnership development A partnership in which alliances and cooperation between groups are developed and maintained to accomplish objectives that are mutually beneficial to both parties.

Patent Exclusive rights to an invention.

Patent medicines Potions and pills that were touted as cures during the 19th century.

Perceptual analyzer a computerized tool used to measure participant opinion of a message; usually used in a focus group setting.

Personal interview An interaction between a spokesperson and journalists.

Pert chart A graphic that illustrates how the tasks, tactics, and activities of a project will flow.

Photo-op Carefully planned news events that yields an effective photograph or video.

Pitch letter A letter that invites print and broadcast news editors and producers to cover an event, or offers them a news interview with a spokesperson; sometimes used as cover letters for news media kits.

Politics The process by which people and groups make decisions and the process that gets officials elected to government.

Polychronic time Many things happen at the same time and many people are involved in many things at a time.

Power distance The extent to which the less powerful members of organizations and institutions (like the family) accept and expect that power is distributed unequally.

Presentation aid A presentation support tool that adds value, clarity, and depth to a presentation; examples include PowerPoint, video or film graphics, etc.

Press agent model A public relations model in which an organization tells an audience what the organization wants the audience to believe; incorporates little or no research to determine the audience's needs, interests, or inclinations to agree to the organization's objectives.

Primary audiences Audiences that have the biggest effect on an organization.

Primary research Research that involves firsthand investigation, tests, or surveys.

Probability sampling A survey sampling technique that involves random selection. It is considered accurate and rigorous and may represent the population well.

Problem statement A clear and concise statement of the problem facing an organization or individual, providing as much information about who, what, when, where, and why as possible.

Production costs Expenses incurred when working with outside vendors who design and produce many of the campaign or program materials; include printers, graphic designers, advertising costs, catering, and event equipment.

Professional responsibility model A model that tries to balance the interests of the client or company with interests of the public. It holds that the public relations practitioner's first loyalty is to his or her client or company and that he or she best serves the public interest by avoiding or minimizing harm to all those affected by the client's or company's actions.

Propaganda The spread of biased information or falsehoods to promote a cause or serve an agenda; also the title of a book by public relations trailblazer Edward Bernays.

Proponents Those who support the organization's goals and mission.

PR plan A document that outlines the work to be accomplished and an overview of how that work will be accomplished. Also known as *communication plan* or *strategic communication plan.*

PR proposal A document developed by an outside practitioner for the purpose of winning the proposed PR work.

Proxemics The study of the human use of space.

Psychographics The emotional and behavioral characteristics of an audience.

Public awareness campaigns Campaigns designed to bring issues, concerns, opportunities, or problems to the attention of members of the public who may be affected.

Public information model A journalistic approach to public relations that offers information about an organization that is truthful and accurate but usually leaves out damaging or harmful information about the organization.

Public relations An applied discipline within the field of communication that uses strategic thinking, planning, research, and practice to help an organization or person establish and manage mutually beneficial relationships and interact with audiences that ensure success or failure; position an organization, person, or issue favorably within the marketplace of ideas; and/or affect the attitudes, opinions, and behaviors of the targeted audience or audiences.

Public Relations Society of America World's largest public relations society, founded in 1947.

Public service advertising Free advertising time and space run by news publications and stations as a community service; often a part of nonprofit communication campaign strategy. Called public service ads (PSAs) when placed in print media, but public service announcements (PSAs) when on radio or television.

Public space The area in which interaction is anonymous and impersonal.

Publicity The dissemination of messages to the mass media for the purpose of gaining positive attention for an organization, individual, product, or service. It is also sometimes used to refer to the result of these efforts.

Publics Groups with which organizations or individuals seek to have mutually beneficial relationships; also known as *audience.*

Purposive (judgmental) sampling A survey technique in which researchers sample with a purpose in mind for the experiment, usually involves a specific group of people.

Qualitative research Research that uses individual and group interviews to gather non-numerical findings that cannot be used to estimate "how many" or forecast but can help researchers understand the "why" of behaviors.

Quantitative research Research that uses statistics and probability to collect and analyze numerical data that are utilized to answer questions such as how many, how often, to what extent, etc., for the purpose of forecasting behaviors, events, or quantities.

Questionnaire The document containing the questions for a survey onto which the interviewer enters a respondent's answers during personal interviews.

Random sampling A manner for selecting participants that can vary from a computer-generated list of numbers, to a random number list, to putting all the numbers in a drum, spinning them and then drawing the numbers—much like winning lottery numbers are drawn.

Random-digit-dialing sampling An automated method of randomly dialing telephone numbers.

Recursive A process that can repeat itself indefinitely.

Relativist One who makes ethical decisions based on his own value system and beliefs of what is right or wrong; in ethics the belief that right or wrong is dependent on time, place, culture, etc.

Release letters Letters that give permission for full and unrestricted use of the elements that make up collateral material; releases are secured from sources of images, audio, and quotations.

Request for proposal (RFP) A proposal request distributed by an organization seeking assistance.

Research The careful and systematic study, investigation, and collection of data for the purposes of knowing, describing, and understanding.

Research instruments Tools used to conduct audience research, such as questionnaires, screeners, and moderator's discussion guides.

Research plan A plan that delineates the manner in which a research study will proceed and timelines and resources needed.

Resonance theory A theory that says messages must resonate with information the audience already has stored in order for new information to instigate a desired behavior.

Return on Investment ROI Shorthand for the business concept of return on investment, the financial profit or other gain an organization achieves relative to the cost of the activities in which resources were invested.

Sample An example of a larger group of people.

Sample size The size of the sample of a population.

Sampling error A mistake in sampling represented by the difference between the sample and the population, making the sample unrepresentative of the population.

Sarbanes-Oxley Act U.S. legislation that created stiff reporting standards for public U.S. companies and accounting firms.

Screener A document provided to a research facility that identifies participant eligibility criteria for the purpose of recruiting participants in a research study.

Secondary audiences Audiences that have some effect on an organization.

Secondary research Research that involves collection of previously published data or data collected by others.

Securities and Exchange Commission (SEC) Federal agency that protects investors in public companies by overseeing the companies' financial activities

Segmentation *See* Market segmentation.

Self-administered questionnaire Survey instruments that are completed by the respondent and not an interviewer.

Self-efficacy theory The attribute of performing the necessary behavior to change one's environment. People with high self-efficacy believe they have the ability to change their environment to affect a change they desire. People with low self-efficacy believe that they are incapable of changing their environment.

Semantic differential technique A scaling method that allows survey respondents to gauge their answers at a point on a range of possible answers.

Situationalist One who makes ethical decisions based upon a current situation and circumstance.

Slander Injuring another's reputation; sometimes limited to spoken injury.

Sleeper effect The effect of a message having more impact on attitude change after a long delay than when the message is first heard.

Small-group communication A discussion among 3 to 15 participants to solve a problem or to accomplish a specific objective.

Snake-oil salesman Charlatan; derived from publicity stunts of 19th-century sellers of patent medicines.

Social marketing The application of consumer marketing principles to social issues to accomplish social change.

Social media The activities that result from the integration of technology and social interaction in the creation and combination of words, images, videos and audio.

Social network sites (SNS) Internet services where individuals can create profiles, develop a list of users, and view and access their lists and those of others using the service such as Facebook, Linkedin, MySpace, and Bebo.

Social responsibility model A model that says companies have a responsibility to the society in which they operate and should act accordingly.

Social space The area in which people are comfortable conducting everyday interactions with both acquaintances and strangers.

Solicited proposal A proposal written in response to an RFP (request for proposal) distributed by an organization seeking assistance.

Sound bite A very short, 7- to 15-minute quote from a newsmaker recorded on audiotape for use in an audio news release (ANR).

Speeches Carefully prepared talks or presentations written to a formula and designed to have an impact when delivered to an audience assembled to hear the speaker.

Spin The tendency to distort the truth so that the subject at hand is perceived as favorably as possible—more favorably than the truth would cause it to be perceived.

Spiral of silence concept The concept that the opinion of the majority dominates and will eventually silence the opinion of the minority because nonconformity threatens the minority with isolation.

Sponsored films and videos Films and videos produced by organizations to introduce themselves to a key audience and explain their mission and activities; also used as training and communication tools, especially for field personnel who are geographically removed from headquarters.

Still photography A photograph; a powerful PR tool because it can be used to augment a news release and to help frame a story.

Strategic communication The delivery of a message to a specific audience to elicit an intended response.

Strategic communication plan *See* PR plan.

Strategic planning The process by which organizations, like individuals, determine what they want to achieve and how they intend to achieve it.

Stratified sampling A survey technique used to help insure the sample includes desired subgroups.

Summated ratings Ratings that provide statements in a range such as "strongly approve" to "strongly disapprove" with a weight of 1 to 5 attached to each.

Survey research The systematic gathering of information from respondents for the purpose of understanding and/or predicting some aspect of the behavior of the population of interest; uses scientific sampling and questionnaire design to measure the preferences, activities, and habits of a population with statistical precision.

Systematic sampling A probability sampling method in which every Nth numbered record, name, etc. is selected from a list; also called the Nth name selection technique.

Target audiences People most likely to buy or use a company's product.

Task leader A person responsible for managing the implementation a particular task area of a project such as events, media relations, or partnership development.

Teflon president Term coined by congresswoman Patricia Schroeder to describe President Ronald Reagan because no criticism seemed to stick to him.

Telephone focus group A market research technique in which a small group of people connected by telephone is led by a moderator, and specific questions are discussed about a topic.

Theatre testing A qualitative research method that brings a large group of respondents into a room that is arranged theatre style for the purpose of getting their responses to audio or audiovisual materials.

Theory A series of assumptions that explains how something works and what happens during and as a result of the work or process; can examine events and situations to explore how variables are related in order to explain and predict.

Trade libel An intentional false written or spoken statement that disparages a business, product, or property. Also known as *trade disparagement.*

Trademark Word, phrase, logo, symbol, color, sound, or smell used by a business to identify a product and distinguish it from those of its competitors.

Traditional audiences Customers, members, and employees who have had a long and ongoing relationship with an organization.

Triads A type of customized in-depth interview in which three people who have different perspectives on the same topic are interviewed simultaneously.

Twitter A web-based blogging service that allows users to send short (140 characters or less) messages to update other users.

Two-way asymmetrical model A model that emphasizes a change in behavior of audiences only in accord with the objectives and goals of the organization; does not incorporate understanding of the target audience.

Two-way symmetrical model A model that holds that public relations provides a forum for discussion among groups with different interests or values; uses research to better understand the target audience and resolution of disputes.

Uncertainty avoidance The extent to which the members of a culture feel threatened by uncertain or unknown situations.

Uncommitted Neither support nor oppose the organization and may not know the organization exists.

Uncontrolled media Messages that cannot be controlled in terms of timing, or distribution after they have been released; examples include print news releases, video releases, media kits, op-eds, and radio actualities.

Unique selling proposition (USP) Any feature that distinguishes a company or product from the competition.

Unsolicited proposal A proposal submitted to an organization when the practitioner has knowledge about the organization's possible needs or issues facing the organization, but an official RFP has not been issued.

Usability/readability testing A qualitative research method used to predict how easy it is for a person to understand written materials and the ease of using certain materials.

Uses and gratification theory A collection of studies that suggests that consumers of media actively select and use the media to meet their needs.

Videoconference focus group A market research technique in which a small group of people connected by videoconferencing technology is led by a moderator, and specific questions are discussed about a topic.

Video news releases (VNRs) A 90-second to 3-minute news story of carefully constructed images and sound bites distributed to television news directors and editors that allows an organization to encourage news coverage of newsworthy material.

Voice of America Spreads U.S. opinion overseas via radio, television and the Internet; was started to spread war propaganda during World War II.

Watergate Political scandal; series of events that began with a botched burglary and ended with Nixon's resignation as U.S. president.

Web log *See* Blog.

Widget Anything that can be embedded into a web page to provide the user with the opportunity to interact with an application.

Wiki A website that allows users to add and edit content.

Word of mouth A highly personal form of communicating, also referred to as "buzz"; results from consumers talking to their friends and family about products, services, and behaviors.

References

CHAPTER 1

Awad, J. F. (1985). *The power of public relations.* New York, NY: Praeger.

Botan, C. (1977). Ethics in strategic communication campaigns: The case for a new approach to public relations. *The Journal of Business Communication, 34*(2).

Elliott, S. (1997). Arnold Communications is leading what may be the biggest campaign against smoking. *The New York Times*, p. C8.

Greyser, S. A. (1974, October). Probing public opinions. *Harvard Business Review.*

Grunig, J., & Grunig, L. (Eds.). (1992). Models of public relations and communication. In *Excellence in public relations and communication management.* Hillsdale, NJ: Routledge.

Henderson, J. K. (1998). Negative connotations in the use of the term "public relations" in the print media. *Public Relations Review, 24*(1).

Hutton, J. G. (1999). The definition, dimensions, and domains of public relations. *Public Relations Review, 25*(2).

Lustig, T. (1986, March). Great Caesar's ghost. *Public Relations Journal*, pp. 17–20.

McClenaghan, J. S. (2000). CEOs and research at small to medium PR firms in selected states. *Public Relations Quarterly.*

McClenaghan, J. S. (2005). PR practitioners and "issues" in the early millennium. *Public Relations Quarterly, (50)*2.

Novelli, W. (2004). From a speech to the Institute for Strategic Communication for Nonprofits at American University School of Communication.

Ponder, S. (1990). Progressive drive to shape public opinion, 1898–1913. *Public Relations Review, (16)*8.

Public Relations Society of America and Florida International University. (2000). *A student's guide to public relations education.* Author. No author.

Rohenberg, R. (1989, July 2). Brits buy up the ad business. *The New York Times Magazine.* Retreived from http://newyorktimes.com

Ryan, M., & Martinson, D. (1990). Social science research, professionalism and public relations practitioners. *Journalism Quarterly, (67)*2.

Streitmatter, R. (1988). The rise and triumph of the White House photo opportunity. *Journalism Quarterly, 65*(4), 981–985.

Wallack, L. 1993. Media advocacy: A strategy for empowering people and communities. *Journal of Public Health Policy*, Newbury Park: Sage.

CHAPTER 2

Becker, L. B., Vlad, T., Olin, D., Hanisak, S. & Wilcox. D. (2008). *2008 annual survey of journalism and mass communication graduates.* Athens: Grady College, University of Georgia.

Bureau of Labor Statistics, U.S. Department of Labor. *Occupational outlook handbook,* 2010–2011 Edition. Author. No author – government document.

Commission on Public Relations Education, Public Relations Education for the 21st Century (2006). *The professional bond—public relations education and the practice.* Author. No author – a commission report.

DeSanto, B. (1996, Autumn). The state of research education in the public relations curriculum. *Journalism and Mass Communication Educator.*

Duncan, T., Caywood, C., and Newsom, D. (1993). *Preparing Advertising and Public Relations Students for the Communications Industry in the 21st Century* (Final Draft, December). Report of the Task Force on Integrated Communications.

Mogel, L. (1998). *Creating your career in communications and entertainment.* Sewickly, PA: GATF Press.

Ostrowsk, H. (2004, December 13). True diversity starts with the appropriate mindset. *PRWeek.*

Public Relations Society of America and Florida International University. (2000). *A student's guide to public relations education.* Author. No author, report.

PRWeek. (2008). Agency Business Report. Author. No author, report.

PRWeek. (2005, February 21). Salary Survey 2005. Author. No author, report.

PRWeek. (2006, February 20). Salary Survey 2006. Author. No author, report.

PRWeek. (2010, March 1). Salary Survey 2010. Author. No author, report.

Raucher, A. R. (1990, Fall). Public relations in business: A business of public relations. *Public Relations Review.*

CHAPTER 3

Adams, S. H. (1905). The great American fraud, *Collier's Weekly*.

Bates, D. (2006). *Public relations from the dawn of civilization*. Public Relations Society of America

Bernays, E. L. (1923). *Crystallizing public opinion*. New York, NY: Boni and Liveright.

Bernays, E. *Propaganda*. New York, NY: H. Liveright.

Crawford, C. (1996). *Recasting Ancient Egypt in the African context: Toward a model curriculum using art and language*. Trenton, NJ: Africa World Press.

Cutlip, S. M. (1994). *The unseen power: Public relations, a history*. Hillsdale, NJ: Erlbaum.

Cutlip, S. (1995). *Public relations history: From the 17th to the 20th century*. Hillsdale, NJ: Erlbaum.

Cutlip, S. M., Center, A. H., & Broom, G. (2000). *Effective public relations*. Upper Saddler River, NJ: Prentice Hall.

Davis, R. (1992). *The press and American politics: The new mediator*. White Plains, NY: Longman.

Ewen, S. (1996). *PR! A social history of spin*. New York, NY: Basic Books.

Fry, S. L. (1991, November). A conversation with Edward L. Bernays, PRSA. *Public Relations Journal*.

Fullerton, R. A. (1990, Fall). Art of public relations: U.S. department stores, 1876–1923. *Public Relations Review, (16)*.

Gleason, M. (1998, December 7). Let's pitch together. *PRWeek*.

Guth, D. & Marsh, C. (2003). *Public relations: A Values-driven approach*. Boston, MA: Pearson.

Hakluyt, R. (1589). *The principal navigations, voyages, traffiques & discoveries of the English nation*. Retrieved from http://digitalcommons.unl.edu

Hariot, T. (1588). *A brief true report of the new found land of Virginia*. Retrieved from http://ebooks.adelaide.edu.au

Hertzgaard, M. (2004). Beloved by the media: Ronald Reagan. *The Nation*.

LaPlant, K. (1999, June). The Dow Corning crisis: A benchmark. *PR Quarterly, (44)*, 32–33.

Lee, I. L. (1906). *Declaration of principles* in Vaughn, S. (2008). *Encyclopedia of American journalism. New York: Routledge*.

Lustig, T. (1986, March). The great Caesar's ghost. Public Relations Journal. *PRWeek*, 2005.

McKay, F. J. (2006, February 19). Propaganda: America's psychological warriors. *Seattle Times*. Retrieved from http://seattletimes.nwsource.com

McKinnon, L. M. The Museum of Broadcast Communications. Retrieved from http://www.museum.tv

Newsom, D., Turk, J. V., & Kruckeberg, D. (2000). *This is PR* (7th ed.) (pp. 226–227). Belmont, CA: Wadsworth/Thompson Learning.

Olasky, M. (April, 1987). The development of corporate public relations: 1850–1930. *Journalism Monographs*.

O'Neill, K. (1991, November). U.S. public relations evolves to meet society's needs. *Public Relations Journal*.

Raucher, A. R. (1990, Fall). Public relations in business: A business of public relations. *Public Relations Review, (16)*3.

Seitel, F. P. (2001). The *practice of public relations*. Upper Saddler River, NJ: Prentice Hall.

Stauber, J., & Rampton, S. (1995). *Toxic sludge is good for you*. Monroe, ME: Common Courage Press.

Streitmatter, R. (1988). The rise and triumph of the White House photo opportunity. *Journalism Quarterly*, 65(4), 981–985.

Tye, L. (1998). *The father of spin: Edward L. Bernays and the birth of public relations*. New York, NY: Crown.

Warner, G. A. (1996). The development of public relations offices at American colleges and universities. *Public Relations Quarterly, (41)*2, 36–40.

Wicker, T. (1991). *One of us: Richard Nixon and the American dream*. New York, NY: Random House.

CHAPTER 4

Balch, G., & Sutton, S. (1997). *Keep me posted: A plea for practical evaluation*. In M. Goldberg, M. Fishbein, & S. Middlestadt (Eds.), *Social marketing: Theoretical and practical perspectives* (p. 62). Mahwah, NJ: Erlbaum.

Collins, J. (2001). *Good to great—Why some companies make the leap . . . and others don't*.

Grunig, J. & Hunt, T. (1984). *Managing public relations*. New York: Holt, Rinehart & Winston.

Smith, R. D. (2002). Strategic planning for public relations. Mahwah, NJ: Erlbaum.

Sutton, S., Balch, G., & Lefebvre, R. C. (1995). *Strategic questions for consumer-based health communications. Public Health Reports, 110*, 725–733.

U.S. Department of Transportation. Traffic Safety facts 2001. National Highway Traffic Safety Administration. DOT HS 809 484. (Table 68, p. 103).

Weinreich, N. K. (1999). *Hands-on social marketing: A step-by-step guide*. Thousand Oaks, CA: Sage.

Wells, W. (1989). *Planning for ROI: Effective advertising strategy*. Englewood Cliffs, NJ: Prentice Hall.

Wheatley, Bob. (2004, February 2). Strategic and tactical behavior shouldn't be confused. *PRWeek*.

CHAPTER 5

Grunig, J. E. (Ed.) (1992). *Excellence in public relations and communication management*. Hillsdale, NJ: Erlbaum.

Guth, D., & Marsh, C. (2003). *Public relations: A values-driven approach*. Boston, MA: Pearson Education.

Hendrix, J., & Hayes, D. (2000). *Public relations cases*. Belmont, CA: Cengage.

Hutton, J. G. (1999). The definition, dimensions, and domains of public relations. *Public Relations Review*, 25(2).

McCleneghan, J. S. (2005). PR practitioners and "issues" in the early millennium. *Public Relations Quarterly*, (50)2.

Smith, R. D. (2002). *Strategic planning for public relations*. Mahwah, NJ: Erlbaum.

Stuart, E. (2007, March 5). Can't tell your Cokes apart? Sue someone. *The New York Times*, BU2.

CHAPTER 6

American Educational Research Association, Ethical Standards. Retrieved from http://aera.net

Babbie, E. (2000). *The basics of social research*. Belmont, CA: Wadsworth.

Dozier, D. M. (1985, Summer). Planning and evaluation in PR practice. *Public Relations Review*, 21–35.

Grunig, L. A. (1990, Summer). Using focus group research in public relations. *Public Relations Review*, 36–49.

Mantera, F. R., & Artigue, R. J. (2000). *Public relations campaigns and techniques*. Boston, MA: Allyn & Bacon.

Rockland, D. (June 23, 2006). Don't be scared: having the ROI conversation with clients. *PRWeek*.

Schenkein/Sherman Public Relations and PR News (1995). Survey on measurement and accountability. In Caywood, C. (1997). New York: McGraw-Hill.

Weinreich, N. K. (1999). *Hands-on social marketing: A step-by-step guide*. Thousand Oaks, CA: Sage.

CHAPTER 7

Jacobellis v. Ohio, 378 U.S. 184 (1964).

Arthur W. Page Society, New York, NY.

Barney, R. D., & Black, J. (1994, Fall). Ethics and professional persuasive communications. *Public Relations Review*, 20, 233–248.

Baker, S., & Martinson, D. L. (2001, Spring and Summer). The TARES test: Five principles for ethical persuasion. *Journal of Mass Media Ethics*, 16, 148–175.

Beder, S. (1998, Summer). Public relations' role in manufacturing artificial grass roots coalitions. *Public Relations Quarterly*, 43, 20–23.

Cutlip, S. M., Center, A. H., & Broom, G. M. (2000). *Effective public relations*. Upper Saddle River, NJ: Prentice Hall.

Thomas, H., (2002, June). Ethics and PR. *Journal of Communication Management*, 6, 209.

The Ethics Resource Center. (2003). *National business ethics survey*. Washington, DC: Author.

Evan, T. J. (1999, Summer). Odwalla. *Public Relations Quarterly*, 44, 15–17.

Fitzpatrick, K. (2002, Spring). Evolving standards in public relations: A historical examination of PRSA's codes of ethics. *Journal of Mass Media Ethics*, 17, 89–110.

Fitzpatrick, K. (2002, Spring). From enforcement to education: The development of PRSA's member code of ethics 2000. *Journal of Mass Media Ethics*, 17, 111–135.

Fitzpatrick, K., & Gauthier, C. (2001, Summer and Fall). Toward a professional responsibility theory of public relations ethics. *Journal of Mass Media Ethics*, 16, 193–212.

Francis, D. R. (2004, June 28). The rocky road to mutual-fund morality. *The Christian Science Monitor* (p. 17+).

Gruning, L. A., Grunig, J. E., & Dozier, D. M. (2002). *Excellent public relations and effective organizations: A study of communication management in three countries*. Mahwah, NJ: Erlbaum.

International Association of Business Communicators, San Francisco, California.

International Public Relations Association, Surrey, United Kingdom.

Jordan, E. J. (1997, Summer). The whole truth and nothing but the truth: Testing the ethics standards of your employees and recruits. *Public Relations Quarterly*, 42, 29.

Josephson, M., Josephson Institute of Ethics, Six pillars of character. Retrieved from http://josephsoninstitute.org

Martinson, D. L. (2000, Fall). Ethical decision making in public relations: What would Aristotle say? *Public Relations Quarterly*, 45, 18–21.

McElreath, M. P. (1993). *Managing systematic and ethical public relations*. Dubuque, IA: Wm. C. Brown.

Newsom, D., Turk, J. V., Kruckeberg, D. (2000). *This is PR* (7th ed.) (pp. 226–227). Belmont, CA: Wadsworth/Thompson Learning.

PR Watch, Center for Media and Democracy, Madison, WI.

Public Relations Society of America. Code of Ethics, New York, NY: Author.

Seib, P., & Fitzpatrick, K. (1995). *Public relations ethics.* Orlando, FL: Harcourt Brace.

Seitel, F. P. (1992). *The practice of public relations.* New York, NY: Macmillan.

Stauber & Rampton, *PR Watch.*

Speakes, L. (1988). *Speaking out: From inside the White House.* New York, NY: Scribner.

Wilcox, D. L., Ault, P. H., & Agee, W. K. (1992). *Public relations: Strategies and tactics* (3rd ed,). New York, NY: HarperCollins.

CHAPTER 8

Associated Press stylebook and briefing on media law. (2009). Washington, DC: Associated Press.

Cott, C. (2002, December 4–10). Everyone's right to spin: Big media back Nike in Supreme Court case. *Village Voice.*

U.S. State Department

Gower, K. K. (2003). Legal and ethical restraints on public relations. Long Grove, IL: Waveland Press.

Heffleu, K. (2009). *Practical media relation advice from legal beat reporters.* New York, NY: Baker & McKenzie. (Law Firm Marketing Institute, www.lawmarketing.com)

Media Law Resource Center. New York, NY.

McElreath, M. (1993). *Managing systematic and ethical public relations.* Dubuque, IA: Wm. C. Brown.

Newsom, D., Turk, J. V., Kruckeberg, D. (2009). *This is PR.* Cengage.

Phillips, M. (2007). *Journalists' view of legal PR.* New York, NY: Zuckerman Spaeder. (Law Firm Marketing Institute, www.lawmarketing.com)

Shapiro, R. (1993). *Using the media to your own advantage.* Thousand Oaks, CA: Sage.

Smith, L. (2001). *Eight best media practices for litigators.* Washington, DC: Levick Strategic Communications. (Law Firm Marketing Institute, www.lawmarketing .com)

Weidlich, T. (2001, March). Making a case for PR. *ABA Journal.*

CHAPTER 9

Ajzen, A., & Fishbein, M. (1980). *Understanding attitudes and predicting social behavior.* City, NJ: Prentice Hall.

Bandura, A. (1977). Self-efficacy: Toward a unifying theory of behavioral change. *Psychological Review, 84,* 191–215.

Barnlund, D. (1970). In K. Sereno & C. Mortensen (Eds.), *Foundations of communication theory* (pp. 83–102). New York: Harper & Row.

Cialdini, R. B. (2001). The science of persuasion. *Scientific American, 284*(2), 76–81.

Cohen, B. (1963). *The press and foreign policy.* Princeton, NJ: Princeton University Press.

Davison, P. (1983). The third person effect in communication. *Public Opinion Quarterly, 47,* 1–15.

Dozier, D., Grunig, L, & Grunig, J. (1995). *Manager's guide to excellence in public relations and communication management.* Mahwah, NJ: Erlbaum.

Entman, R. (1993). Framing: Toward a clarification of a fractured paradigm. *Journal of Communication, 43*(4), 51–58.

Forsdale, L. (1981). The selective processes. In *Perspective on communication* (pp. 109–133). Reading, MA: Addison-Wesley.

Funkhouser, G., & Shaw, F. (1990). How synthetic experience shapes social reality. *Journal of Communication, 40*(2), 75–87.

Grunig, J. (1989). Publics, audiences and market segments: Models of receivers of campaign messages. In Salmon, C. (Ed.), *Information campaigns: Managing the process of social change* (pp. 197–226). Newbury Park, CA: Sage.

Grunig, J. (Ed.). (1992). *Excellence in public relations and communication management.* Hillsdale, NJ: Erlbaum.

Hovland, C. I., Lumsdaine, A., & Sheffield, F. (1949). *Experiments in mass communication.* Princeton, NJ: Publisher.

Hyman, H., & Sheatsley, P. (1947). Some reasons why information campaigns fail. *Public Opinion Quarterly, 11,* 412–423.

Center, A. and Jackson, P. (2002). *Public Relations Practices.* Upper Saddle River, NJ: Prentice Hall.

Klapper, J. (1960). *The effects of mass communication* (Glencoe, IL: Free Press).

Lang & Lang (1966). The mass media and voting. In W. Schramm & D. Roberts (Eds.). *The process and effects of mass communication.* Chicago: University of Illinois Press.

Lariscy, R. & Tinkham, S. (Winter 1999), The sleeper effect and negative political advertising, *Journal of Advertising, 28*(4).

Larson, C. (1994). Consistency. In *Persuasion: Reception and responsibility* (pp. 182–191). Belmont, CA: Wadsworth.

Lewin, K. (1947). Frontiers in group dynamics. *Human Relations, 1*(2), 145.

McCombs, M. (2002). *Setting the agenda: The news media and public opinion.* Cambridge, England: Policy Publishers.

McCombs, M., & Shaw, D. (1972). The agenda setting function of mass media. *Public Opinion Quarterly, 36,* 176–187.

Lippman, W. (1922) *Public opinion.* New York: Harcourt, Brace and Company.

Madden, T. J., Ellen, P. S., & Ajzen, I. (1992, February). A comparison of the theory of planned behavior and the theory of reasoned action. *Personality & Social Psychology Bulletin, 18(1),* 3–9.

Maslow, A. (1954). *Motivation and personality.* New York, NY: Harper & Row.

Mendelsohn, H. (1973). Some reasons why information campaigns succeed. *Public Opinion Quarterly, 37,* 50–61.

Noelle-Neumann, E. (1974). The spiral of silence: A theory of public opinion. Journal of Communication, 24, 43–51.

Packard, V. (1946). Marketing's eight hidden needs. In *The hidden persuaders* (pp. 61–70). New York, NY: Pocket Books.

Prochaska, J. O., & DiClemente, C. C. (1992). Stages of change in the modification of problem behaviors. In M. Hersen, R. M. Eisler, & P. M. Miller (Eds.), *Progress in behavior modification* (pp. 184–218). Sycamore, IL: Sycamore Press.

Rank, H. (1976). Teaching about public persuasion. In D. Dietrich (Ed.), *Teaching and doublespeak.* Urbana, IL: National Council of Teachers of English.

Rogers, E. (2003). *Diffusion of innovations* (5th ed.). New York: Free Press.

Schwartz, T. (1973). The resonance principle. In *The responsive cord* (pp. 2–25). New York, NY: Anchor Press.

Shannon, C. & Weaver, W. (1949). *A mathematical model of communication.* Urbana, IL: University of Illinois Press.

Steele, E., & Redding, W. (1962). The American value system: Premises for persuasion. *Western Speech, 26,* 83–91.

White, D. (1964). "The 'gatekeeper': A case study in the selection of news, In L. Dexter & D. White (eds.). *People, Society and Mass Communications* (pp. 160–172).

CHAPTER 10

Ajzen, I. (1991). The theory of planned behavior. *Organizational Behavior and Human Decision Processes, 50,* 179–211.

Asher, H. (1988). *Polling and the public.* Washington, DC: Congressional Quarterly Press.

Babbie, E. (1999). *The basics of social* research. Belmont, CA: Wadsworth.

Caywood, C. L. (1997). *The handbook of strategic public relations and integrated communication.* New York, NY: McGraw-Hill.

Furman, E. (2005). *Boomerang nation: How to survive living with your parents . . . the second time around.* Old Tappan, NJ: Fireside.

Grunig, J. E. (1992). *Excellence in public relations and communication management.* Mahwah, NJ: Erlbaum.

Grunig, J. E., & Hunt, T. (1984). *Managing public relations.* New York, NY: Holt, Rinehart & Winston.

Laurent, G., & Kapferer, J. N. (1985). Measuring Consumer Involvement Profiles. *Journal of Marketing Research,* 22, 41–53.

Marston, J. E. (1963). *The nature of public relations.* New York, NY: McGraw-Hill.

Smith, R. D. (2002). *Strategic planning for public relations.* Mahwah, NJ: Erlbaum.

SRI Consulting-Business Intelligence, www.sric-bi.com

Wilcox, D. L., Cameron, G. T., Ault, P. H., & Agee, W. K. (2003). *Public relations strategies and tactics* (2nd ed.). Boston, MA: Allyn & Bacon.

CHAPTER 11

Ajzen, I. (1991). The theory of planned behavior. *Organizational Behavior and Human Decision Processes, 50,* 179–211.

Celsi, R. L., & Olson, J. C. (1988). The role of involvement in attention and comprehension processes. *Journal of Consumer Research, 15,* 210–224.

Clark, A. (2003). Before Speaking to Latino Market, Listen to What They Say. *PRWeek.*

Fishbein, M., & Ajzen, I. (1975). *Belief, attitude, intention, and behavior: An introduction to theory and research.* Reading, MA: Addison-Wesley.

Laurent, G., & Kapferer, J. N. (1985). Measuring consumer involvement profiles. *Journal of Marketing Research,* 22, 41–53.

McGuire, W. J. (1976). Some internal psychological factors influencing consumer choice. *Journal of Consumer Research, 2,* 302–319.

Prochaska, J., & DiClemente, C. C. (1983). Stages and processes of self-change of smoking: Toward an integrative model of change. *Journal of Consulting and Clinical Psychology,* 51, 390–395.

Rogers, E., *Diffusion of innovations* (3rd ed.). New York, NY: Free Press.

Silverman, G. (2001). *Secrets of word-of-mouth marketing.* New York, NY: AMACOM Division, American Management Association.

Weinreich, N. K. (1999). *Hands-on social marketing: A step-by step guide.* Thousand Oaks, CA: Sage.

CHAPTER 12

Iacono, E. (2005, November 14). Revolutionizing the clip book. *PRWeek.*

Smith, R. D. (2002). *Strategic planning for public relations.* Mahwah, NJ: Erlbaum.

Weinreich, N. K. (1999). *Hands-on social marketing: A step-by-step guide.* Thousand Oaks, CA: Sage.

Weiss, L. M., Capozzi, M. M., and Prusak, L. (2004, Summer). Learning from the internet giants. *Sloan Management Review, 45,* 79–83.

Wilcox, D. L., Cameron, G. T., Ault, P. H., & Agee, W. K. (2003). *Public relations strategies and tactics* (2nd ed.). Boston, MA: Allyn & Bacon.

CHAPTER 13

Babbie, E. (1999). *The basics of social research.* Belmont, CA: Wadsworth.

Balch, G., & Sutton, S. (1997). Keep me posted: A plea for practical evaluation. In M. Goldberg, M. Fishbein, & S. Middlestadt (Eds.), *Social marketing: Theoretical and practical perspectives* (p. 62). Mahwah, NJ: Erlbaum.

Lindenmann, W. (2003). *Guidelines and standards for measuring and evaluating PR effectiveness.* Gainesville, FL: Institute for Public Relations.

Stacks, D. (2002). *Primer of public relations research.* New York, NY: Guilford Press.

Weiner, M. (2006, April 24). Do right by your research. *PRWeek.*

Weinreich, N. K. (1999). *Hands-on social marketing: A step-by-step guide.* Thousand Oaks, CA: Sage.

CHAPTER 14

Diggs-Brown, B. *The PR styleguide: Formats for public relations practice.* Belmont, CA: Thomson Wadsworth.

Howard, C., & Mathews, W. (1998). *On deadline: Managing media relations* (2nd ed.). Prospect Heights, IL: Waveland.

Hunt, T., & Grunig, J. (1994). *Public relations techniques.* Fort Worth, TX: Holt Rinehart and Winston.

Keene, M., & Adams, K. (1999). *Easy acccess: The reference handbook for writers.* Mountain View, CA: Mayfield.

Lewis, J., & Jones, D. (2001). *How to get noticed by the national media: Your complete guide to high-impact publicity.* Duluth, MN: Trellis.

Lewis, T. (2009, February 2). Making sure that your opinion gets heard. *PRWeek.*

Newsom, D., & Carrell, B. (2007). *Public relations writing: Form and style.* Belmont, CA: Wadsworth.

Tucker, K., & Derelian, D. (1990). *Public relations writing: A planned approach for creating results.* Englewood Cliffs, NJ: Prentice Hall.

CHAPTER 15

Diggs-Brown, B. *The PR styleguide: Formats for public relations practice.* Belmont, CA: Thomson Wadsworth.

Gladwell, M. (2000). *The tipping point: How little things can make a big difference.* New York, NY: Little, Brown.

Hood, J. (2009, January 22). Radio still a strong medium to connect with consumers," *PRWeek.*

Keller, E. (2003). *The influential: One American in 10 tells the other nine how to vote, where to eat, and what to buy.* Chicago, IL: Free Press.

O'Hair, D., Stewart, R., & Rubenstein, R. (2001). *A speaker's guidebook.* Boston, MA: Bedford/St. Martin's.

CHAPTER 16

Diggs-Brown, B. (2007). *The PR styleguide: Formats for public relations practice.* Belmont, CA: Thomson Wadsworth.

Drucker, G. (2006, August 14). Content blurring not VNRs' fault. *PRWeek.*

Interactive Advertising Bureau. (2008, April). *IABB platform status report: User Generated content, social media, and advertising – An overview.* Author.

Universal McCann. (2008, April). *Comparative study on social media trends.* Author.

CHAPTER 17

Adamson, J. (1998, October 5). The Denny's discrimination story—and ways to avoid it in your operation. *Nation's Restaurant News, 32,* 40.

Anderson, S., & Cavanagh, J. (2000). *Top 200: The rise of corporate global power.* Washington, DC: Institute for Policy Studies.

Benjamin, M. (2005, March 28). Giving the boot; Boards with new backbone are dumping imperial CEOs, *US News & World Reports.* Retrieved from http:// usnews.com

Bush, M. (2006, September 10). The PR industry from the outside. *PRWeek.*

Bush, M. (2006, February 24). Volkswagen brings consumer up to speed. *PRWeek.*

Coombs, T. W. (1995), Choosing the right words: The development of guidelines for the selection of the "appropriate" crisis-response strategies. *Management Communication Quarterly, 8*(4), 447–476.

Coombs, T. W. (1999). *Ongoing crisis communication: Planning, managing, and reporting.* Thousand Oaks, CA: Sage.

Cutlip, S. M., Center, A. M., & Broom, G. (2000). *Effective public relations.* Upper Saddle River, NJ: Prentice Hall.

Dilenschneider, R. L. (2000). *The corporate communications bible.* Beverly Hills, CA: New Millenium Press.

ElBoghdady, D. (2004, November 7). Corporate gift packagers: Today's retailers aim big and donate with more care. *The Washington Post*, p. F5.

Fernandez, J. (2004). *Corporate communications: A 21st century primer.* Thousand Oaks, CA: Response Books.

Frank, J. (2005, September 5). Safeguarding reputation. *PRWeek*, Section Profile, 19.

Gordon, A. (2005, October 11). The blogosphere: Google carves new path by blogging to confront issues. *PRWeek*, Analysis section, p. 11.

Hendrix, J. A. (2000). *Public relations case.* Belmont, CA: Cengage.

Holmes, P. (2003, March 10). Boards must assume greater responsibility in dealing with corporate reputation issues. *PRWeek* (p. 9).

Hood, J. (2003, December 15). The PR industry has to pounce on its current opportunity to move up the marketing ladder. *PRWeek*, Editoral Section, 6.

Howard. C. E., & Mathews, W. K. (1998). *On deadline: Managing media relations* (2nd ed.). Prospect Heights, IL: Waveland.

Lipner, I. (2004, October 11). Improving image of PR profession starts at home. *PR News, 60*(39), 1.

O'Brien, K. (2005, December 19). PR pros critique blogs in Peppercome study. *PRWeek,* 2.

Piontek, S. (2005, March 21). Tough season for CEOs. National Underwriter Life & Health.

PRSA (2005). Putting the safety of babies first: Gerber responds to a major tampering incident. *Public Relations Society of America* (Gerber Products Company/Ruder Finn, 1–3).

PRWeek. (2006, August 28). 2006 career guide. *PRWeek, 20,* 31.

Rampton, S. (2002). Ketchum tackles corporate responsibility. *PR Watch, 9*(3).

Rosen, S. (1999, October/November). Riveted. *Communication World, 16*(9), 36.

Schmelzer, R. (2006, October 23). Cause and effect. *PRWeek.*

Solomon, J. (2007, January 20). Senate passes ban on lobbying by some spouses. *The Washington Post*, p. A6.

CHAPTER 18

Bernstein, N. (1996, September 15). Giant companies entering race to run welfare programs. *The New York Times*, p. 1.

Birnbaum, J. (2005, March 30). AARP leads with wallet in fight over Social Security, Bush's plan faces formidable foe. *The Washington Post*, p. A1.

Blackwood, A., Wing, K., & Pollack, T. (2008). *The nonprofit sector in brief: Facts and figures from the nonprofit almanac 2008: Public charities, giving and volunteering.* Washington, DC: Urban Institute Press.

Bonk, K., Griggs, H., & Tynes, E.(1999). *Strategic communications for nonprofits.* San Francisco, CA: Jossey-Bass.

ElBoghdady, D. (2004, November 7). Corporate gift packagers: Today's retailers aim big and donate with more care. *The Washington Post*, p. F5.

Giving USA Report 2010. The Center for Philanthropy, Indiana University.

Hendrix, J. A. (2000). *Public relations cases.* Belmont, CA: Cengage.

Nonprofit almanac 2008. (2008). National Center for Charitable Statistics at the Urban Institute. City, ST: Urban Institute Press.

Nonprofit almanac, INBRIEF. (2001). City, ST: The Independent Sector. Retrieved from *www.afpnet.org*

CHAPTER 19

Brown, D. H. (1976, Summer). Information officers and reporters: Friends or foes? *Public Relations Review.*

Dennis, L. (1995). *Practical public affairs in an era of change.* New York, NY: Public Relations Society of America.

Federal Election Commission News Release (2005). *2004 Presidential campaign financial activity summarized.*

Federal Election Commission News Release (2008). *2004 Presidential campaign financial activity summarized: receipts nearly doubled 2004 total.*

Gallup Poll February 17, 2010.

Jamieson, K. H., & Campbell, K. K. (1997). *The interplay of influence: News, advertising, politics and the mass media* (p. 307). Belmont, CA: Wadsworth.

Joyce, A. (2007, January 1). Help wanted on the Hill: They'd work long hours for little or no pay, yet thousands are inquiring at the Capitol. *The Washington Post*, p. D1.

Pew Center for the People and the Press (2004). November 11, 2004 voters liked campaign 2004, but too much 'mud-slinging' moral values: how important?

Rich, F. (2006). *The greatest story ever sold: The decline and fall of truth from 9/11 to Katrina*. City, ST: Penguin Press.

Trento, S. (1992). *Power house: Robert Keith Gray and the selling of access and influence in Washington*. New York, NY: St. Martin's Press.

CHAPTER 20

Andersen, P. (1994). Explaining intercultural differences in nonverbal communication. In L. Samovar & R. Porter (Eds.), *Intercultural communication* (pp. 229–240). Belmont, CA: Wadsworth.

Ellis, R. J. (1998). *The dark side of the left: Illiberal egalitarianism in America*. Lawrence: University of Kansas Press.

Freitag, A. (2002). International media coverage of the Firestone tire recall. *Journal of Communication Management*, 6(3), 239–255.

Friedman, T. L. (2002). *The world is flat*. New York, NY: Farrar, Straus and Giroux.

Gannon, M. J. (2001). *Understanding global cultures: Metaphorical journeys through 23 nations* (2nd ed.). Thousand Oaks, CA: Sage.

Hall, E. T. (1966). *The hidden dimension*. Garden City, NY: Doubleday.

Hall, E. T. (1976). *Beyond culture*. New York, NY: Doubleday.

Heath, R. L., & Coombs, T. (2006). *Today's public relations: An introduction*. Thousand Oaks, CA: Sage.

Hofstede, G. (1991). *Culture and Organizations*. New York, McGraw-Hill.

Hofstede, G. (1980). *Cultures consequences – International differences in work-related values* (p. 235). Thousand Oaks, CA: Sage.

Hofstede, G., & Bond, M. H. (1988). "The Confucius connection: From cultural roots to economic growth." *Organizational Dynamics 16*(4), 5–21.

Ihator, A. (2000). Understanding the cultural patterns of the world—An imperative in implementing strategic international PR programs. *Public Relations Quarterly, 45*, 38.

Sly, L. (1996, October 2). U.S. names translated: A tricky job: Thirsty in China? Say "sip and be merry." *The Washington Post*, p. A22.

The VNR top ten, CJR, (March, 1991/April, 1991).

United States Information Agency (USIA) archived website http://dosfan.lib.uic.edo/usia/

Zaharna, R. S. (1995). Understanding cultural preferences of Arab communication patterns. *Public Relations Review*, 11, 241–255.

Zaharna, R. S. (2001), In-awareness approach to international public relations. *Public Relations Review, 27*, 135–148.

Index

A

AARP (American Association for Retired People), 16, 74, 398, 400
Abolitionist movement, 57
Above Water Public Relations, 422
Abramoff, Jack, 379, 419
Absolutist, 151
Acanchi, 437
Account director (AD), 244
Accountability, 15
Accounting principles, 246
Accuracy in news releases, 280
Action stage, 188, 189
Actuality, 341
Ad Council, 53
Adams, Samuel, 39–40
Adams, Samuel Hopkins, 41–42
Administrative costs, 246
Adoption of children in Russia (questionnaire), 125
Advertising
    Budgets, 14
    Colonial newspapers, 40
    Origins of modern, 41
Advertising agencies, early, 40
Advertorial, 294
Advocacy advertising, 294
Advocacy newsletters, 291
AED annual report, 312
African Americans
    Anti-drug campaigns, 106
    Challenging assumptions about, 71–72
    No Child Left Behind education law, 159
    Youth highway fatalities, 423
Agency corporate practices, 370
Agenda setting theory, 192
Aging populations, 220
    Drivers, 338
Agnew, Spiro, 55
AIDS campaign messages, 227–228
    Sample ad, 315
American Anti-Slavery Society, 57
American Association of Motor Vehicle Administrators (AAMVA), 338
American Diabetes Association (ADA), 78–79
American Educational Research Association (AERA), 131–133
American Heart Association (AHA), 255, 352
American Humane Society (AHA), 177
American Idol (AI), 10

American League of Lobbyists, 379–380
    Code of ethics, 448–450
American Peanut Council, 142
American Red Cross, 405
American Revolution, 39
American Tobacco Company, 48
American Veterinary Medical Association (AVMA), 398
Analysis
    Informal research, 200
        brainstorming formal research questions, 202–203
        identifying knowledge gaps, 200
        segmenting the audience, 202
        synthesizing data and drawing conclusions, 201
    Use of term, 195
Andretti, Mario, 20
Angelou, Maya, 93
Animal cruelty, 177
Annie E. Casey Foundation, 73
Annual meeting, 381–382
Annual reports, 292–293, 381
    AED sample, 312–314
Annual Survey of Journalism and Mass Communication Graduates, 31
Anti-abortion campaign, 147
Anti-drug campaigns
    Multicultural, 106
    Public service announcements, 71–72, 316
    Sample ad, 316
Anti-tobacco campaign, 356
Anticipating outcomes, 86
AOL, 380
Appropriation, 165
Argyle Communication, 142
Arthur Andersen accounting firm, 144, 145
Arthur W. Page Society, 50, 387
    Guidelines for Internet, 460
Arts, culture, humanities organizations, 400
    Nonprofit status, 395
Asian Americans, Anti-drug campaigns, 106
Associated Press guidelines for reporting polls and surveys, 216–217
Association, 186
Association of Fundraising Professional (AFP) Code, 406
Astroturfing, 59–60
    Ethics considerations, 149
AT&T (American Telephone and Telegraph Company), 50

Attitudes, 102–104
    Opinion polling, 266–267
Attitudinal objectives, 228
Attorney-client model, 152
Audience
    At international level, 435
    Blogs, 286
    Global, 429–430
    Nonprofit sector, 397, 398
    Segmenting, 202
    Television news viewers, 347
    Writing for, 175–176
Audience focus, 7–8
    Understanding audience-focused PR, 104–105
Audience-focused messages, 78
Audience profile, 234–235
Audience research
    Political, 417
    Political communication, 413
Audience segmentation, defined, 205
Audience segmentation table, 202
Audiences, 5
    Characteristics of, 101–104
    Consumer behavior theory, 230
    Ethical decision making, 146
    Formal research, 85
    Future or potential, 100
    General public, 98
    Government and ancillary, 378
    Identifying potential target, 198–199
    Internal/external, 99
    Keen competition in nonprofit sector, 393
    Key, 241
    Key benefits, 235
    Knowing your, 93–95
    Nontraditional, 100
    Preliminary data, 200
    Proponents, opponents, and uncommitted, 100
    Research on, 104–105
    Research questions to ask, 110–111
    Speeches, 336
    Target audience, 95, 199, 217
    Theory for reaching, 188–191
    Traditional, 99–100
    Types of, 98–99
    Working with researchers to help reach, 182
Authority figures, 185
Automobile safety, 103, 370
Awareness and retention model, 179